Critical acclaim for
Understanding Your Users
A Practical Guide to User Requirements Methods, Tools, and Techniques

I wish I'd had this book ten years ago; it would have saved me an awful lot of time. It's the kind of eminently practical guide that I really appreciate, and the case studies are excellent. I highly recommend it!

—**Steve Krug**, *author of Don't Make Me Think!*
A Common Sense Approach to Web Usability

Courage and Baxter propel the reader to the beating heart of user-centered design with this comprehensive and practical compendium of process, methodology, and cutting-edge thinking. The techniques they explain so clearly in this detailed and thorough book provide the power to expose the common myth, opinion, and misunderstanding, and reveal the authentic nature of the true engine of wealth in the information age: your users; the people who use your digital systems.

—**Alan Cooper**, *Founder & Chairman of the Board, Cooper*

Here's a book that could easily become your best friend, whether you're just starting out or are a seasoned professional.

Courage and Baxter cover it all, from hard science to ethics to the finest practical details. You'll find a wealth of case studies and instantly accessible answers to sudden questions— "My test subject just refused to be video taped. What do I do?" —along with many valuable techniques that will be new even to seasoned interaction designers and usability professionals, techniques that I began applying immediately in my own work.

—**Bruce "Tog" Tognazzini**, *Principal, Nielsen/Norman Group*

This is a detailed, step-by-step guide to user requirements gathering, one of the most critical, yet often overlooked stages in product development research. Courage and Baxter effectively draw on real-world experience as well as tried-and-true methods.

—**Christian Rohrer**, *Director, User Experience Research, Yahoo!*

Modestly presented as a "how to" book, this work is much more. It helps to consolidate the new field of interaction design by focusing on a common-sense approach to user research. This is an immensely practical book with enduring value for the interaction designer and the usability professional. With detailed discussions of seven key methods of study, clear examples, well-chosen supporting case studies, and an assessment of the proper use of each method, Courage and Baxter have provided an intelligent pathway for those new to the field and a reference work for experienced professionals. The added benefit—in effect, illustrating the very philosophy of user-centered design that they advance—is the way the authors have placed usability study in a wider context of what comes before and after one studies users. This is a thoroughly accessible and usable book. It may well become a classic of the field.

—**Richard Buchanan**, Ph.D., Professor, Carnegie Mellon
University and President, Design Research Society

Effectively gathering and applying user requirements is one of the most critical areas of focus in today's companies. This invaluable resource provides comprehensive and practical guidance on a variety of methods—including strategies, tactics, tips, and templates— enabling readers to more efficiently apply techniques in their own organizations.

—**Janice Rohn**, Vice President, User Experience, World Savings Bank

In Understanding Your Users, Catherine and Kathy give usability practitioners a thorough and practical handbook for conducting user research. They provide details necessary for planning, preparing, conducting, analyzing, and presenting the research for a variety of techniques. Their insights and advice on what to do when something unexpected occurs will be particularly invaluable for those just starting out their careers in user research or those interested in trying out an unfamiliar user research technique.

Peppered with checklists, case studies, and practical advice offered in this book, you will immediately increase your ability to conduct user research that yields quality and reliable results.

—**Pawan Vora**, Principal, Inov Information Designs

UNDERSTANDING YOUR USERS

A Practical Guide to User Requirements Methods, Tools, and Techniques

The Morgan Kaufmann Series in Interactive Technologies

Series Editors: Stuart Card, PARC; Jonathan Grudin, Microsoft; Jakob Nielsen, Nielsen Norman Group

UNDERSTANDING YOUR USERS

A Practical Guide to User Requirements Methods, Tools, and Techniques

Catherine Courage and Kathy Baxter

ELSEVIER

AMSTERDAM · BOSTON · HEIDELBERG · LONDON
NEW YORK · OXFORD · PARIS · SAN DIEGO
SAN FRANCISCO · SINGAPORE · SYDNEY · TOKYO
Morgan Kaufmann Publishers is an imprint of Elsevier

MORGAN KAUFMANN PUBLISHERS

Publishing Director	Diane D. Cerra
Publishing Services Manager	André Cuello
Editorial Coordinator	Mona Buehler
Project Manager	Anne B. McGee
Cover Design	Uday Gajendar
Cover Image	Getty Images
Text Design	Yvo Riezebos Design
Composition	SNP Best-set Typesetter, Ltd.
Illustration	Dartmouth Publishing, Inc.
Copyeditor	Keyword Publishing Services Ltd.
Proofreader	Keyword Publishing Services Ltd.
Indexer	Keyword Publishing Services Ltd.
Interior printer	Hing Yip Printing Co., Ltd.
Cover printer	Hing Yip Printing Co., Ltd.

Morgan Kaufmann Publishers is an imprint of Elsevier.
500 Sansome Street, Suite 400, San Francisco, CA 94111

This book is printed on acid-free paper.

Library of Congress Cataloging-in-Publication Data
Application submitted.

ISBN: 1-55860-935-0

For information on all Morgan Kaufmann publications, visit our Web site at www.mkp.com or www.books.elsevier.com

Printed in China
04 05 06 07 08   5 4 3 2 1

CONTENTS

4 SETTING UP FACILITIES FOR YOUR USER REQUIREMENTS ACTIVITY 106

6 DURING YOUR USER REQUIREMENTS ACTIVITY 208

8 SURVEYS 312

9 WANTS AND NEEDS ANALYSIS 370

10 CARD SORTING 414

11 GROUP TASK ANALYSIS 458

12 FOCUS GROUPS 514

PART 4 WRAPPING UP 635

14 CONCLUDING YOUR ACTIVITY 636

PREFACE

How to use this book

Usability refers to the effectiveness, efficiency, and satisfaction with which users can achieve tasks when using a product. A usable product is easy to learn and remember; is efficient, visually pleasing, and pleasant to use; and enables users to quickly recover from errors and accomplish their tasks with ease. In order to make a product usable, those involved in product development must employ usability methods to ensure optimal usability. User requirements methodologies are methods that can be used in the early stages of product development to help fulfill this goal.

This book is designed to be an easy-to-read "how-to" guide on user requirements gathering methods in the real world. It teaches seven distinct user requirements gathering methods and also covers pre- and post-method considerations, such as recruiting, facilitating group activities, negotiating with product developments teams/customers, and getting your results incorporated into the product. To help illustrate the material and methods presented in this book, we refer to a fictitious travel website called "TravelSmart.com" throughout the book. In addition, we have included real-world case studies to show how these methods have been applied in industry.

This book has five main parts.

Part 1: What You Need to Know Before Choosing an Activity

Often people are not aware of all the factors they should consider before choosing a requirements activity. Chapters 1 through 4 will introduce you to user requirements and the factors you need to consider. They cover such critical topics as:

- The difference between user requirements and other types of requirements
- Getting buy-in from the product team to conduct user requirements activities
- Product/domain research
- Learning who your end user really is, including creating personas and scenarios
- Legal and ethical issues
- Creating an environment to conduct user requirements activities.

Part 2: Get Up and Running

Once you have decided to conduct a user requirements activity, the preparation process begins. Much of the preparation that must be done is the same regardless of the activity that you will conduct. Chapters 5 and 6 focus on this groundwork so that you are fully prepared to execute your activity. This work includes:

- Creating a proposal and protocol for your activity
- Recruiting
- Piloting
- Welcoming the participants
- Moderating the activity.

Part 3: The Methods

Chapters 7 through 13 focus on user requirements gathering techniques. Each chapter focuses on a different method and variations on that method. For each of these methods, you will learn step by step how to prepare for the activity, conduct the activity, and analyze the data. Materials, templates, and checklists are provided to get you using the techniques in no time! Lessons learned and method modifications are discussed as well so that you can adapt a method to suit your needs and avoid making costly mistakes. The methods covered are:

- Interviews
- Surveys

- Want and needs analysis
- Card sorting
- Group task analysis
- Focus groups
- Field studies.

In addition, usability experts have been recruited to provide real-world case studies which are presented at the end of each chapter, to show the method in action.

Part 4: Wrapping Up

Once you have conducted an activity and analyzed the data, your job is not done. You must communicate your results clearly to your product team/customer or else the data are worthless. In Chapter 14, we discuss how to effectively report and present your results to ensure that they are incorporated into the product.

Part 5: Appendices

We also include appendices with additional information that will be of great value as you begin your user requirements methods. The appendices are:

- Resources for learning about usability (Appendix A)
- A list of helpful usability training sources for those new to user requirements (Appendix B)
- A list of resources to help you create a facility for conducting user requirements activities (Appendix C)
- A list of resources that can recruit participants, conduct user requirements sessions, and/or rent facilities to you (Appendix D)
- Requirements for creating a participant recruiting database (Appendix E)
- Affinity diagramming discussion (Appendix F)
- An overview of qualitative data analysis tools (Appendix G)
- A report template for your findings (Appendix H)
- Glossary of terms (Appendix I)
- A bibliography of references (Appendix J).

Targeted Readers

This book has something to offer whether you are new to usability or a seasoned professional.

New to usability

You may be a student of usability or human factors, a designer, a member of a product development team, or have a role in marketing. Regardless of your level of knowledge of usability or job title, this book will enable you to effectively run a variety of user requirements activities so that you can ensure that your users' needs are represented in your product. Because this book is designed as a "how-to" guide, we step you through every aspect of the activity, from preparation to presentation of the results.

We have also included an appendix entitled *Learn about Usability*, which can provide you with valuable resources and references as someone new to the field.

Usability professional

If you are a seasoned usability professional, this book can provide you with some additional user requirements activities that you may not be familiar with. Usability professionals are always looking to add new methods to their toolbox. In addition, this book can act as a reference guide for some of those methods you may not have conducted in a while, or you may see some modifications of a method you had never thought of. Finally, we have packed the book with research to demonstrate short-comings and strengths of the different methods, as well as case studies so you can see how your peers are executing these methods.

Usability promoter

Many of us within product development organizations are faced with the task of promoting the importance of usability and user requirements gathering. This book will help provide you with some ammunition. The real-world case studies located within the chapters demonstrate how these methods have been used successfully within companies to improve their products.

ACKNOWLEDGMENTS

We never could have imagined the number of hours that this book would require and it could not have been completed without the support of countless individuals. Joe Dumas's untiring encouragement and expertise as both a reviewer and colleague cannot be measured. We owe him an immense debt of gratitude. Howard Tamler, Jon Meads, and Robin Kinkead were pivotal as reviewers and we thank them for all of their time and insightful feedback. We would also like to thank Stephanie Rosenbaum, Ross Teague, and Bonnie Nardi for their reviews of selected chapters. A tremendous thank you is due to each of our case study contributors for sharing their unique and compelling user requirements stories. Their experiences are wonderful additions to the book. And of course, we cannot forget Dan Rosenberg, Oracle's VP of the Usability and Interface Design Group. He provided us with the time, resources, and words of encouragement to make this book possible. We would also like to thank our wonderful colleagues, friends, and management at Oracle and eBay for their support, ideas, and flexibility. In particular, we would like to thank Michelle Bacigalupi for her feedback and encouragement and Uday Gajendar for his superb original cover design. We would also like to extend our thanks to Diane Cerra for motivating us to write this book, and everyone at Morgan Kaufmann for their assistance throughout this process. On a personal note, we would like to individually acknowledge friends and family.

Kathy: I spent nearly every weekend and many a vacation writing while my husband, Joe Balderrama, remained patient and supportive. He did whatever it took to give me the time, energy, and love to make the book happen. I must also thank my mother, Karen Fulton, who has always been the single greatest cheerleader my entire life. Her strength set the example that I have lived my life by. Finally, I must thank my dear friends, family, and co-workers for listening, supporting, and encouraging me along the way.

Catherine: I would like to say thank you to all my friends and family who motivated, and inspired me throughout this process. A special thank you to my husband, Ian, for being my greatest enthusiast and for making me smile, and to my parents, Mary and George, for encouraging me in all my endeavors.

PART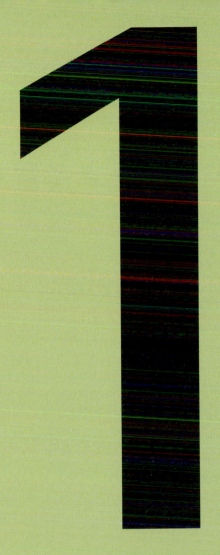

(WHAT YOU NEED TO KNOW BEFORE CHOOSING AN ACTIVITY)

CHAPTER 1

INTRODUCTION TO USER REQUIREMENTS

Introduction

User requirements refers to the features/attributes your product should have or how it should perform from the users' perspective. **User-centered design** is a discipline for collecting and analyzing these requirements. This chapter introduces the basic concepts behind user requirements and the processes involved in capturing them. We discuss what user-centered design is, the different requirements **stakeholders** collect during product development, and how to get buy-in for your user requirements activities. The chapter also provides an overview of the methods presented in this book.

At a Glance

> User-centered design
> A variety of requirements
> Getting stakeholder buy-in for your activity
> The methods

User–centered Design

User-centered design (UCD) is a product development approach that focuses on the end users of a product. The philosophy is that the product should suit the user, rather than making the user suit the product. This is accomplished by employing techniques, processes, and methods throughout the product lifecycle that focus on the user. If you are new to **usability** you should refer to Appendices A (page 678) and B (page 688) at the end of this book to learn about usability resources and classes that can help bring you up to speed.

Principles of User-centered Design

There are three key principles of UCD (Gould & Lewis 1985):

An Early Focus on Users and Tasks

The first principle focuses on the systematic and structured collection of users' requirements. That is the focus of this book. We will teach you how to effectively collect users' requirements using a variety of methods.

To maximize the usability of a product, the user should be involved from the product's inception. The earlier the user is involved, the less repair work needs to be done at the final stages of the lifecycle (e.g., after a usability test). The UCD process should begin with user requirements gathering. By collecting user requirements, you can gain an understanding of such things as what your users really want and need, how they currently work or how they would like to work, and their **mental models** or mental representations of their domain. This information is invaluable when creating a superior product.

Empirical Measurement of Product Usage

The focus here is on ease of learning and effective, error-free use. This can be assessed early in the lifecycle via usability testing of prototypes. Metrics such as errors, assists, and task completion rates gauge this. In a usability test, users are given a prototype or the final product and asked to complete a series of typical tasks using the product. This activity allows you to identify usability issues with your product. Then changes are made to improve the product before its release.

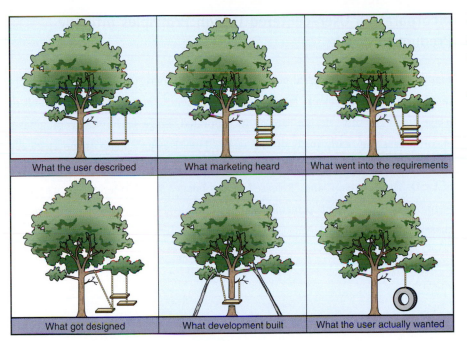

Image based on cartoon #5 at http://www.usability.uk.com/

What the user described	What marketing heard	What went into the requirements
What got designed	What development built	What the user actually wanted

SUGGESTED RESOURCES FOR ADDITIONAL READING

This book does not dive into the detailed process of usability testing, but there are plenty of great books that do. These include:

- Barnum, C. M. (2002). *Usability Testing and Research*. New York: Longman.
- Dumas, J. S. & Redish, J. C. (1999). *A Practical Guide to Usability Testing*, 2nd ed. Exeter, UK: Intellect Books.
- Nielsen, J. (1994). *Usability Engineering*. San Francisco, CA: Morgan Kaufmann.
- Rubin, J. (1994). *Handbook of Usability Testing*. New York: John Wiley & Sons.

Iterative Design

The final principle recommends that requirements are collected and the product is designed, modified, and tested repeatedly. You do not go through the development cycle once; you continue to iterate and fine-tune with each cycle until you get it right. No one gets all the information the first time, no matter how expertly you execute each usability activity.

Incorporating User-centered Design Principles into the Product Lifecycle

Figure 1.1 illustrates the ideal product lifecycle with these UCD processes incorporated. The key elements of "an early focus on users," "empirical measurement of usage," and "iterative design" are all incorporated. Stage 1, the "Concept" phase, encompasses the "early focus on the user." The "Design" phase (stage 2) ideally incorporates the "early focus on the user" and "empirical measurement" principles of UCD. The "Develop" and "Release" phases (stages 3 and 4) tend to focus on the "empirical measurement" principle of UCD. Sample activities in each phase are discussed in this section.

Figure 1.1:

Product lifecycle with UCD processes incorporated

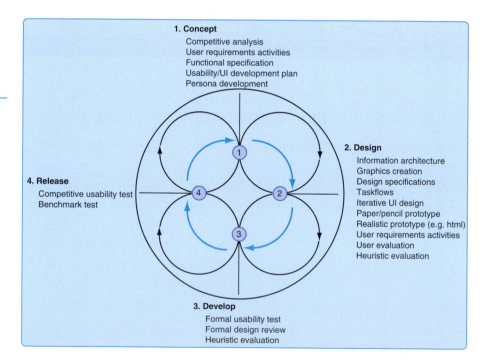

1. **Concept**
   Competitive analysis
   User requirements activities
   Functional specification
   Usability/UI development plan
   Persona development

2. **Design**
   Information architecture
   Graphics creation
   Design specifications
   Taskflows
   Iterative UI design
   Paper/pencil prototype
   Realistic prototype (e.g. html)
   User requirements activities
   User evaluation
   Heuristic evaluation

4. **Release**
   Competitive usability test
   Benchmark test

3. **Develop**
   Formal usability test
   Formal design review
   Heuristic evaluation

Stage 1: Concept

This is the idea phase of your product. You are:

- Developing usability goals and objectives
- Creating user profiles and personas
- Executing user requirements activities, such as interviews, field studies, task analysis, etc.

Stage 2: Design

At this stage, you begin using the information collected in stage 1 to create iterative designs. Some usability activities include:

- User walkthroughs of low-fidelity prototypes (e.g., paper)
- Heuristic evaluations
- Execution of user requirements activities, such as focus groups, interviews, card sorts, etc.

Stage 3: Develop

The developers or engineers now begin to create the product. Some usability activities include:

- Preparation, planning and execution of pre-product release heuristic evaluations
- Preparation, planning and execution of pre-product release usability testing.

Stage 4: Release

The last stage is when your product is released to the public or customer, or within your organization. This stage often blends both user requirements activities with empirical measurement. In software environments, formal usability tests are typically executed on the live code. In addition, requirements collection for the next product release often begins at stage 4, to gauge users' feedback on the product that has been released in the real world. Some stage 4 activities include:

- Usability testing
- Surveys or interviews to gain feedback on released code
- Site visits to see the product being used in its environment.

The third principle of UCD – "iterative design" – is employed throughout the entire cycle, as well as within each stage of the process. For example, you may do a wants and needs (W&N) session in the concept phase. This activity will begin your user requirements collection, but may open up new questions so you may run a follow-up activity such as a group task analysis (GTA). You will then use the results of the analysis to go back and revise and refine or iterate your user requirements document based on your new data.

SUGGESTED RESOURCES FOR ADDITIONAL READING

If your company has not adopted a user-centered design process within its product lifecycle, you have a larger issue on your hands. Conducting a few user requirements activities will not lead to a cure. You will need to employ a change management strategy in order to affect the organization structure, processes, and culture of your company. This is no small task. There are a variety of books and papers that we can recommend if you fall into this category. These include:

- Bias, R. G. & Mayhew, D. J. (eds) (1994). *Cost-justifying Usability*. San Francisco: Morgan Kaufmann.
- Bloomer, S. & Croft, R. (1997). Pitching Usability to your Organization, *Interactions* 4(6), Nov./Dec., 18–26.
- Kotter, J. (1996). *Leading Change*. Boston: Harvard Business Press.
- Rohn, J. & Braun, S. (1993). Structuring Usability within Organizations. Presented at the Usability Professionals' Association Conference, Redmond, WA, 21–23 July.
- Sato, S. & Panton, A. (2003). Using a Change-Management Approach to Promote Customer-centered Design. Presented at the Designing for User Experiences Conference, San Francisco, 5–7 June.
- Schaffer, E. (2004). *Institutionalization of Usability: A Step-by-Step Guide*. New York: Addison-Wesley.

A Variety of Requirements

Thanks to market pressure and a growing awareness of usability, many product teams now realize the importance of understanding their users and the consequences that result when users are unable to utilize products with maximum ease. As a result of this awareness, many companies have incorporated some of the UCD process into their product lifecycles. For many companies, usability begins and ends with the usability test.

There is a clear difference between usability testing and user requirements gathering. Usability testing determines whether a given solution is usable. Requirements gathering provides insight into the many possible solutions and allows a person to select and investigate the best solution from the users' perspective. The difference between a good designer and the outstanding designer is the latter's vision of solutions. Without requirements gathering, your vision is seriously limited.

Although usability testing is a critical part of an effective user-centered lifecycle, it is only one component of the UCD. This book is focused on the requirements gathering stage, which often receives less attention than usability testing, but is equally important. By requirements, we mean the features/attributes the product should have or how it should perform. Requirements can come from a variety of sources – marketing, product development, end users, purchasing decision-makers, etc. All sources have valid requirements and they must be taken into consideration by the product team. For example, if you are building a website for booking travel, some user requirements might include:

- All pages must download in 5 seconds or faster.
- Users must register with the site before making purchases.
- The site must be available in English, Spanish, and French.
- The site should appeal to all demographics of users.
- Users should not require training.

We next describe the different types of requirements you may encounter. By understanding a product's "competing" requirements, you can better position the user requirements for inclusion in the product.

The Product Team's Perspective

The requirements gathering phase is the period when the product team must do its initial research in order to determine the direction of the product. They must collect requirements from a variety of sources (e.g., sales, marketing, managers in your company, customers, end users) and use this information to determine what functionality will be included in the product, the technology that will be used, the task flows they will model, etc. This stage is critical in creating a basis for the design. Poor requirements collection will impact the remaining stages of the product lifecycle depicted in Figure 1.1. You will end up with a misguided product that won't sell, or will be unusable and useless to the users and/or the company that purchases it.

There are a variety of different requirements that factor into product development and there is often confusion between them. Figure 1.2 illustrates some of the many requirements and sources that a product team must deal with.

Figure 1.2:

Requirements sources (image based on Weigers 1999)

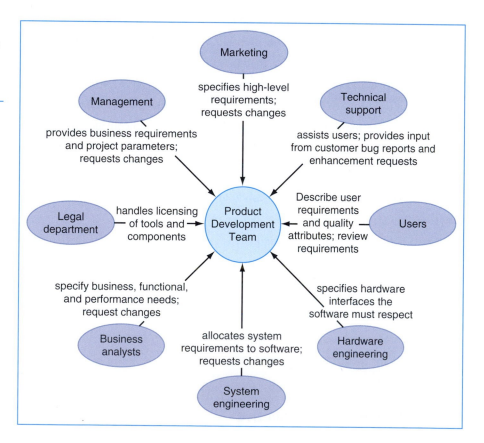

We often encounter teams who say "We have already collected our user requirements," but in reality they have collected functional or marketing requirements, not actual user requirements. Below we discuss business, marketing, and sales requirements because they are often confused with user requirements. It is important to note that each of these is important, but they are not user requirements. There may be overlap, but it is critical for all of the different sources of requirements to be independently collected and then prioritized as a group. You cannot assume that what the sales person wants to see in the product is the same as what the end user wants to see in the product. In order to collect the different requirements effectively, you must be able to distinguish between them.

DILBERT reprinted by permission of United Feature Syndicate, Inc.

Business Requirements

The people who are considering purchasing your product have requirements for that product. These people are typically corporate professionals or executives. We often refer to them as "the decision-makers." Their requirements often reflect the current business practices of their company or new practices they want to adopt to employ cost savings. They want to make sure that the product matches their requirements. If you want to keep these customers, being aware of their business requirements is very important. Sometimes these requirements overlap with the users' requirements, but often business requirements tend to be more high-level and/or technical.

Marketing and Sales Requirements

The marketing and sales departments want to ensure that the product sells and their requirements reflect this goal. They may have requests for features or functions that they think customers want, that competitors have or don't have, etc. Marketing requirements tend to be at a higher level rather than detailed. Marketers are not interested in sending a message about the minute details of the product; they want to send high-level messages to potential customers that will lure them to the product. For example, for a travel website they may have a requirement that the application should have more airline choices than all other competitors, or that it will find you the lowest airfare guaranteed.

The sales representatives are in the field with customers day-in and day-out so the requirements they seek are frequently based on what they are hearing from their customers during product demos. Keep in mind that they are usually demonstrating the product to purchasing "decision makers" and not end users. These requirements tend to be more detailed than marketing requirements. They may have requirements such as "It needs to be fast" or "It needs to look like the number-one travel website in the marketplace." It is important to remember that these requirements may be very customer-specific and not applicable or scalable to other current (or future) customers.

Sales and marketing departments do not typically collect detailed information regarding what the user must be able to do with the product, how they must be able to use it, and under what circumstances they must be able to use it; however, some marketing and sales requirements do represent end user requirements. Consequently, you will likely see some overlap between the user requirements and what sales and marketing have uncovered. The reality is that if the product doesn't do what users want, it doesn't matter how usable it is. Marketing and sales folks often talk to end users and sometimes they even talk to them about usability, even if only at a high level. Mostly, they talk to users about features and capabilities. This is valuable information. Its weakness is that the information they collect is often incomplete, and they almost always collect it in "demo mode" (i.e., selling rather than listening). They work hard at trying to understand users, but because it is not their primary goal they don't have enough time to gather true user requirements. In addition, they may encourage new features to be included in the product because the latest technology is easier to sell, not because users want it.

SUGGESTED RESOURCES FOR ADDITIONAL READING

We do not delve into the processes for collecting these other types of requirements as this book is focused on user requirements. However, if you would like to learn more about this important topic there are a number of books available that deal with the collection and management of these types of requirements. One such book is:

- Weigers, K. E. (1999). *Software Requirements*. Redmond, WA: Microsoft Press.

User Requirements

Just like product development, marketing, and sales, you want your product to sell – it's what pays your salary! If you are creating the product for use in your organization, you will want users to be more productive and satisfied. Consequently, you need to listen to what your customers, marketing, managers, and sales people have to say. Of course, selling the product is just part of the effort. But before the product is sold, you want to make sure that end users can actually use it and that it contains the features they need. If you ignore this important goal, increased training and support or decreased user productivity will lead to unsatisfied customers, and that can harm future sales or decrease renewed licenses or product upgrades. It can also lead to a poor reputation and no new customers.

As was discussed above, you may think you understand what the end users want and need because other sources have told you on their behalf. This is the number-one mistake that product teams make. In reality, purchasing decision-makers, sales, and marketing may think that users interact with the product in a certain way, but because they (decision-makers, sales, and marketing) are not the true end users, they are frequently mistaken. In other cases, they receive information from one single source that has spoken to the end user, but much gets lost in the translation and interpretation by the time the information gets to you. Figure 1.3 illustrates many of these problematic communication paths from which the product team receives "user information."

Figure 1.3:

Communication paths from the user to the product team (image based on Weigers 1999)

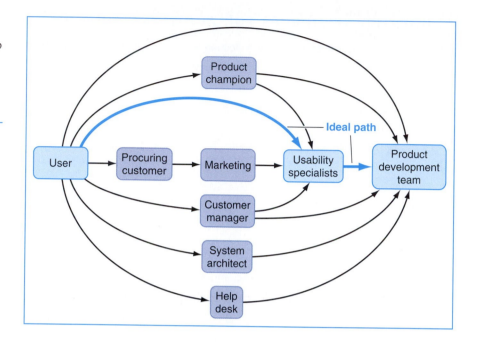

As a result you must talk to the actual users, the people who will use the product at the end of the day, to gain an understanding of their perspective and needs. This understanding includes their tasks, goals, context of use, and skills.

By addressing your users' requirements you can create a product that fulfills their needs. This fulfillment will in turn:

- Increase sales and market share due to increased customer satisfaction and increased ease of use
- Decrease training and support calls that result from user interfaces that don't match the users' mental model
- Decrease development time and cost by creating products that contain only the necessary functionality.

Getting Stakeholder Buy-in for Your Activity

It can be difficult to convince people to support user requirements activities with limited time and budgets. Today's products must be developed on tighter and tighter budgets and deadlines. Below are some of the arguments you may encounter and how to address them. We also discuss ways to prevent this resistance from occurring in the first place.

Arguments and Counter Arguments

 We simply don't have the time or money for such a study."

This will probably be the first response you will hear when proposing such an activity to a product team unfamiliar with user requirements. The reality is, schedules slip. Even if you cannot get the information in to influence the upcoming release of the product, there will be future releases where your data can be used. You want your information to make an impact as soon as possible but do not let schedules prevent you from collecting the information altogether. There are also a variety of methods that can be used to collect information. Some, such as the wants and needs analysis, group task analysis or card sort, can collect the information within an hour or two and you can complete the data analysis in just as little time. You may also want to show documented cases where products went wrong and could have been saved by conducting user requirements activities – see Hackos & Redish (1998) for a plethora of case studies. Better understanding your users can also provide a competitive edge.

SUGGESTED RESOURCES FOR ADDITIONAL READING

The book below contains a plethora of case studies of real-world products that went wrong and could have been saved by conducting a field study.

- Hackos, J. T. & Redish, J. C. (1998). *User and Task Analysis for Interface Design.* New York: John Wiley & Sons.

Sales owns the customers. We don't want to ruin any potential deals. We don't want to make the customer unhappy by pointing out what our product doesn't do."

If you are working on a commercial product, you will likely hear lots of arguments against letting you go near customers. In all of our years of gathering user requirements and conducting usability tests, we have never caused our company to lose a deal or caused a customer to be unhappy with our products. If anything, we have improved relationships between customers and our product development teams because we understand many of the requests customers have been making. Customers may not understand the true cause of their difficulties and have made requests that do not adequately address their problems. The product team may be responsive in making the requested changes; but if the root cause is not understood, more damage can be done to the product. If customers perceive that the product development or sales team is not meeting their needs, this will lead to unhappy customers and frustrated developers or sales people. When you conduct user requirements studies, customers see that your company is trying to understand them and their needs. This will only result in grateful customers. In the end, if you cannot get access to customers, there are other ways of accessing end users (refer to Chapter 5, Preparing for Your User Requirements Activity, "Recruitment Methods" section, page 173).

You'll make promises we can't keep. You'll let out confidential information."
Obviously, you do not want to make promises to customers (whether you know you can keep them or not). You are there simply to collect data. Also, you are not there to share confidential information about the new feature/product/service you are developing. If it is obvious to your participants what you are working on based on your questions, **confidential disclosure agreements** (refer to Chapter 3, Ethical and Legal Considerations, "Legal Considerations" section page 103) can be put in place to keep them quiet. To calm stakeholders' fears, develop a standard script and pass it by everyone for review.

We have information already. Why collect more?"
It can be hard to win support for your study when everyone is telling you they know it all already. The product team may have already conducted their own "focus groups," or the marketing department may have already interviewed potential users, or the sales team may have already conducted their own "site visits." Often, these are product demos or QA tests, asking users whether they prefer A or B. Product teams sometimes give users a "click sheet" to walk through a prototype to get users' impressions. This is not the kind of

data you want to build from. Find out who did the studies, who the users were, and the techniques used. You want unbiased, empirical data. State that all their information is good and you do not intend to replace it; you simply need additional information to supplement what they have learned. You need new details. Show how the information you plan to collect will be different. For example, you want to interview actual end users, not purchasing decision-makers; or you want to learn how users currently complete tasks, not get feedback on a prototype.

"We are introducing a different process, so don't waste your time studying the current process."

You need to understand how people currently work so that you can leverage the good and leave the bad behind. You also want a **transfer of training**. You could end up designing something that is incompatible with the user's current environment – even if your product/system/process is better. You need to understand what challenges you may end up facing when changing the process. Maybe people like the way things are, even if they are inefficient. You also need to understand the ripple effect of your changes. You may end up inadvertently affecting other groups/systems/customers.

"This product/process/service is completely new. There is nothing to observe."

There has to be a manual or automated process currently in place. How was a need for the product determined in the first place? If the potential users do not exist for you to study, who will buy the product? There is always someone or something you can learn from to inform your designs; it just may not be obvious at first.

"Everyone does it differently so there is no point studying a few users."

There will always be individual differences; that is why you want to study a range of users and environments whenever possible. The differences may also be smaller than everyone assumed. If the differences are large, perhaps you can determine the most efficient process. Maybe you can find a pattern in the differences. At the very least, you can identify alternative ways your product should support users.

    We're changing just one part of the system/product/environment. We don't need to study more than that."

You need to understand the context that the change fits into. Users do not work in isolation. Systems are much more interrelated than most people realize. The most successful systems are developed when all parts integrate seamlessly – and this cannot happen if you consider each part in isolation.

    We do need this method, the product is only for our own organization."

You will often hear this from managers of internal products. But the productivity hit is actually twice as bad when an unusable product is implemented in your organization. The end users are less productive and they depend on the support of people in your organization to help them.

Chapter 14, the concluding chapter, contains a great case study about a company called Calico Commerce (no longer in business) that illustrates the kinds of resistance that one often encounters when planning user requirements activities and selling the results (see page 666).

Preventing Resistance

The best way to combat resistance is to avoid it all together. Two ways to accomplish this are:

- Get stakeholder involvement
- Become a virtual team member.

Get Stakeholder Involvement

One of the key themes that is reiterated throughout this book is "getting your product team (or stakeholders) involved." You want them to feel ownership over the activities that you conduct. You want to have their agreement and buy-in that the user requirement activities will benefit their product. If they do not believe in what you are doing, or are skeptical, then they will likely be hesitant to implement your recommendations after the execution of your activity. To gain acceptance for user requirements collection you need to involve them in all stages of the activity from the preparation stages through to the recommendations stage.

Become a Virtual Team Member

If you are not organizationally a member of the product team, you will want to virtually become a member. From the moment you are assigned to the project you will want to work to become an active, recognized member of the product development team. You want to be perceived as part of the team, otherwise it is too easy to be forgotten in the distribution of critical information or in a meeting that is deciding directions without critical input that you can provide.

If you work in a consulting capacity, the product development team may view you as an outsider. Even if you are a dedicated resource to that product, the developers or management may not view you as a team member because of your unique skillset. Deliverables such as your activity proposals and activity findings may not be taken with the same sense of ownership if you are not seen as "one of them." The product team may even feel that you are not knowledgeable enough about the product to be taken seriously. Clearly, this is a detriment to your work.

The ideal situation is when you can become a virtual member of their team. You need to be as knowledgeable about the product and the factors that feed into the process as possible. You want to be perceived as someone who contributes to developing solutions for the product, rather than just identifying problems with existing solutions. This may require you to develop more technical expertise or force you to attend weekly staff meetings that do not always apply to usability and design. You will need to gain the respect and trust of the team and this takes time. You are not there to sabotage their hard work; you are there to help them develop the best product they can. In order to do this you need to understand how the user requirements fit into the big picture. Of course, user requirements are critical for a successful product, but you must be willing to acknowledge that they are not the only requirements. In order to increase your influence this is critical.

The earlier you can get involved the better. The more time you spend with the team and the more familiar you become with the product, the more the team will respect you and your effort. This anecdote from a professional colleague illustrates how important being a member of the group can be:

"I was once working on a project as a contractor for a major software firm. Unfortunately, as a contractor, I was a second-class citizen and was not invited to many of the design discussion meetings that the software engineers held. After a while it became clear that I was no longer up to date on what features and capability that the product was to provide and was unable to contribute to how they should be realized as a user process. In spite of that, the project manager thought that I should still be able to design a user interface. After a while it became evident that things weren't going to change and it made more sense to leave the effort than to remain on and charge them without being able to do the work they were paying for."

Here are some quotes to help you and your organization understand just how important user requirements collection is (Marcus 2002):

- "Incorporating ease of use into your products actually saves money. Reports have shown it is far more economical to consider user needs in the early stages of design, than it is to solve them later. For example, in *Software Engineering: A Practitioner's Approach*, author Robert Pressman shows that for every dollar spent to resolve a problem during product design, $10 would be spent on the same problem during development, and multiply to $100 or more if the problem had to be solved after the product's release." (IBM 2001)

- "One [well-known] study found that 80 percent of software life-cycle costs occur during the maintenance phase. Most maintenance costs are associated with 'unmet or unforeseen' user requirements and other usability problems." (Pressman 1992)

- "When systems match user needs, satisfaction often improves dramatically. In a 1992 Gartner Group study, usability methods raised user satisfaction ratings for a system by 40%." (Bias & Mayhew 1994)

- "Although software makers don't seem liable to the same sorts of litigation as, for example, a manufacturer of medical equipment, poor usability may be an element in lawsuits. For example, the Standish Group reported that American Airlines sued Budget Rent-A-Car, Marriott Corporation, and Hilton Hotels after the failure of a $165 million car rental and hotel reservation system project. Among the major causes of the project's disintegration were 'an incomplete statement of requirements, lack of user involvement, and constant changing of requirements and specifications,' all issues directly within usability's purview." (Standish Group 1995)

In addition, it has been discovered that inaccurate user requirements are responsible for up to 60% of the errors in software production alone (Weinberg 1997). Another study found that 63% of large software projects significantly overran various estimates when planning (Lederer & Prasad 1992). They cited 24 different reasons for the inaccuracies in the estimates, and the four with the highest responsibility were related to a lack of poor user requirements gathering! The reasons stated were:

- **Frequent requests for changes by users**
- **Overlooked tasks**
- **Users' lack of understanding of their own requirements**
- **Insufficient user analyst communication and understanding.**

The Methods

One of the big myths surrounding user requirements gathering is that it takes too much time and money. This is not usually true. There are activities that can be conducted in as little as two hours, while others can be designed to take two months. Each type of activity provides different information and has different goals. There are a variety of user requirements methods to match any schedule and budget. Regardless of your budget or time constraints, in this book you can find a user requirements activity that will answer your questions and improve the quality of your product. These methods are:

- Interviews
- Surveys
- Wants and needs analysis
- Group card sort
- Group task analysis

- Focus group
- Field visits.

The methods were chosen because each offers a different piece of the picture that describes the end user. In addition to teaching you how to conduct each of these methods, this book discusses user identification and recruitment, moderation techniques, and incorporation of user requirements into the product. We also discuss our own lessons learned and modifications for each method. Finally, case studies are provided so that you can see how other usability professionals have leveraged these techniques to support their products. You can benefit from their lessons learned.

In this section is a brief description of each method. Table 1.1 below compares the methods.

Table 1.1:

Comparison of user requirements techniques presented in this book

Method	Purpose	Advantages	Level of effort	Relative time
Interviews (Chapter 7)	Collecting in-depth information from each of several users	• A skilled interviewer can collect a lot of information from each user • Flexible; you can ask follow-up questions & delve into more detail than with surveys or focus groups	• If you are not a skilled interviewer, training is required • It takes time to interview enough users	Medium (phone interviews) to high (on-site interviews)
Surveys (Chapter 8)	Quickly collecting quantitative data from a large number of users	• Collect information from a large number of users simultaneously • If designed correctly, it can be quick & easy to analyze the data • Relatively cheap	• The evaluator must be skilled in creating unbiased surveys (this requires training) • If it is posted to the web, little effort is required to distribute it	Medium
Wants and needs analysis (Chapter 9)	Collecting a prioritized list of users' perceived wants and needs	• Can prepare for, conduct, and analyze data from the activity in short period of time & with few resources	• Group moderations take moderate effort • Recruiting enough users can be resource intensive • Effort to conduct & analyze data is low	Low
Card sort (Chapter 10)	Identifying how users group information or objects to	• Relatively simple technique to conduct • If run as group, can collect data from	• It can be intense to come up with list of information or objects & definitions	Low (group card sort)

Table 1.1 – *Cont'd*

Method	Purpose	Advantages	Level of effort	Relative time
	inform product information architecture	several users at once • Encourages the product team to better understand their own product by breaking the product down & defining each component	• Effort to conduct the activity is low • Effort required to analyze data varies depending on tool, number of cards, & number of participants	Medium (individual card sort)
Group task analysis (Chapter 11)	Understanding how users complete a specific task & issues surrounding that task	• Develop a task flow that works for multiple users/ companies • Quick to conduct • Relatively cheap	• Group moderation is high effort • Fast turnaround on results • Analyzing the data is low effort	Low
Focus groups (Chapter 12)	Assessing user attitudes, opinions, & impressions	• Recruiting enough users can be resource intensive • Collect data from several users simultaneously • Group discussion often sparks new ideas	• Group moderation takes moderate effort • Summarizing the data is relatively low effort	Low
Field studies (Chapter 13)	Learning about the users, their environment, & tasks in context	• Not dependent on what someone says they do • Can collect a plethora of rich data • Ecological Validity	• Arranging the visits, conducting them, & then analyzing the data requires a higher level of effort than any of the previous methods	Medium to high

Interviews

Interviews are one of the most frequently used user requirements gathering techniques. In the broadest sense, an interview is a guided conversation in which one person seeks information from another. There are a variety of different types of interviews you can conduct, depending on your constraints and needs. They are incredibly flexible and can be used as a solo activity or in conjunction with another user requirements activity (e.g., following a card sort). Interviews can be leveraged when you want to obtain detailed information from individual users that you cannot obtain through another activity (e.g., group task analysis, survey, etc.).

The end result of a set of interviews is an integration of perspectives from multiple users. If you conduct interviews with multiple user types of the same process/

system/organization, you can obtain a holistic view. Finally, interviews can be used to guide additional usability activities.

Surveys

Surveys allow you to ask every user the same questions in a structured manner. Users can complete them in their own time and from the comfort of their home or work. Since they can be distributed to a large number of end users, you can typically collect much larger sample sizes than with interviews or focus groups. In addition, you can get feedback from end users around the world; however, response rates can vary from 1% (charity surveys) to 95% (census surveys).

Unlike interviews, surveys should not ask users a lot of open-ended questions because that will decrease the response rate. Use surveys when you have a good idea of the most likely answers an end user would like to select from. Providing set responses for users to choose from will allow you to collect quantitative rather than qualitative data.

Wants and Needs Analysis

The W&N analysis provides information about the kinds of content, features, and characteristics users want and need in a product. This **brainstorming** activity works for any product or service and results in a prioritized list of users' wants and needs. This technique can be used to both validate current feature plans as well as to learn about new features that users would find valuable. Although it can be used at any time, this technique provides the most benefit when used during the conceptual stage of product development.

The W&N analysis can be conducted in about an hour and it takes even less time to analyze the data from a session, making this technique light on resources, but powerful in terms of results. Most often, the results of this activity are fed directly into the product's functional specification and design documentation.

Card Sort

A card sort is used to inform or guide the development of the information architecture of a product. For example, it can help determine the tab and sub-tab structure in applications. It can also provide information when deciding how to lay out displays and controls on an interface.

To conduct the technique, cards describing objects or concepts in a product are sorted into meaningful groups by each participant. By aggregating the sorts created by several users, we can learn how closely related each of the concepts are. This method tells us how a product's features should be structured to match the users' expectations about how those features are related. This technique can be conducted with individuals or with a group of users working individually. If a group is used, the data can be collected in two hours or less and then analyzed with one of several automated tools available today.

Group Task Analysis

This method is used to gain an understanding of the steps users take to complete a particular task and the sequence in which they take those steps. Users work in small groups of four to six people and discuss the steps involved in completing a particular task (e.g., booking a vacation). By having people from different companies work together, you end up with a task flow that works for everyone. The flows generated by the activity are used to determine the task flows in a product. The activity takes about two hours and the results are analyzed in even less time – making the group task analysis ideal for those short on time and resources.

Focus Group

In a focus group, eight to ten end users are brought together for an hour or two to provide information in response to a series of questions, or to provide their subjective response to product demonstrations/concepts. Often, participants are given tasks to complete with prototypes of the product so that they may have a better frame of reference from which to speak. Presenting the questions or product to a group usually sparks group discussion and can provide more information than interviewing individuals alone.

Focus groups are one way to gather information about a target audience that you have very limited information about, but they are better suited to the generation of ideas rather than evaluation and analysis. You can also discover problems, challenges, frustrations, likes, and dislikes among users; however, you cannot use focus groups to generalize the exact strength of users' opinions, only that they are adverse to or in support of a concept or idea. If conducted well, a focus group can provide a wealth of useful information in a short period.

Field Study

The term "field study" is a larger category of usability activity that can include contextual inquiry, on-site interviews, simple observations, and apprenticeship. During a field study, a researcher visits end users in their own environments (i.e., home or workplace) and observes them while they are working. Field studies can last anywhere from a couple of hours to several days depending on the goals and resources of your study.

Using this technique, a usability professional gains a better understanding of the environment and context surrounding the user's work. By observing users in their own environment, you can capture information that affects the use of a product – including interruptions, distractions, and other task demands – and additional context that cannot be captured or replicated in a lab environment. Field studies can be used at any point during the product development lifecycle but are typically most beneficial during the conceptual stage.

*   *   *

These seven methods provide you with a variety of options. Some techniques can be intensive in time and resources (depending on your design), but provide a very rich and comprehensive data set. Others are quick, low-cost, and provide the answers you need almost immediately. In addition, each of these techniques can provide different data to aid in the development of your product or service.

It is important that you choose the correct activity to meet your needs. In Table 1.1 above we outline each of the activities proposed in this book and take you through what it is used for, its advantages, and the level of effort, cost, and time required relative to the other methods.

CHAPTER 2

BEFORE YOU CHOOSE AN ACTIVITY: LEARNING ABOUT YOUR PRODUCT AND USERS

Introduction

When working with a product team, your first objectives are to learn about the product and the users. It is key for you to ascertain as much as possible about the existing product in terms of its functionality, competitors, customers, etc. In addition, you need to assess what is currently understood about the users and begin to create user profiles. This information will enable you to choose appropriate user requirements activities so that you can ultimately improve your product. In this chapter we will detail how to collect product information from a variety of sources and how to make sense of the information readily available to you. We will also discuss how to create user profiles, personas, and scenarios, and how to use these as design tools. Finally, we present two excellent case studies. The first illustrates how to conduct a competitive analysis and the second details the successful use of personas.

At a Glance

> Learn about your product
> Learn about your users
> Pulling it all together

Learn About Your Product

Before you even begin working with a single user, you need to understand the domain you are working in. We cannot stress enough how important it is to do your homework before jumping into one of the **user requirements** activities described in this book. You may be extremely pressed for time and think you can learn the domain while you are collecting data from users. Big mistake! You will need to answer many questions for yourself. What are the key planned or available functions of the product? Who are the competitors? Are there any known issues with the product? Who are the product's perceived users? In addition to helping you collect effective requirements, this knowledge will also earn you necessary respect and trust from the product team (refer to Chapter 1, Introduction to User Requirements, "Become a Virtual Team Member" section, page 19).

Limiting your homework to speaking with the product team is often not enough. We hope that the product team you are working with is composed of experts in the domain and that they have done their homework as well. Unfortunately, this is not always the case. Particularly with new products, the product team is learning about the users and the domain at the same time you are. It is important to interview the product team and learn everything you can from them, but you must also supplement that information with data from other sources. In addition, the more you know about the product and domain, the more respect you get from the product team. You may never know as much as some of the product managers; however, there are always some fundamentals they will expect you to know or to pick up quickly. In the very beginning you can get away with being naive; but with time, **stakeholders** will expect you to understand what they are talking about.

In this chapter, you will read about a variety of sources that you can use to learn about the product you are dealing with, and your end users. Keep in mind that this section is not intended to tell you what to do *instead* of collecting user requirements. It is intended to tell you about some of the research you will want to conduct *before* you even consider running a user requirements activity. In addition, we have included two very enlightening case studies, one related to gaining a better understanding of your product, and the other to gaining a better understanding of your users. The first study is from Diamond Bullet Design and it discusses a competitive analysis that was done to compare online business school libraries. The second study is from Microsoft and it details the process of creating and using personas.

If you do not have a background in **usability**, you will need to be aware of some of the founding principles. You need to understand what questions can be answered by a usability activity and what questions should be answered by a design professional. We strongly recommend that you refer to Appendix A (page 678) to learn about usability resources available to you as well as Appendix B (page 688) for a list of usability training courses. If you require supplemental assistance, you can refer to Appendix D (page 698) for a list of usability consultants that can work with you.

Data are out there that can help you learn a lot about the product. In this section, we tell you how you can use log files, marketing, customers, and general research to help you become a domain expert. Regardless of whether this is a brand new product or a new release of an existing product, there is still a lot of existing information that can help you.

At a Glance

> Use your product
> Networking
> Customer support comments
> Log files
> Your marketing department
> Early adopter or partner feedback
> Competitors

Use Your Product

It may sound trite, but the best way to learn about your product is to use it (if it already exists). In the case of a travel website, you should search for a hotel and flight, make a reservation, cancel your reservation, ask for help. Stretch the product to its limits.

Networking

You are surrounded by people who know about your product and domain, you just have to get to know them. Start by finding out whether your company has a usability group (that is if you are not a part of such a group). Meet the people who support your product and read their usability reports. If you are unable to watch a live activity, ask to view tapes of previous activities for your product and related products. What previous usability issues were encountered? What user requirements have been documented so far?

You should also meet the content writers for the company. These are the folks who create the user manuals and online help (for websites and web applications). What is difficult to document – either because it is difficult to articulate or because the product is so complicated to explain?

If your company offers training courses, attend classes. Speak with the folks who teach the courses. What is hard to teach? What types of question are users asking? What tips (not documented) are the instructors offering?

Customer Support Comments

If you are working on a product that already has an existing version and your company has a Help Desk or Customer Support Group, you can learn a great deal about your product by visiting that department.

People rarely call or e-mail in compliments to tell a company how wonderful their product is, so those calls pertain to issues that you should become familiar with. If you can access logs of customer questions, problems, and complaints over time, you will see trends of difficulties users are encountering. Perhaps the user's manual or Help isn't helpful enough. Perhaps the product has a bug that wasn't captured during QA. Or perhaps users do not like or cannot figure out a "feature" the product team thought every user had to have. This can give you a sense of where you will need to focus your efforts to improve the product.

Users may not be able to accurately describe the problem they are having or may misdiagnose the cause. Likewise, customer support may not have experience with the product under consideration. Although this should never be the case, it often is. If the support staff are not very familiar with the product in question, they may also misdiagnose the cause of the customer's problem or may not capture the issue correctly. This means that, once you have a log of customer feedback, you may need to conduct interviews or field studies with users to get a full understanding of the issues.

Log Files

If you are responsible for the usability of a website, web server **log files** may provide an interesting perspective for you. When a file is retrieved from a website, server software keeps a record of it. The server stores this information in the form of text files.

The information contained in a log file varies but will typically include: the source of a request, the file requested, the date and time of the request, the content type and length of the transferred file, the referring page, the user's browser and platform, and error messages. Figure 2.1 shows a sample of a server log file.

Programs are available that can analyze log files and produce usability data. However, you will likely need to work with your organization's IT department to have useful information captured in your server log file in order to conduct usability analysis.

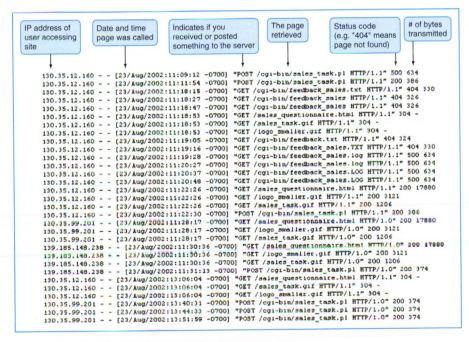

Figure 2.1:

Sample server log file

Information that can be captured includes:

- Unique ID for each visitor so you can see who is returning
- Click path (i.e., the pages users visit and the sequence in which they visit them)
- Time spent per page
- Where visitors leave the site (what page)
- Actions taken (e.g., purchases made, downloads completed, information viewed).

There are some issues or limitations that you should be aware of when interpreting the data you collect from log files.

- The log files often contain an **Internet Protocol** (IP) address temporarily assigned by an **Internet Service Provider** (ISP) or a corporate **proxy** server. This prevents unique identification of each user.
- Browser **caching** leaves gaps in the recorded **click stream**. If a page is cached, the log files do not record the second, third, or 100th time it is visited during the user's stay at your site. It also fails to capture the pages called when the Back browser button is used. Consequently, the last page recorded in the log file may not be the last page viewed if the user exited on a previously cached page. As a result, you cannot be sure what the "exit page" was for the user.
- Log files record when a request was made for a page but not when the transfer was completed. Also, if a user spends 30 minutes on a single page, you don't know why. Did the user walk away or look at another site or program, or was the user viewing the page the entire time?
- You cannot be sure whether the user completed his/her goal (i.e., purchasing, downloading, looking for information) if you don't know the user's goal. Perhaps the user wanted to buy three CDs but could find only one. Perhaps the user was looking for information and never found it.

You can work with your IT department to address each of these issues, but it takes time and knowledge of *what you need* versus *what can be captured*. External companies like WebTrends (www.netiq.com/webtrends/default.asp) can be hired to capture web usage data. These companies are a great source of basic usage data once you have a website running (e.g., number of hits per hour or per day, what page the user came from, how the user got here, time spent on the home page, number of excursions to other pages, time spent on each page, ads clicked on). They can collect data on almost any user action you want to keep track of.

Examining the time users spend per page is a more meaningful measure than the number of **hits** per page. When analyzing time data in a log file, it is best to use **median** rather than average times because the median is less susceptible to **outliers**.

In addition to capturing information about user motivation, you can learn about visitor profiles and activity from log files. However, it is best to study log files over a long period to discover data that compliments or spurs studies in greater depth. For example, you can identify areas of a site for further testing.

SUGGESTED RESOURCES FOR ADDITIONAL READING

The article below provides lots of helpful information about analyzing log file data, including working with your IT department to capture the information you need.

- Kantner, L. (2001). Accessing Web Site Usability from Server Log Files. In R. Branaghan (ed.), *Design by People for People: Essays on Usability*, pp. 245–261. Chicago: Usability Professionals' Association.

Fuller and de Graaff's (1996) carefully designed study details how you can deter-mine user motivation based on time data. This paper contains a great deal of detail about analyzing usability from server log files and we encourage you to review the paper if you are interested in learning more about user motivation and log files.

- Fuller, R. & de Graaff, J. J. (1996). Measuring User Motivation from Server Log Files. Available at: www.microsoft.com/usability/webconf/fuller/fuller.htm.

Below are two excellent websites that you can refer to when studying log files. They each contain a variety of articles that can answer every question regarding server log files.

- Usability.gov: server log analysis (http://usability.gov/serverlog/index.html) provides FAQs for analyzing server log file data, a list of helpful websites, and additional articles.
- http://webdesign.about.com/sitesearch.htm?terms=log%20 files&SUName= webdesign&TopNode=3042&type=1 provides a list of articles about using log files to analyze your website.

Your Marketing Department

Frequently, your company's marketing department will conduct focus groups or competitive analysis to determine the need for a product and how best to promote and place it. Although this information is meant to drive sales, it is an excellent source to learn about the product, as well as potential customers and competitors.

Unfortunately, you do not always learn a lot about end users. Marketing information should not be confused with user requirements. The data from the marketing department *can* reflect the end users' needs, but not always. Marketing collects information about the value and perceived worth of a product, whereas usability professionals collect information about how something is used and how the product's worth is realized.

Additionally, the information you collect from the marketing department is only part of the information needed when creating a user profile. It is often missing contextual information about circumstances and environment that can affect a user's decision to use and how to use your product. This is often the case for products that are to be used by corporations rather than an individual (e.g., Human Resources applications versus a website designed to sell books to the public). In the case of corporate products, the marketing department is typically interested in the business needs of the marketplace (i.e., companies that could be potential buyers) rather than the end users. Regardless, this information can be very helpful to you when you are starting out.

When you contact the marketing department, you may want to ask them questions such as:

- Where are you collecting your data?
- Who are our competitors?
- What is the profile of people you have spoken with, and how did you find them?
- What activities have you conducted (e.g., focus groups, surveys)?
- When is your next activity scheduled?
- Have you conducted a competitive analysis?
- What are the requirements you have collected?

Early Adopter or Partner Feedback

Frequently, companies will align themselves with a small number of customers in the early stages of development. These customers may play an active role in the design of the product and become partners in the process. They may implement early versions of the product on a small scale in their own companies. This relationship is beneficial to all parties. The customers get to help design the product to meet the needs of their own companies. On the other side, the product team gets early feedback and the company can ask for references when selling the product to others.

The feedback early adopters provide can be enlightening because the product can be implemented and used in a real-world setting (as opposed to testing in the lab). You can leverage these existing relationships to learn about the product space and some of the product's known issues. However, when you are ready to move on to the next stage and collect user requirements, be wary of basing all of your user requirements on the few existing customers. You should obtain user requirements from a variety of users (refer to "Learn About Your Users" section, page 41).

Competitors

You can learn a lot from your competitors. A competitive analysis can be an effective way to gain an advantage over your competitors. It is beneficial to conduct a competitive analysis when you are creating an entirely new product or simply entering a new product domain. It can also be a great strategy if your product is failing, but your competitor's product is thriving. It is wise to periodically check out your competition to see where you stand with the rest of the pack. Some companies have product analysts whose primary job is to keep tabs on the competitors and the market. Get to know this person and learn everything he or she knows. If the product does not have a product analyst, this is something that you can do.

Tip

When leveraging your competitor's successes, keep in mind copyright laws and intellectual property rights. If you are not sure where the line is between public domain and intellectual property, consult a lawyer or your company's legal department.

Do not limit yourself to direct competitors. You should also examine **surrogate products**. These products may or may not compete directly with your product but they have similar features to your product and should be studied to learn about your strengths and weaknesses. For example, if you are adding a shopping cart to your travel website, check out companies that have shopping carts, even if they don't compete with you (e.g., online book stores). Some people make the mistake of thinking their product or service is so innovative that no one else does it; therefore, they skip competitive analysis. No product is so revolutionary that there isn't someone out there to learn from.

Traditional competitive analysis focuses more on cost, buying trends, and advertising. A usability competitive analysis is more concerned with the user experience (user interface, features, user satisfaction, overall usability). The goals of both types of competitive analysis are to learn from your competitors and snag a strategic advantage. Below we will concentrate on conducting a usability competitive analysis.

To identify your competitors, speak with the product team, sales or marketing department, conduct a web search, read trade magazines, and conduct user surveys, interviews, or focus groups. Market analysts and researchers – such as CNet, ZDNet, Gartner, Anderson, Forrester, and IDC – can be a great way to collect information about your product's market space and competitors. These companies identify and analyze emerging trends in products and their impact on business.

Keep in mind primary competitors as well as secondary competitors. A secondary competitor can be a smaller company with a less threatening product offering, one having only a few features in common with your product, or one competing indirectly with your product. For example, the bricks and mortar travel agency does not compete directly with your online travel company but it is an alternative that should not be ignored.

Once you have identified your competitors, you should ascertain their:

- Strengths
- Weaknesses
- Customer base (profile of users, size of customer base, loyalty, etc.)
- Availability

- Functionality and unique features
- Reputation
- Requirements (hardware, software, etc.).

In gathering this information, it is extremely helpful to access some of the competitors' products. If a product can be bought off the shelf, or is an easily accessible website, this should not be a problem. However, some products or services are sold only directly to companies. Most major software companies state in their licensing agreement that you are not allowed to conduct competitive tests against their product. They also state that you cannot show the installation of the product (or the product in use) to a competitor company.

If you are able to evaluate the competitor product yourself, you should identify a set of core tasks with which to compare your product (if you have one at this stage) and the competitor's. This is particularly important if you plan to include functionality from the other product, because you may learn that a function doesn't work well. Take numerous screenshots or photos and record your interaction as you conduct the evaluation.

Whether or not you are able to access the product yourself, surveys (Chapter 8, page 312), interviews (Chapter 7, page 246), focus groups (Chapter 12, page 514), and wants and needs analyses (Chapter 9, page 370) will be valuable ways to learn about users' perceptions of the product. By conducting these kinds of activities with users of your competitor's products, you can learn about the strengths, weaknesses, and key features of these products. In a competitive analysis, the majority of your effort should be spent mining the competitor's product for ideas (e.g., functionality, user interface style, widgets, task structure, terminology).

There are a number of companies available to measure the usability or user satisfaction of a website (e.g., Vividence, Biz Rate, OpinionLab). They can do this for your site or for your competitor's site. These companies send actual or target customers to any website (i.e., yours or a competitor's) and then collect qualitative, quantitative, and behavioral data as users pursue actual tasks in a natural environment, such as their own homes and offices. Most companies allow clients to easily analyze both the quantitative and qualitative data gathered during an evaluation. This approach can be quite beneficial, but it is often expensive and requires that users can easily access the website. If the web-based product must be purchased or is behind a firewall, you will have to provide the users with access. In the case of a competitor that sells licensed software, this option is not possible.

As you conduct your competitive analysis, it is helpful to create a grid comparing your product against the competitor's (see Table 2.1). List the key features, design strengths and weaknesses, usability scores or issues . . . anything you can learn. Tracking this information over time will show you how your product compares and how the market may be changing.

Table 2.1:

Grid comparing TravelSmart.com against three competitors

	TravelSmart.com	TravelCrazy.com	WillTravel.com	Corner Travel Store
Unique features	• Client recommendations • Chat board	Customer loyalty program	Travel agent on call	Personalized service
Design strengths	• Short 3-step process • Shows price comparison	• Useful travel guides • Customer and expert ratings	• Shows price comparison • Travel alerts and recommendations	• Frequent customer program • Phone access or in person
Design weakness	• Must know 3-letter airport code • Customer support/Help is hidden	• Cluttered display with too many options • Confusing search UI	Search results are inconsistent and not reliable	No web access
Customer base	2500 users	500,000 users	150,000 users	Customer size unknown
Satisfaction score	68	72	Not available	Not applicable
Requirements	• Section 508 compliant • Accessible on all browser types	• Internet Explorer 5.5 only • Flash required	Accessible on all browser types	No require-ments
Core features:				
Research locations	✗	✗	✗	✓
Air travel	✓	✓	✓	✓
Rental car	✓	✓	✓	✓
Hotel reservations	✓	✗	✓	✓
Train tickets	✓	✓	✗	✓
Bus tickets	✗	✓	✗	✓
Travel packages	✓	✓	✓	✓

Learn About Your Users

At a Glance

> User profile
> Personas
> Scenarios

If you do not understand who your users (or potential users) are, your product is doomed to failure. The single most critical activity to developing a quality product is understanding who your users are and what they need, and documenting what you have learned. This begins by developing a **user profile** – a detailed description of your users' attributes (job title, experience, level of education, key tasks, age range, etc.). These characteristics will typically reflect a range, not a single attribute (e.g., ages 18–35). Your users should fall within those ranges. A user profile will help you understand who you are building your product for, and will help you when recruiting for future usability activities.

Once you have developed a thorough user profile, you can develop **personas** (exemplars of your end user) and **scenarios** (a day-in-the-life of your end user).

- Personas are designed to help keep specific users in focus during design discussions.
- Scenarios help you test your system and to build functionality into your product that users will actually want to use.

Table 2.2 compares these three types of user documents. You may have very little information to develop these initially – that is why you conduct user requirements activities. As you conduct user requirements activities, you will collect information to feed back into the user profiles, personas, and scenarios (see Figure 2.2). Figure 2.2 illustrates the relative time to spend at each stage of the cycle. Please note its iterative nature; you should always feed the results of requirements activities back into your initial understanding of your users. User profiles, personas, and scenarios are discussed in detail in the following sections.

Table 2.2:

Comparison of user profiles, personas, and scenarios

Document	Definition	Purpose	Content
User profile	Detailed description of your users' attributes	To ensure that you know who you are developing your product for, and who to recruit for usability activities	• Demographic data • Skills • Education • Occupation
Persona	A fictional individual created to describe the typical user based on the user profile	To represent a group of end users during design discussions, and keep everyone focused on the same target	• Identity and photo • Status • Goals and tasks • Skill set • Requirements and expectations • Relationships
Scenario	Story that describes how a particular persona completes a task or behaves in a given situation	To bring your users to life, test to see if your product meets the users needs, and develop artifacts for usability activities (e.g., tasks for usability tests, day-in-the-life videos for focus groups)	• Setting • Actors • Objectives or goals • Sequence of events • Result

Figure 2.2: *Illustration of the relative time to spend at each stage of the lifecycle. This is the ideal case with multiple iterations*

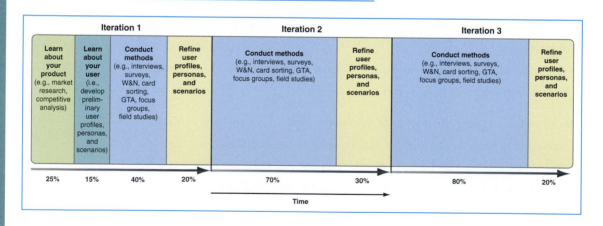

Keep in mind as you learn about your users that you should not focus on only the "best" or most experienced users. Someone who is considered an expert on a system may not be an expert on all parts of the system. It is much more likely that an individual will leverage only key areas of the product over and over while ignoring other parts. You should consider a range of users to ensure that your product works for at least 80% of your user population. However, it is not impracticable to target 90–95% of the population. If a consumer product has one million users and 2% of them call customer support for a usability problem that could have been identified via more research, you have just earned an additional 20,000 calls. If each call costs the company $6, preventing those 20,000 calls would save $120,000! As a final note, making a change to the product that enables only 80% of the users to use the new release, where 90% of the users could use it in the previous version, is a very bad thing. Guidelines like "80% use" are just that – guidelines. Other factors must be taken into consideration when deciding what the acceptable level of usability is for your product.

Step 1: User Profile

At a Glance

> Finding information to build your user profile
> Understanding the types of users
> Creating a user profile

The first step in understanding your users is to create a user profile.

Finding Information to Build Your User Profile

Before you can conduct a user requirements activity, you need users. It is vital to get the right users, otherwise the data you collect are not only worthless, they can actually harm your product, your credibility, and the credibility of usability activities. But who are your users? What are their goals?

You should begin by developing a user profile. This is a detailed description of your users' attributes (job title, experience, level of education, key tasks, age range, etc.).

For example, the typical users might be between 18 and 35 years of age, have job titles like "Travel Specialist," "Travel Agent," or "Travel Assistant," and work for travel agencies with fewer than 50 employees.

Creating a user profile is an iterative process. You will likely have some idea of who your users are at first, but this will probably not be detailed and may even be just a guess. But it is a place to start. The example above is just our first, best guess of who our travel agent user might be. You can capture the initial information to build your user profile from:

- Product managers
- Functional specifications
- Industry analysts
- Marketing studies
- Market analysts
- Customer support
- Competitive benchmarking and analysis
- Census bureau
- Surveys.

Once you have an initial stake in the ground, you can develop a phone screener and begin recruiting for your user requirements activity (refer to Chapter 5, Preparing for Your User Requirements Activity, "Recruiting Participants" section, page 156). As you conduct your activities and learn more about the end users, you should come back to the user profile and update it. Your first guess may have been slightly off center. At the very least it probably is not as detailed as it could be.

Understanding the Types of Users

You need to define what you mean by "user." Most people consider the individuals who will interact directly with the product as their users, but you may need to consider other individuals as well:

- The manager of your direct user
- The system administrator who configures the product for the direct user
- People who receive artifacts or information from the system
- People deciding whether they will purchase your software

- People who use competitors' products (you want to convert them to use your product).

Try to categorize your users into one of three categories: primary, secondary, and tertiary. **Primary users** are those individuals who work regularly or directly with the product. **Secondary users** will use the product infrequently or through an intermediary. **Tertiary users** are those who are affected by the system or the purchasing decision-makers. All of these individuals have an interest in the product. This does not mean that you have to conduct user requirements activities with the secondary and tertiary users, but you should at least know who they are. If the tertiary decision-makers do not purchase your product, the primary users will never use it. If the secondary system administrators cannot figure out how to customize and implement the product, the primary users will have a painful experience with it.

It is also important to realize that a single user may have several roles and sometimes these roles can have contradictory needs. For example, many online auction users are both buyers and sellers. Buyers want to pay the least they can while sellers want to get as much as they can, and a single auction site must support both these contradictory roles without harming either. Additionally, the product should behave similarly for both roles – users should not have to learn a different interaction model, navigation, terminology, etc. based on their role. Only the information presented and some of the functions available should be different.

Creating a User Profile

There are several characteristics you need to consider in order to develop a thorough user profile. We provide an *ideal* list of characteristics below, but you will likely not have access to all of this information. As you do further research and conduct additional user requirements activities, you will fill in these blanks, but you may never find the answers to some of the questions. Ideally, you should determine not only the typical or most frequent level for each of the characteristics, but also the range and the percentage of users who fall along that range. As a final note, some of the characteristics on page 46 are more important than others in regards to your product and situation. Prioritize the characteristics and spend the majority of resources capturing information on those key characteristics for your product. For example, if a human resources administrator enters in the wrong social security number into a financial application, you might not get paid. This is terrible, but if a medical professional enters in the wrong social security number in an electronic chart, you might get the wrong medication. This is much more serious so it is important to understand not only the tasks a user does but the consequences of a possible error. Figure 2.3 shows a sample user profile.

- *Demographic characteristics* – age, gender, location, socio-economic status
- *Occupation experience* – current job title, years at the company, years of experience at that position, responsibilities, previous jobs and job titles
- *Company information* – company size, industry
- *Education* – degree, major, courses taken
- *Computer experience* – computer skills, years of experience
- *Specific product experience* – experience with competitors' products or other domain-specific products, usage trends
- *Tasks* – primary tasks, secondary tasks
- *Domain knowledge* – the users' understanding of the product area
- *Technology available* – computer hardware (monitor size, computing speed, etc.), software, other tools typically used
- *Attitudes and values* – product preferences, fear of technology, etc.
- *Learning style* – visual learner, audio learner, etc.
- *Criticality of errors* – in general, the possible consequences of a user's error.

Figure 2.3: *Sample user profile for a travel agent*

Travel Agent (primary) Characteristic Ranges	
Age:	25–40 years (Average: 32 years)
Gender:	80% female
Job Titles:	Travel agent, Travel specialist, Travel associate
Experience Level:	0–10 years (Typical: 3 years)
Work Hours:	40 hours per week; days and times depend on the company
Education:	High school to Bachelors degree (Typical: some college)
Location:	Anywhere in the U.S. (Predominantly mid-west)
Income:	$25,000–$50,000/year; depends on experience level and location (Average: $35,000/year)
Technology:	Some computer experience; high speed internet connection
Disabilities:	No specific limitations
Family:	Single or married (Predominantly married with 1 child)

Once you determine the range of responses for each of the characteristics and the percentage of users along that range, you will want to categorize your users into groups based on their similarities. Some groupings you may use are:

- Age (child, young adult, adult, older, etc.)
- Experience (novice, expert)
- Attitudes (first adopters, technophobe)
- Primary task(s) (buyer, seller).

You can use an **affinity diagram** to organize the characteristics into groups (see Appendix F, page 714). The groups should be significantly different from each other in order to justify them as different user types. As with many things, this is more of an art than a science and there are rarely clearly marked boundaries that put every user in one group or another. Having multiple stakeholders take part in the affinity diagram exercise can help when creating these groups and also assures stakeholder buy-in from the very beginning (refer to Chapter 1, Introduction to User Requirements, "Getting Stakeholder Buy-in for Your Activity" section page 14).

Now that you have a handle on your user population, you can develop personas, scenarios, and a recruitment screener (refer to Chapter 5, Preparing for Your User Requirements Activity, "Recruiting Participants" section, page 156). As you collect user requirements over time, you can add the information into your personas and scenarios to make them more robust and realistic. Composing a persona or scenario may even point out areas where you need more information and help you identify user requirement activities you need to conduct.

Step 2: Personas

At a Glance

> Benefits of personas
> Things to be aware of when creating personas
> Creating a persona

*"According to my Zip Code, I prefer non-spicy foods, enjoy tennis more
than golf, subscribe to at least one news-oriented periodical, own between thirty and
thirty-five ties, never buy lemon-scented products, and have a power tool
in my basement, but none of that is true."*

Alan Cooper developed a method called "Goal-Directed Design" in which personas
are a key part. Personas were first introduced to the world in Cooper's 1999 book
The Inmates are Running the Asylum.

Benefits of Personas

Personas take a user profile and then fill in details to create a "typical" user. A
persona is simply a fictional individual created to describe a specific user. Since you
cannot possibly speak with every end user, you must create a model that can represent those end users.

There are many benefits to using personas. Because it can be difficult to feel connected to an abstract description of something, personas give your users life and
help team members feel connected to them. They also get everyone on the same
page by encouraging all team members to think about the same persona, instead of
each individual working towards his or her own vision of who the end user is. Trying

to build a product for the generic "user" is like trying to hit a moving target. Without a specific target to focus on, "the user" can change from the expert to the novice to your grandmother, all in the midst of a single conversation. Designing for a small set of personas will assure greater success of hitting that target. A persona can be used in meetings as a discussion tool (e.g., "Mary would never use that feature"), in cognitive walkthroughs, **storyboarding**, role-playing, and other usability activities. Finally, personas can also help new team members quickly learn who the end user is. You should create at least one persona per user type (e.g., one for the travel agent, one for the travel customer).

Things To Be Aware of When Creating Personas

You may want to develop multiple personas for each user type. This will help you cover the range of characteristics for each user type. For example, if one of your user types is a "novice travel agent," you may want to create multiple "novice" personas: one at a small company, one at a large company, one who received formal training, one who was self-taught, etc. By limiting your vision to just one persona, you may end up filtering out valuable data from end users who do not match that one profile. For example, if we did not create a persona for the self-taught travel agent, team members might assume all travel agents receive formal training and make all their design decisions based on that fact. Having multiple personas for each user type will prevent people from building the product around a single user and help develop a product that works for all of your users. However, you should keep the set of personas manageable. It is a balancing act. If you have too many personas to represent one user type, they will simply blur together in everyone's mind and diminish their benefits. You want your personas to be memorable. Three primary personas is a common recommendation.

You must also make sure that the personas you devise are specific to the product or feature you are developing. As we mentioned above, not all users use all parts of a product or system; therefore, it is unrealistic to assume that the same persona will work for all parts of your product. In the second case study at the end of the chapter, the authors warn about the dangers of persona reuse.

As a final note, we want to stress that personas should never replace conducting usability activities with your end users. Personas should be based on the data from usability activities. In most cases you cannot have users present with you all the time, so personas act as placeholders in cases where you cannot speak with your end users. They allow the users' voice to be heard even when they are not physically present. Of course you should still conduct user requirements activities wherever possible.

Creating a Persona

There are several components to a persona. You can add as much detail to each of these areas as you have, but you may not be able to fill in all areas at first. The details will come from the information in your user profile. Just as developing a user profile is an iterative process, so is persona development. As you conduct user requirements activities, you should take what you learn to validate and beef up your personas. When creating a persona, it should be fictional but describe attributes from real users. Provide details and maintain authenticity. The list below is an idealized list – you may not have all the information below. Fill in what you can.

- *Identity.* Give this user a first and last name. Provide an age and other demographic information that would be representative of the user profile. Include a picture as well. If you have a face to go with the name, the persona is more realistic and easier to associate with.
- *Status.* Is this a primary, secondary, tertiary, or **anti-user** of your system?
- *Goals.* What are this user's goals? Do not limit yourself to goals related to your specific product.
- *Skill set.* What is the background and expertise of your user? This includes education, training, and specialized skills. Again, do not limit yourself to details related to your specific product.
- *Tasks.* What are the basic or critical tasks the user conducts? What is the frequency, importance, and duration of those tasks? More detailed task information is included in scenarios (see below).
- *Relationships.* Understanding with whom the user associates is important. Including relationships in the persona keeps you thinking about secondary and tertiary stakeholders.
- *Requirements.* What does your user need? Including quotes will really drive those needs home.

- *Expectations.* How does the user think the product works? How does the user organize the information in his or her domain/job?
- *Photograph.* Include a photo in your persona to put a human face to your end user.

Just as there are several types of user profiles, there are several types of personas: primary, secondary, tertiary, and the anti-users (or **negative users**). The primary, secondary, and tertiary users have been described. An anti-user is one who would not buy or use your product in any way. You want to keep this persona in mind to warn you when you are getting off track. For example, if you are designing a product for an expert user but find more and more instruction text, tutorials, and help dialogs creeping into the product, you should check your anti-user persona (a novice user in need of a "walk up and use" product) to see whether this product would now work for him/her. If so, you are on the wrong track. You want to be sure that you are designing for the primary user while considering the secondary and tertiary users. You should be aware of the anti-users but do not design for them. Figure 2.4 shows a persona for a travel agent.

Name:	Alexandra Davis
Age:	32
Job:	Travel agent at TravelSmart.com for the last three years
Work hours:	8 am to 7 pm (Mon–Sat)
Education:	B.A. Literature
Location:	Denver, Colorado
Income:	$45,000/yr
Technology:	PC, 1024 × 768 monitor, T1 line
Disabilities:	Wears contacts
Family:	Married with 8-year-old twin daughters
Hobbies:	Plan trips with her family
Goals:	Double her productivity every year. Travel to every continent at least once by age 35.

Alexandra is a self-described "Workaholic" which makes it difficult for her to find time to spend with her family. However, she "wouldn't give any of it up for the world!" She has been married to Ryan for the last seven years and he is a stay-at-home dad.

Figure 2.4: Sample persona for a travel agent. © Getty Images. Reprinted with permission

Continued

Figure 2.4 – *Cont'd*

She loves the perks she gets working for TravelSmart.com. She is able to travel all over the world with her family at a substantially reduced rate. This is very important to her and she wouldn't work those kinds of hours without such perks.

Alexandra began working as a travel agent right after college. She has used every system out there and is amazed at how difficult they are to use. Speed is the name of the game. "Clients don't want to sit on the phone and listen to typing for five minutes while I look up all the available five-star hotels in Barbados. I need that information with few keystrokes and all on one screen. Don't make me page through screen after screen to see the rates for all the hotels."

Alexandra loves helping clients design their dream vacation! She helps to take care of all of their travel needs – including choosing destinations, booking airfares, arranging car rentals, booking hotels, and arranging tickets for attractions. Clients often send Alexandra postcards and pictures from their destinations because they are so grateful for all her help. She appreciates the fact the TravelSmart.com offers clients the opportunity to do it all themselves or to seek out the help of a professional. She feels that travel agents are sorely under-appreciated. "Of course people can make travel reservations on any website today. There are tons of them out there and they all offer pretty much the same deals. But if you don't know anything about your destination, you could easily pick a bad hotel because their advertising literature is out of date, or you could pay too much because you don't know what to ask for. Travel agents do so much more than book flights!"

Step 3: Scenarios

At a Glance

> Benefits of a scenario
> Things to be aware of when creating scenarios
> Creating scenarios

Scenarios, often referred to as "use cases," are stories about the personas you have just created. A good scenario begins with a persona and then adds more detail based on your user requirements activities. The story describes how a particular persona completes a task or behaves in a given situation. It provides a setting, has actors, objectives or goals, a sequence of events, and closes with a result.

Benefits of a Scenario

Scenarios are another way to bring your users to life during product development. They can be used to test a system during early evaluation. Is this a system that meets your users' needs? Does it satisfy the goals and fit in the user's workflow? You can also use scenarios to create "day-in-the-life" videos. These are useful artifacts for focus groups (refer to Chapter 12, page 514).

Things To Be Aware of When Creating Scenarios

Scenario development can be time-consuming. It is not necessary to create a library of scenarios that cover every conceivable task or situation the end users might encounter. Focus on developing scenarios for the primary tasks users will encounter, and then, if there is time, move to secondary tasks. Never let user profiles, personas, or scenarios replace usability activities with actual users. You need data from real users to build your product and to keep your profiles, personas, and scenarios fresh. People change over time. Their needs, expectations, desires, and skills are not permanent – so your scenarios shouldn't be either.

Creating Scenarios

Scenarios normally include descriptions about:

- The individual user (i.e., the persona)
- The task or situation
- The user's desired outcome/goal for that task
- Procedure and task flow information
- A time interval
- Envisioned features/functionality the user will need/use.

You may also want to include exceptions. What are some of the rare events that happen? (Remember, frequency does not equate to importance!) By understanding the extreme or infrequent situations users encounter, you may identify situations where your product would be obsolete or even problematic. You could also identify key features that would benefit your end users.

Using the list of tasks in the user profile and/or persona, choose the critical tasks and begin creating scenarios with your stakeholders. In one scenario, describe the ideal way the persona might complete a given task. In another scenario, describe a problem (or problems) the persona might encounter while completing this task and how the persona would react. Continue building a set of scenarios for each of your personas until you feel you have covered the functionality of your product and the tasks/situations users encounter. As with user profiles and personas, you should use the information from user requirements activities to validate your scenarios and add more information to them.

Scenarios should not describe individual widgets. For example, you should avoid things like "... and then Mary selected her preferred hotel from the droplist" or "Mary scrolled to the bottom of the page and clicked the 'Submit' button." Instead, you should describe the basic actions, like "Mary selected her preferred airline" or "Mary submitted the information." Below is an example of a very simple scenario:

Sally needs to plan a vacation for her family. She decides to hop on Travel-Smart.com and do both the research and reservations there. She begins by researching the top family-friendly destinations as recommended by TravelSmart.com customers. She wants to compare the travel time, travel costs, hotel costs, hotel availability, and amusement activities for each destination. For each of those criteria, Sally gave a weighting to help her make her decision. She finally settled on the destination that required the least travel time, cheapest travel costs, moderate hotel costs, good availability, and a large selection of activities for the whole family. From that spot, Sally begins searching for the flights and hotels that meet her criteria. She decides to save those results for later because she wants to be sure the whole family is in agreement before she makes the reservations with her credit card.

Tip

The topic of your scenario is your foundation to build upon. The topic should not be so broad that it results in a 32-page scenario. Similarly, it should not be so focused that it represents only a small percentage of users or tasks. It will likely take several iterations before you get it right. Work with your team members to make sure the set of topics for your scenarios are clear and represent the majority of users and tasks/situations.

Scenarios can be more sophisticated depending on the information you have collected. Often they will start out small – based on the information you were able to collect initially – and then expand to give more detail as you gather data from user requirements activities.

One scenario proponent suggests there are five types of scenario components (McInerney 2003). To help you cover a large portion of the users, tasks, functionality, and situations, make sure that your set of scenarios covers these five components. All of the scenario elements we listed above (e.g., the individual, task, desired outcome, envisioned features) will still be included in the scenarios, but also make sure that your set of scenarios includes the five components or topics below:

1. *Process lifecycle.* Take a large-scale process and break it down into several steps. Each step should be represented by a different scenario. Using our travel example, the process might be booking a vacation. The steps (and therefore, individual scenarios) might be Research Locations, Create Itinerary, Book Plane Ticket.

2. *Audience segments.* Your scenarios should examine the different user types (or audience) and their experiences, goals, skills, patterns of use, etc. Using our travel example, scenarios might include "Travel agent booking vacation for client," and "Traveler booking his/her own vacation."

3. *Product functions.* A product may have very different features/functions that support different, unrelated tasks. Your set of scenarios should cover the range of features/functions your product supports. Scenarios for a travel website may focus on "Viewing recommendations," and "Creating a personal profile."

4. *Variants of a class of task situation.* A single task (or goal) may be accomplished by different means. Ideally, the set of scenarios should examine those variants for each task. If your task is Book Plane Ticket, some scenarios might include "Buy a ticket for a full flight" or "Buy a ticket with Frequent Flyer Miles."

5. *Methods for performing a task.* This scenario component is similar to *Product functions* above. A single task is selected and alternate features/functions/ methods for accomplishing that task are examined. If the task is Book Plane Ticket, the scenarios might include "Book ticket on the web," "Book ticket with travel agent," or "Book ticket over phone with airline."

Each individual scenario does not have to include all five components, but the set of scenarios for a persona should. In other words, do not select one type of topic and ignore the other four. One partial set of scenarios might be as set out in Figure 2.5 – this would result in six separate scenarios. When you are first creating your user profile you may be able to develop only a simple scenario, but with further research it should expand into more detailed scenarios.

Figure 2.5: *A partial set of six scenarios*

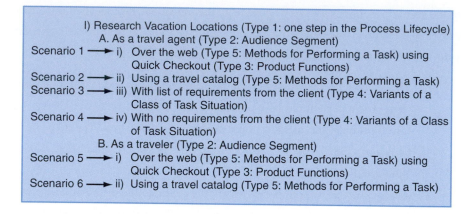

To make scenarios more consistent between each other and more complete, a template is recommended for each scenario. One possible template is provided below (McInerney 2003). The sections include:

- *Title.* This provides a general description of the situation. Avoid being too specific or character driven. For example, "Sally needs to research locations for a family vacation" should be worded instead "Research vacation locations."

- *Situation/task.* In a paragraph or two, describe the initial situation, the challenge facing the user, and the user's goal. Do not discuss how the user will accomplish his/her goal yet – that is covered next.

- *Method to address the situation.* Either in a bullet list or a task flow diagram, describe how the users cope with the situation. There are many ways in which the user could accomplish a given task. The task flow should show the different possibilities in about 5 to 15 steps. This section should be generic and technology neutral (don't include specific design elements). The specific technology is discussed next.

- *Execution path.* In a narrative form, describe how the task is completed and the user's goal is reached. Now you can discuss specific features or technology used. You will likely have multiple "Execution path" sections – one for each possible way of accomplishing the task shown in the "Method to address the situation" step above. Alternatively, you may want to illustrate how different designs would accomplish each task. This section should be updated as design decisions are made. The other parts of the scenario will remain relatively unchanged over time.

Figure 2.6 is a detailed scenario using the template described above.

Title: Traveler researches a vacation

Situation: Sally needs to plan a vacation for her family. She doesn't know where they can afford to go or where the family might have the best time.

Method to address the situation:

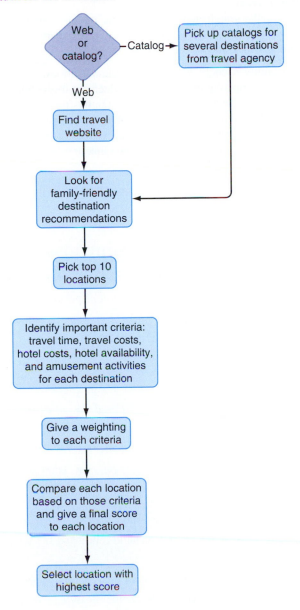

Figure 2.6: *Portion of a detailed scenario using the template proposed by McInerney (2003)*

Continued

Figure 2.6 – *Cont'd*

Execution path:

Step 1: Web or catalog?
Sally has never researched travel online before, but she has some computer experience and decided to save money by doing the research herself.

Step 2: Find travel website.
Sally goes on a popular search engine and types in "travel." She receives a flood of results but the featured website caught her eye: TravelSmart.com. She liked the brief description provided and decided to check it out.

Step 3: Look for family-friendly destination recommendations.
On the front page, the top 10 hot spots were provided but those didn't seem very family-friendly. Sally typed into the search box, "family-friendly destinations." The results provided a link to several pages on the site, including "Tips for parents traveling with children," and "Things to look for in a family-friendly hotel." She continued looking through the results and found a link to a chat board discussion on family-friendly destinations.

<Note: This scenario would continue until all steps were described.....>

SUGGESTED RESOURCES FOR ADDITIONAL READING

Check out Chapter 9 of *The Inmates are Running the Asylum* and Chapter 5 of Cooper and Reimann's book for a deeper discussion of personas:

- Cooper, A. (1999). *The Inmates are Running the Asylum*. Indianapolis, IN: Sams.
- Cooper, A. & Reimann, R. (2003). *About Face 2.0: The Essentials of Interaction Design*, 2nd ed. New York: John Wiley & Sons.

To learn more about scenarios and their role in design, check out the following:

- Carroll, J. M. (2000). *Making Use: Scenario-based Design of Human-Computer Interactions*. Cambridge, MA: MIT Press.
- Rosson, M. B. & Carroll, J. M. (2002). *Usability Engineering: Scenario-based Development of Human-Computer Interaction*. San Francisco, CA: Morgan Kaufmann.

We described above the five scenario topics and a scenario template you may want to consider. To learn more about the five scenario topics and the template, see the paper below:

- McInerney, P. (2003). Getting More from UCD Scenarios. Paper for IBM MITE. Can be found at http://www-306.ibm.com/ibm/easy/eou_ext.nsf/Publish/50? OpenDocument&../Publish/1111/$File/paper1111.pdf.

Pulling It All Together

In this chapter, we have covered various sources you can turn to in order to learn more about your product domain and end users. Doing your homework is critical to the success of your product! It provides a solid foundation from which to build your future usability activities and can save you a great deal of time and money further down the road.

CASE STUDY A

Derren Hermann and Tom Brinck of Diamond Bullet Design share with us their recent experience of conducting a competitive analysis to inform their redesign of a business school library website. They walk us through the process of identifying websites for the analysis, how they evaluated the sites and used that information for their redesign. They also pass on their valuable lessons learned.

Competitive Intelligence: Mining Design Concepts from Business School Libraries

Derren Hermann and Tom Brinck, Diamond Bullet Design (www.diamondbullet.com)

The Problem

The Michigan Business School, along with our design firm Diamond Bullet, had recently completed a major redesign of the school's central website (Brinck et al. 2003), and at the school the Kresge Business Administration Library was ready for a significant upgrade to their site to accomplish these goals:

- Integrate the design with the newly redesigned business school website
- Make information and resources easier to find
- Achieve a design that reflects the best of practice in online library services.

The Kresge website consisted of approximately 140 pages (Figure 2.7). The site's primary function was to enable people to select and access over 70 online databases. These databases can be searched for articles, books, journals, corporate information, stock information, and a wide variety of other topics. In addition, the library site provides details on the library's hours, services and policies, access to reference assistance, School

Figure 2.7:

The Michigan Business School wished to update this older version of the Kresge Library website. The current site can be viewed at www.bus.umich.edu/ KresgeLibrary

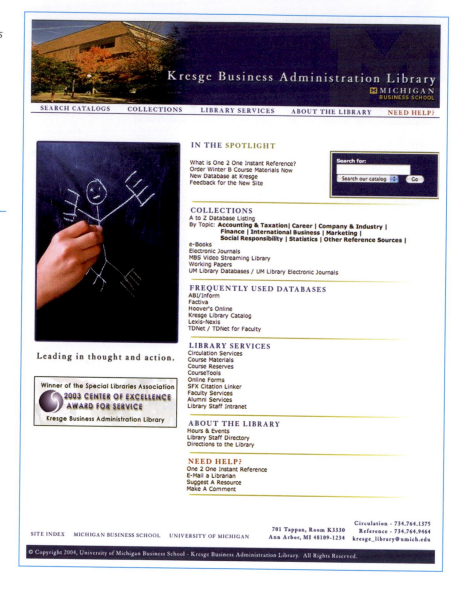

publications, and course materials. The site's most frequent users are business school students, faculty, library staff, and the school staff. Additional user groups include alumni, the broader university community, and the general public.

With a large number of heterogeneous resources available, there was a significant concern that people doing research were not able to locate the most effective resource and were often unaware that given resources even existed. As a first step, the library conducted a survey of site users with 376 respondents. The survey indicated what resources were most desired and what people liked and disliked from the site. However, a survey doesn't effectively provide *specific* solutions to improve the site.

Our Approach

While we – as a consulting firm hired to design and develop the primary school website – were quite familiar with the business school as a whole, the library domain itself was rich, complex, and specialized. Understanding the wide range of searchable databases provided on the library site was a challenge that immediately suggested reviewing other library websites to see what organizational options had been explored. In addition, we spent considerable time with library staff to understand the types and organization of the information they provide.

Analysis of the competition proved to be an excellent shortcut that quickly provided a range of viable design solutions: organizational schemes, labeling, layout, functionality, and content. This enabled us to avoid spending time on exploring ineffective approaches in the design space.

Our goal in performing any competitive analysis is to identify features and design ideas from related products to create a new product that is demonstrably better, and which is more considered and complete than it might have been because we have examined the design thinking behind other products currently in use. A broad outline of our approach to this project was the following:

- Identify the competitors
- Inventory and rate each competitor
- Derive design recommendations
- Expand the competitor list
- Revisit competitors throughout the design process.

The primary competitive review took approximately 40 hours, but it was further elaborated and revisited throughout the design process as we discovered detailed areas of interest.

Before the competitive analysis had even begun, we set the groundwork by establishing our target audiences, short typical usage scenarios, and a list of high-priority tasks the site would need to support. After a quick review of the competitors we had identified, we identified evaluation criteria and then visited each competitor. On each competitor's site, we stepped through the pages of the site, seeking their approaches to supporting users in the principal tasks and gathering evidence to support a high or low rating on each of our criteria. In the process, we collected a set of observations about what constituted an effective solution and built up a set of recommendations based on those observations.

Identifying Competitors

Kresge staff provided an initial list of five competitors that exhibited characteristics they found desirable. We then added five more that represented the libraries of other well-known business schools. After our primary analysis we found a large online index of business school library sites around the world (*www.lib.berkeley.edu/BUSI/businessLibs.html*). Using this list, we opened windows onto *every* listed site and did a cursory review of each, saving a few standouts for deeper analysis. Few of these sites are really considered "competitors," for the simple reason that many of these institutions work collaboratively or target different audiences. The choice of comparison sites was really to find any that had useful ideas to draw from. The ten primary sites we reviewed for our analysis were:

- MIT Libraries
  libraries.mit.edu
- Northwestern University Library
  www.library.northwestern.edu
- UCLA Library
  www.library.ucla.edu
- Vanderbilt Walker Management Library
  www.mba.vanderbilt.edu/walker
- Harvard Baker Library
  www.library.hbs.edu
- Stanford Jackson Library
  wesley.stanford.edu/library
- Lippincott Library at Wharton (Penn)
  www.library.upenn.edu/lippincott
- Columbia Business & Economics Library
  www.columbia.edu/cu/lweb/indiv/business
- Duke University Ford Library at Fuqua School of Business
  www.lib.duke.edu/fsb/index.htm

- Thomas J. Long Business & Economics Library – UC Berkeley
  www.lib.berkeley.edu/BUSI.

An additional international site we located later that was helpful was Macquarie University Library, at *www.lib.mq.edu.au.*

Evaluation Criteria

We defined a set of evaluation criteria that would help us establish the best of practice elements for online library services (Table 2.3).

Criteria	Definition	Examples
Site features	Items promoted on site, usually on home page	Featured news, quick links, online chat
Items of note	Unique and innovative elements or issues with the site	Missing meta tags, audience-oriented approach, unusual layout
Top-level navigation	The main navigation of the site at the top 1–2 levels	About Us, Services, Research Materials, Help
Utility links	Links common to all pages of the site, usually at bottom of pages	Site map or index, Contact Us, Policies
External links	Links to other websites within the university	University home page, other campus libraries

Table 2.3:
Evaluation criteria applied to business school library websites

One of our main areas of focus was the organization and presentation of each library's electronic resources (the searchable databases). We broke down our analysis of this section into the following subsections:

- *Categorization* – the organizational scheme of resources including labeling and grouping
- *Types of resources* – the various resource types, like journals or electronic books, offered by a library
- *Subjects* – the topics used to categorize resources
- *Individual entries* – the descriptive fields, like title and access notes, attached to an individual resource entry
- *Features* – additional features worthy of note associated with the presentation and organization of resources.

Furthermore, we evaluated each site within the following areas according to a rating scale ranging from 1 to 5 (poor to excellent):

- *Aesthetic appeal* – overall visual organization, balance, color scheme, contrast, imagery, and design identity
- *Layout* – consistency, organization, balance, visual hierarchy, and use of space
- *Navigation* – consistency, labeling, organization, presentation, and functionality
- *Utility features* – quantity and quality
- *Site features* – quantity, quality, uniqueness, and presentation
- *Help/Instruction* – quantity of help options, embedded help options, display, organization, quality, and presentation
- *Electronic resource presentation* – organization, presentation, labeling, browsing, and searching options
- *Usability and accessibility* – how effectively and efficiently a person can utilize the site in order to meet his or her needs regardless of their abilities.

Below is a summary of observations we made of the other business libraries to illustrate the types of issues we looked at and ideas those sites generated. These observations provide a sense of conventions and design solutions used on library sites. In the requirements phase, the features that are observed are used to suggest features that may be requirements for our own design. In addition, the lack of features suggests valuable opportunities for distinguishing our own design solution. At later points in the design, specific design approaches suggest common design solutions, organizational schemes, and terminology to use. The benchmarks provide a qualitative way to assess whether proposed feature sets and designs would compare favorably against competitors.

Our Observations

The most common features that we found on the home pages of the sites evaluated included a prominently displayed news or featured items section, quick links (drop-down menus of shortcuts), online chat with a librarian, and the library's contact information.

Usability and Accessibility

The majority of the sites showed little attention to web usability and accessibility issues. For example, only six of the ten sites included alternate text for images, and none of the sites provided back-up functionality for JavaScript in case a user has their scripting turned off in their browser preferences. Other items lacking from the majority of the sites included missing meta tags (hidden meta data that provides keywords and descriptions of each page – a surprise to us that library websites would lack this type of markup), and a lack of breadcrumb links (which indicate a page's position within the overall website).

Navigation Categories

Almost all of the sites reviewed included an audience-oriented approach to organization, clearly indicating the resources and services that are available to each of their audiences (e.g., faculty, students, alumni). The most common top-level navigation items included *Services*, *Resources*, *Help*, and *About Us*. Other common options were *Catalogs*, *Course Information*, *Career Information*, and a *News* or *Featured Items* section.

Categorization of Online Databases/Electronic Resources

Library websites typically contain anywhere from a couple dozen searchable databases to well over one hundred. These databases, often called "Electronic Resources," allow people to search library catalogs, journal articles, corporate financial data, and a wide variety of other data from an extremely diverse group of information providers, each with unique searching interfaces.

The categorization schemes for the databases were quite similar for each site. All sites included the alphabetical A through Z listing of resources. The other most common approaches included organization by resource type (e.g., books versus journals) and by subject. Interestingly, fewer than half of the sites evaluated included the ability to search the databases by keyword. Only one site, MIT, allowed users to search for databases by provider.

A variety of resource types were used to categorize electronic resources. While ideally it is the decision of the library staff to determine the level of specification in their classification system, articles, journals, and newspaper articles were the most common resource type categorizations. Others of note included electronic books, statistical sources, biographical sources, dictionaries and thesauri, directories, encyclopedias, government, market research, reference sources, research guides, search engines, and working papers.

While some of the library sites in this analysis covered more than business-related areas, only subjects broadly related to business were analyzed. The most common business subjects included economics, psychology, management, law, finance, marketing, and social sciences.

Each individual entry listing for an electronic resource includes descriptive information to help users determine whether it is the resource to meet their needs. The more extensive the information, the better equipped users are to make an informed decision. All of the sites included the title, URL, a description, and access information with each entry. (Owing to the heterogeneity of these resources, many have different access privileges, serving different subsets of the user population.) Other common fields included the dates of coverage, help and research guides, the type of resource or format, the resource provider or publisher, related subjects, and the frequency of publication.

Ratings

Sites were rated on a scale of 1 to 5, where 1 represented "poor" and 5 represented "excellent" (Table 2.4 on page 67). With eight categories, the highest total possible score was 40. These scores were subjectively determined by a single evaluator (one of the present authors). For our purposes, a qualitative rating was sufficient to clarify that some sites substantially differentiated themselves from others, and this table helped guide the writing of recommendations by helping to emphasize which sites we could revisit to refine our ideas on a particular design issue or find a good example to emulate.

The Individual Libraries

Below we discuss the results for each school's website.

MIT

The MIT Libraries' website received the highest ratings of all for its clear, simple, and easy-to-use approach. There are no extraneous elements to clutter the pages. The focus is on presenting information in a clear and consistent manner that allows for targeted searches as well as browsing. The site nicely categorizes the different research resources (Figure 2.8 on page 68 shows an organization of databases by type or format of the resource) and provides a variety of help options, explaining for instance how to conduct research online and all other means of getting help, through face-to-face assistance, phone, e-mail, chat, and so forth (Figure 2.9 on page 68). Furthermore, the site is organized in a manner that allows for a variety of information-seeking preferences and approaches.

Table 2.4: *Ratings assigned to each library's website, according to several design criteria*

	MIT	Northwestern	UCLA	Vanderbilt	Harvard	Stanford	Penn	Columbia	Duke	UC Berkley
Aesthetic appeal	5	3	3	2	3	2	2	2	2	1
Pages layout	5	3	3	2	3	2	3	3	3	2
Site navigation	4	3	3	3	2	3	3	3	2	2
Utility features	5	3	2	1	2	2	4	4	1	2
Site features	3	3	3	2	4	3	3	2	4	3
Help and instruction	5	4	4	2	3	2	4	4	3	3
Resources presentation	4	4	4	2	4	3	4	4	3	3
Usability & accessibility	4	2	3	2	2	2	2	3	2	3
Total score	35	25	25	16	23	19	25	23	20	19

Figure 2.8:

MIT "Search Our Collections" section

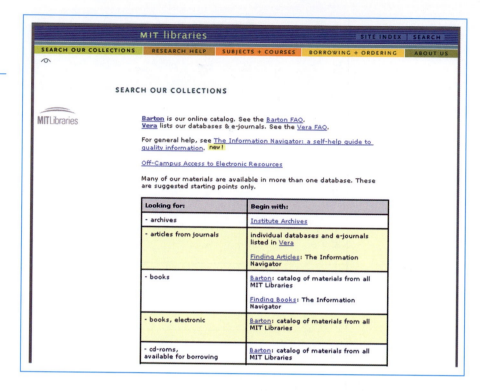

Figure 2.9:

MIT "Research Help" section

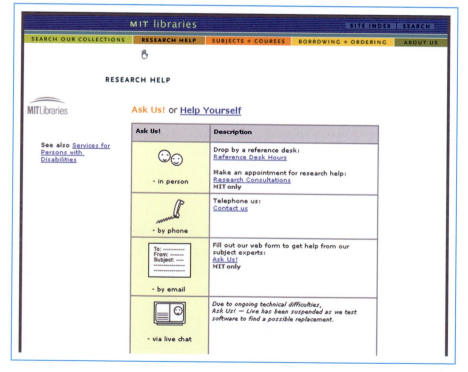

Northwestern

The Northwestern, UCLA, and Penn websites all include excellent presentation of their electronic resources and excellent help instruction. Northwestern allows browsing electronic sources by type, field of study, and/or title along with plenty of explanatory text (Figure 2.10). The site also includes a well-organized help section.

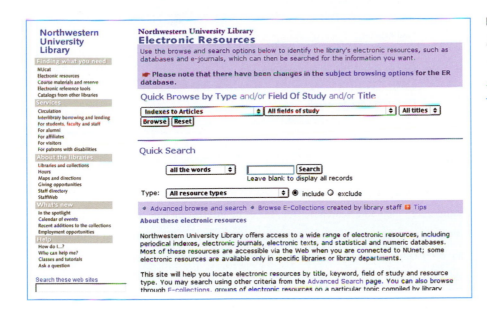

Figure 2.10:

Northwestern's "Electronic Resources" section

UCLA

UCLA Library offers electronic resources organized by online materials, books, articles, research guides by subject area, and help with research. Furthermore, they include embedded help icons with each section that include a wealth of useful information (Figure 2.11).

Their interface of multiple drop-down menus seems to be potentially confusing, but it suggests an alternative we might not have otherwise considered that manages the complexity of a large number of options. In this spirit, competitive analysis is primarily an idea-generation exercise – we don't necessarily conclude that the competitors have designed a "good" or "correct" interface, and our own design cannot be assumed to be well designed just because it imitates another. Competitive analysis does not remove the need for evaluating and refining our own designs, preferably through user testing and related techniques.

Figure 2.11:

UCLA Library "Resources Search" selections (with embedded help)

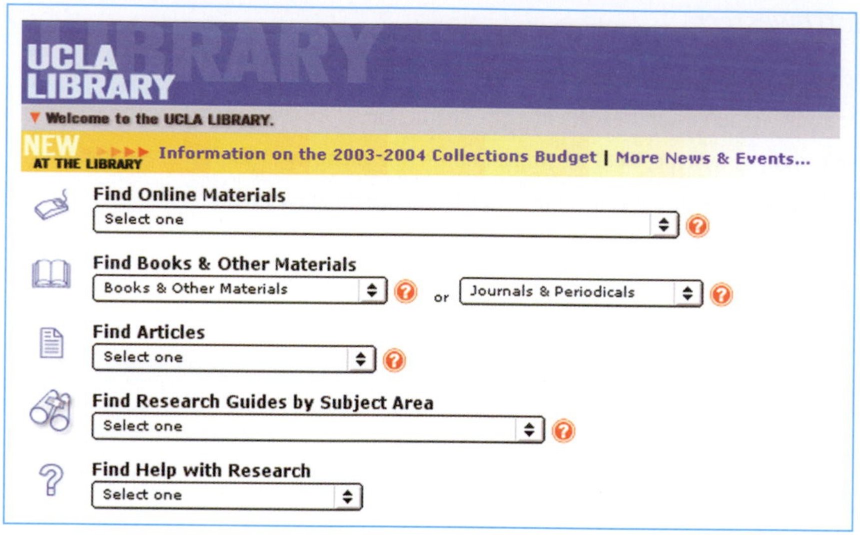

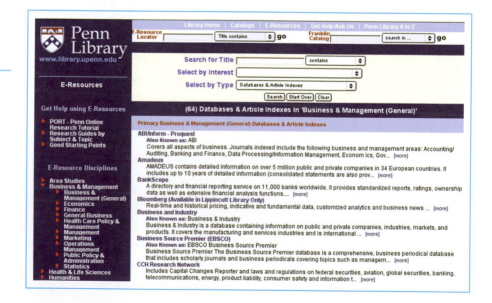

Penn

The Penn Library site offers a variety of search and browse options for electronic sources (Figure 2.12), including search by title, select by interest or type, browse by alphabetical listing, browse by area of discipline, search e-resources, and search the catalogs. Plus, they offer help sections for using their e-resources: an online research tutorial, research guides by subject and topic, and instruction on good starting points.

Figure 2.12:

Penn Library e-resources section

The Penn site provides abstracts for each resource that include the ability to view more information about the resource – including other names for the resource, the URL for the resource, who is allowed to use the resource, a description of the resource, and topics or subjects to which the resource is relevant (Figure 2.13).

This detailed list of specific information features is one of the most valuable aspects to a competitive analysis, as it ensures a more complete consideration of possible information we can provide for our own users. While we may not duplicate all the components of a

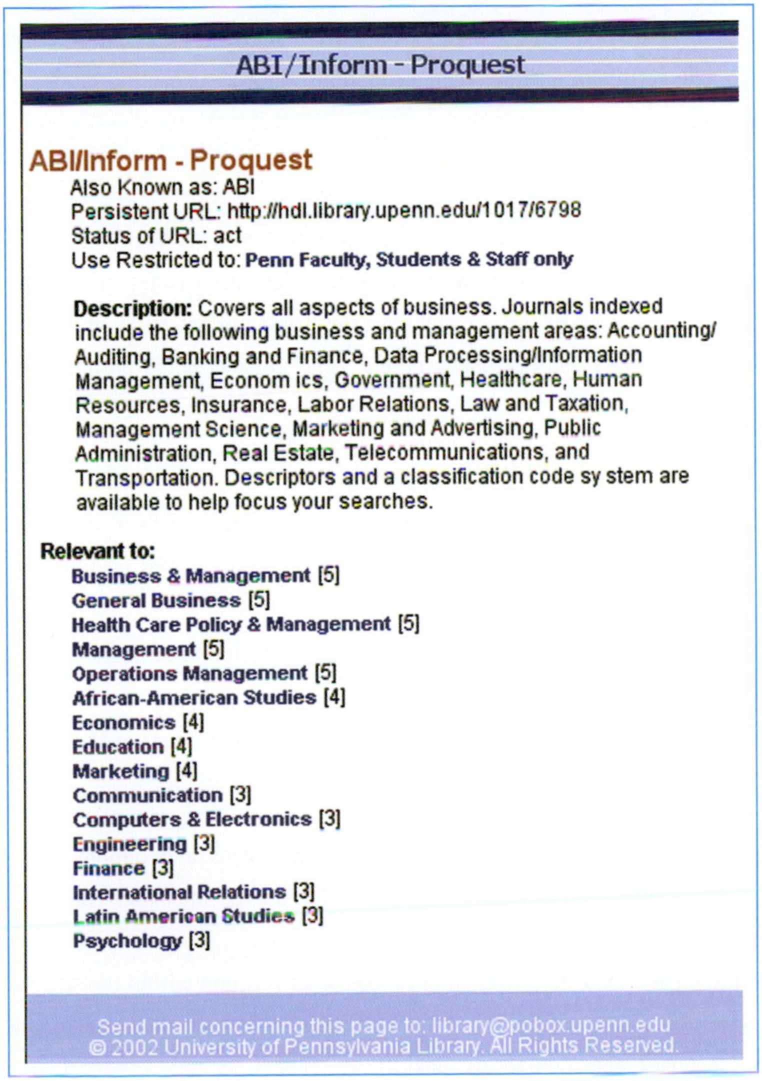

ABI/Inform - Proquest

ABI/Inform - Proquest

Also Known as: ABI
Persistent URL: http://hdl.library.upenn.edu/1017/6798
Status of URL: act
Use Restricted to: **Penn Faculty, Students & Staff only**

Description: Covers all aspects of business. Journals indexed include the following business and management areas: Accounting/ Auditing, Banking and Finance, Data Processing/Information Management, Econom ics, Government, Healthcare, Human Resources, Insurance, Labor Relations, Law and Taxation, Management Science, Marketing and Advertising, Public Administration, Real Estate, Telecommunications, and Transportation. Descriptors and a classification code sy stem are available to help focus your searches.

Relevant to:
Business & Management [5]
General Business [5]
Health Care Policy & Management [5]
Management [5]
Operations Management [5]
African-American Studies [4]
Economics [4]
Education [4]
Marketing [4]
Communication [3]
Computers & Electronics [3]
Engineering [3]
Finance [3]
International Relations [3]
Latin American Studies [3]
Psychology [3]

Send mail concerning this page to: library@pobox.upenn.edu
© 2002 University of Pennsylvania Library. All Rights Reserved.

Figure 2.13: *Penn Library detailed resource information*

competitor's product, by creating an inventory of all possibilities, we can prioritize and select the ones appropriate to us.

Design Recommendations

The results of this analysis provided a variety of recommendations for the Kresge Library website. These are some highlights of those recommendations, based on observations like those listed above. Note that these are *not* meant to be *absolute requirements*. These recommendations are grounded in analysis of the possibilities of the information structure, examination of common practices, and a qualitative consideration of their benefits for the target audience. We followed this competitive analysis with user interviews and testing to help corroborate these recommendations and to explore the rationale behind uncertain ones.

General Site Features

- Prominently display the latest news highlights on the home page.
- Include a quick-links drop-down menu to the most used pages or sections of the website on all pages of the site and limit the list of options to 15 at most.
- Include the library address, phone number, and possibly hours on all pages of the site.

Usability and Accessibility

- Follow web accessibility standards and guidelines, at least the Section 508 standards (*www.section508.gov*), to meet the needs of disabled users. This includes the proper implementation of alternate text for images.
- Provide alternate functionality for when users have scripting turned off so that drop-down menus will still function properly.
- Include keyword and description meta tags for the major pages of the site.

Navigation

- Include audience-oriented sections covering the needs and options available to students, faculty and staff, alumni, the University of Michigan community, and campus visitors.
- Include breadcrumbs to provide a better sense of location within the site for users.
- Provide utility links at the bottom of each page of the site – including site index, help, feedback, and "Contact us" links.

- Provide links to the University of Michigan, the Business School, and the main campus library below the utility links on all pages of the site.

Electronic Resources

- Categorize databases (electronic resources) by type, topic/subject, and alphabetical ordering. Include more extensive information about each resource, including usage privilege restrictions.
- Use at least the following *category fields* to organize electronic resources: alphabetical, resource type, relevant subjects, and keywords for searching capabilities.
- Use at least the following *resource type fields* to organize electronic resources: articles, journals, electronic books, newspaper articles, and other types identified by library staff.
- Use at least the following *subject fields* to organize electronic resources: economics, management, marketing, finance, company profiles, law, company financials, industry research, and statistics.
- Use at least the following *individual entry field descriptors* to organize electronic resources: access privileges, dates and coverage, help and/or guides, types or formats, provider or publisher, relevant subjects, and frequency of publication.
- Include a drop-down menu of the most popular database resources on either the home page of the site or the entry page to electronic resources section of the site and limit the list to 15 at the most.

Note that these recommendations are derived from a variety of aspects of our evaluation. The "general site features" reflect a set of common practices observed online. The "usability" and "navigation" recommendations are grounded in strengths and weaknesses we observed on other sites. Finally, our approach of doing an inventory of other sites was particularly informative in the structure of the online databases/electronic resources, where we can list suggested fields to structure the information.

Lessons Learned

This competitive analysis provided essential information to the design task. Our clients at the library were enthusiastic in reading the analysis. Even beyond the scope of the current site redesign, this analysis provided a snapshot of what was going on in their industry that gave insight toward longer-term strategies.

One of the lessons we learned from this particular analysis was to be more systematic at the very beginning of the process in reviewing *all* of the competitors. Choosing examples from the top 10 business schools was effective at finding sites that were generally better than average; but when we found a comprehensive list of all the competitors and reviewed them, we identified some additional ones with very useful ideas. These were added to our recommendations but did not receive a thorough review due to time limitations.

We also want to address some common confusions about competitive analysis. While the approach outlined here can be combined with a more traditional business analysis of competitors' financial and market positions, we have a *very* different focus on identifying detailed design characteristics. Our approach applies to many kinds of product design, but it is particularly appropriate in the complex domain of software and website design where design options are intricate and not always obvious.

In addition, this approach of *mining design ideas* is distinct from techniques of competitive user-testing, where benchmarks are established in user-testing to determine whether your design is better or worse than competitors'. Competitive user-testing is a useful extension of our qualitative ratings, and helps predict whether your product will be well-received in the market; but user-testing a competitor's product primarily provides information about the flaws in a competitor's product, which is far less useful in design iteration than testing your own product. We find that in the early stages of design, a more economical and insightful approach is to analyze and inventory the competitor's product, as described here, to establish requirements and set a design direction for your own product.

Reference

Brinck, T., Ha, S., Pritula, N., Lock, K., Speredelozzi, A. & Monan, M. (2003). Making an iMpact: Redesigning a Business School Website around Performance Metrics. In *DUX 2003, Designing User Experiences*, San Francisco, CA, June, pp. 1–15.

CASE STUDY B

A team from Microsoft provides us with a superb case study of how they have used personas with great success for a very large project with a vast number of users. They describe their approach to developing personas and how they are used throughout the company. They also share with us the benefits and risks they have discovered when using personas.

Personas: A Case Study by Microsoft Corporation

John Pruitt, Trish Miner, Tracey Lovejoy, Robert Graf, Tjeerd Hoek, & Shanen Boettcher, Microsoft Corporation

This case study describes our approach and experience with personas, an interaction design technique introduced by Alan Cooper's 1999 book, *The Inmates are Running the Asylum*. In over three years of use, we have extended Cooper's technique to make personas a powerful complement to other usability and product design methods. We have used personas on a wide range of projects from small to large. This case study focuses on the latter in an attempt to illustrate how far the method can be taken, given adequate resources and attention. We don't propose that what we describe is the best or most appropriate use of personas; it is simply a description of what we did and how it affected our development team and the product we were working on. The main goal of this effort was to help the development team identify and understand its target audience; aiding in design and development decisions.

The Challenge

Microsoft Corporation released the first version of the Windows® operating system for desktop computers in November of 1985, and since that time, several additional versions have been released. The product development team for Windows platform development is now working on the next version of Microsoft® Windows®, code name "Longhorn."

Developing a new version of the operating system is a multi-year, complex, and expensive effort. For example, the Windows® 2000 operating system took three and a half years to develop at an estimated cost of $2 billion. While there are over 6000 people in our product division, the actual number of people actively working on a particular release changes greatly over time. The process starts with several hundred members and grows to several thousand at the peak of the effort, which of course, happens across multiple years during the development cycle. Like those in most software companies in the industry, the development team is comprised of many disciplines and job roles – developers, quality assurance testers, program managers, designers, technical writers, product planners, user researchers, user assistance specialists, marketing professionals, and countless others.

Our Approach to Personas

There are three main points from the above description that are important to our persona effort. Our development cycle is quite long, so maintaining long-term focus on a clear target is important. Our team is very large, and thus, getting everyone moving down the same path is difficult. As our team changes over time, there is a regular need for new people to become educated on the product goals and target audience in an effective way.

Not surprisingly, when asked who they are building our product for, and why, many members of the product team would say something like "We're building it for everyone – the new version will have the latest technology that runs better and faster." Also, while they may not have consciously thought about it, members of the product team tend to have a "typical" user or set of users in mind while doing product design. A major goal of the personas effort for the Longhorn release is to have every team member designing for the same explicit and focused set of target users, rather than trying to design for everyone, or designing for the variety of individual users they tend to think about.

Historically, our product team had regularly included market research, traditional usability and user-centered design techniques as part of its product definition and development activities. Though personas and other representations of users had not been used broadly on our team, other product teams at our company had been using them for several years. Thus, by the time we began our team's personas effort, the persona methodology used around Microsoft had matured significantly. Several previous persona efforts had suffered from four basic problems:

- The characters were not believable; either they were obviously designed by committee (not based on data) or, if data were used to define them, the relationship to the data was not clear. This led to a certain lack of use by some product team members, and even total objection to the method outright.

- The characters were not communicated well. Often the main communication method was a resumé-like document – blown up to poster size and posted around the hallways – that was not easily understood or remembered. The result here was that most people on the product team didn't know much about the personas. Thus there was really no sense of shared understanding or language.

- There were no explicit uses of the personas beyond discussion in design meetings. In particular, there was typically nothing that spoke to all disciplines or was applicable during all stages of the development cycle. As a result, many people on the team, including those that understood the personas and wanted to use them, were not able to deeply utilize them in their work efforts.

- Persona projects were often grass-roots efforts with little or no high-level support (such as people resources for creating and promoting personas, budget for posters or other materials to make the personas visible, or a mandate from team leaders to use the personas). Thus, in many cases, persona use was limited to a select few and typically died out over time.

The personas method used in our current development cycle was evolved specifically to address these problems. And fortunately, because of the persona "buzz" around the industry, the general notion had become more familiar and fairly well accepted by the development team. In fact, the executives and leaders of the development team asked us to investigate the possibility of creating personas rather than our having to convince the team that personas would be useful.

Our Experience in Creating and Using Personas

The team for our persona creation and validation effort consisted of roughly 22 people – several technical writers, several usability engineers, four product planners, and two market researchers – and took about three months. After our personas were created, the ensuing persona campaign involved the part-time efforts of several usability engineers, ethnographers, graphic designers, and product planners, and the campaign is ongoing at the time of writing this case study (roughly two and a half years). A high-level description of our process and activities follows.

However, before moving on, it is important to note that not every persona effort needs to involve so many people over such a long period. We believe that you can go deep or go cheap. That is, you can benefit from these methods even if you do not have the ability to spend many resources and much time on generating them. Obviously the deeper you go, the more articulate and valuable your knowledge of your users will become. And of course, you don't need the personas method to gain this kind of knowledge, but the method does help make it happen.

To create the personas, we divided the 22-person team into sub-teams so that each persona to be created would have two or more dedicated people to do the work. Based on the advice of other persona "practitioners," we wanted to keep the set of characters down to a manageable number – roughly six personas – which meant that we knowingly left out segments to help drive priorities and focus. Also, we were given the directive from our executive staff that we must address three broad customer sets: consumers, large enterprises, and a new, growing market for us, small businesses. Related to these three broad customer sets, our market research team had previously executed several large-sample, quantitative market segmentation analyses. One in particular was our customer taxonomy 2000 – well-known and regularly referred to by our product planners, market researchers, and executive staff. Such analyses typically provide cohesive, differentiable and identifiable groups of users (i.e., segments) with common characteristics: common demographics, attitudes, behaviors, etc. In each of our three major markets, we chose two or three of the most important segments to be developed into personas. The relative importance of the various segments was determined by market size, historical revenue, influence, and strategic or competitive placement. With these segments as a starting point, the bulk of our persona creation effort during the following two to three months focused on collecting, consuming, and filtering data from other previously executed user research. This body of research included field studies, focus groups, surveys, interviews, and other market research from both internal and external sources.

Because our personas effort drew on many research studies, we divvied up the research documents for consumption, with each team member becoming well acquainted with only a few studies. We then held "affinity" sessions where we physically cut out data points and interesting/relevant facts from the results documents and pinned them to a wall to form groups of related findings across studies. The resulting groups of findings were used in writing narratives that attempted to "tell the story of the data." As we wrote the personas' stories, we used qualitative data and observational anecdotes wherever possible. We also strived to support each and every detail in our personas explicitly with user data.

Although we did not create a set of international personas, we included international market information in each of our personas by having field reps in each market review our personas, highlighting key differences.

We created a single "foundation" document for each persona which was used as a storehouse for information about that persona (key attributes, photos, relevant data points, reference materials, etc.). More specifically, the foundation document contained goals, fears, and typical activities that would motivate and justify scenarios that were soon to appear in feature specs, vision documents, story boards, and so forth. (See Figure 2.14 for the standard table of contents of a foundation document.) Links between persona characteristics and the supporting data were made explicit in the foundation documents using the "Comment" feature in Microsoft® Word. Thus, these documents contained copious

Overview – Patrick Blakeman (the consultant)
  Get to know Patrick, his business and family.
A Day in the Life
  Follow Patrick through a typical day.
Work Activities
  Look at Patrick's job description and role at work.
Household and Leisure Activities
  Get information about what Patrick does when he's not at work.
Goals, Fears, and Aspirations
  Understand the concerns Patrick has about his life, career, and business.
Computer Skills, Knowledge, and Abilities
  Learn about Patrick's computer experience.
Market Size Influence
  Understand the impact people like Patrick have on our business.
Demographic Attributes
  Read key demographic information about Patrick and his family.
Technology Attributes
  Get a sense of what Patrick does with technology.
Technology Attitudes
  Review Patrick's perspective on technology, past and future.
Communicating
  Learn how Patrick keeps in touch with people
International Considerations
  Find out what Patrick is like outside the U.S.
Quotes
  Hear what Patrick has to say.
References
  See source materials for this document.

Figure 2.14:

Table of contents for an example foundation document

footnotes, comments on specific data, and links to research reports that support and explain the personas' characteristics.

In the last month of the three-month development phase, and once the basic persona descriptions were written, we set up "reality check" field studies with participants who matched the personas on high-level characteristics to see how well they matched on low-level characteristics. We did this because our creation method utilized multiple data sources, many of which were not directly comparable or inherently compatible. We wanted to make sure that through this process we didn't inadvertently match characteristics that were either incompatible or not representative. As it turned out, our personas descriptions were largely on track, though we did do a small amount of rewriting where it seemed appropriate. (We discuss these site visits a bit more later.)

At this point, our persona descriptions had become stable and we were getting close to the point of sharing them broadly with our team. Up to this point, we had been using stock photos to put a face on each persona. Other persona efforts at our company had avoided stock photo galleries because they typically offer only one or two shots of a given model. Also, many of the images in stock photo galleries were simply "too professional"; the people looked like models, not like typical customers. So, we recruited a few local people to serve as models and held one- to two-hour photo shoots to get visual material to illustrate and communicate each persona.

Once the basic persona documents and materials were in place, we organized multiple kick-off meetings to introduce the personas to the team at large. These meetings not only included descriptions of the personas, but also introduced the basic persona method and provided details about how different roles on the team could use them. (We discuss more on this latter part shortly.) From that point, communicating our personas took the form of a multifaceted, multimodal, and ongoing campaign. Of course, the foundation documents described earlier were made readily available to anyone on the team who wished to review them, but they were not considered the primary means for delivering information. Instead, we created many variations of posters, flyers, and handouts spread out over many months and years. We even created a few gimmicky (and popular) promotional items (e.g., squeeze toys, beer glasses, magnetic whiteboards) – all sprinkled with persona images and information.

It is important to note here that the use of costly media is not critical to the success of the communication campaign. Our own materials ranged in quality and cost depending on the availability of resources at the time that we were producing them. For example, some of our posters were merely nicely formatted Word documents printed on tabloid-size paper. The more important aspect of the persona campaign was that the information in the personas was communicated in "consumable" chunks that suited the people being communicated to. Not surprisingly, e-mail and intranets are heavily used at our company. To capitalize on this, we started an ongoing "persona fact of the week" e-mail campaign; where details about the personas were slowly but regularly revealed and reinforced. As a quirky promotional gimmick, each persona got a real e-mail address which we used occasionally to send "thank you" notes to the development team from specific personas as certain features were being developed. We created an internal website to host the foundation documents and provide links to supporting research, related customer data, and scenarios – as well as links to a host of tools for using the personas (screening material for recruiting usability test participants, spreadsheet tools, comparison charts, posters and photos, etc.). The top-level pages of the website featured high-level summaries of the personas – the information we felt was most important for all team members to know – instead of simply linking to the foundation documents. All persona illustrations and handout materials included the URL to the persona website to enable team members to access the detailed supporting documentation (including the foundation documents).

Figure 2.15 shows two basic persona posters created to enhance the team's general understanding of our personas. The first one allows for the comparison of important characteristics across four of the personas. The second one communicates the fact that our personas are based on real people. It attempts to provide a sense of the essence of one of the personas by providing quotations from real users who are similar to that persona. (Some of the poster images presented here are intentionally blurred to hide proprietary information.) Figure 2.16 shows a poster that provided information about how customers think about security and privacy; also using real quotes from real people who fit our various persona profiles.

As mentioned earlier, we instruct our team in specific persona use and try to provide tools to help when possible. Cooper describes persona use mostly as a discussion tool – asking

Figure 2.15:

Two persona posters: one comparing characteristics across personas; the other presenting real quotations from users that fit the profile of one of our personas

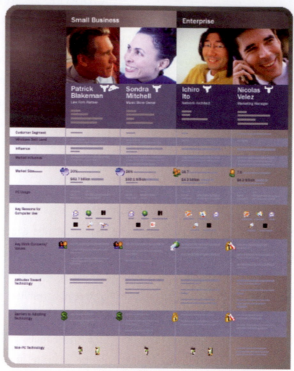

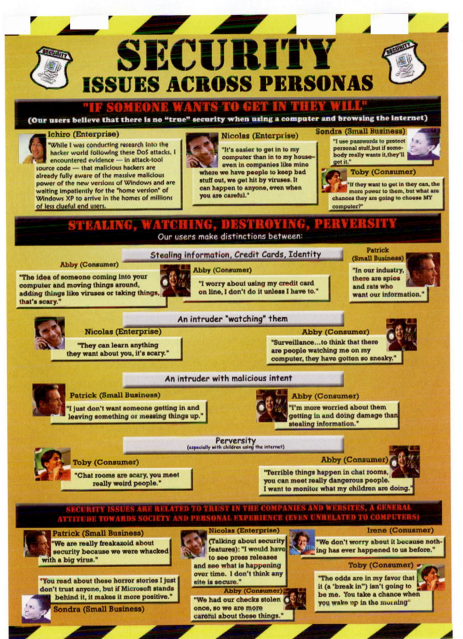

Figure 2.16:

A more targeted poster communicating aspects of security and privacy across our personas

questions of your personas, such as "Would Patrick use this feature?" This is valuable, but we have generated some additional persona-oriented activities and incorporated them into specific development processes. We created a few spreadsheet tools (discussed below) and document templates for clearer and consistent persona utilization. We have strongly encouraged our product team to utilize the personas as they write vision documents, create storyboards, and generate feature specification documents. In doing so, they have typically written short scenarios that extended the personas by extrapolating from their basic characteristics (e.g., "walk-through" scenarios that illustrate how a certain feature would be used). It is interesting to note that our persona foundation documents do not contain all, or even most, of these feature scenarios. There are literally hundreds of feature specification documents that get created over time (several months to several years) by a wide variety of team members. Each feature specification document might contain as many as 15 scenarios (though most contain only three or four). Thus, over time, some growing portion of the persona information exists outside of their core definitions (i.e., outside of the "foundation" documents). Because of this, we collected persona scenarios from across the product team in a spreadsheet that enabled us to track and "police" the use of the personas. We did this by combing through each of the feature specification documents and manually pasting the scenarios into a spreadsheet. With simple filters and pivots on this spreadsheet, we were able to roughly gauge the direction of a product as it is developed (e.g., How many scenarios are written for Toby vs. Abby? Are all of the Abby scenarios appropriate to Abby's core persona?).

We use a spreadsheet tool that we call the "feature–persona weighted priority matrix" that can help our team prioritize proposed features for the product. Figure 2.17 shows an

Figure 2.17:

A feature–persona weighted priority matrix

	Persona 1	**Persona 2**	**Persona 3**	
Weight:	50	35	15	**Weighted sum**
Feature 1	0	1	2	65
Feature 2	2	1	1	150
Feature 3	−1	1	0	−15
Feature 4	1	1	1	100
Etc.	–	–	–	–

abstract version of a feature–persona weighted priority matrix. Such a matrix can be executed in a rigorous fashion or somewhat casually. Of course, the more rigor that is applied, the more you can trust the outcome.

There are three steps in creating such a matrix. First, weights are given to each persona that represent how important each persona is to your product. For our product, these weights were derived from measures of market size, and historical and projected revenues. Next, the planned features of the product are scored. In the example, the scoring in the feature rows is as follows:

- Minus 1 – the persona is confused, annoyed, or in some way harmed by the feature
- Zero – the persona doesn't care about the feature one way or the other
- Plus 1 – the feature provides some value to the persona
- Plus 2 – the persona loves this feature or the feature does something wonderful for the persona even if the person doesn't realize it.

Ideally, these scores are derived from user research (e.g., focus groups or surveys) in which your proposed features are shown to participants and measures of appeal etc. are taken. In our particular case, the scoring was done by a committee of people on our team that had thorough knowledge of the personas and supporting data as well as a good understanding of the proposed features. In such a case, though, care must be taken so that such scores are not full of personal bias and misunderstanding.

Finally, a weighted sum is calculated. In the example, the weighted sum of feature 1 is calculated as follows: $(0 \times 50) + (1 \times 35) + (2 \times 15)$. Once completed, the rows (i.e., the features) are then sorted according to the weighted sum showing which features are most important for the team to develop. Our team then used the results to determine which features we would pursue and which features should be dropped – or at least reconsidered. In the example, it is clear that features 2 and 4 should be made a high priority for the development team, while feature 3 should probably be dropped.

It is stressed to the team that this tool is not "golden," it is a guide; exceptions can and should be made, when appropriate for strategic or business reasons. That is, meeting end-user needs is not the only thing that makes a product or business successful. Our team needs to be aware of cost, time to market, competitive products, key influential people (e.g., a well-known product reviewer), and any other factors that influence the purchase and adoption of our products. So, these factors can all be included in the exception-making process. The point here is that the inclusion or exclusion of features is much more explicit and understandable to the broader team.

Our design teams have made use of the personas also as inspiration for visual design by doing creative visual explorations based on the personas. More specifically, they have created branding and style collages by cutting and pasting images that "feel like" our personas from a variety of magazines onto poster boards (see Figure 2.18). They then used these boards to create a variety of visual treatments for several feature areas of the product (see Figure 2.19). These explorations were then used in focus groups to aid in understanding what aspects of the designs were appealing to users and how they worked together to form the visual style.

We wanted our personas to have value beyond feature definition and design; to extend their value into the feature development phase. To do this we needed to create screeners that would allow us to identify and recruit real people who matched the personas and bring them into the development process via user-centered design methods like focus groups, participatory design sessions, advisory panels, user research surveys, usability lab evaluations, etc.

As discussed earlier in this case study, the first user research we conducted with real representatives consisted of site visits for the purpose of doing a "reality check" of our understanding of each persona. Our first attempt at recruiting these representatives made it evident that the screener criteria needed to be carefully selected to identify only the most important characteristics that clearly defined a persona and discriminated between different personas. Any additional nonessential criteria had the potential to dramatically reduce the number of qualified respondents.

For example, we planned to do five home visits to meet, interview, and observe Abby-Toby pairs – two of our personas that represent a mother and a son. On the surface the criteria seemed simple enough: we were looking for a woman with at least two years of college, 40–50 years old, and with a son aged 14–16 years. Additionally, the mom and son needed to self-rate their PC experience within predefined ranges and have an Internet-connected PC in the household. Recruiting proved very difficult; surprisingly, we couldn't find one such household after making nearly 50 calls.

Further investigation revealed that there was a multiplicative effect of the percentage representation of the specific criteria within the general population. A quick check of the

Figure 2.18:

A persona-focused style collage

Figure 2.19:

A design exploration based on the style collage in Figure 2.18

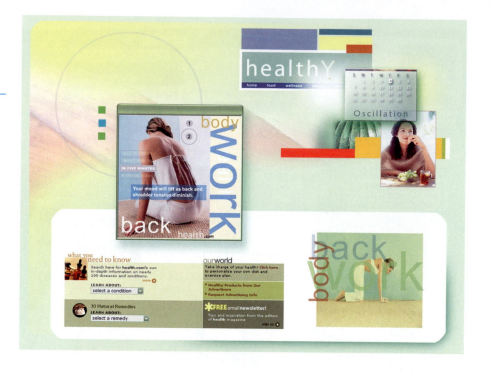

census bureau's age data showed that women from 40–49 years of age comprise 15% of the population and males from 15–19 (a four-year age span) comprise 7.5%. Since we were looking for a three-year span we reduced the percentage by three-fourths, estimating the percentage at 5.6%. The probability of finding a household that met both of these simple criteria was estimated by multiplying 15% and 5.6%, which yielded a probability 0.0084 (approximately 8 hits in 1000).

Realizing that writing effective and useful screeners would not be an easy task, we conducted several meetings with stakeholders from around the team to identify and agree upon the minimum essential defining criteria for each persona. Our goal was to identify the largest possible pool of candidates from which to recruit. We reduced the Abby screener to six criteria, removed the gender, age, and educational requirements, and used a response scale to make the requirements softer and more flexible.

Some teams needed additional criteria to meet the needs of their feature domain. For example, though not particularly core to the Abby persona, it made sense to recruit only those "Abby"s with an interest in home networks to conduct usability studies on home networking products. We allowed optional refinements to be added to the persona screeners to accommodate this need. However, the core criteria had to be met first. The home-networking "Abby"s had to be a proper subset of all "Abby"s.

After agreeing upon the criteria for all six personas, we created a spreadsheet to help our recruiters identify usability participants by asking the minimum number of questions. We did this to avoid the need to ask all screener questions on all phone calls. The spreadsheet implemented a branching flow chart we created to show the shortest route for identifying any given persona. Since personas were mutually exclusive, we were able to skip large portions of questions that would be irrelevant for any given branch.

We used these screeners for our next major user research activity. We used an outside agency to recruit and manage an online panel of over 6000 persona representatives. We created the panel to conduct quick turn-around quantitative research with a large population of persona representatives. We would send surveys every two weeks to one or more of these personas.

During the recruiting process, the outside agency reported that three of our screeners were excessively restrictive. One screener was qualifying less than 1% of potential candidates. They also reported question-by-question qualification percentages, so we could focus on the most problematic questions. We reconvened meetings with the appropriate stakeholders to review and relax the criteria by eliminating questions or by allowing a wider range of answers on the response scales. The agency had recorded all responses and could automatically recompute the effect of these modifications without having to resubmit the questions to the panel. Eventually, we got all qualifications rates between 8% and 27%. The modified screeners that resulted from this research became the new standard for other user research activities.

Though it is clear that creating participant recruiting screeners was a much more difficult task than we had assumed, the results proved to be well worth the effort. Not only were we able to recruit participants who were similar to our personas for ongoing usability, ethnographic, and market research; we were also able to categorize, analyze, and report our findings by persona. This served as a tremendously effective means of communicating the essence of personas and the value of usability research for the development team at large. Seeing real examples of our personas in the usability lab or in the field had an amazing effect on participating team members. Also, based on the findings of our various research endeavors, we have continued to enrich our persona definitions with new information.

Finally, other disciplines within our team have used the personas to a lesser extent to fill their need for user definition. For example, our quality assurance test team has used the personas to organize "bug bashes" as well as to select and refine scenarios for their automated testing. Similarly, one of our technical writing groups used the personas to plan and write "how to" and reference books for the popular press. In doing so, they expanded the persona definitions based on their own research endeavors to include notions of learning style, book usage patterns, and so forth, to enrich how they wrote for the specific audiences.

Lessons Learned

Our experience has identified several benefits and risks associated with persona use, as explained below.

Benefits of Personas

It is clear to us that personas can create a strong focus on users and their work contexts. Though we have not tried to rigorously measure the impact of our personas, there are several indications that the method has had an impact.

- First, the development team and executives have generally perceived the personas and their effect on the product as useful and positive. As a result, we have seen the persona approach go from scattered use in the company to widespread adoption. We have also had partner teams building related but different products, adopting and adapting our personas in an effort to enhance cross-team collaboration, synergy, and communication.

- Second, our personas are actually being used in the design and development process. A wide range of team members, both inside and outside of our product team – from line-level developers and designers to company executives – know about, design for, and discuss the next version of our product in terms of the personas. Our personas are seen everywhere and are used broadly. For example, they are seen in feature specs, vision documents, storyboards, demo-ware, design discussions, and "bug bashes." They are used even by VPs arguing for user concerns in product strategy meetings.

- Third, our team appears to know who our target audience is. Prior to the personas, asking team members about our target audience generally resulted in a different answer from every person asked.

- Fourth, the personas have generally raised awareness of user-centered design. That is, not only have our development teams engaged with personas, but correspondingly they have engaged with our other user-centered activities. Our persona campaign generated a momentum that increased general user focus and awareness.

The act of creating personas has helped us make our assumptions about the target audience more explicit. Once created, the personas have helped make our decision-making criteria for the product equally explicit – Why are we building this feature? Why are we building it like this? Without personas, our development teams routinely made decisions about features and implementation without recognizing or communicating their underlying assumptions about who would use the product and how it would be used. The "feature–persona weighted priority matrix" described earlier is a good example of how the personas have helped clarify our decision-making. Using that tool regularly results in "pet" or favored features (or even seemingly important features) being pushed down in the priority list. When this happens, our team members have to be very explicit with their reasoning to get a feature back in the plan.

Personas are a medium for communication; a conduit for information about users and work settings derived from ethnography, market research, usability studies, interviews, observations, and so on. Once a set of personas is familiar to a team, a new finding can be instantly communicated: "Sondra cannot use the search tool on your web page." This communication style has an immediacy lacking from the finding "A subset of participants in the usability study had problems with the search tool" – especially for team members who now, for all intents and purposes, see Sondra (the persona) as a real person. We have found this to be extremely powerful for communicating results and furthering our teammates' understanding of the personas.

Finally, personas focus attention on a specific target audience. The method helps establish who is and consequently who is *not* being designed for. Personas explicitly do not cover every conceivable user; they help focus sequentially on different kinds of users. For example, a quality assurance engineer can test a product one day focusing on Patrick scenarios and another day focusing on Abby scenarios. As stated in the previous section, this works for testers and other product team members, in "bug bashes" for example. An experienced tester reported feeling that he was identifying "the right kind" of problems in drawing on knowledge of a persona in guiding his test scripts and activities.

Risks of Personas

Getting the right persona or set of personas is a huge challenge. Cooper argues that designing for any one external person is better than trying to design vaguely for everyone or specifically for oneself. This may be true, and it does feel as though settling on a small set of personas provides some insurance; but it also seems clear that personas should be developed for a particular effort. In making choices it becomes clear that the choices have consequences. For example, they will guide participant selection for future studies and could be used to filter out data from sources not matching one of the persona profiles.

Related to this is the temptation of persona reuse. After the investment in developing personas and acquainting people with them, it may be difficult to avoid over-extending their use when it would be better to disband one cast of characters and recruit another one. It can be good or bad when our partner teams adopt or adapt our personas. Different teams and products have different goals, so the personas are stretched a bit. So far, the stretching around our company has been modest and closely tied to data (because our target customers do indeed overlap), but it is a concern.

In addition, marketing and product development have different needs that require different persona attributes, and sometimes different target audiences. Marketing is generally interested in buyer behavior and customers; product development is interested in end-users. We've had some success in collaborating here, but there are rough edges.

Finally, we have seen a certain level of "persona mania" within our organization and others. Personas can be overused. At worst, they could replace other user-centered methods, ongoing data collection, or product evaluation. Readers of this case study might conclude that we have gone overboard regarding our persona effort. It is important to note that the things we have described here have happened over several years. Not everything was created up front. There are periods of persona focus and periods where we do many other types of UCD-oriented work. We know that personas are not a panacea. We believe personas should augment and enhance – augment existing design processes and enhance user focus. We have found that personas can enhance user testing and other evaluation methods, field research, scenario generation, design exploration, and solution brainstorming.

Persona use does require decision-making. It isn't a science. If not used appropriately, any powerful tool can take one down the wrong path, as in lying with statistics or using unrepresentative video examples. Personas are one such powerful tool. It is up to all of us together to develop effective and appropriate ways to use them.

Acknowledgments. Many people contributed to the personas effort described in this case study. We thank Kelly Fisher, Manish Sharma, Dave Ciuba, Kris Tibbetts, Lisa Olfert, Louise Kapustka, Leslie Scott, Scott Ottaway, Steve Scallen, Stacy Lewis, Karen Carncross, Colleen Dunham, Kent Sullivan, Shannon Kallin, Nelle Steele, Craig Hally, Jenny Lam, Greg Melander, Mark Ligameri, Heesung Koo, Dan Black, Neil Powell, and Hillel Cooperman. We also thank Jonathan Grudin for encouraging us to publish our experiences with personas as well as reflecting with us on the method.

CHAPTER 3

ETHICAL AND LEGAL CONSIDERATIONS

Introduction

Before conducting any kind of user activity there are a number of ethical and legal considerations that you must be aware of. You are responsible for protecting the participants, your company, and the data you collect. These are not responsibilities that should be taken lightly. This chapter applies to ALL readers. Even if you are "just" doing research, if it involves human participants, this chapter applies to you. In this chapter, we will inform you of what you need to know before conducting a user activity to make sure you collect valuable data without legal or ethical harm.

Ethical Considerations

Because we live in a litigious society, you must be cautious not to behave in a manner that could result in your company or yourself being sued by a disgruntled participant. The best way to do that is by treating the participant ethically. Every company/organization that gathers data from people should have a set of policies and practices in place for ethical treatment. If they do not, then you should implement them for your group or organization. Remember, you are the advocate of the user. It is your responsibility to protect the participants' physical and psychological wellbeing when they have kindly volunteered to help you by sharing their time, experience, and expertise. In the case where the participant is a customer, you have the added responsibility of protecting and promoting the customer's relationship with your company. A poor experience in your usability activity could result in lost revenue. You can be certain that your company will not support future usability activities once that has occurred.

As a final (but important) consideration, you should protect the data you are collecting. You do not want to bias or corrupt the data. If this happens, all of your time, money, and effort will be wasted when the data have to be discarded. The data you use in making design decisions must be valid and reliable or you risk doing more harm than good – poor data can result in bad design decisions. With this being said, if data are compromised, it is always possible to recruit more users and collect more data, but it is much harder to restore the dignity of a participant who feels coerced or ill-treated, or correct a damaged business relationship. So keep in mind that the participants' wellbeing is always your top priority. Figure 3.1 illustrates this priority by placing the participant at the highest point.

In this section, we discuss some of the key ethical considerations to keep in mind when running any usability activity.

Figure 3.1:

Triad of ethical

considerations

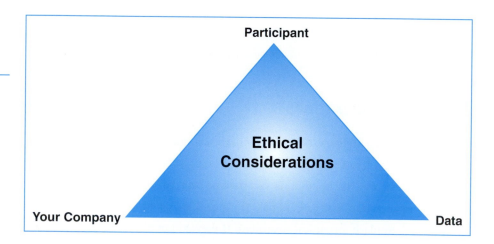

96   Ethical Considerations

SUGGESTED RESOURCES FOR ADDITIONAL READING

For more detail about any of the points below, please refer to the APA's *Ethical Principles of Psychologists and Code of Conduct*. You can request a free copy from the APA Order Department, 750 First Street, NE, Washington, DC 20002-4242, or by phone (202-336-5510). You can also download a free copy from the web at www.apa.org.

You can also refer to:

- American Psychological Association (1995). *Publication Manual of the American Psychological Association*, 4th ed. Washington, DC: APA.

At a Glance

> The right to be informed

> Permission to record

> Create a comfortable experience

> Appropriate language

> Anonymity

> The right to withdraw

> Appropriate incentives

> Valid and reliable data

> Acknowledge your true capabilities

> Data Retention and documentation

> Debrief

The Right To Be Informed

Any participant in a study has the right to know the purpose of the activity he or she is involved in, the expected duration, procedures, use of information collected (e.g., to design a new product), incentives for participation, the participant's rights as a part of the study, and any risks, discomfort, or adverse effects. (The final three often apply in medical or psychological studies, but should never apply to a usability activity.) This information should be conveyed during the recruitment process (refer to Chapter 5, Preparing for Your User Requirements Activity, "Recruitment Methods" section, page 173) and then reiterated at the beginning of the activity when the informed consent form (see Figure 3.2) is distributed and signed by the participant. The participant signs this form to acknowledge being informed of these things and agreeing to participate. If you are working with participants under the age of 18, a parent or guardian must sign the informed consent form.

Figure 3.2:

Sample informed consent form

Statement of Informed Consent

Purpose:
You have been asked to participate in a <**insert activity**> for <**insert product or project name**>. By participating in this activity, you will help us make our product easier to learn and use. This activity is meant to help us develop our product; it is not intended to test your individual performance in any way.

Evaluation Procedure:
You will be asked to <**insert summary statement of task(s) participants will accomplish**>. While you work, I will videotape your interactions and record your comments.

Confidentiality:
We will use the data you give us, along with the information we collect from other participants, to develop our product. To ensure confidentiality, we will not associate your name with your data. This session will be videotaped.

Breaks:
There <**will/will not**> be a scheduled break. However, you may take a break at any time.

Freedom to Withdraw:
You may withdraw from the activity at any time without penalty.

- -

If you agree to these terms, please indicate your acceptance by signing below:

Signature: _____

Printed name: _____ _____

Date: _____

If participants have a misperception about the purpose of the activity (e.g., believing that it is a job interview), the participant must be corrected immediately and given the opportunity to withdraw. Participants should also have the opportunity to ask questions, and to know whom to contact with further questions about the study or their rights. Without the participants, you could not conduct your study. Remember the participants in your study must be treated with the utmost respect. This applies to *all* methods described in this book.

Permission to Record

Before recording the voice or image of any individual, you must obtain permission. This can be accomplished with the consent form in Figure 3.2. The recording must not be used in a manner that could cause public identification or harm. Inform participants during recruitment that they will be audio or video recorded. Some individuals are not comfortable with this, so you do not want to wait until the participant arrives to find that out. Although it is rare, we have had a couple of participants leave before the activity even began because they refused to be taped.

Create a Comfortable Experience

Participants in your study should never feel uncomfortable, either physically or psychologically. This includes simple things like offering regular bathroom breaks, beverages, and comfortable facilities. And of course this includes treating the participants with respect at all times. If your user requirements activity involves any type of completion of tasks or product use (e.g., having users complete tasks on a competitor product), you must stress to the participant that the *product* is being evaluated, not them. Using a particularly difficult or poorly designed product can be stressful. If a participant performs poorly, never reveal that his or her answers are wrong or that something was done incorrectly. You need to be empathetic and remind participants that any difficulties they encounter are not a reflection on their own abilities but on the quality of the product they are using.

Appropriate Language

Part of treating participants with respect is understanding that they are not "subjects." Of course, you would never address a participant by saying "What do you think, subject number 1?" You should also show the same respect when speaking about them in their absence or in documentation. The APA *Publication Manual* referred to earlier recommends that you replace the impersonal term "subjects" with a more descriptive term when possible. You do not want to use the participants' names for reasons of anonymity (see below); however, *participants*, *individuals*, or *respondents* are all better alternatives to "subjects." The people who agree to provide you with their time and expertise are the foundation of a successful study. Without them, nearly every activity listed in this book would be impossible. We strongly recommend that readers review the fourth edition of the APA *Publication Manual* to better understand language bias, both written and spoken.

Anonymity

Participants have a right to anonymity. You are required to keep their information confidential and you should never associate a participant's name with his/her data or other personally identifiable information unless the participant provides such consent in writing. Do not write participants' names on any data forms (e.g., surveys, notes) or videotapes. Instead, you should always use a participant ID (e.g., P1, participant 1, user 1).

If the participants are employees of your company, you have a special obligation to protect their anonymity from their managers. Never show tapes of employees to their managers. This rule should also apply to their colleagues.

The Right To Withdraw

Participants should feel free to withdraw from your activity without penalty. If a participant withdraws part way through the study and you do not pay the person (or pay only a fraction of the original incentive), you are punishing him/her. Therefore, you are obligated to pay all participants the full incentive, whether they participate in the full study or not.

Appropriate Incentives

You should avoid offering excessive or inappropriate incentives as an enticement for participation as such inducements are likely to coerce the participant (refer to

Chapter 5, Preparing for Your User Requirements Activity, "Determining Participant Incentives" section, page 159). We realize that the incentive is part of the reason why most people participate in usability activities, but the incentive should not be so enticing that anyone would want to participate regardless of interest. The main reason for participation should be interest in influencing your product's design. In other words, don't make anyone an offer they can't refuse.

Valid and Reliable Data

The questions you ask participants and your reactions to their comments can affect the data you collect. In every activity, you must ensure that the data you collect are free from bias, accurate, **valid**, and **reliable**. You should never collect and report data that you know are invalid or unreliable. You must inform **stakeholders** about the limitations of the data you have collected. And of course, you must *never* fabricate data.

Along the same lines, if you learn of someone who is misusing or misrepresenting your work, you must take reasonable steps to correct it. For example, if in order to further an argument, someone is inaccurately quoting partial results from a series of focus groups you conducted, you must inform everyone involved of the correct interpretation of the results of the study. If people question the integrity of your work, your efforts are all for naught.

You should remove yourself from situations in which a conflict of interest may affect your actions. For example, it is ill-advised to get feedback on your own designs because your objectivity is affected. Although many companies hire individuals to act as both designer and usability specialist with the expectation that they will evaluate their own designs, this is unwise. Due to your bias, your results will not be valid.

Acknowledge Your True Capabilities

You should provide services, make recommendations, and conduct research only within the boundaries of your competencies. In your job role, this may require you to seek out additional training or resources. You should always inform individuals of the boundaries of your knowledge and skills, should you be placed in a situation that is outside your areas of expertise. For example, if you are asked to run a usability activity and you know nothing about usability, you should not attempt to wing it. If you do not have the time to learn what is necessary to run the activity, you should contract it out to a professional who can.

We provide the training and tools in this book to help you learn how to collect user requirements, but we also encourage you to supplement this with additional courses and mentoring. See Appendices A (page 678) and B (page 688) to learn more about usability resources and training.

Finally, you should not delegate work to individuals whom you know do not have the appropriate training or knowledge to complete the task. For example, not only should you be well-versed in the background and mechanics of a wants and needs analysis before conducting one, you must also ensure that the person who acts as your scribe is also appropriately trained.

Data Retention and Documentation

Retain the original data collected only for as long as it is relevant. This will typically be the period of time that you are working on a particular version of the product. You will want to retain the data in case you need to reference it at a later date for clarification purposes. It can also be very useful to provide continuity in the event that someone must take over usability support for the product.

It is important to accurately record the methods of any study you conduct (refer to Chapter 14, Concluding Your Activity, "Reporting Your Findings" section, page 652). This will allow anyone to understand exactly how you collected the data and what conclusions were drawn. This history is also critical for all stakeholders – and especially anyone that is new to the product team. You would be amazed at how often a "brand new" idea really isn't brand new. Those reports can prevent repetition of the same mistakes every time a new team member comes on board.

Debrief

If a participant was not aware of the full intent of the study (i.e., its purpose) before it began, you should attempt to debrief him/her about the nature, results, and conclusions of the study. Typically in a usability activity, the participants are told why the information is being collected (e.g., to help design a usable product, to learn more about a domain, to collect user requirements) so this is not an issue. However, in the case of a customer this could mean asking participants at the end of the study whether they wish to be contacted regarding the results of the activity once the product has shipped.

Legal Considerations

It is very important for you to protect your company whenever you run any kind of usability activity. For example, you want to run sound studies and treat your participants with respect. You do this for ethical reasons, but also to protect your company from being sued. By following the basic rules of ethics discussed above you should avoid such circumstances.

In addition to protecting your company from law suites, you also want to protect the confidentiality of your products. As a company, you do not typically want the world to know too early about the latest and greatest products you are developing. In most cases, this information is deemed highly confidential. When you run user requirements activities you are exposing people outside of your company to a potential or existing product. It may not be the product itself, but ideas relating to that product. Regardless, it is imperative that your participants keep the information they are exposed to confidential so that it cannot be used to create competitor products. In order to protect your company's product you should have all participants sign a **confidential disclosure agreement** (CDA). This form is a legal agreement in which the participant signs and thereby agrees to keep all information regarding the product and session confidential for a predefined period. You should work with a legal department to create a CDA that is appropriate for your purposes and to ensure that it will protect your company.

Figure 3.3 shows a sample CDA to help you get a sense for the kind of information that this document should contain. Again, we do not advise that you take this document and start using it at your company. It is imperative that you have a legal professional review any CDA that you decide to use.

Figure 3.3:

Basic confidential

disclosure agreement

<Company letterhead>

Confidentiality Agreement

Thank you for agreeing to give us your feedback on <describe project non-specifically>. The concepts you will be exposed to, and the information concerning them, are confidential and have not been released to the public. In exchange for participating in our design process and for seeing these unreleased concepts, you agree to keep the information you see or hear confidential until <name of company> releases that information to the public. You agree not to disclose this information to any third parties or use the information for any purpose other than this development process.

This agreement will cover discussions we intend to have with you on <date, place>.

To indicate your acceptance of these terms and your agreement to keep them confidential, please sign below (and return a copy to us if this agreement is being signed before our meeting).

We greatly appreciate your participation in our design process. Only by learning the needs of people like you can <company name> design systems that are useful. Thank you for your participation.

Signature _____   Date _____

Printed name _____

Signature for <company name>_____   Date _____

Tip

Make sure that any document you give to participants (legal or otherwise) is easy to read and understand. Handing participants a long, complicated document full of legal terms will unnecessarily frighten them, and some may refuse to sign without having a lawyer review it.

Pulling It All Together

In this chapter, we have introduced you to the legal and ethical issues to take into consideration when conducting a usability activity. By treating participants legally and ethically, you will protect them, your company, and your data – all of which are critical for successful user requirements collection.

CHAPTER 4

SETTING UP FACILITIES FOR YOUR USER REQUIREMENTS ACTIVITY

Introduction

You may already have access to a **usability** lab at your company or your client's site. If so, it was most likely built with the intent of conducting one-on-one usability evaluations. Will this lab work for collecting **user requirements**? Yes and no. For individual activities (i.e., interviews, solo card sort), your current set-up may be fine. However, it is unlikely that a "standard" usability lab is able to accommodate group activities (e.g., focus group, wants and needs analysis). Since standard labs are typically the size of an office, they are just too small.

Now that you have decided to pursue user requirements gathering, you may be wondering whether a permanent space needs to be built to conduct these activities. The answer is no. It is great if you have the budget, but it is not absolutely necessary. In this chapter, we discuss the options for setting up facilities to conduct a user requirements activity. We look at the pros and cons for each option, as well as what you should be aware of when making your selection. In addition, this chapter includes a case study from a usability specialist at Imagitas who was faced with the challenge of building a facility for user requirements activities, as well as usability testing.

Tip

Wherever you conduct usability activities, be sure to create and post some signs outside the room indicating that an activity is in session and whether or not people may enter the room. If you can secure the door to prevent entry, that's even better. This will prevent people from barging in and disrupting your session.

At a Glance

> Using your company's existing facilities
> Renting a marketing or hotel facility
> Building a permanent facility

Using Your Company's Existing Facilities

Depending on the size of your company, you may have a few choices of existing facilities to conduct user requirements activities. The most important factor when choosing a room for your session is whether it can comfortably accommodate groups of about 12 people, plus a couple of moderators. It should be flexible enough to allow multiple activity configurations. For example, it should allow everyone to sit around one large table for **brainstorming** with enough room for you, the scribe, and a whiteboard or flip charts at the front of the room – see Figure 4.1 for two possible configurations.

Figure 4.1:

Table set-up for W&N analysis or a focus group. The "U" shape allows all participants to see each other easily, as well as the moderator – but an oval shape will work as well

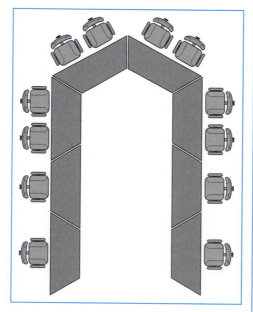
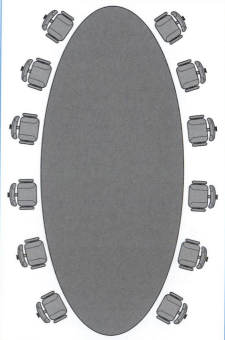

This arrangement will accommodate a wants and needs (W&N) analysis (Chapter 9, page 370), a focus group (Chapter 12, page 514), and group card sorting (Chapter 11, Group Task Analysis, page 458). It should also allow you to bring in smaller tables for a group of six users to collaborate on a task flow – see Figure 4.2 for two possible configurations. A large conference room is the most likely candidate for these purposes.

Many companies have a video-conferencing facility. This is usually a large room with a web camera, networking capability, a large table, and several chairs. Some cameras in these facilities are voice-activated and move towards the direction of the speaker. There will be a delay between when the speaker begins talking and when the camera focuses on the speaker, so they are really designed for conferences in which speaker changes are infrequent; however, it can still work for you.

Individual activities (e.g., interviews) can be conducted in a conference room, or you may choose a more intimate location that is quiet, such as an empty office. What-ever location you choose, it does not need to be permanently devoted to user activities. As long as you can get access to the room when needed, and no one disturbs your activities, there is no reason why a good conference room or office should be locked up when not in use for their primary purpose.

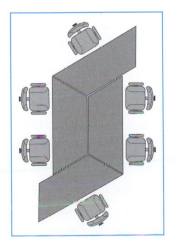
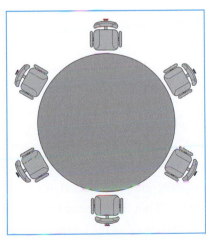

Figure 4.2: *Table set-up for a group task analysis (GTA). A round table works just as well, but these configurable tables can be expanded for longer task flows*

When using your company's existing facilities you may be tempted to leave enough space in the back of the room for observers, but you must resist this temptation. It is important to keep the observers in a room that is separate from participants. Participants will feel very self-conscious if there are people in the room who are not taking part in the activity but simply watching them. You can either transmit an image of the session live to a TV in the next room, or you can record the activity for later viewing by product team members. Either way, you will need at least one video camera and a microphone to record the activities and conversations. A videographer is also necessary to control the camera since it is highly unlikely that the camera can be placed in one location that will capture the entire group for the duration of your session (refer to Chapter 6, During Your User Requirements Activity, "Recording and Note-taking" section, page 226).

Renting a Marketing or Hotel Facility

You can rent a room from a marketing research vendor. Rooms are available in most major cities in the US and the western world. The benefit of this option is that the activity is being held on neutral territory. Participants may feel free to be more honest in their statements if they are not sitting in the middle of the company's conference room.

These firms typically set up for focus groups with one camera and an observation room. These full-service facilities may offer focus group moderators for an additional fee. They will also typically recruit and provide food for your session. If you do not conduct user requirements activities frequently and cannot acquire the funds for a permanent lab, this is a good option. For a list of some market research vendors, see Appendix D (page 698).

If you do not have marketing research vendors in your area, you may wish to go to the nearest hotel and reserve a meeting room. As was noted above in "Using Your Company's Existing Facilities," you should not have observers in the same room as the participants, and you will need to set up video equipment to record the session. Some hotels will not let you bring in your own video camera, so make sure you ask about this when making the reservation. It is essential to capture your session for future reference – so if the hotel will not allow you to bring in your own camera, find another location.

Building a Permanent Facility

Usually the most difficult thing to convince a company of is to give you a permanent space to build your lab. The budget to purchase the equipment is usually easier to get approved, but committing a space that could otherwise be used as a conference room or a set of offices is quite difficult. However, there are several benefits to having a dedicated usability lab:

- It tells/reminds people in your company that they have a usability group – one important enough in the company's agenda to get their own lab room (hopefully in a prominent location near the main entrance so that participants can get to it easily).
- You do not have to ask someone for permission to use the facility to conduct your usability activity; or worst yet, get evicted from the facility by a higher ranking individual during your activity, for a high-priority meeting!
- You do not have to transport the audio-video equipment and other materials from one room to another because you can keep them there permanently. Not only will this save your back and time, it will prevent damaging equipment during transport.
- You will have your *own* room in which to analyze your data, and to post **affinity diagrams** (see Appendix F, page 714) and session artifacts without fear of someone removing them. You will have also a ready location to hold meetings and presentations.

Components of a Devoted User Requirements Facility

At a Glance

> Equipment for your facility:

>> Tables

>> Chairs

>> One-way mirror

>> Adjustable lighting

>> Video cameras

>> Microphones

>> Computer and monitors

>> VCR/DVD recorder

>> Scan converter

>> Screen-capture software

>> Sound-proofing

>> Mixer

>> Datalogging software

>> Computer projector and screen

>> Cables

>> Television/video monitor

>> Equipment cart

>> Whiteboards or walls that you can tape paper to

>> Space for refreshments

>> Storage space

If your company is supportive of creating a permanent room devoted to user requirements gathering, you are in luck! Not to worry, you don't have to feel overwhelmed by the daunting task of figuring out what a "scan converter" is or what type of mixing board you should choose. There are many companies that can help you assess your needs (and your budget) and build the lab of your dreams – but you should at least be knowledgeable about the equipment available and its purpose (see Appendix C, page 694). We have provided price ranges for some of the equipment listed below to give readers a general idea of the cost, but you should keep in mind that these are only estimates and valid at the time of publication. Technology often drops in price over time, and you may be able to find the equipment on discount web sites. But do keep in mind that often you get just what you pay for, so saving money in the short term may cost you in the long term.

Caution

Like prices, technology itself also changes. Use this chapter as a starting point, but also do some research on what is new to the market. Check with the companies listed in this chapter and Appendix C (page 694) to hear about their latest offerings.

Tip

Remember that "pre-owned" equipment is an option. Some large companies periodically update their equipment, and when they do, they sell back their old equipment. Other companies, when hitting on hard times, have had to sell back their lab equipment and disband their usability group. Buy the equipment from *reputable* companies that you know will stick around to offer support, and make sure they offer guarantees. A warranty/guarantee is worth the additional cost. If you are really looking to save money, you can often find equipment on eBay (www.ebay.com).

Tables

One of the most useful purchases you can make is configurable tables, as sketched earlier in Figures 4.1 and 4.2. These tables have rollers with locks on them so that they can be pushed from one arrangement to another quickly and easily and then locked in the chosen position.

Chairs

Try to find chairs that are stackable (for storing in tight places) and easy to move. The chairs should be well-made so that participants can comfortably sit for a two-hour session. If the participants are uncomfortable, you will not be getting their best. Chairs with armrests are more comfortable but also take up more room. If you are in a tight space, you might be better off skipping the armrests but keep in mind that comfortable participants are happy participants.

One-way mirror

If you have the luxury of dividing a space into two halves – a user half and an observer half (also known as the control room) – a one-way mirror is necessary. Obviously this allows stakeholders to watch a session without being seen by the participants. Unfortunately, it can be expensive to purchase and install a one-way mirror (the cost depends on the size of the room and the construction required).

Remember that you will need to keep the control room dark, but not so dark that you cannot see your hand in front of your face. You can have low levels of light and it will still be extremely difficult for participants to see through. However, keep in mind that reflective surfaces (e.g., television screens, white paper, white clothes) in the control room can sometimes be seen even when the lights are very low.

Tip

If you have a separate room where observers can watch from behind a one-way mirror, paint the walls of this room a dark color. This reduces reflection and makes it more difficult for participants to see the observers.

Adjustable lighting

Because the activities in the lab will vary, different levels of lighting may be necessary. For example, you might want the lights out if you are showing slides or a video, but you will want the room well lit if you are conducting a brainstorming activity. Dimmer switches, and lights that can be turned on independently throughout the room, will allow you to provide as much or as little light as needed. However, dimmer switches for fluorescent lights can be very expensive (several hundred dollars each). You should also provide dimmer switches in the observation room so that very low levels of light can be achieved to ensure the participants will not see the observers during a user requirements activity. Task lighting can be very helpful for solo card sorting tasks and other activities.

Video cameras

Purchasing a video camera that has pan-tilt control (i.e., allowing horizontal and vertical movement) will be an excellent investment. Alternatively, a sturdy tripod with two-way pan-tilt control will cost less than $20.

At the very least, the camera should have an analog output (RCA or coaxial) and a microphone – but S-Video output is even better. A VHS camera costs around $200, a Hi-8 camera over $250, and a MiniDV around $300. Since Hi-8 is not compatible with VHS and is now outdated technology, we do not recommend it. We recommend a MiniDV with IEEE1394 (or FireWire) output because this will allow you to send the digital video signal directly to the computer for editing without loss of quality; however, this will cost you about $800–$2000. MiniDV tapes cost $8–12, but if you send the signal directly to a mixer or desktop they are not necessary. You could just record the image from the VCR (using VHS or S-VHS tapes), or post the digital video on a website for stakeholders to view. The issue of analog versus digital recording is reviewed later in this chapter (see page 126).

Mounting the video cameras from the ceiling is optimal. They are then less intrusive, and you do not have to worry about someone knocking them over. This is also extremely useful when conducting a group task analysis; being able to capture an overhead view of the flow while it is being constructed will put observers right in the middle of the action! Good quality dome cameras have remote pan/tilt/zoom capabilities and are perfectly silent. Of course, you will not be able to use the cameras in other rooms or in field studies.

Microphones

Handheld microphones can be purchased for less than $10. Flat-profile, omni-directional microphones pick up sound from all directions and are best suited for group activities – a microphone can be shared between several participants. They go virtually unnoticed by participants, which is ideal when you do not want to make people self-conscious about being recorded. However, they pick up sound well for only a couple of feet, so you will likely need three to six of them for a group of 12. The microphones could be placed either close to the users (e.g., on the table top) or suspended from the ceiling using a boom. Omni-directional, uni-directional, and hanging microphones cost between $120 and $300.

Lavaliere microphones are ideal for the moderator who is often on the move. They offer improved audio quality but they require a mixer to receive the wireless signal. You should be able to find one for $30.

Computer and monitors

A laptop or single workstation will likely be sufficient in the user-half of the lab. This can be used if you need to conduct a slide show or demonstrate a software product. An additional laptop or workstation in the control room allows a coworker to take notes during the activity. At the very least, ensure that plenty of outlets are installed so that stakeholders can bring in laptops to take their own notes during a session.

VCR/DVD recorder

A standard VCR that can record VHS-quality audio and video input will work fine. If you have the budget, you could go for a higher-end VCR that records S-VHS input. A dual-deck VCR allows you to do basic video editing – i.e., you play the original tape, record it to the second tape, and stop the recording during sections you do not wish to include. You can find a dual-deck VCR for less than $200, but you could spend $1000 or more if you wished. An even better solution is to record directly to MPEG-1 or MPEG-2 format or to purchase a consumer-grade DVD recorder.

Scan converter

A scan converter allows you to capture the image from a computer monitor and record it for viewing on a TV. Unless you frequently conduct focus groups in which you demo products on the computer, or do participatory design activities on the computer, a scan converter is unnecessary. However, if you will also conduct software/web usability tests in this facility, a scan converter will be necessary.

The image you capture for viewing on the TV will *not* be as high quality as what you see on the computer screen – TV technology simply is not up to par with computer monitors. However, should you choose to purchase a scan converter you will need to know the refresh rate and resolution of the computer(s) you will be connecting to. Low-end scan converters can support computer resolutions of 640×480 pixels and a vertical refresh rate of 60 Hz. High-end scan converters can support workstation computers with resolutions up to 1600×1280. The refresh rates for these scan converters are usually defined by the horizontal, rather than the vertical, refresh rate. Scan converters range in price from about $100 to $30,000, although you wouldn't want one that cost under $1500. Scan converters over $20,000 are actually professional movie quality and unnecessary for your purposes.

A cheaper way of recording computer screen activity is by plugging a VCR cable directly into the TV-out port of the computer's video card. You can record directly to tape. The best resolution you can hope for will be 800×600 pixels, but you will probably be limited to 640×480. Keep in mind though, VHS has only 240 lines so a higher resolution does not add any quality to your screen recordings. Most people move towards software-based screen capture because it does not have that limitation (see next section).

Screen-capture software

You can purchase software that captures the image on a computer hard drive while a participant works (i.e., no scan converter necessary). Products like TechSmith's *Morae*™ and *Camtasia*®, Hyperionic's *HyperCam*®, *ScreenCorder 2.1*™, and Lotus *ScreenCam*® can be purchased from $30 to $150. They allow you to edit the images to create a highlights video (a visual summary of actions the user made or comments by users). Many of these tools have free trial versions so you can see which one best suits your needs. At the time of the publication of this book, a nice analysis of the tools can be found at www.boxesandarrows.com/archives/print/002919.php.

Sound-proofing

Whether or not you have a separate control room, it is wise to have sound-proofing in your lab. At a minimum, it blocks out conversations from the hallway or surrounding offices. In addition, it keeps the confidential discussions within the lab. If you do have an observation room (i.e., control room), sound-proofing is necessary between this room and the participant room, so that any discussions in the control room between the observers are not heard by the participants.

To ensure quality sound-proofing, double glass one-way mirrors with a bit of space for air between the two mirrors will work well.

The cost of sound-proofing will vary depending on the size of the room and the materials used. Having separate entrances to the two rooms will also ensure that sound does not travel through the door. Double walls between the control room and the users' room, with a little space between the walls, also ensures good sound-proofing.

Regardless of the quality of sound-proofing, it is always a good idea to ask the observers to be as quiet as possible.

Mixer

A mixer will allow you to mix multiple inputs from the cameras and a computer or computer projector in the users' room. A mixer will also permit a picture-in-picture (PIP) display (see Figure 4.3). Instead of purchasing a mixer, you can buy an individual PIP for less than $200 – but it will limit you to placing the picture in one of four corners and may allow you to resize it to only two different sizes. A mixer (over $600) will allow you to move the PIP anywhere on the screen and make it any size, including filling the screen completely with one image or the other. Output from the mixer is fed into a monitor to view what is being recorded to the VCR.

Figure 4.3:

Picture of the results of a mixer

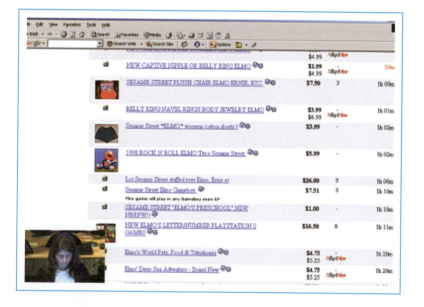

Datalogging software

Special software for taking notes during the session is not required – although it is extremely valuable to have a program that time-stamps each entry to match the corresponding video. If you want to create a highlights tape to showcase particular user comments, you can check the datalog and then go to the exact section of the recording.

Some datalogging products available today are *ObServant* (by User Works), *Usability Activity Log v2.3* (by Bit Debris Solutions), *Observational Coding System Tools* (by Triangle Research Collaborative Inc.), and *The Observer 5.0* (by Noldus Information Technology). These tools support customizable functions so that you can create codes for specific user actions (e.g., each time a user gets a phone call, each time the user checks e-mail). This allows faster note-taking and allows you to categorize behavior for easy analysis. Some tools come with analysis functions, while for other tools, the notes are saved as ASCII or RTF (rich text files) and can be exported to a spreadsheet or statistical analysis program.

Unfortunately, some datalogging applications available today are not intuitive and are really designed more for usability testing than for requirements gathering activities. Make sure you do your homework and insist on a free trial period before investing in any application. Some things to look for in a data-logging application:

- Automatic clip extraction of digital recordings based on comments and codes
- Free form text note-taking *and* structured coding
- Searching digital video files.

In the majority of cases, a simple text editor or spreadsheet (most will give you time-stamps) will do just fine to record users' comments and unique events.

Computer projector and screen

If you would like to demo software, show day-in-the-life videos, or do participatory design, it is most convenient to display your computer image on a screen. Mounting the projector in the ceiling saves space and prevents people from accidentally knocking it over, but it also prevents you from using the projector in other rooms. Computer projectors cost anywhere from $850 to over $3000, so unless you have the money to buy several projectors, we do not recommend a ceiling mount.

Cables

You will likely need a variety of cables to connect all the equipment we are describing. Long RCA cables and power strips cost real money and should be budgeted for. Depending on your set-up, you will likely spend $70 or more.

Although clerks at electronics stores may recommend the highest quality, gold-plated cables, the quality difference in the signal is usually not noticeable. Remember that the people selling you those cables are likely working for commission rather than for your best interests. If you plan to send the video signal from one room to another, you might want to consider purchasing shielded (closed-circuit) video cables. They will protect the signal from interference from other electronic equipment but will cost around $200.

> **Tip**
>
> Label those cords! Most black cords look alike. If a piece of equipment is misbehaving or needs to be replaced, you don't want to spend an hour tracing back every cord to figure out which one is the one you need.

Television/video monitor

If observers are watching from another room, a television is necessary to show what you are recording. Make sure it has RCA inputs. A 13 in TV is usually fine for one to two observers. You can find one for around $60, depending on the quality desired.

Equipment cart

If you have been unable to convince your company to give you a space that is yours alone, and large meetings or a teleconference requires use of the space, you may wish to move the equipment out – to prevent curious individuals from altering your settings or unintentionally breaking your hard-earned equipment. You will need a sturdy, high-quality equipment cart on wheels (around $200). Do not try to save money by buying a cheaper cart only to have all your equipment crash to the floor! You can keep the equipment permanently stored on the cart, so when it comes time to relocate you simply unplug the cables and roll away. Alternatively, you may want to opt for a "portable lab." For around $6000, you can get a digital VCR (miniDV), two FireWire cameras, two tripods, multiple effects mixer, and cables, all in an aluminum briefcase with wheels.

Whiteboards or walls that you can tape paper to

Some conference room walls are covered in carpet or fabric to provide a level of sound-proofing. Unfortunately, this makes it almost impossible to tape anything to it. Additionally, some walls are so dense that you cannot use push-pins. For capturing brainstormed ideas, posting brainstorm rules, displaying paper prototypes, etc., you will need a surface from which you can hang paper. Unless you have a whiteboard to write on, or a smooth surface to tape paper to, you will need multiple easels.

Electronic whiteboards can be purchased for anywhere from $1200 to $5000, but these are usually too heavy to carry from meeting to meeting. A more portable and cheaper solution is purchasing a "capture bar" that attaches to a regular whiteboard or flip chart for $350–$900 (see Figures 4.4 and 4.5). Virtual Ink's *Mimio*, Electronics for Imaging's *eBeam*, and Interlink Electronics Inc.'s *FreeBeam* are three portable solutions. The capture bar uses sonic receivers to track movements on the whiteboard or flip chart. Regular markers fit into special holders that emit a very faint buzzing sound at a specific frequency whenever you press down to draw on the whiteboard. A special eraser works in a similar fashion. Once you have finished

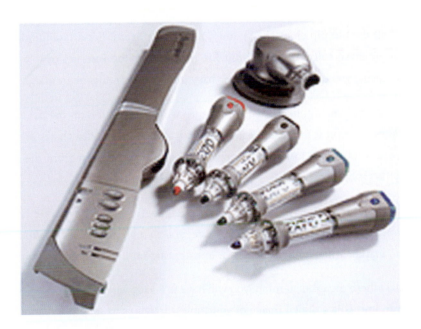

Figure 4.4:

Close-up of equipment to turn a regular whiteboard into an electronic whiteboard (Mimio)

Figure 4.5:

Display of how the equipment captures and transmits the image (eBeam)

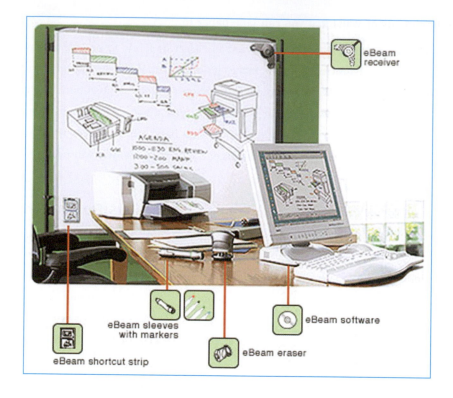

writing or drawing, a digital image is captured and then sent to a laptop or computer. Once you have saved the image, you can erase the text on the whiteboard (or pull off the old flip chart sheet) and do it all over again. For an additional fee, you can purchase software to transmit the images over the Internet or to a PDA. Unfortunately, you cannot edit, copy, or paste the text since this is an image.

In the end, you will still likely need to type up what was written on the board. For this reason, we find it faster and easier to just capture text on flip charts and take them back to our desk to retype, or have someone else copy text from the board during the session.

As a final note, you will have to calibrate the system before use. The marker holders sometimes require a lot of pressure to activate, and changing the angle at which you hold the marker will slightly alter how a line appears on the computer/laptop.

With all of these thoughts in mind, you will have to decide whether the price is worth having an immediate digital image of your notes/drawings to send out to others.

Space for refreshments

It is always nice to offer at least a light snack and drinks during group sessions, especially those conducted during dinnertime. Obviously, you need to be sure there is enough room to set the refreshments out of the way so they do not get bumped into while allowing participants to easily access them.

Storage space

A closet is often forgotten when designing a lab. Space is at a premium and you may be thinking it is more important to use that space for additional observers. A small storage closet with a lock will allow you to keep all of your materials (e.g., sticky notes, easels, flip charts, markers, incentives) and additional chairs locked away so that others do not "borrow" them. Obviously, you want this closet next to your lab so that you do not have to haul chairs or an armful of materials back and forth between sessions. Also, if you must move your equipment out of the lab from time to time (see "Equipment cart" discussion above), the storage closet is a convenient place to lock it away.

Lab Layout

We strongly recommend having a "user" room and a "control" room in your lab configuration (see Figure 4.6). As we mention throughout the book, you do not want stakeholders in the same room with participants. Being viewed by a crowd can be disturbing for participants. Additionally, observers often have a very difficult time not interacting with participants or having conversations among themselves regarding the interesting things they are observing. Additionally, participants can be distracted by all the equipment and monitoring going on.

Figure 4.7 shows a typical two-room layout. If you are unable to build this type of layout, but you do have access to a second room, you can do a wireless transmission (via a VHF transmitter) to another television for $100–200. It will not work well around corners, and you have to be careful of what is in the way of the signal.

Figures 4.8 through 4.10 show room configurations for different types of activities. Your room configuration may be significantly different, but the elements for an ideal lab are present in these images.

Figure 4.6:

An observation room. In this photo, you can see the one-way mirror, the usability engineer's computer for datalogging, VCR, mixing board, and an overhead TV so that stakeholders can see what the participant is doing

Figure 4.7:

Typical two-room lab layout

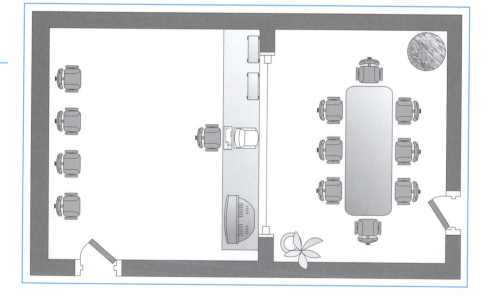

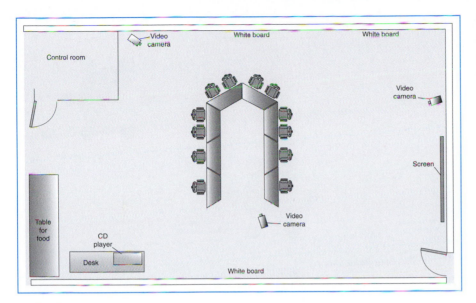

Figure 4.8:

Sample layout for a brainstorming activity

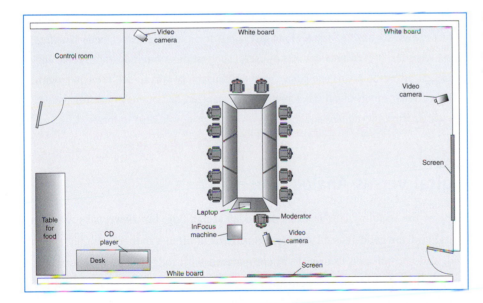

Figure 4.9:

Sample layout for a focus group

Figure 4.10:

Sample layout for a group task analysis

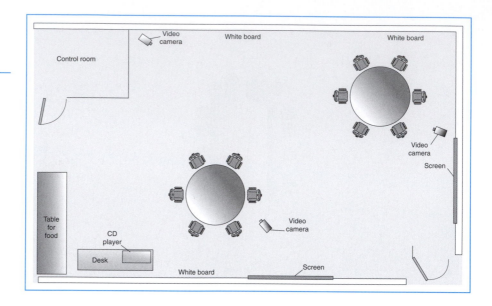

SUGGESTED RESOURCES FOR ADDITIONAL READING

For more tips and useful resources, visit the Usability Special Interest Group website (http://www.stc.org/sig_description.asp?ID=21). It provides a list of book chapters and websites. It even provides lists of useful suggestions from industry experts, and contact information for companies who build usability labs or sell the equipment. The information on this site is sometimes reorganized, so you may need to conduct a search from the home page (http://www.stc.org/sig_info.asp) to locate it.

Digital versus Analog Labs

Many of the usability labs in existence today are analog, but newer labs are going digital and for good reason! Analog equipment is often expensive, highly specialized, and complicated to operate in comparison with today's digital options. Intel spent well over $20,000 to equip their former analog lab and under $5000 for a superior digital solution (Jones & Bullara 2003).

In analog labs, a scan converter (refer to page 116) is necessary to present a computer image on a television monitor, severely deteriorating the quality of the image. Most often, text on the screen is completely illegible. In addition, creating a highlights tape is time-consuming and requires a skilled editor. If you are not familiar with the technical aspects of building a lab, speak with vendors and consultants who specialize in building labs to determine which solution is best for your particular needs.

Analog Recording

If the analog signal you are recording is S-Video, you will need to use an S-VHS or Hi-8 tape for recording. Unfortunately, most consumer VCRs in North America read only composite video signals (the lowest quality video signal), which means they cannot read S-VHS or Hi-8 tapes. Consequently, remote stakeholders will be unable to view your tapes. Additionally, S-VHS and Hi-8 tapes are expensive (about $8 each). The best quality analog video signal is called "component," but it is typically used only in professional video production (very expensive!). Computer monitors use a form of component video, and most consumer DVD players can read it – but you would be better off to go with a digital solution (see later). Figure 4.11 shows a typical analog recording set-up.

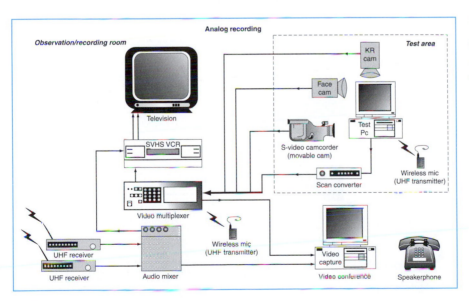

Figure 4.11:

A standard analog recording set-up

Digital Recording

To go digital, you will need a computer with a lot of processing power and plenty of memory, a large hard drive, a VGA-out splitter, USB 2.0 ports, a FireWire card (IEEE 1394 port), a multichannel sound card, and an analog video capture/output card. Additionally, you will need screen-capture software (as described earlier), microphone(s), and a tripod-mounted camcorder with FireWire (IEEE 1394) output to capture visual images of the participant in action. Optionally, you may also want to get a CD or DVD writer for archiving videos (unless you plan to store them all on a very large server), a USB 2.0 or FireWire monitor-mounted camera to capture participants' facial expressions while working on the computer, a remote pan-tilt head for the video camera, and multimedia editing software (often provided with DVD recorders). CDs and DVDs run to about $1 to $3 each today – much cheaper than their tape counterparts. With digital, you also have the benefits of making your videos accessible from the web, and the ability to edit them with ease (compared to VHS tapes). See Figure 4.12 for a digital recording solution.

It is ideal to record the source video in an uncompressed format and then re-render the final video in a compressed format (MPEG) to save it on DVDs. This can be done by reducing the frame rate, the resolution of each video frame, and/or the

Figure 4.12:

A digital recording solution

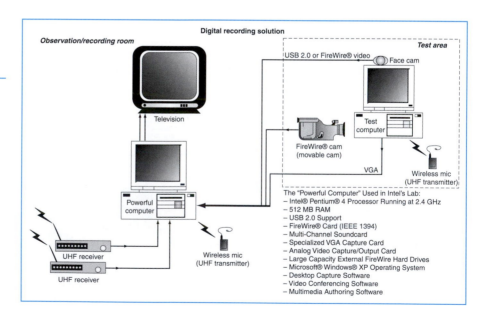

audio quality, or by using a compressor/decompressor. Uncompressed video takes up about 13 GB/hour so a compressed file is far more manageable.

Tip

Appendix C (page 694) lists a few companies that provide usability lab equipment, build usability labs, and/or consult on lab design (current at time this book went to press). Many of these companies also rent portable labs. When selecting a vendor, you should go with a company that has a brick and mortar presence, as well as good reviews and customer recommendations. You want a company that will be around to back up their service and help you work out any kinks in the system. The reliability and support will be worth the extra money spent!

Pulling It All Together

User requirements can be quick and easy to run and do not require expensive, high-tech usability labs. We have offered solutions for any budget, as well as resources to build the lab of your dreams!

CASE STUDY

Aimee McCabe was given the opportunity to build a usability lab at her company. She wanted to be sure she could conduct user requirements activities, as well as usability tests in her new environment. To work within a constrained budget, she did much of the homework herself rather than using a consultant. She shares with us her experience and extremely helpful lessons learned.

Designing an Innovative Cost-effective Usability Lab

Aimee McCabe, Usability Specialist, Imagitas

Impetus for a Usability Lab

In 1999, Imagitas decided to expand one of their offline (print) products to be online and also launch a government information website. Usability studies were essential because these online products involved millions of people transacting with the government. At that time our research department had already educated upper management about the importance of user-centered design (UCD) for our print products. For example, we conducted many focus groups around the country to get consumer feedback, and we did a large "habits and practices" study with a representative sample of small businesses, by telephone. Because UCD was philosophically accepted at Imagitas, conducting usability studies and adding a usability lab did not require a shift in the culture of the company. It was just a matter of expanding the research team and building the inhouse capabilities.

Though I was in the right environment, time, and place to design a usability lab, I continued to evangelize UCD by conducting inhouse seminars on usability, as well as paper prototyping to educate clients, designers, developers, and marketing teams. Later, this would prove valuable in that many of these team members would attend usability studies and debriefing sessions and were open to changes that needed to be made to improve the usability of the website.

Fortunately, my company was moving to a new location within a year, so the next steps were to research and propose lab specifications for budget approval. Originally, I spoke to a consultant who wanted to charge $10,000 just to create the audio-visual equipment specification list and electrical layout of the usability lab. Because I had the time and wanted to save money, I decided to research and design the lab myself. This process allowed me to focus on the usability lab environment for the comfort and use of the test participants, usability specialists, and clients.

Research to Design the Usability Lab

My goal was to design and build an innovative, cost-effective usability lab. First I gathered information and researched existing labs by reading books such as Jeffrey Rubin's *Handbook of Usability Testing: How to Plan, Design and Conduct Effective Tests* – to learn what was needed to have a good testing environment. That book does an excellent job illustrating various room setups using both text and diagrams that show a range of equipment that can be used.

I enrolled in Bentley College's "Information Design Program" and took Joseph Dumas' Usability Testing course. Bentley's new usability lab and teaching room was an inspiration, but I did not have the budget to duplicate such an expensive environment. I visited other usability labs to see and learn from usability specialists who had gone through the process of building and using a lab. I wanted to know "what worked well" and "what not so well" in lab layout and equipment, as well as finding out about audio-visual vendors and staff requirements.

Networking was essential in getting access to prestigious usability labs and face time with usability specialists who were so kind to share their experiences and knowledge. I was able to talk with various usability specialists in the Greater Boston area who gave me personal tours of their usability labs and answered many of my lab layout and A/V electronic equipment questions. I was able to learn about their lab designs and equipment successes and challenges. For example, I chose a specific brand microphone for our lab because of a recommendation – and it was the best decision for excellent sound quality. Hearing the test participant and moderator is essential to gathering good data.

I also talked with other usability specialists at conferences (e.g., Usability Professional Association), seminars, and local meetings (Greater Boston/Special Interest Group Computer Human Interaction). After gathering all this helpful information, I started to draft my usability lab layout and specifications, and to compile a "wish list" of technical capabilities.

Approval of Usability Lab and Equipment

After drafting my usability lab specifications, I met with our facilities director because she was working closely with the architects who were designing our new workspace. She was very supportive in allowing me to design the layout of my lab, although I was allotted only three rooms in the architectural plans. I had originally planned on four rooms, two being observation rooms – one for the usability lab and another for the focus group room. The facilities director also had first round of budget approval and challenged me to be cost-effective. She recommended that I use a local audio-visual vendor for the lab equipment, installation, and maintenance. This would later prove valuable, especially for quick turnaround on technical and maintenance support.

With the restriction to three rooms, I came up with the idea of making the center room the observation room for both the usability lab and the focus group room, with one-way mirrors on both sides of the observation room (see Figure 4.13). Blackout curtains were installed in case we needed to close one of the mirrors.

Figure 4.13:

Room layout of the usability lab facility

Usability Lab	Observation Room	Focus Group/Executive Observation Room
13' x 16'	13' x 18'	13' x 18'

Figures 4.14, 4.15, and 4.16 show general views of the three rooms. The appendix to this case study lists the furniture and equipment, and shows detailed layouts of the three rooms.

Next I designed the focus group room to have the dual purpose of an executive observation room for usability testing. I accomplished this by having a real-time connection to the usability lab computer electrically networked to the focus group room. Then we connected a video projection machine for those clients who wanted to make phone calls and use their laptops computers during testing sessions. They could remotely watch/listen to the usability tests without interrupting the usability specialists and clients in the observation room taking notes.

Now that we had one central observation room, we needed only one audio-visual recording system, and this saved thousands of dollars. As a result I was able to purchase high-end equipment. Interestingly, we finished with a much better lab because I was forced to work with three rooms.

Figure 4.14:

The users' room, showing the one-way mirror

Figure 4.15:
Observation room view of the users' room

Figure 4.16:
The focus group and executive room, showing the one-way mirror

Another challenge was the physical location of the usability lab in the company space. Ideally, the test participants should have the least amount of exposure to your company as possible so as not to bias their feedback. Placing the lab close to the main entrance and near bathrooms are important, along with no evidence of company branding or employees. Our assigned space for the lab was far from the main entrance, but we were able to minimize the test participants' exposure to the company by having them walk down an unobtrusive hallway. On test days, I use this "hallway walking time" to talk with the test participants and get feedback on the driving directions to our company. This helps me establish a rapport with them and is a nice segues to start the usability study.

I also worked closely with the facilities director to ensure the usability lab environment was designed for the comfort of the test participants, researchers, and clients (e.g., comfortable chairs, good air ventilation, refrigerator for drinks).

Next I spoke with the A/V vendor about the usability lab specifications – including the picture-in-picture (PIP) video format that would record both the test participant using the computer and real-time computer screen capture (scan converter; see Figure 4.17). Also, I wanted the ability to record on S-VHS (Super-VHS) a paper prototyping or card sort session from above with a document camera and the test participant(s) from the side.

My usability lab specifications and budget were approved. They were approximately $68,000 for the A/V electronic equipment and installation, $8000 for a one-year support plan (unlimited phone and onsite visits) and a two-hour training session, plus $25,000 for the architectural design specifications, which included sound-proofing, two one-way mirrors, a heating ventilation air conditioning (HVAC) system, electrical and phone outlets, network wiring, and lighting.

Figure 4.17:

Usability test control panel screen

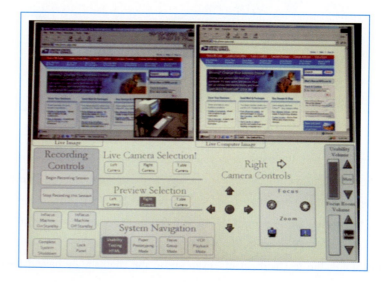

Additionally, we were able to use existing computer equipment for the usability lab, and VCRs (for tape duplications), a stationary video camera, and microphones from our old focus group room for our new room. Since the new usability lab was constructed during the building renovations that were being made for the relocation of our company, it saved additional time and money. Also, the company was able to depreciate the lab equipment expense over the life of the equipment.

Building the Usability Lab

Again, because my company was moving to a new location that was being completely renovated, the A/V vendor was able to get access to the building during construction, which made it easier to lay the electrical network. I worked closely with an A/V programmer to design the user interface for the touch panel. My goal was to make it so simple to use that we would not need a staff A/V technician. Instead, a research specialist could quickly and easily set up and adjust the camera/video/sound controls without interrupting a usability test session.

Because I had no other usability lab control touch panel interface models to reference, I paper prototyped the touch screen user interface and tested it with a colleague. This was an opportunity to be innovative and design a completely user-centered A/V control panel for a usability specialist to operate their own lab equipment. As a result, with the touch of a few panel buttons (in less than a minute), the A/V equipment can be set up for a usability test, focus group, paper prototyping, or card sorting session.

When designing this usability lab, I always kept the test participants', usability specialists', and clients' needs in mind to ensure a comfortable environment. Even though I started with a good mental concept of the lab function and design, I was open to changes based on feedback from other usability specialists and the A/V vendor. Because the usability lab was not going to be built immediately, I was able to spend months gathering information before I finalized the specifications.

The Launch and Afterwards

To build excitement after the usability lab was built, we announced the "Grand Opening" in the company newsletter and invited people to attend testing sessions. Employees and clients were given private tours of the lab, where we demonstrated the innovative audio-visual capabilities and talked about user-centered design. We also conducted training sessions on usability basics and how to observe a usability test before each testing day. My philosophy is to empower all observers with the tools to understand users' needs so they can contribute to solving usability issues.

Our new usability lab helped us to conduct usability studies to make online products easy to use. Most importantly, we improved the user experience for successful government transactions, which generates revenue and saves money. As a result, in June 2003, the website we designed and tested received the e-Gov 2003 Explorer Award for exceptional delivery of government services through its Internet Channel.

I am very fortunate to work for a company and client who believe in the UCD process. After using the usability lab for a year, we upgraded the audio-visual VHS system to record on DVD, for about $2500. Now clients are able to watch the usability test sessions from their computer instead of using a VCR, and the digital format is easier to edit for high-lights of the study.

Lessons Learned

- Educate people about usability and encourage them to observe test sessions. It is enlightening to watch "real users" who, for example, are unable to complete an online transaction, get frustrated and leave your website. In a short period one can easily see how costly it could be to launch a poorly designed product.

- Visit usability labs and talk with specialists so that you can learn from their mistakes and successes.

- Place the lab close to the main entrance and near bathrooms, along with no evidence of company branding or employees. Then the test participants have least amount of exposure to your company so as not to bias their feedback.

- Find a good, local, audio-visual vendor who can support your technical needs and provide quick turnaround on equipment maintenance.

- Design the lab to be upgradeable to new technology (e.g., video to DVD).

- Be flexible and creative with the limitations and resources that you have (e.g., budget, space, technology).

- Include independent temperature controls in each room – rooms tend to get warmer with more people.

- Design the rooms for the comfort of the test participants, usability specialists, and clients by selecting comfortable chairs and having good air ventilation. Install a refrigerator for drinks.

Finally, do not be discouraged by roadblocks – they will certainly occur somewhere in the process of building and implementing your usability lab. Focus on creative lab design solutions.

Acknowledgments. I thank the following people and organizations for their support – my usability lab could not have been designed and built without their invaluable knowledge, expertise, and kindnesses: Kelly GordanVaughn (American Institutes of Research, Concord, MA); Joseph Dumas and William Gribbons (Bentley College, Waltham, MA); Rulie Chou (Fidelity Investments, Boston, MA); Taki Fragopoulos, Amy Holt, and Jared Mallory (Group-Comm Systems Inc., Newton, MA); Susan Blumenfeld, Patty Dew, Chris Manos, Brett Matthews, and Scott Matthews (Imagitas, Waltham, MA). Photographs are by Holly Yang and Johannes Wong.

Appendix

The Users' Room

See Figure 4.18.

- *Construction environment:*
  Good ventilation (quiet fan)
  Thermostat
  Diffused lighting
  Sound-proofing
  Off-white paint color on walls
  One-way mirror (93 in × 52 in, placed 32 in from the floor)
  Window with blinds.
- *Electronic equipment:*
  Electrical outlets and internet/server connections
  Computer with Internet network (both high-speed and dial-up)
  Phone connections
  Computer desk
  Printer and table
  Two pivotal hidden cameras (unobtrusive)
  Stationary overhead document ceiling camera (unobtrusive)
  Desktop microphone (unobtrusive)
  Intercom speaker from observation room.

Figure 4.18:

Users' room layout (13 ft × 16 ft)

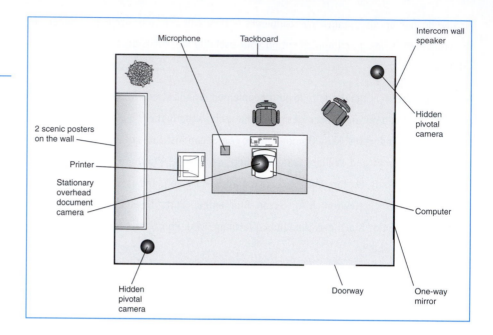

- *Furniture:*

  Tack board (8 ft × 4 ft)

  Two comfortable adjustable chairs with wheels

  Phone

  Credenza with cabinet (73 in × 24 in × 29 in)

  Artificial 6 ft Ficus tree for the corner of the room

  Coat hooks on wall

  Two scenic posters on wall

  Wastebasket.

The Observation Room

See Figure 4.19.

- *Construction environment:*

  Good ventilation (quiet fan)

  Thermostat

  Diffused lighting

  Sound-proofing

  Off-white paint color on walls

  One-way mirror (93 in × 52 in, placed 32 in from the floor).

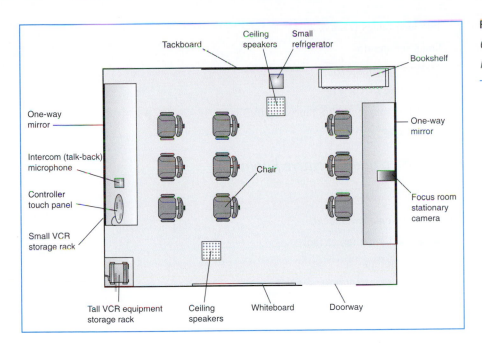

Figure 4.19:

Observation room layout (13 ft × 18 ft)

- *Electronic equipment:*

  Electrical outlets

  Computer with Internet network (both high-speed and dial-up)

  Phone connections

  Projection screen (white wall space)

  Ceiling-mounted video projection machine (displays real-time computer screen image)

  Scan converter

  LCD 15 in touch panel (A/V controls)

  Audio-video recording system with picture-in-picture

  Four VHS recorders (later upgraded to one DVD recorder)

  Intercom (talkback) microphone connected to users' and focus group rooms.

- *Furniture:*

  Tall (7 ft) VCR and A/V equipment storage rack

  Short (2 ft) VCR equipment storage rack

  Phone

  Fifteen comfortable adjustable chairs with wheels

Two long tables (72 in × 20 in)

Small refrigerator

Tackboard (8 ft × 4 ft)

Whiteboard (8 ft × 4 ft)

Shelf for storage of VHS tapes and DVD disc

Wastebasket.

Focus Group and Executive Room

See Figure 4.20.

- *Construction environment:*

  Good ventilation (quiet fan)

  Sound-proofing

  Off-white paint color on walls

  Thermostat

  Diffused lighting

  Window with blinds

  One-way mirror (93 in × 52 in, placed 32 in from the floor).

Figure 4.20: *Focus group and executive room layout (13 ft × 18 ft)*

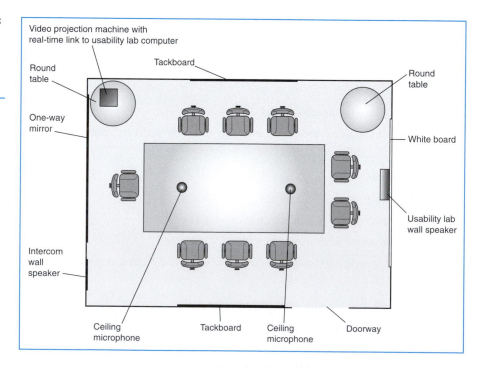

- *Electronic equipment:*

  Phone

  Video projection machine (displays real-time computer screen image)

  Electrical outlets

  Computer with Internet network (both high-speed and dial-up)

  Phone connections

  Audio system (unobtrusive microphones)

  Intercom speaker from observation room

  Speaker with connection to users' room.

- *Furniture:*

  Whiteboard (8 ft × 4 ft)

  Tackboard (8 ft × 4 ft)

  Phone

  Fifteen comfortable chairs

  Large conference table (8 ft long)

  Two small round tables

  Wastebasket.

Suggested Reading

Bias, R. G. & Mayhew, D. J. (eds) (1994). *Cost-Justifying Usability*. San Francisco, Morgan Kaufmann.

Dumas, J. S. & Redish, J. C. (1999). *A Practical Guide to Usability Testing*, 2nd ed. Exeter, England: Intellect Books.

Nielsen, J. (1994). *Usability Laboratories: A 1994 Survey*. Available at: www.useit.com/.

Mayhew, D. J. (1999). *The Usability Engineering Lifecycle: A Practitioner's Handbook for User Interface Design*. San Francisco: Morgan Kaufmann.

Rubin, J. (1994). *Handbook of Usability Testing: How to Plan, Design and Conduct Effective Tests*. New York: John Wiley & Sons.

Scanlon, T. (1999). Usability Labs: Our Take. *User Interface Engineering Eye For Design*, July/Aug.

Tognazzini, B. (AskTog Columns) (2000) *If They Don't Test, Don't Hire Them*. Available at: www.asktog.com/.

PART 2

(GET UP AND RUNNING)

CHAPTER 5

PREPARING FOR YOUR USER REQUIREMENTS ACTIVITY

Introduction

Presumably you have completed all the research you can before involving your end users (refer to Chapter 2, Before You Choose an Activity, page 28) and you have now identified the **user requirements** activity necessary to answer some of your open questions. In this chapter, we detail the key elements of preparing for your activity. These steps are critical to ensuring that you collect the best data possible from the real users of your product. We cover everything that happens or that you should be aware of prior to collecting your data – from creating a proposal to recruiting your participants.

At the end of this chapter you will find a fascinating case study from Kaizor Innovation that focuses on international research studies. Specifically, the study details issues relating to using western research methods in China.

At a Glance

> Creating a proposal
> Deciding the duration and timing of your session
> Recruiting participants
> Tracking participants
> Creating a protocol
> Piloting your activity

Creating a Proposal

A usability activity proposal is a roadmap for the activity you are about to undertake. It places a stake in the ground for everyone to work around. Proposals do not take long to write up but provide a great deal of value by getting everyone on the same page.

At a Glance

> Why create a proposal?
> Sections of the proposal
> Sample proposal
> Getting commitment

Why Create a Proposal?

As soon as you and the team decide to conduct a user requirements activity, you should write a proposal. A proposal benefits both you and the product team by forcing you to think about the activity in its entirety and determining what and who will be involved. You need to have a clear understanding of what will be involved from the very beginning, and you must convey this information to everyone who will have a role in the activity.

A proposal clearly outlines the activity that you will be conducting and the type of data that will be collected. In addition, it assigns responsibilities and sets a time schedule for the activity and all associated deliverables. This is important when preparing for an activity that depends on the participation of multiple people. You want to make sure everyone involved is clear about what they are responsible for and what their deadlines are. A proposal will help you do this. It acts as an informal contract. By specifying the activity that will be run, the users who will participate, and the data that will be collected, there are no surprises, assumptions, or misconceptions.

Tip

If you are conducting multiple activities (e.g., a card sort and wants and needs analysis for the same product), write a separate proposal for each activity. Different activities have different needs, requirements, and time-lines. It is best to keep this information separate.

Sections of the Proposal

There are a number of key elements to include in your proposal. We recommend including the following sections.

History

The history section of the proposal is used to provide some introductory information about the product and to outline any **usability** activities that have been conducted in the past for this product. This information can be very useful to anyone who is new to the team.

Objectives, measures, and scope of the study

This section provides a brief description of the activity that you will be conducting, as well as its goals, and the specific data that will be collected. It is also a good idea to indicate the specific payoffs that will result from this activity. This information helps to set expectations about the type of data that you will and will not be collecting. Do not assume that everyone *is* on the same page.

Method

The method section details how you will execute the activity and how the data will be analyzed. Often, members of a product team have never been a part of the kind of activity that you plan to conduct. This section is also a good refresher for those who are familiar with the activity, but perhaps it has been a while since they have been involved in an activity of this particular type.

User profile

In this section, detail exactly who will be participating in the activity. It is essential to document this information to avoid any misunderstandings later on. You want to be as specific as possible. For example, don't just say "students"; instead state exactly the type of student you are looking for. This might be:

- Between the ages of 18 and 25
- Currently enrolled in an undergraduate program
- Has experience booking vacations on the web.

It is critical that you bring in the correct user type for your activity. Work with the team to develop a detailed user profile (refer to Chapter 2, Before You Choose an Activity, "User Profile" section, page 43). When you write your proposal, it is possible that you may not have met with the team to determine this. If that is the case, be sure to indicate that you will be working with them to establish the key characteristics of the participants for the activity. Avoid including any "special users" that the team thinks would be "interesting" to include but are outside of the user profile.

Recruitment

In this section, describe how the participants will be recruited. Will you recruit them, or will the product team do this? Also, how will they be recruited? – Will you post a classified advertisement on the web, or use a recruitment agency? Will you contact current customers? In addition, how many people will you recruit?

You will need to provide answers to all of these questions in the recruitment section. If the screener for the activity has been created, you should attach this to the proposal as an appendix (see "Developing a Recruiting Screener", page 161).

Incentives

In your proposal, specify how the participants will be compensated for their time and how much (see "Determining Participant Incentives", page 159). Also, indicate who will be responsible for acquiring these incentives. If the product team is doing the recruiting, you want to be sure the team does not offer inappropriately high incentives to secure participation. (Refer to Chapter 3, Ethical and Legal Considerations, "Appropriate Incentives" section, page 100, for a discussion of appropriate incentive use.) If your budget is limited, you and the product team may need to be creative when identifying an appropriate incentive.

Responsibilities and proposed schedule

This is one of the most important pieces of your proposal – it is where you assign roles and responsibilities, as well as deliverable dates. Be as specific as possible in this section. Ideally, you want to have a specific person named for each deliverable. For example, do not just say that the product team is responsible for recruiting participants; instead, state that "John Brown from the product team" is responsible. The goal is for everyone to be able to read your proposal and understand exactly who is responsible for what.

The same applies to dates – be specific. You can always amend your dates if timing must be adjusted. It is also nice to indicate approximately how much time it will take to complete each deliverable. If someone has never before participated in one of these activities, he or she might assume that a deliverable takes more or less time than it really does. People most often underestimate the amount of time it takes to prepare for an activity. Sharing time estimates in your proposal can help people set their own deadlines.

Once the preparation for the activity is under way, you can use this chart to track the completion of the deliverables. You will be able to see at a glance what work is outstanding and who is causing the bottleneck.

Tip

If possible, do not propose to run your activity on a Monday or Friday. These days have the highest rates for no-shows.

Sample Proposal

The best way to get a sense of what a proposal should contain and the level of detail is to look at an example. Figure 5.1 offers a sample proposal for a card sorting activity to be conducted for our fictitious travel website. This sample can be easily modified to meet the needs of any activity.

Figure 5.1:

*Example of a card
sorting proposal*

TravelSmart.com
CARD SORT PROPOSAL
Jane Adams
Usability Specialist

Introduction and History

TravelSmart.com is a website that will allow travelers to book their travel on-line at discount prices. The key features for the first release will include:

- Searching for and purchasing airline tickets
- Searching for and booking hotels
- Searching for and booking rental cars

A Wants and Needs Analysis was conducted for this product in February of this year. Student participants brainstormed features that they want and need in an ideal discount travel site. The report of this activity can be found on the TravelSmart.com internal usability webpage. The results of the Wants and Needs Analysis will be used to create cards for a Card Sort activity.

This document is a proposal for a group Card Sort activity, which will be conducted in the Usability Research Laboratory with students currently enrolled in college. The Card Sort will be carried out through the coordinated efforts of the TravelSmart.com product team and the Usability and Interface Design team.

Objectives, Measures, and Scope of Study

Card sorting is a common usability technique that discovers a user's mental model of an information space (e.g., a website, a product, a menu). It generally involves representing each piece of information from the information space on an individual card and then asking target users to arrange these cards into groupings that are meaningful to them. This activity has two objectives:

- To help establish the high-level information architecture for the main functions of TravelSmart.com for student users
- To learn about any problematic terminology in TravelSmart.com.

The following data will be collected:

- Students' categorization schemas for travel objects and actions
- Category naming information
- Alternative terminology identified by participants
- Demographic information for each respondent (e.g., university, frequency of travel, web experience)

The information collected from this activity will be used to architect the TravelSmart.com website specifically targeted towards students.

Figure 5.1 – *Cont'd*

Method

Cards

There will be a set of objects represented on cards for participants to sort into categories. A term and a corresponding definition will be printed on each card, along with a blank line for participants to write in an alternate/preferred term for the definition.

Procedure

The card sort will be conducted in the usability lab on the evenings of March 25th and 27th. *<Sometimes the specific dates have not been determined at the time of the proposal. You should at least make a guess – e.g., the end of March>*

- After signing consent and non-disclosure agreements, participants will be given the set of "object" cards.
- Participants will first read each card and make sure that they understand the meaning of each term and definition. The test administrator will clarify any unfamiliar terms.
- Participants may rename any card they wish by writing the new term on the blank line.
- Next, participants will sort the cards into "groups that make sense to them." Participants will be informed there is no wrong way to sort the cards, no limit to the number of groups or cards in a group, and to work individually.
- Blank cards will be included in the set for participants to include any concept they feel is missing from the set.
- After sorting the cards, participants will give each group a name describing the group.
- Finally, participants will staple or clip groups together and give them to the administrator.

After the session is completed the data will be analyzed using cluster analysis software. The Usability and Interface Design team will conduct the analysis and provide design recommendations to the product team.

User Profile

Participants must meet the following criteria in order to participate:

- Be a student currently enrolled in one or more college classes
- Be at least 18 years of age
- Not work for a TravelSmart.com competitor

Recruitment

Usability intern, Mark Jones, will perform the recruiting for the Card Sort. An advertisement will be posted on a local web-based community bulletin board to solicit potential participants. Participants will be screened using the screener questionnaire (*You should attach this to the proposal if it has been created.*), and a total of 17 participants will be scheduled (15, plus 2 in case of attrition).

Continued

Figure 5.1– *Cont'd*

Compensation

Participants will receive $75 in AMEX gift checks for their participation. These incentives will be paid for and acquired by the Usability and Interface Design group.

What the usability team needs from the TravelSmart.com team

The usability team requires the following commitments from the TravelSmart.com product team:

- Work with usability team to develop objects list with definitions
- Attendance by at least one member of the product team to observe each session
- Review and approve user profile (see above)
- Review and approve screener
- Review and approve study proposal (this document)

What the usability team will provide

The usability team is committed to providing the following:

- Usability engineer, Jane Adams, to conduct the study
- Usability intern, Mark Jones, to recruit participants
- Acquisition and distribution of incentives for participants
- Detailed study plan (this document)
- Data collection and analysis
- Summary report with recommendations
- Presentation to your staff/manager

Proposed Schedule

	Work package	Owner	Estimated time-to-complete	Date forecast	Status
1	Provide object terms and definitions	Jane (UI team) and Dana (Product team)	2 days	March 1	COMPLETED March 3
2	Request incentives for 17 participants	Jane (UI team)	1 hour	March 1	COMPLETED March 1
3	Book laboratory space	Jane (UI team)	1 hour	March 1	COMPLETED March 1
4	Meet with UI team to finalize proposal	Jane (UI team) and Terry (Product team)	1 hour	March 20 (firm)	As of March 27, not yet completed
5	Recruit 17 participants (15 + 2 extra for attrition)	Mark (UI team)	1 week	Mar 17–21	TBD
6	Print labels for cards and create card sets	Jane and Mark (UI team)	6 – 10 hours	Mar 17 – Apr 21	TBD

Figure 5.1 – *Cont'd*

7	Conduct session 1	Jane (UI team)	1 hour	March 25 6:00 – 8:00 *<if known>*	TBD
8	Conduct session 2	Jane (UI team)	1 hour	March 27 6:00 – 8:00 *<if known>*	TBD
9	Analyze data and produce high-level findings for OSS team	Jane (UI team)	1 week	Mar 28 – Apr 4	TBD
10	Create draft report	Jane (UI team)	1 week	Mar 28 – Apr 4	TBD
11	Review and comment on report	Jane (UI team) and Terry (Product team)	1 week	Apr 4–11	TBD
12	Publish final report	Jane (UI team)	1–2 weeks	Apr 10–21	TBD

Getting Commitment

Your proposal is written, but you are not done yet. In our experience, if **stakeholders** are unhappy with the results of a study they will sometimes criticize one (or more) of the following:

- The skills/knowledge/objectivity of the person who conducted the activity
- The participants in the activity
- The tasks/activity conducted.

Being a member of the team and earning their respect (refer to Chapter 1, Introduction to User Requirements, "Preventing Resistance" section, page 18) will help with the first issue. Getting everyone to sign off on the proposal can help with the last two. Make sure that everyone is clear, before the activity, about all aspects of the study to avoid argument and debate when you are presenting the results. This is critical. If there are objections or problems with what you have proposed it is best to identify and deal with them now.

You might think that all you have to do is e-mail the proposal to the appropriate people. This is exactly what you do *not* want to do! Never e-mail your proposal to all the stakeholders and hope they read it. In most cases, your e-mail attachment will not even be opened. The reality is that everyone is very busy and most people do not have the time to read things that they do not believe to be critical. People may not believe your proposal is critical, but it is.

Instead, organize a meeting to review the proposal. It will likely take less than an hour. Anyone involved in the preparation for the activity or who will use the data should be present. At this meeting, you do not need to go through every single line of the proposal in detail, but you do want to hit several key points. They include:

- *The objective of the activity.* It is important to have a clear objective and to stick to it. Often in planning, developers will bring up issues that are out of the scope of the objective. Discussing it up front can keep the subsequent discussions focused.

- *The data you will be collecting.* Make sure the team has a clear understanding of what they will be getting.

- *The users who will be participating.* You really want to make this clear. Make sure everyone agrees that the user profile is correct. You do not want to be told after the activity has been conducted that the users "were not representative of the product's *true* end users" – and hence the data you collected are useless. It may sound surprising, but this is not uncommon.

- *Each person's role and what he/she is responsible for.* Ensure that everyone takes ownership of roles and responsibilities. Make sure they truly understand what they are responsible for and how the project scheduled will be impacted if delivery dates are not met.

- *The time-line and dates for deliverables.* Emphasize that it is critical for all dates to be met. In most cases, there is no opportunity for slipping.

Tip

Add a cushion to your deliverable dates. We often request deliverables a week before we absolutely need them. Then, if deliverables are late (which they often are), it's OK.

Although it may seem overkill to schedule *yet another* meeting, meeting in person has many advantages. First of all, it gets everyone involved, rather than creating an "us" versus "them" mentality (refer to Chapter 1, Introduction to User Requirements, "Preventing Resistance" section, page 18). You want everyone to feel like a team going into this activity. In addition, by meeting you can make sure that everyone is in agreement with what you have proposed. If they are not, you now have a chance to make any necessary adjustments and all stakeholders will be aware of the changes. At the end of the meeting, everyone should have a clear understanding of what has been proposed and be satisfied with the proposal. All misconceptions or assumptions should be removed. Essentially, your contract has been "signed." You are off to a great start.

Deciding the Duration and Timing of Your Session

Of course, you will need to decide the duration and timing of your session(s) before you begin recruiting your participants. It may sound like a trivial topic, but the timing of your activity can determine the ease or difficulty of the recruiting process. For individual activities, we offer users a variety of times of day to participate, from early morning to around 8 pm. We try to be as flexible as possible and conform to the individual's schedule and preference. This flexibility allows us to recruit more participants.

For group sessions it is a bit more challenging because you have to find one time to suit all participants. The participants we recruit typically have daytime jobs from 9 am to 5 pm, and not everyone can get time off in the middle of the day – so the time recommendations below focus on this type of user. Of course, optimal times will depend on the working hours of *your* user type. If you are trying to recruit users who work night shifts, these recommended times may not apply.

We have found that conducting group sessions in the periods 5–7 pm and 6–8 pm works best. We like to have our sessions end by 8 pm or 8:30 pm as we have found that, after this time, people get very tired and their productivity drops noticeably. Their motivation also drops because they just really want to get home. Also, a group activity can be quite tiring to moderate.

Because most people usually eat dinner around this time, we have discovered that providing dinner shortly *before* the session makes a huge difference. Participants appreciate the thought, and enjoy the free food; and their blood sugar is raised so they are thinking better and have more energy. As an added bonus, participants chat together over dinner right before the session and develop a rapport. This is valuable because you want people to be comfortable in sharing their thoughts and experiences with each other. The cost is minimal (about $60 for two large pizzas, soda, and cookies) and it is truly worth it. For individual activities that are conducted over lunch or dinnertime you may wish to do the same.

User requirements activities can be tiring for both the moderator and the participant. They demand a good deal of cognitive energy, discussion, and active listening to collect effective data. We have found that two hours is typically the maximum amount of time you want to keep participants for most user requirements activities. This is particularly the case if the participants are coming to your activity after they have already had a full day's work. Even two hours is a long time, so you want to provide a break when you see participants are getting tired or restless. If you need more than two hours to collect data, it is often advisable to break the session into smaller chunks and run it over several days or evenings. For some activities, such as surveys, two hours is typically much more time than you can expect participants to provide. Keep your participants' fatigue rate in mind when you decide how long your activity will be.

Recruiting Participants

Recruitment can be a time-consuming and costly activity if not done correctly. Below are some tips that should save you time, money, and effort. This information should also help you recruit users who better represent your true user population.

Tip

Never include supervisors and their own employees in the same session. Not only are these different user types, but employees are unlikely to contradict their supervisors. Additionally, employees may not be honest about their work practices with their supervisors present. Finally, supervisors may feel it necessary to "take control" of the session and play a more dominant or expert role in the activity to save face in front of their employees. The issues are similar when you mix user types of different levels within a hierarchy, even if one does not report directly to the other (e.g., doctor and nurse).

At a Glance

> How many participants do I need?
> Determining participant incentives
> Developing a recruiting screener
> Creating a recruitment advertisement
> Recruitment methods
> Preventing no-shows
> Recruiting international participants
> Recruiting special populations

How Many Participants Do I Need?

This is one of the hardest questions to answer for any usability activity, and unfortunately there is no straightforward answer. In an ideal world, a user requirements activity should strive to represent the thoughts and ideas of the entire user population by involving every user. In a slightly more practical world, an activity would be conducted with a representative **sample** of that population, so that the results are highly predictive of those of the entire population. This type of sampling is done through precise and time-intensive sampling methods. In reality, this is typically done only in academic, medical, pharmaceutical, and government research (e.g., Census Bureau surveys), but not in typical product development activities. This book is focused on user requirements, so a detailed discussion of statistics is not appropriate. If statistical accuracy is essential for you, we suggest that you refer to a book devoted to statistics or research and design.

SUGGESTED RESOURCES FOR ADDITIONAL READING

If **statistically significant** results and accuracy are critical, we recommend that you become familiar with the basics of statistics. A good introductory book is:

- Keppel, G., Saufley, W. H., & Tokunaga, H. (1992). *Introduction to Design and Analysis: A Student's Handbook*, 2nd ed. New York: W. H. Freeman.

In the world of product development, **convenience sampling** is typically used. When employed, the sample of the population used reflects those who were available (or those you had access to), as opposed to selecting a truly *representative* sample of the population. Rather than selecting participants from the population at large, you recruit participants from a convenient subset of the population. For example, research done by college professors often uses college students for participants instead of representatives from the population at large.

Convenience sampling reflects the reality of product development. Typically, you need answers and you needed them yesterday. This means that you do not have the time or resources to get responses from hundreds of randomly selected users. So how many responses are enough? Because the appropriate sample size varies with each method, we will not explore a discussion of specific numbers in this section. In each method chapter, we suggest participant sample sizes based on our own practices and the practices of many usability professionals we consulted with while writing this book.

The unfortunate reality of convenience sampling is that you cannot be positive that the information you collect is truly representative of your entire population. We are certainly not condoning sloppy data collection, but as experienced usability professionals are aware, we must strike a balance between rigor and practicality. For example, you should not avoid doing a survey because you cannot obtain a perfect sample. However, when using a convenience sample, still try to make it as representative as you can.

Determining Participant Incentives

Before you can begin recruiting participants, you need to identify how you will reward people for taking time out of their day to provide you with their expertise. You should *always* provide your participants with an incentive to thank them for their time and effort. The reality is that it also helps when recruiting; but you don't want your incentive to be the sole reason why people are participating, and you should not make the potential participants "an offer they cannot refuse" (refer to Chapter 3, Ethical and Legal Considerations, "Appropriate Incentives" section, page 100).

Tip

Offering large incentives may encourage dishonest individuals to participate in your study. They may not be truthful about their skills, or they may quickly take you up on your offer of "free to leave at any time without penalty" offer. Make the incentive large enough to thank people for their time and expertise, but nothing more.

Generic users

When we use the term "generic users," we are referring to people who participate in a usability activity, but have no ties to your company. They are not customers and they are not employees of your company. They have typically been recruited via an electronic community bulletin board advertisement or an internal database of potential participants, and they are representing themselves, not their company, at your session (this is discussed further in "Recruitment Methods" below). This is the easiest group to compensate because there is no potential for conflicts of interest. You can offer them whatever you feel is appropriate. Some standard incentives include:

- One of your company products for free (e.g., a piece of software)
- A gift certificate (e.g., an electronics store, a department store, movie pass)

- Gift checks
- Charitable donations in the participant's name.

Cash is often very desirable to participants, but it can be difficult to manage if you are running a large number of studies with many participants. Obviously, you will want to make sure that you have a secure place to store this. Also, if you are working for a large company that requires purchase orders to track money spent, you will not be able to place a purchase order for cash. If you work for a smaller company this may be a manageable option.

In our experience we have found a gift check to be a great alternative to cash. We typically purchase gift checks from American Express. They can be bought in denominations of $10 up to $100. These gift checks can be used like travelers' checks. Participants can spend them at any place that takes American Express, or they can be cashed/deposited at a bank. We have found that these work well for both participants and ourselves.

With regard to how much to pay participants, this varies a great deal. In the San Francisco Bay area we typically use the formula of $50 per hour; however, we vary this formula depending on how difficult the particular user profile is to recruit or how specialized their skill set is. For example, we may pay students $75 for a two-hour study, but pay doctors $200 for the same session. One thing to keep in mind is that you want to pay everyone involved in the *same* session the same amount. We sometimes come across the situation where it is easy to get the first few participants, but difficult to get the last few. Sometimes we are forced to increase the compensation in order to entice additional users. If you find yourself in such a situation, remember that you must also increase the compensation for those you have already recruited. A group session can become very uncomfortable and potentially confrontational if, during the activity, someone casually says "This is a great way to make $100" to someone who you offered a payment of only $75. You do not want to lose the trust of your participants and potential end users – that isn't worth the extra $25.

For highly paid individuals (e.g., CEOs), you could never offer them an incentive close to their normal compensation. For one study, a recruiting agency offered CEOs $500 per hour but they could not get any takers. In these cases, a charitable donation in their name sometimes work better. For children, a gift certificate to a toy store or the movies or a pizza parlor tends to go over well (just make sure you approve it with their parents first). Some companies have even offered savings bonds to children, although the parents usually appreciate them more than the kids do.

Customers or your own company employees

If you are using a customer or someone within your company as a participant, you will typically not be able to pay them as you would a generic end user. Paying customers could represent a conflict of interest because this could be perceived as a payoff. Additionally, most activities are conducted during business hours so the reality is that their company is paying for them to be there. The same is true for employees at your own company. Thank customer participants or internal employees with a company logo item of nominal value (e.g., mug, sweatshirt, keychain).

If sales representatives or members of the product team are doing the recruiting for you, make sure they understand what incentive you are offering for customers and why it is a conflict of interest to pay customers for their time and opinions. We recently had an uncomfortable situation in which the product team was recruiting for one of our activities. They contacted a customer that had participated in our activities before and always received logo gear ("swag"). When the product team told them their employees would receive $150, they were thrilled. When we had to inform the customer that this was not true and that they would receive only swag, they were quite offended. No matter what we said, we could not make the customer (or the product team representative) understand the issue of conflict of interest and they continued to demand the same payment as other participants. After we made it clear that this would not happen, they declined to participate in the activity. You never want the situation to get to this point.

Developing a Recruiting Screener

Assuming you have created a user profile (refer to Chapter 2, Before You Choose an Activity, "User Profile" section, page 43), the first step in recruiting is to create a detailed phone screener. A screener is composed of a series of questions to help you recruit participants who match your user profile for the proposed activity.

Screener Tips

There are a number of things to keep in mind when creating a phone screener. They include:

- Do not screen via e-mail
- Work with the product team
- Keep it short
- Use test questions
- Collect demographic information
- Eliminate competitors
- Provide important details
- Prepare a response for people who do not match the profile.

Do not screen via e-mail

It is important for you to talk to the participants, for a number of reasons. Firstly, you want to get a sense of whether or not they truly match your profile, and it is difficult to do this via e-mail. You really need to have a discussion with the individuals. Secondly, you want to make sure that the participants are clear about what the activity entails and what they will be required to do (see "Provide important details", page 165). If you send this information via e-mail, you cannot be sure that they read and understood those details. Thirdly, you want to get a sense of an individual's personality. If someone sounds and behaves in a weird fashion on the phone it is probably because they *are* weird. Fourthly, you will discover that some people are simply interested in the money or that they are trying to sell themselves to you in order to get a job at your company. You want to avoid recruiting these types of people and a phone call can help you do this.

Work with the product team

We cannot emphasize too strongly how important it is to make sure you are recruiting the right users. Your screener is the tool to help with this. Make sure that the product team helps you to develop it. Their involvement will also help instill the sense that you are a team working together, and it will avoid anyone from the product team saying "You brought in the wrong user" after the activity has been completed.

Keep it short

In the majority of cases, a screener should be relatively short. You do not want to keep a potential participant on the phone for more than 10 or 15 minutes. People are busy and they don't have a lot of time to chat with you. You need to respect that fact. Also, you are very busy and the longer your screener is, the longer it will take you to recruit your participants.

"I'm not trying to sell you anything, sir. I'm doing market research, and all I ask is two or three hours of your time to answer a few thousand questions."

Use test questions

Make sure that your participants are being honest about their experience. We are not trying to say that people will blatantly lie to you (although occasionally they will), but sometimes people may exaggerate their experience level, or they may be unaware of the limitations of their knowledge or experience (thinking they are qualified for your activity when, in reality, they are not).

When recruiting technical users, determine that they have the correct level of technical expertise. You can do this by asking test questions. This is known as knowledge-based screening. For example, if you are looking for people with moderate experience with HTML coding, you might want to ask "What is a CGI script and how have you used it in the past?"

Collect demographic information

Your screener can also contain some further questions to learn more about the participant. These questions typically come at the end, once you have determined that the person is a suitable candidate. For example, you might want to know which university the person attends and whether he/she is full-time or part-time. The university and the student status will not rule the person out from participating, but it is some relevant information that you can compile about the participants that you brought in for the activity. You can use this demographic information to determine the diversity of your population of participants.

Eliminate competitors

Always, always, find out where the potential participants work before you recruit them. You do not want to invite employees from companies that develop competitor products. This usually means companies that develop or sell products that are anywhere close to the one being discussed. Assuming you have done your homework (refer to Chapter 2, Before You Choose an Activity, page 28), you should know who these companies are. You might imagine that, ethically and legally, this would never happen, but it does. We did have a situation where an intern recruited someone from a competitor to participate in an activity; as luck would have it, the participant canceled later on. If this happens to you, call the participant and explain the situation. Apologize for any inconvenience but state that you must cancel the appointment. People will usually understand.

Sending the participants' profiles to the product team after recruitment can also help avoid this situation. The team may recognize a competitor that they forgot to tell you about. If you are in doubt about a company, a quick web search can *usually* reveal whether the company in question makes products similar to yours.

Provide important details

Once you have determined that a participant is a good match for the activity, you should provide the person with some important details. It is only fair to let the potential participants know what they are signing up for. (Refer to Chapter 3, Ethical and Legal Considerations, page 94, to learn more about how to treat participants.) You do not want there to be any surprises when they show up on the day of the activity. Your goal is not to trick people into participating, so be up-front. You want people who are genuinely interested. Here are some examples of things you should discuss:

- Obviously, let them know the logistics: time, date, and location of the activity.
- Tell them exactly how they will be compensated.
- Let them know whether it is a group or individual activity. Some people are painfully shy and do not work well in groups. It is far better for you to find out over the phone than during the session. We have actually had a couple of potential participants who declined to participate in a session once they found out it was a group activity. They simply didn't feel comfortable talking in front of strangers. Luckily, we learned this during the phone interview and not during the session, so we were able to recruit replacements. Conversely, some people do not like to participate in individual activities because they feel awkward going in alone.
- Make them aware that the session will be videotaped. Some people are not comfortable with this and would rather not participate.
- Emphasize that they must be on time. Late participants will not be introduced into an activity that has already started (refer to Chapter 6, During Your User Requirements Activity, "The Late Participant" section, page 211).
- If your company requires an ID from participants before entry, inform them that they will be required to show an ID before being admitted into the session (see "The Professional Participant," page 189).
- Inform them that they will be required to sign a consent/confidential disclosure agreement, and make sure that they understand what these forms are (refer to Chapter 3, Ethical and Legal Considerations, "Legal Considerations" section, page 103). You may even want to fax the forms to the participants in advance.

Prepare a response for people who do not match the profile

The reality is that not everyone is going to match your profile, so you will need to reject some very eager and interested potential participants. Before you start calling, you should have a response in mind for the person who does not match the profile. It can be an uncomfortable moment, so have something polite in mind to say, and include this in your screener so you do not find yourself lost for words. Simply thank the person for his/her time and interest in the study, and kindly state that he/she does not match the profile for this particular activity. It can be as simple as "I'm sorry, you do not fit the profile for this particular study, but thank you so much for your time." If the person seems to be a great potential candidate, encourage him or her to respond to your recruitment postings in the future.

Sample Screener

Figure 5.2 is a sample screener for the recruitment of students for a group card sorting activity. This should give you a sense of the kind of information that it is important to include when recruiting participants.

Figure 5.2:

Example of a recruitment screener

**TravelSmart.com Card Sort
Recruitment Screener
March 25 and 27, 6:00–8:00 pm**

Start of Call

Hello, this is _____ from TravelSmart.com's usability group. I'm responding to your e-mail regarding the usability activity for students. Let me tell you a little about the activity, and then if you're interested, I'll need to ask you a few questions. Is that ok? Great!

This will be a **group activity**, where you would be helping us design a travel website. The activity will begin at 6:00 pm on either Tuesday, March 25 or Thursday, March 27, and will last for about 1 hour. This takes place at TravelSmart.com in San Francisco. *<Describe the location briefly.>* Participation is on a paid basis. Are you interested in participating?

- **Yes** – ask the next series of questions
- **No** – thank the person and then end the call.

Figure 5.2 – *Cont'd*

Great! I have a few questions to ask you to see whether you fit the profile of the individuals we need for this session. After talking with you, I will take your information back to the team for review, and then I will call you back to let you know whether your background is a good fit, and to schedule you.

I. Background Information

Name: _____ Daytime Phone: _____

E-mail: _____

1. Have you participated in Travelsmart.com usability testing before? _____ Yes _____ No
   If yes, when/what activity? _____ *<If yes, check the participant database for comments and to determine how much they have been paid this calendar year.>*

2. Are you currently enrolled as a student? _____ Yes _____ No *<If no, end the call.>*
   _____ Undergraduate _____ Graduate

3. At which college or university? _____ *<Participants should be from a mix of schools.>*

4. Department/Major? _____ *<Participants should be from a mix of departments/majors.>*

5. Are you a full time or part time student? _____ Full _____ Part *<Informational only.>*

6. Have you booked travel on the web before? _____ Yes _____ No *<If no, end the call.>*

7. How many trips have you booked in the last 12 months? _____ *<If less that 2, end the call.>*

8. Are you currently employed outside of your school? _____ Yes _____ No
   If Yes, company name: _____ *<Must not be TravelSmart.com competitor – e.g., CheapTravel.com.>*
   Job title: _____ *<Informational only.>*

II. Computer Experience

9. How long have you been using the web? _____ *<If less than 6 months, disqualify.>*

10. How long have you been using a computer? _____ *<If less than 1 year, disqualify.>*

III. Confidentiality agreement, permission to tape, and verify identity

[*If the participant meets all criteria, please ask the additional questions that follow.*]

I also have some questions to make sure you understand and are comfortable with our procedures before you come in:

- Are you willing to sign a standard consent form, which acknowledges that you agree to participate, and confidential disclosure form, which states you agree not to share the details of the session with anyone for a period of 3 years?
   _____ Yes _____ No *<If no, disqualify.>*

Continued

Figure 5.2 – *Cont'd*

- Are you willing to be videotaped? (Thevideo's purpose is so we cango back and capture more detailed notes. Videos are seen internally only by members of the product and usability teams who are interested in what you have to say.)
  _____ Yes _____ No <*If no, disqualify.*>
- The compensation is $75 in American Express gift checks (used like travelers checks). In order to pay you, we will require that you show us a government-issued ID. We are required to make sure that the name on the gift check matches the name of the person we are paying. <*Make sure that the name the person has given you will match the name on the driver's license.*> Are you willing to bring your driver's license or a passport?
  _____ Yes _____ No <*If no, disqualify.*>

Based on the screener answers in section (I, II, & III) choose one of the following responses:

It looks like your profile is a match for this activity, and if you'd like, I'll go ahead and schedule you for a time.

or

It looks like you might fit the profile for this study, but I will have to check with the product team before I can know for sure. I will check with the team and get back with you as to whether or not we can go ahead and schedule you for this study.

or

I'm sorry, you do not fit the profile for this particular study, but thank you so much for your time.

IV. Availability

For which session(s) would you be available?

Tuesday March 25 @ 6:00 pm ___available ___not available ___not sure

Thursday March 27 @ 6:00 pm ___available ___not available ___not sure

Thank you for taking time to share your information. I will now take your information to the team, and will call you soon to let you know whether you would be a match for this particular study.

V. Scheduling

It looks like your profile is a match for this activity, and I'd love to schedule you for a time.

<*Schedule participant and verbally confirm date and time.*>

Great! Let me give you some information about where to go, and I will follow that up with an e-mail confirmation along with a map to TravelSmart.com.

- *Participation contact:* Mark Jones, Phone: 555 555-6655
- *Location:* 123 Fake Street, San Francisco, CA 94105
- *Directions:* Hwy 280 (North or South, depending on where they're coming from) to King Street exit. Go straight and take a left on Third Street to Harrison. You can park in the lot on your right, or in any parking garage for free.

Figure 5.2 – *Cont'd*

Other Instructions:

- Wait in lobby of the building to be escorted to session room.
- Participants will be escorted in starting at 5:40 pm for light dinner/snacks (so come early!). *<Inquire whether they are vegetarian, if you feel comfortable asking this.>*
- Allow plenty of time, as traffic can be very bad! Because we will begin the activity right at 6:00 pm, <u>late arrivals may not be able to join the session</u>, as it would delay everyone else. *<Emphasize this.>*
- Also, on some occasions we need to cancel sessions. We don't expect this, but if this does happen you will be contacted as soon as possible before your session.
- Please remember your driver's license, or we cannot let you into the session!
- I will call you again just before your scheduled appointment to remind you of the evaluation and confirm your attendance. If for some reason you need to cancel or reschedule, please call me as soon as possible! Thank you and we look forward to seeing you on *<Insert time & date>*!

Creating a Recruitment Advertisement

Regardless of the method you choose to recruit your participants, whether it is via a web posting or an internal database of participants (discussed later in "Recruitment Methods"), you will almost always require an advertisement to attract appropriate end users. Depending on your method of recruiting, you or the recruiter may e-mail the advertisement, post it on a website, or relay its message via the phone. Potential participants will respond to this advertisement or posting if they are interested in your activity. You will then reply to these potential participants and screen them.

There are several things to keep in mind when creating your posting.

At a Glance

> Provide details

> Include logistics

> Cover key characteristics

> Don't stress the incentive

> State how they should respond

> Include a link to your in-house participant database

Provide details

Provide some details about your study. If you simply state that you are looking for users to participate in a usability study, you will be swamped with responses! This is not going to help you. In your ad, you want to provide *some* details to help narrow your responses to ideal candidates.

Include logistics

Indicate the date, time, and location of the study. Obviously, by doing so, those who are not available will not respond. You want to weed out unavailable participants immediately.

Cover key characteristics

Indicate some of the key characteristics of your user profile. This will pre-screen appropriate candidates. These are usually high-level characteristics (e.g., job title, company size). You do not want to reveal all of the characteristics of your profile because, unfortunately, there are some people who will pretend to match the profile. If you list all of the screening criteria, deceitful participants will know how they should respond to all of your questions when you call.

For example, let's say you are looking for people who:

- Are over 18 years of age
- Have purchased at least three airline tickets via the web within the last 12 months
- Have booked at least two hotels via the web within the last 12 months
- Have booked at least one rental car via the web within the last 12 months
- Have experience using the TravelSmart.com website
- Have a minimum of two years' web experience
- Have a minimum of one years' computer experience.

In your posting you might indicate that you are looking for people who are over 18, enjoy frequent travel, and have used travel websites.

Don't stress the incentive

Avoid phrases like "Earn money now!" This attracts people who want easy money and those who will be more likely to deceive you for the cash. Incentives are meant to merely compensate people for their time and effort, as well as to thank them. An individual who is attending your session only for the money will complete your activity as quickly as possible and with as little effort as possible. It really isn't worth your time and money to bring those individuals in to participate. Trust us.

State how they should respond

We suggest providing a generic e-mail address for interested individuals to respond to rather than your personal e-mail address or phone number. If you provide your personal contact information (particularly a phone number), your voice-mail and/or e-mail inbox will be jammed with responses. Another infrequent but possible consequence is being contacted by desperate individuals wanting to participate and wondering why you haven't called them yet. By providing a generic e-mail address, you can review the responses and contact whomever you feel will be most appropriate for your activity.

It is also nice to set up an automatic response on the e-mail account, if it is used solely for recruiting purposes. Keep it generic so you can use it for all of your studies. Here is a sample response:

> "Thank you for your interest in our usability study! We will be reviewing interested respondents over the next two weeks and we will contact you if we think you are a match for our study.
>
> Sincerely,
>
> The TravelSmart.com Usability Group"

Include a link to your in-house participant database

If you have an in-house participant database, you should point participants to your web questionnaire, at the bottom of your ad (see Appendix E, page 704).

Be aware of types of bias

Ideally, you do not want your advertisement to appeal to certain members of your user population and not others. You do not want to exclude true end users from participating. This is easy to do unknowingly based on where you post your advertisement or the content within the advertisement.

For example, let's say that TravelSmart.com is conducting a focus group for frequent travelers. To advertise the activity you have decided to post signs around local colleges and on college web pages because students are often looking for ways to make easy money. As a result, you have unknowingly biased your sample to people who are in these college buildings (i.e., mostly students) and it is possible that any uniqueness in this segment of the population may impact your product. Make sure you think about bias factors when you are creating and posting your advertisement.

This type of bias, created by those who do not respond to your posting, is referred to as **non-responder bias**. The "non-responders" are the people who do not respond to your call for participation. Of course there will always be suitable people who do not respond, but if there is a pattern (e.g., those who are not students) then this is a problem. To avoid non-responder bias, you must ensure that your call for participation is perceived equally by all potential users and that your advertisement is viewed by a variety of people from within your user population.

One kind of bias that you are unable to eliminate is **self-selection bias**. You can reduce this by inviting a random sample of people to complete your survey, rather than having it open to the public; but the reality is that not all people you invite will want to participate. Some of the invited participants will self-select to not participate in your activity.

Sample Posting

Figure 5.3 is a sample posting to give you a sense of how a posting might look when it all comes together.

> **Tip**
>
> After a potential participant has been screened, sending the completed screener to the product team for their approval *before* the participant is scheduled can be a good idea. This works well in cases in which the qualifications are particularly complex, or when you want to make sure that the product team agrees that the participants were truly potential users.

Figure 5.3:

Example of a

recruitment ad

Attention Frequent Travelers!

Interested in participating in an activity to help design a discount travel website?
We will be conducting a usability study on March 25 and 27 at the TravelSmart.com
Usability Labs in San Francisco, CA (King Street exit). Participation will involve
approximately one hour of your time on one day and is on a paid basis.

To participate in the study, you should meet the following requirements:

- Enjoy frequent travel
- Have experience with travel websites
- Be over 18 years of age.

If you are available and would like to be part of this activity, please reply via e-mail to
travel_usabilty@travelsmart.com with the subject line "Travel study".

You also must include:

- **Your name**
- **Age**
- **Indicate the travel website that you have experience with**
- **Phone number**

We will contact you within the next two weeks if you are an appropriate match.
If you are also interested in participating in future usability activities at
TravelSmart.com, please complete the form located at
http://travelsmart.com/usability.htm.

Recruitment Methods

There are a variety of methods to attract users and each method has its own strengths
and weaknesses. If one fails then you can try another. In this section, we will touch
on some of these methods so that you can identify the one that will best suit your
needs.

At a Glance

> Advertise on community bulletin board sites

> Create an in-house database

> Use a recruiting agency

> Make use of customer contacts

Advertise on Community Bulletin Board Sites

Web-based community bulletin boards allow people to browse everything from houses to jobs to things for sale. We have found them to be an effective way to attract a variety of users. We will typically place these ads in the classified section under "Jobs." You may be able to post for free or for less than $100, depending on the area of the country you live in and the particular bulletin board. The ad is usually posted within 30 minutes from when you submit it. One of the advantages of this method is that it is a great pre-screen if you are looking for people who use the web and/or computers. If they have found your ad, you know they are web users!

If you are looking for people who are local, use a site that is local to your area. Sites such as your local newspaper website or community publications are good choices. We have had great success using Craig's List in the San Francisco Bay area (see Figure 5.4). It has often proved to be one of our most successful methods of recruitment. If you do not have access to any web publications in your area, or if you want

Figure 5.4:
Craig's List in the San Francisco Bay Area (www.craigslist.org)

people who do not have web experience, you could post your advertisement in a physical newspaper.

Create an In-house Database

You can create a database within your company where you maintain a list of people who are interested in participating in usability activities. This database can hold some of the key characteristics about each person (e.g., job title, years of experience, industry, company name, location, etc.). Prior to conducting an activity, you can search the database to find a set of potential participants who fit your user profile. See Appendix E (page 704) for a discussion of how to set up such a database.

Once you have found potential participants, you can e-mail them some of the information about the study and ask them to e-mail you if they would like to participate. The e-mail should be similar to an ad you would post on a web community bulletin board site (see Figure 5.3 on page 173). State that you obtained the person's name from your in-house participant database, which he/she signed up for, and provide a link or option to be removed from your database. For those who respond, you should then contact them over the phone and run through your screener to check that they do indeed qualify for your study (refer to "Developing a Recruiting Screener," page 161).

Use a Recruiting Agency

You can hire companies to do the recruiting for you. They have staff who are devoted to finding participants. These companies are often market research firms but, depending on your user type, temporary agencies can also do the work. In the San Francisco Bay area we have used Nichols Research (www.nichols-research.com) and Merrill Research (www.merrill.com). Fieldwork (www.fieldwork.com) is another company that has offices sprinkled throughout the United States. You can contact the American Marketing Association (www.marketingpower.com) to find companies that offer this service in your area. Appendix D (page 698) contains a list of companies that can recruit for activities, conduct them, and rent facilities.

Sounds great, doesn't it? Well, it certainly can be. We have found that a recruiting service is most beneficial when trying to recruit a user type that is difficult to find.

For example, we needed to conduct a study with physicians. Our participant database did not contain physicians and an electronic community bulletin board posting was unsuccessful. As a result, we went to a recruiting agency and they were able to get these participants for us.

An additional benefit to using recruiting agencies is that they usually handle the incentives. Once you cut a purchase order with the company, you can include money for incentives. The recruiting agency will then be responsible for paying the participants at the end of a study. This is one less thing for you to worry about.

You might ask: "Why not use these agencies exclusively and save time?" One of the reasons is cost. Typically they will charge anywhere from $100 to $200 to recruit each participant (not including the incentives). The price varies depending on how hard they think it will be for them to attract the type of user you are looking for. If you are a little more budget conscious, you might want to pursue some of the other recruiting options; but keep in mind that *your* time is money. A recruiting agency might be a bargain compared to your own time spent recruiting.

Also, in our experience, participants recruited by an agency have a higher no-show rate. One reason for this is that not all agencies call to remind the participants about the activity the day before (or on the day of) the study. Additionally, using a recruiting agency adds a level of separation between you and the participants – if you do the recruiting yourself, they may feel more obligated to show up.

We should note, however, that not all usability professionals we have spoken with share our negative experience with recruiting agencies. Some have told us that their no-show rates have been very low when working with recruiting agencies.

Some recruiting agencies need more advance notice to recruit than we normally need ourselves. Some agencies we have worked with required a one-month notice to recruit so they had enough resources lined up. Consequently, if you need to do a quick, lightweight activity, an agency might not be able to assist you, but it never hurts to enquire.

Lastly, we have found that agencies are not effective in recruiting very technical user types. Typically, the people making the calls will not have domain knowledge about the product you are recruiting for. Imagine you are conducting a database study and you require participants who have an intermediate level of computer programming knowledge. You have devised a set of test questions to assess their knowledge about programming. Unless these questions have very precise answers (e.g., multiple-choice), the recruiter will not be able to assess whether the potential participant is providing the correct answers. A participant may provide an answer that is close enough, but the recruiter doesn't know that. Even having precise multiple-choice answers doesn't always help. Sometimes the qualifications are so complex that you simply have to get on the phone with candidates.

Regardless of these issues, a recruiting agency can be extremely valuable. If you decide to use one, there are a few things to keep in mind.

At a Glance

> Provide a screener
> Ask for the completed screeners to be sent after each person is recruited
> Ensure that they remind the participants
> Avoid the professional participant
> You can't always add them to your database

Provide a screener

You will still need to design the phone screener and have the product team approve it. The recruitment agency will know nothing about your product, so the screener may need to be more detailed than you would normally provide. Indicate what the desired responses are for each question, and when the phone call should end because the potential participant does not meet the necessary criteria. Also provide a posting, if they are going to advertise to attract participants.

Be sure to discuss the phone screener with the recruiter(s). Don't just send it via e-mail and tell them to contact you if they have any questions. You want to make sure that they understand and interpret each and every question as it was intended. Even if you are recruiting for a user with a non-technical profile, make sure you do this. You may even choose to do some role-playing with the recruiter. Only when the recruiter begins putting your screener to work will you see whether he/she really understands it. Many research firms will employ a number of people to make recruitment calls. If you are unable to speak with all of them then you should speak with your key point of contact at the agency and go through the screener.

Ask for the completed screeners to be sent after each person is recruited

This is a way for you to monitor who is being recruited and to double-check that the right people are being signed up. You can also send the completed screeners along to members of the product team to make sure they are happy with each recruit. This has been very successful for us in the past.

Ensure that they remind the participants

It sounds obvious, but reminding participants of your activity will drastically decrease the no-show rate. Sometimes recruiting agencies recruit participants one to two weeks before the activity. You want to make sure that they call to remind people on the day before (and possibly again on the day of) the activity to get confirmation of attendance. It is valuable to include reminder calls in your contract with the recruitment agency, which also states that you will not pay for no-shows. This increases *their* motivation to get those participants in your door.

Avoid the professional participant

Yes, even with recruitment agencies, you must avoid "the professional participant." A recruitment agency may call on the same people over and over to participate in a variety of studies. We have encountered this. The participant may be new to you but could have participated in three other studies this month. Although the participant may meet all of your other criteria, someone who seeks out research studies for regular income is not representative of your true end user. They will likely behave differently and provide more "polished" responses if they think they know what you are looking for.

You can insist that the recruitment agency provide only "fresh" participants. To double-check this, chatting with participants at the beginning of your session can reveal a great deal. Simply ask: "So, how many of you have participated in studies for the ABC agency before?" People will often be proud to inform you that the recruiting agency calls on them for their expertise "all the time."

> ## Tip
>
> Include a screener question that asks whether a person has participated in a usability study or a market research group in the last six months and, if so, how many. If the answer is more than one, you should consider disqualifying that person.

You can't always add them to your database

You may be thinking that you will use a recruiting agency to help you recruit people initially and then add those folks to your participant database for future studies (see Appendix E, page 704). In many cases, you will not be able to do this. Some recruiting agencies have a clause in their contract that states that you cannot enlist any of the participants they have recruited unless it is done via them. Make sure you are aware of this clause, if it exists.

Make Use of Customer Contacts

Current or potential customers can make ideal participants. They truly have something at stake because, at the end of the day, they are going to have to use the product. As a result, they will likely not have problems being honest with you. Sometimes they are brutally honest.

Typically, a product team, a sales consultant, or **account manager** will have a number of customer contacts with whom they have close relationships. The challenge can be convincing them to let you have access to them. Often they are worried or concerned that you may cause them to loose a deal or that you might upset the customer. Normally, a discussion about your motives can help alleviate this problem.

Start by setting up a meeting to discuss your proposal (see "Getting commitment," page 153). Once the product team member, sales consultant, or account manager understands the goal of your user requirements activity, they will hopefully also see the benefits of customer participation. It is a "win–win" situation for both you and the customer. Customers love to be involved in the process and having their voices heard, and you can collect some really great data. Another nice perk is that it can cost you less, as you typically provide only a small token of appreciation rather than money (see "Determining Participant Incentives," page 159).

Despite your efforts, it is possible that you will be forbidden from talking with certain customers. You will have to live with this. The last thing you want is to make an account manager angry, or cause a situation in which a customer calls up your company's rep to complain that they want what the usability group showed them, not what the rep is selling. The internal contacts within your company can be invaluable when it comes to recruiting customers – they know their customers and can assist your recruiting – but they have to be treated with respect and kept informed about what you are doing.

If you decide to work with customers, there are several things to keep in mind.

At a Glance

> Be wary of the angry customer
> Avoid the unique customer
> Recruiting internal employees
> Allow more time to recruit
> Make sure the right people are recruited

Be wary of the angry customer

When choosing customers to work with, it is best to choose ones who currently have a good relationship with your company. This will simply make things easier. You want to avoid situations that involve heavy politics and angry customers. The last thing you or your group needs is to be blamed for a spoiled business deal. However, deals have actually been *saved* as a result of intervention from the usability professionals – the customer appreciated the attention they were receiving and recognized that the company was trying to improve the product based on their feedback. If you find yourself dealing with a dissatisfied customer, give the participants an opportunity to vent; however, do not allow this to be the focus of your activity. Providing 15 minutes at the beginning of a session for a participant to express his/her likes, dislikes, challenges, and concerns can allow you to move on and focus on the desired requirements gathering activity you planned.

When recruiting customers, if you get a sense that the customer may have an agenda, plan a method to deal with this. Customers often have gripes about the current product and want to tell someone. One way to handle this is to have them meet with a member of the product team in a separate meeting from the activity. The usability engineer needs to coordinate this with the product team. It requires additional effort, but it helps both sides.

Avoid the unique customer

It is best to work with a customer that is in-line with most of your other customers. Sometimes there are customers that have highly customized your product for their unique needs. Some companies have business processes that differ from the norm or industry standards. If you are helping the product development team collect user requirements for a "special customer," this is fine. If you are trying to collect user requirements that are going to be representative of the majority of your user population, you will not want to work with a customer that has processes different from the majority of potential users.

Recruiting internal employees

Sometimes your customers are people who are internal to your company. These can be the hardest people of all to recruit. In our experience, they are very busy and just don't feel it is worth their time to volunteer. If you are attempting to recruit internal participants, we have found it extremely effective to get their management's buy-in first. That way, when you contact them, you can say "Hi John, I am contacting you because your boss, Sue, thought you would be an ideal candidate for this study." If their boss wants them to participate they are unlikely to decline.

Allow more time to recruit

Unfortunately, this is one of the disadvantages of using customers. Typically, customer recruiting can be a slow process. There is often corporate red tape that you need to go through. You may need to explain to a number of people what you are doing and whom you need to participate. You also need to rely on someone within the company to help you get access to the right people. The reality is that although this may be your top priority, in most cases it is not their's, so things will always move more slowly than you would like. You may also have to go through the legal department for both your company and the customer's in order to get approval for your activity. Confidential disclosure agreements may need to be changed (refer to Chapter 3, Ethical and Legal Considerations, "Legal Considerations" section, page 103).

Make sure the right people are recruited

You need to ensure that your company contact is crystal-clear about the participants you need. In most cases, the contact will think that you want to talk to the people who are responsible for purchasing or installing the software. Make sure the person understands that you want to talk to the people who will be *using* the software after it has been purchased and installed. It is best not to hand your screener over to the customer contact. Instead, provide the person with the user profile (refer to Chapter 2, Before You Choose an Activity, "User Profile" section, page 43) and have him/her e-mail you the names and contact information of people seeming to match this profile. You can then contact them yourself and run them through your screener to make sure they qualify.

It is important to note that companies often want to send their best and brightest people. As a result it can be difficult to get a representative sample with customers. You should bring this issue up with the customer contact and say: "I don't want only your best people. I want people with a range of skills and experience."

Also, don't be surprised if the customer insists on including "special" users in your study. Often, supervisors will insist on having *their* input heard before you can access their employees (the true end users). Even if you don't need feedback from purchasing decision-makers or supervisors, you may have to include them in your activity. It may take longer to complete your study with additional participants, but the feedback you receive could be useful. At the very least, you have created a more positive relationship with the customer by including those "special" users.

Preventing No-shows

Regardless of your recruitment method, you will encounter the situation where people who have agreed to participate do not show up on the day. This is very frustrating. The reason could be that something more important came up, or the participant might have just completely forgotten. There are some simple strategies to try and prevent this from occurring.

Provide contact information

Participants are often recruited one to two weeks before the activity begins. When we recruit, participants are given a contact name and phone number and told to contact this person if they will not be able to make the session for any reason. We understand that people do have lives and that our activity probably ranks low in the grand scheme of things. We try to emphasize to participants that we really want them to participate, but we will understand if they cannot make the appointment. We really appreciate it when people take the time to call and cancel or reschedule. It allows us an opportunity to find someone else, or to reschedule. It is the people who just do not appear that cause the most difficulty.

Remind them

The day before, and on the day of the activity, contact the participants to remind them. Some people just simply forget, especially if it is on a Monday morning! A simple reminder can prevent this.

Try to phone people rather than e-mail them, because you need to know whether or not they will be coming. If you catch them on the phone you can get this immediately. Also, you can reiterate a couple of very important points to them. Remind them that they must be on time for the activity, *and* they must bring a valid driver's license or they will *not* be admitted to the session. If you send an e-mail, you will have to hope that people read it carefully and take note of these important details. Also, you will have to wait for people to respond to confirm. Sometimes people do not read your e-mail closely and they do not respond (especially, if they know they are not coming). If participants cannot be reached by phone, and you must leave a voice-mail, remind them about the date and time of the session, and all of the other pertinent details. Ask them to call you back to confirm their attendance.

Over-recruit

Even though you have provided your participants with contact information to cancel and you have called to remind them, there are still people who will not show up. To counteract this problem, you can over-recruit participants. It is useful to recruit one extra person for every four or five participants needed.

Sometimes everyone will show up, but we feel this cost is worth it. It is better to have more people than not enough. When everyone shows, you can deal with this in a couple of ways. If it is an individual activity, you can run the additional sessions (it costs more time and money but you get more data) or you can call and cancel the additional sessions. If participants do not receive your cancellation message in time and they appear at the scheduled time, you should pay them the full incentive for their trouble.

If everyone shows up for a group activity, we typically keep all participants. An extra couple of participants will not negatively impact your session. If there is some reason why you cannot involve the additional participants, you will have to turn them away. Be sure to pay them for their trouble.

Some people double-book every slot for an individual activity. They will involve the first person who arrives, and if the second person shows up then he/she will be paid but turned away. Unless you are under a very strict deadline, or the user profile is expected to have a very high no-show rate, we do not recommend using this method – primarily because you have to spend twice as long recruiting and pay twice as much for your participants. Also, it is never very nice to have to turn people away. You do not want to set yourself up so that you are potentially turning away half of your participants. That is no way to create a loyal following of participants.

Recruiting International Participants

Depending on the product you are working on and its market, you may need to include participants from other countries. You cannot assume that you can recruit for *or* conduct the activity in the same manner as you would in your own country. Below are some pieces of advice to keep in mind when conducting international user requirements activities (Dray & Mrazek 1996).

- Use a professional recruiting agency in the country where you will be conducting the study. It is highly unlikely you will know the best places or methods for recruiting your end users.

- Learn the cultural and behavioral taboos/expectations. The recruiting agency can help you, or you can check out several books specifically for this. Refer to "Suggested Resources for Additional Reading" on page 186 for more information.

- If your participants speak another language, unless you are perfectly fluent you will need a translator. Even if your user speaks your language, you will need a translator. The participants will likely be more comfortable speaking in their own language or could have some difficulty understanding some of your terminology if they are not fluent. There are often slang or technical terms that you will miss out on, despite being well-versed in the foreign language.

- If you are doing in-home studies in Europe, in some countries not only is it unusual to go to someone's home for an interview or other activity, it is also unusual for guests to bring food to someone's home. Since you are a foreigner, or because the study is unusual, bringing food will likely be accepted.

- Punctuality can be an issue. For example, you must be on time when observing participants in Germany. In Korea or Italy, however, time is somewhat relative – appointments are more like suggestions and very likely will not begin on time. Keep this in mind when scheduling multiple visits in one day.

- Pay attention to holiday seasons. For example, you will be hard pressed to find European users to observe in August since many Europeans go on vacation at that time. Countries with a large Islamic population will likely be unavailable during Ramadan.

Recruiting is just the tip of the iceberg when it comes to conducting international field studies. You cannot simply apply a user research method in a foreign country in the same way that you would in your own country. At the end of this chapter you will find a fascinating case study from *Kaizor Innovation* that discusses issues relating to applying western research methods in China. If you plan to conduct international user requirements activities you will gain a tremendous amount of beneficial information that can be applied to your particular situation.

SUGGESTED RESOURCES FOR ADDITIONAL READING

Here are some additional resources you may find valuable when preparing for international user studies.

Hofstede's "five cultural dimensions" and Hall's "proxemic theory" have been used in cultural anthropology, sociology, and cultural user interface studies for many years. These frameworks can help you understand a country's business etiquette and culture prior to conducting your study and may help you analyze your findings following your visit.

- Hofstede, G. (1991). *Cultures and Organizations: Software of the Mind – Intercultural Cooperation and its Importance for Survival.* New York: McGraw-Hill.
- Hall, E. T. (1976). *Beyond Culture.* New York: Anchor Books.

For a recent example of how researchers applied these frameworks to understand cultural differences in product use, check out:

- Kim, S., Kim M. J., Choo, H., Kim, S. H., & Kang, H. J. (2003). Cultural Issues in Handheld Usability: Are Cultural Models Effective for Interpreting Unique Use Patterns of Korean Mobile Phone Users? In *Proceedings of the Usability Professionals' Association 2003 Conference.* Scottsdale, AZ, 23–27 June.

The website below provides the results of Geert Hofstede's "five cultural dimensions" for 57 national and regional cultures, and charts of the dimensions by predominant religion:

- http://geert-hofstede.international-business-center.com.

The websites below have a high-level discussion of Hall's model of context, space, and time in relation to human behavior and interaction:

- http://www.csiss.org/classics/content/13 and http://www.cs.ur.edu/~gnick/bvdh/edward_t_hall_great_.htm.

Recruiting Special Populations

There are a number of special considerations when recruiting special populations of users. These populations can include such groups as children, the elderly, and people with disabilities. This section discusses some things to consider.

Transportation

You may need to arrange transportation for people who are unable to get to the site of the activity. You should be prepared to arrange for someone to pick them up before the activity and drop them off at the completion of the activity. This could be done using taxis, or you could arrange to have one of your employees do it. Also, if it is possible, you should consider going to the participant rather than having him or her come to you.

Escorts

Some populations may require an escort. For example, in the case of participants under the age of 18, a legal guardian must accompany them. You will also need this guardian to sign all consent and confidential disclosure forms. You may also find that adults with disabilities or the elderly may require an escort. This is not a problem. If the escort is present when the user requirements session is being conducted, simply ask him/her to sit quietly and not interfere with the session. It is most important for the participant to be safe and feel comfortable (refer to Chapter 3, Ethical and Legal Considerations, "Ethical Considerations" section, page 95). This takes priority over everything else.

Facilities

Find out whether any of your participants have special needs with regard to facilities as soon as you recruit them. If any of your participants have physical disabilities, you must make sure that the facility where you will be holding your activity can accommodate people with disabilities. You will want to ensure that it has parking for the handicapped, wheelchair ramps, and elevators, and that the building is wheelchair accessible in all ways (bathroom, doorways, etc.). Also keep in mind that the facility may need to accommodate a dog if any of your participants use one as an aid.

If you are bringing children to your site it is always a nice idea to make your space "kid friendly." Put up a few children's posters. Bring a few toys that they can play with during a break. A few small touches can go a long way to helping child participants feel at ease.

Tracking Participants

When recruiting via an electronic community bulletin board posting, recruiting agency, or an in-house database, there are a number of facts about the participants that you need to track. To help you accomplish this, set up a database that lists all of the participants that you use. This can be the beginning of a very simple participant database. You will want to track such things as:

- The activities they have participated in
- The date of the activity
- How much they were paid
- Any negative comments regarding your experience with the participant (e.g., "user did not show up," "user did not participate," "user was rude")
- Any positive comments (e.g., "Joe was a great contributor")
- Current contact information (e-mail address, phone number).

You may also want to check with your legal department whether you can collect participants' social security numbers. It is a great piece of information to have because it is a unique identifier for each participant. However, it tends to deter participation. May people are very protective of this information (as they should be!) and would rather not participate if it requires providing their social security number. This may also cause participants to distrust your motives.

At a Glance

> Tax implications
> The professional participant
> Create a Watch List

Tax Implications

If any participant is paid over $600 in one calendar year in the United States, your company will be *required* to complete and submit a 1099 tax form. Failure to do so can get your company (and possibly even the person who hands out the money) into serious trouble. This is a real headache and you will do yourself a big favor by avoiding this. To do so, you will need to track how much each participant has been paid each calendar year. Once a participant reaches the $600 mark, move him/her to a Watch List (see below). This list should be reviewed by the recruiter prior to recruiting.

The Professional Participant

Believe it or not, there are people who seem to make a career out of participating in usability activities and market research studies. Some are just genuinely interested in your studies, but others are genuinely interested in the money. You definitely want to avoid recruiting the latter.

We follow the rule that a person can participate in an activity once every three months or until he or she reaches the $600/year mark (see "Tax Implications," page 188). Unfortunately, there are some people who don't want to play by these rules. We have come across people who have changed their names and/or job titles in order to be selected for studies. We are not talking about subtle changes. In one case, we had a participant who claimed to be a university professor one evening and a project manager another evening – we have compiled at least nine different aliases, phone numbers, and e-mail addresses for this participant! The good news is that these kinds of people tend to be the rare exception.

By tracking the participants you have used in the past, you can take the contact information you receive from your recruits and make sure that it does not match the contact information of anyone else on your list. When we discover people who are using aliases, or who we *suspect* are using aliases, we place them on a Watch List (see below).

We also attempt to prevent the alias portion of the problem by making people aware during the recruiting process that they will be required to bring a valid government-issued ID (e.g., drivers license, passport). If they do not bring their ID, they will not be admitted into the activity. You need to be strict about this. It is not good enough to fax a photocopy or send an e-mail of the license before or after the activity. The troublesome participant described above actually altered her driver's license and e-mailed it to us to receive the incentive she had been denied the night before.

Create a Watch List

The Watch List is an important item in your recruiting toolbox. It is where you place the names of people you have recruited in the past, but do not want to recruit in the future. These people can include:

- Those who have reached the $600 per calendar year payment limit (you can remove them from the watch list on January 1st)
- Those who have been dishonest in any way (e.g., used an alias; changed job role without a clear explanation)
- Those who have been poor participants in the past (e.g., rude; did not contribute; showed up late)
- Those who did not show up for an activity.

Figure 5.5:

A warning poster

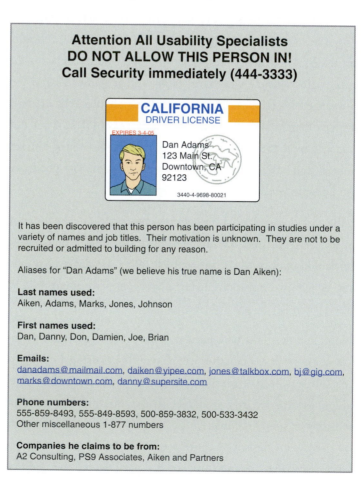

The bottom line is that you want to do all you can to avoid bringing in undesirable participants. Again, in the case of our troublesome participant, she managed to sweet-talk her way into more than one study without a driver's license ("I left it in my other purse," and "I didn't drive today"). As a result, we posted warning signs for all usability engineers in our group. We even included her picture from the forged ID she e-mailed us. See Figure 5.5 on page 190 for an example of a "Wanted" poster.

Creating a Protocol

A protocol is a script that outlines all procedures you will perform as a moderator and the order in which you will carry out these procedures. It acts as a checklist for all of the session steps.

The protocol is very important for a number of reasons. Firstly, if you are running multiple sessions of the same activity (e.g., two focus groups) it ensures that each activity and each participant is treated consistently. If you run several sessions, you tend to get tired and may forget details. The protocol helps you keep the sessions organized and polished. If you run the session differently for each activity, you will impact the data that you receive for each session. For example, if the two groups receive different sets of instructions, each group may have a different understanding of the activity and hence produce different results.

Secondly, the protocol is important if there is a different person running each session. This is never ideal, but the reality is that it does happen. The two people should develop the protocol together and rehearse it.

Thirdly, a protocol helps you as a facilitator to ensure that you relay all of the necessary information to your participants. There is typically a wealth of things to convey during a session and a protocol can help ensure that you cover everything. It could be disastrous if you forgot to have everyone sign your confidential disclosure agreements – and imagine the drama if you forgot to pay them at the end of the session.

Finally, a protocol allows someone else to replicate your study, should the need arise.

Sample Protocol

Figure 5.6 is a sample protocol for a group card sorting activity. Of course, you need to modify the protocol according to the activity you are conducting, but this one should give you a good sense of what it should contain.

Figure 5.6:

Example of a protocol

TravelSmart.com Card Sort Protocol

Before participant arrives:

- Lay out food
- Turn on CD player (background music while people are coming in and getting settled)
- Distribute name tags, pens, consent form/CDA
- Turn on VCR and put tape in to record the activity
- Make sure you have protocol, cards, envelops, staples, rubber bands, extra pens, and incentives

After participant arrives:

- Ask for ID
- Offer something to drink and eat
- Explain about video, observers behind the one-way mirror, and breaks
- Explain CDA/consent form, and name tags
- Collect signed paperwork and ask assistant to make copies
- Begin video recording
- Explain who we are and the purpose of the activity
- Indicate that we are not members of the development team. We did not develop the content we will be working with today, so feel free to be honest.

Facilitator says:

"We are in the process of designing a travel website targeted at college and university students. Today, you are here to help us develop the structure of the interface. There are several pieces of information or objects that we would like for you to group into meaningful piles. This will help us to group the information in our product so that it is easy to find.

I am going to present each of you with a stack of cards. On each card is a term and a corresponding definition. I would like for you to review each card and tell me if the definition does not make sense or if you disagree with the term we have provided. For example, you might say 'I have heard of this before but I call it something else.' At that point, I will ask if there is any one else who calls this object by a different name. I

---

would like for you to make any changes to the definition or the term directly on the card. Also, if you do not use this object or if you have never heard of it before, please write 'I never use this' or 'I have never heard of this before' directly on the card. After you have reviewed all of the terms, please sort the objects together into meaningful groups. There is no limit to the number of groups or number of cards in a group. Also, we'd like you to work individually. There are NO wrong answers. If you believe that an object *needs* to be in more than one group, you can create a duplicate using one of the blank cards.

Once you have divided all of your cards into groups, please use the blank cards to give each group a meaningful name. This could be a word or a phrase. If you need more blank cards, please let me know. Also, please let me know if you have any questions!"

<Do a quick sorting example on the whiteboard. If people understand then hand out the set of cards and let them begin to sort. Sit quietly at the front of the room and answer any questions.>

Finishing Up

- As people begin to finish their sorts, ask them to staple each group together and place them in a pre-marked envelope. If a group is too big to be stapled, use a rubber band.
- As participants finish, thank them for their time, pay them, and escort them back to the lobby.
- Be sure to collect each participant's visitor's badge.

Figure 5.6 – *Cont'd*

Piloting Your Activity

A pilot is essentially a practice run for your activity. It is a mandatory element for any user requirements activity. These activities are complex, and even experienced usability specialists always conduct a pilot. You cannot conduct a professional activity without a pilot. It is more than "practice," it is debugging. Run the activity as though it is the true session. Do everything exactly as you plan to for the real session. Get a few of your co-workers to help you out. If you are running a group activity that requires 12 people, you do not need to get 12 people to participate in the pilot. (It would be great if you could, but it usually is not realistic or necessary.) Three or four co-workers will typically help you accomplish your purpose. We recommend running a pilot about three days before your session – this will give you time to fix any problems that crop up.

Conducting a pilot can help you accomplish a number of goals.

Is the audio-visual equipment working?

This is your chance to set camera angles, check microphones, and make sure that the quality of recording is going to be acceptable. You don't want to find out after the session that the video camera or tape recorder was not working.

Clarity of instructions and questions

You want to make sure that instructions to the participants are clear and understandable. By trying to explain an activity to co-workers ahead of time, you can get feedback about what was understandable and what was not so clear.

Tip

Avoid sensitive or personal topics. It should go without saying, but it is unwise to discuss extremely sensitive or personal topics like politics, sex, or morals in any usability activity. Obviously, these are topics that are sometimes uncomfortable or cause heated discussion between friends and family. It is not appropriate for you to ask participants to discuss them in front of strangers and on camera. The pilot is a good time to make sure that you have not included any questions that could possibly offend or embarrass participants.

Find bugs or glitches

A fresh set of eyes can often pick up bugs or glitches that you have not noticed. These could be anything from typos in your documentation to hiccups in the product you plan to demo. You will obviously want to catch these embarrassing oversights or errors before your real session.

Practice

If you have never conducted this type of activity before, or it has been a while, a pilot offers you an opportunity to practice and get comfortable. A nervous or uncomfortable facilitator makes for nervous and uncomfortable participants. The more you can practice your moderation skills the better (refer to Chapter 6, During Your User Requirements Activity, "Moderating Your Activity" section, page 220).

The pilot will also give you a sense of the timing of the activity. Each usability activity has a pre-determined amount of time, and you need to stay within that limit. By doing a pilot you can find out whether you need to abbreviate anything.

Tip

Have a back-up plan for things that you can foresee going wrong. For example, technology can sometimes be a problem area. If you plan to show slides on the laptop, have printouts as well in case the projector or laptop acts up. If you are demonstrating a prototype or code that is known to be unstable, have a plan in place in case it goes down. Perhaps you can show screenshots instead, or maybe you will need to change the format of the activity entirely. Just remember to be flexible and realize that things don't always go according to plan. The reality is that if things go wrong, you may have to use a less-polished but still serviceable method to get the data.

Who should attend?

If this is the first time you have conducted this type of activity, it is advisable to have someone experienced in your pilot session. He or she will be able to give you feedback about what can be improved. After the pilot, if you do not feel comfortable executing the activity due to inexperience as a moderator, you will seriously want to consider having someone experienced (a co-worker or consultant) step in for you. You can then shadow the experienced moderator to increase your comfort level for next time. (Appendix D, page 698, has a list of vendors that could execute the activity for you.)

Members of the product team should attend your pilot session. They are a part of your team for this activity, so you want them to be involved at every step – and this is an important step. Even though they have read your proposal (see "Getting Commitment," page 153), they may not have a good sense of how the activity will "look." The pilot will give them this sense. It also gives the product team members one last chance to voice any concerns or issues. Be prepared for some possible critical feedback. If you feel their concerns are legitimate, you now have an opportunity to address them.

Ironically, the pilot is the one session to which you may feel uncomfortable inviting team members, because you may be nervous and because events do go awry at pilots. But if you explain the nature and purpose of pilots to the team and set their expectations, they can help you without you feeling threatened.

Pulling It All Together

Preparation is the key to a successful user requirements activity. Be sure to get the product team involved in the preparation immediately and work together as a team. In this chapter, we have covered all the key deliverables and action items that you and your product team will need to complete in order to prepare for a successful user requirements activity.

CASE STUDY

International studies add another layer of complexity to any user requirements activity. Recruiting is just the tip of the iceberg. You must be aware of all of the complicating factors when you are *preparing* for your activity. User research techniques based on Western models of thought must be adapted for Asian models of thought if conducting user research in China. In this case study, Elaine Ann presents some fascinating and insightful recommendations drawn from field studies in China that can be applied to other international studies.

Cultural Differences Affecting User Research Methods in China

Elaine Ann, Founder/Director, Kaizor Innovation

China, with its 1.3 billion population – over four times the population of the United States – has an average and continuing growth of 8% GDP every year. Since China opened its doors to the world in 1981, it has risen to become the largest emerging consumer power.

China's immense market and growing demands for all types of products and services have attracted many multinational foreign companies competing to enter the market to claim a share of the pie. However, products imported into China will need to adapt to the differences in Chinese culture and lifestyle. This requires an in-depth understanding of the Chinese psyche and behavioral patterns affecting product requirements and design. User research is an important tool to inform product development teams.

To date, user research methods originating from the US are based on a Western model of thought. A typical user research study begins by recruiting respondents from the target market segment through market research companies or the client's existing customer database. Then a team of user researchers and designers plan and formulate interview questions and observational requirements prior to the research study. Depending on the context of use for the product or services, the study might take place at the respondent's home, workplace, or mobile environment. During the visit, the entire process might be photographed or videotaped for documentation. Following the study, the research team analyzes the observations and insights to formulate strategies informing product development or marketing teams.

This process and methodology can lead to cross-cultural conflicts and misinterpretation of data when applied to China without considering the fundamental differences in culture. This case study discusses the assumptions Western user research methodologies are based on and how they conflict with the Chinese model of thought and way of working. Based on our initial user research experiences in China with Hewlett-Packard conducted from a bi-cultural point of view, there is reason to believe that user research methods will require adaptation if conducted in China for results to be accurate and meaningful.

As Hewlett-Packard's research is highly confidential, this case study discusses only the insights on user methodologies based on the research experience without referring to the actual content of the study.

Difference between Chinese and Western Models of Thought

Table 5.1 gives an overview of the difference between Chinese and Western models of thought. This fundamental difference has important effects on user research methodologies and results. When employing Western methods, it cannot be assumed that the Chinese will respond in the same way as Western respondents do.

Table 5.1:

Comparison of Chinese and Western models of thought

Chinese model	Western model (US)
Confucius	Plato
Collectivist society	Individualistic society
Hierarchical social order, all men are not equal	Equality
Authoritarian	Democratic
Relationship-oriented	Logic and scientific inquiry of the "truth"
Indirect and implicit communication	Direct verbal communication
Practical	Philosophic
Family	Self
Relationship-based trust	Positivism
Harmony & balance	Truth

As our research team is bi-cultural – combining Chinese cultural upbringing and received Western education and design training – our insights stem from both Chinese traditional cultural values and Western design and research professional practice. We have observed during our user research studies in China that certain assumptions and methods might need to be adapted for the Chinese context (see Table 5.2).

Table 5.2:

Comparison of research methods

Assumptions of Western user research methods	Cultural differences in China
Rely on Chinese local language translators to interpret information	Local mainland Chinese translators with a communist upbringing might not be familiar with the Western or capitalist ways of working and concepts. Translators outside the domain of design and user research might misinterpret information and important concepts
Recruit respondents randomly from a market segmentation database to ensure objectivity	As China is a relationship-oriented society, research teams might encounter difficulty in recruiting when "knocking on the door cold." Chinese people do not respond well to strangers as the social structure differentiates "in-groups" (friends/family) from the "out-groups" (strangers)
Ask questions in an objective or scientific way, inquiring about the "truth"	Chinese people are more interested in maintaining a harmonious relationship when interacting with each other. Researchers asking a similar question repeatedly in multiple ways with an inquisitive attitude might come through as an offensive interrogation to the Chinese

Assumptions of Western user research methods	Cultural differences in China	Table 5.2 – Cont'd
• Treat respondents as "subjects" of study (users) • Keep emotionally distant from respondents to maintain objective results	The separation between "friendship" and "business" dealings in the US might come through as an insincere gesture and create distrustful feelings in the Chinese towards Westerners. In China, friendship is a prerequisite to dealing with business and money.	
Assume respondents will verbally express themselves communicating truthful feelings or opinions	Chinese traditional education is dogmatic and requires the young to be obedient and silent to show respect for teachers, elderly, and superiors. This upbringing discourages openness in verbal communication. Chinese will refrain from giving criticisms openly in public, especially to strangers, and say the "appropriate thing" so as not to offend, giving the opposite party "face"	
Assume respondents will participate creatively in the making of artifacts revealing deeper inner thoughts	Chinese education traditionally does not encourage the expression of individual creativity but to excel in imitating the master of classics. Chinese thinking also tends not to challenge the norm but to conform to social expectations and benefits of the group, therefore stifling individual ideas and expressions	
Assume findings can be accurately analyzed and interpreted from a Western point of view	Data collected from user research studies will need to be accurately interpreted to be valuable to foreign companies. The very same observations might yield very different insights depending on the cultural "lens" it's viewed through	

Adapting Western User Research Methods in China

This section discusses in detail the four key areas that researchers need to take into consideration when applying user research methods in China.

Language Translation versus Conceptual Translation

Cultural difference: Differences in cultural concepts and domain knowledge.

An often overlooked factor in cross-cultural research is the assumption that hiring local translators shuttling information between two different cultures will yield the same research results. It is important to note that domain and cultural knowledge of the translator and his/her understanding of the relevance of the research results applied to design are critical for accurately interpreting conceptual differences. Simply translating between languages word for word will guarantee misrepresentation of information, as well as skewing research findings.

For example, in the US the concept of "industrial design" (such as practices under IDSA, Industrial Design Society of America) is an umbrella term referring to the design of all types of products – consumer goods as well as heavy industrial machinery. In China, the same term refers mainly to the designing of heavy industrial machinery, including aerospace design involving much more engineering knowledge; the term "product design" is mainly used for consumer goods. The department of "industrial design" at Beijing University of Aeronautics and Astronautics is much more engineering driven and would be considered as engineering in the US.

Here is another example. Tsing Hua University (Beijing), one of the top design schools in China, showcased a design exhibit organized by the British Council, titled in English as "Designed for Use." However, the exhibit title was translated into Chinese as "Easy to Use Design" (see Figure 5.7) Here, two diverse concepts were mistaken as equivalent, and

Figure 5.7:

Language translation versus conceptual translation. On this exhibit card, "Designed for Use" in English has been translated to "Easy to Use Design" in Chinese

neither side notices the difference without a conceptual bridge and domain knowledge in the field of design. Although each word was translated correctly, the underlying meaning and concept was completely misinterpreted.

Recruiting Respondents

Cultural difference: Relationships (Guan-Xi) as prerequisites to businesses in China.

As a standard practice in respondent recruitment in the US, a market research or recruiting company might be hired to sample randomly from a targeted segment of users as respondents. This requires recruiting firms to pick up the phone and cold call potential or past customers from a database list. Western respondents will most likely welcome the opportunity to give feedback to corporations on their products/services in return for monetary rewards and will also be comfortable with researchers paying visits to their homes.

In the Chinese context, however, this method can have its difficulties. The Chinese society is built on "Guan-Xi" – relationships and networks of friends and family. As a society built upon Confucius's Five Cardinal Relationships (Wu Lun; see Figure 5.8 on page 202), "In the Chinese world it is relationships, not law, that provide the security necessary to do business" (Blackman 1997). In conducting user research in China, researchers must recognize the inherent social structure that Chinese people operate in. China is a collectivist society (see Figure 5.9 on page 202) and a person's very existence is "defined by a bilateral relationship with another person." Whether it's traditional Confucius belief of close bonding with one's family, or the communist way of adhering to one's party "unit," either way Chinese people operate collectively in having close relationships with an immediate group (in-group). Everyone else out of this network is considered a stranger (out-group) unless he or she is referred by someone trusted.

In recruiting for respondents, we in the West have a much higher rate of success by relying on personal networks and relationships. As non-objective as it may seem to the West, connections will play a large part in recruitment in China if information gathered is to be reliable, for the following reasons (page 203):

Figure 5.8:

*Confucius's Five
Cardinal Relationships*

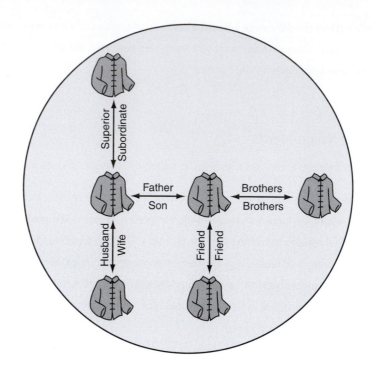

Figure 5.9:

*Collectivist versus
individualist society*

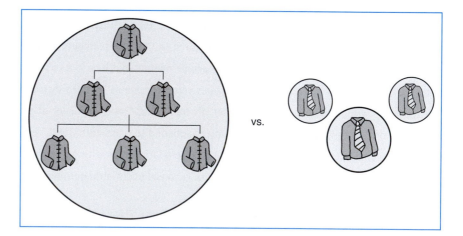

- Building trust – friendship before business
- Privacy of the home
- Reluctance in disclosing truthful feelings to strangers.

Building Trust

As Blackman, a researcher of Western–Asian business relationships at the University of Dallarat says (1997):

> "In developing business relationships in China, establishing a long-term relationship of friendship and trust is a pre-requisite to building business relationships."

Chinese people place much more trust in knowing someone personally or through a close friend/relative and trust their inner circle much more than acquaintances (Bond 1991). Thus, recruiting randomly as in Western methodologies without referrals have a much higher risk of "no shows," non-responsiveness, or superficial feedbacks.

One respondent in this research who is a personal contact insisted that she invites the research team for lunch as we are guests visiting "her soil" – a courteous Chinese gesture for welcoming visitors. The research visit was also seen more as a friendship favor than business dealing. Another respondent known indirectly made comments in Chinese expressing impatience in dealing with the "lao wai" (translated as "old outsiders" = foreigners) during the research.

Since friendship is a basis before any business dealings in China, this stark contrast with the West can be a problem when foreign researchers or companies expect to be able to recruit easily based on monetary rewards. The value put on relationships in Chinese society overrides any monetary returns. In some cases, even with compensation, the Chinese might not be willing to hassle over dealing with strangers unless it is a referral from a friend or an established associate.

In addition, the Western way of treating research studies as business and objective study devoid of any continuation of personal friendship after the research might leave the Chinese to feel being "used" and viewing Westerners as being very "practical." Subsequent requests on future research might be refused if such feelings of "take and leave" are created amongst the Chinese respondents.

Privacy of the Home

The Chinese are more private when it comes to exposing their homes to complete strangers. When introduced through a friend or relative, the visit becomes a much more friendly experience than an offensive one.

It is also a courteous gesture for the Chinese to tidy up the home before visitors arrive, so as to hide the unpresentable. One of our respondents mentioned that he had tidied his home prior to our research team arriving, as his place is normally a mess and there is usually a lot of junk. This factor of Chinese cultural courtesy should be especially noted for research teams to remind Chinese users *not* to clean their homes if they want to obtain a more "truthful" view of the person's living environment. Although in the West it is also a courteous gesture to tidy the home before visitors arrive, it is much more so in Chinese culture and considered shameful and inappropriate otherwise.

Reluctance in Disclosing Feelings Truthfully

Another disadvantage in recruiting without personal references or connections in China is that respondents might be less truthful in disclosing real feelings or opinions in front of people whom they do not consider as their in-group. Remarks might therefore be more superficial, giving a more publicly acceptable answer rather than true opinions. Therefore research studies will have a higher risk of collecting inaccurate information. However, as a friend, one might be much more helpful and communicate more truthful feedback.

Interviewing Methods and Observational Research

Cultural difference: Scientific/rational of the West versus intuitive/subjective mentality of the Chinese.

The Chinese traditionally believe in the importance of maintaining a harmonious relationship between "heaven, earth, and man" for mankind to exist in peace with nature. However, in the West (especially in the US) a scientific culture of attempting to understand nature and "truth," calls for research methods to emphasize on "objective" analysis and proof (Leong & Clark 1999). This stark contrast reveals itself in user research as the Chinese place much more importance on maintaining harmonious feelings amongst each other rather than trying to understand a subject matter objectively (see Figure 5.10).

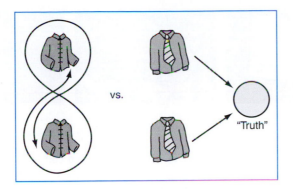

Figure 5.10:
Relationship-oriented culture versus scientific inquiry of the "truth"

During our research studies, in some cases, Chinese users became frustrated when questions asked by Westerners were posed in a "scientific" way – repeating a similar question in multiple ways in order to validate the answer. Some Chinese users are also surprised and responded with awe that an "obvious" answer to a question needed to be asked. This interviewing technique of direct questioning to validate findings can appear offensive as the Chinese view repeated questioning as either mistrust in what they have already answered or a challenge to their intelligence.

The treatment of people as "users" and subjects of study could also offend. Observational research methods such as videotaping and photographing to document the research can be offensive to some Chinese, especially when they are dealing with strangers. Relationships need to be treated with much sensitivity and respect.

Cultural Insights

Cultural difference: Cultural insights beyond research findings.

Cultural insights from user research are also important in interpreting findings. Without the background to understand cultural differences, findings might not be well understood.

An example is the power of celebrities or a publicly known figure appearing in advertising in China. In the US, celebrities might be chosen mainly to represent or advertise for certain brands related to their profession or image. For example, Michael Jordan, a famous basketball player in the US, advertises sports products (Nike) or healthy-living foods (Kellogg's). In China, a publicly known figure or celebrity will be seen advertising for a

Figure 5.11:

The same Chinese celebrity advertises unrelated brands

multitude of unrelated products. For example, Gi Gi Leung, a famous Hong Kong Chinese celebrity, advertises cell phones, juice drinks, cosmetics, and computers (see Figure 5.11).

This cultural understanding is important to business strategies as product sales in China can be influenced purely by a reputable spokesperson. Trust for a brand is placed more in the person promoting the product than in the company or even the product quality alone. In a relationship-driven society, comments and opinions from an authoritative and respected figure overpowers all logic.

Another example of cultural insight is the "one-child policy" implemented in China in 1979. This can have important implications for product development strategies. To Western cultures, the "one-child policy" might seem undemocratic and violate human rights. However, without understanding China's internal problem, judgments can be made falsely. "The rapid population growth that occurred after the Communist Party came to power had put a strain on the government's efforts to help its people. So in an attempt to combat the widespread poverty and improve the overall quality of life, the one-child policy was gradually adopted" (http//axe.acadiau.ca/~043638z/one-child/). On average, a mainland Chinese family has two parents and four grandparents looking after one child, leading to the raising of "little emperors." This phenomenon provides opportunities for companies to develop products taking advantage of the power-relations of this type of social structure. An example is developing toys or products targeted to the single child.

Lessons Learned

- When usability professionals conduct any user research methods propounded in this book in another country, they should take some time to understand the broader culture in which they will be working.
- It is clearly important to have translators capable of communicating in both languages fluently as well as interpreting conceptual and cultural differences and domain knowledge.

- Establish a network of friends in China with continued relationships to smoothen the recruitment process for more accurate research results.
- Adapt for less intrusive research methods, obtaining insights reading "in between the lines".

Acknowledgment. This material is from "Cultural Differences Affecting User Research Methods in China" by Elaine Ann. IDSA 2003 National Educational Conference, Industrial Design Society of America (IDSA), New York, © 2003. Reprinted with permission from *Eastman National IDSA Education Conference Proceedings*, the annual educational publication of the Industrial Designers Society of America; e-mail: idsa@idsa.org; website: www.idsa.org.

References

Blackman, C. (1997). *Negotiating China: Case Studies and Strategies.* St Leonards, NSW: Allen & Unwin.

Bond, M. H. (1991). *Beyond the Chinese Face: Insights from Psychology.* New York: Oxford University Press.

Leong, B. D. & Clark, H. (1999). Culture-based Knowledge Towards New Design Thinking and Practice. Presented at an International Conference, Tuusula, Finland.

Suggested Reading

Zink, J. China's One-child Policy. http://axe.acadiau.ca/~043638z/one-child/.

Mou, Zong-san (1963). *Characteristics of Chinese Philosophy* [in Chinese]. Taiwan Student Bookstore.

Nisbett, R. E., Peng, K., Choi, I., & Norenayan, A. (2001). Culture and Systems of Thought: Holistic vs. Analytic Cognition, *Psychological Review*, 108, 291–310.

Seligman, S. D. (1990). *Dealing with the Chinese: A Practical Guide to Business Etiquette.* London: Mercury House.

The West in Distress: Resurrecting Confucius's Teachings for a New Cultural Vision and Synthesis [in Chinese]. Hong Kong: Chinese University Press.

CHAPTER 6

DURING YOUR USER REQUIREMENTS ACTIVITY

Introduction

In the previous chapter you learned how to lay the groundwork and prepare for any activity. Getting the right participants and preparing for the activity is critical; but what happens during the activity is just as important, if not more so to the success of your activity. In this chapter, we cover the fundamentals that you must be aware of in order to execute a successful **user requirements** activity.

At a Glance

> Welcoming your participants
> Dealing with late and absent participants
> Warm-up exercises
> Inviting observers
> Introducing your think-aloud protocol
> Moderating your activity
> Recording and note-taking
> Dealing with awkward situations
> Pulling it all together

Welcoming Your Participants

Asking participants to arrive about 15 minutes before the session is due to begin (30 minutes if you are serving dinner) allows enough time for participants to get some food, relax, and chat. In the case of a group session, it also provides a buffer in case some participants are running late. We tell participants during recruitment (refer to Chapter 5, Preparing for Your User Requirements Activity, "Recruitment Methods" section, page 173): "The session starts at 6:00 pm; please arrive 30 minutes ahead of time in order to eat, and to take care of administrative details before the session starts. Late participants will not be admitted into the session."

During this pre-session period, you can introduce yourself, give a quick overview of the session's activities, and explain the **confidential disclosure agreement** and **consent form** (refer to Chapter 3, Ethical and Legal Considerations, page 94). Playing an audio CD during this time can provide a casual atmosphere and is more pleasant than the sound of uncomfortable silence or of forks scraping plates.

If it is a group session, during this pre-session period, a co-worker should be in the lobby by a "Welcome" sign on a flip chart to greet and direct participants as they arrive. Such a sign might read: "Welcome to the participants of the TravelSmart.com focus group. Please take a seat and we will be with you shortly." This sign lets participants know they are in the right place and directs them what to do in the case that the greeter is not present. If your location has a receptionist, to avoid confusion, provide the receptionist with your participant list and make sure the receptionist asks all participants to stay in a specified location. We have had the distressing task of trying to locate a wayward participant when a receptionist was trying to be helpful and sent the participant off in the wrong direction to find us. This doesn't start the session off on the right foot. If your location does not have a receptionist, put up a large sign that specifies where participants should wait in case people arrive while others are being escorted to the activity location.

It saves time and effort to bring participants to the session location in groups of four or five. Make sure to ask participants if they need to use the bathroom along the way to avoid having to make multiple trips back and forth.

Tip

Once your participants are in the room where the activity will take place, you should not leave them alone. Participants may get lost if wandering the halls during a break or in your absence, and you will have to waste time trying to find them. Also, for security reasons it is not wise to allow non-employees to roam your company's premises. Someone should always escort participants to bathroom while someone else stays in the room with any remaining participants.

Dealing with Late and Absent Participants

You are sure to encounter participants who are late or those who simply do not show up. In this section we discuss how to deal with and prevent these situations.

At a Glance

> The late participant
> You can't wait any longer
> Including a late participant
> The no-show

The Late Participant

You are certain to encounter late participants in both group and individual activities. We do our best to emphasize to participants during the recruiting phase that being on time is critical – and if they are late, they will not be admitted to the session. We emphasize this again when we send them e-mail confirmations of the activity and when we call them back to remind them about the session the night before. It is also a good idea to make them aware of any traffic or parking issues in your area that may require extra time.

However, through unforeseen traffic problems, getting lost, and other priorities in peoples' lives, you will often have a participant who arrives late despite your best efforts. Thanks to cell-phones, many late participants will call to let you know they are on their way. If it is a group activity and you have some extra time, you can try to stall while you wait for the person to show up. If it is an individual activity your ability to involve a late participant may depend on the flexibility of your day's schedule. We typically have a one-hour cushion between participants, so a late participant is not a problem. Thanks to your cushion you should be able to accommodate him/her.

For group sessions, we will typically build-in a 15-minute cushion knowing that some people will arrive late. It is not fair to make everyone wait too long just because one or two people are late. If it is an evening session and we are providing food, we ask participants to arrive 30 minutes earlier than the intended session time to eat. This means that if people arrive late, it will not interfere with your activity. They will just have less time (or no time) to eat.

Tip

If you are conducting a group activity and waiting for late participants, doing a creative exercise is one way to stall for time (see "Warm-up Exercises," page 215). There is no need to wait for every last participant before you start "priming the pump."

You Can't Wait Any Longer

In the case of a group activity, at some point you will need to begin your session whether or not all of your participants are present. The reality is that some participants never show, so you don't want to waste your time waiting for someone who is not going to appear.

After 15 minutes, if a participant does not appear, leave a "late letter" (see Figure 6.1) in the lobby with the security guard or receptionist. For companies that don't have someone employed to monitor the lobby on a full-time basis, you may wish to arrange ahead of time to have a co-worker volunteer to wait in the lobby for 30 minutes or so for any late participants. Alternatively, you can leave a sign (like the "Welcome" sign) that says something like: "Participants for the SmartTravel.com

Dear Participant:

Thank you for signing up for tonight's group activity. Unfortunately, you have arrived too late to participate in this evening's session. The session was scheduled for *<insert start time>*, and we delayed the start time until *<insert last check time>* hoping to include as many people as possible. However, at *<insert last check time>* we had to begin the session. We have a lot of material to cover in a short time, and it would be disruptive to stop and repeat the instructions for late arrivals once we have started. Doing so would slow down the entire group, pushing the end of the session beyond *<insert end time>*. We hope you understand that it would be unfair to those who arrived on time if we asked them to stay beyond their committed time.

We understand that many circumstances such as traffic, work, and home life can cause a delay in arrival. We regret that we have to turn away those who struggled to get here this evening, but it is the only fair thing we can do for the entire group. To thank you for taking the time to try and make it to the session we would like to compensate you with *<insert incentive>*.

We are sorry that you were unable to join us this evening, but we hope that you will consider participating in a user activity in the future. We really do value your input.

Sincerely,
<Your name, job title, phone, e-mail>

Figure 6.1:

Example of a letter for latecomers

Focus Group: The session began at 5 pm and we are sorry that you were unable to arrive in time. Because this is a group activity, we had to begin the session. We appreciate your time and regret your absence."

You should provide an incentive in accordance with the policy you stated during recruitment. If you do not plan to pay participants if they are more than 15 minutes late, you should inform them of this during recruitment. However, you may wish to offer a nominal incentive or the full incentive to participants who are late as a result of bad weather, bad traffic, or other unforeseeable circumstances. Just decide prior to the activity, inform participants during recruiting, and remain consistent in the application of that policy.

Inform the security guard or receptionist that late participants may arrive but you cannot include them in the activity. Or, as mentioned, you can also assign someone to wait in the lobby and fulfill this role. Tell him/her to hand out the late letter and incentive to the participant if they should show up. Make sure you tell whomever is waiting to greet the late participants to ask for identification before providing the incentive (refer to Chapter 5, Preparing for Your User Requirements Activity, "The Professional Participant" section, page 189). It is also advisable to have that person ask the participant to sign a sheet of paper confirming that the incentive was received.

As an additional alternative, leave the late participant a voice-mail on the cell-phone and home or work phone. State the current time and politely indicate that because the person is late, he/she cannot be admitted to the session. Leave your contact information and state that the person can receive an incentive (if appropriate) by coming back to your facility at his/her convenience and showing a driver's license (if ID is one of your requirements).

Including a Late Participant

There are some situations where you are unable to turn away a late participant. These situations may include: a very important customer who you do not want to upset, or a user profile that is very difficult to recruit and you need every participant you can get.

Again, for individual sessions (e.g., interviews) we typically have about an hour cushion between participants so a latecomer is not that big a deal. For group sessions, it is a little more difficult to include latecomers. If they arrive just after the instructions have been given, you (or ideally someone working with you) can pull them aside and get them up to speed quickly. This is by no means ideal, but it can be done fairly easily and quickly for most user requirements activities.

If the participant arrives, the instructions have been given, and the activity itself is well underway, you can include them, but you may have to disregard their data. Obviously, if you know you are going to throw away the person's data, you would only want to do this in cases where it is politically necessary to include the participant, not for cases where the participants are hard to get. In cases where participants are hard to come by, make sure you reschedule the participant(s). Don't waste their time and yours by including them and then throwing away the data. But do keep in mind if you reschedule them that participants who are late once are more likely to be late again or be no-shows. If it is an activity such as a group task analysis (refer to Chapter 11, Group Task Analysis, page 458) where adding a participant in the middle of the flow can have a serious impact, you may want to consider having the user create their own flow independent of the group. In these cases, you will need a co-worker to do more than give instructions; he or she will have to moderate the session and collect the data.

The No-show

Despite all of your efforts, you may encounter no-shows. These are the people who simply do not show up for your activity without any warning. We have found that for every 10 participants, one or two will not show up. This may be because something important came up and you are the lowest priority, or the person may have just completely forgotten. Chapter 5 discusses a number of measures that you can take to deal with this problem (refer to Chapter 5, Preparing for Your User Requirements Activity, "Preventing No-shows" section, page 182). Essentially:

- Provide recruited participants with your contact information so that they can contact you if needing to cancel or reschedule.
- Remind participants of the activity and ask them to re-confirm a day or two prior to the activity.
- Whatever number of participants you decide upon, recruit about one extra participant for every five that you would like to attend. This is to account for late cancellations (which don't leave you enough time to recruit someone else) and no-shows.

Warm-up Exercises

When conducting any kind of user activity, ensure that your participants are comfortable and feeling at ease before you begin. When conducting an individual activity, start out with some light conversation in the lobby and as you move towards your destination. Comment on the weather; ask whether the person had any trouble with traffic or parking. Keep it casual. When you sit down to begin the session, start with an informal introduction of yourself and what you do. Ask the participant to do the same. Also find out what you should call the person, and then use first names if appropriate.

Ensuring that participants are at ease is extremely important for group activities. Each person will typically need to interact with you and everyone else in the room, so you want to make sure they feel comfortable with this. This is particularly important when the group has not worked together before. Typically, we give people colorful markers and nametags or name tents. We ask them to write their names and draw something that describes their personality on the tag. (For example, if I like to play golf, I might draw some golf clubs on my nametag.) During this time, the moderators should also create nametags for themselves. Once everyone has finished this, the moderators should explain what they have drawn on their own nametags and why. This will help to put the first participant at ease when he/she describes his/her nametag, and so on around the room. Any type of warm-up activity that gets people talking will do.

The nametag activity is great because it serves a two-fold purpose: it helps everyone relax, and it helps you get exposure to each person's name. You will want to use people's names as much as possible throughout the session, to make the session more personal.

You can use any kind of warm-up activity that you feel works best for you. Some people like to have people spend a few minutes talking about what they like and dislike about the current product they are using. Whatever activity you use, you should keep in mind that this is not intended to take a long time. You just want to do something to get everyone talking and to get those creative juices flowing. Fifteen minutes should be plenty of time to accomplish this.

Inviting Observers

By the term "observer" we mean someone who does not have an active role during the activity. If you have the appropriate facilities, invite **stakeholders** to view your user requirements sessions. Having appropriate facilities means that the observers are watching, but their presence is not known to the participants (e.g., behind a one-way mirror). To learn about setting up facilities that are appropriate for observers, see Chapter 4 (refer to Chapter 4, Setting up Facilities for Your User Requirements Activity, page 106).

Having observers in the same room as the participants will only serve to distract, disrupt, and/or intimidate participants. We recently conducted a focus group where the product team wanted to have 15 members of the team sitting in the back of the room. This was more than the number of participants in the session! After explanation of the potential for disruption (e.g., from whispering, getting up to take calls, or going to the bathroom) they were happy to observe from another room.

Development teams often think they know all of the user requirements, but sometimes they need to attend to see how much or how little they know. Observers can learn a lot about what users like and dislike about the current product or a competitor's product, the difficulties they encounter, what they want, and why they think they want it by observing user requirements activities. Watching a **usability** activity has a far greater impact than reading a usability report alone.

Another advantage of inviting observers is team-building. You are all part of a "team" so stakeholders should be present at the activities too. Also, it helps stakeholders understand what you do and what value you bring to the team – and that builds credibility. It is also wise to record sessions for anyone who may not be able to attend, as well as for your own future reference.

When you invite observers it is a good idea to set expectations up-front:

- Tell observers to come early and enter in a manner so that they are not seen by the participants.
- They will need to be quiet. Often, rooms divided by a one-way mirror might not be fully sound-proofed.
- They should turn off their cell-phones. Answering calls will disturb other observers and sometimes the signal from a cell-phone can interfere with the recording equipment. It can be difficult to get busy people (especially executives) to turn off their phones; but if they understand that the signal can interfere with the equipment, they will usually oblige.

Tip

For group activities, we usually order extra food so there is enough left over for the observers to enjoy after the session. The promise of cookies is usually enough incentive for the observers to hang around until the very end!

It is not good practice to allow participants' managers to observe the session. This request is most often made when we are conducting activities with customers because the managers want to see for themselves what their employees are contributing to the product's design. If participants know or believe that their boss is watching, it can dramatically impact what they do or say. For example, in a group task analysis, if participants know they are being watched by their boss, they may say that they do things according to what company policy dictates but this may not be the truth. You need to capture the truth. It is great to have customers interested in your activity, but explain to them that their presence may intimidate the participant, and that you will summarize the data for them (without specific participant names) as well as discuss the details after the session. We find that with this explanation they are typically understanding and accept your request not to observe. If you are unable to avoid this situation for political reasons (e.g., a high-profile customer that insists on observing), you may have to allow the supervisor to observe and then scrap the data. For ethical reasons you will also want to let the participant know he/she is being observed by the supervisor.

Introducing Your Think-aloud Protocol

A think-aloud protocol is the process of having participants speak what they are thinking as they complete a task. They tell you about the steps in the task as they complete them, as well as their expectations and evaluation statements. This technique is typically used for usability tests, but it can also be quite beneficial for certain user requirements activities where you are working with one person at a time – for example, individual card sorts (refer to Chapter 10, page 414) and field studies (refer to Chapter 13, page 562).

You get an understanding of why the user is taking the actions that he/she takes, and the person's reactions to and thoughts about what he/she is working with. For example, in the case of a card sort, you can learn about why the person groups certain cards together and why he or she thinks certain cards do not belong.

Before asking participants to think-aloud, it can help to provide an example. It is best to use an example that reflects what they will be working with. If they will be completing tasks on the web, say, demonstrate an example with a web-based task. We often use the example of trying to find a blender on an e-commerce website. If the participant will be working with a physical product, then demonstrate the think-aloud protocol with a physical object (e.g., a stapler). Remember that the instructions to the participant should model what you want them to do. So if you want them to describe expectations, model that for them. If you want them to express feelings, model that for them. During the demonstration, the facilitator works through the task and the participant observes him/her using the protocol. Below is an example of a think-aloud protocol demonstration using a stapler (Dumas & Redish 1999):

> **"Now as you work on the tasks, I am going to have you do what we call 'think out loud.' What that means is that I want you to say out loud what you are thinking as you work. Let me show you what I mean. I am going to think out loud as I see whether I need to replace the staples in this stapler. 'OK, I am picking it up. It looks like an ordinary stapler. I would expect that there would be some words or arrows that show me how it opens. I don't see any here. I am disappointed in that. Well I am going to pull it apart here. I think that this is how it opens. It seems easy to pull apart, that's good. I can see there are staples in it. So I am going to close it. That was pretty much how I expected the stapler to work.'**
>
> **Do you see what I mean about thinking out loud? I am going to give you some practice by telling me out loud how you would replace the tape in this tape dispenser."**

We don't generally comment on the specifics of what they say. It is almost always just a play-by-play of steps. But we do listen to the loudness of the participant's voice. Many participants talk quietly as if it were a private conversation instead of a recorded session. If they are quiet, we say, "That was just what I want you to do, but remember you are speaking to the microphone, not just to me. You may have to talk a bit louder. Don't worry, I will remind you if I can't hear you."

Moderating Your Activity

Excellent moderation is key to the success of any activity. Even when participants are provided with instructions, they do not always know exactly what you are looking for, so it is your job to remind them. Also, many of these activities are in the evening and people are tired after work – it will be your job to keep them energized. A moderator must keep the participants focused, keep things moving, make sure everyone participates equally, and ultimately ensure that meaningful data are collected.

When people think of moderation they might think of managing a group of people. Moderation of a group is the most complex, but moderation is also important for individual activities. There are a few rules that apply to both types, such as staying focused and keeping the activity moving. Some common individual and group moderating scenarios are discussed below. If you would like to take a class in moderating skills, or you are interested in having an outsider moderate the activity for you, Appendices B (page 688) and D (page 698) have some pointers.

Tip

It is ideal for the moderator to have some domain knowledge, particularly if a complex topic is being discussed. If you have domain knowledge this will enable you to follow up and delve deeper into important issues and to give little attention to things that are unrelated or unimportant to the discussion. Chapter 9 discusses a lesson learned where the moderator and scribe lacked domain knowledge and as a result the session lesson was less than ideal (refer to Chapter 9, Wants and Needs Analysis, "Lessons Learned" section, page 412).

At a Glance

> Have personality
> Ask questions
> Stay focused
> You are not a participant
> Keep the activity moving
> Keep the participants motivated and encouraged
> No critiquing
> Everyone should participate
> No one should dominate
> Practice makes perfect

Have personality

The participants should feel at ease around you, the moderator. Be personable and approachable. Also, remember to smile and look them in the eyes. You may be tired and have had a terrible day, but you cannot let it show. You need to emanate a happy and positive attitude. Before the session begins, while people are coming in or eating dinner, chat with them. You do not need to talk about the activity, but participants often have questions about your job, the product, or the activity. Getting to know the participants will help you get a sense for the type of people in the room, and it will get them comfortable speaking to you.

Ask questions

Remember that you are not the expert in the session, the participants are, and you should make them aware of that fact. Let them know that you will be stopping to ask questions and get clarification from time to time. The participants will undoubtedly use acronyms and terminology with which you are not familiar, so you should stop them and ask for an explanation rather than pushing on. There is no point collecting data that you do not understand.

You also want to make sure that you capture what the user is *really* saying. Sometimes the best way to ensure that you understand someone is to listen reflectively ("active listening"). This involves paraphrasing what the participant has said in a non-judgmental, non-evaluative way, and then giving the participant a chance to correct you if necessary.

At other times, you will need to probe deeper and ask follow-up questions. For example, Joe may say "I would never research travel on the web." If you probe further and ask "Why?" you may find out that it is not because Joe thinks it would be a bad idea to research travel on the web; it's just that he never conducts travel research because he spends all of his vacation time at his condo in the Florida Keys.

Stay focused

Do not let participants go off on a tangent. Remember that you have a limited amount of time to collect all of the information that you need, so make sure that participants stay focused on the topic at hand. Small diversions, if relevant, are appropriate, but try to get back on track quickly. You can make comments such as "That is really interesting, but perhaps we can delve into that more at the end of the session, if we have time."

Another strategy is to visually post information that will help keep people on track. For example, if you are running a group task analysis, write the task in the top of the task flow. If people get off topic, *literally* point back to the task that is written down and let them know that, although their comments are valuable, they are beyond the scope of the session. If you are running a focus group or a wants and needs analysis, do the same by visually displaying the question via a projector or on a flip chart. You can also periodically repeat the question to remind people what the focus of the discussion is.

You are not a participant

Remember that you are the moderator! It is critical that you do not put words into your participants' mouths. Let *them* answer the questions and do not try to answer for them. Also, do not offer your opinions because that could bias their responses. This may sound obvious, but sometimes the temptation can be very hard to resist. We have seen this most frequently in group task analyses where participants are working together to create a task flow. As a moderator, your hands should be empty. You do not want to write anything or touch any of the cards. If the participants see that you are doing the work, they will often be happy to allow you to take over. If you fall into this trap, at the end of the session you will end up with a flow that represents *your* thinking instead of that of the end users.

Keep the activity moving

Often, people stay focused on the goal or question presented in the activity, but they go into far more detail than necessary. You need to control this, otherwise you might never finish the activity. It is OK to say to them: "I think I now have a good sense of this topic, so let's move on to the next topic because we have a lot of material to get through today." After making a statement such as this once or twice during the session, people will typically get a sense of the level of detail you are going after. You can also let them know this up-front in your introduction: "We have a lot to cover today, so I may move along to the next topic in the interests of time."

Keep the participants motivated and encouraged

On average, a user requirements activity lasts for about two hours. This is quite a long period of time for a person or a group of people to be focused on a single activity. You must keep people engaged and interested. Provide words of encouragement as often as possible. Let them know what a great job they are doing and how much their input is going to help your product. A little acknowledgment goes a long way. Also keep an eye on your participants' energy levels. If they seem to be fading, you might want to offer them a break or offer up some of those left-over cookies to help give them the necessary energy boost. You want everyone to have a good time, and to leave the activity viewing it as a positive experience. Try to be relaxed, smile often, and have a good time. Your mood will be contagious.

No critiquing

As the moderator, you should never challenge what participants have to say. This is crucial, since you are there to learn what *they* think. You may completely disagree with their thoughts, but you are conducting an end user activity and you are not the end user in this situation. You may want to probe further to find out why a participant feels a certain way; but at the end of the day, remember that, in this session, *he or she* is the expert; not you. Collect these thoughts and ideas and you can validate them later, if necessary.

At the beginning of a session, stress that there is to be no critiquing of input. Also, emphasize to the participants that this is not an evaluation. All ideas are correct and you welcome all their thoughts and comments. Inevitably, someone cannot resist critiquing another person's ideas. Be sure to post this as a rule to help remind your participants. Let them know that it is OK to have different ideas, but there are no wrong ideas. Usually if you remind people of this, they will let everyone have their say.

Everyone should participate

In a group activity, it can take a great deal of energy to draw out the quiet members, but it is important to do so. If you have a focus group of ten people and only five are contributing, that essentially cuts your effective participant size in half. You must get everyone involved and the sooner you do this the better. Call quiet members out by name and ask them their thoughts: "Jane, what do you usually do next?" If things don't improve you could try moving towards a round-robin format (i.e., everyone participates in turn). This can be an effective solution for group activities like a focus group; however, it is not ideal for every activity (e.g., a group task analysis). If you start off doing a round-robin, you may not need to continue it for the whole activity; just a couple of turns may help people feel more comfortable about speaking up.

No one should dominate

It is very easy for an overbearing participant to dominate the group and spoil the group dynamic. It can take a great deal of skill and tact to rein in a dominating member without embarrassing him/her. When you notice that a participant is beginning to dominate, call on others in the group to balance things out. If you are standing in the middle of the group (e.g., in a U-shaped table formation), use body language to quieten down the dominant user. Turn your body so that the dominant one cannot get your attention, focus fully on a quieter participant, and avoid eye contact. If things do not improve, gently thank the overbearing person for earlier ideas and let him/her know that now other participants need to contribute. If it is clear that the participant will not work with others, give the group a break. Take the strong-willed member to the side and remind him/her that this is a *group* activity and that everyone should participate equally. You can tell the person that he or she might be asked to leave. Alternatively, you can provide the user with his/her incentive with thanks and provide a graceful exit. It is certainly the exception rather than the rule that things get this bad, but it is good to have a plan of action in mind in case they do.

Another technique that works well in group sessions is to ask for participants to raise a hand before speaking, and to have an assistant note any hand that goes up and make sure that person gets called on eventually. By forcing participants to wait until they are called on, you have a means to eliminate interruptions. This is particularly effective when the group size is over ten. All the participant has to do is raise a hand briefly, which is noted, and then they *will* be called on as soon as there is a break in the action. Ideally, you do not want to have to resort to this; but if overbearing participants cannot control themselves, you will have to resort to a more structured session.

Practice makes perfect

Moderating activities is definitely an art. The bottom line is that it takes practice and lots of it! We still find that we learn new tricks and tips and also face new challenges with each session.

We recommend that people new to moderating groups watch videotapes of the activity they will be conducting and observe how the facilitator interacts with the participants. Next, they should shadow a facilitator. Being in the room as the activity is going on is a very different experience from watching a video. Also, a beginner should practice with co-workers who are experienced moderators. Set up a pilot session so that you can practice your moderating skills before the real activity. Have your co-workers role-play. For example, one person can be the dominant participant, one can be the quiet participant, one can be the participant who does not follow instructions, etc. You can videotape the sessions and watch them with an experienced moderator to find out how you can improve. Another great idea is to be a participant in focus groups. Find a local facility that runs and/or recruits for them and contact them to get on their participant list. That way you can observe professional moderators at work.

Having said that, you must find your own style. For example, some people can easily joke with participants and use humor to control the overbearing ones: "If you don't play well with the others, I will have to take your pen away!" Other people are not as comfortable speaking in front of groups and have difficulty using humor in these situations. In those cases, trying to use humor can backfire and might come across as sarcasm. Find an experienced moderator to emulate – one whose personality and interaction style are similar to yours.

Recording and Note-taking

There are a few options when deciding how to capture information during your activity.

At a Glance

> Take notes

> Use video or audio recording

> Combine video/audio and note-taking

Take Notes

Taking notes on a clipboard is one obvious choice. One of the benefits of taking notes during the session is that you can walk away from the activity with immediate data and you can begin analysis (see Figure 6.2 for a sample of notes). You are also signaling to the participants that you are noting what is being said. It is good to show the participants that you are engaged in the activity, but they might be offended if you are not taking notes when the participants feel they are saying something particularly noteworthy.

A potential problem with taking notes is that you can get so wrapped up in being a stenographer that you have difficulty engaging the participants or following up. You could also fail to capture important comments because the pace of a discussion can be faster than your note-taking speed. If you choose to take notes yourself during a session, develop shorthand so that you can note key elements quickly (see Figure 6.3 for some sample shorthand). Also, do not try to capture every comment verbatim – paraphrasing is faster.

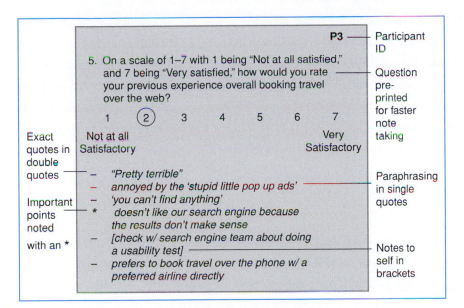

Figure 6.2:

Excerpt of notes taken during an interview

```
Participant #1: P1
Because: b/c
With: w/
Within: w/i
By the way: btw
At: @
As a matter of fact: aamof
Not Applicable: N/A
No comment: NC
```

Figure 6.3:

Sample shorthand for note-taking

For some activities, such as focus groups and group task analyses, the moderating is so consuming that it is simply not possible for you to take effective notes. Then, a better option is to have a co-worker take notes for you. If appropriate, you might wish to take some high-level notes yourself to highlight key findings, but leave all the details for a co-worker to capture.

As mentioned, the great benefit of notes is that you have an immediate record to begin data analysis. The note-taker can be in the same room with you or behind the one-way mirror if you have a formal lab set up (refer to Chapter 4, Setting up Facilities for Your User Requirements Activity, "Building a Permanent Facility" section, page 111). It can also help to have an additional pair of eyes to discuss the data with and come up with insights that you might not have had yourself.

If the note-taker is in the same room, you may or may not want to allow the person to pause the session if getting behind in the notes or not understanding what a participant has said. This can be very disrupting to the session, so ideally you want an experienced note-taker. The person should not attempt to play court stenographer: you are not looking for a word-by-word account, only the key points or quotes. The moderator should keep the note-taker in mind and ask participants to speak more clearly or slowly if the pace becomes too fast.

Tip

Like the activity moderator, the note-taker needs to have domain knowledge, particularly if a complex topic is being discussed. If the note-taker understands what he or she is writing, it is much easier to condense what is being said. Also, an awareness of the domain means that the note-taker will have an understanding of what is important to capture versus things that are known or unrelated.

Use Video or Audio Recording

The benefit with recording is that you do not *have* to take notes, so you can focus solely on following up on what the participants say. The recordings capture nuances in speech that you could never capture when taking notes. Video recording also has the benefit of showing you the participants (as well as your own) body language. You can also refer back to the recording as often as needed. Some tools today can even analyze multimedia files (see Appendix G, page 722).

If you choose to rely solely on video or audio recording and not to take notes during the session, you will either have to listen to the recording and make notes, or send the recording out for transcription. Transcription is expensive and it takes time (it is charged per hour of transcription, not per hour of recording). Depending on the complexity of the material, the number of speakers, and the quality of the recording, it can take four to six times the duration of the recording to transcribe. In the San Francisco Bay area in 2004, a professional transcription company charged about $42 per hour of transcription – so the cost to transcribe a single two-hour interview can run between $168 and $252. Searching the phone book, you may be able to find individuals who transcribe "on the side" and charge significantly less than professional companies.

Getting tapes transcribed is *not* the same thing as taking notes during the session. Shorthand notes pull out the important pieces of information and leave behind all the noise. If you get transcripts you will need to read through them and summarize. We recommend getting transcripts of the session *only* when you need a record of who said what (e.g., for exact quotes or documentation purposes). Regulated industries (e.g., FDA) may also require such documentation.

Finally, you should be aware that recording the session can make some participants uncomfortable, so they may not be forthcoming with information. Let the participants know *when you recruit them* that you plan to record. If a person feels uncomfortable, stress his or her rights, including the right to confidentiality. If the person still does not feel comfortable, then you should consider recruiting someone else or just relying on taking notes. In our experience, this outcome is the exception rather than the rule.

Tip

Aim to audio record as a minimum, but videotaping is best. You may miss subtler points after the session when listening to audio recordings to create your notes. For example, reasons for pauses may be unknown when listening to audio. With video it would be obvious that the pauses were due to the fact, say, that the participant's instant message window kept popping up and this had to be attended to each time. Videotape also allows further analysis of both verbal and physical behavior.

Video Tips

- If you choose to video record there are several things to keep in mind. Ideally, record from a separate room (i.e., behind a one-way mirror). If this is not possible, have someone who already has a role in the activity also take on the responsibility for the video, to avoid introducing additional people into the room.

- It is not necessary to have someone behind the camera the entire time – that will only serve to distract. Simply set up the video camera to get a shot that includes the participant's face and leave it until you are required to do something with it (e.g., start the video, insert a new tape).

- If you are conducting a group activity, the camera-person should focus on the group as a whole rather than zooming in on each individual. Attempting to focus in on each speaker is difficult with large groups, and anyone watching the video afterwards will get motion sickness.

Combine Video/Audio and Note-taking

As with most things, a combination is usually the best solution. Having a co-worker take notes for you during the session while it is being recorded is the optimal solution. That way you will have the bulk of the findings, but if you need clarification on any of the notes or user quotes, you can refer back to the recording. This is often necessary for group activities. Because so many people are speaking during a group activity, and because conversations can move quickly, it can be difficult for a note-taker to capture every last detail. An audio- or videotape of the session is extremely important for later review. It will allow you to go back and get clarification in areas where the notes may not be clear or where the note-taker may have fallen behind. In addition, although it is rare, recordings do fail and your notes are an essential back-up.

Dealing with Awkward Situations

Just when you think you've seen it all, a participant behaves in a way you could never have expected! The best way to handle an awkward situation is by preventing it all together. However, even the best-laid plans can fail. What do you do when a user throws you a curve ball? If you are standing in front of a group of 12 users and there is a room of eight developers watching you intently, you may not make the most rational decision. You must decide before the situation ever takes place, how you should behave to protect the user, your company, and your data. Refer to Chapter 3, Legal and Ethical Considerations, page 94, to gain an understanding of these issues.

In this section we look at a series of several uncomfortable situations and suggest how to respond in a way that is ethical and legal, and which preserves the integrity of your data. Unfortunately, over the last several years we have encountered almost every single one of these awkward situations. They have been divided by the source of the issue (i.e., participant or product team/observer). We invite you to learn from our painful experiences. There are also some awkward situations that relate to late participants. These situations are discussed in the "Dealing with Late and Absent Participants" above.

Tip

If you find yourself in an awkward situation and you cannot decide whether a participant should be paid, err on the side of caution and pay up. In most cases, a disruption in your study is not the fault of the participant, so they should not be penalized. Even if the person *is* the cause of the awkward situation, saving $100 is not worth the potential for confrontation.

Extra Caution Required with Customers

If you are working with customers and an awkward situation arises, you need to treat the situation with utmost care. For example, if you discover during a session that a participant is not the correct user type and that person is *not* a customer, you can typically explain the situation, tell the participant that, due to the error, their involvement will not be required, and pay them. However, if the person is a customer it is not always that easy. Typically, you will need to involve the person in the session somehow. Turning away or dismissing a customer who is excited about being involved in your activity could potentially damage your relationship with that customer. You may not be able to use the data you collect, but it is more important to include the customer, than risk harming your relationship.

When working with customers, we typically try to have extra product team members available and a back-up plan in place, so that if something goes wrong (e.g., recruitment of a customer who is the wrong user type, a customer with an agenda that differs from your planned activity) we ask product team members to attend to the customers. For example, in a group session if a customer is disruptive or the wrong user type, we have a co-worker or product team member conduct a separate session with the user while the main session continues. We recently had this situation during a group task analysis in which the product team recruited people from a key customer. We were assured that the surprise participants met the user profile, but after a brief conversation at the beginning of the session we knew they were not. Luckily, a co-worker was standing by to interview those individuals. We gathered some wonderful insights from those interviews, the different user profile did not derail the group task analysis, and the relationship with the key customer was saved.

In most cases, participants are not sure exactly what they are going to be doing as a part of your activity, so they happily go along with whatever you propose. So just remember that keeping your customer happy will have to take precedence over the quality of your data. If you have thought through the potential problems in advance, you should be able to have a happy customer and good data.

Participant Issues

The Participant is Called Away in the Middle of the Test

Situation: You are half way through interviewing a participant when her cell-phone rings. She answers it and says it's her child calling. She states that she must go but will be back in 45 minutes to finish the interview. What do you do?

Response: Thank her for her time, pay her, and let her know that it will not be necessary for her to return. It is not ethical to withdraw compensation if the participant leaves early. To force her to stay is not only unethical but the participant would clearly be distracted during the remaining questions. A participant is free to leave without penalty at any point, so remember to compensate her for her expertise and effort. It would be impossible to allow her to return in the case of a group activity as she would have missed too much of the session. In the case of an individual activity it would be possible to allow her to return, but the 45-minute delay between questions would differentiate her data from that of other participants.

To prevent this from happening, it is always a good idea to ask participants to turn off their cell-phones and pagers before the activity begins. If the participant states she is expecting an important call and cannot turn off the phone, do not press the issue further because it may only serve to distract or upset the participant. Be prepared in the future by over-recruiting so that the loss of one or two participants does not affect the integrity of the dataset.

The Participant's Cell-phone Rings Continuously

Situation: The participant is a very busy person (e.g., doctor, database administrator). She is on call today and cannot turn off her cell-phone for fear of losing her job. You reluctantly agree to let her leave the phone on. Throughout the session, her pager and phone buzz, interrupting the activity. Each call lasts only a couple of minutes but it is clear that the participant is distracted. This user type is really hard to come by so you hate to lose her data. Should you allow the activity to continue, or ask her to leave?

Response: It is obvious that the user is distracted and it won't get better as the session continues. If this is an individual activity, you may choose to be patient and continue. However, if this is a group session where the user is clearly disturbing others, have a collaborator follow the participant out during the next call. When she finishes her call, ask her to turn the phone and pager off because it is causing too much distraction. If this is not possible, offer to allow her to leave now and be paid, since it seems to be a very busy day for her. In our focus group with doctors, one of the participants spent more time in the hallway on his cell-phone than in his chair. The other participants were clearly annoyed and distracted. When given the choice to turn his phone off or leave, he surprisingly chose the former. Unfortunately, his mind wasn't on the discussion and he didn't participate in the rest of the session.

If you know your user type is in a highly demanding job, you should inform potential participants during the screening process that they will have to turn their cellphones and pagers off for the duration of the activity (refer to Chapter 5, Preparing for Your User Requirements Activity, "Developing a Recruiting Screener" section, page 161). If the potential participant will be on duty the day of the session and cannot comply with the request, do not recruit him/her. Otherwise you are inviting trouble. When the participants arrive for the activity, ask everyone to turn their cellphones and pagers off. They agreed to give you one or two hours of their time and you are compensating them for it. It is not unreasonable to insist they give you their full attention, especially if you made this request clear during the screening process.

Tip

A humorous way to get users to comply is to ask everyone who has a cell-phone to get it out and show it to the person on their right. After you have seen everyone who has a phone, ask them – on the count of three – to turn them off! Users sometimes groan at the trick but find it amusing. Too many participants, when asked to turn off a phone if they have one, will either ignore the request by saying it's already off or they will genuinely think it is off when it is not.

The Wrong Participant is Recruited

Situation: During an activity, either it becomes painfully obvious or the user lets it slip that he does not match the user profile. The participant has significantly less experience than he originally indicated, or does not match the domain of interest (e.g., has the wrong job to know about anything being discussed). It is not clear whether he was intentionally deceitful about his qualifications or misunderstood the requirements in the initial phone screener. Should you continue with the activity?

Response: Is the participant different on a key characteristic? If you and the team agree that the participant is close enough to the user profile to keep, continue with the activity and note the difference in the report.

If the participant is too different, your response depends on the activity. If it is a group activity where the participants do not interact with one another (e.g., a group card sort), note the participant and be sure to throw his data out. If it is a group activity that involves interaction among the participants, you will have to remove the participant from the session. The fact that the person is a different user type could derail your session entirely. Take the participant aside (you do not want to embarrass him/her in front of the group) and explain that there has been a mistake and apologize for any inconvenience you may have caused. Be sure to pay the participant in full for his effort.

If it is an individual activity, you may wish to allow the participant to continue with the activity to save face, and then terminate the session early. It may be necessary to stop the activity on the spot if it is clear the participant simply does not have the knowledge to participate and to continue the activity would only embarrass the participant further. Again, pay the participant in full; he or she should not be penalized for a recruiting error.

If the participant turns out to work for a competitor, is a consultant who has worked for a competitor and is likely to return to that competitor, or is a member of the press, you need to terminate the session immediately. Remind the person of the binding confidentiality agreement, pay him, and escort him out. Put him on the watch list immediately (refer to Chapter 5, Preparing for Your User Requirements Activity, "Create a Watch List" section, page 190).

Follow up with the recruiter to find out why this participant was recruited (refer to Chapter 5, Preparing for Your User Requirements Activity, "Recruitment Methods" section, page 173). Review the remaining participant profiles with the team/recruiting agency to make sure that no more surprises slip in. Make sure the recruiter clearly understands the user profile before proceeding to recruit any others. To better prepare for any usability activity, create the user profile and screener with the development team. In addition, review and approve each user with the team as he or she is recruited.

A participant thinks he is on a job interview

Situation: The participant arrives in a suit and brings his resumé, thinking he is being interviewed for employment at your company. He is very nervous and asks about available jobs. He says that he would like to come back on a regular basis to help your company evaluate its products. He even makes reference to the fact that he needs the money and is grateful for this opportunity to show his skills.

Response: This situation can be avoided by clarifying up-front when the participant is recruited that this is *not* a job interview opportunity, and in no way constitutes an offer of employment (refer to Chapter 5, Preparing for Your User Requirements Activity, "Developing a Recruiting Screener" section, page 161). If the participant attempts to provide a resumé at any point in the conversation, stop the activity and make it clear that you cannot and will not accept it. It is best not to even agree to forward a resumé to the appropriate individual. The participant may incorrectly assume that your agreement to forward it comes with your recommendation. You may then receive follow-up phone calls or e-mails from the participant "to touch base about any job opportunities." When the economy is tough, you will likely encounter this situation more than once.

Given that the participant is already in your activity, you need to be careful not to take advantage of a person who is obviously highly motivated but for the wrong reasons. In this case, the activity should be paused and you should apologize for any misunderstanding, but make it clear that this is not a job interview. Reiterate the purpose of the activity and clarify that there is no follow-on opportunity for getting a job at your company which can be derived from his participation. The participant should be asked whether he would like to continue now that the situation has been clarified. If not, the participant should be paid and leave with no further data collection.

A Participant Refuses to be Videotaped

Situation: During recruiting and the pre-test instructions, you inform the participant that the session will be videotaped so that you can go back to pick up any comments you may have missed. The participant is not happy with this. She insists that she does not want to be videotaped. You assure her that her information will be kept strictly confidential but she is not satisfied. Offering to turn the videotape off is also not sufficient for the participant. She states that she cannot be sure that you are not still taping her and asks to leave. Should you continue to persuade her? Since she has not answered any of your questions, should you still pay her?

Response: Although this rarely occurs, you should not be surprised by it. It is unethical to coerce the participant to stay. You may want to ask if she would be willing to be audiotaped instead. This is not ideal but at least you can still capture her comments. If she still balks, tell her that you are sorry she does not wish to continue but that you understand her discomfort. You should still pay the participant. If you have a list of participants to avoid, add her name to this list (refer to Chapter 5, Preparing for Your User Requirements Activity, "Create a Watch List" section, page 190). Alternatively, if the participant agrees to stay, if the user type is difficult to find, and/or if you are dealing with a customer, you may wish to rely on notes and not worry about the video or audio recording.

To avoid such a situation in the future, inform all participants during the phone screening that they will be audio- and/or videotaped and must sign a confidentiality agreement (refer to Chapter 5, Preparing for Your User Requirements Activity, "Developing a Recruiting Screener" section, page 161). Will this be a problem? If they say that it is, they should not be brought in for any activity.

A Participant is Confrontational With Other Participants

Situation: While conducting a group session, one of the participants becomes more aggressive as time goes by. He moves from disagreeing with other participants to telling them their ideas are "ridiculous." Your repeated references to the rule "Everyone is right – do not criticize yourself or others" is not helping. Unfortunately, the participant's attitude is rubbing off on other group members and they are now criticizing each other. Should you continue the session? How do you bring the session back on track? Should you remove the aggressive participant?

Response: Take a break at the earliest opportunity to give everyone a chance to chat and cool off. Since you are the focus of most participants at this moment, you will need a co-worker to assist you. Have the co-worker quietly take the participant outside of the room and away from others, to dismiss him. The co-worker should tell the participant that he has provided a lot of valuable feedback, thank him for his time, and pay him. Alternatively, you may wish to tell him the real reason he is being asked to leave, thereby emphasizing your commitment to fostering acceptance and non-judgmental behavior. We typically do not take this approach because things may get confrontational and you will then need to devote time and energy to this confrontation. When you restart the session, if anyone notices the absence of the participant, simply tell the group that he had to leave early. It is never easy to ask a participant to leave, but it is important not only to salvage the rest of your data but also to protect the remaining participants in your session.

A Participant Takes Over the Group

Situation: At the beginning of a group task analysis, a user decides to "lead" the group and begins developing the entire flow himself. You have stopped him once and let the entire group know that they must work together to develop the flow. In addition, you have encouraged the other group members to get involved and asked specific members their thoughts on the flow so far. Unfortunately, the overbearing participant seems undeterred by this brief interruption and continues to dominate the group. How do you give control back to the group? Should you allow the participant to stay?

Response: Take a break and have a co-worker take the participant outside the room. You have a couple of options here. The collaborator can give him his own set of materials (make sure you have an extra set made) and allow him to work on his own. Alternatively, the collaborator can thank the participant for all of his input, provide his incentive, and escort him out. Whatever the solution, the participant should leave happy and never feel scolded or humiliated in front of the other participants.

After the break, inform the participants that the absent participant left early. You should then undo any of the work the assertive participant has done alone and ask the remaining participants to continue.

It is important to be an assertive, but not overbearing, moderator during these difficult sessions. You must draw out the reserved participants and quiet down the aggressive participants so it does not get to this point. It is common for some people to assume that every group "needs a leader" and nominate himself or herself. We have noticed that highly trained or technical users tend to have more dominating personalities. If you will be conducting a group activity with highly skilled users, beef up your moderations skills by practicing with your colleagues (see "Moderating Your Activity" on page 220). Consider having a co-worker assist you, since two people correcting the overbearing participant may be more effective.

A Participant is Not Truthful About Her Identity

Situation: You recognize a participant from another activity you conducted but the name doesn't sound familiar. You mention to her that she looks familiar and ask whether she has participated in another study at your company. She denies that she has ever been there before, but you are convinced she has. Should you proceed with the test or pursue it further?

Response: Ask every participant for ID when you greet them. If a participant arrives without *some* form of ID, apologize for the inconvenience and state that you cannot release the incentives without identification. If it is possible, reschedule the activity and ask the participant to bring ID next time.

When recruiting, you should inform participants that you will need to see an ID for tax purposes, as well as for security purposes (refer to Chapter 5, Preparing for Your User Requirements Activity, "Developing a Recruiting Screener" section, page 161). In the US, the Internal Revenue Service requires that companies complete a 1099 form for any individual who receives more than $600 from you in a year. For this reason, you need to closely track whom you compensate throughout the year. During recruitment, you may say to participants:

> **"In appreciation for your time and assistance, we are offering $100 in American Express gift checks. For tax purposes, we track the amount paid to participants and so we will be asking for ID. We also require ID when issuing a visitor's badge. If you can simply bring your driver's license with you, we will ask you to present it upon arrival."**

Repeat this in the phone or e-mail confirmation you provide to participants. For participants being dishonest about their identity (in order to participate in multiple studies and make additional money), this will dissuade them from following through. You will probably get a call back from the participant saying that he or she is no longer available. For honest participants, it reminds them to bring their license with them, as opposed to leaving it in the car or at home.

If the information provided does not match the information on the driver's license, you will have to turn the participant away. Then, copy the information from the ID next to the "alternative" information provided by the participant. Place both identities on your Watch List (refer to Chapter 5, Preparing for Your User Requirements Activity, "Create a Watch List" section, page 190).

A Participant Refuses to Sign Confidential Disclosure Agreement and Consent Forms

Situation: You present the usual confidential disclosure agreement (CDA) and consent form to the user and explain what each form means. You also offer to provide copies of the forms for the participant's records. The participant glances over the forms but does not feel comfortable with them, particularly the CDA. Without a lawyer, the participant refuses to sign these documents. You explain that the consent form is simply a letter stating the participant's rights. The CDA, you state, is to protect the company since the information that may be revealed during the session has not yet been released to the public. Despite your explanations, the participant will not sign the documents. Should you continue with the activity?

Response: Absolutely not. To protect yourself and your company, explain to the participant that, without her signature, you cannot conduct the activity. Since the participant is free to withdraw at any point in time without penalty, you are still required to provide the incentive. Apologize for the inconvenience and escort her out. Be sure to place her on your Watch List (refer to Chapter 5, Preparing for Your User Requirements Activity, "Create a Watch List" section, page 190).

Prevent this situation by informing participants during recruitment that they will be expected to sign a confidentiality agreement and consent form (refer to Chapter 5, Preparing for Your User Requirements Activity, "Developing a Recruiting Screener" section, page 161). Offer to fax participants a copy of the forms for them to review in advance. Some participants (particularly VPs and above) cannot sign CDAs. Their company may have a standard CDA that they are allowed to sign and bring with them. In that case, ask the participant to fax you a copy of their CDA and then forward it to your legal department for approval in advance.

If the legal department approves of their CDA, you may proceed. However, if a participant states during the phone interview that he/she cannot sign any CDA, thank the person for his/her time but state that the person is not eligible for participation.

Fire Alarm Sounds in the Middle of a Test

Situation: While in the middle of a test, a fire alarm sounds. It is a false alarm but the participant still seems unnerved. After evacuating the building, the participant states he would like to continue with the activity, but you are not sure whether the alarm disturbed the participant such that he will not be able to concentrate. Should you let the activity continue? If so, do you use the data?

Response: After security allows you to return, take a break and offer the participant something to drink. Let him know that he provided a lot of valuable feedback, that he is not obligated to stay, and that he will be paid in full regardless. If the participant seems more at ease and is still eager to continue, allow him to proceed. Compare his data to the other participants to determine whether he is an **outlier**.

Product Team/Observer Issues

The Team Changes the Product Mid-test

Situation: You are conducting a focus group for a product that is in the initial prototype stage. The team is updating the code while the focus groups are being conducted. In the middle of the second focus group, you discover the team has incorporated some changes to the product based on comments from the previous focus group. Should you continue the focus groups with the updated product, or cancel the current focus group and bring in replacements so that all users see the same product? How do you approach the team with the problem?

Response: Ask the participants to take a break at the least disruptive opportunity and go to speak with the developers in attendance while your co-moderator attends to the group. This will give you time to determine whether the previous version is still accessible. If it is, use it. If the previous version is not available, it is up to you whether you would like to get some feedback on the new version of the prototype, or you might attempt to continue the focus group with activities that do not rely on the prototype. Be sure to document the change in the final report. Meet with the team as soon as possible to discuss the change in the prototype. Make sure the team understands that this may compromise the results of the activity. If they would like to do an interactive design approach, they should discuss this with you in advance so that you may design the activity appropriately.

As a rule, make sure that you inform product teams of "the rules" before any activity. In this case, before the activity you would inform them that the prototype must stay the same for all focus group sessions. Be sure to inform them "why" so that they will understand the importance of your request. Let them know that you want to make design changes based on what both groups have to say, not just one. Remember that this is the product team's session too. You can advise them and tell them the consequences, but be aware that they may want to change it anyway and it is your job to analyze and present the results appropriately (even if this means telling stakeholders that the data are limited because of a decision the team made).

In some cases, the team finds something that is obviously wrong in the prototype and changes it after the first session. Often this is OK. But they should discuss it with you prior to the session. If they don't discuss it with you and you find out during the session, it doesn't always invalidate the data if it is something that should be changed in any case. When working with a team you must strike a balance between being firm but flexible.

An Observer Turns on a Light in the Control Room During Your Activity

Situation: You are interviewing a participant in the user room while the team is watching in the control room. During the interview, one of the team members decides to turn on a light because he is having trouble seeing. The control room is now fully illuminated and the participant can see there are five people in the other room watching intently. Should you try to ignore the people in the other room and hope it does not draw more attention to the situation, or should you stop the interview and turn off the light?

Response: The participant should never be surprised to learn that people are in the control room observing the activity. At the beginning of every activity, participants must be made aware that "members of our staff sometimes observe in the other room." It is not necessary to state the specific number of people in the other room or their affiliation (e.g., usability group, development team). Participants should also be warned that they may hear a few noises in the other room, such as coughing or a door closing but they should just ignore it. Their attention should be focused on the activity at hand. Some people like to show the participant the control room and the observers prior to the session. We typically do not adopt this approach because participants can become intimidated if they *know* that a large group of people are observing.

In the situation above, if the participant is not facing the other room and has not noticed the observers, do not call attention to it (someone may turn the light off quickly). This actually happened to one of our co-workers. Thanks to a datalogger with Ninja-like speed, the lights were turned off before the participant even noticed. However, if the participant has seen the observers, simply ask the observers to turn off the light and apologize to the participant for the disruption. After the participant has left, remind the team how one-way mirrors work and explain that it may affect the results if the participants see a room full of people watching them. Participants may be more self-conscious about what they say and may not be honest in their responses. If you notice that the participant's responses and behavior change dramatically after seeing the observers, you may have to consider throwing away the data.

Product Team/Observers Talk Loudly During an Activity

Situation: While interviewing a participant in the user room, the team in the control room begins talking. As time goes by, the talking grows louder and the team begins laughing. The participant appears to be ignoring it, but the noise is easily audible to you so the participant must be able to hear it too. In addition, the datalogger is having difficulty hearing what the participant is saying and fears the participant can hear the conversation. Should you or the datalogger interrupt the interview to ask the team to be quiet and possibly draw more attention to it, or should you continue to ignore the noise?

Response: This situation can be avoided if you ask the developers to maintain quiet before you leave the control room to conduct the interview (see "Inviting Observers," page 216). You must clearly explain to the observers that the room is *not* completely sound-proof and that silence is extremely important during an activity. If this is unsuccessful, act quickly. Having another member of your team in the control room (usually a datalogger) is also helpful because that individual can prevent the situation from getting out of hand. Hopefully, your datalogger will tell them to quiet down and remind them that the room is not sound-proof. However, if the volume increases enough for you to become aware of it, excuse yourself to "get something in other room" (e.g., another pen, your drink, the participant's compensation). When you step into the other room, inform the observers that you can hear them. Politely tell them that the interview can be very revealing so they probably want to pay close attention. If there is an important conversation that they must have, they should excuse themselves and speak in another office or lobby – but not out in the hallway because the user may be able to hear them there too.

If there are multiple sessions, observers may think that they have heard it all after the first participant. As a result, they start talking and ignoring the session. Explain to them that *every* participant's feedback is important and that they should be taking note of where things are consistent and where they differ. Be nice but firm. You are in charge. Observers are rarely uncooperative.

We had the unfortunate situation once when a participant actually said "I can hear you laughing at me." Despite assurances that this was not the case, the participant was devastated and barely spoke a word for the rest of the session. Amazingly, the observers in attendance were so caught up in their own conversation that they did not hear what the participant said!

Pulling It All Together

In this chapter, we have given you ingredients that will help you conduct any of your user requirements activities effectively. You should now be able to deal with participant arrivals, get your participants thinking creatively, moderate any individual or group activity, and instruct your participants how to think aloud. In addition, we hope that you have learned from our experiences and that you are prepared to handle any awkward testing situation that may arise. In the following chapters we delve into the methods of a variety of user requirements activities.

PART 3

(THE METHODS)

CHAPTER 7

INTERVIEWS

Introduction

Interviews are one of the most frequently used **user requirements** gathering techniques. In the broadest sense, an interview is a guided conversation in which one person seeks information from another. There are a variety of different types of interviews you can conduct, depending on your constraints and needs. They are flexible and can be used as a solo activity or in conjunction with another user requirements activity (e.g., following a card sort).

In this chapter, we discuss when to use interviews, things to be aware of when conducting interviews, how to prepare for and conduct an interview, as well as how to analyze the data. We spend a good deal of time concentrating on constructing interview questions and how to interact with participants to get the best data possible. These processes are critical to a successful interview. Finally, we close this chapter with our own lessons learned and an illustrative case study by Microsoft.

At a Glance

> When should you conduct interviews?
> Preparing to conduct an interview
> Conducting an interview
> Data analysis and interpretation
> Communicate the findings

When Should You Conduct Interviews?

Many usability activities do not provide you with the opportunity to have detailed discussions with users (e.g., group task analyses, surveys). Interviews can be leveraged anytime in the **user-centered design** (UCD) lifecycle when you want to obtain detailed information from individual users (e.g., to understand the biggest challenges users face in their work and how they would like to work differently). Interviews are excellent for innovation. If you are looking to develop a new product or service, interviews allow you to conduct an outcomes analysis and retrieve the kind of detailed feedback from users necessary for product innovation.

Interviews can also help you prepare for another **usability** activity. Perhaps you do not know enough about the domain and tasks in order to run a group task analysis (see Chapter 11, page 458); or you can conduct a series of open-ended interviews to identify the most frequent responses to questions in order to build a closed-ended survey (see Chapter 8, page 312); or you may use the results of the interviews to design questions for a wants and needs analysis (see Chapter 9, page 370). Finally, you can conduct interviews following another usability activity to better understand your results (e.g., why participants responded a certain way on your survey).

The end result of a set of interviews is an integration of perspectives from multiple users. It is your best opportunity to understand and explore a domain and current usage in depth. If you conduct interviews with multiple user types of the same process/system/organization, you can obtain a holistic view.

Interviews, Survey, or Focus Group?

An interview is *not* appropriate if you are looking for information from a large sample of the population. One-on-one interviews can take significant time to conduct and more resources than a survey (see Chapter 8, page 312). There may be times when you need to collect large samples of data to feel more confident that the results you have obtained can be applied to the user population as a whole (not just the people you have interviewed). If you are in need of a large data set, surveys are a better option. (Refer to Figure 7.1 for a checklist of questions to determine whether interviews or surveys are best for your study.) However, interviews provide detailed information that you could not capture in a survey. You are able to follow-up

To Choose Interviews Versus Surveys

1. Does the task require interaction with the respondents? If there must be a two-way conversation, or if there are several contingencies where the question to be asked depends on a previous response, interviews will be required and survey collection isn't feasible.

2. Is there the likelihood of interaction between the tendency to respond and the issues or topics being measured or assessed? If such interaction is present, serious nonresponse bias precludes the use of surveys and requires interviews.

3. To what degree are accurate, timely mailing lists of *qualified* respondents available? Lacking one or more mailing lists that: (*a*) include a full representation of the population to be surveyed and (*b*) exclude unqualified individuals, interviewing will be necessary.

4. Must the activity be conducted in a *specific* location, such as a store or polling place, or at a specific time such as in the morning or on a particular weekend? If so, interviews are needed.

5. Can the respondents provide and *record* their own responses, or must the recording be done by a fieldworker? The more complex and intricate the recording of the data, the less likely a survey will provide satisfactory data.

6. Is it more important to collect a large amount of data from each of a small number of respondents, or to obtain a more limited amount of data from each of a very large number of respondents? In general, the larger the sample required, the more appropriate a survey becomes.

7. Are the respondents widely dispersed over a broad geographic area or concentrated in groups in a confined area? The more widely dispersed, the less appropriate interviewing becomes, because of the cost of travel or of long distance telephone calls.

8. Would respondents be more embarrassed or threatened by talking to someone than merely recording their own responses? Is complete anonymity very necessary? The higher the degree of psychological threat and need for anonymity, the more appropriate the survey becomes.

on responses and clarify participants' statements, which isn't possible in a survey.

A focus group is another alternative if you are looking for multiple points of view in a shorter period of time (see Chapter 12, page 514). A focus group can create synergy between participants and enable you to conduct **brainstorming**. In an interview, you can spend more time understanding a single participant's needs, thoughts, and experiences as compared to a focus group. You can also cover more topics and do not have to worry about participants influencing each other's responses. In a focus group, you are typically limited in the number of questions you can ask and the depth of discussion with each participant because you want to hear from each participant equally.

In conclusion, use a survey when (a) you need a large number of responses, (b) questions can be answered adequately from a selection of options, and (c) you want to cover a large geographic region in a short period. Use a focus group when (a) you need data from several participants in a short period, (b) you want to cover only a few questions without a lot of depth from each participant, and (c) the topics are not sensitive or likely to be influenced by the opinions of others. But in cases where you want a lot of detail from end users and large numbers of participants is not of primary importance, interviews cannot be beaten (see Figure 7.2).

Figure 7.2:

Pros and cons of interviews

Interviews are good for ...
- Collecting rich, detailed data
- Collecting information to design a survey or other usability activity
- Getting a holistic view of the system

Interviews are not as good for ...
- Collecting data from large samples of people
- When you need to collect data very rapidly
- Collecting information on highly sensitive topics

Interviews, focus groups, and surveys are all very valuable user requirements methods. Be clear about your objectives and the kind of data you are seeking and choose the activity that best suits your needs.

Things To Be Aware of When Conducting Interviews

As with all user requirements activities, there are some factors that you should be aware of before you jump into the activity. In the case of interviews, these include bias and honesty.

Bias

It is easy to introduce bias into an interview. A skilled interviewer will know how to word questions that do not encourage a participant to answer in a manner that does not reflect the truth. This takes practice and lots of it. Later, we discuss in detail how to avoid introducing bias into the wording of your questions (see page 265) and into your interactions with participants (see page 271).

Honesty

Individuals who are hooked on performance metrics, or who question the value of "anecdotal" data, may frown upon interviews. Sometimes people ask how you know a participant is telling the truth. The answer is that people are innately honest. It is an extremely rare participant who comes into your interview with the intention of lying to you or not providing the details you seek.

However, there are factors that can influence a participant's desire to be completely forthcoming. Participants may provide a response that they believe is socially desirable or more acceptable rather than the truth. This is known as social desirability. Similarly, a participant may describe the way things are supposed to happen rather than the way things actually happen. For example, a participant may describe the process he or she uses at work according to recommended best practice, when in actuality the participant uses shortcuts and workarounds because the "best practice" is too difficult to follow – but the participant does not want to reveal this. Make it clear that you need to understand the way he or she *actually* works. If workarounds or shortcuts are used, it is helpful for you to understand this. And of course, remind the participant that all information is kept confidential – the employer will not receive a transcript of the interview.

A participant may also just agree to whatever the interviewer suggests in the belief that it is what the interviewer wants to hear. Additionally, a participant may want to impress the interviewer and therefore provide answers that increase his/her image. This is called prestige response bias. If you want the participant to provide a certain answer, he or she can likely pick up on that and oblige you. You can address these issues by being completely honest with yourself about your stake in the interview. If you understand that you have a stake in the interview and/or what your personal biases are, you can control for them when writing questions. You can also word questions (see "Write the Questions," page 262) and respond to participants in ways that can help mitigate these issues (e.g., do not pass judgment, do not invoke authority figures). You should be a neutral evaluator at all times and encourage the participant to be completely honest with you.

Be careful about raising sensitive or highly personal topics. A survey can be a better option than interviews if you are seeking information on sensitive topics. Surveys can be anonymous, but interviews are much more personal. Participants may not be forthcoming with information in person. For more discussion on this topic, see "Asking the tough questions," page 281.

If the participant is not telling the complete truth, this will usually become apparent when you seek additional details. A skilled interviewer can identify the rare individual who is not being honest, and disregard that data. When a participant is telling a story that is different from what actually happened, he or she will not be able to give you specific examples but will speak only in generalities.

> **Tip**
>
> With continued prodding, a dishonest participant will likely become frustrated and attempt to change the subject. If you doubt the veracity of a participant's responses, you can always throw away the data and interview another participant. Refer to "Know when to move on," page 288.

Outcomes Analysis

In brainstorming sessions, focus groups, and interviews, users are sometimes asked for solutions to problems or challenges they identify. Unfortunately, users are often not well-versed in the technical requirements to implement such solutions (emergent technologies), and they are limited by their own personal experience. To deal with this issue, you can conduct interviews in the form of "outcomes analysis." The sidebar on page 253 describes what outcomes analysis is and how to use it.

Outcomes Analysis

A company's Research & Development (R&D) department should be charged with the responsibility for developing new, innovative solutions – not the customers. Giving the responsibility of innovation to your customers can result in several problems (Ulwick 2002):

- The development team will make small, iterative changes to the product, rather than drastic, pioneering changes because participants do not have the technical knowledge to suggest such radical improvements

- Since people are limited by their experiences, participants will typically suggest features or changes available in your competitors' products that are not in yours. These additions may not drastically improve your product but it will simply bring you up to par with your competitors – something you could have done with a simple competitive analysis (see Chapter 2, Before You Choose an Activity, "Competitors" section, page 37).

- Participants may have needs they are not even aware of, so leaving innovation to what users report can leave entire areas of potential innovation undiscovered.

- Most users leverage less than 10% of a software product's overall capability. By adding more and more features to a product simply because participants brainstormed them (as they were asked to do) may cause users to resent paying additional money for a product full of features they don't actually need or use.

Limiting your questions to participants to the outcomes they need to achieve and allowing the developers to create the solutions can prevent the problems listed above. There are five steps to this process:

Plan outcome-based interviews

Prior to the interviews, deconstruct the processes or tasks users do associated with your product or service. This could be done via a group task analysis (see Chapter 11, page 458). As with any user requirements technique, recruit only true end users and strive for a diverse user population.

Capture desired outcomes

The interviewer must understand the difference between outcomes and solutions and ask the appropriate probes to weed out the solutions while getting to the outcomes (see example below). Participants should discuss every aspect of the process or task they complete when using your product or service. The interviewer will have to take descriptions by participants, translate them into hypothesized outcomes, and then validate them with participants. About 75% of the participants' desired outcomes can be identified in the first two-hour interview (Ulwick 2002). Another 15–20% can be captured in a second interview and another 5–10% in the third interview.

Participant: "All the flight times presented on a Palm 7." [Solution]

Interviewer: "Why would you like the flight time presented on a Palm 7? What would that help you do?" [Probe for outcome]

Participant: "I travel a lot so I need to see when flight times change and I take my Palm 7 with me everywhere." [Outcome]

Interviewer: "So you would like to have access to flight times from anywhere?" [Rephrasing to confirm outcome]

Participant: "Exactly." [Confirmation]

Organize the outcomes

Following the interviews, make a comprehensive list of all the captured outcomes and categorize them by steps in the process or activity users complete.

Rate the outcomes for importance and satisfaction

Send out a survey listing the outcomes identified in the interviews to as many end users as possible. Ask them to rate each outcome in terms of importance and their satisfaction that each outcome is currently being met (e.g., Likert scale with ratings of "not at all important" to "very important" and "not at all satisfied" to "very satisfied"). Compute a score for each outcome using the following formula:

Importance + (Importance − Satisfaction) = Opportunity

The "opportunity score" provides a more accurate result than traditional gap analysis. Gap analysis simply subtracts satisfaction from importance. It does not take into account the magnitude of importance of an outcome. See the example below:

Desired Outcome	Importance	Satisfaction	Opportunity
Speak with a live travel agent while booking travel	4.2	0	8.4
Get the lowest price available	8.2	4.0	12.4

Gap analysis would give both these outcomes the same score (4.2), neglecting the fact that getting the lowest price is considerably more important to users than speaking with a travel agent. If TravelSmart.com spent the same amount of resources on a solution to address both outcomes, users would not be more pleased (or well-served) with the resulting product than if the company had put more resources into delivering the lowest price.

Use the outcomes to jump-start innovation

Now that you have opportunity scores for each desired outcome, you know where R&D, marketing, and development should be spending their resources. In addition to developing new concepts for evaluation, you can use the results to identify whether different segments of your user population put different weights on each outcome. Perhaps it appeared initially that your user population was homogeneous in their desired outcomes, but once you examined the opportunities by user type you realized that your user population values each outcome differently. This can help you better position your product and target each user type appropriately. You may even find areas of product development that will not get you the bang for your buck everyone expected, and identify new areas of innovation that no one ever considered (even the end users!).

Preparing to Conduct an Interview

Now that you understand what interviews are and when to conduct them, we are going to discuss how to prepare for one. This includes selecting the type of interview to conduct, wording the questions, creating the materials, training the interviewer, and inviting observers.

First, Table 7.1 is a high-level timeline for you to follow when preparing for an interview. These are approximate times based on our personal experience and should be used only as a guide. It could take longer or less time for each step depending on a variety of factors – such as responsiveness of the development team, access to users, and resources available.

Table 7.1:

Preparing for the interview session

When to complete	Approximate time to complete	Activity
As soon as possible	1–2 weeks	☐ Meet with team to identify questions ☐ Meet with team to develop user profile
After identification of questions and user profile	1 week	☐ Create and distribute activity proposal
After the proposal has been agreed to by all stakeholders	1–2 weeks	☐ Word questions appropriately and distribute to co-workers for review
After development of the questions	2 weeks	☐ Identify and recruit users ☐ Assign roles for the activity (e.g., note-taker, interviewer) ☐ Prepare interview materials ☐ Acquire location ☐ Acquire incentives ☐ Prepare documentation (e.g., confidentiality agreement, consent form)
1 week before activity	2 days	☐ Conduct pilot ☐ Make necessary changes to questions and procedure based on pilot
Day before interview	1 hour	☐ Call and confirm with participant(s) ☐ Remind stakeholders to come and observe the activity (if appropriate)
Day of interview	1 hour	☐ Set up location with all materials necessary

Are You Ready?

Before you begin *any* user requirements activity there are a number of things that you must be familiar with. Because these elements are common to all user requirements activities, they have been covered in the earlier chapters – but now is a good time to double-check the list. If you are not familiar with one of the items you can refer to the earlier chapter to brush up or familiarize yourself with that element.

Chapter 1: Introduction to User Requirements
- ☐ **Get stakeholder buy-in for your activity** (see page 14)

Chapter 2: Before You Choose an Activity
- ☐ **Learn about your product** (see page 29)
- ☐ **Learn about your users** (see page 41)

Chapter 3: Ethical and Legal Considerations
- ☐ **Create consent forms** (see page 98)
- ☐ **Create confidential disclosure agreements** (see page 103)

Chapter 4: Setting up Facilities for Your User Requirements Activity
- ☐ **Create or acquire a facility for your activity** (see page 106)

Chapter 5: Preparing for Your User Requirements Activity
- ☐ **Develop an activity proposal** (see page 146)
- ☐ **Determine the time of day and duration of your session** (see page 155)
- ☐ **Recruit participants** (see page 156)
- ☐ **Develop an activity protocol** (see page 191)
- ☐ **Pilot your activity** (see page 193)

Chapter 6: During Your User Requirements Activity
- ☐ **Record and take notes during your activity** (see page 226)

At a Glance

> Identify the objectives of the study
> Select the type of interview
> Decide now how you will analyze the data
> Write the questions
> Test your questions
> Players in your activity
> Inviting observers
> Activity materials

Identify the Objectives of the Study

When developing questions for interviews, it is easy to add more and more questions as stakeholders (i.e., product team, management, partners) think of them. That is why it is important for everyone to agree upon the purpose and objectives of the study from the beginning. This should be included in your proposal to the stakeholders and signed off by all parties (refer to Chapter 5, Preparing for Your User Requirements Activity, "Creating a Proposal" section, page 146). As you and the stakeholders determine the type of interview to conduct and brainstorm questions for the interview, use the objectives of the study as a guide. If the type of interview suggested or the questions offered do not match the objectives that have been agreed upon, the request should be denied. This is much easier to do once the proposal has been signed off, rather than trying to get the agreement halfway through the process.

Select the Type of Interview

There are three main types of one-on-one interview:

- Unstructured (or open-ended)
- Structured
- Semi-structured.

They vary by the amount of control the interviewer places on the conversation.

In an unstructured interview, the interviewer will begin with talking points but will allow the participant to go into each point with as much or little detail as he/she desires. The questions or topics for discussion are open-ended, so the interviewee is free to answer in any manner, and the topics do not have to be covered in any particular order.

A structured interview, on the other hand, is the most controlled type. The interview may consist primarily of closed-ended questions and the interviewee must choose from the options provided. Open-ended questions may be asked, but the interviewer will not delve into the participant's responses for more detail or ask questions that are not listed on the script. This type of interview is similar to conducting a survey verbally and is used by organizations like the Census Bureau and Bureau of Labor Statistics.

Tip

A caution is warranted when using only closed-ended questions. Participants may have an opinion or experience different from the options offered. If you do not provide an "out" (e.g., "None of the above"), the participant will be forced to provide an inaccurate answer. Because closed-ended questions are more typical in surveys, you can find a discussion of the different types of closed-ended question and their uses in Chapter 8, Surveys, "Response format" section, page 324.

A semi-structured interview is clearly a combination of the structured and unstructured types. The interviewer may begin with a set of questions to answer (closed- and open-ended) but deviate from that set of questions from time to time. The interview does not have quite the same conversational approach as an unstructured one.

When determining the type of interview to conduct, keep the data analysis and objectives of the study in mind. By first deciding the type of interview you plan to conduct, you know the type of questions you will be able to ask. As with any method, there are pros and cons to each type of interview (see Table 7.2). Make sure that all stakeholders understand these, and that everyone is in agreement about the way to proceed.

Interview type	Type of data received	Pros	Cons
Unstructured	Qualitative	• Rich data set • Ability to follow up and delve deeper on any question • Flexible • Useful when you don't know what answers to expect	• Difficult to analyze • The follow-up questions may not be consistent across participants • Talkative participants may prevent you from covering everything you are interested in • Quiet participants may not give you enough information
Semi-structured	Combination	• Provides both quantitative and qualitative data • Provides some detail and an opportunity to follow up	• Takes some additional time to analyze participants' comments • Not as consistent across participants as the structured interview
Structured	Quantitative	• Faster to analyze • Questions asked are consistent across participants • You can generally ask more questions than in an unstructured interview	• You may not understand why you got the results you did because participants were not given an opportunity to explain their choice

Interviews via phone or in person?

Regardless of the type of interview you select, you have the option of conducting the interviews in person or over the phone. Although it is more convenient for both participant and interviewer to conduct the interviews via the phone and skip the travel time, there are a few disadvantages to conducting phone interviews.

- One study found that participants on the telephone ended the interviews before participants in face-to-face interviews did (Johnson, Hougland, & Clayton 1989). It can be difficult to keep participants on the phone for more than 20 minutes.

- Participants were more evasive, agreed with the interviewer more quickly, and were more hesitant to reveal sensitive information about themselves.

- If you are cold-calling participants (i.e., not a pre-scheduled interview), the biggest challenge may be keeping the participant's attention. If you do not have the participant in a quiet location, it is easy for their co-workers or children to come in during your interview for a "quick" question.

- You cannot watch the participant's body language, facial expressions, and gestures, which can provide important additional information.

- Phones can be perceived as impersonal and it is more difficult to develop a rapport with the participant and engage him/her over the phone. Web conferencing tools are available so that you may show artifacts to participants if appropriate, but you still cannot gain the personal connection over the phone and computer.

Figure 7.3 is a nice checklist that can help you determine whether a phone interview is appropriate or not.

Figure 7.3:
Checklist to determine whether a phone interview is appropriate for your study (Alreck & Settle 1995)

To Choose Telephone Versus In-Person

1. Must the data be collected at some special location outside the home or workplace, such as a shopping center, polling place, meeting, or event? If so, personal interviews will be required.

2. Does the interview task require showing the respondent something? If so, telephone interviewing is precluded and personal interviews are required.

3. Must the respondents be seen to judge if they're qualified to respond? If there's a quota based on the physical appearance or observed behavior of respondents, personal interviews will be necessary.

4. Are interviewers likely to include or exclude certain types of people, based on their appearance or visible characteristics, contrary to quota specifications? If such selection bias is likely, telephone interviews are more appropriate.

5. Is there a likelihood of psychological threat or intimidation in a personal encounter with an interviewer? If so, the more remote telephone interviewing method is indicated.

6. Is contamination of responses by the respondents' companions during the interview session likely? If so, telephone interviewing is more appropriate because others are less likely to overhear the conversation or interrupt it.

7. Will the interview take an exceptionally long time? If so, personal interviews are preferred because greater rapport and cooperation can be achieved with personal presence.

8. Does the telephone directory or other telephone number list serve as an adequate sample frame? If not, telephone interviews are precluded.

9. Are the respondents spread throughout a wide geographic area? If so, time and travel costs for personal interviews are likely to be prohibitive and long distance telephone interviews are advisable.

10. Is there the necessity for very rapid data collection? If so, telephone interviews can normally be completed much more quickly than interviewing in person.

Decide Now How You Will Analyze the Data

Whether you are asking closed-ended or open-ended questions, there are tools available to help you analyze your data. For a discussion of how to analyze open-ended questions, see "Data Analysis and Interpretation" (page 293). For a discussion of how to analyze closed-ended questions, refer to Chapter 8, Surveys, page 312.

Most people do not analyze interview data electronically. If you choose to do so, you need to allow time to purchase the software and learn how to use it. We strongly advise entering sample data from your pilot interviews into the tool and analyzing it (refer to Chapter 5, Preparing for Your User Requirements Activity, "Piloting Your Activity" section, page 193). This will help to determine whether the tool will meet your needs, or whether you need to adjust the questions.

Write the Questions

It is now time to identify all the questions to ask. You may want to do initial brainstorming with all stakeholders (members of the product team, the usability group, marketing). You will likely end up with questions that are out of the scope of the proposed activity, or questions that are best answered by other activities. You may also end up with more questions than you could possibly cover in a single interview. If this is the case, you will either need to conduct multiple sessions or trim down the number of questions to fit into a single session.

Tip

We do not recommend conducting interview sessions beyond two hours. However, dedicated participants or customers may be willing to stay for longer interviews if you provide regular breaks and keep the session interesting.

The next step is to word the questions so that they are clear, understandable, and impartial.

"*Next question: I believe that life is a constant striving for balance, requiring frequent tradeoffs between morality and necessity, within a cyclic pattern of joy and sadness, forging a trail of bittersweet memories until one slips, inevitably, into the jaws of death. Agree or disagree?*"

Brevity

Questions should be kept short – usually 20 words or less. It is difficult for people to remember long or multiple-part questions. Break long, complex questions into two or more simple questions.

Wrong: "If you were waiting until the last minute to book a plane ticket to save money and the only seats available were on the red-eye flight or had two layovers, what would you do?"

Right: "If you were paying for the ticket on a four-hour airplane trip, would you take a late-night/dawn-arrival flight that cost half as much? *<answer>* Would you accept a change of planes with a two-hour delay? *<answer>* What if you saved a quarter of the direct-flight fare?"

Clarity

Avoid **double-barreled questions** that address more than one issue at a time. Introducing multiple issues in a question can be confusing. The example below addresses multiple issues: the frequency of traveling, the frequency of booking travel online, and the purpose for booking travel online. These should be asked separately.

Wrong: "Do you regularly book your travel online to save money?"

Right: "How often do you travel? *<answer>* What proportion of that do you book online? *<answer>* Why do you book travel online?"

Vague questions, too, can cause difficulty during an interview. Avoid imprecise words like "rarely," "sometimes," "usually," "few," "some," and "most." Individuals can interpret these terms in different ways, affecting their answers and your interpretation of the results.

Wrong: "Do you usually purchase plane tickets online?"

Right: "How often do you purchase plane tickets online?"

A final challenge to creating clear questions is the use of **double negatives**. Just as the name implies, double negatives insert two negatives into the sentence, making it difficult for the interviewee to understand the true meaning of the question.

Wrong: "Do you no longer book travel on TravelSmart.com because they do not offer travel rewards?"

Right: "Why did you stop using TravelSmart.com? *<answer>* What was the main reason?"

Avoiding bias

As we mentioned earlier, there are a number of ways in which you might introduce bias into questions. One way is with **leading questions**. These assume the answer and may pass judgment on the interviewee. They are designed to influence a participant's answers.

Wrong: "Most of our users prefer the new look and feel of our site over the old one. How do you feel?"

Right: "How do you feel about the visual appearance of this website?"

Wrong: "Would you agree that it is more convenient to book travel online rather than through a travel agent?"

Right: "What is the greatest advantage to you of booking travel online? *<answer>* What is the greatest disadvantage? *<answer>* How does booking online compare to booking through a travel agent?"

Leading questions are rather obvious and easy to pick up on. **Loaded questions** are subtler in their influence. They typically provide a "reason" for a problem in the question. This frequently happens in political campaigns to demonstrate that a majority of the population feels one way or another on a key issue.

Wrong: "The cost of airline tickets continues to go up to cover security costs. Do you think you should have to pay more when you buy your ticket, or should the government start paying more of the cost?"

Right: "How much are you willing to pay for your plane ticket to cover additional security at the airport?"

The question above suggests that the reason for increasing travel costs is increased security costs. It is clear how the interviewer in the first (wrong) question would like the participant to answer. This is also an example of a question based on a false premise. The example implies that the government has not paid for additional security costs and should now start to do so. These types of question begin with a hypothesis or assumption that may not be fully accurate or can be easily misinterpreted. Not only is this type of question unethical, but the data you get in the end are not valid.

The final type of bias is **interviewer prestige bias**. In this case, the interviewer informs the interviewee that an authority figure feels one way or another about a topic and then asks the participant how he or she feels.

Wrong: "Safety experts recommend using a travel agent instead of booking your travel online. Do you feel safe using travel websites?"

Right: "Do you feel that booking travel online is more or less confidential than booking through a travel agent?"

Predicting the future

Do not ask participants to predict the future. Usability specialists, designers, marketers, and product managers are all guilty at some point of asking potential or current users to predict whether they would like a specific product feature or not. Until people have actual experience with a service or feature, they may not know what works for them or what they may actually like.

Wrong: "What are your thoughts about a new feature that allows you to instant message a travel agent with any questions as you book your travel?"

Right: "Would you like to correspond with a travel agent while you are booking travel? *<answer>* What are some ways that you would like to correspond with a travel agent while you are booking travel?"

The "wrong" question above would be a problem if the participant was unfamiliar with instant messaging. In that case, you would want to speak in broader terms and ask the participant to discuss communications methods with which he/she is familiar.

Rather than asking participants to predict the future or develop a solution to a perceived problem, it is best to limit your questions to desired outcomes. This interviewing technique is known as "outcomes analysis" (see discussion on page 253). What are the current issues users are encountering, and what is the goal or outcome they would like to achieve?

Inaccessible topics

You have screened your participants against the user profile but you still may encounter one who cannot answer all of your questions. A participant may not have experience with exactly what you are asking about, or may not have the factual knowledge you are seeking. In these cases, be sure a participant feels comfortable saying that he or she does not know the answer or does not have an opinion. Forcing a participant to choose an answer will only frustrate the participant and introduce error into your data.

Begin the interviews by informing participants that there are no right or wrong answers – if they do not have an opinion or experience with something, they should feel free to state that. Keep in mind that interviewees are often eager to please or impress. They may feel compelled to answer and therefore make a best guess or force an opinion that they do not actually have. Encourage them to be honest and feel comfortable enough to say they cannot answer a particular question.

Depending on memory

Think about the number of times you have booked a rental car in the last three years. Are you confident in your answer? Interviewers and surveys often ask people how frequently they have done a certain task in a given period. If the question seeks information about recent actions or highly memorable events (e.g., your wedding, college graduation), it probably won't be too difficult. Unfortunately, people are often asked about events that happened many years ago and/or those that are not memorable.

What is key is the importance or salience of the event. Some things are easily remembered because they are important or odd and require little effort to remember them. Other things are unmemorable – even if they happened yesterday you would not remember them. In addition, some memories that seem real may be false. Since most participants want to be "good" interviewees, they will try hard to remember and provide an accurate answer, but memory limitations prevent it. Under-reporting of events or inaccurate reporting frequently happens in these cases.

In addition to memory limitations, people have a tendency to compress time. This response bias is known as **telescoping**. This means that if you are asking about events that happened in the last six months, people may unintentionally include events that happened in the last nine months. Over-reporting of events will result in these cases.

To help mitigate these sources of error you should avoid questions covering unmemorable events. Focus the questions on salient and easy-to-remember events. You can also provide memory aids like a calendar. Finally, if you are truly interested in studying events over a period of time, you can contact participants in advance and ask them to track their behaviors in a diary (see Chapter 13, Field Studies, "Incident diaries" section, page 588). This means extra work for the participant, but the data you receive from those dedicated individuals who follow through will likely be far more accurate than from those who rely on memory alone.

Other types of wording to avoid

Avoid emotionally laden words like "racist" and "liberal." Personal questions should be asked only if absolutely necessary, and then with much tact. This includes questions about age, race, and salary. Figure 7.4 describes how to identify questions that might be perceived as threatening.

Jargon, slang, abbreviations, and geek-speak should be avoided unless you are certain that your user population is familiar with this terminology. Speaking in the user's language is important (as long as you understand it). And of course, take different cultures and languages into consideration when wording your questions (refer to Chapter 5, Preparing for Your User Requirements Activity, "Recruiting

To Identify Threatening Questions

1. Does the question ask about financial matters? This society judges people by what they earn and own, and most people fear the IRS above all else.
2. Does the question challenge mental or technical skill or ability? People often fear looking stupid or inept in their own eyes or to others.
3. Will the question reveal self-perceived shortcomings? People are highly sensitive to their inability to accomplish personally or socially desirable goals.
4. Is the question about *social status* indicators? Those with low-level educations, jobs, neighborhoods, and the like may be defensive about such questions.
5. Does the question focus on sexuality, sexual identity or behavior? Sexuality is a very private topic and many are embarrassed by even the mention of sex.
6. Does the question refer to consumption of alcohol or illegal drugs? Many will deny or understate such consumption or be insulted by the suggestion of use.
7. Are personal habits the topic of the question? Most people don't like to admit their inability to form or to break personal habits.
8. Does the question address emotional or psychological disturbance? Such illnesses are far more threatening to people than physical ailments.
9. Is the topic of the question associated with the *aging process*? Indicators of aging arouse fear and anxiety among many people of all ages.
10. Does the question deal with death or dying? Morbidity is often a forbidden topic and many refuse even to think about their own or their loved ones' death.

Figure 7.4:

Checklist to determine whether a question might be perceived as threatening (Alreck & Settle 1995)

International Participants" section, page 184). A direct word-for-word translation can result in embarrassing, confusing, or misinterpreted questions.

Figure 7.5 provides a checklist of dos and don'ts in question wording.

DO:

- Keep questions under 20 words
- Address one issue at a time
- Word questions clearly
- Keep questions concrete and based on the user's experience
- Limit questions to memorable events or ask participants to track their behavior over time in a diary
- Provide memory aids like calendars to help participants remember previous events
- Use terms that are familiar to the user

Continued

Figure 7.5:

Dos and don'ts in question wording

Figure 7.5 – *Cont'd*

> Use neutral terms and phrases
> - Ask sensitive or personal questions only if necessary
>
> ***DON'T:***
> - Force users to choose an option that does not represent their real opinion
> - Ask leading questions
> - Ask loaded questions
> - Base questions on a false premise
> - Use authority figures to bias questions
> - Ask users to predict the future
> - Ask users to discuss unmemorable events
> - Use jargon, slang, abbreviations, geek-speak
> - Use emotionally laden words
> - Use double negatives
> - Ask sensitive or personal questions out of curiosity

Test Your Questions

It is important to test your questions for clarity and validity (i.e., are you really asking what you think you're asking). If you are conducting an unstructured interview, test your list of topics or talking points. Begin with members of your team who have not worked on the interview so far. The team members should be able to summarize the type of information you are looking for in a question. If the co-worker incorrectly states the information you are seeking, you need to clarify or reword the question. Find someone who understands survey and interview techniques to check your questions for bias.

Once the questions have passed the test of co-workers, conduct the interview with a couple of actual participants. How did the participants react to the questions? Did they answer your question, or did it seem like they answered another question? Was everything clear? Were you able to complete the interviews within the allotted time frame?

Players in Your Activity

In addition to end users, you will require three other people to run the sessions. In this section we discuss the details of all the players involved in an interview.

The participants

We recommend interviewing approximately six to ten participants of each user type, with the same set of questions. This is a general guideline and there are several factors to take into consideration.

One factor to consider is the diversity of the user population. If you believe that a particular user type is homogeneous, you can interview fewer participants (five to six) because the results will be extremely similar. But you must be careful not to generalize too soon from a small set of interviews. If you have the resources and you are continuing to learn new insights with each user, it is useful to conduct additional interviews. Alternatively, if your subject matter is complex and/or highly varied in potential response, or if you believe that a particular user type is quite diverse, you should interview more participants (ten or more) to understand the variety of opinions and experiences present. Obviously, if you are unsure about the diversity of your user group, you can begin with a small number of interviews and continue to recruit participants until you feel you have gained a full understanding. Once you begin to hear the same responses over and over with very little new information, you can stop interviewing new participants.

The final thing to consider is the number of user types you have. You will likely find it more beneficial to conduct a few interviews with each user type rather than many interviews with only one user type. Only you know what resources you have available to conduct your studies, so you must weigh the resources available with the questions you need to answer.

There is no magic formula for determining the number of participants to interview – the final answer is: "it depends." (Refer to Chapter 2 to learn about identifying your users, creating a user profile, page 43.)

The interviewer

The task of the interviewer is to elicit responses from the participant, examine each answer to ensure that he or she understands what the participant is really saying, and then paraphrase the response to make sure that the intent of the statement is captured. In addition, the interviewer needs to know when to let a discussion go off the "planned path" into valuable areas of discovery, and when to bring a fruitless discussion back on track. The interviewer needs to have sufficient domain knowledge to know which discussions are adding value and which are sapping valuable time. He or she also needs to know what follow-up questions to ask on-the-fly to get the details the team needs to make product decisions.

We cannot stress enough how important it is for interviewers to be well-trained and experienced. Without this, interviewers can unknowingly introduce bias into the questions they ask. This will cause participants to provide unrepresentative answers or to misinterpret the questions. Either way, the data you receive are inaccurate and should not be used. People new to interviewing may wish to take an interviewing workshop – in addition to reading this chapter – to better internalize the information. (See Appendix B, page 688 for a list of individuals/companies offering training courses.)

We recommend finding someone who is a skilled interviewer and asking him/her to review your questions. Then practice interviewing him/her. The more you practice this skill, the better you will become and the more confident you can be in the accuracy of the data you obtain. Co-interviewing with a skilled interviewer is always helpful.

Finally, although we all hate to watch ourselves on video or listen to ourselves on a tape recorder, it is helpful to watch/listen to yourself after an interview. Even experienced interviewers fall into bad habits – watching yourself on tape can make you aware of them and help break them. Having an experienced interviewer watching or listening to the tape with you helps because he or she can point out areas for improvement.

The note-taker

You may find it useful to have a co-worker in the same room or another room who is taking notes for you. This frees you from having to take detailed notes. Instead you can focus more of your attention on the interviewee's body language and cues for following up. (Refer to Chapter 6, During Your User Requirements Activity, "Recording and Note-taking" section, page 226 for more details on capturing the data.)

The videographer

Whenever possible, video record your interview session. (Refer to Chapter 6, During Your User Requirements Activity, "Recording and Note-taking" section, page 226 for a detailed discussion of the benefits of video recording.) You will need someone to be responsible for making the recording. In most cases, this person simply needs to start and stop the tape, insert new tapes as needed, and keep an eye out for any technical issues that arise.

Inviting Observers

As with other usability techniques, we do not recommend having observers (e.g., co-workers, product team members) in the same room as the participant during the interview. If you do not have the facilities to allow someone to observe the interviews from another room, but you do want stakeholders to be present, it is best to limit the observers to one or two individuals. Any more than this will intimidate the person being interviewed. The observers should be told explicitly, prior to the session, not to interrupt the interview at any time.

Tip

Spend some time prior to the interview informing the observers about the importance of asking unbiased questions and the impact different types of bias can have on the data you collect. You may even choose to do some role-playing with the observers, having them interview you. Identify any biased questions they ask and tell them how the question would be asked without bias. Once observers understand the difficulty of asking unbiased questions and the impact biased questions have on the data, you will find they will be much more likely to respect your request for their silence.

It is up to you if you would like to leave time at the end of the interview for observers to ask follow-up questions. However, the questions observers ask should follow the same guidelines discussed above (e.g., avoid bias, keep them brief). Since you cannot control what the observers say, we recommend asking them to write questions on paper and then pass them to you at the end of the session. You then have the opportunity to reword a loaded or double-barreled question. Or you can work with the observer prior to the session to devise a set of follow-up questions that they may ask if time permits. This works well in cases where you do not have the domain knowledge to ask and follow up on technical questions.

Activity Materials

You will need the following materials for an interview (the use of these will be discussed in more detail in the next section):

☐ Protocol
☐ List of questions for interview
☐ Method of note-taking (laptop and/or paper and pencil)
☐ Method of recording (video or audio recorder)
☐ Comfortable location for participant, interviewer, note-taker, and video equipment
☐ Memory aids (e.g., calendar) – optional
☐ Artifacts to show the participant – optional.

Conducting an Interview

At a Glance

> The five phases of an interview
> Your role as the interviewer
> Monitoring the relationship with the interviewee
> Dos and don'ts

You are now prepared to conduct an interview. In this section, we walk you through the steps.

First, Table 7.3 covers in general the sequence and timing of events to conduct an interview. It is based on a two-hour session and will obviously need to be adjusted for shorter or longer sessions. These are approximate times based on our personal experience and should be used only as a guide.

Interviewing is a skill and takes practice. You should observe the five phases of an interview and monitor the interviewing relationship throughout.

Approximate duration	Procedure
5–10 minutes	Introduction (welcome participant, complete forms, give instructions)
5–10 minutes	Warm-up (easy, non-threatening questions)
85–100 minutes	Body of the session (detailed questions) *This will vary depending on the number of questions.* *This is the upper limit of what we recommend.*
5–10 minutes	Cooling-off (summarize interview, easy questions)
5 minutes	Wrap-up (distribute incentives, thank participant, escort him/her out)

Table 7.3:

Timeline for an interview (approximate times)

The Five Phases of an Interview

Whether the interview lasts ten minutes or two hours, a good interview is conducted in phases. There are five main phases to be familiar with.

The introduction

This should not be too long. If it is over ten minutes, you are probably giving the participant too many instructions and other things to remember. Begin by introducing yourself and any observer(s) in the room. If there are people watching in another room, mention their presence in generic terms. Next, state the purpose of the interview and why the participant has been asked to participate. Be sure to ask permission to audio or video record the session. Explain any confidentiality agreements and consent forms that must be signed. This is the first opportunity you have to encourage participants to answer honestly and feel free to say when they cannot answer one of your questions. Don't forget to thank the participants for coming. The following is a sample introduction:

"My name is Jane Doe and I work for TravelSmart.com. Thank you for coming in today! We will spend the next hour talking about your experience booking travel online."

"I understand that you are a current customer of TravelSmart.com and that you signed up for our Customer Participation Program. We would like to learn how we could improve our site to better suit our customers' needs."

"We have a couple members of the product development team in another room watching this session, and – if you do not mind – I would like to make a recording. This will allow me to go back at a later time and review your comments so that I am not distracted from our conversation by taking notes."

"I am not a member of the product team. I am a neutral evaluator, so nothing you say today will hurt my feelings. Your honest opinions can only help us improve our product. If you do not have an opinion or cannot answer any of the questions I ask, please feel free to say so."

"Since this product is not on the market yet, you will need to sign a non-disclosure agreement in which you promise not to discuss this product with anyone until it is put on the market, or until two years from now."

"You are free to leave at any time. Please stop me at any point if you have questions."

Warm-up

Always start an interview with easy, non-threatening questions to ease the participant into the interview. You can confirm demographic information (e.g., occupation, company), how the participant first discovered your product, etc. You may even allow the participant to vent his or her top five likes and dislikes of your product. The participant should focus his/her thoughts on your product and forget work, traffic, the video cameras, and so on. This is best done with easy questions that feel more like a conversation, and less like a verbal survey or test.

Five to ten minutes may be sufficient for the warm-up, but if the participant is still clearly uncomfortable, this could be longer. However, do not waste the participant's time (and yours) with useless small talk. The warm-up should still be focused on the topic of the interview.

Body of the session

Begin with general questions and move into more detailed ones. This should be the bulk (about 80%) of your interview time with the participant.

Cooling-off

Your interview may have been intense with very detailed questions. At this point, you may want to pull back and ask more general questions or summarize the interview. Ask any follow-up questions in light of the entire interview. Five to ten minutes should be sufficient.

Wrap-up

You should demonstrate that the interview is now at a close. Some people like to do this by closing a notebook and putting away their pens (if they were taking notes), changing their seat position, or turning off the tape recorder. This is a good time to ask the participant whether there are any questions for you. Thank the person for his/her time, and compensate the participant for their time and expertise, as agreed beforehand.

Your Role as the Interviewer

Interviewing can be an intense activity for the interviewer. Even though the participant is providing the information you are seeking, you cannot be a passive interviewer. You know the information you are seeking and it is your job to help the participants provide that information. "Active listening" means that you must judge if each response has adequately addressed your question, be on the lookout for areas of deeper exploration, and monitor the interviewing relationship throughout.

Do not interrupt

One of the biggest mistakes in interviewing is interrupting the participant. Don't let your enthusiasm for the topic or time constraints make you forget your manners. You never want to complete participants' thoughts for them or put words in their mouths. Give each participant time to complete his/her thought. If you do not have enough information after adequate silence, then follow-up with another question or restate the participant's answer (see "Reflecting," page 288). Of course, if the participant is struggling with a word and you are sure you know what the participant is trying to say, offer the word or phrase the participant is searching for, especially if the participant says, "It's on the tip of my tongue. Do you know what I'm talking about?"

Keep on track

It is easy for unstructured interviews to go off track. The participant may go into far more detail than you need but not know that. A participant may also digress to topics that are outside the scope of the study. It is your job to keep the participant focused on the topic at hand and move on to the next topic when you have the information needed. Below are some polite comments to get participants back on track or to move them on to a new topic:

> **"I can tell that you have a lot of detail to provide about this but, because of our time constraints, I need to cover a new topic. If we have time at the end, I would like to come back to this discussion."**

> **"That's really interesting. I was wondering if we could go back to topic XYZ for a moment . . ."**

> **"I'm sorry, I am going to interrupt you for a moment. A moment ago, you were discussing XYZ. Can you tell me more about that?"**

Silence is golden

Another big mistake in interviewing is attempting to fill every silence. An interviewee may need to think about whether a particular answer is appropriate or how to word it. A participant may also wonder how much detail you are looking for. In that case, he or she will likely provide a brief answer and then wait to see whether you move on. If you do not, the participant has been "given permission" to provide more detail. Some people recommend counting to ten before either moving on to the next question or probing for more detail. However, this extended silence can be uncomfortable for both you and the participant. Counting to five should provide adequate time for the participant to continue without inserting uncomfortable silence. Also, pay attention to the participant's body language (e.g., sitting forward, poised to make another statement) to determine whether he/she has more to say.

It is possible to go too far with your pauses and risk giving participants the silent treatment. That is why **acknowledgment tokens** are so important. Acknowledgment tokens are words like "oh," "ah," "mm hm," "uh huh," "OK," and "yeah" that carry no content. Since they are free of content, they are unobtrusive and require almost no processing by the participant, so he or she can continue unimpeded with a train of thought. These devices reassure participants that you hear them, understand what is being said, and want them to continue. Speakers expect a reaction from listeners, so acknowledgment tokens complete the "conversational loop" and keep the interviewing relationship a partnership, rather than a one-way dialog. Tokens like "mm hm" and "uh huh" are called "continuers" because they are not intrusive or directive. Tokens like "OK" and "yeah" imply agreement, which you may not want to imply to participants, revealing your personal opinions (Boren & Ramey 2000).

Remain attentive

Have you had the experience where someone has been talking for the past several minutes and you have no idea what he/she has been saying? If you are tired or bored, it is easy to zone out. Obviously, this is a faux pas in any conversation but particularly so in an interview. If you are tired or bored, there is a good chance that the participant is too.

Take a break at a logical stopping point. This will give you a chance to walk around and wake up. Evaluate how much you have engaged the participant in the interview. If this is an unstructured interview, you should be engaging the participant frequently for clarification, examples, and reflection (refer to these topics below). If it is a highly structured interview, the interviewee's answers should be short, followed by your next question. In either case, you should be engaging in the interview (without interrupting the participant, of course). After the break, take a moment to ask the interviewee to briefly summarize his/her last response. This will help the interview pick up where it left off and get you back on track.

Tip

Running multiple interviews in one day may speed up the information gathering process but it will also leave you exhausted. We recommend running no more than two two-hour interviews per day. Conducting three or more interviews per day for several days will likely leave you exhausted and degrades the quality of your data.

If you are going from city to city conducting interviews and must conduct, for example, seven interviews in two days, you don't have much of a choice. In this case, we recommend bringing a colleague with you to take notes during the interviews. Alternating the roles of note-taker and interviewer can give you both a modest break. At least you will not have to be fully "switched on" for every interview (encouraging participants, following up on questions).

Also, be sure to allow a small break between interviews. The more time you can give yourself the better. You will need enough time to get up, stretch your legs, take a bathroom break, and grab a beverage. Allow yourself time to eat, too, because if you cram all of your interviews back, to back, your energy is sure to run out. We hope it goes without saying, but *never* eat your lunch while interviewing a participant; that is rude and distracting.

If you have conducted several interviews on the same topic before, it is easy to assume that you have heard it all. What new information could the sixth participant provide? If you think you already know the answers to the questions, you can find yourself hearing what you want to hear or expect to hear, and thereby miss new information. Every participant has something unique to provide – although it may not be significant enough to warrant additional interviews. If you have conducted several interviews and feel confident that you have gained the required information, do not recruit additional participants. However, once the participant is in the door, you owe him/her the same attention that you gave the very first participant. Keep an open mind and you will be surprised at what you can learn.

Asking the tough questions

Sometimes you may need to ask questions that are embarrassing or cover sensitive topics. As we mentioned earlier, this is best done via surveys; but if you think there is a need to ask a difficult question in an interview, wait until you have developed a rapport with the participant. When you ask the question, explain why you need the information. This lets the participant know that you are asking for a legitimate reason and not just out of curiosity. The participant will be more likely to answer your question and relieve any tension. For example:

> "This next question is about the range your salary falls in. I'm asking this only because we believe that people who fall within specific salary ranges are sometimes more or less likely to book their travel online. To help us understand this, we are asking everyone about their salary range – if they feel comfortable. Would you mind stating which of the following ranges your salary falls in?"

Using examples

No matter how hard you try to make your questions clear, a participant may still have difficulty understanding exactly what you are asking. Sometimes rewording the question is not sufficient and an example is necessary for clarification. Since the example could introduce bias, you want to do this as a last resort. Having some canned examples for each question and then asking co-workers to check those examples for bias will help immensely.

Give the interviewee a moment to think about the question and attempt to answer it. If it is clear that the participant does not understand the question or asks for an example, provide one of the canned examples. If the participant still does not understand, you could either provide a second example or move to the next question.

> **Wrong:** "What are some of the discount airlines, such as Jet Blue, that you prefer to travel on?"
>
> **Right:** "Have you traveled on a discount (lower fare) airline? *<User does not understand what you mean by discount airlines; read a complete list of discount airlines.>* If you have, which ones do you prefer to travel on?"

Watch for generalities

Interviewees will often speak in general terms because they believe it is more useful to provide summary descriptions or typical situations rather than specific examples. This is usually the result of a generalized question (see below):

> **Interviewer:** "Tell me what happens when you call the agent on-call."
>
> **Participant:** "When you call the agent on-call, you wait and wait and wait. They don't pick up."

If you are looking for specific, detailed answers, do not ask generalized questions. Ask for **significant events**. Since the best indicator of the present is the past, ask the interviewee to describe a particular past event that best exemplifies the situation. Keep in mind our earlier discussion about memory limitations and telescoping (see page 268). Below is a sample interview asking for a significant event:

Generalized question →

> **Interviewer:** "What has been your experience booking travel online?"
>
> **Participant:** "Oh, I always have a terrible time. Either I can't remember my password or the session times-out before I can make my decision so I have to start all over. It's always something."

Follow-up for a significant event →

> **Interviewer:** "Can you tell me what was particularly frustrating about the last time you tried to book travel online?"
>
> **Participant:** "Well, the last time wasn't so bad. I know my session always ends up timing-out before I can finish so this time I was prepared. I did research on the flight and hotel in advance so that I could enter in all the information quickly. I logged in, selected the airline I wanted, entered in the flight dates, times, and then chose the flight that I knew I wanted. That went very quickly. I couldn't book the hotel though. I knew which hotel I

wanted but the dates I needed were not showing up as available. That annoyed me since I had already called the hotel to check for availability. I ended up having to leave the site and just book the hotel over the phone. I didn't get any kind of discount, so that sucked."

Do not force choices

Do not force opinions or choices from participants. If you ask an interviewee to make a choice from a list of options, but he/she says that it does not matter, or all of them are fine, you could probe to learn more about each option. By asking the participant to verbalize (and therefore think more about) each option, he or she may then show more of a preference for one option over others. However, if the participant states that all options *are* equal, do not force him/her to make choice. Likewise, if the participant states that he/she does not have an opinion on something, forcing him/her to elaborate will only generate annoyance (see example below).

Interviewer: "Which of the following customer rewards would you most like to receive when booking a certain number of trips with TravelSmart.com?"

- **10% discount on your next plane ticket**
- **Free upgrade on a car rental or plane ticket**
- **Free night at the hotel of your choice**
- **3% cash rebate**

Participant: "All of those sound good to me!"   ← Participant may not have understood that a single response was desired

Interviewer: "Do you have a preference for one over the other?"   ← Interviewer restates question

Participant: "No. They are all about equal."

Interviewer: "Can you tell me the pros and cons you can see with each option?"   ← Interviewer tries to determine if participant has a preference

Watch for markers

Sometimes participants throw out **markers**. These are key events to the participant that you can probe into for more rich information. You should search for more detail *only* if you believe it will provide relevant detail to your study – and not out of curiosity. Below is an interview excerpt with a marker and appropriate follow-up:

Marker →

> **Interviewer:** "Can you tell me about a difficult time you had using TravelSmart.com?"
>
> **Participant:** "Well, it was right after my aunt passed away. I needed to get a plane ticket back home quickly, but I couldn't get any on your site."
>
> **Interviewer:** "You mentioned your aunt had just passed away. What made it difficult to get a plane ticket at that time?"
>
> **Participant:** "I just knew I needed to get home quickly. Unfortunately, the seats would have cost a fortune since it was last-minute travel. I heard that airlines offered bereavement discounts but I couldn't figure out how to do that on your site. I did a search on your site but I couldn't find anything. I was hoping that you had an on-call agent like WillCall.com, but you didn't."
>
> **Interviewer:** "What happened next?"
>
> **Participant:** "I was so stressed out that I ended up leaving your site and going to WillCall.com instead. They were able to get me the discount pretty quickly."

Interviewer detects marker and seeks relevant information

The participant provided the marker of her aunt passing away. That was critical to her. She was stressed out and couldn't find the information she needed. She wanted someone to personally help her and provide some support, but the website could not do it. Consequently, she now has a strong negative memory of TravelSmart.com and a positive one of the competitor. Following-up on that marker allows us to better understand the context of what happened and why the experience was so difficult for the participant. If the participant drops such a marker inadvertently and does not feel comfortable elaborating on it, he/she will let you know the topic is off-limits.

Select the right types of probe

Your probes for detail should be as unbiased as your initial question to the participant. There are closed-ended and open-ended probes, just like the initial question you asked. A closed-ended probe would be something like: "Were you using Netscape or Internet Explorer?" An open-ended probe might be: "Tell me about the browser(s) you use." Keep all probes neutral and do not ask the participant to defend his/her choices.

Wrong: "Why did you do that?"

Right: "Can you tell me more about your decision?"

Table 7.4 provides an excellent comparison of different types of biased and unbiased probes, as well as what makes each probe biased.

Some interviewers recommend "playing dumb" to get more detail out of participants. By downplaying what you know, participants will be more explicit and may want to impress you with their knowledge. This may work in some cases, but if you slip and reveal in a question or probe that you know more than you are letting on, the participant can feel betrayed, duped, or patronized. This will clearly harm the interviewing relationship. As a result, we recommend being honest about what you know and understand – but make it clear that the participant is the expert, not you. Your knowledge may be limited and the participant is there to increase your knowledge.

Table 7.4: *Biased and unbiased probes (adapted from Dumas & Redish 1999)*

Ask:	Instead of:	Why:
Can you tell me what you are thinking right now? What are you trying to do?	Are you thinking _____? Are you trying to _____?	Even though you may think you know what they are thinking (that may be why you are asking the question), you do not want to put words into their mouths, because you may be wrong. Remember, you do not want participants to know your opinions about what you are questioning them on.
What are you thinking? Can you explain to me what you are trying to do? Can you explain to me your train of thought right now? (After the task is ended) Why did you try to _____?	Why are you _____? Are you trying to _____ because _____? Are you trying to_____?	By asking participants why they are doing something, they may feel that you are asking them to justify their actions, and, therefore, think that they are going about the task incorrectly. It is, however, acceptable to ask a participant why they went about a task in a certain way after the task has been ended, or at the end of the test if future tasks have components similar to the task you are questioning them about.
Did you find the product easy or difficult to use? Were the instructions clear or confusing? Were error messages helpful or hindering?	Did you find the product easy to use? Did you find the product difficult to use? Were the error messages helpful?	Trying to get someone to express an opinion on a specific usability attribute is not always easy. Therefore, you may find that you need to guide participants by specifying the attribute you want them to react to. It is important to use both ends of the spectrum when you do this so that they do not perceive you as encouraging either a positive or negative answer. Also, by doing so, you will encourage a more informative response. Instead of responding "No (it was not easy)," they are more likely to say "I found it very difficult to use," or "it was pretty easy." You then can follow up by asking them "why?"
What are you feeling? How did you feel when you were doing _____?	Are you feeling confused? Are you feeling frustrated?	Sometimes, participants need to stop and think—maybe to try to remember how a similar product worked. Though they may appear confused or frustrated, they may just be contemplating. Everyone expresses themselves differently, so we take a risk by trying to guess what they are thinking.

Table 7.4 – *Cont'd*

Ask:	Instead of:	Why:
Would you change anything about this (product, screen, design, etc.)?	Do you think ___ would improve the product?	Unless the design team is considering a particular design change, you should never suggest what changes participants should talk about.
Are there any changes you would make to ___ to make it easier to use?	If we changed ___ to ___ do you think that it would be easier to use?	Always let participants express their own ideas. And, if there is a design change that the design team feels will improve the product, ask them to react to it only after they have made their suggestions and only after you let them know that their input is considered valuable.
How do you feel about (that error message, the organization of the screen, the way the procedure is described in the manual, etc.)?	Was the (error message, the organization of the screen, the description of the procedure, etc.) confusing?	Even though you may think you know what they are thinking (that may be why you are asking the question), you do not want to put words into their mouths, because you may be wrong.
Do you have any reactions to (that error message, the organization of the screen, the way the procedure is described in the manual, etc.)?	Are you confused by the (error message, the organization of the screen, the description of the procedure, etc.)?	Remember, you do not want participants to know your opinions about what you are questioning them on.
Do you have any comments on the (appearance, size, feel, feedback, etc.) of ___?	Do you like the (appearance, size, feel, feedback, etc.) of ___?	

Watch your body language

Your tone and body language can affect the way a participant perceives your questions. Be alert to your biases. Is there an answer to your question that you would like the participant to provide? Is there an answer you expect? Your expectations and preferences can be conveyed in your tone, body language, and the way you phrase questions, probes, and summaries. For example, looking bored or not making eye contact when you disagree, or sitting on the edge of your seat and nodding vigorously when the participant is confirming your suspicions, will clearly reveal your biases. Your biases are even conveyed in the responses that you do not follow up on. Watching yourself on videotape can help you identify those biases. If you are alert to your biases, you can better control them.

Know when to move on

Knowing when to let go is as important as knowing when to follow up. A participant may not be as forthcoming as you would like, or maybe the person is just plain lying. As rare as that is, you should know how and when to move on. Remember: this is an interview, not an interrogation. Even if you suspect that the participant is not being completely honest, continued badgering is as rude as calling the participant a liar. Once it is clear that the participant cannot provide the details you are looking for, drop the line of questioning and move on. If necessary, you can throw out that participant's data later. For ethical reasons, you must remember to treat the participant with respect, and part of that is knowing when to let a topic of discussion drop.

Reflecting

To verify that you understand what the participant has told you, it is essential to summarize, reword, or reflect the participant's responses. You are not probing for more detail but confirming the detail you already have. It is not necessary to do this after every response, especially if the response is brief and straightforward as in structured interviews. However, if the participant's response has been lengthy, detailed, or not completely clear, you should summarize and restate what the participant has said and check for accuracy. A reflection of the earlier interview excerpt (see page 284) is provided below:

> **"I just want to make sure that I have captured your experience correctly. You needed to purchase tickets for immediate travel and you were looking for a bereavement discount. You couldn't find information on bereavement discounts or an agent to assist you at TravelSmart.com, so you went to WillCall.com because you knew they had an agent on call. They were then able to get you the tickets at a discount. Does that summarize your experience correctly?"**

Reflections help build rapport by demonstrating that you were listening and understood the participant's comments. They can also be used to search for more information. The participant may clarify any incorrect information, or provide additional information, when responding to your summary.

At no time should you insert analysis into your summary or in response to a participant's statement. In other words, do not try to provide a solution to a problem the participant has had, explanations for why the product behaved as it did, or why you think the participant made a certain choice. In the example above, you would not want to inform the participant where she could have found the bereavement discount on your site. You are not a counselor and you should not be defending your product. You are there to collect information from the interviewee – nothing more. Ask for observations, not predictions or hypotheses.

Empathy and antagonism

When you are speaking with someone – even if it is someone you barely know – doesn't it make you feel better to know that the other person understands how you feel? A skilled interviewer is able to empathize with the participant without introducing bias. Keep in mind that this is not a conversation in the traditional sense; you are not there to contribute your own thoughts and feelings to the discussion. In the earlier example, the interviewer could have shown empathy by stating: "That [bereavement] must have been a difficult time for you." An inappropriate response would have been: "I know exactly how you feel. When my grandmother passed away, I had to pay an arm and a leg for my plane ticket." The interview is not about you. You do not have to be a robot, devoid of emotion, in order to prevent bias. Make eye contact and use your body language to show the participant that you are engaged, that you understand what he/she is saying, and that you accept the participant regardless of what he or she has said.

It should be unnecessary to say, but some interviewers actually make the mistake of disagreeing with participants. Just as in sales the customer is always right, in usability the participant is always right. None of your questions, probes, or reflections should insinuate that you disagree with what the participant has said. You do not want to insult the participant and disrupt the remainder of the interview. Even if the interviewee's understanding of how a product works is incorrect, you do not want to say: "Actually, that's wrong." You are there to collect information and your thoughts and opinions are irrelevant. If for the purposes of accurate data collection, you need to correct some factual data the participant has mistaken, find a diplomatic way to provide the correct information.

Transitions

Your questions or topics for discussion should transition smoothly from one topic to another. This will allow participants to continue on a track of thought and the conversation will appear more natural. If you must change to a new topic of discussion and there is not a smooth transition, you can state: "That's excellent information you've given me. While I make a note of it, can you think about how you would *<introduce different topic>*?." This lets the participant know that he or she should not be looking for a connection or follow-up from the last question. If the participant believes that you are trying to probe more deeply into the previous topic, he or she may get confused or misinterpret your next question. A simple transition statement gives closure to the last topic and sets the stage for the next one.

Avoid negative connectors like "but" and "however." These might signal to a participant that he or she has spoken too long or has said something incorrect. The person is likely to be more cautious when answering the following questions.

Monitoring the Relationship with the Interviewee

Like all user requirements activities, interviews are a giving and taking of information. Since it is one-on-one, the relationship is more personal. To get the most out of participants, it is important to monitor the relationship and treat the participant ethically. You want to make sure that the participant is comfortable, engaged, and trusting. If the participant does not feel you are being honest or is wondering what the motivation is behind your questions, he/she will be guarded and will not provide the full details you are looking for.

Watch the participant's body language

Does the participant seem tense, nervous, bored, or angry? Is he/she looking at the clock or is his/her attention lapsing? Do *you* feel tense? If so, the participant likely feels tense too. You may have jumped into the detailed, difficult, or sensitive questions before you established a good rapport. If possible, go back to easier questions, establish the purpose and motivations of the study, and be sure that the participant is a willing partner in the activity. If a particular line of questioning is the problem, it is best to abandon those questions and move on. A break may even help. Sometimes a participant is just having a bad day and nothing you say or do will help. At that point, ending the interview can be the kindest act possible for the both of you.

SUGGESTED RESOURCES FOR ADDITIONAL READING

Although you should pay attention to a person's body language to determine whether he/she is tired, uncomfortable, or annoyed, we do not advocate anything more than that. Body language is ambiguous; a person may be staring at the floor through shyness. It is more important to note *changes* in behaviors over time, rather than a singular action/behavior. To learn more about what people's gestures and body language might mean, refer to:

- Argyle, M. (1988). *Bodily Communication*, 2nd ed. London: Methuen.
- Nance, J. (2001). *Conquering Deception*. Irvin–Benham Group, LLC.

Fighting for control

If you find yourself competing with the participant for control of the interview, ask yourself why. Is the participant refusing to answer the questions you are asking, or is he/she interrupting before you can complete your questions? Just as the interview is not about your thoughts or opinions, it is not up to the participant to ask the questions or drive the interview. At some point, the participant misunderstood the guidelines of the relationship. Begin with polite attempts to regain control, such as:

> **"Because we have a limited amount of time and there are several topics that I would like to cover with you, I am going to need to limit the amount of time we can discuss each topic."**

If the participant refuses to be a cooperative partner in the interviewing relationship and you do not feel you are obtaining useful information, simply let the participant go on and then write off the data. In extreme cases, it is best for all parties to end the interview early. If you have recorded the session, watch or listen to it with a colleague to see whether you can identify where the interviewing relationship went awry and how you can avoid it in future.

Hold your opinions

Even though the interview is not about you, if the participant directly asks your opinion or asks you a question, you do not want to seem evasive because it could harm the rapport you have established. If you believe your response could bias the participant's future responses, your reply should be straightforward:

> **"Actually, I don't want to bias your responses so I can't discuss that right now. I really want to hear your honest thoughts. I would be happy to talk about my experiences after the interview."**

If you are sure the question and your response will not have an effect on the remainder of the interview, you can answer the question but keep it brief.

Tip

If you look at a transcript of a bad interview, one of the first clues you might see is a one-to-one ratio of participant comments to interviewer comments/questions, especially in an unstructured interview. However, an abundance of participant comments does not necessarily indicate a successful interview. It is your job to keep the participant focused and not allow him/her to delve deeply into irrelevant topics or go beyond the scope of the study.

Dos and Don'ts

We have provided a lot of recommendations about how to conduct a successful interview. For easy referral, some of the key tips are summarized in Figure 7.6.

DO:

- Divide the interview into the five major phases
- Ask personal or sensitive questions only after you have developed a rapport with the participant and state why you need this information
- Use acknowledgment tokens to keep the participant talking and in control
- Ask the participant to describe the qualities of each choice, if the person does not have a preference
- Provide background information only if necessary and keep that information factual
- Be alert to your biases and remain neutral
- Know when to stop probing for detail
- Reflect as accurately as possible what the participant has told you
- Empathize with the participant
- Provide transitions between different topics
- Monitor the interviewing relationship
- Keep the participant focused on the topic
- Choose an effective method for recording data

DON'T:

- Jump into detailed or sensitive questions without first developing a rapport with the participant
- Assume you know the participant's response
- Interrupt the participant, put words in his/her mouth, or complete his/her sentences
- Force participants to make choices or have an opinion
- Attempt to fill every silence
- Insert your own observations or analysis in the reflection
- Disagree with the participant or state that he/she is wrong
- Provide information about yourself, your opinions, or similar experiences
- Allow a poor interviewing relationship to continue unchecked

Figure 7.6:

Dos and don'ts when conducting an interview

Data Analysis and Interpretation

Data should be analyzed shortly after conducting each interview. As with any activity, the longer you wait to get to the analysis, the less you will remember about the session. The notes will be more difficult to interpret and you will have to rely heavily on the recordings. The more you have to rely on the recordings, the more time it will take you to analyze the data. Hold a debrief session as soon as possible with your note-taker and any other observers to discuss what you learned. Review the recording to fill in any gaps or expand on ideas if necessary, and add any additional notes or quotes. If the session is still fresh in your mind it will not take as long to review the recording.

You can either wait until you have conducted all the interviews before analyzing the data, or you can do preliminary analysis following each interview. We recommend the latter because it can give you insights for future interviews. You may want to delve into more detail on questions, or remove questions that are not providing value. And as any usability professional can attest to, stakeholders often ask for results before a study is complete. It can help if you have something more substantial to give them than just a few interesting quotes that stand out in your mind.

Categorizing

If you are conducting structured or semi-structured interviews, you can begin by tallying the responses to closed-ended questions. For example, how many people so far have selected each option in a multiple-choice question, or what is the average rating given in a **Likert scale** question? Chapter 8 has a detailed discussion of closed-question data analysis (see Chapter 8, Surveys, "Data Analysis and Interpretation" section, page 348).

If you are conducting unstructured interviews, you can begin by identifying potential categories. What is the range of responses you are getting to each question? What is the most frequent response? Regardless of the type of interview, you can select some illustrative quotes to represent each category of response.

Affinity Diagram

An affinity diagram is probably the most useful method for analyzing interview data. Similar findings or concepts are grouped together to identify themes or trends in the data. A detailed discussion of what an affinity diagram is, how to create one, and how to analyze the data from one is provided in Appendix F, page 714. This data analysis technique applies to other methods as well, such as focus groups and field studies.

Qualitative Analysis Tools

Several tools are available for purchase to help you analyze qualitative data. They look for patterns or trends in your data. Although these tools hold a lot of potential, none of the seasoned usability professionals we have spoken with have used these tools. If you would like to learn more about the available tools, what they do, and where to find them, refer to Appendix G, page 722. As with affinity diagrams, this data analysis technique can be applied to other methods.

Communicate the Findings

In this section we discuss some of the ways in which interview data can be effectively communicated. There are a few different ways that you can present the data. It all depends on the goals of your study, how your data stacks up, and the method you feel best represents your data. In the end, a good report illuminates all the relevant data, provides a coherent story, and tells the stakeholders what to do next.

Preparing to Communicate Your Findings

The specific data that you communicate to product teams can vary depending upon the activity you conducted, but some elements of *how* you communicate the results are the same regardless of the method. Because these strategies are common to all user requirements activities, they are discussed in detail in Chapter 14, Concluding Your Activity, page 636. We recommend that you read that chapter prior to relaying your results to your stakeholders. Topics discussed include:

- ☐ **Prioritization of your findings** (see page 638)
- ☐ **Creating an effective presentation** (see page 644)
- ☐ **Writing valuable reports for different audiences** (see page 652)
- ☐ **Ensuring the incorporation of your findings** (see page 660)

Over Time

Your interview may cover a period of time, such as asking a travel agent to describe his/her day from the first cup of coffee in the morning through turning off the computer monitor at the end of the day. Or you may ask someone a series of questions that cover the first six months of training on the job.

If your questions cover a period of time, it makes sense to analyze the data along a timeline. Use the results from your initial categorization to start filling in the timeline. In our travel agent example, what is the first thing that the majority of travel agents do in the morning? What are the activities that fill their days? Then use individual anecdotes or details to fill in gaps and provide interesting information that does not fit neatly into a category. It can be those additional details that provide the most value.

By Topic

Your questions may not follow a timeline but simply address different topics related to a domain or user type. In these types of interview, you may wish to analyze and present the data per question. Provide the range of answers for each question and the average response. Alternatively, you can group the data from multiple questions into larger categories and then discuss the results for each category. An affinity diagram is most helpful in these types of interviews to identify higher-level categories, if they exist (see Appendix F, page 714).

By Participant

If each participant and his/her results are widely different, it can be difficult to categorize the data. This may be the result of difficulties with your user profile and recruiting, or it may be intentional in the case where you want to examine a variety of user types. It may make more sense to summarize the results per participant to illustrate those differences. Similarly, you may choose to analyze the data per company (customer), industry, or some other category membership.

Vehicles for Communicating Your Results

As with any of the usability techniques described in this book, you may wish to archive the methods and results of your study in a usability report, along with an Executive Summary to provide a quick synopsis of the results. (Refer to Chapter 14, Concluding Your Activity, page 652 to learn more about reporting usability results.) The following are some additional methods for communicating your results:

- Create a poster that summarizes the results in either a time-based or topic-based manner. Include particularly illuminating quotes to make it more interesting, and remind the audience that these results are from the mouths of real users.

- Use the results to build or improve your personas and scenarios (see Chapter 2, Before You Choose an Activity, "Learn About Your Users" section, page 41).

- Identify follow-up activities that can be built based on the results of your interviews (e.g., a survey).

- Create a table of recommendations that summarizes the issues uncovered and recommendations for next steps (see Table 7.5). This table should be easy to quickly scan and understand. It may not be as easy to construct as if you had conducted a usability test, but it is still possible. The best recommendation may be "Investigate further." Without that recommendation, however, the product team may stall and have no idea how to proceed.

Issue	Recommendation
The most frequently stated difficulty participants had with our site was finding information using our search facility.	• Search team should work with the UI group to identify methods for improving the search engine and display of search results.
Nine out of ten participants asked for an on-call agent to help when they had a difficulty.	• Conduct a usability evaluation of site to improve overall usability. • Provide a FAQ based on the results of the interviews and questions we have received via e-mail to date. • Investigate the feasibility of providing on-call agents.
When asked for additional services we can provide, half the users suggested being able to arrange transportation to and from the airport (taxi, hotel shuttle, etc.).	• Investigate the feasibility of purchasing shuttle tickets from our site. • Ask associated hotels that provide shuttles to and from airports whether we can arrange this service online.

Table 7.5:

Sample table of recommendations

Lessons Learned

We conducted a series of interviews at hospitals in Houston, Texas and Cardiff, Wales. We interviewed doctors, nurses, and other staff members throughout the hospitals. We kept small notebooks with us to jot down important points to follow up, but we relied almost exclusively on audio recorders. Unfortunately, during transcription we discovered one tape from each hospital was blank. There is no way to know what happened, but those interviews are lost forever. Check and recheck your equipment. Is the light on, indicating that it is recording? Is the tape progressing? Monitor the time you have been recording. If it is a 30-minute tape, it had better flip over or stop at the 30-minute mark. If not, you haven't been recording the entire time. Also, replay sections of the tape during breaks. If you find that the audio was not recorded, the conversation should be fresh enough in your mind that you can jot down a few notes to fill in the blanks. If you're very lucky, you may be able to interview the participant again.

Pulling It All Together

We began by discussing the best uses for interviews and the different types of interviews (structured, unstructured, and semi-structured). Proper wording of questions in interviews was then discussed in detail. If the questions in an interview are constructed poorly, the results of your study will be biased or will not provide the information you need. We also discussed how to conduct an interview, including the five phases of an interview, your role as an interviewer, and recording the data from the interviews. Finally, methods for analyzing the data and presenting your results were discussed.

The results from your interviews can be incorporated into documentation such as the Detailed Design Document. Ideally, additional user requirements techniques should be used along the way to capture new requirements and verify your current requirements.

SUGGESTED RESOURCES FOR ADDITIONAL READING

The book below is a detailed resource for anyone conducting interviews. The author provides lots of sample interviews and indicates good and bad points in the interviewers' techniques. We recommend this for anyone wanting a standalone resource for interviewing.

- Weiss, R. S. (1994). *Learning from Strangers: The Art and Method of Qualitative Interview Studies*. New York: Free Press.

CASE STUDY

Donna Andrews provides an illuminating case study about a series of interviews she conducted for the MSN8 Dashboard. She provides detailed information about designing the interviews, conducting them, taking notes, and analyzing the data. She even describes the results they found and her own lessons learned.

Preparing and Conducting On-site Interviews

Donna Andrews, Microsoft Corporation

The MSN8 Dashboard is a way for users to keep personally relevant links and real-time information available on their desktop (see Figure 7.7 on page 300). It contains a set of "tiles" from which users can select – such as "stocks" and "weather" – to see real-time information, or "movies" to navigate to particular movie sites on the Internet. For a new, similar feature in a future version of Windows, we were interested in whether the Dashboard, or a different, internal product called Sideshow, provided more useful and usable model for users.

Sideshow offered a similar user interface to Dashboard (a bar that sits lengthwise at the edge of the screen – for convenience I will call them both "bars") but offered different content, a different method of choosing and adding content, and a different interaction model. The feature team decided to set up a "trial period study" in which participants compared Sideshow and Dashboard over a period of months, and then interview the participants about their experiences.

Reasons for Choosing the Semi-structured Interview

We chose a trial period and semi-structured interviews for several reasons. First of all, because the purpose of Dashboard and Sideshow is to allow users to remain peripherally aware of personally important information at all times, a lab study was inappropriate. Each bar comes with a variety of tiles that the user can choose from, and the user can choose to install as many or as few of those on the bar as they wish. Participants would need ample time to find the types of tiles available in each bar, decide which might be relevant or interesting, and learn to customize the user interface at will. A trial period also provided users a chance to use the interface in the manner it was intended – at

Figure 7.7:

Sideshow (left) and
Dashboard

periodic intervals and in very short bursts of attention – potentially a few seconds at a time, rather than in a short, concentrated period of time.

Secondly, the purpose of both bars is to provide information at a quick glance. It would be extremely difficult to "observe" participants using the bars because each "use" might last only a few seconds, and come at long intervals. In addition, there would be no way to know which tiles were being viewed, which information available in that tile was being gleaned, and what value the information provided the user once it had been viewed. Furthermore, since the bar is always available and visible, it may provide some peripheral awareness benefits that would be entirely unobservable by us but might be consciously realized by users over a period of time.

Finally, we were as interested in participants' reactions to the bar as we were in what aspects of the bar they used and how often they used it. Their impressions, observations, and ideas could be extremely valuable in helping us to understand how to shape the new product but are literally impossible to observe. The only way to get at that type of information is to allow the users to experience the product first-hand in their own environments, and then encourage them to speak freely about their experiences.

There are drawbacks to the type of trial period study used here. Participants' statements about their use of the bars had to be taken at face value. Sometimes participants had trouble remembering the specifics of a situation that had happened weeks previously, or were unable to recount clearly the troubles they had early on once they had surmounted any "learning curve" issues.

Therefore it was decided that the best method for gathering user requirements would be to allow participants to use each bar on their own, in whatever way they found most suitable, and conduct an interview after a set period of using each one.

Study Setup

Seven people participated in the study. Participants were recruited through the Microsoft Usability recruiting pool and were screened to be members of the seven "personas" created by the feature team (refer to Chapter 2, Before You Choose an Activity, "Step 2: Personas" section, page 47). We made three visits to each participant.

- During the first visit we installed the first bar (three used Dashboard first and four used Sideshow first) and conducted a semi-structured interview about computer use as well as their use of and interest in other forms of digital technology (e.g., digital photos, digital media). This interview was written and conducted by a Project Manager in the usability group and was not part of the structured interview process detailed here.

- The second visit was approximately eight weeks later, to give participants time to learn how the product worked, customize it, and get used to using it; and also to give me time to complete a full round of visits and write up the data before beginning another. At the second visit, I returned with one or two members of the product team (or occasionally, members of related or partner teams – program managers, developers, testers, product designers, and writers all attended), and interviewed participants about their use of the first bar. After that interview the first bar was uninstalled and the second one was installed.

- After another period of approximately eight weeks, we made our third and final visit. Again participants were interviewed. Since eight weeks is a long time between visits, I gave participants a small notebook to record any experiences, thoughts, or comments that they wanted to remember to share when I returned. Several used the notebook; others made notes on their computer. One participant provided us with six to eight pages of typed notes and ideas at each visit.

I chose to do a "within subjects" style design, having all participants use both bars, because with only seven participants we didn't feel we would be able to draw strong enough conclusions from a "between subjects" design. We were afraid that if participants saw only one bar, they would all "like" the bar they used. Since it is something of a new concept, with nothing to compare it to, users might not be as critical as we wanted them to be. It was felt that giving them experience with both styles of bar might spark their critical interest and imagination more, and make them better able to express preferences for the types of things they found useful or irrelevant, convenient or annoying.

All participants were compensated at each visit with an item of Microsoft software.

Planning and Writing the Interview

I asked the team designing Sideshow to brainstorm a list of questions they wanted user information on. I already had a fairly complete list of questions I anticipated asking, but asking for input and participation in the planning created an interest in the project among the team, and buy-in that the results would be useful and "worth waiting for."

I combined the team's questions with my own and wrote a final list of questions. I couched the questions explicitly in terms of the characteristics of the two bars in the study, so that I could ask the same questions about both bars and get comparable information about each. For example, one of the questions the feature team wanted to ask was "What types of information should we show in our product?" I translated this into a series of questions that could be answered about each individual bar. Here is an example of this.

Information Need: "What Kind of Information Should We Have in the Bar?"

1. Which bar parts did you use most?

2. Why did you use them? How did you use the information?

3. Which parts were most useful? Were there some parts that were useful at one time but not later?

4. Which parts did you enjoy using the most? (Which were your favorite parts?) Why?

5. Which parts have you added to your bar? Why?

6. Which parts have you removed? Why?

7. Was there information you wanted to add to your bar that you weren't able to? Why did you want to have access to that kind of information?

The careful reader will have noticed that the questions in this list have a significant amount of overlap. The tiles that got used most were likely to be the tiles that were either the most useful or the most enjoyable. The tiles that participants took the time to remove from the bar were likely to be neither useful nor enjoyable. The reason for creating questions that might have overlapping answers or references was that it allowed me, as the interviewer, to ensure that nothing was overlooked in the interview process.

On the other hand, asking a series of overlapping questions directly would undoubtedly cause participants to repeat themselves. I therefore included a "general" question (in this case, "Tell me what you think about all the different tiles you have on the bar."). By asking this general question first, I was able to get answers to many of the more specific questions without having to ask them directly, and follow up with any questions the participant had not touched on.

Also, asking a more general question allows the interviewer to get a sense of what the participant thinks is important. In many cases, this may not be the same information the interviewer or the product team considers important. Understanding participants' priorities helps the team consider whether they are asking the right questions and prioritizing correctly.

In the end, I had nine general questions, with anywhere from three to twenty more specific, sometimes overlapping, questions.

Interview Preparation

In preparation for conducting the interviews, I created an "interview outline." Each page of the packet had only one general question and its related questions. The rest of the page was left blank for note-taking. Main headings were the general questions and subheadings were the detailed questions, the answers to which could comprise the answer to the more general question. By keeping questions on a similar topic together, and keeping each topic on a separate page, it was easy to see at a glance whether any aspects of the topic had not been addressed yet and I needed to ask follow-up questions.

Conducting the Interviews

All the interviews were conducted at the participants' homes, in close proximity to the computer on which the user interface in question was installed. This allowed me and accompanying team members to see the bar – to see what parts they had added, what information they were monitoring, and the manner in which they had organized the bar – and to use it as a reference for the interview. This last was especially valuable, as participants often did not know technical names for the areas or features they wanted to refer to. Having the bar visible made it easier for participants to point to or even re-enact situations they had difficulty explaining. It also served as a "memory jog" for participants' answers. The interview differed from a "contextual inquiry" in that I did not ask the participants to "use the bar" while I watched, merely to recount their experiences with using it.

I was very interested in learning participants' subjective reactions to both of the products they tried. A very real danger of interviewing is that by focusing too strictly on the predetermined questions the interviewer may overlook information participants offer on their own, because it may not fit into our prepared set of questions. In order to avoid this, I began each interview with a very general question that allowed the user to be as general or as specific as he or she wanted. The question I asked was a sort of "role play" question, in which I asked the participant to imagine that I was a friend who had just noticed this feature on the person's desktop, and asked him or her to explain to the friend what it was. This allowed participants to single out whatever aspects of the user interface or functionality were important to them. I followed this up by asking the general questions from my outline, and then specific questions only when I wanted more information.

Another danger I wanted to avoid was leading the participants in such a way that they told me what they thought I wanted to hear, rather than what they really thought. One benefit of individual interviews over focus groups is that generally individual participants feel freer to speak their mind because they are not influenced by outspoken members of the group. However, if the interviewer asks questions that suggest a personally held opinion, this benefit can be nullified as the participant attempts to be agreeable – a natural human desire. In order to avoid leading participants, the general questions were all phrased less as questions and more as a direction to "tell me about" a particular feature. For example, rather than asking "Did you like the bar?", I asked: "Tell me what you thought of the bar." Such a question merely asks for an opinion without betraying my own.

I was very glad to have members of the feature team accompany me on these visits, but this could occasionally present problems, chief among them being physical space. Several of the participants had their computers in rather small rooms; it was sometimes a juggle to find chairs for all of us, and in at least one case a team member had to stand for most of the two-hour visit. I tried to make sure I took only one companion on visits when I knew the quarters would be cramped, but sometimes two team members felt they simply "had to" come on that particular visit, either for scheduling reasons or because they were interested in a specific "persona." When I confirmed with the participant the day before I always let them know how many people would be joining me, so there would be no surprises.

Before the visit, I briefed the team members going with me on how I planned to conduct the interview, and asked them to write down any questions they came up with and hold them until the end, because it was possible that the question would be answered along the way. I did this not because I wanted to stifle my companions, but to avoid overwhelming the participant with the feeling of being interrogated. When we arrived, I would introduce the people with me (including their job titles), and explain that they were very interested in the participant's opinions. While I set up the camera, the team members would chat with the participant, asking about his or her job and family, and often discussing artifacts in the room such as pictures. By the time we began the interview, a comfortable atmosphere had been established and we never felt we had any problems with participants feeling intimidated.

All visits were videotaped. Taping of all interviews is an absolute must because even the best listeners and note-takers can benefit from hearing the interview again later. A good-quality audiotape is often sufficient for this. In our case, video allowed us to capture not only the participants' comments but also see what parts of the bar they were referring to when they spoke. Participants often use deictic words such as "this one" when describing things, and without the video to be able to know exactly what they were referring to it would have been virtually impossible to reconstruct what they were talking about. Even so, it was sometimes necessary for me to ask the participants to point to the portion of the bar they were referring to, in order to really understand their answers.

Asking Clarifying Questions

During each interview, there were times when participants' comments were unclear. A participant might start talking about a feature sounding very favorable and then finish sounding quite unfavorable. Or, a participant might seem to say that she had succeeded in accomplishing something with the bar but a moment later seem to say exactly the opposite. Sometimes comments were simply vague. These are common situations in all interviews.

When this happens, the interviewer may feel that he or she shouldn't ask for clarification, at the risk of making the participant feel to blame for the lack of clarity. In fact, asking for clarification can send a very favorable signal to the participant. It indicates that the interviewer is listening carefully, and that the participant's ideas are worthy of comment, discussion, and follow-up. Of course, for our own understanding of user issues also, it is very important to ask the participant to clarify. If an interviewer is too shy to ask for clarification, he or she runs the risk of jumping to incorrect conclusions about user needs for the product or feature.

In this study I used two ways of asking for clarification, both of which were useful. One was to "summarize" what I understood the participant to mean. I began by saying something like "Ah, this is interesting, let me see if I've got this right," and then paraphrased what the person had said. This method has the potential side-effect that the participant may feel uncomfortable disagreeing if in fact you haven't grasped the correct meaning, but I found participants quite willing to correct errors in my summary.

Another method I used was to ask the participant for specific examples. This method was especially useful when contradictions appeared to arise. Sometimes I asked the participant to recount an example from his or her experience; other times I asked them to show me by reproducing the experience for me.

Taking Notes

Taking notes during an interview is a tricky process. No matter how organized one is, or how good at interpreting user comments, the note-taking procedure can be overwhelming – especially during a lengthy interview (each of these lasted approximately 90 minutes). I am not sure that I have yet found the most useful method for taking notes, and there were certainly many pitfalls in the procedure adopted. In this section I outline the method used and why I chose to take notes in this manner. I also describe the problems that arose, and suggest some possible remedies.

I recorded answers longhand on the page that contained the questions as I asked them. When I asked a question, I recorded the outline number for that question and then wrote the participant's response. In theory, this allowed me to easily link answers to the questions. What I discovered, though, was that all participants followed a "train of thought" that didn't conform to my nice outline. Often they would start out answering my question but end up answering a question I hadn't asked yet, or even elaborating on something that really related more to a question I had asked earlier. Therefore an answer that I might have labeled "4c" might detail some information that I wanted to include as part of an answer to 5a or 2b. When a response "wandered" onto the topic of another question, I initially tried quickly to find the question number that they seemed to be answering, but I soon gave this up because it took too long and took my attention away from what the participant was saying. After a few unsuccessful attempts to tie answers to the right questions during the interview, I abandoned the idea and just wrote comments as they came, and only actively looked for the "right" place to record answers when I was ready to ask a new question. After the interview was over, I could re-read the answers and comments and tie them to the questions to which they were most relevant.

Many usability engineers prefer to type notes directly on a laptop computer if they have one. This has the benefit of saving a step – notes do not have to be typed up later. I chose not to do so for several reasons. First of all, the screen space available on a laptop is small, and I needed to be able to view both my questions and participants' answers as I typed them. Secondly, although I type quickly, my accuracy is fairly low; and having to back-space or delete in order to make typed notes even remotely coherent adds long amounts of "blank space" to the interview. Finally, the logistics of dealing with both the video camera and a laptop in what was often a very confined space may seem a small thing but it can often be aggravating. Any one of these hurdles may be minor and easily over-come for the interviewer who is a better window manager, a better typist, or a better manager of paraphernalia. For me, however, the overhead was too high, so I chose to take notes the old-fashioned way.

As much as possible, I took notes verbatim, in order to keep myself from trying to inter-pret too much on the spot, and to be sure that I didn't miss anything. This was some-times difficult as participants spoke quickly, so I developed many shorthands and symbols for the various features of the user interface and actions related to it that participants repeated often (such as capital "B" for bar, capital "T" for tile, up and down arrows for turning the bar on and off, etc.). One problem was that vague or unclear comments unnec-essarily became part of my notes. As much as possible, I stopped writing as soon as I felt the need to clarify something, and began again as soon as I was sure I had understood the answer or comment. A benefit of the verbatim notes was that I had plenty of "quotes" from participants to share with the product team and to spice up the report.

Of course it was inevitable that I occasionally missed a comment. When that happened, I quickly looked at my watch and wrote down the exact time. I could then go back to the videotape and go straight to that portion of the tape to find what I had missed. I also encouraged team members who accompanied me on these visits to take their own notes, as a back-up. However, I found their notes were generally confined to design ideas or fixes that they noticed as the interview progressed and were usually related specifically to their job, rather than notes on the actual interview, and so these were of limited value to me. On the other hand, I did find it very useful to debrief after each visit with the team members who had gone, to compare notes and memories and discuss our key take-aways from the session. This again increased the buy-in of the team and helped us all to under-stand more the experience they had heard about first-hand.

Tying Up Loose Ends

I didn't want the final interview to seem "anti-climactic," leaving the participants with no sense of how much they had helped us or how we were using their information. In order to give the participants (and myself) a sense of closure to the whole study, I took several pictures with me on the last visit showing possible designs for the Windows bar feature, which incorporated some of their ideas and comments. After the regular interview, I showed these to the participants and got their reactions to the designs. All the participants appreciated the "sneak peak" and, I think, felt pleased to see how their experiences had been translated into concrete designs.

Analysis

Analyzing qualitative data is a time-consuming process, no matter how you do it. Software packages exist which are meant to aid in qualitative analysis (QA), but these packages are often cumbersome, require more time to learn than the researcher is able to devote, and in many cases do not significantly improve the researcher's ability to produce a quality report.

In this study, I chose to make use of the features in Microsoft Word that allow you to find instances of text, and to copy and paste. The first step, however, was to transfer the notes from my longhand pages to a Word document. While this may seem a time-consuming and unnecessary step that could be bypassed by simply typing notes from the start rather than writing them, forcing oneself to retype every note has clear benefits. First of all, it required me to review every word of the notes, allowing me to think about the context in which the comments were made and interpret the significance of the comments. Secondly, it allowed me to find patterns in responses that I might have overlooked otherwise, which allowed me to cross-reference answers between different questions and between different participants. The act of typing up my notes provided an excellent review of the interviewing during which I drew fresh inferences and conclusions.

I typed each comment under the question to which it was most related, and if the participant had wandered and addressed a different issue, I copied it under that question too. I created separate interview reports for each participant, and called these the "participant data."

I also took the comments from the individual interview reports and created a "summary" document that included the answers from all seven participants. For example, under the question "What did you like about the sidebar" I listed all seven participants' answers (next to their names, and always in the same order). This allowed me to look at all answers to any question and decide whether there was a common theme or trend running through all participants' comments. I had one set of answers for the Dashboard, and another set for Sideshow. I called this the "question data." When writing up the report for the product feature team, this organizational method proved much more useful, as I could glance at a given question and tell immediately how many participants had answered in similar ways.

Every time I thought I saw a pattern to participant responses, I wrote it down in very general terms (e.g., "Participants liked the stocks tile" or "Participants had more trouble adding tiles to one bar than the other"). I copied relevant quotes from the summary document and pasted them under these general statements, refining the general statements to be more specific as I continued to comb through the data (e.g., "5 out of 7 participants"). These general statements and the supporting comments became the basis of my report.

The Results

The data we obtained in this study helped us make decisions about how a feature in a future version of Windows similar to Sideshow or the Dashboard should work. We found that participants expressed preferences for some aspects of each bar. For example, both bars use "flyout" windows to display additional information, but the windows in Sideshow were considered much more useful than those in the Dashboard. On the other hand, the Dashboard's mechanism for adding and removing tiles from the bar was more intuitive than Sideshow's.

However, not everything that participants said they liked made it into the plans for the upcoming feature. For example, six of the participants expressed a preference for Sideshow's "hover and show" method of displaying the flyout windows over the Dashboard's "click and show" method. On the other hand, the hover method caused everyone to experience occasional instances of flyouts appearing when they weren't wanted, either because the mouse accidentally strayed to the right side of the screen, or because the participant was trying to access the right edge of a document with the mouse (usually to use the scrollbar) and accidentally called up the flyout window. Despite the fact that most participants said they preferred the hover interaction, the ubiquitous nature of unwanted flyouts and the fact that at least one participant found this irritating enough to say she didn't like the hover interaction led the team to the conclusion that for the public at large the hover interaction would cause too much interference with other tasks, and so the decision was made to adopt the Dashboard's click interaction model.

Lessons Learned

- Begin with general questions and follow-up with specific questions. Asking specific questions first may lead the participant into talking about only what he or she thinks you want to hear about.

- Don't feel you need to ask every question on your list. Let the participant talk, and then follow up with those that are essential.

- Videotape everything, if possible. Audiotapes are insufficient in situations where participants constantly refer to things with vague references. Be sure to get permission.

- Involve your product team early and often. Encourage team members to accompany you and debrief after each visit with those who do. This will increase their buy-in to the need for research. Also, understanding what they are taking away from the interview will help you understand their priorities better.

- Understand your own note-taking skills in deciding whether or not to type or write. Taking notes on the laptop may save a step, but slow or inaccurate typing drags down the interview. Additionally, the second step of typing up notes is a great double-check.

Acknowledgments. I wish to express my sincere thanks to Shannon Kallin who initially conceived of and began planning this study but was unable to see it to completion. Thanks also to J. J. Cadiz, Gavin Janke, Andrew Brenner, Tracey Lovejoy, and Kent Sullivan.

Suggested Reading

Cadiz, J., Venolia, G., Jancke, G., & Gupta, A. (2002). Designing and Deploying an Information Awareness Interface. *Proceedings of the 2002 ACM Conference on Computer Supported Cooperative Work* (CSCW), New Orleans, LA, 16–20 November, pp. 314–323.

CHAPTER 8

SURVEYS

Introduction

Surveys can be an extremely effective way to gather information about your users. A well-designed survey can enable you to gather a plethora of information that can help you to design a product that will meet your users' needs. The problem is that a valid and reliable survey can be very difficult to design; yet surveys are *perceived* as very easy to create. It's just a bunch of questions right? Well yes, but the questions you choose and how you ask them are critical. A poorly designed survey can provide meaningless or – even worse – inaccurate information. In this chapter, we hope to enlighten you about this process. Surveys can provide you with great data, but you must be familiar with the rules of creation, collection, and analysis. In this chapter, we cover the key topics that are important to consider when designing a survey and analyzing the data. In addition, we share an industry case study with you to show how a survey was used by eBay to collect **user requirements**.

At a Glance

> When should you use a survey?
> Things to be aware of when using a survey
> Creating and distributing your survey
> Data analysis and interpretation
> Communicate the findings

When Should You Use a Survey?

Whether it is for a brand new product or a new version of a product, a survey can be a great way to start your user requirements gathering. In the case of a new product, surveys can be used to:

- Help you identify your potential user population
- Find out what they want and need in the product you are proposing
- Find out at a high level how they are currently accomplishing their tasks.

In the case of an existing product, a survey can help you to:

- Learn about the user population and their characteristics
- Find out users' likes and dislikes about the current product
- Learn how users currently use the system.

Also, whether it's for a new or existing product, surveys are a way to reach a larger number of people than the other methods typically allow. Surveys can be provided to users as a standalone **usability** activity or as a supplement to other user activities (e.g., following a card sort).

SUGGESTED RESOURCES FOR ADDITIONAL READING

Because survey creation is so complex, many books have been written solely on the subject of survey creation and analysis. In this one chapter we are unable to dive into the detail that those books cover. So if you are brand new to survey design or would like to learn more after reading this chapter, below are two books that we would recommend.

If you plan to conduct a survey that is very complex or will have large financial impact, we strongly urge you to read these two books before creating your survey. We cannot stress enough how complex survey creation can be. Making a mistake on your survey could cost you or your company significant revenue. Each book dives in to all the details associated with a more complex survey. Such topics include sample selection methods and statistical analyses.

- Alreck, P. L. & Settle, R. B. (1995). *The Survey Research Handbook*, 2nd ed. Burr Ridge, IL: Irwin Professional Publishing.
- Salant, P. & Dillman, D. (1994). *How to Conduct Your Own Survey*. New York: John Wiley & Sons.

Things To Be Aware of When Using a Survey

As with any user requirements technique, there are always factors that you must be aware of before you conduct a survey study.

Response Bias

A survey relies on self-reports. Sometimes respondents may answer questions based on how they think they should be answered, rather than truly expressing their own opinions. This phenomenon of providing socially desirable answers rather than truthful answers is known as **social desirability**.

Social desirability tends to be more of a problem in interviews rather than surveys, because surveys are usually anonymous whereas in an interview the interviewee must answer directly to the interviewer. However, it is still a factor that one must be aware of in surveys. Also, in most cases, surveys designed for product development will not contain questions that are deemed socially intrusive. If you are able to provide your respondents with complete anonymity, this will decrease the impact of **response bias**.

Response Rate

The unfortunate reality of surveys is that not everyone is going to respond. Experienced survey researchers give response rate estimates of anywhere between 20% and 60%. In our experience, you are likely to get a response rate closer to 20%, unless you have a very small, targeted population that has agreed to complete your survey ahead of time. However, there are some things you can do to improve the response rate.

- Include a personalized cover letter or header at the top of the survey to provide information about the purpose of the study and how long it will take.
- Reduce the number of **open-ended questions**.
- Keep it short.
- Make the survey attractive and easy to comprehend.
- Make the survey as easy to complete and return as possible. For example, if you are sending surveys in the mail, include a self-addressed envelope with pre-paid postage.
- Follow up with polite reminders.
- Consider offering a small incentive for their time. For example, we like to offer participants a $5 coffee card for completing a survey. It may not seem like much but you would be surprised at how the response rates skyrocketed once the coffee card was offered.
- Contacting non-respondents in multiple modes has been shown to improve response rates. For example, if potential respondents were initially contacted via e-mail, try contacting the non-respondents via the phone.

Creating and Distributing Your Survey

Are You Ready?

Before you begin *any* user requirements activity there are a number of things you must be familiar with. Because these elements are common to all user requirements activities they have all been covered in the earlier chapters, but now is a good time to double-check the list. If you are not familiar with one of the items you can refer to the earlier chapter to brush up or familiarize yourself with that element.

One of the biggest misconceptions about a survey is the speed with which you can prepare for, collect, and analyze the results. A survey can be an extremely valuable method, but it takes time to do it correctly. In this section we will discuss the preparation required for this user requirements method.

Preparation Timeline

Table 8.1 contains approximate times based on our personal experience and should be used only as a guide. If you are new to survey design the length estimate will likely be much longer. For example, it may take you double the time to create the questions, build the survey, and analyze the data. In addition, the length of time for each step depends on a variety of factors – such as responsiveness of the product team, access to users, and resources available.

Surveys require significant preparation. Below, we discuss how to compose your questions, build your survey, and then pilot the survey.

Table 8.1:

Preparation timeline for

a survey

When to complete	Approximate time to complete	Activity
As soon as possible	1–2 weeks	☐ Meet with team to identify questions ☐ Meet with team to develop user profile
After identification of questions and user profile	1 week	☐ Create and distribute activity proposal
After the proposal has been agreed by all stakeholders	1–2 weeks	☐ Word questions appropriately and distribute to co-workers for review ☐ Determine data analysis method
After the questions are finalized	2 weeks	☐ Identify potential respondents ☐ Acquire incentives ☐ Prepare any documentation (e.g., consent form) ☐ Create the questionnaire either electronically or on paper
1 week before the survey distribution	2 days	☐ Pilot the survey ☐ Make necessary changes
After a successful pilot	1 week	☐ Distribute the survey
7–10 days after distribution	1 day	☐ Distribute follow-up reminders if appropriate
After receiving the completed questionnaire	1 day	☐ Send thank you notes and incentives (if appropriate)

At a Glance

> Identify the objectives of your study

> Players in your activity

> Compose your questions

> Determine now how you will analyze your data

> Building the survey

> Considerations when choosing a survey distribution method

> Distributing your survey via the web, e-mail, or paper

> Test your survey

Identify the Objectives of Your Study

Do not just jump in and start writing your survey. You need to do some prep work. Ask yourself:

- Who is the survey for? (Refer to Chapter 2, Before You Choose an Activity, "Learn About Your Users" section, page 41.)
- What information are you looking for (i.e., what questions are you trying to answer)?
- How will you distribute the survey and collect responses?
- How will you analyze the data?
- Who will be involved in the process?

It is important to come up with answers to these questions and to document your plan. As with all user requirements activities, you should write a proposal that clearly states the objectives of your study. (Refer to Chapter 5, Preparing for Your User Requirements Activity, "Creating A Proposal" section, page 146 for a discussion on creating proposals.) The proposal should also explicitly state the deliverables and include a timeline. Because you normally want to recruit a large number of participants (20–30 or more), it can be resource-intensive to conduct a survey study. There are more participants to recruit and compensate, as well as more data to analyze than for most user requirements activities. As a result, it is important to get your survey right the first time and get sign-off by all stakeholders. A proposal can help you do this.

Players in Your Activity

As with every user requirements activity, there are players involved in the execution of the activity. However, a survey is different from the other activities described in this book because – unless it is a part of another activity – you are typically not present as the survey is completed. As a result, there is no moderator, no scribe, no videographer, etc. The players are your participants, but now we will refer to them as respondents.

The first thing to determine is the user profile (refer to Chapter 2, Before You Choose an Activity, "Learn About Your Users" section, page 41). Who do you plan to distribute this survey to? Are they the people registered with your travel website? Are they using your product? Are they a specific segment of the population (e.g., college students)? Who you distribute your survey to should be based on what you want to know. The answers to these questions will impact the questions you include.

For example, let's say that the hypothetical website TravelSmart.com plans to add some new functionality to its website and their objective is to see what users think of this proposed functionality before it is created. A good target audience might be those registered with the website. Let's suppose that as a part of the Travelsmart.com registration process, users indicate whether they are willing to receive e-mail from your company. You can e-mail a survey to everyone that indicated they are interested in receiving e-mail from TravelSmart.com. Alternatively, you may choose to randomly invite people using your site to complete your survey via a pop-up that is triggered to appear at a certain frequency from a given page on the site.

In the product development world, usability professionals usually target 20–30 responses per user type. If you are able to get more participants that is great, and we definitely encourage you to do so; but the reality is that time and resources may prevent you from doing so (refer to Chapter 5, Preparing for Your User Requirements Activity, "How Many Participants Do I Need?" section, page 157 for a more detailed discussion of sample size.)

Compose Your Questions

This is the most important part of the process. You need to determine what information you need, and how to ask the right questions. Recommendations in this section will also help increase completion rates for your survey. This stage is the same regardless of how you plan to distribute your survey (e.g., paper, web). However, the formatting of your questions may vary depending on the distribution method. The stage of "building" your survey and the impact of different distribution methods is discussed later in this chapter.

At a Glance

> Keep it short
> Asking sensitive questions
> Question format and wording
> Avoiding pitfalls
> Standard items to include

Keep It Short

One of the key pieces of advice is to *keep the survey short*. If you ignore this rule, you are doomed to fail because no one will take the time to complete your survey. The general rule is no more than two, nicely spaced, sides of a single sheet of paper. A dense two-page survey is actually worse than a five-page survey with the questions well spaced. Dense surveys take longer to read and it can be difficult to distinguish between questions. And you should stick to a 12-point font. For web surveys, the guideline of 20–25 questions is often provided. In terms of time, 20 minutes is the most you want people to spend completing your survey. If you can adhere to these rules then your survey will have a much greater chance of being completed. Following the steps described below of brainstorming and then reducing your question set will help you achieve this.

Brainstorm initial questions

Start with brainstorming of all the potential questions that you might like to ask. As with any brainstorm, begin by blue-skying it (i.e., anything is possible). Once you have your complete list, only then begin to narrow down the set. By approaching survey development in this manner (rather than coming up with 20 questions and thinking you are done), you will make sure that all the critical questions are identified in time to include them in the study. It is great to go through this process with all team members who have a stake in the survey (refer to Chapter 1, Introduction to User Requirements, "Preventing Resistance" section, page 18). Working alongside stakeholders, you will be able to hit on all the important areas where you need to get answers.

It is a good idea to write the potential questions on a whiteboard or flip chart as they are generated. Keep them in view of the stakeholders at all times so they can review them and think of new ideas or to make sure that nothing has been missed. Don't worry about the exact wording of the questions at this point. Also, don't worry about the format of the questions yet (e.g., multiple-choice, open-ended). There will be time to deal with this important issue later.

Reduce the initial question set

It is now time to reduce your initial question set. This is the tough part. Continue to work as a group to do this. If you have taken your blue sky to the limit, some of the questions may be eliminated quickly. Put an X next to the questions as they are eliminated. Don't erase them since you may change your mind later.

When it becomes difficult to reduce the question set, for each question ask: "How will the answer to this question inform our study objectives?" If it won't, then eliminate it. Some questions may provide interesting information, but if it is not going to aid your product's design or development, then drop it. Let's say the key objective of your study is to decide whether or not to implement a "best price guaranteed" policy. As a member of the TravelSmart.com team, you may want to ask respondents their occupation. This might be interesting information to have; but if whether someone is a doctor, a mechanic, or a teacher has nothing directly to do with your study objective, it would be an easy one to eliminate. However, a question such as "Do you ever shop around at multiple websites for the best travel prices?" would be kept because it fulfils the key objective. The answer to this question could impact your decision of whether or not to implement the "best price guaranteed" policy that you are considering.

If you are still above the limit for the number of questions, an additional method for narrowing down your list is to look at the time to implement. All of the questions may impact the design of your product, but if some of them will impact versions further down the line, those can be put aside. It is better to limit the range of the questions to immediate impact and get a large number of responses, rather than covering a broader product impact and reducing the number of completed surveys.

As a final resort, rate the questions. Give each person on the brainstorming team a collection of colored stickers, and tell them they can assign their vote to each question. Green stickers count for 3 votes, yellow for 2, and red for 1. Everyone goes to the wall and sticks stickers on the questions they value most – it's a vote. At the end you take the top 15–20 questions with the most votes, but the team has all participated in the process and owns it.

Asking Sensitive Questions

Both interviews and surveys have pros and cons with regard to asking sensitive questions. In an interview, you have the opportunity to develop a rapport with the respondent and gain his or her trust. But even if the respondent does trust you, he/she may not feel comfortable answering the question in person. If your survey is anonymous, it is often easier to discuss sensitive topics that would be awkward to ask face to face (e.g., age, salary range). However, even in anonymous surveys, people may balk at being asked for this type of information.

Ask yourself whether you really need the information – that it is not just out of curiosity or because you think the question is "standard." If the answers to these questions will help you better understand your user population and therefore your product, provide a little verbiage with the question to let respondents know *why* you need this information. For example: "To help us improve our incentive program, we would like to know the following information." Above all, never make these fields "required" or "mandatory" for completion in a survey. Participants will either refuse to complete your survey or they will purposely provide inaccurate information just to move forward with the survey. Finally, do not ask these questions toward the front of the survey as they might turn some people off immediately. Wait until you have their trust and they have put some time into answering the other questions.

Question Format and Wording

Once you have come up with your list of questions, you will need to determine their wording and format. By "format" we are referring to how the respondents are expected to respond to the question, as well as the layout and structure of your survey. Participants are far more likely to respond when they perceive your survey as clear, understandable, concise, of value, and of interest. The questions and how they are presented are key in accomplishing this.

Based on an illustration from The Christian Science Monitor. www.csmonitor.com

Tip

It is a good idea to start thinking about your data analysis at this stage. Make sure you know how you will analyze the data for each format of question you use. It is not imperative that you have all of your data analysis methodologies worked out before you distribute the survey, but it can help to start thinking about it even at this early stage. Refer to "Determine Now How You Will Analyze Your Data," page 333.

Response format

For each of your questions you must decide the format in which you want the participant to respond. One of the first things you need to determine is whether the questions will be open-ended or closed-ended. **Open-ended questions** allow the users to compose their own responses; for example: "What are the features that are

most important to you in a travel website?" **Closed-ended questions** require participants to answer the questions by either:

- Providing a single value or fact
- Selecting all the values that apply to them from a given list
- Providing an opinion on a scale.

One of the advantages of open-ended questions is that they are much easier to create.
As a result, inexperienced survey creators are often tempted to use them for the
bulk of their survey. However, in the world of survey design, open-ended questions
typically do not fare well, for a number of reasons:

- Open-ended questions make data analysis tedious and complex.
- Because respondents use their own words/phrases/terms, responses can be
  difficult to comprehend and you typically will not have an opportunity to follow
  up and clarify with the person who responded.
- They can make the survey longer to complete, thereby decreasing the return
  rate.

The bottom line is, do *not* ask essay questions. A survey that asks the user to make
only check marks or write single rating digits has a much higher chance of being
completed and returned. As a result, we do not recommend using open-ended questions at all in surveys, unless the input is limited to very brief and simple answers;
for example: "Which cities have you flown to in the past 2 years?"

Since open-ended questions are best reserved for interviews, refer to Chapter 7 to
learn more about wording those questions (see Chapter 7, Interviews, "Write the
Questions" section, page 262).

There are three main types of closed-ended question responses to choose from:
multiple-choice, rating scales, and ranking scales. Each serves a different purpose
but all provide data that can be analyzed quantitatively.

Multiple-choice questions

Participants are provided with a question that has a selection of pre-determined
responses to choose from. In some cases, participants are asked to select multiple
responses and in other cases they are asked to select single responses.

- *Multiple-response.* Participants can choose more than one response from a list of options. For example:

> "What types of travel have you booked online? Please select all that apply."
>
> ☐ **Airline tickets**
> ☐ **Train tickets**
> ☐ **Bus tickets**
> ☐ **Car rental**
> ☐ **None of the above**

- *Single-response.* Participants are provided with a set of options from which to choose only one answer. For example:

> "How often do you book travel online?"
>
> ☐ **Once a month**
> ☐ **4–6 times per year**
> ☐ **1–3 times per year**
> ☐ **I never book travel online**

- *Binary.* As the name implies, the respondent must select from only two options. For example: "Yes/No," "True/False," or "Agree/Disagree." This is not just a type of single-response question. With single-response questions, you want to provide respondents with the most likely options to choose from. You are acknowledging that the answer may not be black or white. With binary questions, you are forcing participants to drop all shades of gray and pick the answer that best describes their situation or opinion. It is very simple to analyze data from these types of questions, but you introduce error by not better understanding some of the subtleties in their selection. For example, someone may have no opinion, or may partially agree and disagree.

Rating scales

There are a variety of scale questions that can be incorporated into surveys. Likert and ranking are two of the more common scales. For a detailed discussion of the many scales that can be used in survey design, consult Alreck and Settle's book *The Survey Research Handbook* (see "Suggested Resources for Additional Reading," page 315).

The Likert scale is the most frequently used rating scale. Participants are provided with a scale and asked to select the most appropriate rating. Providing five to nine levels in the Likert scale is recommended. You may wish to provide anchors for every number, or anchor only the end points. You should also consider whether or not to allow a middle-position for users to settle on a neutral point. Some usability professionals prefer to remove the neutral point since they believe that people tend to gravitate towards neutral positions and they want to force respondents to come down on one side of the fence or the other. Be aware that if a participant truly does not have a preference one way or the other, forcing him/her to make a choice will introduce error into your results.

Below is an example of a Likert scale with a middle-point and two anchors.

> "How would you rate your previous experience booking travel over the web?"
>
> | 1 | 2 | 3 | 4 | 5 | 6 | 7 |
> |---|---|---|---|---|---|---|
> | **Not at all satisfactory** | | | | | | **Very satisfactory** |

Another type of rating scale question asks users to give a priority rating for a range of options. For example:

> "Rate the importance of each of the following features in a travel site from 1 to 4, with 1 being not at all important and 4 being very important."
>
> ___ Low prices
>
> ___ Vast selection
>
> ___ Chat and phone access to a live travel agent
>
> ___ A rewards program for purchases

In this rating question, you are not comparing the options given against one another. As a result, more than one option can have the same rating.

SUGGESTED RESOURCES FOR ADDITIONAL READING

The following has a wonderful and detailed discussion of wording Likert rating scale questions:

- Dumas, J. (2001). Usability Testing Methods: Subjective Measures – Measuring Attitudes and Opinions. In *Design by People for People: Essays on Usability*, pp. 107–117. Chicago: Usability Professionals' Association.

Ranking scales

This type of scale question gives participants a variety of options and asks them to provide a rank for each one. Unlike the rating scale question, the respondent is allowed to use each rank only once. In other words, the respondent cannot state that all four answers are "most important." For example:

> "Rank the importance of each of the following features in a travel site from 1 to 4, with 1 being most important."
>
> ___ Low prices
>
> ___ Vast selection
>
> ___ Chat and phone access to a live travel agent
>
> ___ A rewards program for purchases

The rank scale differs from a rating scale presented above because the respondent *is* comparing the options presented *against* one another to come up with a unique ranking for each option.

Avoiding Pitfalls

When selecting the answers for a respondent to choose from (regardless of the type of question format), avoid vague options like "few," "many," and "often." Participants will differ in their perception of those options and it will be difficult for you to quantify them when you analyze the data.

In addition, if you are providing a range of answers to choose from, it is best to keep ranges equal in size and never allow the ranges to overlap (e.g., "0–4," "5–10," "11–15").

You should consider providing an "out" option to respondents on each question. This could include "None of the above," "No opinion," "Not applicable," and "Other." It is possible that you did not think of all the possible options that a participant may want to choose from. If you provide "Other" as an option, you may wish to provide a blank space for the participant to insert his/her own answer. This changes the question from closed-ended to open-ended. You will likely have to analyze the free-response answers by hand, but it is worth it to learn what options you may have missed.

Question wording

Your choice of words for survey questions is critical. The wording of survey questions can impact peoples' responses. Whether your questions are open-ended or closed-ended, they should be clear and unbiased. For a detailed discussion of question wording, see Chapter 7, Interviews, "Write the Questions," page 262. Figure 8.1 is a summary of dos and don'ts to consider when wording your survey questions.

Figure 8.1:

Dos and don'ts in question wording

DO:

- Keep questions under 20 words
- Address one issue at a time
- Word questions clearly
- Provide precise options in closed-ended questions
- Equally space the range of options in closed-ended questions
- Ask users to discuss desired outcomes
- Provide background information only if necessary and keep that information factual
- Keep questions concrete and based on the user's experience
- Limit questions to memorable events or ask participants to track their behavior over time in a diary
- Provide memory aids like calendars to help participants remember previous events
- Use terms that are familiar to the user
- Use neutral terms and phrases
- Ask sensitive or personal questions only if necessary

DON'T:

- Force users to choose an option that does not represent their real opinion
- Ask leading questions
- Ask loaded questions
- Base questions on a false premise
- Use authority figures to bias answers
- Ask users to predict the future
- Ask users to create solutions
- Ask users to discuss unmemorable events
- Use jargon, slang, abbreviations, geek-speak
- Use emotionally laden words
- Use double negatives
- Ask sensitive or personal questions out of curiosity

Tip

In this chapter, we recommend piloting after you have built your survey, but it is also helpful to run a pilot after you have created your question list (see "Test Your Survey," page 346). This can help you make sure you are asking all of the necessary questions and that your questions make sense. Doing so now can prevent you from having to rebuild your survey later. Once you are satisfied with your survey questions and format, build the survey, pilot it again, and distribute it.

Standard Items to Include

There are certain elements that every survey should contain, regardless of topic or distribution method.

Title

Give every survey a title. The title should give the participant a quick sense of the purpose of the survey (e.g., "TravelSmart.com Customer Satisfaction Survey"). Keep it short and sweet. If you can think of a name to entice respondents, that is even better.

Instructions

Include any instructional text that is necessary for your survey as a whole or for individual questions. The more explicit you can be, the better. For example, instructions that apply to the whole survey might be: "Please complete all of the following questions and return the completed survey in the enclosed self-addressed, postage-paid envelope." An instruction that applies to an individual question might read: "Of the following, check the *one* answer that most applies to you." Of course, you want to design the survey form and structure so that the need for instructions is minimized. A lengthy list of instructions either won't be read or will inhibit potential respondents from completing the survey.

Contact information

There are many reasons why you should include contact information on your surveys. If a potential respondent has a question prior to completing the survey (e.g., When is it due? What is the compensation? Who is conducting the study?), he/she may choose to skip your survey if your contact information is not available.

Others may have questions in the middle of the survey. If the survey was distributed via the web or e-mail, then an e-mail contact address would be a safe choice. If you have distributed your survey via the mail, provide a phone number as contact information, unless you are certain that your user population has e-mail access. It is important to note that this could be a problem for surveys sent out to a very large audience. If 5% of the respondents have questions and the survey went out to 10,000 people, then you would get 500 requests to answer. You would need to have someone devoted to make sure requests are responded to. It is a much better idea to test your survey extensively if it is going out to large numbers. But providing an option for questions would be reasonable for surveys going out to a small audience (100–200).

If your survey was distributed via mail with a self-addressed envelope, it is still wise to include the return address on the survey itself. Without a return address on the survey, if the return envelope is lost, people will be unable to respond. And last but not least, providing your contact information lends legitimacy to the survey.

Purpose

In a line or two, tell participants why you are conducting the survey. Ethically, they have a right to know (refer to Chapter 3, Ethical and Legal Considerations, "The Right To Be Informed" section, page 97). Also, if you have a legitimate purpose, it will attract respondents and make them want to complete the survey. A purpose could read something like:

> "TravelSmart.com is conducting this survey because we value our customers and we want to learn whether our travel site meets their needs, as well as what we can do to improve our site."

Time to complete

People will want to know at the beginning how long it will take to finish the survey before they invest their time into it. You don't want respondents to quit in the middle of your 15-minute survey because they thought it would take five minutes and now they have to run to a meeting. It is only fair to set people's expectations ahead of time and respondents will appreciate this information. If you do not provide it, many potential respondents will not bother with your survey because they do not know what they are getting into.

Confidentiality and anonymity

Data collected from respondents should always be kept confidential, unless you explicitly tell them otherwise (refer to Chapter 3, Ethical and Legal Considerations,

"Anonymity" section, page 100). Confidentiality means that the person's identity will not be associated in any way with the data provided. You should make a clear statement of confidentiality at the beginning of your survey.

Anonymity is different from confidentiality. If a respondent is anonymous, it means that even *you*, the researcher, cannot associate a completed survey with the respondent's identity. Make sure that you are clear with respondents about the distinction. Web surveys, for example, are typically confidential but not anonymous. They are not anonymous because you could trace the survey (via an IP address) back to the computer from which it was sent. This does not necessarily mean that the survey is not anonymous because someone may use a public computer, but you cannot make this promise in advance. So just be sure ahead of time that you can adhere to any confidentiality and/or anonymity statements that you make.

Determine Now How You Will Analyze Your Data

Those who are new to survey methodologies have a tendency to wait until the data has been collected before they consider how it will be analyzed. An experienced usability professional will tell you that this is a big mistake. It can cost you valuable time after the responses have been collected and you may end up ignoring some of your data because you are not sure what to do with it or you do not have the time required to do the analysis that is necessary.

By thinking about your data analysis *before* you distribute your survey, you can make sure that your survey contains the correct questions and you will be able to answer some key questions for yourself.

- What kind of analysis do you plan to perform? Go through each question and determine what you will do with the data. Identify any comparisons that you would like to make and document this information. This can impact the question format.
- Are there questions that you do not know how to analyze? Perhaps you should remove them. If you keep them in your survey, you will know going into the analysis that you will need to do some research or contact a statistical professional.

- Will the analysis provide you with the answers you need? If not, perhaps you are missing questions.

- Do you have the correct tools to analyze the data? If you plan to do data analysis beyond what a spreadsheet can normally handle (e.g., beyond means, standard deviations), you will need a statistical package like *SPSS*™ or *SAS*™. If your company does not have access to such a tool and will need to purchase it, keep in mind that it may take time for a purchase order or requisition to go through. You don't want to hold up your data analysis because you are waiting for your manager to give approval to purchase the software you need. In addition, if you are unfamiliar with the tool, you can spend the time you are waiting for the survey data to come in to learn how to use the tool.

- How will the data be entered into the analysis tool? This will help you budget your time. If the data will be entered manually, allot more time. If the data will be entered automatically via the web, you will need to write a script. If you don't know how to do this, it may take time to learn.

By answering these questions early on, you will help ensure that the data analysis goes smoothly. This really should not take a lot of time, but by putting in the effort up front, you will also know exactly what to expect when you get to this stage of the process and you will avoid any headaches, lost data, or useless data.

Summary for Composing Your Questions

We have provided a lot of information to keep in mind when creating your survey. Figure 8.2 references the key points for convenience.

Figure 8.2:

Checklist for survey creation

☐ Brainstorm all the questions you have with stakeholders.
☐ Narrow down the question set to 20–25.
   ☐ For each question, ask whether it will help you design or improve your product.
   ☐ If you need to narrow the list of questions further, determine the timeframe the questions will impact.
☐ Determine the format of the questions.
   ☐ Open-ended or closed-ended?
   ☐ Avoid open-ended questions because they reduce the completion rate for surveys.

Figure 8.2 – *Cont'd*

- ☐ For closed-ended questions, determine the format:
    - ☐ Single choice from one or more options
    - ☐ Multiple choice from one or more options
    - ☐ Providing an opinion on a scale
    - ☐ Rank a set of options.
- ☐ Avoid vague options.
- ☐ Keep ranges equal in size and never allow the ranges to overlap.
- ☐ Consider providing an "out" option.
- ☐ Keep questions short, clearly worded, and unbiased.
- ☐ Ask sensitive or highly personal information only if necessary.
- ☐ Make sure the standard information is included (i.e., title, instructions, contact information, purpose, time to complete, statement of confidentiality and/or anonymity).
- ☐ Determine how you will analyze the data *before* you distribute the survey.

Building the Survey

Now that you have composed your questions, you can move on to the next stage, which is building the survey in the format in which it will be distributed (e.g., paper, web, e-mail). There are a number of common elements to keep in mind when building your survey, regardless of the distribution method. These will be discussed first. Then we look at elements unique to each distribution method.

Common Survey Structure Elements

How your survey is constructed is just as important as the questions that it contains. There are ways to structure a survey to improve the response rate and reduce the likelihood that respondents will complete the survey incorrectly.

Reduce clutter

Whether you are creating your survey electronically or on paper, avoid clutter. The document should be visually neat and attractive. Think minimalist. Include a survey title and some instructional text, but avoid unnecessary headers, text, lines, borders, boxes, etc. As we mentioned earlier, it is imperative that you keep your survey short. Adhering to the rule of two sides of a single sheet of paper does not mean that you should jam as many questions onto each side as possible. Provide sufficient white space to keep the survey readable and one question distinguishable from another.

Strike a balance between the amount of white space and the need to include all of your questions.

Color selection

Do not go crazy with color. You do not want a loud and vibrant survey or one that has a plethora of different colors. It should be pleasing to the eye but simple. Use a neutral color for the background (white or beige) and then choose a color with high contrast to the background for your questions. Black on white is always a safe choice. You may want to throw in one additional color to draw participants' attention to certain things such as required fields or instructional text, but keep in mind participants who are color-blind. You can use bold and/or underline to effectively differentiate elements if necessary, rather than using additional colors.

Font selection

You may be tempted to choose a small font size so that you can fit in more questions, but this is not advisable. If your population includes those over 45 years of age, a small font size will not be appreciated. A 12-point font is the smallest recommended. If you are creating a web survey, choose fonts that are comparable to these sizes. For web surveys, set relative rather than absolute font sizes, so that users can adjust the size via their browsers.

Font style is another important consideration. Choose a font that is highly readable. Standard *serif fonts* (fonts with tails on the characters, such as Times New Roman), or *sans serif fonts* (fonts without tails on the characters, such as Arial or Verdana) make for good choices. Avoid decorative or whimsical fonts, for example **ALGERIAN** and *Monotype Corsiva*, as they tend to be much more difficult to read. Choose one font style and stick with it.

Tip

NEVER USE ALL CAPS AS IT IS VERY DIFFICULT TO READ.

Consistency

To make your survey as easy to use as possible, minimize the number of different types of response formats. You should select the question format that best provides you the information you need but remember that providing several different question formats can confuse respondents.

If you use scales, keep them as consistent as possible. For example, do not make the value "1" represent "Strongly agree" on some scales and "Strongly disagree" on others; this will confuse respondents and potentially introduce errors into your data analysis. Also, if your survey is paper or e-mail-based, reduce the number of branching questions. For example: "If you answered 'Yes' to this question, proceed to question 5. If you answered 'No,' proceed to question 6." The more branches that are included, the greater the likelihood that people will make mistakes. If your survey is web-based and you would like to include branching, you can program the survey to advance to the next appropriate question based on the participant's answer to the previous question.

Use a logical sequence and groupings

Place your questions in a logical order and use groupings that are meaningful. For example, group all of the demographic questions together rather than spreading them throughout the survey. Likewise, keep questions related to a specific feature together. For example, if some of the questions in your survey are related to searching, group them together. This is less confusing for respondents and allows them to concentrate on one topic at a time.

It is also a good idea to start with the simple questions first and then move towards the more complex ones. Let participants start out with the easy stuff to get them into the swing of things. Another strategy is to start with the really interesting questions to draw your respondents in and make them want to complete your survey. You know your users best, so adopt the strategy that you think will work best for them. Again, if you have to include sensitive or personal questions, leave them until the end of the survey.

Summary for Building Your Survey

We have provided a lot of information to keep in mind when building your survey. Below is a bullet list to reference the key points:

- Reduce clutter.
- Limit your survey to three colors.
- Use an easy to read 12-point font.
- Minimize the number of different types of response formats.
- Avoid branching questions.
- Ask your questions in a logical sequence and group related information.

Considerations When Choosing a Survey Distribution Method

This section discusses a variety of factors that apply to each of the distribution methods. This information should enable you to make the appropriate distribution choice based on your needs. Table 8.2 is a summary.

Table 8.2:

Comparison of survey distribution methods

	Web	E-mail	Paper
Approximate cost	$0.88 per survey	Unknown	$2.07 per survey
Aids in data entry	Yes	Possibly	No
Interactivity capabilities	Yes	No	No
Easy for participants to respond	Yes	Yes	More effort required
Data received rapidly	Yes	Yes	Slower
Consistency	Can be a problem	Can be a problem	Not a problem
Security	Highest threat	Medium threat	Low threat
Respondent privacy	Moderate privacy	Least privacy	Highest degree of privacy
Computer expertise	Required	Required	Not required

Cost

It had been found that web-based surveys are cheaper to conduct than paper-based ones. One study found that the average cost of a paper survey was $2.07, while the average cost for the web survey was $0.88 (Schaefer 2001). The cost of e-mail surveys is undetermined. Be aware that spam blockers may prevent some of your e-mail surveys from reaching recipients.

Data Entry

One of the major advantages of a web-based survey is that it assists you in your data entry. With a paper or e-mail survey, when you get your responses, you have to parse the data if it is electronic or manually enter it into your analysis tool or spreadsheet. This method is tedious and is prone to errors during the transition. With a web-based survey, the data can be automatically downloaded into a spreadsheet or data analysis package. This will create *tremendous* time savings for you and it also reduces the chances for errors.

Interactivity

E-mail and paper-based surveys do not offer interactivity. The interactivity of the web provides some additional advantages.

Validation

The computer can check each survey response for omitted answers and errors when the respondent submits it. For example, it can determine whether the respondent has left any questions blank and provide a warning or error message to make the person aware of this. If a respondent has entered letters in a field that required a numeric response, it can show the error.

Allow for more complex designs

With careful design, a web-based survey *can* help you to make a detailed or large survey simple from the users' point of view. For example, it was mentioned earlier that the number of branching questions should be minimized because they can make a survey quite complex. By using the web, you have the ability to include branching questions without the respondent even being aware of the branch (see Figure 8.3).

Figure 8.3:

A survey with

branching

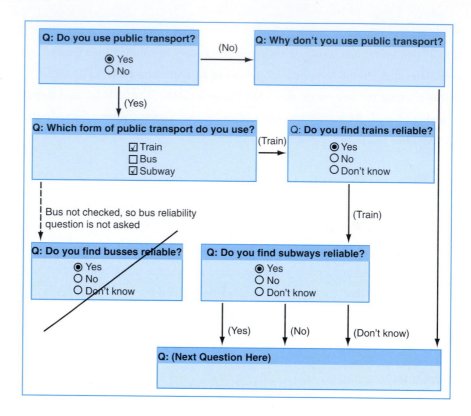

For example, let's say that the question asks whether a participant uses public transit and the response to this question will determine the set of questions the person will be required to answer. You could choose a design where once respondents answer the question, they are required to click "Next." When they click "Next," they will be seamlessly brought to the next appropriate set of questions based on the response they made on the previous page. The respondents will not even see the questions for the alternative responses.

More intuitive design

Web widgets can help make your survey more intuitive. Widgets such as droplists can reduce the physical length of your survey and can clearly communicate the options available to the user. Radio buttons can limit respondents to one selection, rather than multiple, if required (see Figure 8.4).

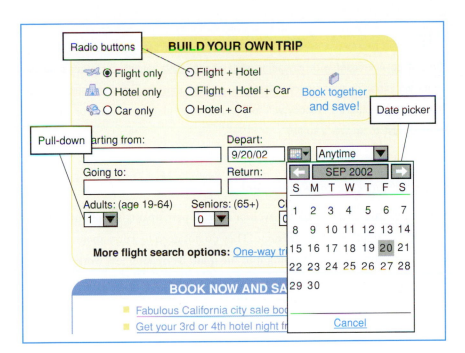

Figure 8.4:

Examples of web widgets

Tip

Scrolling droplists should be avoided where possible. They hide the list of answers, and some people will visually focus on the top couple of entries and not see a more suitable answer lower on the list. Avoid long lists of radio buttons that would force the user to scroll back and forth to view all of the options.

Progress indicators

If the survey is broken into multiple pages, status indicators can (and should) be included to let respondents know how far along they are and how many more questions they have left to complete (see Figure 8.5).

Figure 8.5:

Progress indicator

> ## Tip
>
> Do not go overboard with cascading style sheets, Java applets, or other plug-in-requiring extras on your survey unless you are sure that the recipients already have the necessary plug-ins. Nobody will load yet another plug-in, or wait for an applet to load, just to answer a survey.

Amount of Work for the Respondent

After completing a survey via the web or e-mail, participants simply need to click "Submit" or "Send" and they are done. They do not need to worry about putting the survey in an envelope and dropping it in the mail. By making less work for the participants, you improve your chances of getting more responses.

Data Delivery

Responses are received via the web or e-mail much faster than with the traditional mail survey. You must incorporate the time for the survey to be returned to you via the postal system when using paper-based surveys.

Consistency

By the term "consistency" we are referring to how the participant sees the survey. This is not an issue for paper-based surveys because you have total control over the way the questions appear. In the case of e-mail, participants may have their e-mail program customized so that their e-mail appears in a format that is different from the norm of wrapping text with a white background and black text. You cannot control this and it could possibly impact your results. In the case of the web, you will need to take additional time to ensure that your survey is accessible from all the browser types your population may be using. In the majority of cases, this will be Netscape® and Internet Explorer®. View your survey in both browsers and test the data collection in both. You want your survey to look as consistent as possible in both browsers. If the survey appears or behaves differently in different web browsers, it could impact your results. As with e-mail, you will not be able to control any specific customizations that respondents make to their browsers.

Security

Security is less of a concern for paper and e-mail, but is a major consideration for the web. You must make sure that your data is secure. In most cases, your web-based survey will be outside of a **firewall**, so it is important to ensure that outsiders cannot access the information you collect. Work with your company's system administrator to determine whether this will be a problem for you.

Privacy

Respondents may be hesitant to complete your survey because they are concerned about their privacy. This is usually not an issue for a paper-based survey since the person can remain anonymous (other than the postmark on the envelope). In the case of e-mail, privacy is a big issue. The respondent is sending the survey back via an e-mail address that is tied directly to the person. In the case of the web, even though respondents may not be entering their names, you can capture a computer's IP address and that can make people uncomfortable. Assure respondents up front that all information collected from them will remain confidential and that their information will not be associated with any results or sold to any third parties.

Computer Expertise

Obviously, computer expertise is not an issue for paper-based surveys, but it is an issue for e-mail and, especially, web-based surveys. If your participants have varying levels of computer experience, this could impact your survey results. If your survey has a simple design and uses standard web widgets – such as pull-downs, check boxes, etc. – a low level of web expertise is required. However, if you anticipate that some of your respondents will have very little web experience, consider a paper-based survey.

Distributing Your Survey via the Web, E-mail, or Paper

The mechanism you choose to distribute your survey will depend in many cases on your user type. If you suspect that some potential respondents will not have access to computers, you should avoid an online survey because it will create a **sampling** bias. A traditional mail survey would be the better choice in this situation. However, if this is not an issue for your user population, we recommend using a web-based survey because it is both cost- and time-effective.

Creating a Web-based Survey

There are a number of things to keep in mind when creating a web-based survey.

- When creating a web-based survey, do not begin the process by writing your questions in HTML (hypertext markup language). It takes much more time to make changes in the code than it does in a word processor or on paper.
- If your survey is longer than a single sheet of paper, you will want to consider breaking it up into multiple pages on your website, rather than having one extremely long scrolling page.
- Use "Next" and "Back" navigation to allow respondents to move between the different pages of the survey in case they want to skip sections or go back and make changes.
- Avoid horizontal scrolling. This is frustrating to users and will increase the time necessary to complete the survey.
- Avoid flashing icons or animations. Your goal is not to make the survey look "cool" but to make it clear and easy to complete. Don't distract respondents with dancing images. Remember – keep it simple!
- Include a progress indicator to let respondents know how close they are to completing the survey (see Figure 8.5). Some professionals have the philosophy that if your survey is so many pages that it needs a progress indicator, it's too long. Instead of using a progress indicator, they say, shorten the survey. In most cases this is likely a valid point; but we have seen surveys where only one question was presented per page due to graphics that were associated with questions. In such cases the progress indicator is useful. It is also a good idea to include a "Save for later" or "Finish later" button so that users can save their work if interrupted in the middle of completing the survey.
- Avoid "special requirements." For example, do not force respondents to download plug-ins or special viewers. Not many people will want to complete your survey if you do.

Web-based survey development tools

There are commercially available web-based survey tools that can help you create your survey without you having to write a single line of code, and they will collect the responses for you. They provide you with summary data, and most will allow you to download the raw data if you would like to conduct further analyses. Some of the tools available today are:

- InstantSurvey (www.netreflector.com/instantsurvey.shtm)
- QuestionBuilder (www.questionbuilder.com)
- Sparklit (www.sparklit.com)
- SurveyMonkey (www.surveymonkey.com)
- WebSurveyor (www.websurveyor.com)
- Zoomerang (www.zoomerang.com).

Keep in mind that these aids do not relieve you of the responsibility of identifying the questions and wording them appropriately. That will still be your job.

Creating an E-mail Survey

If you do not have the budget or the ability to create a web-based survey, then an e-mail survey is an option. If you decide to distribute your survey in this way, make sure that it is embedded *in* the e-mail rather than as an attachment. That way, respondents can hit "Reply" and complete the survey within the e-mail. Do not expect people to download an attached document, complete the survey, save it, then reattach it and send it back to you. This takes more time and effort than many participants are willing to provide, and some may not be willing to open an attachment for fear of computer viruses. Also, do not ask respondents to reply to a different address. Make the process as simple as possible.

Creating a Paper-based Survey

If your user population typically does not have access to the web, traditional paper (i.e., mail survey, hand-carrying to recipients, handing out at trade shows) is your best bet. Also, if you are conducting a scientific survey, mail is a good choice because it is easier to obtain a random sample of the population.

Again, make the process as easy as possible for respondents. Include a self-addressed, postage-paid envelope. Allow time in your schedule to do this as it takes considerable time to make copies of your survey and to stuff and address a large number of envelopes. As your data is on paper rather than in an electronic format so you will need to manually enter the data into an analysis tool. Do a trial data entry early on using one of your completed pilot surveys so you can get a sense of just how long this will take. Experienced usability professionals know this always takes longer than expected. It is better to be aware of this ahead of time so you can budget the extra time into your schedule.

Test Your Survey

The value of running a pilot or pre-testing your user requirements activity is discussed in Chapter 5 (refer to "Piloting Your Activity" section, pape 193). However, testing your survey is so important to its success that we want to discuss the specifics here in more detail. Keep in mind that once you send the survey out the door, you will not be able to get it back to make changes – so it is critical to discover any problems before you reach the distribution stage.

You may be thinking: "Well, my survey is on the web, so I can make changes as I discover them." Wrong. If you catch mistakes after distribution, or realize that your questions are not being interpreted in the way intended, you will have to discard the previous data. You cannot compare the data before and after edits. This means that it will take more time to collect additional data points and may cost more money.

When running your pilot, you want to make sure that someone who matches your user profile completes the survey, not just co-workers. Colleagues can help you catch typos and grammatical errors, but unless they are domain experts, many of the questions may not make sense to them. Using someone who fits the user profile will help you confirm that your questions are clear and understandable. For example, if your co-worker completes a survey designed for a nurse, he/she will likely not understand the questions (unless he/she also works in this domain) and as a result will not be able to help you determine if your questions are appropriate. A pilot will enable you to do the following:

- Catch embarrassing typos and grammatical errors
- Determine the time it takes to complete the survey (if it is too long, now is your chance to shorten it)
- Determine the comprehensibility of the format, instructions, and questions
- In the case of a web survey, determine (a) whether there are any broken links, or bugs, and (b) whether the data are returned in the correct or expected format.

A modified version of a technique referred to as **cognitive interview testing** can be valuable when pre-testing your survey. We say a "modified version" because formal cognitive interviewing can be quite labor-intensive. It can involve piloting a dozen or more people through iterative versions of your survey and then undertaking a detailed analysis. Unfortunately, in the world of product development, schedules do not allow for this. The key element of this technique that will benefit you in evaluating your survey is the **think-aloud protocol**.

Think-aloud protocol or "verbal protocol" as it is often called – is described elsewhere in this book (refer to Chapter 6, During Your User Requirements Activity, "Introducing Your Think-aloud Protocol" section, page 218). If you have ever run a usability test, you are likely familiar with this technique. When applied to survey evaluation, the idea is that you have someone complete your survey while literally thinking aloud, as you observe. As the participant reads through the questions they tell you what they are thinking. The person's verbal commentary will allow you to identify problems, such as questions that are not interpreted correctly or that are confusing. In addition, during the completion of the survey, you can note questions that are completed with incorrect answers, skipped questions, hesitations, or any other behaviors that indicate a potential problem understanding the survey. After the completion of the survey, you should discuss each of these potential problem areas with the pilot participant. This is referred to as the retrospective interview. You can also follow up with the pilot respondent and ask for his/her thoughts on the survey: "Did you find it interesting?" "Would you likely fill it out if approached?" This is sure to provide some revealing insights. This type of pilot test can provide you with a wealth of information to help you improve your survey.

> ## SUGGESTED RESOURCES FOR ADDITIONAL READING
>
> If you would like to learn more about cognitive interviewing, we can refer you to a couple of references:
>
> - Forsyth, B. H. & Lesser, J. T. (1991). Cognitive laboratory methods: A taxonomy. In P. P. Biemer, R. M. Groves, L. E. Lysberg, N. A. Mathiowetz, & S. Sudman (eds), *Measurement Errors in Surveys*, pp. 393–418. New York: John Wiley & Sons.
> - Willis, G. B. (1999). *Cognitive Interviewing: A "How To" Guide* (found April 2004 at http://appliedresearch.cancer.gov/areas/cognitive/interview.pdf).

After you run your pilot, you will want to go back and make changes. It is wise to then run another pilot test. Continue with this process until you run a pilot that does not elicit any new problems. This process can be time-consuming, but it is worth every minute, as it will spare you from headaches that would have arisen later on down the road when they are very difficult (or impossible) to correct.

If you will be conducting a survey that is going to require a large number of responses (over 100), and you plan to conduct some complex data analysis, it is a nice idea to conduct a pilot with a group of 10 or so participants. Keep in mind that some of those people can be co-workers. This will allow you to test your data analysis methods.

Data Analysis and Interpretation

You have collected all of your survey responses, so what's next? Now it is time to find out what all of those responses are telling you.

Initial Assessment

Your first step (if this did not happen automatically via the web) is to get the data into the tool that you are going to use. Microsoft® Excel®, *SPSS*, and *SAS* are some of the well-known programs that will enable you to accomplish your analyses. Typically, the data will be entered into a spreadsheet. The rows will be used to denote each participant and the columns will be used to indicate each question. Some statistical packages allow you to enter only numeric values so you may need to do some coding. For example, if you asked people whether they were male or female, you would not be able to enter male or female into the spreadsheet; you would have to use a code for each response, such as "male = 1" and "female = 2." Figure 8.6 illustrates a sample of data entered in a spreadsheet format.

Participant no.	Q1 –Gender	Q 2 – Salary	Q3 – Age	Q4 – Years of web experience
1	1	55 000	34	9
2	1	65 000	39	5
3	2	100 000	41	4
4	2	58 000	22	5
5	1	79 000	33	7

Figure 8.6:

Sample data entered into a spreadsheet

Once you have your data in the spreadsheet, you should scan it to catch any abnormalities. This is manageable if you have 100 or fewer responses, but it can be more difficult once you get beyond that. Look for typos that may have been generated at your end or by the participant. For example, you might find in the age column that someone is listed as age "400," when this is likely supposed to be "40." If you have the paper survey to refer to, you can go back and find out whether there was a data entry error on your part. If data entry was automatic (i.e., via the web), you cannot ethically make any changes. Unless you can contact that respondent, you cannot assume you knew what he/she meant and then change the data. You will have to drop the abnormal data point or leave it as is (your stats package will ignore any empty fields in its calculation). You may also find that some cells are missing data. If you entered your data manually, the ideal situation is to have a co-worker read out the raw data to you while you check your spreadsheet. This is more reliable than "eyeballing" it; but because of time constraints, this may not be possible if you have a lot of data.

Types of Calculation

Below we discuss the most typical forms of data analysis for closed-ended questions. Because we do not recommend open-ended questions for surveys we do not go into detail about how to analyze the data from them in this chapter. A discussion can be found in Chapter 7, Interviews, "Data Analysis and Interpretation" section, page 293.

The types of calculation that you will carry out for most surveys are fairly straight-forward. They do not require advanced statistical knowledge. There are complex statistics that can be executed to extract subtleties in the data if you have responses from enough participants, but they are typically not necessary in the case of product design. If you are interested in analysis beyond what is covered below, consult Alreck and Settle's book *The Survey Research Handbook* (see "Suggested Resources for Additional Reading," page 315).

The key calculations that will be of importance to you for closed-ended questions can easily be calculated by any basic statistics program or spreadsheet. Our goal is not to teach you statistics, but to let you know what the common statistics are and why you might want to use them. These types of calculations can be illustrated effectively by using graphs and/or tables. Where appropriate, we have inserted some sample visuals.

SUGGESTED RESOURCES FOR ADDITIONAL READING

If you have never taken a course in statistics, or are unfamiliar with the metrics discussed in this section, we recommend that you become familiar with the basics by reading an introductory statistics text. A good introductory book is:

- Keppel, G., Saufley, W. H., & Tokunaga, H. (1992). *Introduction to Design and Analysis: A Student's Handbook*, 2nd ed. New York: W. H. Freeman.

At a Glance

> Mean
> Median
> Mode
> Measures of dispersion
> Frequency
> Measures of association
> Complex stats

Mean

The mean is the average of the scores in the population. It is probably the most frequently used calculation in survey analysis. It equals the sum of the scores divided by the number of scores. For example, you might want to know the mean amount of web experience of your respondents, or their mean age. If the ages in your sample were

19, 19, 21, 22, 25, 25, 29, 32, 37, 37, 37, 38, 40, 41, 45

the average age was 31.13 years (467 divided by 15). Figure 8.7 illustrates how you might want to display related means.

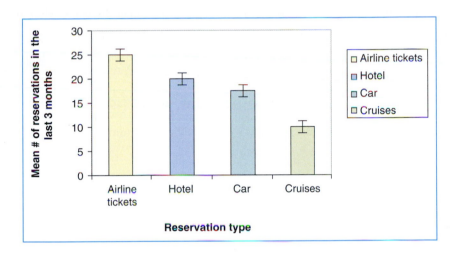

Figure 8.7:

Graph of mean number of bookings in the last three months

Median

The median of your sample is the point that divides the distribution of scores in half. Numerically, half of the scores in your sample will have values that are equal to or larger than the median, and half will have values that are equal to or smaller than the median. So, if the ages in your sample were

19, 19, 21, 22, 25, 25, 29, 32, 37, 37, 37, 38, 40, 41, 45

"32 years" would be the median age. The median is the best indicator of the "typical case" when your data are skewed.

Mode

The mode is the score in the population that occurs most frequently. The mode is *not* the frequency of the most numerous score. It is the value of that score itself. So, if the ages in your sample were

19, 19, 21, 22, 25, 25, 29, 32, 37, 37, 37, 38, 40, 41, 45

"37 years" would be the mode age because it appears most frequently. The mode is the best indicator of the "typical case" when the data are extremely skewed to one side or the other.

Measures of Dispersion

As discussed above, it is useful to know the average (mean) of your data, but it is also helpful to have an idea of the "spread" or dispersion of the data around the mean.

Maximum and minimum

The *maximum* indicates how far the data extend in the upper direction, while the *minimum* shows how far the data extend in the lower direction. In other words, the minimum is the smallest number in your data set and the maximum is the largest. So, if the ages in your sample were

19, 19, 21, 22, 25, 25, 29, 32, 37, 37, 37, 38, 40, 41, 45

"19 years" is the minimum age and "45 years" is the maximum.

Range

The *range* is the maximum value minus the minimum value, so it indicates the spread between the two extremes. So, if the ages in your sample were

19, 19, 21, 22, 25, 25, 29, 32, 37, 37, 37, 38, 40, 41, 45

the range is 45 minus 19, which equals 26 years.

Standard deviation

The standard deviation (SD) is a measure of the deviation from the mean. The larger the standard deviation, the more varied the responses were that participants gave. It is easily calculated by any spreadsheet program, so we will not go into the details here. The standard deviation is represented by the I-shaped device on each bar of the graph, as in Figure 8.7.

Frequency

The frequency is the number of times that each response is chosen. This is one of the more useful calculations for survey analysis. This kind of information can be used to create graphs that clearly illustrate your findings. It is nice to convert the frequencies to percentages (see Figure 8.8).

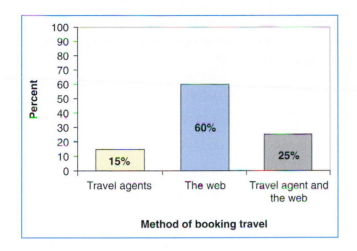

Figure 8.8:

Graph of frequencies for the methods of booking travel

Measures of Association

Measures of association allow you to measure the relationship between two survey variables. Two of the most common measures of association are comparisons (or cross-tabulation) and correlation.

Comparisons

Comparisons are by far the most common measure of association for surveys. It can be insightful to find out how answers to one question are related to the responses to another question. Comparisons allow you to see these relationships. For example, let's say we had a question that asked people whether they made hotel reservations via the web. As a comparison, we want to see whether the answer to this question relates to whether or not they book cars on the web.

For our first question – "Have you ever booked a hotel on the web?" – the response was

Yes	No
73%	27%

For the 73% who responded "Yes," we want to determine how they answered the question "Have you ever booked a rental car on the web?" The breakdown can be seen as follows:

Yes	No
69%	31%

For the 27% who responded "No" to the first question, we want to determine how they answered the question "Have you ever booked a rental car on the web?" This breakdown can be seen below:

Yes	No
20%	80%

From this comparison, it appears that users who book hotels online are likely to also book rental cars online, while users who do not book hotels online are also unlikely to book cars online. This is an example of cross-tabulation.

Graphs are a great way to visualize these comparisons (see Figure 8.9). Microsoft Excel can help you complete this kind of comparison via "pivot tables." A pivot table is an interactive table that enables you to quickly summarize large amounts of data. It allows you to rotate its rows and columns to see different summaries of the source data, filter the data by displaying different pages, or display the details for areas of interest. Microsoft Excel's Help explains how to create this kind of table.

Figure 8.9:

Graph comparing people who book hotels and cars on the web versus those who do not

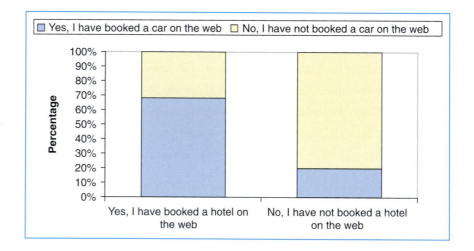

Correlations

Correlations are another measure of association. They are used to measure the degree to which two variables are related. It is important to note that correlations do not imply causation (i.e., you could not state that the presence of hotel deals caused people to book a hotel).

Correlation analysis generates a *correlation coefficient*, which is the measure of how the two variables move together. This value ranges from 0 (indicating no relationship) to plus or minus 1. A positive number indicates a positive correlation, and the closer that number is to 1, the stronger the positive correlation. By "positive correction," we mean that the two variables move in the same direction together. For example, you might have a positive correlation that indicates that if people book hotels they are also likely to book airline tickets.

Conversely, a negative number indicates a negative correlation, and the closer that number is to –1, the stronger the negative correlation. By "negative correction," we mean that the two variables move in opposite directions together. For example, you may discover the negative correlation that if people book package vacations, they usually do not book a rental car. Below is an example of a negative correlation illustrated with data.

For our first question – "Do you use the internet at home?" – the response was

Yes	No
64% (16 of 25 respondents)	36% (9 of 25 respondents)

For the question "Do you use a travel agent?" the response was

Yes	No
32% (8 of 25 respondents)	68% (17 of 25 respondents)

We want to determine whether the responses to these two questions are related, so we calculate a correlation coefficient. Figure 8.10 illustrates the breakdown of the data. Microsoft Excel or any stats program can easily calculate correlation coefficients for you, so we will not go into the details.

The correlation coefficient for this data set equals –0.91, which indicates that those who use the Internet at home tend not to use a travel agent. It does not mean that use of the Internet *causes* people to avoid using travel agents. It simply implies that there is a relationship between the two items.

Figure 8.10:

Data from two survey questions

Participant no.	Do you use the internet at home?	Do you use a travel agent?
1	yes	no
2	yes	no
3	yes	no
4	yes	no
5	yes	no
6	yes	no
7	yes	no
8	yes	no
9	yes	no
10	yes	no
11	yes	no
12	yes	no
13	yes	no
14	yes	no
15	yes	no
16	yes	no
17	no	yes
18	no	yes
19	no	yes
20	no	no
21	no	yes
22	no	yes
23	no	yes
24	no	yes
25	no	yes

Complex Stats

Again, if you are interested in analysis beyond what is covered above, such as statistical measures of association and causality, Alreck and Settle's book on survey design details types of calculations, such as analysis of variance, discriminate analysis, regression analysis, and correlation analysis (see "Suggested Resources for Additional Reading," page 315). We recommend that interested readers review this book to learn more.

Communicate the Findings

Preparing to Communicate Your Findings

The specific data that you communicate to product teams can vary depending upon the activity you conducted, but some elements of *how* you communicate the results are the same regardless of the method. Because these strategies are common to all user requirements activities, they are discussed in detail in Chapter 14, Concluding Your Activity, page 636. We recommend that you read that chapter prior to relaying your results to your stakeholders. Topics discussed include:

- ☐ **Prioritization of your findings** (see page 638)
- ☐ **Creating an effective presentation** (see page 644)
- ☐ **Writing valuable reports for different audiences** (see page 652)
- ☐ **Ensuring the incorporation of your findings** (see page 660)

The most important thing to keep in mind when presenting survey results is to make the results as visual as possible. You want those reviewing the findings to be able to see the findings at a glance. Bar charts, line graphs, and pie charts are the most effective ways to do this. Most statistics packages or Microsoft Excel will enable you to create these visuals with ease.

Obviously, you will need to explain what the results mean in terms of the study objectives, as well as any limitations in the data. If the results were inconclusive, highly varied, or not representative of the true user population, state this clearly. It would be irresponsible to allow people to draw conclusions from results that were inaccurate. For example, if you know your sample was biased because you learned the product team was sending only their best customers the link to your survey, inform the stakeholders that the data can be applied only to the most experienced customers. It is your responsibility to understand whom the survey is representing and what conclusions can be drawn from the results. Sometimes the answer is: "Further investigation is needed."

Lessons Learned

The deployment of several surveys has taught us a few lessons. The first involves getting access to end-users. The last lesson learned involves asking open-ended questions in a survey.

Accessing End Users

Be sure you have a population available that will complete your survey. In one instance, we worked with a product team that assured us they had contacted their customers and that the customers were willing to complete the survey. When we deployed the survey, the response rate was abysmal and the responses were incredibly inconsistent. Part of the problem was our lack of understanding of the users' job roles and titles. As a result, we stopped the survey and worked with the team to research users' job roles and titles. The most important lesson learned here is to confirm that you know your user population. Unfortunately, sometimes it takes a failure to demonstrate what you or the product team *doesn't* know. Additionally, if you plan to work with customers, confirm their interest in participating and have a backup plan in the event they do not follow-through.

A situation similar to the one above happened with a different product team. This time, the team wanted to understand their student users in the UK. Since we are not located in the UK, we were depending on our customers in the UK to distribute the surveys to their students. Before we began developing the survey, we knew we needed agreement from the customers themselves to distribute the survey – not just an assurance from the product team. When the rubber hit the road, we were unable to get the customers to agree to distribute the surveys because they did not feel that the results would provide enough benefit to them. They insisted that we conduct a usability test on the current product and didn't want to "waste" their students' time completing a survey. Despite the fact that the product team and usability group strongly agreed on the need for the information from the survey to improve future versions of the product, without support from the customers themselves we could not complete the surveys in the timeframe required. The only bright side was that we did not waste a great deal of time and effort developing a survey that was doomed to fail from the beginning. If you are depending on someone else to distribute your survey, obtain all assurances that your "supporter" will follow-through before you code a word of it, and then develop a backup plan if possible.

Asking Open-ended Questions

Make sure you ask only those questions that you plan to analyze the data for and that will provide meaningful responses. We once worked with a team that insisted on including a plethora of open-ended questions. We warned the team about the additional time it would take to analyze the responses. They ensured us that they had the bandwidth to do this. It was not until the responses were in that they realized just how much work the analysis of the open-ended questions involved. In the end, they dropped the data to these questions.

Pulling It All Together

In this chapter, we have illustrated the details of creating an effective survey. You should now be able to create valuable questions and format your survey in a way that is easy to understand and that attracts the interest of the potential respondents. You should also be equipped to deploy your survey, collect the responses, and analyze as well as present the data. You are now ready to hit the ground running to create a survey that will allow you to collect the user requirements that you need.

CASE STUDY

Kelly Braun provides a wonderfully detailed case study about how eBay uses surveys to inform the design of their website. She shares with us how they created their questions, shows a sample survey, discusses the use of survey vendors, and describes the data analysis. She also gives helpful hints about creating and deploying surveys online.

Using Online Surveys to Quantify Usability Issues

Kelly Braun, Senior Manager, eBay Usability Group

eBay's Usability Group has found that online surveys can be powerful tools in the user-centered design (UCD) process. We have used surveys to gather user requirements for new features and to obtain feedback on both newly launched and future designs. This case study presents an international research effort that used surveys to assess the general "usability health" of four international eBay sites. It also discusses some of the issues we have encountered while running surveys at eBay.

eBay is the World's Online Marketplace™ providing a venue for people to buy and sell goods around the world. One way in which eBay differs from most e-commerce sites is that all items offered for sale are being sold by individuals or businesses, but not by eBay itself. There are currently over 16 million items a day available on eBay and users continue to add approximately 2 million new items a day. Most e-commerce sites focus only on how to help people find and buy items; eBay also has to focus on helping people list items for sale.

The eBay Usability Group proactively monitors the usability of the site. We conduct regular in-lab site usability reviews that test the usability of the buying and selling processes with a wide range of participants – including those who have never used eBay before. We gather a great deal of qualitative information during these site reviews, but we also wanted to quantitatively measure the impact of usability issues on the site. We have used surveys to gather this quantitative data.

Our Approach

In general, we believe that surveys are not effective at uncovering usability issues. Surveys need to present the hypothesized usability concerns so that users can choose those responses. Providing open-ended response fields can help you gather new data; however, this relies on the user to articulate the problem. We have found that surveys are very useful for quantifying usability issues that have been previously identified.

For this project, we decided to create a survey that displayed in a pop-up window as users left the site. When users exited the site, we asked what they thought about the eBay experience they had just completed. We chose a pop-up exit survey because the experience would be fresh in users' minds and it would not interrupt their buying or selling activities.

Creating the Questions

We had recently completed field studies and in-lab usability studies in the United States (www.ebay.com), Germany (www.ebay.de), Italy (www.ebay.it), and Taiwan (www.tw.ebay.com). We used the data from these field and lab studies to create the questions for the surveys. The pop-up survey allowed us to ask very targeted questions based on what page the person had just left. For instance, if the user left the site on the final page of registration, we presented questions about the registration process. We also created surveys for intermediate steps along a particular process so that we could ask specific questions about steps within that process. For instance, if a person left the registration process on the page where they needed to enter a credit card, we could include "I am uncomfortable putting my credit card online" as an answer choice for why they left the site.

First, we identified the processes and the pages within those processes that we wanted to investigate. We identified more than 30 pages where we wanted to know why a user might leave the site. Since this research was being conducted in four languages, we ended up creating (and managing) over 120 surveys. We created a framework for the surveys that included questions that were asked in every survey as well as answer choices that were unique to each survey. By controlling the standard questions we were able to look at some data across all processes and all countries. By creating unique answer choices per flow we were able to investigate the specifics and thus make the survey contextual and more usable for the respondent.

One of the processes we chose to survey was finding an item to buy on eBay. One way to find items is to type keywords into the search box located on most pages. The user is then presented with a search results page. Typically, users look at the returned list of items and then click on one item of interest. Clicking on the title of this item takes them to the description of the item that the seller has listed for sale. People usually go back and forth between the search results page and individual items until they find the item they want to buy.

We created a survey that was delivered to every 100th person who left the eBay website from the search results page. We ensured that users received only one exit survey no matter where they exited the site.

Figures 8.11A and B are a representation of the survey we presented when people exited the search results page. This survey was presented on two pages because it looked too long and daunting all on one page. We took the last three questions (13 through 15) that were also the most complicated-looking and put them on the second page, with a message stating that these were the last questions. Participants clicked on the "Next" button after question 12. Questions 1–12 were part of the standard questions, while 13–15 were specific to the Search process flow.

This may seem like a long and complex survey; however, we have learned from previous experience that eBay users are motivated to tell us what they think about eBay. Of the people who started this survey, 88% of them completed it.

Figure 8.11A:

First page of the web survey

Thank you for visiting eBay! Your feedback is extremely important to us and we want to understand how we can make your eBay experience better. The information that you provide will be used strictly within eBay's Privacy Policy.

1. Overall, how satisfied were you with your eBay visit?

- ○ Very satisfied
- ○ Satisfied
- ○ Neither satisfied nor dissatisfied
- ○ Dissatisfied
- ○ Very dissatisfied

2. In the past 3 months, how many times have you bid on or bought an item on eBay?

- ○ I have never bid on or bought an item
- ○ 1–3 times
- ○ 4–9 times
- ○ 10–19 times
- ○ 20 times or more

3. How likely are you to bid on or buy an item on eBay in the next 3 months?

- ○ Definitely will
- ○ Probably will
- ○ Might or might not
- ○ Probably will not
- ○ Definitely will not

4. Were the item(s) you were looking for today available on eBay?

- ○ Yes
- ○ No

5. Today on eBay, did you bid on or buy an item?

- ○ Yes
- ○ No

6. What was the <u>main</u> reason for ending your eBay visit today?

- ○ I am the highest bidder right now/I bought an item(s)
- ○ I bid on an item(s), but someone outbid me

Figure 8.11A –

Cont'd

○   I am planning on returning later to place a bid/buy an item(s)

○   I was just browsing or researching information

○   I could not find an item that I wanted to bid on/buy

○   I am not comfortable buying from an individual

○   Using eBay is too difficult

○   Using eBay takes too much time

○   eBay's pages take too long to load

○   Other _____

7. **We are particularly interested in getting your feedback on how easy it was to use eBay. Which of the following <u>contributed</u> to your decision to end your eBay visit today? (Choose all that apply)**

☐   I have no other reasons besides the main reason above

☐   eBay's pages are too cluttered

☐   Finding items on eBay is difficult

☐   I do not understand how auctions work on eBay

☐   I have to complete too many steps to buy an auction item

☐   Placing a bid on eBay is difficult

☐   There is too much text on eBay's pages

☐   There are too many links on eBay's pages

☐   Finding my way around eBay is difficult

☐   Understanding eBay's text is difficult

☐   eBay has too many features

☐   In general, eBay is not easy to use

8. **The following are other common reasons why people might leave eBay. Which of the following apply to you? (Choose all that apply)**

☐   I have no other reasons

☐   eBay does not have enough unique items

☐   eBay's pages take too long to load

☐   I am unable to get help on eBay when I need it

☐   eBay does not have the items I was looking for

☐   I do not like waiting for an auction to end

☐   I do not want to buy from individuals

☐   I need more information on the item(s) before I buy (e.g., shipping costs)

☐   I was concerned that the item(s) I found might not be authentic

☐   The item(s) I found were not in the condition I wanted

☐   The price of item(s) was too high

☐   There is no one to turn to in case of fraud

Continued

Figure 8.11A –

Cont'd

9. What was the <u>main</u> purpose of your visit to eBay today?

○ I was looking for a specific item to bid on/buy

○ I was just browsing eBay

○ I was researching product prices and information

○ I was completing purchase of an item that I had won

○ I wanted to sell an item

○ Other _____

10. When did you first visit eBay?

○ This is my first visit

○ Less than 1 month ago

○ 1–3 months ago

○ 4–6 months ago

○ 7–12 months ago

○ More than 12 months ago

11. When did you register on eBay?

○ I am not registered on eBay

○ Less than 1 month ago

○ 1–3 months ago

○ 4–6 months ago

○ 7–12 months ago

○ More than 12 months ago

12. In the past 3 months, how many times have you listed an item to sell on eBay?

○ I have never listed an item to sell

○ 1–3 times

○ 4–9 times

○ 10–19 times

○ More than 20 times

Figure 8.11B

Second page of the

web survey

13. eBay enables you to find items by using our search feature. To what extent do you agree or disagree with the following statements:

Strongly disagree	Disagree	Neither agree nor disagree	Agree	Strongly agree	
○	○	○	○	○	The search results I received were relevant a majority of the time
○	○	○	○	○	In general, when I entered a search term I received too many results
○	○	○	○	○	eBay's search helps me find items quickly
○	○	○	○	○	eBay's search is similar to other sites I use
○	○	○	○	○	eBay's search results pages are easy to use
○	○	○	○	○	eBay's search results pages are well-organized
○	○	○	○	○	eBay's search results pages load quickly

14. eBay allows you to narrow down and sort your list of search results. Which of the following were you aware of? (Choose all that apply)

I was aware that I could ...

- ☐ Narrow my search results to specific categories
- ☐ Search for items within a specific category
- ☐ Search for items based on specific characteristics, such as size and color
- ☐ Search for items that are sold by sellers in Asia and Europe
- ☐ Search the title and full description of items at the same time
- ☐ Select to view only Auction or Buy-It-Now items
- ☐ Sort items by price or end time
- ☐ Customize my search using special criteria like price range

15. Which of the following would you use if available on eBay?(Choose all that apply)

I would ...

- ☐ Narrow my search results to specific categories
- ☐ Search for items within a specific category
- ☐ Search for items based on specific characteristics, such as size and color
- ☐ Search for items that are sold by sellers in Asia and Europe
- ☐ Search the title and full description of items at the same time
- ☐ Select to view only Auction or Buy-It-Now items
- ☐ Sort items by price or end time
- ☐ Customize my search using special criteria like price range

Survey Vendors

We completed this research using a self-service survey vendor. Self-service vendors usually offer the ability to create your own survey and provide basic tools for data analysis. Many self-service vendors also provide professional services such as survey creation and more complex data analysis for a fee. On average, a self-service survey with 1200 respondents costs $2000, assuming we do all the analysis ourselves.

Full-service vendors create, field, and analyze the survey for you. While the self-service option can be five to ten times less expensive, you will need to invest your time and effort. For more complex analyses that the self-service tools do not provide, you may want to bring in a consultant.

For most surveys we need only basic statistics like means and standard deviations, and identifying whether there are **statistically significant** differences within the results. For this project, we wanted to create a model that could quantify the effects of addressing specific findings. We hired a consultant to build a regression-based model that helped us prioritize which issues to address first.

Self-service survey vendors usually offer basic statistics capabilities, but you should double-check that their tools can do the analysis you need or can put the data into a format you can use. One of the biggest surprises we had working with self-service vendors was discovering that some do not understand the research side of surveys. For instance, we found one vendor who could present the survey questions in random order but could not randomize the responses within a question. Re-ordering the response choices is a common need in surveys – doing so eliminates the bias of people choosing the first response. For our needs, randomized order for response choices is much more important than randomized question order. This vendor focused their resources on creating the survey delivery technology but they did not have market research resources to tell them whether the functionality they were building made sense to a researcher.

We ran these surveys for a set period of time. Most self-service survey vendors offer pricing options of either paying per number of respondents or paying for the amount of time the survey runs regardless of the number of responses. We did not want our users to be presented with a pop-up that said "Sorry the survey is closed," so we opted for the pay-per-time option for this project.

Since we were running these surveys internationally, we wanted to find a vendor who could support multiple languages. Here we found two types of vendor: those who have the capability to adapt their survey creation tools into different languages, and those who provide an English-only interface for creating the surveys, but support the survey elements (buttons, etc.) in various languages. One of the most important factors for us when creating international surveys is the amount of customization permitted within the standard survey elements. For instance, one vendor provided a standard "Thank you" message at the end of the survey. When eBay's linguistic team reviewed the Italian message they felt the translation was inappropriate. The survey provider told us there was no opportunity for us to customize this final message, so we had to choose another vendor.

One of the most difficult things for us was finding a survey vendor who could handle the traffic we knew this survey would generate. Even when we present the pop-up survey to a subset of our users (1 in 100), we have brought down vendor sites. If you are planning to put a link on your website to a survey, our advice is to involve the folk who run the technical operations of your site. They will be able to identify potential problems with a vendor's traffic capabilities.

We deliver surveys to our users in one of three ways: by posting links to the survey on the site, by sending e-mail invitations, and via pop-up on-exit surveys. Exit surveys generate the most traffic to a vendor's site because the survey loads into every pop-up window, regardless of whether or not the person chooses to respond to the survey. With links in e-mails or links on the site, users initiate the survey only if they have some intention of taking the survey. If you use a vendor who cannot handle traffic from your e-mail or site link invitations, don't even consider doing an exit survey with them.

Analyzing the Data

Once we successfully gathered all of this survey data, we needed to analyze it. The self-service survey tool provided the basic statistics so that we could see how many people responded to each answer choice. We were also able to look at basic cross-tabulations which helped us answer questions like "Of the people who said they did not bid on or buy an item today (question 5), how many also responded: 'I was just browsing or researching today' to question 6?" For more complex data analysis, we hired consultants to help us answer questions like "Of the people who did not bid or buy (question 5), and who also said they left the site because 'Using eBay is difficult' (question 6), which options in question 7 (a list of possible usability issues) did they choose, and did those options vary by country site?"

The consultants created statistical models to help us understand the magnitude and the impact of issues on the overall usability of the site. This model was able to provide an estimate of the positive impact of improving usability issues, as well as an estimate of potential losses that could occur if existing usability decreased. These data were helpful for prioritizing what issues should be addressed first, as well as providing input for analyzing return on investment.

Findings

While we cannot discuss the bulk of our findings, one of the most interesting things we found was that there were no differences in the direction of the data between country sites. Language and cultural differences did not play a role in how people were trying to find items on the site.

Lessons Learned

We have found that surveys can be an effective tool to assist usability engineers to quantify usability issues. Here are a few things to keep in mind that we think will help you be successful with your survey efforts:

- Have a thorough understanding of what you want to learn from the research before you create a survey. You need to understand the issues in order to create the most effective survey with targeted questions and responses. You also need to understand what information you want to get from your respondents in order to identify the data analysis you will need.
- Apply the same experimental design standards to surveys that you would to usability testing. Surveys are not a fishing expedition where you hope the users will guide you to an answer.

- Get buy-in from all stakeholders before launching the survey. We went through an extensive iterative process to refine the surveys for this project. It was time-consuming but it also ensured that when the surveys were complete we had answers to everyone's research questions. When you are putting this much effort into a project you don't want people asking, "Did you consider asking about x?" after you have your data collected.

- Carefully choose the vendor based on the features and amount of support you need for the project. Problems with a vendor can make your job much harder than it needs to be. We experienced problems with the vendor not being able to handle the traffic on our site. This forced us to reduce the rate at which we presented the survey, which, in turn, required the survey to run a few days longer than expected.

- If the survey will be launched from your site, ask your webmaster or other technical expert to review the survey company's technology. Any third-party that interfaces with our site must go through a stringent technical evaluation.

- If you will need assistance with data analysis and intend to bring in a consultant, make sure the consultant reviews the survey before you launch it. The consultant can ensure that the structure of your survey permits the data analysis you need.

- When calculating the cost of a survey done in-house with a self-service vendor, be sure to include your time and the time of anyone else on the team needed to create, field, and analyze the survey. It might be more cost-effective to send the survey out to a full-service vendor.

Acknowledgments. I should like to thank Sonia Wong from the Product Management Group who devised the survey framework and ensured that this enormous international effort ran smoothly. I also thank Paul Fu from the Usability Group and Teri Morris from Project Management who worked tirelessly on the technical details and implementation of over 120 surveys.

CHAPTER 9

WANTS AND NEEDS ANALYSIS

Introduction

A wants and needs (W&N) analysis is an extremely quick, and relatively inexpensive, **brainstorming** method to gather data about user needs from multiple users simultaneously. It provides you with a structured methodology to obtain a prioritized list of initial **user requirements**. In its simplest form, user requirements gathering involves asking users what they want or need. Brainstorming is one of the tools that has been used successfully for many years to get a wealth of ideas from a variety of sources. Brainstorming with users is the key component of the W&N analysis; but the analysis has an added benefit compared to brainstorming alone because it incorporates a prioritization step that allows you to identify the most important wants and needs from the entire pool of ideas that were generated.

This method is ideal when you are trying to scope the features or information that will be included in the next (or first) release of the product. It enables you to find out what your users want and need in your product. Finally, by adding features based on the prioritized list, product teams can prevent **feature-creep** (i.e., the tendency to add in more and more features over time).

In this chapter, we discuss when to use this method, how to prepare for and conduct a wants and needs analysis session, as well as how to analyze and present your findings. We also share some of the lessons we have learned while using this method over the years. Finally, we provide a case study from industry to illustrate the benefits of this method in the real world.

At a Glance

> When should you conduct a wants and needs analysis?
> Things to be aware of when conducting a wants and needs analysis
> Preparing for a wants and needs analysis
> Conducting a wants and needs analysis
> Data analysis and interpretation
> Communicate the findings
> Modifications

When Should You Conduct a Wants and Needs Analysis?

A wants and needs analysis is a quick way to gather or confirm basic user requirements. This method can be used in the beginning of the product lifecycle to guide development, or in the middle of the lifecycle to determine changes to make to the product. It is always best to do this gathering early in the product development lifecycle, but sometimes product development proceeds without a clear understanding of requirements. You will quickly realize that a team needs this information when conversations that revolve around deciding what features to include keep cropping up and no resolution can be reached. This is a good sign that you ought to suggest that the team "confirm" their understanding of the user requirements. W&N is a perfect tool for this because it is quick and the team finds out what users really need.

Things To Be Aware of When Conducting a Wants and Needs Analysis

IBM's *Ease of Use* website (www-306.ibm.com/easy) provides a series of brainstorming questions you can ask users to help design a website. Some of the questions are: "What activities would you like to perform?", "What information would you like to get from this site?", and "How would you like to accomplish a particular task?" However, one should be aware that:

- People don't always know what they *really* would like and are not good at estimating how much they will like a single option
- There are always variables that people do not take into consideration
- What people say they do and what they actually do may be different.

That is why the questions you ask users cannot be for:

- Ill-defined problems (e.g., problems that are broad or unclear)
- Complex emotions (e.g., hatred)
- Things with which users have no experience.

In the wants and needs analysis you are asking users what they want or need, but the questions are well-defined and about things users already have some amount of experience with.

It is critical to note that a W&N analysis is only the beginning, not the end. It should be used as a jumping off point and not as your sole source of information. You should also use other methods detailed in this book, as well as supplementary information from product teams and marketing to tell a complete story (refer to Chapter 1, Introduction to User Requirements, "A Variety of Requirements" section, page 8). By beginning your requirements gathering process with an activity such as the W&N, you can assess what is really important to the users and then plan future activities to drill into these things.

DILBERT reprinted by permission of United Feature Syndicate, Inc.

Preparing for a Wants and Needs Analysis

Are You Ready?

Before you begin *any* user requirements activity there are a number of things you must be familiar with. Because these elements are common to all user requirements activities they have all been covered in the earlier chapters, but now is a good time to double-check the list. If you are not familiar with one of the items you can refer to the earlier chapter to brush up or familiarize yourself with that element.

Chapter 1: Introduction to User Requirements
- ☐ **Getting stakeholder buy-in for your activity** (see page 14)

Chapter 2: Before You Choose an Activity
- ☐ **Learn about your product** (see page 29)
- ☐ **Learn about your users** (see page 41)

Chapter 3: Ethical and Legal Considerations
- ☐ **Create consent forms** (see page 98)
- ☐ **Create confidential disclosure agreements** (see page 103)

Chapter 4: Setting up Facilities for Your User Requirements Activity
- ☐ **Create or acquire a facility for your activity** (see page 106)

Chapter 5: Preparing for Your User Requirements Activity
- ☐ **Develop an activity proposal** (see page 146)
- ☐ **Determine the time of day and duration of your session** (see page 155)
- ☐ **Recruit participants** (see page 156)
- ☐ **Develop an activity protocol** (see page 191)
- ☐ **Pilot your activity** (see page 193)

Chapter 6: During Your User Requirements Activity
- ☐ **Welcoming participants** (see page 209)
- ☐ **Dealing with late and absent participants** (see page 211)

□ **Warm-up your participants** (see page 215)

□ **Invite observers to watch your activity** (see page 216)

□ **Successfully moderate your activity** (see page 220)

□ **Record and take notes during your activity** (see page 226)

One of the biggest benefits to conducting a W&N is the speed with which you can prepare for, conduct, and analyze the results. In this section, we discuss the preparation required for the activity.

Preparation Timeline

Compared to some of the other user requirements activities, there is not an overwhelming amount of preparation required to conduct a W&N. A W&N session can be prepared for in just a couple of weeks. The most time-intense element is recruiting users. Table 9.1 is a preparation table with the actions you will have to complete in order to prepare for a successful session. The timeline contains approximate times based on our personal experiences and should be used only as a guide. It could take longer or less time for each step depending on a variety of factors – such as responsiveness of the product team, access to users, and resources available.

When to complete	Approximate time to complete	Activity
As soon as possible	1–2 weeks	□ Meet with team to formulate question(s) □ Meet with team to develop user profile
After identification of questions and user profile	1 week	□ Create and distribute activity proposal
After the proposal has been agreed to by all stakeholders	2 weeks	□ Identify and recruit users □ Assign roles for the activity (e.g., moderator and scribe) □ Prepare and/or acquire materials for activity

Table 9.1:

Preparation timeline for a W&N session

Continued

Table 9.1 – *Cont'd*

When to complete	Approximate time to complete	Activity
After the proposal has been agreed to by all stakeholders – *Cont'd*		☐ Acquire location ☐ Acquire incentives ☐ Order food (optional) ☐ Prepare documentation (e.g., letter for late participants, CDA, consent form, list of participants)
1 week before the session	2 days	☐ Run a pilot session or rehearse ☐ Make changes based on the pilot and re-pilot
Day before W&N	1 hour	☐ Call and confirm with participants ☐ Remind stakeholders to come and observe the activity (if appropriate)
Day of W&N	2–3 hours	☐ Create and place "Welcome" sign in lobby ☐ Pick up food (optional) ☐ Set up location with all materials necessary

At a Glance

> Identify the brainstorm question

> Players in your activity

> Inviting observers

> Activity materials

Identify the Brainstorming Question

You should work with the product team to determine the type of information you need and then carefully craft your question. An effective brainstorm session starts with a well thought-out question that summarizes the problem. A well-defined question will enable you to keep your brainstorm session focused.

The question you ask will determine the success of your activity. It is critical that it is not too broad *or* too specific. Let's say you are interested in building a program that allows you to book airline travel. You do not want to make your question so specific that you build in assumptions or narrow your participants' thinking. For example, you don't want to ask your participants "How do you want and need to add flights to your shopping cart?" Right away you are assuming that people want and need a shopping cart, and by inserting the shopping cart metaphor you limit their ideas. Likewise, you would not want to ask them to tell you "the features they want in an ideal system that allows them to book travel" if you are only interested in airline travel. People purchase travel tickets for traveling in ways other than on airplanes (e.g., buses, trains) so you will get a lot of information that is irrelevant to you. The question "What features do you want and need in an ideal system that allows you to purchase airlines tickets?" would be effective for your purposes. Ask yourself what information you need and then word your question to fulfill that need.

Your goal is to gain an understanding of what the users want and need in the product. Rather than allowing the participants to brainstorm about anything they would like, it is more effective to ask the question so that it targets content, tasks, or characteristics of your product. Based on this assumption, the W&N question can be asked in three different forms:

- *Information.* You can ask a question that will tell you the information that users want and need to be found in or provided by the system. A typical content question might be: "What kind of information do you need from an ideal online travel website?" You might receive answers like: hotels available in a given area, hotel prices, airline departure and arrival time, etc.

- *Task.* You can ask a question that will tell you about the types of activities or actions that users expect to be performed or supported by the system. A typical task-based question might be: "What tasks would you like to perform with an ideal hotel reservation system?" Some of the answers you receive might be: book a hotel, compare accommodations between hotels, create a travel profile, etc.

- *Characteristic.* You can ask questions that will provide you with traits users want or need the system to have. For example: "What are the characteristics of an ideal system that lets you book travel online?" Some responses you might receive are: reliable, fast, and secure.

The question you ask should mention "the ideal system" because you do not want participants limited by what they think technology can do. You want participants to think about "blue sky."

It is important to run a pilot or practice session to determine the types of answers you might receive (refer to Chapter 5, Preparing for Your User Requirements

Activity, "Piloting Your Activity" section, page 193). You may think what you are asking is clear, but it is not until your question is posed to people that you will truly know whether you are asking the right question. If the types of answers you receive in your pilot session are not in line with the information you need, then you will need to rephrase your question. If you do not pilot and wait until the session to see whether your question is correct, you may end up wasting time and money. In the "Lessons Learned" section of this chapter (see page 408), there is a great example of just how important piloting is for a W&N session.

Players in Your Activity

Of course you will need end users to take part in your session, but you will also require three people to conduct the session. In this section we discuss the details of all the individuals involved in a W&N session.

The participants

Since the group dynamic is an important component to this method, you should recruit 8–12 end users per session. Groups with more than 12 participants are difficult for a moderator to manage and participants may not have enough opportunity to speak. It is wise to run at least two groups of participants since group dynamics may vary. In addition, this provides you with a higher number of data points and more **reliable** results. Each group should consist of users with the same profile (refer to Chapter 2, Before You Choose an Activity, "Step 1: User Profile" section, page 43). For example, if you are gathering requirements for your travel website, you may like to speak with travel agents and customers who book travel online. These are two different user profiles. As a result, you would want to run two sessions with each profile, making a total of four sessions. The needs of each user type will likely be very different. If you include both user types in the same session, the results obtained will not accurately reflect either user type.

Speaking with especially effective or expert users can provide a wealth of ideas since "lead" users (the people who first use a product and become proficient with it) are often a source of innovation. However, do not limit yourself to experts, because their wants and needs can be different from those of novice or average users. Specifically, things they ask for may be completely unusable by less sophisticated users. As a result it is beneficial to have an understanding of the perspectives of both expert and novice users.

The moderator

One moderator is needed per session to facilitate the brainstorming. The moderator will elicit responses from the group, examine each answer to ensure he/she understands what the user is really asking for, and then paraphrase the response for the scribe (see below). Moderating is not quite as simple as one might think. It takes practice to learn how to manage and illicit information from a large group of users.

Figure 9.1 is a moderator's checklist. For a detailed discussion of the art of moderating, refer to Chapter 6, During Your User Requirements Activity, "Moderating Your Activity" section, page 220.

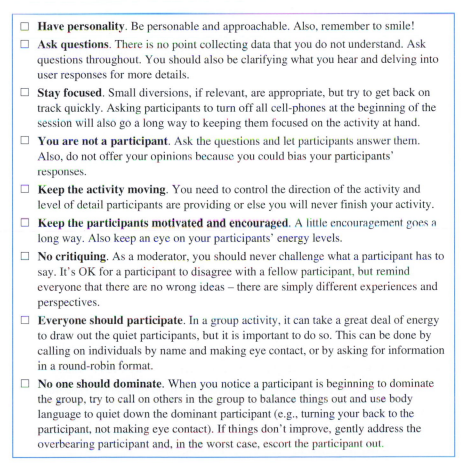

☐ **Have personality**. Be personable and approachable. Also, remember to smile!

☐ **Ask questions**. There is no point collecting data that you do not understand. Ask questions throughout. You should also be clarifying what you hear and delving into user responses for more details.

☐ **Stay focused**. Small diversions, if relevant, are appropriate, but try to get back on track quickly. Asking participants to turn off all cell-phones at the beginning of the session will also go a long way to keeping them focused on the activity at hand.

☐ **You are not a participant**. Ask the questions and let participants answer them. Also, do not offer your opinions because you could bias your participants' responses.

☐ **Keep the activity moving**. You need to control the direction of the activity and level of detail participants are providing or else you will never finish your activity.

☐ **Keep the participants motivated and encouraged**. A little encouragement goes a long way. Also keep an eye on your participants' energy levels.

☐ **No critiquing**. As a moderator, you should never challenge what a participant has to say. It's OK for a participant to disagree with a fellow participant, but remind everyone that there are no wrong ideas – there are simply different experiences and perspectives.

☐ **Everyone should participate**. In a group activity, it can take a great deal of energy to draw out the quiet participants, but it is important to do so. This can be done by calling on individuals by name and making eye contact, or by asking for information in a round-robin format.

☐ **No one should dominate**. When you notice a participant is beginning to dominate the group, try to call on others in the group to balance things out and use body language to quiet down the dominant participant (e.g., turning your back to the participant, not making eye contact). If things don't improve, gently address the overbearing participant and, in the worst case, escort the participant out.

Figure 9.1:

A moderator's checklist

The scribe

A scribe is needed to help the moderator. The sole job of the scribe is to write down what the moderator paraphrases and to number these ideas. The scribe does not question the users or write down anything other than what the moderator states. Pick a co-worker who can write large and clearly enough for everyone to read and who will be able to hold their tongue (see "Lessons Learned", page 407).

Tip

A blue or black marker is the easiest for everyone to read.

The videographer

If videotaping is possible, you will need a co-worker to record the activity. The video-tape can be very helpful after the session if you are referring to the list of brain-stormed ideas and want to obtain more detail. You will find a detailed discussion of how to record and the benefits of videotape in Chapter 6, During Your User Requirements Activity, "Recording and Note-taking" section, page 226. Ideally you should have someone to monitor the video equipment during the session in case something goes wrong; but if that is not possible, set up the shot, hit "Record," and hope that nothing goes wrong.

Inviting Observers

If you have the facilities to allow **stakeholders** to view these sessions, you will find it highly beneficial to invite them. (Chapter 4, Setting Up Facilities for Your User Requirements Activities, page 106 covers how to create an observation area appropriate for observers.) Stakeholders can learn a lot about what users like and dislike about the current product or a competitor's product, the difficulties they encounter, what they want, and why they think they want it. As with any **usability** activity, seeing it with their own eyes has a far greater impact than a report alone. Product teams often think they know the user requirements. They need to attend to see how little or how much they really do know. It is also wise to videotape the W&N sessions for any stakeholder who may not be able to attend, as well as for your own future reference.

Activity Materials

The materials needed are simple and cheap:

- ☐ Blue or black marker for the scribe
- ☐ Self-adhesive flip chart pads for the scribe to write on and post for all to see
- ☐ "Top 5" booklets
- ☐ Materials for a creativity exercise
- ☐ Large room conducive for a group activity.

It is best to write on flip chart paper instead of a whiteboard because you can continue to add paper and post them around the room if you begin to run out of space on the board. In addition, you can take the flip chart sheets back to your desk after the session and transcribe all the ideas.

Tip

To save time, post several flip chart sheets across the wall or whiteboard prior to starting the session. We usually start off with seven or eight sheets.

Conducting a Wants and Needs Analysis

In this section we detail the steps involved in the collection phase of the activity. This is the phase where all of the users are in the room and you now need to conduct the session.

The timeline in Table 9.2 gives the detail of the sequence and timing of events to conduct a W&N session. It is based on a one-hour session and will obviously need to be adjusted for shorter or longer sessions. These are *approximate* times based on our personal experiences and should be used only as a guide, but we have found them to be reliable, regardless of the question or user type.

Approximate duration	Procedure

5 minutes	Welcome the participants:
	    Signing of forms (CDA, consent)
	    Creative exercise/participant introductions

5 minutes	Rules for brainstorming and practice exercise
40 minutes	Brainstorming
10 minutes	Complete W&N booklets

Now that you know the steps involved in conducting a W&N session in outline, we will discuss each step in detail.

At a Glance

> Welcome the participants
> Introduce the activity and brainstorming rules
> Have a practice exercise
> The brainstorming
> Prioritization

Welcome the Participants

This is the time during which you greet your participants, allow them to eat some snacks, ask them to fill out any paperwork, and get them warmed-up for your activity. The details of these stages are described in Chapter 6, During Your User Requirements Activity (refer to "Welcoming Your Participants" section, page 209).

Introduce the Activity and Brainstorming Rules

After the warm-up, we jump into a brief overview of the goal and procedure of the activity. We say something along these lines:

"We are currently designing *<product description>* and we need to understand what *<information, tasks, or characteristics>* you want and need in this product. This will help us make sure that the product is designed to meet your wants and needs. This session will have two parts. In the first part we will brainstorm *<information,*

tasks, or characteristics> of an ideal system; and then in the second part of the activity we will have you individually prioritize the items that you have brainstormed."

After the brief overview, the rules that the participants must follow during the brainstorming session are then presented. We always write these on a flip chart and have them visible during the entire session. If anyone breaks one of the rules, the moderator can point to the rule as a polite reminder.

The brainstorming rules are:

1. This is an *ideal* system so all ideas are correct. Do not edit yourself or others.
2. There is no designing, so do not try to *build* your system.
3. The moderator can ask about duplicates.
4. The scribe writes down only what the moderator paraphrases.

Rule 1: Ideal system, no wrong answers

In the brainstorming phase, we want everyone thinking of an *ideal* system. Sometimes, users do not know what is possible. Encourage them to be creative and remind them that we are talking about the ideal. Because this is the ideal system, all ideas are correct. Something may be ideal for some users and not for others – and that is OK. Don't worry about unrealistic ideas as they will be weeded out in the prioritization phase.

Rule 2: No designing

Some users are steeped in the latest technology and will want to spend the entire session designing the perfect product. Users do not make good graphical or navigational designers; so do not ask them to design.

For example, if a participant says he would like to look up the latest flight information on a Personal Digital Assistant (PDA), we would stop the user and probe for more information. Ask the user why this information must be accessible from a PDA. He may respond, "Well, because I have a PDA that I take everywhere and I want to be able to look up the latest flight information when I am not at my desk." Ah! So the user really wants the information available from anywhere! You would then ask the scribe to write "Available from anywhere." It is your job as the moderator to probe what the user is really asking for and paraphrase that accurately for the scribe. In other words, you are drilling down for the user's ultimate goals or desired outcomes, rather than any particular way of achieving those goals. It is your job, along with the designers and product team, to determine what is technically feasible and to develop designs after the session.

For a discussion of "outcomes analysis" (a technique that focuses on understanding the user's desired outcome); see Chapter 7, Interviews, "Outcomes Analysis" section, page 252.

Rule 3: Moderator checks for duplicates

Another job of the moderator is to check for duplicates. Sometimes users forget that someone made the exact same suggestion earlier. When you point it out to them, users will respond that they had forgotten about it or not seen it. However, there are times when the user *isn't* asking for the exact same thing, it just sounds like it. This is where you must probe for more details and learn how these two suggestions are different from each other so that you can capture what the user is really asking for. It is important to mention this to the participants as a rule so that they do not think that you are challenging their idea – you are simply trying to understand how it differs from another idea.

Rule 4: Scribe writes down only what the moderator paraphrases

This rule is important to set the participants' expectations. Participants may not understand why the scribe isn't writing down verbatim everything they are saying. It isn't because the scribe is rude and doesn't care what the participants are saying. It is because the moderator must understand what the participants really want with each suggestion. What the participant initially says may not be what he or she really wants. The scribe needs to give the moderator time to drill down and get at what the participant is asking for before committing it to paper. Once participants understand this, they will understand that the scribe isn't being rude but is simply waiting for "the final answer."

Have a Practice Exercise

Once everyone understands the rules of brainstorming, we usually do a brief practice exercise. A favorite of ours is: "What tasks do you want and need to perform in an ideal bookstore?" Some answers the group may provide are "search for books," "pay for books," "find out what is new," and "read reviews." This practice exercise should last for only a couple of minutes.

When you believe everyone has a good grasp of the process, you can begin the official activity. One way to make this assessment is to ensure that everyone in the room has given at least one example that you feel answers the practice question appropriately. During the practice, if anyone gets off track (e.g., offering information, rather than a task), this is the time to refer back to the question and/or the rules. Inevitably, if you are asking about tasks people will give you information, and vice versa. It is your job to catch this and ask the user to rephrase a request. For example, using the question noted above, a participant might respond by saying that he/she wants "the books to have a rating given by other readers." This is a great idea, but it is information rather than a task. Ask the participant what the task is that relates to this information. Ask: "Is it that you want to be able to find reviews written by other readers?" Work with the participant to make sure the task is elicited. This is also a good time to make sure that the scribe's writing is large and clear enough for everyone to read.

The Brainstorming

In addition to displaying the participation rules for all to see, the question is also posted for all to see. Before you begin the generation of ideas, make sure that everyone understands the question. If you have a complex or technical question, you may require a brief clarification discussion. Often, because of the multiple meanings that words can have, people say one thing but mean another. It is important to have everyone on the same page.

For instance, if you were doing a W&N to learn more about the manageability needs for your customers' database environments, you would probably want to start off with a discussion of what is meant by "manageability" in a database environment. This discussion can take as little or as long as you feel necessary to get everyone thinking along the same lines.

Tip

Provide participants with paper and a pen so that they can jot ideas down during the brainstorming. Often there is a flurry of ideas being generated and you do not want a participant who is waiting for a chance to jump in to forget their idea(s) while someone else is speaking.

It's now time to jump into the brainstorming session. As the moderator, there is a lot for you to do (also see Chapter 6, During Your User Requirements Activity, "Moderating Your Activity" section, page 220):

- ☐ Make sure everyone is participating.
- ☐ If users digress, bring them back on track by pointing to the question under consideration.
- ☐ Remember to encourage people to think about an *ideal* system. They shouldn't be concerned about the technical constraints, what is available today, or what will be available tomorrow.
- ☐ Check for duplicates.
- ☐ Enforce the ground rules for brainstorming.
- ☐ Make sure everyone can read what is being written.
- ☐ Verify that what is being written accurately summarizes what the participant is asking for.

Also, be sure to keep an eye on the scribe. Make sure the scribe is:

- ☐ Accurately getting your summarizations on paper
- ☐ Keeping up with the pace of the session (if not, slow things down)
- ☐ Writing large and clear
- ☐ Numbering each item as it is added to the list.

Numbering each item will help you identify which idea the user desired. It is especially useful when the handwriting looks like a drunk chicken walked across the page!

Figure 9.2 illustrates a number of important elements of the W&N session. These include:

- The approximate size of the room we use for these sessions
- The table configuration we like to use
- The mirrored observation room to the left.

After about 40 minutes of brainstorming or so, you will notice that the number and quality of ideas tend to decrease. When you ask for additional suggestions, you will probably be met with blank stares. At this point, ask everyone to read through the list of ideas and make sure none is missing. If you are still met with silence, the generation phase is over. It is now time for the prioritization phase.

Prioritization

In the prioritization phase, users spend about 15 minutes picking the most desired items from the pool of brainstormed ideas. They are asked: "If you could have *only* five items from the brainstormed list what items would you pick?" We ask for five choices because we have found that this will elicit the "cream of the crop." We also like asking for five because we often ask two W&N questions during a two-hour usability session. For example, during the first hour we may ask about information desired in an ideal system, and in the second hour we may ask about the tasks desired in that same ideal system. By asking for the top five at the end of each brainstorming portion of the session, it keeps the evening to two hours and it does not exhaust the participants. Choosing the top selections is quite an exhausting procedure for the participants, so the more choices you ask for, the more time and effort it takes.

Figure 9.3:

Typical page of a wants and needs booklet

> **Please identify the top 5 tasks you would like to do with an ideal hotel reservation system.**
>
> Idea #: _____
>
> Idea name: _____
>
> Describe it: _____
>
> _____
>
> _____
>
> Why is it important to you? _____
>
> _____
>
> _____

Participants fill in their answers in a "Top 5 booklet." The booklet asks users to name the item they are choosing, describe it, and state why that item is so important to them (see Figure 9.3). We ask for this additional information to be sure that we are capturing what the users are *really* asking for. People may choose the same item from the brainstormed list, but have completely different interpretations of these items. The descriptions and "why is it important" paragraph will help you detect these differences in the data analysis phase. A brief set of instructions is provided to users:

- Write only one item per page. If more than one answer is provided per sheet, the second answer will be discarded.
- Indicate the number of item from the brainstorming flip chart.
- The five are not ranked and are of equal weight.
- No duplicates are allowed. If anyone votes for the same item more than once, the second vote will be discarded.

- Provide a description of the item.
- State why it is important to you.

Once participants have completed their booklets, you can send them home with thanks and an incentive. If there is another W&N question to answer, give participants a brief break. Typically, you can complete two questions in one two-hour usability session.

Effective Brainstorming Tips

The most effective brainstorm sessions follow some key recommendations. We have adopted a set of strategies that are used by many who conduct usability and market research studies (Kelly 2001). For a list of moderating tips that apply to more than brainstorming, see Chapter 6, During Your User Requirements Activity, "Moderating Your Activity" section, page 220.

Hone the problem
This is the development and fine-tuning of your question. Work with the product team to develop a question that summarizes the problem and keeps your brainstorming focused.

Warm-up – relax
As with other group activities, the warm-up is very important. This is particularly important when the group has not worked together before and most of the group does not have much brainstorming experience. Ideas for creativity exercises can be found in Chapter 6, During Your User Requirements Activity, "Warm-up Exercises" section, page 215.

The sky is the limit
You want to encourage creativity during your session. You want people to think "blue sky" – anything they want! Don't worry; the prioritization step of this technique will ensure that ideas such as "booking your airline travel ticket through osmosis" won't end up in your software requirements document.

Capture and number the ideas

As ideas are being captured on paper, it is useful to number them. This will make it easier for people to refer to points already on the list. It is also extremely helpful in the second stage when the participants are prioritizing their choices. It will also give you a sense of how many ideas you have generated during the session. As an approximation you can use the rate of 100 ideas per hour as a brainstorming rate guideline.

Keep up the momentum

This is referred to as "build and jump." You need to be able to keep the brainstorming alive. One way to do this as a moderator is to help participants "build" on ideas. You can do this by probing further when you think there is more to be uncovered. For example, if we are brainstorming about features in an ideal airline travel site, someone might say that they want to be able to search by price. Well, there are lots of other things people might want to search on, so you should try to build on this idea and ask: "Is there anything else you think you might want to search on?"

Conversely, you also want to be able to "jump." If people are continuing to focus on a certain issue and are getting buried in the minutia, you will want to jump to another topic. Let's say people are getting bogged down in every kind of search criteria they want. This would be a good opportunity to say: "OK, I think we understand that it is important for you to be able to search, but let's now think about what features would help you make your decision of which flight(s) to buy." It can be hard to think of non-biasing questions on the spot. It is best to speak with the team and come up with a list of areas the team would like more information about. Once you have that list, you can write "jump" questions that are non-biasing and then refer to them as needed during the session.

The Doomed Brainstorm

Just as there are ways to have an effective brainstorming session, there are also ways to have an ineffective session. Here are some of the things that you don't want to do when acting as moderator (Kelly 2001).

Don't be too serious

Yes, your report at the end of the day should be serious, but the brainstorming should not adopt this mood. You need to let people be creative. You want them to think about the ideal. Don't suffocate their creativity by telling them that ideas are silly or impossible. With the silly will come the serious. Let people have fun. All ideas are good ideas and all should be treated equally! Ideas that are a little far-fetched at the moment might be within the realm of possibility in the future.

Don't document every detail

Documenting every detail won't get you very far. It will interrupt the natural quick paced flow of the session. You need to learn to summarize the points of interest and move on. The participants should not be required to take any notes: that is the job of the scribe. The participants should focus on the generation of great ideas, not the documentation of them.

Don't limit your session to the elite

Experts can make great contributions, but don't always limit your participants to groups of experts. People who are new to a particular field, or who do not have experience, but interest, make great participants for a brainstorming session. Sometimes the expert is the first person that comes to mind to recruit, but you should keep the average user in mind too. Make sure you identify who will be using your product at the end of the day. Is the person who travels weekly going to be the predominant user of your travel website, or will it be the "average Joe" who travels once or twice a year? If you think that both the expert and novice will use your product, then you should consider including users with a range of experience in your sessions, or multiple sessions with different experience criteria.

Avoid too much structure

Yes, you want to encourage everyone to get involved, but do not make the discussion overly structured. For example, going around the room giving each person time to speak (e.g., round-robin) is going to kill the brainstorming. This approach may work initially if you want to get everyone warmed-up (or in other activities, such as focus groups), but in a true brainstorming session ideas are generated spontaneously. Jim says one thing and it makes Sarah think of something related (**synergy**). If you make Sarah wait until "her turn," she might be side-tracked by the next person's idea and/or the idea may be lost (**production blocking**). Encourage people who are quiet to speak, and those who are speaking too much to settle down – but do not force it. The only exception to the round-robin is if your brainstorming has been done individually on paper (see "Modifications," page 401).

Tame the dominator

An overbearing person who insists on doing all of the talking and/or loves to interrupt others will surely ruin your session. You will need to get this person in check quickly. (Refer to Chapter 6, During Your User Requirements Activity, "Moderating Your Activity" section, page 220 for tips on how to deal with this and other difficult moderating situations.)

Data Analysis and Interpretation

In this section, we describe in detail how to analyze the data from your wants and needs session. One of the great advantages of this method is that you can score the data as quickly as you collected it. In one to two hours you can have the results compiled and entered in an electronic format.

At a Glance

> Create identifiers for each booklet

> Sort based on verbatim content

> Combine groups

> Remove duplicates from each pile

> Determine the percentage of respondents per group

> Combine data from multiple sessions (optional)

> Interpreting the data

Tip

We strongly encourage you to score the data within 24 hours of collecting it, while the discussions that took place that evening are still fresh in your mind. If you recorded the session, you can always go back and review the tape, but that is a time-intensive process that we try to avoid.

It is valuable to have the scribe analyze the data with you. Not only does the analysis go faster, it is helpful to have another set of eyes to decipher difficult handwriting. Also, the scribe was present at the session, so he or she can be helpful as you try to recall details of the evening.

Create Identifiers for Each Booklet

Begin by marking each sheet in your Top 5 booklet with an identifier. For example, write "1" on each sheet of the first booklet, "2" on all the sheets for the second booklet, and so forth. After all forms have been marked with a unique identifier, divide the booklets in half (half for you and half for the person assisting you with the analysis) and separate the forms (i.e., remove the staples from the booklets).

Sort Based on Verbatim Content

Sort the worksheets into groups based on verbatim content. If users provide more than one answer per sheet, ignore the second answer on the page. If you and the

scribe call out each answer as you lay the sheets down, this helps you to locate stacks of identical worksheets. Figure 9.4 shows the worksheets being sorted by the moderator and the scribe. As you can see, you will end up with quite a number of piles, so make sure you have a large working space.

Tip

Use sticky notes to identify each stack as you sort. If you have a large number of groups, it can be easy to get them mixed up or "lose" a group.

Combine Groups

Once all worksheets have been sorted, you will want to combine groups that are similar. For example, you may have three sheets in one stack called "Search by cost" and another stack of two sheets called "Find the best price." Upon closer examination (i.e., reading the selection descriptions and "why it is important") you determine that these piles are both referring to conducting a search to find the best price. As a result these groups can be combined into a category called "Search by Price."

The need to combine groups happens for a number of reasons. Firstly, items may have been duplicated during the brainstorming. As in the above example, the concept is the same but the wording is slightly different. Ideally, this should have been caught during the session, but the reality is that it is often difficult to recall everything that has been said during the session and as a result duplicates sometimes slip in. Also, if the items are phrased differently during the brainstorming you may think the items differ, but when you read the descriptions of the items on the Top 5 forms you realize that they are the same. Or perhaps, after discussion with the product team or domain experts, you realize that items you thought were unique are in fact the same.

Secondly, even though you ask all participants to indicate the number of the brainstormed items they choose, there will be some who don't do this – which may result in the creation of extra piles when you do your first sort. Alternatively, they might not write verbatim what was written on the flip chart. Believe it or not – it happens all the time.

Remove Duplicates from Each Pile

This is when the identifiers from step 1 are used. When you are tallying the votes in the next step ("Determine the percentage of respondents"), you do not want to count multiple votes from the same user. Each user only gets one vote per item – you stated this rule during your session and you need to stick to it. To adhere to this you need to make sure that each pile does not have any repeating identifiers.

Continuing our example above, let's say you have a pile with five worksheets in it. If participant #3 voted for "Search by price" and "Search by cost," her vote would be counted only once in the next step. You know the same participant's vote is in the pile twice because you can see the identifier "3" in the pile two times. Staple the double selection together. You may be tempted to throw one of the votes away, but sometimes each sheet contains different details in the "why is it important" section and you don't want to loose this information. By stapling the sheets together you will remember to count this information only once in the next step.

Determine the Percentage of Respondents Per Group

Once you have determined that all the groups are in the highest-level groupings possible, determine the percentage of respondents per group (i.e., for each group, how many of the total participants chose this item?). To do this, count the number of unique votes and divide by the total number of participants.

For example, if there were 12 participants in your session and four worksheets with unique identifiers in a particular group, the percentage for that group would be calculated like this:

4 worksheets divided by 12 participants = 0.33

0.33 × 100 = 33%

Combine Data from Multiple Sessions

When conducting multiple sessions with the same user profile and question, the data from each session should be analyzed separately and compared. The results should be relatively consistent across sessions, with only slight differences in percentages. When comparing the tables, we use the rule that any item that half of the participants have chosen to be one of their Top 5 sections in one table should appear in the other table.

So, looking at the sample tables in Figure 9.5, we would identify the items in each table that at least half of the participants selected as part of their Top 5. These are highlighted in the example. We would then make sure that these items appear in both tables. If an item has half the vote in one table, but less than half the vote in another table, that is OK – we just want to make sure that it appears in the second table (e.g., "Read hotel reviews" in the example).

It is important to acknowledge that we have not empirically tested the reliability of this method so we do not have hard and fast rules to recommend. This is what we do in practice and we have found it to be effective for us. This is one of the challenges of taking a qualitative method and trying to apply quantitative measures to it.

Group 1

Brainstormed Item	# of user that choose the item as a top 5 selection
Book a room	10 of 10
Look up hotel information	10 of 10
Read hotel reviews	9 of 10
Compare hotels	5 of 10
E-mail a travel agent with questions	2 of 10

Group 2

Brainstormed Item	# of user that choose the item as a top 5 selection
Book a room	10 of 10
Look up hotel information	9 of 10
Compare hotels	7 of 10
Read hotel reviews	4 of 10
Search by price	4 of 10

Figure 9.5:

Comparison of wants and needs Top 5 tables between two sessions

Another thing we do is look at the list of all items brainstormed that evening. Are they similar? They should be. If they are completely different, it is likely that you may have recruited different user types. Examine the users recruited and identify possible differences between the groups. Perhaps you were running sessions with travelers (e.g., prior to the session you did not think that being a frequent traveler or an infrequent traveler would matter) and as it turned out, one session had a majority of frequent travelers while the other had a majority of infrequent travelers. You discover this when you analyze the result from each night's session and see the brainstormed ideas are dramatically different across each night. You may have assumed that the wants and needs were the same for all travelers. The difference in your results would indicate that this might not be the case. To confirm this suspicion, you would need to conduct a session with all infrequent travelers and another session with all frequent travelers. Differences could exist because of group dynamics (e.g., a domineering individual was present in one group, there were just more creative people one night than another, etc.). Perhaps you did not run enough participants to obtain consistency.

Careful research and preparation can usually prevent such errors (refer to Chapter 2, Before You Choose an Activity, "Learn About Your Users" section, page 41). Procedures during each session could also vary and explain differences in results. For example, perhaps there were two moderators and different instructions were given at each session. It can be helpful to review videotapes of the sessions to see where the differences may lie.

It is important for us to note that just because differences were found between sessions, it is does not automatically mean that the moderators did something wrong. As we mentioned earlier, we have not empirically tested the reliability of this method. It is possible that you may find differences in the results between sessions but will not be able to determine the cause. Although we have never found large differences in the results between sessions, if you do and you cannot figure out why, run another session and see whether the results are similar to either of the other sessions.

In the end, however, if the data across each night are similar (which they will be in almost all cases), combine the worksheets from all sessions and rescore. This provides you with a higher number of data points and more reliable results.

Interpreting the Data

Keep in mind that some selections are so obvious that they may not appear in the brainstorming. In our travel example, if no one suggested "Room availability" as an information need, it does not mean that users don't want or need that piece of information – they may simply have assumed that the information would be provided. Or users may simply not have thought about it. You must use your domain knowledge, expertise as the user advocate, and simply your common sense. The ideas you are obtaining through the W&N are a jumping off point, but there is still more research required on your part to verify those needs.

Compare the items that received priority attention from the users to the product's functional specification. The items that received the highest percentage of votes should receive first attention by the product team. Perhaps the team had already planned to incorporate these items into the product. You have just validated their decision. Or you may have a case where the highest priority items were not even on the product team's radar. Go back to the videotape and listen to the discussion around those items. Why did participants suggest those items? Why did they say they were important on the worksheets? This is fundamental information that needs to be shared with the product team.

The information from the W&N session can also be used to hold feature-creep in check. When a developer finds a cool, new feature that he/she really swears the user must have, the team should go back to the W&N results. Did the participants ever discuss this feature? Did it come up in anyone's Top 5? If not, more research should be done before resources are spent including the feature. Too many products become unnecessarily complicated when features are added just because someone thought it would be cool.

Alternatively, **feature-shedding** can also be re-examined with the results of a W&N session. When the product development team starts identifying features to drop, there are many considerations: resources required to build it, business requirements, dependency of other features, etc. One of the considerations should also be user requirements. If a feature that a high percentage of participants selected is on the chopping block, shedding it should be reconsidered. Are there any other features that could be dropped instead?

Communicate the Findings

Preparing to Communicate Your Findings

The specific data that you communicate to product teams can vary depending upon the activity you conducted, but some elements of *how* you communicate the results are the same regardless of the method. Because these strategies are common to all user requirements Activities, they are discussed in detail in Chapter 14, Concluding Your Activity, page 636. We recommend that you read that chapter prior to relaying your results to your stakeholders. Topics discussed include:

- ☐ **Prioritization of your findings** (see page 638)
- ☐ **Creating an effective presentation** (see page 644)
- ☐ **Writing valuable reports for different audiences** (see page 652)
- ☐ **Ensuring the incorporation of your findings** (see page 660)

We present the results of the W&N in a simple table for the product team to review (see Table 9.3). The key elements are:

- Item or category (e.g., cost information)
- Exemplars of the item or category (e.g., price of single room, price of suite, cost of gym access). The exemplars often come from specific examples that people gave during the brainstorm or from details that they provided on the worksheet.
- Percentage of participants who selected that item as a Top 5.

Table 9.3: *Sample results table illustrating the results of two sessions combined into one*

Task	Exemplars	Percentage of users requesting it
Book a room	• Make an advance reservation • Pay for room • Receive confirmation number • Print hotel confirmation	100% (20 of 20)
Look up hotel information	• Cost • Availability • Picture of hotel • Picture of room • Accommodations (e.g., non-smoking, king bed, refrigerator, etc.) • View from room	95% (19 of 20)
Read hotel reviews	• From professional reviewers • From previous guests	70% (14 of 20)
Compare hotels	• Select more than one hotel and compare the price, availability, and accommodations	60% (12 of 20)
Research activities around the hotel	• Find popular tourist attractions within driving distance of hotel • Find activities sponsored at or by the hotel	45% (9 of 12)
Sign up for frequent visitor programs	• Look up frequent flyer programs the hotel contributes to • Sign up for programs that provide rewards for staying at the hotel	25% (5 of 20)

Make the table easy to scan quickly. The table should be ordered from highest to lowest priority. Typically, we will include any item in the table that received at least one vote; however, some people like to include only the items that received at least two votes.

In addition to this table, we include the complete list of brainstormed ideas in our usability report. The brainstormed list can be a source of inspiration or additional features. Since most executives and developers do not read the usability report, the table is the key piece of information. We recommend keeping it to a couple of pages, if possible, and providing a few sentences of recommendation or explanation with the table. This can be posted to a website or it can be enlarged and posted in high-visibility areas for all to see. The most important place to include this information is in the product team's documentation (e.g., functional specification, software requirements document, high-level design document). The W&N can provide a starting point for such documentation and is one piece of a very large puzzle, but it is a valuable piece. Ideally, additional user requirements techniques should be used along the way to capture new requirements and verify your current requirements.

Modifications

Because the W&N analysis is so flexible, a number of modifications can be made to customize it to fit your needs. None of these modifications is better or worse than what we have presented in this chapter; they are simply different. Depending on your particular situation they may suit your specific needs better. Modifications can be made to both the brainstorming phase and the prioritization phase.

The Brainstorming Phase

Below are examples of some of the modifications that can be made during the brainstorming stage of the activity.

Pen-and-paper brainstorming

There are a few ways, other than effective moderation, to address the issues that are a natural part of brainstorming. These issues include social loafing (i.e., the tendency for individuals to reduce the effort they make toward some task when working together with others) and **evaluation apprehension** (i.e., the fear of being evaluated by others). To reduce social loafing, participants can be given several minutes at the beginning of the session to silently write down as many ideas as possible. This can be followed by a round-robin in which each user must read one of the ideas from his/her list. Since each user is accountable for providing a new idea during his/her turn, the user cannot sit back and avoid participating. Users may generate new ideas during the sharing of ideas written, and therefore benefit from the group synergy (i.e., an idea from one participant positively influences another participant, resulting in an additional idea that would not have been generated without the initial idea). You must be sure to follow up with users and understand why they are suggesting the ideas, otherwise, you may never know.

Some studies have shown that people generate more ideas when working separately and then pooling their ideas rather than working as a group (Mullen, Johnson, & Salas 1991; Paulus, Larey, & Ortega 1995). One study found that when college psychology students were allowed to work alone and/or were not held accountable for the number of ideas generated, they actually generated more ideas than those working face to face (Kass, Inzana, & Willis 1995). This method would be particularly effective for someone who did not feel comfortable with his or her moderation skills. It takes a skilled moderator to counteract social loafing and evaluation apprehension (refer to Chapter 6, During Your User Requirements Activity, "Moderating Your Activity" section, page 220). This modification helps to deal with the issue for you. The main disadvantages of this modification is that it can be more time-consuming.

Electronic brainstorming

A group of individuals at University of Arizona created one of the first commercially available electronic brainstorming tools – called *GroupSystems*. Although this system forces all the individuals in the group to be in the same room, current tools are available that allow remote participants to join in on the brainstorming via the web (e.g., Groove, MSN Messenger, Yahoo Chat, Lotus Notes). Such a computer aid can allow users to participate anonymously, thus avoiding evaluation apprehension. Since answers can be typed in simultaneously, no one has to wait to be recognized (i.e., production blocking) and there is no problem with overbearing or expert users jumping queue. However, because most people type more slowly than they speak, **communication speed** is decreased and social loafing often increases.

One study showed that with groups of four or more people, electronic brainstorming produced more ideas than verbal brainstorming; and with groups of eight or more, electronic brainstorming produced more ideas than paper-and-pencil brainstorming (Dennis & Williams 2003). However, you should be aware of the difficulties of using electronic tools for brainstorming. If you wish to have everyone in the same room at the same time, you will need to have one computer per user. So, based on the research findings noted above, to see a benefit over verbal groups you would require four or more computers. To realize a benefit over paper-and-pencil brainstorms you would need eight or more computers. That is quite an expense to incur for brainstorming activities. Also, you will need to train the users how to use the software, and you will have to go in with the awareness that computer problems may arise.

If you choose to go the remote route, be keenly aware that you have no control over who is participating. You cannot be sure that your desired user is actually contributing the ideas on the screen. The security of your brainstorming session is also at risk.

Finally, you will lose the opportunity to ask users why they are suggesting the ideas on the screen. Since it is anonymous, you do not know whom to ask. It is much more difficult to control the quality of responses that get on to the list of brainstormed ideas. If participants begin designing their ideal system, you will not be able to probe deeper into their ideas or get at the core of what they are asking for. Considering the cost, security, lack of contact, and complexity with electronic brainstorming, we do not currently use it, either in a group or over the web; however, others swear by it.

Affinity brainstorming

The Usability Net website (www.usabilitynet.org/home.htm) suggests another modification to brainstorming techniques: Ask users to create an **affinity diagram** as part of the brainstorming. Users should write each idea on a separate sticky note.

Each note is then placed on a large wall or whiteboard. To avoid a chaotic free-for-all, you can ask one participant at a time to post their stickies. As the individual adds a new sticky note, he/she must announce it to the group. This can prevent duplicate sticky notes and can spark ideas for other participants. Similar ideas should be placed in close proximity to each other. Once everyone has posted their ideas, you may identify categories of ideas as a group and then discuss them. One of the advantages of this method is that the sorting portion of the data analysis is done for you during the session. For more information on affinity diagrams, see Appendix F, page 714.

Focus on outcomes

Outcome analysis is a technique that is focused on the outcome that the users want (i.e., what they want the product to do for them), rather than the features or information they desire (Ulwick 2002). This technique is particularly useful when your goal is innovation – the reason being that users can relate only to what they have experience with.

Outcome analysis is typically used in an interview format, but the principles can be applied to a W&N. During the brainstorming phase, the moderator is responsible for translating each brainstormed item into an outcome. For example, let's say you are discussing the ideal tasks that you want and need to perform in a system for booking travel. If a participant says "Search for flight information," you need to translate this into an outcome. What is the ultimate outcome the participant wants from searching for flight information? A reasonable outcome might be to identify a flight that suits his/her schedule and budget. The moderator poses this outcome to the participant to see whether he/she agrees, ensuring there is no misinterpretation. The outcome is then written on the flip chart. The moderator often does the translation rather than the participant because the latter sometimes have a difficult time making this jump. After participants understand that you are looking for outcomes, they may begin brainstorming in terms of the outcomes, not just the tasks. At the end of the session the outcomes are then prioritized.

SUGGESTED RESOURCES FOR ADDITIONAL READING

If your focus is on innovation, outcome analysis is a worthwhile technique for you to explore. More information can be found in Chapter 7, Interviews, "Outcomes Analysis" section, page 252. For a full discussion, see the following paper:

- Ulwick, A. W. (2002). Turn Customer Input into Innovation. *Harvard Business Review*, January, pp. 5–11. Available at:

  http://harvardbusinessonline.hbsp.harvard.edu/b01/en/common/item_detail. jhtml?id=R0201H.

The Prioritization Phase

Below are examples of some of the modifications that can be made during the prioritization stage of the activity.

Adding questions to the Top 5 worksheet

Some people who employ this method use an additional question on the worksheet: "How do you know when the ideal system has the characteristic/task/information?" This is intended to help the evaluator better understand what the user is really asking for and why he/she wants it. That is, you want to understand how a feature will be used or how it contributes value to the user's end goals.

For example, if you are designing an ideal system to transport you to work and you chose "fast" as a characteristic of the system, how would you know that your system is really fast? The answer could be "When I can leave for work five minutes before I need to be there." Unfortunately, no matter how many examples of this question and answer we give during a session, participants never seem to "get it." They understand the examples but have a difficult time applying them to their actual brainstorm at hand. The typical response is "I know I have it when it is there." We also found that participants try to design the system when answering this question and, as we discussed earlier, you shouldn't rely on users to design your system. You may have better luck with this question than we have, so we offer it here for you to try. We find that we capture the desired information about why the participant wants this item in the response to the "Why is it important to you?" question. You may also add any other questions that you think will provide you with beneficial information to understand what the participant is truly looking for.

Top 5, 10, or 15?

As mentioned earlier in the chapter, you do not have to use the "Top 5." You may increase the selection to a participant's top 10 or 15, or whatever number you desire. Due to the desire to extract the "cream of the crop" from the brainstorming, as well as participants' attention and energy levels in the evenings, we find that the "Top 5" works best; but we have increased the number when running a one-hour session with only one brainstorm question. If you are running only one session it can be a nice idea to collect more prioritization information.

Rank the selections

You could ask the users to rank order their selections or rate the importance of each selection. This will give you a more detailed breakdown of the users' priorities. Keep in mind that this will complicate the data analysis. You may choose to state how many people selected an item as their first choice, second choice, etc. Alternatively, you can assign each ranking a point value (e.g., first choice equals five points, second choice equals four points, etc.). Add up the total number of points each item earned and then create your prioritized list from there. The top items don't change with this variation.

Eliminate items from the list

The evaluator can go through the list of ideas generated and remove any that are impractical to implement, duplicates that were not caught earlier, ideas that the product team has already included (or plans to include) in the product, or ideas that do not meet some preset criteria. You can also eliminate "obvious" ideas such as being able to purchase a book from an online bookstore. After the brainstorm is complete, the moderator does this by putting an X next to the items on the list that he/she does not want the participants to include in their Top 5 selections. By removing obvious, impractical, or already implemented ideas, participants will not "waste" their votes on ideas that aren't useful. We recommend using this modification for products that already have a released version or have a detailed and well-researched functional specification.

Another way to handle "obvious" answers is by asking users to select their top five "wants," followed by the selection of their top five "needs." For example, a user may not *need* to read through all the hotel descriptions to find a suitable hotel, but may *want* the travel site to hold information about his/her profile and preferences and then automatically find hotels to match the needs.

Lessons Learned

We have been using the W&N methodology since August, 1999. Over the years, we have learned many things that have helped us improve our techniques. We thought it would be helpful to share these things with you so that you don't make the same mistakes we did.

Scribe Training

Probably the biggest lesson learned was that your scribe must be well trained. That may sound painfully obvious or maybe it sounds trivial. Apparently, all the scribe has to do is write what you say. How hard can it be? How wrong we were! The most common problem is when the scribe tries to be a para-legal and capture every word the participants are saying, rather than writing only what the moderator paraphrases. We have also had occasions where scribes have written down their own ideas! In another case, a scribe stopped writing and began chatting with the participants. "Oh yeah! I hate it when that happens! You know what I hate is . . . ." Usually, it is purely innocent, but it can impact your results. It can be awkward to correct the scribe in front of a group of participants, as well as observers watching from another room.

A scribe must be able to write quickly and clearly, and be able to remember what the moderator paraphrases while the rest of the room is chatting. In addition, the scribe cannot be afraid to say "Slow down – I need to catch up" or "I did not catch that. Could you repeat it?" It isn't an easy task and not everyone can do it. The scribe should take time to watch a W&N session, noting what the other scribe does well and not so well. The pilot or rehearsal session is another important training opportunity. If the scribe does anything incorrectly at that point, it is far less embarrassing to correct him/her there. You can also determine whether the scribe has the *"write* stuff!" If not, you may want to quickly seek out an alternative scribe.

Pilot

As we have mentioned, running a pilot or rehearsal session is important. You would never run a usability test without conducting a pilot session to test your tasks, **protocol**, and timing. So why would you conduct a group activity without running a pilot session? We have found that wording a question for a W&N can be tricky. Is the question too broad or narrow? Does it make sense? Use this opportunity to work any bugs out of your protocol, train your scribe, and do a check of all materials. We have learned that a pilot is an investment well made!

In one particular instance, the following question was not piloted: "What information do you want and need in an ideal mobile device?" This question was posed to a group of field sales representatives and the results that were brainstormed were almost all focused on design. Participants keep referring to their Palm Pilots and cell-phones. As you recall, during a W&N you do not want to focus on design. As hard as the moderator tried, she could not get the group to stop thinking about their current devices. The session was a bust! Had the question been piloted, this could have been avoided. It was determined after the session that the problem was that the question contained the words "mobile device." The next night the question was rephrased to "What information do you want and need when you are out of your office?" This session was a great success! Another lesson learned the hard way.

Pulling It All Together

In this chapter, we have illustrated the details of conducting a wants and needs analysis. You should now be able to determine when this activity is appropriate, prepare for the session, and collect and analyze your data. We hope you have as much success with this activity as we have.

CASE STUDY

The wants and needs analysis is a method that has been used effectively by Oracle's Usability and UI group. In this case study, the method was used to collect user requirements for a new domain that Oracle was diving into – healthcare. This study illustrates how the technique added value to the requirements collection phase of product development.

Understanding Users' Healthcare Wants and Needs

Kathy Baxter, eBay, Inc.

When I worked for Oracle they wanted to learn more about how people select healthcare providers (i.e., physicians). This information would inform the design of their Provider Finder (the search, advanced search, and information page for each provider). We ran a series of wants and needs (W&N) sessions to examine three types of patients: healthy patients, frequent visitors, and patient agents. These types of patient are fundamentally different and we wanted to be sure we understood how those differences might affect the way each user type selected providers. Healthy patients do not need regular medical care and usually go to the doctor only once a year for checkups. Frequent visitors, on the other hand, visited a single physician or multiple physicians on a regular basis. These individuals included pregnant women, chemotherapy patients, AIDS patients, and dialysis patients. Finally, a patient agent is an individual who acts on the medical behalf of another. This could be a parent, a person caring for a seriously ill partner, or an adult child caring for an elderly parent.

Our Approach

It was decided that a W&N analysis would be a great starting point to understand how these types of patients differed in terms of what they want and need in a product that would allow them to choose a healthcare provider. The majority of participants were recruited through an online community job board. The remaining participants were recruited through word of mouth in our department. It took a couple of weeks to recruit all the users, with frequent visitors being the most difficult group to recruit. The wording for ads recruiting participants and the screener to schedule participants had to be worded carefully. We had to respect people's privacy and be considerate of their situation. We could be speaking to someone who is dealing with cancer or taking care of a dying parent. We also had to be mindful of people's potential situation during the W&N session. We needed to avoid probing questions that might embarrass a participant or ask for too much personal information in a group setting. Everything we created was proofread by the product team (many of whom were physicians and registered nurses themselves) as well as by other members of our group.

Each session lasted two hours. All three user types were in separate sessions but were asked the same two questions. In the first hour, participants were asked what information they wanted and needed to know in order to select a new provider. In the second hour, participants were asked what tasks they would perform with an ideal system that would help them manage their healthcare (or the healthcare of a loved one, in the case of patient agents). In this case study, I will discuss only the first question.

Because of the number of user types under investigation and the expense of recruiting so many participants, only one session of 10 participants each was conducted for a total of 30 participants. We hoped we could follow up with additional sessions but were unable to.

Analysis and Findings

The day after each session, the moderator and scribe met for an hour to sort the worksheets and discuss the results. Table 9.4 shows the results for frequent visitors. (For confidentiality reasons, the tables for healthy patients and patient agents are not shown in this study.)

After all three sessions were conducted, we compared the results across groups. We found that the majority of items appearing in the prioritized lists were the same but the percentage of users requesting often differed between groups. This reflected the different priorities of each group.

The largest percentage of users, regardless of group affiliation, wanted to know the qualifications of the provider they were considering. However, the next highest priority need varied between groups. Healthy individuals were concerned about insurance acceptance (70%). Patient agents were equally concerned with knowing the insurance information and location/hospital affiliation (60% each). However, frequent visitors

Piece of information	Exemplars	Percentage of users requesting it
Qualifications	• Experience • Certification • Educational background (degree, major) • Languages spoken • Specialty • Success ratio	90% (9 of 10)
Doctor/patient ratio	• Amount of time provider spends per patient • Amount of time provider keeps patient waiting • How long does it take to get an appointment?	70% (7 of 10)
Communicating with the provider	• Can the provider be reached via e-mail, phone, or in person (appointment) only?	40% (4 of 10)
Style/philosophy	• Attitude toward alternative treatments • Manner/communication style • Seek aggressive treatments or laid back?	40% (4 of 10)
Insurance information	• Type of insurance accepted and not accepted	40% (4 of 10)
Patient feedback	• Satisfaction ratings	30% (3 of 10)
Specialist referrals	• Will the provider make referrals when he/she isn't knowledgeable about something or does he/she try to treat everything? • Is the provider free to make referrals when necessary or does the provider have to get permission first?	30% (3 of 10)
Location	• Address	30% (3 of 10)
Availability of advice nurse	• Do they have a 24-hour advice nurse to answer questions?	20% (2 of 10)
"Black marks"	• Lawsuits/malpractice suits against the provider • Patient mortality rate	20% (2 of 10)
Staff qualifications	–	10% (1 of 10)
Convenience	• Can you get the service close to you during the hours you need for a reasonable price? • Does the provider make house calls?	10% (1 of 10)
Hospital affiliation	• Does this provider belong to a hospital with a good reputation?	10% (1 of 10)
Office hours	–	10% (1 of 10)

Table 9.4:

Prioritized list of information frequent visitors requested when selecting a new provider

preferred to know the doctor/patient ratio rather than insurance acceptance (70% compared to 40%).

We determined that, because the core user requirements were the same across user types, the differences between user types were not significant enough to warrant different interfaces for each user type. This list of information and tasks wanted/needed was added into the functional specification of the product. In addition, these findings were used to determine the fields for the prototype's advanced-search screen that enables users to find a provider. The results were also used to determine what details are displayed when a provider is found.

The W&N analysis was valuable for the product design because participants shared with us their concerns when selecting a healthcare provider. The development team was unaware of many of the concerns participants had and realized they could easily be addressed in the design of the product. This information was used by the team in the generation of their first prototype.

Lessons Learned

We knew it would be difficult to recruit frequent visitors, but we didn't realize how difficult. In addition to the moderator, an intern spent several hours interviewing participants and asking both patient agents and healthy patients whether they could recommend any frequent visitors for the session. We now know that at least three weeks should be allowed to recruit difficult user profiles.

In addition, we would have preferred to break the groups of ten into two groups of five for each user type. That might have made the frequent visitors more comfortable when speaking in front of a smaller group. The added benefit would have been having groups to validate the findings against. It would have taken an additional three days but we think it would have been worth it.

CHAPTER 10

CARD SORTING

Introduction

Creating a product that has a logical **information architecture** is critical to the success of your product. Information architecture refers to the organization of a product's structure and content, the labeling and categorizing of information, and the design of navigation and search systems. A good architecture helps users find information and accomplish their tasks with ease. Card sorting is one method that can help you understand how users think the information and navigation should be within your product.

This method involves writing objects that are in – or proposed to be in – your product (e.g., hotel reservation, rental car agreement) on cards and asking users to sort the cards into meaningful groups. The objects are pieces of information or tasks that are – or will be – in your product. You want to understand how the users think those objects should be organized. You then strive to replicate these groupings in your product. By doing so, users will be able to easily find what they are looking for when using your product.

In this chapter, we discuss uses for card sorting, how to prepare for and conduct a card sort, and how to analyze and present the information. Several modifications are presented at the end to help you customize the method to your particular needs. Finally, a case study by Redish & Associates, Inc. is offered so that you may see how an industry icon has used card sorting with success.

At a Glance

> When should you conduct a card sort?
> Things to be aware of when conducting a card sort
> Group or individual card sort?
> Preparing to conduct a card sort
> Conducting a card sort
> Data analysis and interpretation
> Communicate the findings
> Modifications

When Should You Conduct a Card Sort?

Card sorting is excellent for situations where you want the users' **mental model** to drive the information architecture of the product. You should use it anytime you need feedback about the content, terminology, and organization of your product.

Unfortunately, many developers design products to conform to their own mental model of a domain. They may base their decisions about the information architecture or product's layout on the underlying technology (e.g., the database). In the case of designing a website, some companies mirror their organizational or departmental hierarchy. Users are rarely aware of the developer's point of view, the underlying technology, or the company's departmental organization. As a result, they will have difficulty using a product designed based on those considerations. There have been cases where it has taken us a month of working with the development team to get a list of objects within the product and definitions that everyone can agree upon. This happens when the product is not well defined or each person on the team has a different understanding of the product. The exercise of identifying objects and defining them can be eye-opening for the development team and demonstrate the need for a card sort as well as other **usability** activities.

You can do a card sort for entire sets of information (e.g., a website's entire information architecture) or for subsets of information (e.g., the information within a specific web page). In a large product, different sections have different users. In this case, you will likely want to conduct a card sort on each section by users most likely to use it. Additionally, you can compare novice versus expert mental models.

There are several types of information that you can obtain with a card sort:

- Overall organization of the content or tasks in your product
- Terminology employed by users
- Labels users apply to different categories of information or tasks
- Missing objects
- Unnecessary objects.

Things To Be Aware of When Conducting a Card Sort

Users may not always have optimal mental models (Nielsen & Sano 1994). Designing a system based on flawed user mental models can clearly hamper user performance. For this reason, you should avoid including users in your card sort with no or little experience in the domain of concern. Obviously, if a user does not understand a domain well and have experience in it, that person's mental model will not be as efficient or even correct as that of others who do.

Group or Individual Card Sort?

You need to decide whether to conduct your card sort with several participants at once or one at a time. We conduct these sessions with several participants simultaneously because this allows us to collect large samples of data in a short period. You can conduct a card sort with as many people at a time as you physically have room for. Even though we have a group of participants in the same room at the same time, they are not working together – they are each working individually.

The disadvantage with running several participants simultaneously is that you cannot collect think-aloud data, so you do not know why the users grouped the data the way they did. (Refer to Chapter 6, During Your User Requirements Activity, "Introducing Your Think-aloud Protocol" section, page 218.) Although think-aloud data are helpful, participants typically provide enough information in their description of each group so that the need to collect data quickly and from large samples outweighs the benefit of having think-aloud data.

Some people dislike running a group card sort because they feel that the participants turn it into a race. In our experience this has not been a problem. We encourage people to take their time because we will be there for as long as they need to sort the cards.

If you have the time, a hybrid approach works quite well: After collecting data from a group of participants, run one or two individual card sorts to collect think-aloud data. This additional data can help you better understand the groupings.

Preparing to Conduct a Card Sort

Are You Ready?

Before you begin *any* **user requirements** activity there are a number of things that you must be familiar with. Because these elements are common to all user requirements activities, they have been covered in the earlier chapters – but now is a good time to double-check the list. If you are not familiar with one of the items you can refer to the earlier chapter to brush up or familiarize yourself with that element.

Chapter 1: Introduction to User Requirements
  ☐ Get **stakeholder** buy-in for your activity (see page 14)

Chapter 2: Before You Choose an Activity
  ☐ **Learn about your product** (see page 29)
  ☐ **Learn about your users** (see page 41)

Chapter 3: Ethical and Legal Considerations
  ☐ **Create consent forms** (see page 98)
  ☐ **Create confidential disclosure agreements** (see page 103)

Chapter 4: Setting up Facilities for Your User Requirements Activity
  ☐ **Create or acquire a facility for your activity** (see page 106)

Now that we have presented when and why to conduct a card sort, we will discuss how to prepare for one.

Preparation Timeline

The timeline in Table 10.1 covers in detail the sequence and timing of events to prepare for a card sort. These are *approximate* times based on our personal experience and should be used only as a guide. It could take longer or less time for each step depending on a variety of factors, such as responsiveness of the development team, access to users, and resources available. It can take as long as a month or as little as two days to identify the objects for the sort and develop clear definitions. The time it takes to create the cards depends on the number of cards and participants needed; but on average it can take about three and a half hours to create enough cards for 60 objects and ten participants.

Table 10.1:

Preparation timeline for

a card sort

When to complete	Approximate time to complete	Activity
As soon as possible	1–2 weeks	☐ Meet with team to identify and define objects ☐ Meet with team to develop user profile
After identification of objects and profile	3 hours	☐ Create and distribute proposal
After the proposal has been agreed to by all stakeholders	2 weeks	☐ Identify and recruit users ☐ Prepare materials ☐ Assign roles for the activity (e.g., moderator) ☐ Acquire location ☐ Acquire incentives ☐ Prepare documentation (e.g., CDA, informed consent form) ☐ Order food (optional)
1 week before activity	2 days	☐ Conduct pilot ☐ Make necessary changes to cards and procedure based on pilot
Day before card sort	1 hour	☐ Call and confirm with participant(s)
Day of card sort	3 hours	☐ Create and place "Welcome" sign in lobby ☐ Set up location with all materials necessary ☐ Pick up food (optional)

At a Glance

> Identify objects and definitions for sorting

> Activity materials

> Additional data collected in a card sort

> Players in your activity

> Inviting observers

Identify Objects and Definitions for Sorting

There are several ways to obtain your objects (i.e., pieces of information or tasks) and definitions for sorting. The first and most frequent method is to work with the development team to identify the objects and then develop clear definitions. The creation of definitions can be surprisingly time-consuming since the development team may define things in terms of the way the back-end or technical components of the product works. It is your job to make sure the definitions are clear and easy for participants to understand. Without those definitions, you cannot be sure that you and the participants are on the same page, speaking the same language.

In cases when your product is still in the conceptual stage, you may not have a determined list of content or tasks for the product. While still working with the development team, you may need to supplement your knowledge with input from the marketing department or a competitive analysis (refer to Chapter 2, Before You Choose an Activity, "Learn About Your Product" section, page 29). You may find it beneficial to do a wants and needs (W&N) analysis (see Chapter 9, page 370) to learn about the information or tasks you would like to have in your product. You will need to ensure that, during the brainstorming portion of the W&N analysis, you clearly understand what each idea means so that you can write complete definitions for your card sort.

If a version of the product already exists and your goal is to re-architect the product, you and the team can together identify the possible areas to re-architect. Once you have done this, you can make a list of all the objects contained within these areas. If there are objects that will be omitted in the next release, you should omit these from the card sort. Conversely, if there are new objects that the product team intends to add to the product, you should certainly include these.

Finally, you can also obtain objects for a card sort by asking participants to free-list all the items associated with a given domain (i.e., participants write down every phrase or word associated with a particular topic, domain, etc.). This is a brainstorming activity similar to a W&N analysis and can be done either individually or as a group. The difference is that, in free-listing, you are asking participants to name every "item" they can think of that is associated with a domain – not just the ones they want for a given product or system. Using our travel example from other chapters, we might want to ask participants to name every piece of information they can think of that is associated with making travel reservations. Some responses might be: plane ticket, car rental, hotel room, confirmation number, and frequent-flyer miles.

How many participants are needed for this kind of free-listing activity? The answer is: "It depends." The best way to determine the appropriate number is to conduct the activity with five or six participants, tally the results to see the number of participants identifying each object, and then see how those results change by adding one or two new participants. If the results are stable, no further participants are needed.

The benefit of both the W&N analysis and free-listing is that you obtain information about the users' terminology because they are offering their ideas in their own language.

We have found that it is best to limit the number of objects to be sorted at 90 or less, because participants cannot keep more than that in their mind at one time. However, there are studies where more cards have been used. One study was found to use 500 cards (Tullis 1985)! We would not recommend this. Keep in mind that the more cards there are to sort, the longer it will take for the participants to sort and the more you will fatigue and overwhelm them. In addition, sorts with large numbers of cards will take considerably longer to analyze.

Tip

If you plan to use a computer program to analyze the data, check for any limit to the number of cards or users it can handle. There often is a limit. Sometimes this information is buried in the "Release Notes" or "Known Bugs."

Although it may seem unnecessary to run a pilot session for a card sort, it helps to have several individuals review the objects and definitions on the cards. A fresh set of eyes can find typos or identify confusing definitions and terms. In addition, a pilot can help you get a sense of how long it will take for participants to complete the sort, and determine whether you missed any objects.

Activity Materials

You will need the following materials for a card sort:

☐ 3 in × 5 in index cards (different colored cards is optional)
☐ Printer labels (optional)
☐ Stapler
☐ Rubber bands

☐ Envelopes

☐ Plenty of workspace for a participant to spread out the cards.

Tip

To save time during data collection, card sorts can be conducted as a group. If you are running the sort as a group, you will need three different colors of index cards. When participants are sitting next to each other, it is easy for cards to get mixed up. You don't want to hear participants ask "Are those my cards or yours?" Alternate the colors of the cards between users sitting next to or across from each other.

To create the cards, type the name of the object, a blank space, and the definition of the object on a sticky printer label (see Figure 10.1). You can also add an example of the object, if you feel it will help users understand the object. Make sure that you use at least a 12-point font. It is easy to create a file of the objects and then print out several sheets. You can then quickly stick labels on the cards. Alternatively, you could buy sheets of punch-out index cards and print directly onto the sheets; however, we have found them only in white.

The number of index cards needed (C) can be computed by multiplying the number of objects in the sort (O) by the number of participants you intend to recruit (P):

$$C = O \times P$$

Attributes of the Hotel Room	Vacation Packages
The various benefits or accommodations of the hotel room. Some examples include: non-smoking, mini bar, king size bed, ocean view.	Travel packages that typically include air travel, hotel and rental cars often for a discounted price.
Destinations	Customer Reviews
A list of places where you can arrange to travel to.	Reviews of a product or service written by customers who have used it.

Figure 10.1:

Replication of several cards used in card sorting exercise (reduced size)

So if you have 50 objects and ten participants, you will need 500 index cards. We recommend providing about 20 blank cards per participant for labeling their groups.

Additional Data Collected in a Card Sort

Of course, the main type of data you will collect in a card sort relates to the information architecture, but you can collect additional information. There are five types of changes participants can make to the cards you provide:

- Delete an object
- Add a new object
- Rename an object
- Change a definition
- Place an object in multiple groups.

Any of the changes that participants make to the cards must be analyzed manually (covered later – see page 438). Often, the additional information that you obtain by allowing participants to make these changes justifies the additional work. However, it is a decision for you to make.

Delete an object

If a participant does not think an object belongs in the domain, he or she can remove it. For example, if you have the object "School bus" in a card sort for your travel website, a participant may want to remove it because in that person's experience, school buses are never provided as an option on travel websites. Additionally, you may allow participants to delete a card if they do not use the object in real life.

Allowing participants to remove cards reveals whether you are providing users with content or tasks that are unnecessary – which represent "noise" for the user to deal with. It can also reveal whether you (or the development team) have an incorrect perception of the domain (e.g., providing school buses on a travel website). However, you may have a product where all of your features must be included for business reasons. If this is the case you would not want to allow participants to create a "discard" pile.

Add a new object

As participants read through the cards, they begin to understand the depth and breadth of information or tasks your product supports. They may realize that certain information or tasks are missing from the sort, and therefore from your product. Using our travel example, a participant may notice that "Airport code" is missing from the sort and adds it in. Perhaps this was left out because the development team thought that the full name of the airport was more helpful and the airport code is unnecessary. Allowing participants to add cards points out information or tasks that users expect to have in your product. You should also ask users to define any objects they add and state why they are adding them.

Rename objects

As we mentioned at the beginning of the chapter, you can collect information about terminology in a card sort. You might present participants with an object they are familiar with, but in their opinion the name of the object and definition do not match up. Sometimes differences exist between companies or different parts of the country, or there is an industry standard term that you were not aware of. Technical jargon or abbreviations that we are not aware of are sometimes used in the workplace, or users may simply have another term for the object in their workplace. By allowing participants to change the names of your objects, you collect information about terminology that you may not have had before.

Change a definition

Providing a definition for each term ensures that everyone is on the same page. This is critical when asking participants to organize information. If everyone has a different understanding of the objects they are sorting, there will be no consensus in the organization of the cards. Sometimes, the definitions provided are incomplete or not quite right, so allow participants to make additions, deletions, or word changes to the definitions. For example, you may have defined a certain object as "standard" or "best practice" but the participants point out that the object is just one of many practices and not necessarily the best practice or even the standard. This is important for you to know.

Place an object in multiple groups

Sometimes participants tell you that a single object belongs in multiple locations. In order to do this, a participant would need to create a duplicate card. This adds some complexity to the data analysis but you may want to collect this information (see "Data Analysis and Interpretation," page 432). You want to understand where an object *best* fits, so ask participants to place the card provided in the best group. Then, ask them to create as many duplicate cards as necessary and place them in the additional locations.

Players in Your Activity

Of course you will need end users to take part, but you will also require other people to help conduct the activity. In this section, we discuss the details of all the players involved in a card sort session.

The participants

A study recently conducted with 168 participants found that a card sort with only 20–30 participants can yield an average correlation coefficient of well over 0.9 (Tullis & Wood 2004). Beyond 30 participants, you get diminishing returns. We typically run one or two group sessions with 10–12 participants of the same user type. If you are short on time and resources, however, run six or eight participants and analyze the data. Add an additional couple of participants and see whether the addition of each new user changes the groupings (this is a good time to collect think-aloud data). If the results are stable and the major groups do not change, there is no need to run additional participants.

All participants should meet the same **user profile** (refer to Chapter 2, Before You Choose an Activity, "Learn About Your Users" section, page 41). If you wish to compare user types (e.g., novice versus expert), we recommend using the analysis technique above (i.e., run six or eight of each type, analyze the data, add a couple more, see how the groups change, determine whether more participants are needed). It is not advisable to mix user types. If different user types sort information differently, you may need to create a different interface for each user type. Mixing the user types in the same sort washes out those differences and could result in an interface that no one can use. Refer to Chapter 5, Preparing for Your User

Requirements Activity, "Recruiting Participants" section, page 156 for more information.

The facilitator

Only one facilitator is needed for the activity, whether it is conducted as a group or individually. If you run a group, it helps to have a co-worker as an extra pair of hands but that is optional. The job of the facilitator is to provide initial instructions, distribute the materials, answer any questions along the way, and then collect the materials. If run as a group, the majority of the session is spent sitting quietly, answering any questions, and making sure people are not comparing their sorts. If run individually, the facilitator must be familiar with the think-aloud protocol and how to instruct participants in it (refer to Chapter 6, During Your User Requirements Activity, "Introducing Your Think-aloud Protocol" section, page 218). The facilitator will also need to take notes of what a participant is thinking, and it is advisable to record the session in case you miss something.

The videographer

If you are conducting the card sort as a group, there is no discussion to videotape, but if conducting the sort individually, it is beneficial to record so that you can capture the think-aloud data. You will find a detailed discussion of videotaping tips and the benefits of videotape in Chapter 6, During Your User Requirements Activity, "Recording and Note-taking" section, page 226. If you plan to record, make sure that someone takes responsibility for this task. It is ideal if you can have someone to monitor the video equipment during the session in case something goes wrong; but if that is not possible, set up the shot, hit "Record," and hope that nothing goes wrong.

Inviting Observers

If you are conducting the card sort as a group, there is nothing for an observer to see except a room full of people silently grouping cards. If the session is conducted individually, stakeholders will find it interesting to hear why people group objects the way they do. Refer to Chapter 6, During Your User Requirements Activity, "Inviting Observers" section (page 216) for more information.

Conducting a Card Sort

You have prepared for the card sort and now you need to actually conduct the session (see Figure 10.2). Whether conducted with a group or individually, the steps are the same. Some minor differences in instructions are noted below.

Figure 10.2:

The action! As you can see, participants do not need a lot of space

Activity Timeline

The timeline in Table 10.2 shows the sequence and timing of events to conduct a card sort. These are *approximate* times based on our personal experience and should

Table 10.2:

Timeline for conducting a card sort

Approximate duration	Procedure
3 minutes	Welcome participants (introductions, forms)
5 minutes	Conduct a card sort practice
3 minutes	Instructions
30–100 minutes	Card sorting
5 minutes	Wrap-up (distribute incentives, thank participants, escort them out)

be used only as a guide. The overall length of the session will obviously depend on the number of cards to be sorted. As we mentioned earlier, participants can typically sort 50–70 cards in a one-hour session.

Welcome the Participants

This is the time during which you greet your participants, allow them to eat some snacks, ask them to fill out paperwork, and get them warmed-up. The details of these stages are described in Chapter 6, During Your User Requirements Activity, "Welcoming Your Participants" section, page 209.

Practice

Upon their arrival, explain to the participant(s) that the purpose of the activity is to gain an understanding of how people group a set of concepts. We then begin with a practice exercise so that they understand exactly what we will be doing. We typically write about 12–15 types of zoo animals on a flip chart or whiteboard (e.g., grizzly bear, ape, polar bear, monkey). We then ask participants to call out animals that they think belong in the same group (e.g., polar bear and grizzly bear). We circle the items and then ask them to name that group (e.g., bears). See Figure 10.3 for an example.

Card Review and Sorting

Once everyone is comfortable with the concept, distribute the cards and provide some instructions. You can use the following sample script:

"We are currently designing *<insert product description>* and we need to understand how to best organize the *<information or tasks>* in the product. This will help users of the product find what they are looking for more easily.

"On each of the cards we have written a *<piece of information or task>* in our proposed product, along with a description of it. Please read through all of the cards and make sure both the terms and definitions make sense. If the terms or definitions do not make sense, please make corrections directly on the cards. Use the blank line to rename the object to something that makes more sense to you. In addition, please let me know what changes you are making so I can be sure that I understand what you are writing.

"Once you have reviewed all the cards, you may begin sorting them into groups that belong together. There are no right or wrong answers. Although there may be multiple ways you can group these concepts, please provide us with the groupings that you feel make the most sense. When you are sorting, you may place any cards that do not belong (or that you do not use, do not understand, etc.) in a discard pile, and you may use the blank cards to add any objects that are missing. If you feel that a particular card belongs in more than one location, please place the card provided in the *best* location you believe it fits. Use the blank cards to create as many duplicate cards as necessary and place those in the secondary groups.

"When you have completed your sort, use the blank cards to name each of your piles."

If this is a group card sort, add: "Please do not work with your neighbor on this. We want to understand how *you* think these cards should be grouped. We do not want a group effort – so please don't look at your neighbors' cards." If this is an individual sort, state: "I would like for you to think-aloud as you work. Tell me what you are thinking as you are grouping the cards. If you go quiet, I will prompt you for feedback." (Refer to Chapter 6, During Your User Requirements Activity, "Introducing Your Think-aloud Protocol" section, page 218, for more information.)

Whenever participants make a change to a card, we strongly encourage them to tell us about it. It helps us to understand why they are making the change. In a group session, it offers us the opportunity to discuss the change with the group. We typically ask questions like

"John just made a good point. He refers to a 'travel reservation' as a 'travel booking.' Does anyone else call it that?"

or

"Jane noticed that 'couples-only resorts' is missing. Does anyone else book 'couples-only resorts?'"

If anyone nods in agreement, we ask him/her to discuss the issue. We then ask all the participants who agree to make the same change to their card(s). Participants may not think to make a change until it is brought to their attention, otherwise they may believe they are the only ones who feel a certain way and do not want to be "different." Encouraging the discussion helps us decide whether an issue is pervasive or limited to only one individual.

Participants typically make terminology and definition changes while they are reviewing the cards. They may also notice objects that do not belong and remove them during the review process. Most often, adding missing cards and deleting cards that do not belong are not done until the sorting stage – as participants begin to organize the information.

Labeling Groups

Once the sorting is complete, the participants need to name each of the groups. Give the following instructions:

> "Now I would like for you to name each of your groups. How would you describe the cards in each of these piles? You can use a single word, phrase, or sentence. Please write the name of each group on one of the blank cards and place it on top of the group. Once you have finished, please staple each group together, or if it is too large to staple, use a rubber band. Finally, place all of your bound groups in the envelope provided."

Tip

We prefer to staple the groups together because we do not want cards falling out. If your cards get mixed with others, your data will be ruined; so make sure your groups are secured and that each participant's groups remain separate! We mark each envelope with the participant's number and seal it until it is time to analyze the data. This prevents cards from being confused between participants.

Data Analysis and Interpretation

There are several ways to analyze the plethora of data you will collect in a card sort exercise. We describe here how to analyze the data via programs designed specifically for card sort analysis as well as with statistical packages (e.g., *SPSS, SAS, Statistica*™) and spreadsheets. We also show how to analyze data that computer programs cannot handle. Finally, we walk you through an example to demonstrate how to interpret the results of your study.

When testing a small number of participants (four or less) and a limited number of cards, some evaluators simply "eyeball" the card groupings. This is not precise and can quickly become unmanageable when the number of participants increases. Cluster analysis allows you to quantify the data by calculating the strength of the perceived relationships between pairs of cards, based on the frequency with which members of each possible pair appear together. In other words, how frequently did participants pair two cards together in the same group? The results are usually presented in a tree diagram or **dendrogram** (see Figures 10.4 and 10.5 for two examples). This presents the distance between pairs of objects, with 0.00 being closest and 1.00 being the maximum distance. A distance of 1.00 means that none of the participants paired the two particular cards together; whereas 0.00 means that every participant paired those two cards together.

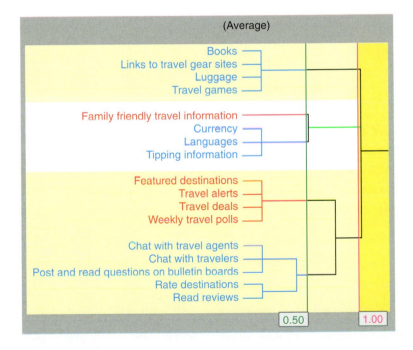

Figure 10.4:

Dendrogram for our travel website using EZCalc

Figure 10.5:

Tree diagram of WebCAT data analysis for an e-mail system

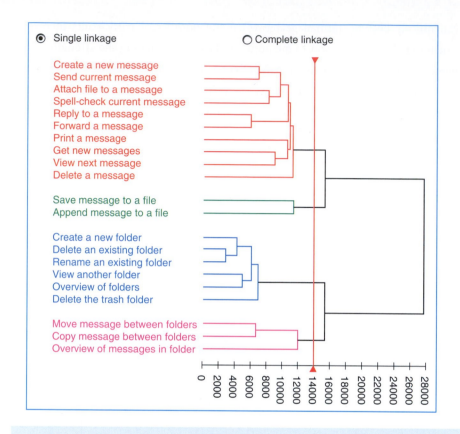

Brief Description of How Programs Cluster Items

Cluster analysis can be complex, but we can describe it only briefly here. To learn more about it, refer to Aldenderfer & Blashfield (1984), Lewis (1991), or Romesburg (1984).

The actual math behind cluster analysis can vary a bit, but the technique used in most computer programs is called the "amalgamation" method. Clustering begins with every item being its own single-item cluster. Let's continue with our travel example. Below are eight items from a card sort:

Hotel reservation	Airplane ticket	Rental auto	Rental drop-off point
Frequent-guest credit	Frequent-flyer miles	Rental pick-up point	Featured destinations

Participants sort the items into groups. Then every item's difference score with every other item is computed (i.e., considered pair-by-pair). Those with the closest (smallest) difference scores are then joined. The more participants who paired two items together, the shorter the distance. However, not all the items are necessarily paired at this step. It is entirely possible (and in fact most probable) that some or many items will not be joined with anything until a later "round" or more than two items may be joined. So after "round 1," you may have:

- Hotel reservation *and* Frequent-guest credit
- Airplane ticket *and* Frequent-flyer miles
- Rental auto, Pick-up point, *and* Drop-off point
- Featured destinations

Now that you have several groups comprised of items, the question is: "How do you continue to join clusters?" There are several different amalgamation (or linkage) rules available to decide how groups should next be clustered, and some programs allow you to choose the rule used. Below is a description of three common rules.

Single linkage

If any members of the groups are very similar (i.e., small distance score because many participants have sorted them together), the groups will be joined. So if "Frequent-guest credit" and "Frequent-flyer miles" are extremely similar, it does not matter how different "Hotel reservation" is from "Airplane ticket" (see "round 1" groupings above); they will be grouped in "round 2."

This method is commonly called the "nearest neighbor" method, because it takes only two near neighbors to join both groups. Single linkage is useful for producing long strings of loosely related clusters. It focuses on the similarities among groups.

Complete linkage

This is effectively the opposite of single linkage. Complete linkage considers the most dissimilar pair of items when determining whether to join groups. Therefore, it doesn't matter how extremely similar "Frequent-guest credit" and "Frequent-flyer miles" are; if "Hotel reservation" and "Airplane ticket" are extremely dissimilar (because few participants sorted them together), they will *not* be joined into the same cluster at this stage (see "round 1" groupings above).

Not surprisingly, this method is commonly called the "furthest neighbor" method, because the joining rule considers the difference score of the most dissimilar (i.e., largest difference) pairs. Complete linkage is useful for producing very tightly related groups.

Average linkage

This method attempts to balance the two methods above by taking the average of the difference scores for all the pairs when deciding whether groups should be joined. So the difference score between "Frequent-guest credit" and "Frequent-flyer miles" may be low (very similar), and the difference score of "Hotel reservation" and "Airplane ticket" may be high but, when averaged, the overall difference score will be somewhere in the middle (see "round 1" groupings above). Now the program will look at the averaged score to decide whether "Hotel reservation" and "Frequent-guest credit" should be joined with "Airplane ticket" and "Frequent-flyer miles," or whether the first group is closer to the third group, "Rental auto" and "Rental pick-up point."

SUGGESTED RESOURCES FOR ADDITIONAL READING

If you would like to learn more about cluster analysis, you can refer to:

- Aldenderfer, M. S. & Blashfield, R. K. (1984). *Cluster Analysis*. Sage University paper series on Quantitative Applications in the Social Sciences, #07-044. Beverly Hills, CA.
- Lewis, S. (1991). Cluster Analysis as a Technique to Guide Interface Design. *Journal of Man–Machine Studies*, 10, 267–280.
- Romesburg, C. H. (1984). *Cluster Analysis for Researchers*. Belmont, CA: Lifetime Learning Publications (Wadsworth).

You can analyze the data from a card sort with a software program specifically designed for card sorting or with any standard statistics package. We will describe each of the programs available and why you would use it.

At a Glance

> Analysis with a card sorting program
> Analysis with a statistics package
> Analysis with a spreadsheet package
> Data that computer programs cannot handle
> Interpreting the results

Analysis with a Card Sorting Program

At the time of publication, there are at least four programs available on the web that are designed specifically for analyzing card sort data:

- IBM's *USort/EZCalc*®
  (www-3.ibm.com/ibm/easy/eou_ext.nsf/Publish/410)
- NIST's *WebCAT*®
  (http://zing.ncsl.nist.gov/WebTools/WebCAT/overview.html)
- *WebSort* (www.websort.net/) which uses *EZCalc* to analyze the data
- *CardZort/CardCluster* (http://condor.depaul.edu/~jtoro/cardzort/cardzort.htm)

Data analysis using these tools has been found to be quicker and easier than using manual methods (Zavod, Rickert, & Brown 2002).

Analysis with a Statistics Package

Statistical packages like *SAS*, *SPSS*, and *Statistica* are not as easy to use as specialized card sort programs when analyzing card sort data; but when you have over 100 cards in a sort, *USort/EZCalc* and *WebCAT* cannot be used. A program like *SPSS* is necessary, but any package that has cluster analysis capabilities will do.

Analysis with a Spreadsheet Package

Most card sort programs have a maximum number of cards that they can support. If you have a very large set of cards, a spreadsheet (e.g., Microsoft Excel, Lotus™ Notes) can be used for analysis The discussion of how to accomplish this is complex and beyond the scope of this book. You can find an excellent, step-by-step description of analyzing the data with a spreadsheet tool at www.boxesandarrows.com/archives/analyzing_card_sort_results_with_a_spreadsheet_template.php.

Data that Computer Programs Cannot Handle

Computer programs can be great, but they often do not do all of the analysis for you. Below are some of the issues that we have encountered when using different electronic programs. Although the data analysis for these elements is a little awkward, we think the value that the data bring makes them worth collecting.

Adding or renaming objects

One of the basic requirements of cluster analysis is that all participants must have the exact same set of cards in terms of name and number. If participants renamed any of the objects or if they added any cards, you will not be able to add this information into the program. You will need to record this information for each participant on a sheet of paper and analyze it separately. The number of cards added or changed tends to be very small but it is an extra step to take. Returning to our earlier example, you notice that participant 1 added the object "airport code." Write this down and then tally the number of other participants who did the same thing. At the end, you will likely have a small list of added and renamed objects, along with the number of participants who made those changes. Based on the number of participants who added it, you can assess its importance.

Group names

The group names that participants provide are not presented in the analysis. You will need to record the pile names that participants suggested and do your best to match them to the results. We typically write down the names of each group for each participant and look for similarities at the end. How many participants created an "Airline Travel" group? How many created a "Hotel" group? When examining the dendrogram, you will notice clusters of objects. See if there is a match between those clusters and the names of the groups that participants created.

Duplicate objects

As we discussed earlier, sometimes participants ask to place an item in multiple locations. Because the computer programs available do not allow you to enter the same card more than once and you must have the same number of cards for each participant, include the original card in the group the participant placed it. The duplicate cards placed in the secondary groups will have to be examined and noted manually.

Deleted objects

EZCalc is the only program we are aware of that can handle discards automatically. Many computer programs cannot deal with deleted cards. For these programs, if you have allowed participants to create a discard or miscellaneous pile of cards that they do not believe belong in the sort, there is a workaround you need to do. You cannot enter this collection of discarded cards as a group into a computer program since the cluster analysis would treat these cards as a group of objects that participants believe are related. In reality, these cards are not related to any of the other cards. Place each rejected card in a group by itself to demonstrate that it is not related to any other card in the cluster analysis. For example, if participants placed "Frequent Flyer Miles," "Companions," and "Meal Requests" in the discard pile, you should enter "Frequent Flyer Miles" in one group, "Companions" in a second group, and "Meal Requests" in a third group.

Interpreting the Results

You now have a collection of rich data. The dendrogram displays groups of objects that the majority of participants believe belong together.

Changes that participants make to cards can make interpretation of the results tricky. When a deleted object is repeatedly placed in a group by itself (or left out, in the case of *EZCalc*), you may see it on a branch by itself or loosely attached to a group that it really doesn't belong with. Additionally, if participants place an object in multiple groups, they may not have agreed on the "best" location to place it. Consequently, you may find the object is living on a branch by itself or loosely attached to a group that it really doesn't belong with. You must use your knowledge of the domain or product to make adjustments when ambiguity exists. Use the additional data you collected like new objects, group names, changed terminology, and think-aloud data to help interpret the data.

Let's walk through our travel example and interpret the results of our dendrogram shown earlier in Figure 10.4. Using our domain knowledge and the group labels participants provided in the card sort, we have named each of the clusters in the dendrogram (see Figure 10.6). We appear to have four clear groups: "Products," "Resources," "News," and "Opinions."

It is important to note that the card sort methodology will not provide you with information about *type* of architecture you should use (e.g., tabs, menus). This decision must be made by a design professional. Instead, the tree diagram demonstrates

Figure 10.6:

Dendrogram of a travel website card sort with group names added

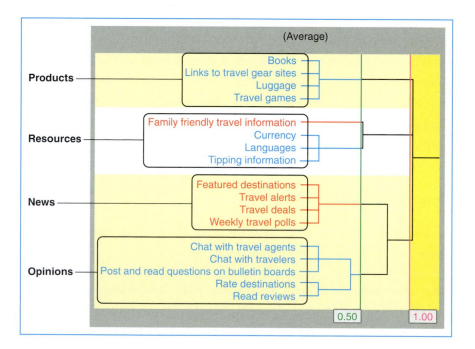

how participants expect to find information grouped. In the case of a web-based application with tabs, the tree may present the recommended name of the tab and the elements that should be contained within that particular tab.

Now you should examine the list of changes that participants made (e.g., renamed cards, additional cards) to discover whether there is high agreement among participants.

- What objects did participants feel you were missing?
- What objects did participants feel did not belong?
- What are all of the terminology changes participants made?
- What definitions did participants change?
- What items did users want in multiple locations?

Use this information to determine whether your product needs to add or remove information or tasks in order to be useful to participants. You may recommend to the team that they conduct a competitive analysis (if they haven't already) to discover whether other products support such functionality. Similarly, use the information about deleted objects to recommend that the team examine whether specific information or tasks are unnecessary.

Terminology can be specific to a company, area of the country, or individual. With each terminology change, you will need to investigate whether it is a "standard" – and therefore needs to be incorporated – or whether there are several different possible terms. When several terms exist, you will want to use the most common term but allow your product to be customized so that it is clear to all your users.

Finally, examine the definition changes. Were the changes minor – simply an issue of clarification? If so, there isn't anything to change in your product. If, however, there were many changes, you have an issue. This may mean that the product development team does not have a good grasp of the domain, or that there is disagreement within the team about what certain features of the product do.

Communicate the Findings

Preparing To Communicate Your Findings

The specific data that you communicate to product teams can vary depending upon the activity you conducted, but some elements of *how* you communicate the results are the same regardless of the method. Because these strategies are common to all user requirements activities, they are discussed in detail in Chapter 14, Concluding Your Activity, page 636. We recommend that you read that chapter prior to relaying your results to your stakeholders. Topics discussed include:

- ☐ **Prioritization of your findings** (see page 638)
- ☐ **Creating an effective presentation** (see page 644)
- ☐ **Writing valuable reports for different audiences** (see page 652)
- ☐ **Ensuring the incorporation of your findings** (see page 660)

When we present the results of a card sort analysis to executives or teams, we present the actual dendrogram generated by the application (as in Figure 10.6) and a simple table to review (see Figure 10.7). We also present a table of changes that participants made to the cards (added objects, deleted objects, terminology changes, and definition changes) and any sketches the designers may have produced to illustrate the recommendations. (Refer to Chapter 14, Concluding Your Activity, "Reporting Your Findings" section, page 652, to learn more about reporting usability results.)

As with all of the other user requirements methodologies, the card sort is a valuable addition to your software requirements documentation. These results can be incorporated into documentation such as the Detailed Design Document. Ideally, additional user requirements techniques should be used along the way to capture new requirements and verify your current requirements.

Tab name	Objects to be located within the tab
Resources	Tipping information Languages Currency Family friendly travel information
News	Travel deals Travel alerts Featured destinations Weekly travel polls
Opinions	Read reviews Post and read questions on bulletin boards Chat with travel agents Rate destinations
Products	Travel games Luggage Books Links to travel gear sites

Figure 10.7:

Travel card sort table of recommendations

Modifications

Below are a few modifications on the card sorting technique we have presented. You can limit the number of groups users can create, use computerized tools for the sort instead of physical cards, provide the groups for users to place the cards in, ask users to describe the items they would find in a particular category, or physically place groups that are related closer to each other.

Limit the Number of Groups

You may need to limit the number of groups a participant can create. For example, if you are designing a website and your company has a standard of no more than seven tabs, you can ask participants to create seven or fewer groups. Alternatively, you can initially allow participants to group the cards as they see fit; then, if they create more than seven groups, ask them to regroup their cards into higher-level groups. In the second case, you should staple all the lower-level groups together and then bind the higher-level groups together with a rubber band. This will allow you to see and analyze both levels of groupings.

Electronic Card Sorting

There are tools available that allow you to have the users sort the cards electronically rather than using physical cards (i.e., *USort*, *WebCAT*, *Classified*, *WebSort*, *Socratic CardSort*, *CardZort*). Electronic card sorting can save you time during the data analysis phase because the sorts are automatically saved in the computer. Another advantage is that, depending on the number of cards, users can see all of the cards available for sorting at the same time. Unless you have a very large work surface for users to spread their physical cards on, this is not possible for manual card sorts. Electronic sorting has the disadvantage that, if you run a group session, you will need a separate computer for each participant. This means money and potential technical issues. In addition, you need to provide a brief training session to explain how to use the software. Even with training, the user interface may be difficult for users to get the hang of.

Some tools support remote testing which allows you to gather data from users anywhere. However, users may have a more difficult time without a facilitator in the room to answer questions.

Unfortunately, none of the computer-based programs provides a definition with the objects. Also, they do not allow users to add, delete, or rename the objects. In our opinion, this is a serious shortcoming of the tools and the reason why we do not use them.

SUGGESTED RESOURCES FOR ADDITIONAL READING

The paper below provides a nice comparison of some of the automated card sorting tools available (at the time of publication) if electronic card sorting is of interest to you:

- Zavod, M. J., Rickert, D. E., & Brown, S. H. (2002). The Automated Card-sort as an Interface Design Tool: A Comparison of Products. *In Proceedings of the Human Factors and Ergonomics Society 46th Annual Meeting*, Baltimore, MD, 30 September–4 October, pp. 646–650.

Pre-name the Groups

You may already know the buckets that the objects being sorted must fit into. Going back to our website example, if you cannot completely redesign your site, you may want to provide participants with the names of each tab, section, or page of your site. Provide participants with a "placemat" for each group. The placemat should state the name of the group and provide a clear description of it. Participants would then be tasked with determining what objects fit into the predetermined groups.

To go one step further, you may have the structure for your entire application already laid out and simply want to find out whether you are correct. Applications like *Classified*® by Information and Design and UCDesign (www.infodesign.com.au/usabilityresources/classified/default.asp) and Socratic Technologies' *Socratic Card-Sort* (www.sotech.com/main/eval.asp?pID=123) can help you assess this (see Figures 10.8 and 10.9). These applications present users with the category names you pick and ask them to drop the predefined objects into the most appropriate category. Because the program appears to scold users when they do not place objects in the groups the product team chose ("Incorrect – please try again") and because it eventually trains users to think like the product team, we do not use *Classified*.

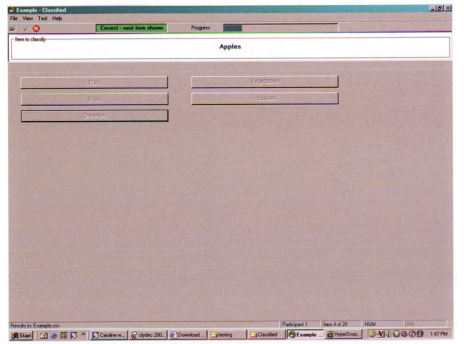

Figure 10.8a:

Screens from Classified. *If the participant selects the same category you placed the item in, a green box with the word "Correct" is shown*

Figure 10.8b:

Screens from Classified. *– Cont'd. If the participant does not select the same category, a red box with the word "Incorrect" is shown, and the instruction "Incorrect – please try again"*

Figure 10.9:

Spreadsheet containing Classified *output from one participant*

	A	B	C	D	E	F
1	Classified classification output file					
2	Created by Classified version 1.0					
3	Copyright (c) 1998/1999 UCDesign / Information & Design					
4	Classification output file: Example.csv initially created on Monday 22 December 2003 at 1:51:21 PM					
5	Classification input file: Example.txt					
6						
7	**Participant**	**Item**	**Actual Location**	**First Attempt**	**Second Attempt**	**Third Attempt**
8						
9	1	Turmeric	Spices	Spices		
10	1	Brie	Cheeses	Cheeses		
11	1	Haddock	Fish	Fish		
12	1	Apples	Fruit	Fruit		
13	1	Flounder	Fish	Vegetables	Fish	
14	1	Snow peas	Vegetables	Vegetables		
15	1	Coriander	Spices	Spices		
16	1	Spinach	Vegetables	Vegetables		
17	1	Cheddar	Cheeses	Cheeses		
18	1	Paw-paw	Fruit	Fish	Vegetables	Cheeses
19	1	Cod	Fish	Fish		
20	1	Kiwi	Fruit	Fruit		
21	1	Oranges	Fruit	Fruit		
22	1	Plaice	Fish	Spices	Fish	
23	1	Edam	Cheeses	Vegetables	Spices	Cheeses
24	1	Carrots	Vegetables	Vegetables		
25	1	Star anise	Spices	Fruit	Vegetables	Spices
26	1	Beans	Vegetables	Vegetables		
27	1	Nutmeg	Spices	Spices		
28	1	Bananas	Fruit	Fruit		
29						

Lessons Learned

The first time we used *EZSort* (IBM's predecessor to *USort/EZCalc*), we did not know that the program would choke if given over 90 cards. We prepared the material, ran the study, and then entered the data for 12 participants and 92 cards. When we hit the button to compute the results, it blew up. There was no warning and nothing to prevent us from making the mistake. It took extensive investigation to determine the cause of the problem, including contacting the creators of *EZSort*. By that point, there wasn't much we could do. We were forced to divide the data, enter it in chunks, and compute it. This had to be done several times so that the data overlapped. This was a painful lesson to learn. Rest assured that we never use a free program now without thoroughly reviewing the "Release Notes" and website from where we downloaded the program. We also look for other documents such as "Known Bugs."

Pulling It All Together

In this chapter, we have discussed what a card sort is, when you should conduct one, and things to be aware of. We also discussed how to prepare for and conduct a card sort, along with several modifications. Finally, we have demonstrated various ways to analyze the data and used our travel example to show you how to interpret and present the results.

Below, Ginny Redish presents a case study to share with readers how she recently employed a card sort to build the information architecture for a government website.

CASE STUDY

Ginny Redish conducted a card sort for the National Cancer Institute's Division of Cancer Prevention. Since she does not work for the National Cancer Institute, she describes how she worked as a consultant with the development team and gained the domain knowledge necessary to conduct the card sort. She describes in wonderful detail the process of understanding the user profile, identifying the objects for sorting, creating the materials, and recruiting the participants. She provides a unique perspective because she conducted the sort individually with think-aloud protocol and opted not to use cluster analysis software.

How Card Sorting Changed a Website Team's View of How the Site Should Be Organized

Janice (Ginny) Redish, Redish & Associates, Inc.

This case study is about the website of the US National Cancer Institute's Division of Cancer Prevention. When the study began, the division's website focused on its mission and internal organization (see Figure 10.10).

Figure 10.10:

The website before card sorting

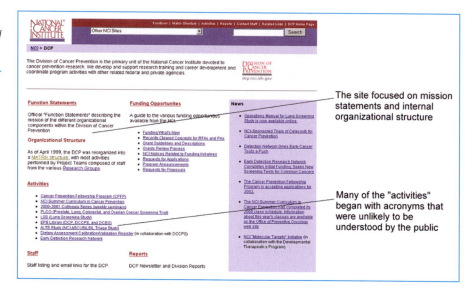

Our Approach

Our Approach

I was brought in as a consultant to help the division's web project team revise the site. They knew it needed to change, and the division's new Communications Manager, Kara Smigel-Croker, understood that it did not have the public focus that it needed.

We began by having me facilitate a two-hour meeting of the division's web project team at which we discussed and listed the purposes of the site and the many user groups the site must serve.

Although the site, at that time, reflected the organization of the division and the research that it funds, the project team agreed that the mission of the website was to be the primary place that people come to for information on preventing cancer.

When we listed audiences, we found many potential users – from the public to medical professionals to researchers to students – and, of course, realized that there would be a wide range of knowledge and experience within each of these audiences.

In addition to listing purposes and audiences, the third activity in our initial meeting was to understand the scenarios that users would bring to the site. I handed out index cards, and each member of the project team wrote a sample scenario. The most interesting and exciting result was that after just our brief discussions of purposes and audiences, 17 of 18 members of the project team wrote a scenario about a member of the public coming for information about preventing cancer, even though, at that time, there was almost no information on the site for the general public! (The 18th scenario was about a graduate student seeking a post-doctoral fellowship – a very legitimate scenario for the website.)

The stage was now set for card sorting. The project team agreed that card sorting was the way to find out how members of the public and medical professionals would look for information on the site.

Planning and Preparing for the Card Sorting

Members of the project team wrote cards for topics. In addition to the topics from each research group and from the office that handles fellowships, we added cards for types of cancer and for articles that existed elsewhere in the many, many National Cancer Institute websites to which we could link.

How Many Cards?

We ended up with 300 cards – many more than we could expect users to sort in an hour. How did we winnow them down? We used examples rather than having a card for every possible instance of a type of topic or type of document.

For example, although there are many types of cancer, we limited the cards to about ten types. For each type of cancer, you might have information about prevention, screening, clinical trials, etc. Instead of having a card for each of these for each type of cancer, we had these cards for only two types of cancer – and our card sorters quickly got the point that the final website would have comparable entries for each type of cancer. Instead of having a card for every research study, we had examples of research studies.

Even with the winnowing, we had about 100 cards – and that was still a lot for some of our users. An ideal card sorting set seems to be about 40 to 60 cards.

What Did the Cards Look Like?

Figure 10.11 shows examples of the cards. Each topic went on a separate 3 in × 5 in white index card. We typed the topics in the template of a page of stick-on labels, printed the topics on label paper, and stuck them onto the cards – one topic per card. We created two "decks" of cards so that we could have back-to-back sessions.

We also numbered the topics, putting the appropriate number on the back of each card. Numbering is for ease of analysis and for being able to have back-to-back sessions. Here's how it worked. In hour 1, participant 1 sorted deck 1. In hour 2, participant 2 sorted deck 2 while someone copied down what participant 1 did, using the numbers on the back of the cards to quickly write down what topics participant 1 put into the same pile. Deck 1 was then reshuffled for use in hour 3 by participant 3, and so on.

With stick-on labels and numbers for the topics, you can make several decks of the cards and have sessions going simultaneously as well as consecutively.

Figure 10.11:

Examples of the cards used

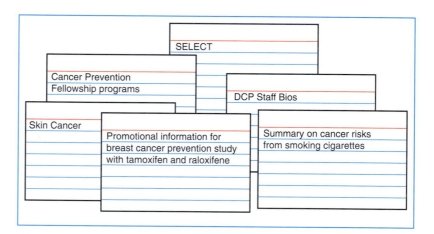

Recruiting Users for the Card Sorting

We had two groups of users:

- Eight people from outside who came one at a time for an hour each
- About 12 people from inside – from the project team – who came either singly or in pairs for an hour each; pairs worked together, sorting one set of cards while discussing what they were doing – like co-discovery in usability testing.

The National Cancer Institute worked with a recruiting firm to bring in cancer patients/survivors, family members of cancer patients/survivors, members of the public interested in cancer, doctors, and other health professionals. Our eight external users included people from each of these categories. The external people were paid for their time.

Conducting the Card Sorting Sessions

The only real logistic need for card sorting is a large table so that the participant can spread out the cards. We held sessions in an empty office with a large desk, in a conference room, and on a round conference table in another office. The conference room table worked best; one participant especially liked the chair on wheels so he could roll up and down next to the table looking at his groupings. Other participants sorted the cards standing up so they could reach along the table to work with the cards they had already put out.

In addition to the deck of cards with topics on them, we also had:

- Extra white cards for adding topics
- Sticky notes for indicating cross-links (when participants wanted a topic to be in two places, we asked them to put it in the primary place and write a sticky note to indicate what other group should have a link to it)
- Cards in a color for putting names on the groups at the end
- Rubber bands for keeping each group of cards together at the end
- Pens for writing new topics, cross-links, and group names.

The instructions for card sorting are very simple. You put the first card on the table. You then look at the second card and decide whether it goes into the same group as the first or not. If yes, you put the two cards together. If no, you start a second pile. And so on. Participants had no difficulty understanding what to do.

We also explained that we were building the home page and navigation for a website. This gave participants a sense of about how many piles (groups) it would make sense to end up with.

Participants were also told that they could:

- Rearrange the cards and groups as they went – that's why the topics are on separate cards

- Reject a card – put it aside or throw it on the floor – if they did not know what it meant or if they did not think that it belonged on the site
- Write a card if they thought a topic was missing
- Write a sticky note if they would put the card in one group but also have a link to it from another group.

We encouraged the participants to think aloud, and we took notes. However, we found that the notes we have from think-aloud in card sorting are not nearly as rich as those we have from usability testing, and that the card sorts themselves hold the rich data. We have since done card sorting studies for other projects in which we have run simultaneous sessions without a note-taker in each – and thus without anyone listening to a think-aloud. (We did not tape these sessions.) In these other projects, several sorters worked at the same time, but each worked independently, in different rooms, with the facilitator just checking in with each card sorter from time to time and doing a debrief interview as each person finished.

When the participants had sorted all the cards, we gave them the colored cards and asked them to name each of their groups. We also asked them to place the groups on the table in the approximate configuration that they would expect to find the groups on the home page of a website.

The Analysis

In this study, we found that we did not need to do a formal analysis of the data to meet our goals of understanding at a high level what categories people wanted on the home page, where on the home page they would put each category, and the general type of information (topics) that they would expect in each category. We did not do a formal analysis with complex cluster analysis software for at least four reasons:

- This was a very small study – eight users.
- We were looking only at the top level of an information architecture. Our interest was the home-page categories with names and placement on the page for those categories and a general sense for the types of information that would go in each category. We were not doing an entire information architecture or putting every underlying piece of content into a category.

- This was just one step in an iterative process. Our goal was to get input for a prototype that we would take to usability testing. The project continued through several rounds of prototypes and usability testing.
- It was obvious as soon as the sessions were over that there was incredibly high agreement among the users on the categories, names, and placements.

If any of these four had not been the case, a formal analysis with one of the available software tools would have been imperative.

We put each person's results on a separate piece of paper – with the group (category) names in the place they would put it (see Figure 10.12).

We spread these pages out on a conference room table and looked them over for similarities and differences. The similarities were very striking, so we took that as input to a first prototype of a new website, which we then refined during iterative usability testing.

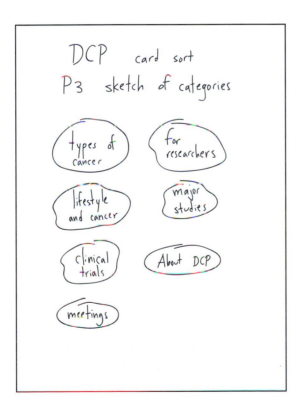

Figure 10.12:

Example sketch of one user's placement and names for categories

Main Findings

Achieving Consensus

Card sorting can produce a high degree of consensus about what a home page should look like. In this case, looking just at the eight external card sorters' topics for the home page:

- Seven had types of cancer or some variant – and they put it in the upper left corner of the page.
- Six had prevention or lifestyle or some variant. This category included topics such as exercise, tobacco cessation, nutrition, eating habits, as well as general information about preventing cancer.
- Five had clinical trials or some variant. They wanted a main entry to all the clinical trials as well as a link to each from the relevant type of cancer.
- Six had *About NCI DCP* or *Administration*. This category included the mission statement, organization chart, directory, etc. Although two of eight also wanted a very brief mission statement with a link in the upper left corner of the home page, all six put the *About . . .* category in the lower right of the page.

Opening Internal Users' Eyes

The technique itself can open the eyes of internal users to the problems with the way the site is currently designed.

The participants from the web project team (the internal users) all started by sorting cards into their organizational groups, creating once again the old website. However, after 5–10 minutes (and sometimes with a bit of prodding to "think about the users and scenarios you wrote in the meeting"), they made comments like this: "How would someone from the public know that you have to look under [this specific research group] to find out about that?"; "The public would want to look up a specific type of cancer"; "The public would want to look up information about diet or nutrition."

In the end, each of the internal users came to very similar groupings as the public. They also realized on their own that information about the organization would not be the most important reason people came to the site. Like the public users, they put the *About . . .* category in the lower right of the page.

If you think of internal users as "developers," you may wonder whether it was wise to let them do the card sorting. Of course, you do not want to have the developers (or internal users) be the only card sorters. The primary audience for the site must be the primary participants in any card sorting study.

In this case, however, the internal users were very curious about the technique. They wanted to try it, too. If we could have set up the card sorting sessions with the project team as observers (as we typically do for a usability test), that might have satisfied their curiosity. However, we did not have the facilities for observation for this particular study, so we decided to let them try the card sorting for themselves.

The danger, of course, was that they would remain in their own frame and not get beyond creating once again the site they knew. Just a little prodding to "think about the users," however, made these internal project team members realize for themselves both that they could put themselves into the users' frame and that, once in that frame, they could see how the users would want the site to be organized. Letting the internal people also do the card sorting might not always be wise; but in this case, for many of them, it was a "light bulb moment" that made them empathize even more with the external users.

Discovering Gaps in Understanding

With card sorting, you can find out about words that users do not know. All of the external card sorters ended up with some cards in a pile of "I can't sort this because I don't know what it means."

The most common cards in that pile were ones with acronyms like ALTS, STAR, SELECT. Others were words like "biomarkers" and "chemoprevention." This was a huge surprise to many of the NCI researchers. It was a critical learning for them; the acronyms refer to clinical trials that the division is funding. Information about these clinical trials is one of the great values of the site, but people will not find the information if it is hidden under an acronym that they do not recognize.

Getting a Better Understanding of Card Sorting

Card sorting is like usability testing in that you have to be concerned about recruiting representative users, but it is logistically easier than usability testing. You need only a conference table, cards, someone to get the user going and – if you are running consecutive sessions – someone to record what each participant has done and reshuffle the cards for another participant. The difficult part of card sorting is deciding on the topics to include and limiting the number of cards by choosing good exemplars of lower-level content rather than including every single article that might be on the site.

What Happened to the Website?

Figure 10.13 is the "after" version that was launched in the summer of 2001. (The current site at www.cancer.gov/prevention is a later update following NCI's adoption of new look and feel standards.)

Figure 10.13:

The website after card sorting, prototyping, and iterative usability testing

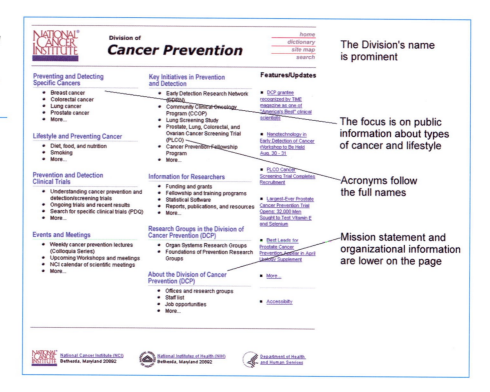

Acknowledgments. My time as a consultant to the NCI Division of Cancer Prevention (DCP) came through my work with the NCI Communication Technologies Branch (CTB) in the NCI Office of Communication. NCI is part of the US National Institutes of Health, Department of Health and Human Services. I thank Kara Smigel-Croker (DCP Communications Manager) for leading this project, and Madhu Joshi (who was a CTB Technology Transfer Fellow at the time) for handling all logistics and support.

CHAPTER 11

GROUP TASK ANALYSIS

Introduction

One critical segment of information required when developing a product is an understanding of how your users do their work – how they complete their tasks, both physically and cognitively. This **procedural knowledge** helps you to ensure that your product reflects ideal or current work practices and information flows. In most cases, you want to model the users' current work practices and identify problematic areas. In order to do so, you must understand all of the critical steps involved in their processes. A group task analysis (GTA) is used to identify the steps users take to complete a particular task, and the sequence of those steps.

You may have an *idea* of the steps users take to complete their tasks, but this is not enough. You need to understand how your users *truly* work. In a GTA, participants work in small groups and discuss the steps involved in completing a particular task (e.g., booking a vacation) in order to create a task flow. The flow(s) generated by the activity are then modeled to develop accurate, usable task flows within your product. The activity takes about two hours and the results are analyzed in even less time; and although the information you obtain is not as rich or context-specific as you would obtain in a field study (see Chapter 13, page 562), the GTA is ideal for those short on time and resources.

In this chapter, we discuss what task analysis is in general and the GTA in particular. You will learn how to prepare for and conduct a GTA, as well as how to analyze the results. Finally, we discuss a few variations on the GTA and our own lessons learned. The chapter concludes with a case study from Oracle that is designed to understand how internet meetings are conducted.

Background to Task Analysis

At its core, a task analysis decomposes a particular job role or task into steps. Task analysis should not be confused with **task allocation**. However, during a task analysis, you may discover information that can help you allocate tasks – such as cognitive workload, skill set, environmental constraints, safety requirements, and functional demands. The following information can be collected in a task analysis:

- Users' overall goals
- How they currently approach the task
- Information needed to achieve goals
- Interdependencies between steps
- Various outcomes and reports that need to be produced
- Criteria used to determine quality and acceptability of these results
- Communication needs of users as they exchange information with others while performing the task or preparing to do so
- Exceptions/emergencies that occur and how they deal with them
- Users' model of the task
- Problems they encounter
- What they like best
- What annoys them
- What changes they would like
- Ideas for improvement.

A variety of task analysis methods exist and a variety of information may be collected depending on the method. Some of the best known ways to do this are through:

- Examination of documentation (e.g., training materials, manuals)
- Interviews (see Chapter 7, page 246)
- Field studies techniques, such as observation or Contextual Inquiry (see Chapter 13, page 562).

The ideal and most reliable way to collect task information is through a combination of the above methods. However, observing several representative users at work and interviewing each one can be time-consuming. It can be difficult to convince product development teams to find time in their schedules for up-front **usability** activities (refer to Chapter 1, Introduction to User Requirements, "Getting Stake-holder Buy-in for Your Activity" section, page 14). In addition, you may not be able to access users in their workplace to observe them. Some companies do not want to let people observe their work practices, for confidentiality reasons or because you may disrupt the workplace. To make things more difficult, marketing departments or sales representatives can be very possessive of their customers. They fear you may cause customers to become dissatisfied with their current product and demand changes; or worst yet, they fear you could blow a deal they are trying to make with the customer. Finally, documentation is often confidential, incomplete, or simply inaccurate. Just because the training materials tell workers to complete a task in a certain fashion does not mean that they actually do it that way. Workers frequently find workarounds to make their jobs easier or more efficient. We have faced these challenges time and again. As a result, we utilized the group task analysis (GTA).

SUGGESTED RESOURCES FOR ADDITIONAL READING

If you are interested in learning about some of the other types of task analysis methods, below are several books that examine different methods.

Cognitive task analysis focuses on the knowledge and thinking that people engage in when attempting a task. This includes methods like GOMS (Goal, Operators, Methods, and Selection), PARI (Prediction, Action, Result, Interpretation), and DNA (Decompose, Network, and Assess). To learn more about cognitive task analysis, we recommend:

- Gordon, S. & Gill, R. (1997). Cognitive Task Analysis. In C. Zsambok & G. Klein (eds), *Naturalistic Decision Making*, pp. 131–140. Mahwah, NJ: Lawrence Erlbaum.

There are a variety of books describing task analysis in general. Below are just a few:

- Hackos, J. T. & Redish, J. C. (1998). *User and Task Analysis for Interface Design.* New York: John Wiley & Sons.
- Kirwan, B. & Ainsworth, L. K. (eds) (1992). *A Guide to Task Analysis: The Task Analysis Working Group.* London: Taylor & Francis.
- Luczak, H. (1997). Task Analysis. In G. Salvendy (ed.), *Handbook of Human Factors and Ergonomics*, pp. 340–416. New York: John Wiley & Sons.

Overview of Group Task Analysis

The group task analysis is an abbreviated version of a method known as the "bridge session" (Dayton, McFarland, & Kramer 1998). The "bridge session" is a great, but time intensive task analysis method that produces three key results:

- A user-centered task flow
- A set of abstract task objects
- A paper prototype of a graphic user interface (GUI).

It has three major dependent sequential steps:

- Task analysis
- Task-to-object mapping
- Object-to-GUI mapping.

This process requires three full days from an interdisciplinary team of at least five **stakeholders**: user, project manager, usability engineer, developer, and designer.

Although this method sounds great on paper, and the creators have had much success with it, we have been unable to get a team of five people to commit their time for three full days. In addition, our users are brought in from outside, so we are concerned that they might be overwhelmed by the often-contentious opinions of four company employees and that their voices might not be heard.

SUGGESTED RESOURCES FOR ADDITIONAL READING

To learn more about the bridge session methodology, we recommend the following:

- Dayton, T., McFarland, A., & Kramer, J. (1998). Bridging User Needs to Object Oriented GUI Prototype via Task Object Design. In L. Wood (ed.), *User Interface Design: Bridging the Gap from Requirements to Design*, pp. 15–56. Boca Raton, FL: CRC Press.

To address these constraints, we have adopted a modified method called the "group task analysis." We decided to focus on the task-analyzing portion of the session and to let the users create the entire task flow without the influence of the product team. By doing this, we complete only a third of the process but we are able to collect a wealth of valuable task flow information and reduce the session time from three days to two hours. We then transfer this flow to our team of professional designers who translate it into design.

The GTA provides an abundance of information in a very short period and does not suffer from many of the constraints of other task analysis methods (e.g., getting access to workplaces, inaccurate documentation). To give you a high-level understanding, the GTA provides a group of users with a set of steps the product development team thinks users take to complete a given task. Users are asked to validate those steps, include missing steps, place them in the order they accomplish them, and provide additional details about the task. Users work together to develop a task flow they can all agree upon.

When to Use a Group Task Analysis

As with any task analysis method, the GTA can be conducted at any point in the product development lifecycle; however, it can have the greatest impact at the very beginning of a product development lifecycle. Below are five situations in which you would want to leverage the GTA during product development.

Validating task information

Sometimes, developers cannot make a decision, they cannot agree on the steps users take, or they keep changing their minds about how the product should work because they don't understand how users work. Each developer, manager, or product analyst may imagine he or she is the only one who has a "true" understanding of the end user. You are the neutral third party who can solve these problems. It is actually easy to sell product development teams on doing this activity when the team is faced with these kinds of issues. You can state that you simply want to "confirm" what they already know by collecting some additional "clarifying" details. When offered the opportunity to validate their own perspective, most team members will happily work with you.

New domain or adding new functions

It is ideal to conduct a task analysis when you are creating a product in a new domain or if you would like to add new functionality to an existing product. For example, let's say that you have learned from a wants and needs analysis (see Chapter 9, page 370) that customers want online chat capabilities with live travel agents on your travel site. As far as you are aware, this has not been done before. As a starting point, it would be useful to gain an understanding of how people currently interact with their travel agents. What information do they want to know? How do they normally obtain this information? Do they make multiple calls? Do they always want to speak with the same agent? By understanding how and why users currently interact with travel agents, you can better support the transition to this new feature. With complex tasks, an understanding of the current process is critical since you want to support a transfer of training.

Automating tasks

Another valuable use for this technique is to analyze users' moving from a manual to an automated task. For example, you know some of your potential northerly customers travel south each spring to new sunny destinations. Most of these customers start to research prices and destinations at the beginning of each year to decide where to travel that year. How would you automate this task so that their research is done for them each year? A group task analysis can help provide insight into the current manual process. You could bring in users and find out how they are currently conducting this research. Learn about the steps they take. Find out what they like and dislike about their current process. Let's say you learn that at the beginning of each year they pick up the latest travel package catalogs and then they surf the web. Use this information to create the ideal flow for their needs. Perhaps you could have users fill-in their general travel preferences and e-mail address on your website. You could then e-mail them the latest and greatest travel links that match their preferences at the beginning of each year. In addition, a group task analysis will help you understand the key functions you will need in your automated travel research system.

Competitive analysis

If you would like to introduce a product into a market where a strong competitor already exists, you can conduct a group task analysis to find a competitive advantage. By collecting information about the way users complete a task with the competitor's product, you can learn what steps users dislike and/or where the product is less efficient. By developing a product that automates the disliked steps or makes a task more efficient, you can create a competitive advantage. Conversely, you can learn what users really like about the current competitor. It is important for you to understand what is successful about the current standard and leverage that. For example, if you discover that users love the toll-free phone number available to them on the leading travel site, TravelWise.com, you will want to include such a feature in your product. Additionally, if the competitor has become the standard, you may not want to differentiate your product so much that a transfer of training is not possible.

To learn more about conducting a competitive analysis, refer to Chapter 2, Before You Choose an Activity, "Competitors" section, page 37.

Improving your product

The GTA can be very helpful when you need to fix an unsuccessful product. Similarly to identifying the weaknesses in a competitor's product, you can identify problem areas in tasks completed with your product.

In a usability test of your product you may have learned where a problem area exists, but you are not sure how to fix it or why it is a problem. Bring in current users of the product and have them focus on the steps of the task that they find inefficient or problematic. You may want to ask users to work with your product prior to conducting the GTA so that it is fresh in their mind. By conducting such an activity you may discover that the version of the travel site you released in Japan is failing because the translation is very poor and users are unable to get the information they need about the available travel destinations.

Benefits of the Group Approach

Many of the task analysis techniques in use today restrict data collection to individual users. As the name implies, the group task analysis allows data to be collected from a group of users, typically four to six at a time. Even though people are working together as a group on the flow, you are not encouraging **groupthink**. As participants develop a flow, they are encouraged to discuss their individual situations and any differences between participants are noted. Participants are not influenced to agree with something just because the rest of the group thinks it should be that way.

There are many benefits to collecting task information from several users at once.

- Describing procedural knowledge is difficult for many people, so asking individual users how they complete a task can result in missed steps, or users may provide only the most common situations. By working as a group, users must describe to each other the way they work. Information that users may not have thought about sharing while working alone is verbalized and unique situations are often identified.

- Because users must come to a consensus on the flow, you are not forced to combine several disparate flows into something you *think* may work for everyone. You can feel confident that the flow the group develops represents a common way in which they can all complete the task. Remember, you are not creating a product for one user.

- Within about two hours you can collect a complete flow that represents data from up to six users. This is over six times faster than collecting individual flows and having to analyze the data afterward. Obviously, the complexity of the task and the level of detail you are interested in will dictate the length of the session – but in our experience, two hours is adequate for even complex tasks.

Things To Be Aware of When Conducting a GTA

Contextual Inquiry and similar field studies that get you into the user's environment provide extremely valuable insights into the context of the user's tasks and the environment in which they are conducted (refer to Chapter 13, Field Studies, page 562). Unfortunately, as mentioned earlier, it can be difficult to get access to a single user's environment, much less several users' sites. In addition, product development teams rarely include the time in their development cycle necessary to conduct such studies. Although we always try to conduct field studies when we want to better understand a user's tasks, context of use, and environment, there are times when "discount" methods are necessary.

In addition to the tremendous time savings that result from conducting this type of activity as compared to a field study, you also obtain information from up to six different users (and companies) at a time. However, there are several limitations you should keep in mind when conducting a GTA.

Loss of context

The data you get will not be as rich as the data you can obtain from a field study. You lose the context of the task and surrounding data when you conduct studies outside of their true environment. This is a cost that comes with the benefits of a "discount" technique. However, we use probes, moderation skills, and group discussion to bring out as much detail about a task as possible.

Missed steps

Users may miss a step or incorrectly describe a step because it can be difficult for users to verbalize what they do. Some steps are so automatic, ingrained, or subtle in a user's mind that the person does not even think to tell you about them. Again, this is where group discussion and moderation skills are essential. What is the probability that all six individuals will forget or misstate the exact same step? It is pretty unlikely, so by asking participants to describe the details around each step, many of the subtleties are drawn out.

What users *say* they do versus what they *actually* do

What people say they do, and what they actually do, may be different. Sometimes users will tell you how they are "supposed" to accomplish their task, not how they actually "do" their task. For example, someone may tell you that she books her hotel online, but it may turn out that she provides her secretary with the information and the secretary actually books it online. There are a couple of ways to help prevent this problem.

First, make sure the user understands that you are interested in reality, not what the instruction manual states or how the boss thinks the task should be done. This awareness will help to make sure that your data are authentic. As a moderator, listen for verbal cues like "we are supposed to . . ." or "I'd like to do it this way . . ."; cues such as these tell you that the user is deviating from the way he/she actually works.

Secondly, assure the users that their data will be kept confidential. Their managers will not know that they are not completing their task according to company policy.

Forgetting exceptions

Participants usually mention typical cases but do not think of exceptions. It is your job as the moderator to make sure that these exceptions come to light. For example, if no one mentions that they compare the prices across several websites before purchasing a ticket online, but you suspect this is something users do, you will need to probe to verify or disprove your suspicion.

As you can see, moderation is a critical component to the success of a GTA. It can also be helpful if you ask participants to bring in artifacts of the task. For example, ask participants to bring in an e-mail confirmation about their hotel booking or any other materials they may have printed out or used as supplements the last time they used the web to make travel reservations.

Finally, while direct observation can remove many of the above issues, frequently it is not an option. When time, resources, or access to users' environments is not possible, the GTA is a good alternative with many benefits.

Types of Data You Can Collect

During the GTA session users are asked to "build a bridge" from a trigger to an end point. Along the way, they identify steps, the order that they accomplish them, decisions that are made, additional information needed, exceptions, pain points, and other people involved in the task. Even though users must build consensus while creating the flow, this technique still allows you to capture individual differences. You can identify steps that are unique to a particular user or steps that are situation-dependent.

The GTA can provide a plethora of information that other task analysis techniques take significantly longer to collect. Let's look at this information while thinking of the sample task "Booking a hotel online."

Triggers

What is the trigger that makes users start the task? Why are they doing this task? It is not enough to understand how a task is done; you must also understand *why* a task is done. In our example of booking a hotel, it might be "going on a business trip" or "going on a family vacation." These are specific triggers – but at a general level, the user is about to take a trip and needs somewhere to stay.

End points

How does the user know when the task is complete? In the case of booking a hotel online, the end point or goal for the user could be "receive a hotel confirmation number." Your product should support that end point and provide users with a confirmation number. If you do not support the end point, users may not be sure they are done and worry they have not actually booked the hotel. At that time, users may abandon your site and call the hotel directly or go to a competitor's site.

Standard steps

This information tells you about every step that the users typically take in order to complete the task – steps that your product should support. For example, when I book my hotel, some possible steps are: searching for hotels, reading reviews, locating nearby attractions, etc. These are all features we would want to include in our product. Leaving out reviews, for example, would mean that users would have to go to another site to find that information and may find that staying with our site isn't worthwhile.

Decision points

It is important to understand the forks-in-road that users encounter. What choices do they have to make? We must be sure to include those options in our product and provide users with the information necessary to make an educated decision. Leaving out those options, or providing inadequate information, will leave users dissatisfied and may even convince them to abandon your product. Using our example, a critical decision point would be "Does the hotel meet all (or enough) of my criteria? If so, I will make a reservation. If it does not, I will repeat my search at another hotel." You must be sure that the site provides enough information (or options) about each hotel for the user to decide whether a particular hotel meets his/her criteria.

The sequence of steps that users take

This specifies the order that these steps occur. This will be important when you are creating the task flows for your product. In our example, if I were going to book a hotel, the first thing I would do is search for hotels in the city of interest and within a certain price range. I would then check the address of a particular hotel to see whether it was within walking distance to the places I am interested in visiting. Next, I would check to see whether there were rooms available on the required dates, with the options I prefer (e.g., king size bed, non-smoking). I am now at a decision point as to whether or not to book the hotel.

If we determined that this is a common flow, we would want to design our site to follow that same flow. If we determined that people conduct these steps in different sequences, we would want our design to have the flexibility to allow this.

Exceptions

These are steps that only some users take, or that they take only in certain cases. This is what helps avoid groupthink. You can also determine whether there are steps that are conditional. For example, if I was booking a hotel for business, I may not be so concerned about price, or I might have to choose from a limited set of hotels that my company has deals with. Even though there may be a most common task path, when designing our site we will want to include different filters in our search facilities to support various conditions even if some of these steps are infrequent.

Steps that users dislike

This can inform you about the problems your users currently deal with, and help you develop a product that eliminates these issues. For instance, users may hate websites that make them register before even searching for hotels available. In this case, when designing our travel website, we would want to hold off registration until users were ready to actually make a reservation – rather than alienating them before they even get to use our product.

Additional information

This additional information pertains to a step within the flow. It may be about materials needed or the context of the action taken. You can and should find out whether there are additional pieces of information or materials required for certain steps within the flow.

For example, a step in the flow may be "Get recommendations." During the group discussion, you learn that participants always get recommendations from friends about good places to stay. They also rely on travel books, so they would be referencing these things when conducting a search. So the additional information you should capture for that step is: "Ask friends and look in travel books." Can we include recommendations from other customers or a travel expert feature on our website? Could we add links to, or partner with, other sites that offer the additional travel information that users are looking for?

Actors

An actor is a person or people, other than the target user, responsible for a step in the task. From this, you would learn about whom else is involved in this task, what steps they are responsible for, and what their role is. Actors are additional users that you must take into consideration when designing your product.

For example, some users will call their travel agent once they find the hotel they are interested in, because they don't feel comfortable entering credit card details on the web. Consequently, we may want to make a customer service representative available for users to call. It might also be helpful if users could share their screen or information they have looked up with the travel agent so they do not have to repeat all the details to the agent.

Tip

Although it sounds obvious, the more information you attempt to collect along the way, the more time it will take users to complete the GTA. Make sure you allot enough time for users to give you the detail you are looking for. If you are dealing with a complex task or want a plethora of details from users, allot at least two hours.

Preparing to Conduct a Group Task Analysis

Are You Ready?

Before you begin *any* **user requirements** activity there are a number of things that you must be familiar with. Because these elements are common to all user requirements activities, they have been covered in the earlier chapters – but now is a good time to double-check the list. If you are not familiar with one of the items you can refer to the earlier chapter to brush up or familiarize yourself with that element.

Chapter 1: Introduction to User Requirements
- ☐ Get **stakeholder** buy-in for your activity (see page 14)

Chapter 2: Before You Choose an Activity
- ☐ Learn about your product (see page 29)
- ☐ Learn about your users (see page 41)

Chapter 3: Ethical and Legal Considerations
- ☐ Create consent forms (see page 98)
- ☐ Create confidential disclosure agreements (see page 103)

Chapter 4: Setting up Facilities for Your User Requirements Activity

☐ **Create or acquire a facility for your activity** (see page 106)

Chapter 5: Preparing for Your User Requirements Activity

☐ **Develop an activity proposal** (see page 146)

☐ **Determine the time of day and duration of your session** (see page 155)

☐ **Recruit participants** (see page 156)

☐ **Develop an activity protocol** (see page 191)

☐ **Pilot your activity** (see page 193)

Chapter 6: During Your User Requirements Activity

☐ **Welcoming participants** (see page 209)

☐ **Dealing with late and absent participants** (see page 211)

☐ **Warm-up your participants** (see page 215)

☐ **Invite observers to watch your activity** (see page 216)

☐ **Successfully moderate your activity** (see page 220)

☐ **Record and take notes during your activity** (see page 226)

Now that you understand what a GTA is and when to use it, it is time to plan and prepare for your GTA.

Preparation Timeline

The timeline in Table 11.1 covers in detail the sequence and timing of events to prepare for a GTA. These are *approximate* times based on our personal experience and should be used only as a guide. It could take longer or less time for each step depending on a variety of factors, such as responsiveness of the development team, access to users, and resources available.

Table 11.1:

Preparation timeline for a GTA

When to complete	Approximate time to complete	Activity
As soon as possible	2 weeks	☐ Meet with team to develop user profile ☐ Meet with team to develop the task(s) ☐ Meet with team to identify the potential steps and decisions points, as well as the granularity of the flow you are looking for
After the task and steps have been determined	1 week	☐ Create and distribute a proposal
After the proposal has been signed off by all stakeholders	1 week	☐ Identify and recruit users ☐ Assign roles for the activity (e.g., note-taker, interviewer) ☐ Prepare and/or acquire location ☐ Acquire incentives ☐ Order food (optional) ☐ Prepare documentation (e.g., letter for late participants, CDA, informed consent form, list of participants)
1 week before activity	2 days	☐ Conduct pilot ☐ Make necessary changes to cards and procedure based on pilot
Day before GTA	1 hour	☐ Call and confirm attendance with participants ☐ Remind stakeholders to come and observe the activity (if appropriate)
Day of GTA	2–3 hours	☐ Create and place "Welcome" sign in lobby ☐ Pick up food (optional) ☐ Set up location with all materials necessary

At a Glance

> Determine the task of interest

> Identify the task steps

> Players involved in the activity

> Inviting observers

> Activity materials

Determine the Task of Interest

So, the product development team has come to you and asked you to help them better understand a problematic task flow; or perhaps you have identified a problematic flow via a usability test and have suggested a GTA to the team. There may even be several tasks of interest. You should first identify which tasks are of most importance and determine how many sessions you can conduct in the given timeframe and with your current resources. If you are unsure, you can conduct a wants and needs (W&N) analysis to identify the most important tasks for users (see Chapter 9, page 370).

Once you have identified at a high level what task or tasks are of interest, it is important to properly scope them. You do not want a task of such broad scope that users cannot possibly provide you with enough details in one session (about two hours) to be of value. You also do not want such a small task that users get caught up in minute details. Work with the product development team to identify the key areas of difficulty, or ask them to list their specific questions. This will help you determine the scope. Using our travel example, some sample tasks might be:

- Book a hotel online
- Redeem your frequent-flyer points to book travel
- Conduct a price comparison between different rental car companies.

Identify the Task Steps

Develop a list of proposed steps and decision points that you and the team think users take in order to accomplish the task. Provide these steps and decision points as a jumping-off point. In addition to helping users get started, this will provide them with an understanding of the level of detail you are looking for in the task analysis. (Asking users to identify steps from scratch forces them to use much more cognitive energy and they often have a difficult time getting started.) The steps the team provides are not meant to bias the users, they are meant to be a starting point. They are also critical in enabling users to understand the level of detail that you are looking for. You don't want to provide users with every step and decision you think they make. You do not want to overwhelm the users with a stack of 50 steps – we recommend starting with 10–25 steps, depending on the complexity of the task. Users will have the opportunity to discard any steps that do not belong in the task flow and to add any that are missing.

In developing the product specifications or documentation, you or the team may have created task scenarios that you can refer to when generating the steps. (Refer to Chapter 2, Before You Choose an Activity, "Step 3: Scenarios" section, page 51.) Alternatively, you can interview subject matter experts on the team or research similar products. The list of steps may not be complete or 100% accurate, but even with a new feature or product you can develop a first stab at steps you think the users take. For example, if you were looking at the task of booking a hotel online, some of the possible steps might include:

- Search for all the hotels in the area
- Look for reviews on the hotel
- Determine price
- Look for deals or discounts for the hotel
- Determine the amenities at each hotel.

Some of the decision points might be:

- Does the hotel have rooms available?
- Is this price acceptable?
- Is it located near sites of interest?

Include "controversial" steps if appropriate. Are there steps that you believe the users take but the product team disagrees (or vice versa)? If so, include those to see whether participants include them in the flow or discard them.

What is the granularity of the information you want users to provide? That depends on the information you need. If you are looking for a very detailed task flow, you should provide users with very detailed steps. If you are more concerned with the task at a high level, provide more generic steps. For example, if looking for a high-level review of booking a hotel online, provide steps like:

- Find the hotel you want
- Book the appropriate date
- Print registration confirmation.

If you want a very detailed look at the same task, provide steps and decision points like:

- Research hotels in the area
- Determine your price point
- Determine the features you desire
- Determine the level of quality you desire
- Do a price and quality comparison between hotels in the area
- Does the hotel match the desired criteria? (decision point)
- Does the hotel have rooms available? (decision point)
- Login to the site
- Enter dates desired
- Enter credit card information
- Print the booking confirmation.

Obviously, you want to gain the buy-in of all the stakeholders in the product (refer to Chapter 1, Introduction to User Requirements, "Getting Stakeholder Buy-in for Your Activity" section, page 14). Make sure that product management, your management, and any other stakeholders are in agreement with the task(s) and steps you will provide to users. You do not want someone from the team to tell you after the session has been run that the data are wrong because they believe you used the wrong steps.

Players Involved in the Activity

In addition to participants, two additional roles are key to the success of a GTA: the moderator and a videographer.

The participants

Four to six end users (all matching the same user criteria) should be recruited to work together on the same task. It is too difficult to moderate more than six users in this type of hands-on activity. We strongly recommend collecting data from at least two groups of users. As with any group activity, group dynamics can affect the quality and quantity of data collected. One group may provide more details than the other, or one group may be dominated by a participant and the perspective of the flow could be different. Collecting data from a large number of participants helps ensure representative task flows are collected. Refer to Chapter 5, Preparing for Your User Requirements Activity, "Recruiting Participants" section, page 156 for more details on recruiting participants.

The moderator

The moderator is the person who works with the users to facilitate completion of the task. (In Chapter 6, During Your User Requirements Activity, "Moderating Your Activity" section, page 220, we discuss the key elements of moderating any user requirements activity.) This is a critical role and it can determine the success of your GTA. If no one in your group has experience doing this type of activity, we recommend that you conduct several practice sessions and tape them. Watch them together and critique each other. Some questions to ask each other are:

- What do you think I was trying to achieve with that intervention?
- How did it affect the participants? How well did it work?
- How could it have been done differently? How well would that have worked?
- What would you have done at that point? Why?

If there is someone in your group who is proficient at moderation or who has conducted a GTA before, ask that person to conduct a session while you "shadow" him/her. Standing next to the person, watching body language, and listening for clues as to why the person intervened when he/she did is valuable. You should also ask the expert to shadow you the first time you run a session. If the session is not going well, the expert can always step in and save the data. The expert can then follow up with specific recommendations about your performance. Practice, practice, practice. This isn't brain surgery – but if it is not done well, you can bias the data or simply have a very uncomfortable evening.

The videographer

The moderator will be completely occupied moderating the session, so that same individual should not be recording the session. (In Chapter 6, During Your User Requirements Activity, "Recording and Note-taking" section, page 226, you will find a detailed discussion of videotaping tips and the benefits of recording the session.) Ask a co-worker to do the recording and focus on getting the best picture and audio quality possible.

Videotaping a GTA is not easy. What do you focus on? You can't see what people are writing, people talk over one another, you can only see the task flow sheet from above. And most often you cannot see enough detail unless you zoom in. So why bother? To be honest, most of the recording will not be of great value because of the factors just mentioned. If you do not have an overhead camera, you will need to mount the video recorder above the table and zoom in so that the observers are able to read the steps, decision points, and sticky notes. However, there will likely be times when the observers cannot see anything (e.g., writing is too small, participant is blocking the camera).

However, when the flow is finalized, one person from the group walks through the flow in its entirety. This is what you need to make sure you capture. Make sure that no one is obstructing the camera and ask the participants to speak slowly and clearly. Zoom in on the flow. This video segment will allow you to refer back to the session if a sticky note is not clear or you cannot remember why users placed steps in the order they did. It also allows people who could not be present to understand the flow that was generated from the activity.

Inviting Observers

As with many user requirements sessions, it is great to have all stakeholders (e.g., product management, developers, management) come and observe the session in a separate room. As just mentioned, there will be times when the observers cannot see the flow.

The most important aspect though, is the audio. Observers will get a chance to hear some great audio and will gain an understanding of how the activity really works. Development teams are always amazed at the details they hear, such as pain points and considerations that users must make when completing a task. They learn an enormous amount through the participant discussions. Provide observers with the task, list of steps and decision points provided, as well as a summary of the participants. This will help the audience follow along and feel more engaged.

For a more detailed discussion about inviting stakeholders to your sessions, refer to Chapter 1, Introduction to User Requirements, "Getting Stakeholder Buy-in for Your Activity" section, page 14.

Activity Materials

Below is a checklist of materials you will need to conduct a GTA. The use of each material is explained in more detail in the procedure, but this provides you with a quick overview of the materials needed:

☐ The working canvas – a large, non-sticky flip chart (20 in × 20 in)
☐ At least one thin marker or colored pen for each user
☐ Steps printed on rectangles
☐ Decision points printed on diamonds
☐ Blank rectangles and diamonds
☐ Four different colored sticky notepads
☐ Clear tape
☐ Large room conducive to a group activity
☐ Video camera to record the session
☐ Large circular table to comfortably seat six people
☐ List of steps and decisions points (for observers)
☐ Summary profile of participants (for observers).

The working canvas

You will need something to create your flow on. We find that placing sheets from a large flip chart on the table works well. A large, non-adhesive flip chart should provide enough paper for several sessions. Additional flip charts placed on easels are used to capture assumptions, abbreviations, terms, or other things that you learn during the session.

Steps and decision points

Each step or decision point is printed on an individual slip of paper – steps on rectangles and decision points on diamonds (see Figure 11.1). Using slips of paper rather than asking users to write them directly on the flip chart paper allows users to move them around and make changes as they see fit. We have found that the following sizes work well:

■ Each step should be printed on a rectangle that is approximately 3 in × 2 in.

- Each decision point should be printed on a diamond that is approximately 3 in × 3 in in size.
- Use a font about 16–20 points.

Numerous blank rectangles and diamonds should also be created to allow users to write in the steps or decision points you have missed.

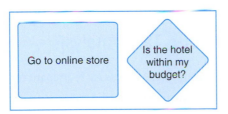

Notepads

You will need four different colored sticky notepads. Light colors are best because it makes the writing easier to read. We use:

- Yellow notes to capture additional information about a step
- Pink notes to identify steps users dislike, and why
- Blue notes to indicate exceptions – steps that not every user completes or steps that are taken only in certain cases
- Green notes to indicate when someone other than the user completes a step (i.e., an actor).

Things to write with

You will also need to provide four to six colored pens or fine-tip markers for users to write with. Even though pencils allow users to undo "mistakes," they are often too difficult for people to read.

Tape it down

Clear tape is used to secure the steps, decision points, and sticky notes to the paper after the flow has been finalized. Obviously, you do not want the participants' hard work to blow away during later review of the task flow.

Facilities

Finally, you really need a large room with a large circular table that allows six people to work around comfortably. Chairs without arms are ideal as the arms take up space and can get in the way. The participants must spend a couple of hours together working very closely. If users are uncomfortable or feel awkward stepping on each other, they will not work together well. Bring the best out in your users by making them comfortable.

Conducting a Group Task Analysis

You are now familiar with the steps necessary to prepare for a group task analysis. You are ready to conduct your first GTA!

Activity Timeline

The timeline in Table 11.2 shows in detail the sequence and timing of events to conduct a GTA. It is based on a two-hour session and obviously will need to be adjusted for shorter or longer sessions. These are *approximate* times based on our personal experience and should be used only as a guide.

A GTA can be tiring for both the moderator and the participant. It requires a good deal of cognitive energy, discussion, and negotiation. We have found that two hours

Table 11.2:

Timeline for conducting a GTA

Approximate duration	Procedures
5 minutes	Welcome participants (introductions, forms)
5 minutes	Creative exercise/participant introductions
5 minutes	Demonstrate the GTA method to participants using a simple example
5 minutes	Instructions
70 minutes	Group work
10 minutes	Break
15 minutes	Final walkthrough with participants
5 minutes	Wrap-up (distribute incentives, thank participants, escort them out)

is the maximum amount of time you want to keep participants for this type of activity. We have attempted to conduct GTAs for two flows in a two and a half hour period. The data we collected for the second flow were much less detailed. People discussed things much less and compromised much more easily. We have also had an extremely difficult time getting participants to add information on the different sticky notes for the second flow. It would have been better to conduct the session across two nights and get more detailed flows as a result. Granted, it would have cost more money and taken more time, but the better quality of the data would have been worth it. If you are forced to conduct a GTA for more than one flow in a session, keep the flows high level and do not ask for a lot of detail on the first flow. The more you ask for on the first flow, the less you will get for the second flow.

Now that you know the steps involved in conducting a GTA at a high level, we will discuss each step in detail.

At a Glance

> Welcome the participants
> Train the participants
> Moderate the group
> Review the task
> Debrief

Welcome the Participants

This is the time during which you greet your participants, allow them to eat some snacks, ask them to fill out paperwork, and get them warmed-up for your activity. The details of these stages are described in Chapter 6, During Your User Requirements Activity, "Welcoming Your Participants" section, page 209 and "Warm-up Exercises" section, page 215. A warm-up exercise is particularly helpful for a GTA because participants must work together to build consensus on the task flow. If they are not comfortable with each other, they won't speak up when they disagree.

Train the Participants

After you complete a warm-up exercise you should move on to a training exercise. Few users have ever created a task flow, so training is necessary for this activity to succeed. We begin by working with the group to develop a simple flow. We often use the example of "Making toast." This is not meant to take long (5–10 minutes), but it should introduce participants to the main concepts of the activity. Because this warm up needs to be relatively fast, there are no predefined steps and the moderator writes on a flip chart as steps are generated.

Figure 11.2:

Sample task flow for making toast

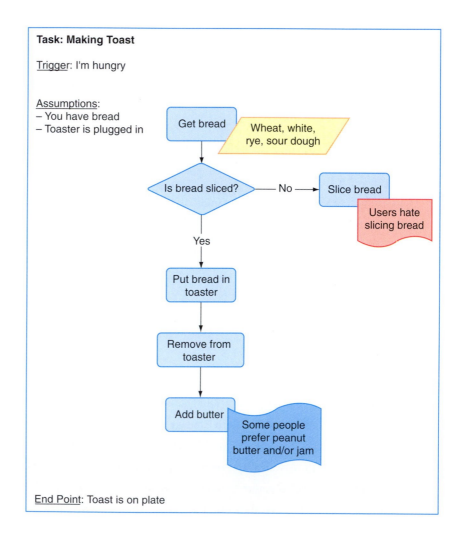

Write the task, "Making toast," at the very top of a flip chart or whiteboard. Ask users what would "trigger" them to make toast (e.g., "I'm hungry"). Users should call out their answers, and once it looks like everyone agrees on the trigger, write the trigger below the task. Next, ask users how they know they are done making toast (i.e., an "end point"). These answers may vary much more than for the trigger (e.g., "I am eating the toast" or "I am no longer hungry"). Write down the end point that most participants agree upon (remember, this practice session should take only a minute). Finally, tell users to build a "bridge" of steps between the trigger and end point. Ask users what the first step is they take to make toast (e.g., "Get the bread"). Draw a rectangle around each step.

As you proceed with the flow, you may notice users disagreeing about the detail of the flow on an area that is not of particular concern to you. For example, they may ask "Is this a two or a four slice toaster?" You are not concerned about the details of the appliance. This is where you can introduce the concept of "assumptions." For example, the moderator should say: "Let's assume it's a four-slice toaster, the toaster is out, and plugged in. I am going to write that down on our list of assumptions." Be sure to include some decision points along the way and draw a diamond around each one so they understand the concept of decision points. Figure 11.2 (page 484) illustrates a sample task flow. The yellow figures are for "additional information," the blue are for "exceptions," and the pink ones are for "disliked steps."

Present the steps and task

Once you feel comfortable that the users have the hang of it, explain that they will be doing the same thing with a different task (e.g., "Booking a hotel online"). Write the task on a whiteboard or folio sheet so that it is in clear view of all participants. Next, hold up the steps and decision points you have provided for the users and explain that you have taken a first stab at guessing how they normally complete this task. Emphasize that this is only a guess and you may be wrong, so they should feel free to throw away any steps or decision points that do not belong in the flow. In addition, they should include any steps or decision points that you may have missed. They should also reword or alter steps as they see fit.

Also, tell participants that you are interested in reality – not what the instruction manual tells them to do or how their boss thinks they should do their job. This awareness will help to ensure that your data are authentic. In addition, remind the participants that their data will be kept confidential. Below is a sample script you might want to use:

> "We have just completed a task flow for making toast. Now I would like for you to do the same thing for *<insert task name>*. We have identified some steps that we *think* you take to *<insert task name>*, but these are only a best guess. [*Hold up steps and decision points you created.*] You are the experts.

> "Just like in our example, we would like you to identify a trigger and end point for *<insert task name>* and then build a bridge of steps between them. We need you to throw away any incorrect steps that you do not take. Just because the step is in the packet, it does not mean that you must incorporate it. In addition, we may be missing some steps or decisions that you normally make. If that is the case, please write them on the blank pieces we have included. If you find any steps that are pretty close but not quite right, please correct them. We are interested in what you do in real life, not just what a user manual or boss *says* you should do."

Present the legend

Next, it is time to introduce the sticky note legend to participants. You are presenting them with several different pieces of paper, all with different meanings. You cannot expect them to keep this wealth of information straight in their heads, so introduce a "legend" of sticky notes (see Figure 11.3). Tape each sticky note on a flip chart or whiteboard and write its purpose on it (e.g., "Additional Information" is written on the yellow sticky note). Describe the purpose of each sticky note. If there are no questions, you are ready to begin. Keep the legend in view so that participants can refer to it if necessary. You can use the script below:

> "You need to work together as a group to develop a task flow that you can all agree upon. As you work, we will ask you questions along the way. That information will be captured on four different colors of sticky notes. [*Point to legend.*] When you identify a step, we will ask you for additional information – like why you take that step and what materials you need to complete the step. That 'additional information' is captured on yellow sticky notes. If there are steps that you do not like to take or are difficult, please indicate that on pink sticky notes. If there are steps that only one or two of you take, we will capture that on blue sticky notes. Also,

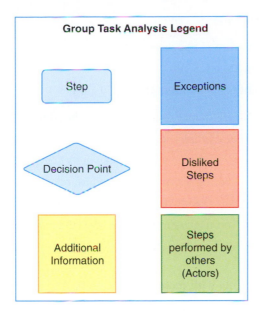

if you take a certain step only in certain special situations, that should be noted on blue sticky notes as well. Those are called 'exceptions.' Finally, if there is someone else that takes part in completing a step, like a manager or co-worker, please indicate that on green sticky notes. Don't worry about having to memorize all of this. We are here to help you along the way."

Present the assumptions

Ask whether anyone has any questions about the task or what you have explained so far. Once you feel comfortable that everyone in the group has a solid grasp of what they will be doing, you can then present the participants with any assumptions that may be associated with the task. As with the task, write the assumptions on a folio sheet or whiteboard in clear view of all participants.

Tip

To save time, write all the tasks and known assumptions on a flip chart before the session.

Possible assumptions are:

- Travel is for pleasure not business.
- You are traveling to a US city.
- You do not want to spend more than $200 a night.

You will also find that additional assumptions may be added to your list as the task analysis progresses. For example, someone may say that he or she likes to book the hotel and airfare together because you can often get a cheaper deal that way. If you are not interested in learning about booking an airfare or about vacation packages, then you could add "You already have your transportation to the city arranged" to the assumptions list. You use assumptions to steer the participants away from any information that you are not interested in.

Present the participants with materials

Spread the steps and end points out on the table and instruct the participants to work together to create a task flow they can all agree upon. Be sure each participant has his/her own set of materials (i.e., marker, blank rectangles and decision points, and several sticky notes of each color). The purpose is to encourage users to be active participants in the session. A participant should never have to ask another group member for materials. Each should be empowered to contribute equally to the flow.

Instructions to the participants

Before the participants jump in, summarize the instructions you have given so far:

- *Work together as a group to build a flow that everyone agrees upon.* This is not an individual activity. Teamwork is critical to the success of your GTA. Make sure the participants understand that they will be working as a team to create one task flow that they can *all* agree upon. They will need to openly discuss their thoughts, ideas, and opinions and be able to compromise to create one ideal flow.
- *Place the steps and decision points in the order that you normally complete them.* Make it clear to the participants that they need to build a bridge between the trigger and end point. To do this, they will use the steps, decision points, and sticky notes provided.

- *Throw out steps and decision points that do not fit and add any that are missing.* You do not want to confine the participants to the steps and decision points that you have created. First of all, many of the steps that you have provided may be incorrect or irrelevant in their situation. Also, you will likely be missing steps. We have never run a GTA yet where users have not added steps and do not expect that we ever will.

- *Include additional information on sticky notes.* Remind the participants about the sticky notes. These tend to get overlooked. Emphasize to participants that this is an important part of the process and that you really need this additional information to build a superior product.

Identify the trigger and end point

Next, ask a member of the group to write the task at the top of the page. Then ask the group to identify the trigger. Ask a different participant to write down the trigger that everyone agrees upon. For example, in the case of our sample task, a trigger may be "I am going on vacation to another city and need somewhere to stay." The trigger helps you gain an understanding of the user's goal. Why would they do this task?

Now, ask for an end point. Ask a third participant to write down the group's end point. For example, in the case of our hotel task, an end point might be "I receive an e-mail confirmation that the hotel is booked." The trigger and end point help to scope the task for the participants. Once they are defined, they need to build a bridge of steps between the two points. Make sure to ask different people in order to encourage participation from the start. If the group believes there are a couple of possible triggers and/or end points, both should be written down; however, the group should not spend a lot of time debating the triggers or end points. The majority of the activity should be spent building a bridge between a trigger and its end point.

Moderate the Group

As with other usability techniques, good moderation is critical to the success and quality of data collected by the GTA. However, because the GTA is such an intense activity, moderation is particularly vital for this activity. Figure 11.4 is a

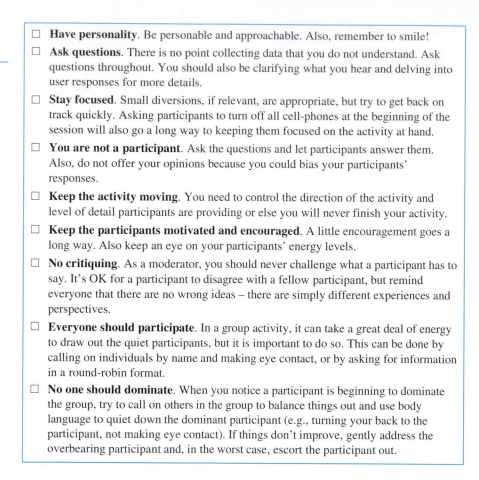

Figure 11.4:

Moderator's checklist

☐ **Have personality**. Be personable and approachable. Also, remember to smile!

☐ **Ask questions**. There is no point collecting data that you do not understand. Ask questions throughout. You should also be clarifying what you hear and delving into user responses for more details.

☐ **Stay focused**. Small diversions, if relevant, are appropriate, but try to get back on track quickly. Asking participants to turn off all cell-phones at the beginning of the session will also go a long way to keeping them focused on the activity at hand.

☐ **You are not a participant**. Ask the questions and let participants answer them. Also, do not offer your opinions because you could bias your participants' responses.

☐ **Keep the activity moving**. You need to control the direction of the activity and level of detail participants are providing or else you will never finish your activity.

☐ **Keep the participants motivated and encouraged**. A little encouragement goes a long way. Also keep an eye on your participants' energy levels.

☐ **No critiquing**. As a moderator, you should never challenge what a participant has to say. It's OK for a participant to disagree with a fellow participant, but remind everyone that there are no wrong ideas – there are simply different experiences and perspectives.

☐ **Everyone should participate**. In a group activity, it can take a great deal of energy to draw out the quiet participants, but it is important to do so. This can be done by calling on individuals by name and making eye contact, or by asking for information in a round-robin format.

☐ **No one should dominate**. When you notice a participant is beginning to dominate the group, try to call on others in the group to balance things out and use body language to quiet down the dominant participant (e.g., turning your back to the participant, not making eye contact). If things don't improve, gently address the overbearing participant and, in the worst case, escort the participant out.

summary of the main requirements. (Refer to Chapter 6, During Your User Requirements Activity, "Moderating Your Activity" section, page 220, for a detailed discussion.)

There are some moderation strategies that are specific to the GTA. We discuss these below.

A fine balance

As a moderator, you will need to work hard to make sure that everyone participates and to probe to ensure that you get as much information from the participants as possible. The moderator must remind users of the importance of including the sticky notes for additional data about the flow (i.e., additional information, exceptions, disliked steps, actors). At the same time, the moderator must remember to step back and let the *users* work. You do not want to do the participants' work for them. Believe us – they will often be happy to let you do this! The moderator should not write *anything*, instead insisting that participants write down their own thoughts/ideas. It can be tempting to get involved in building the flow but be sure to keep your hands empty at all times. This is critical to the success of your GTA and we cannot stress it enough. This helps get everyone involved, and members take more ownership of the final product when they have directly contributed to it. Also, it avoids your preconceived notions and biases from entering the flow. You may have provided users with the steps and decision points, but you do not want to influence the sequence or information captured on the sticky notes as well.

Tip

When you ask participants probing questions and you hear them say things like "I don't know. What do you think?" or "You're in charge here. Whatever you think is best," you have a problem. The participants are not "owning" the flow and you have probably taken too much control. Look for body language like folded arms, staring off into space, or refusal to engage in the activity. This is different from a shy user – this is a disinterested user. As moderator, you must give control of the flow back to the users. One way to do this is by giving participants a quick break. When they return to the table, remind them that they are the experts here and not you. It may even be necessary to tear down any flow that has been put in place and ask the users to start over. The day isn't lost – you will just have to work a little harder to get things back on track.

Keep participants seated while you remain standing

Ask participants to sit down for most of the session. They may need to stand up to write or to reach for materials, but they should spend the majority of the time sitting down. Dominating participants tend to stand over others. Suggesting to the dominating participant that the people may have difficulty seeing around him/her can politely persuade a participant to sit down. You, however, should remain standing

Figure 11.5:
A GTA session in action. The moderator is the only one standing. Everyone else has their own materials and the moderator is there only to ask questions, not to participate in building the flow

and keep moving so that you can gain a perspective from all viewpoints (see Figure 11.5). Hovering over someone can make him/her very nervous and less likely to participate.

Listen closely

Listen closely to what the participants are saying. If you hear participants providing important information, be sure to have them write it on a sticky note. Do not wait until the flow is finished to capture additional information. Users are exhausted by the end and are ready to go home. Additionally, listen for abbreviations or jargon used by participants. Ask them to explain what the abbreviation or jargon means and then write that information on the flip chart.

Keep it moving

Participants can easily get bogged down in details. If you suspect this is happening, or if people ask you how detailed they should get, ask them: "How important is this step to you or the task?" You can help set the "tone" of the flow with the steps you provide at the beginning. If you are looking for a more general flow, make the steps you provide higher level. If you want a lot of detail, make your steps very granular.

Also be sure to keep your eyes on the clock since you need to leave time at the end for participants to walk through the completed flow. You cannot expect participants to stay a second later than you initially proposed.

Signs a Group is Getting Bogged Down

- The flow is not progressing.
- They keep coming back to the same two steps and arguing over which comes first.
- They are creating a plethora of very detailed steps between two higher level steps.
- They begin debating what a particular step or term "really" means.

Review the Task

Once everyone agrees the flow is completed, give participants a break. They need to step away from the flow and rest their eyes. Now would be a good time to offer them fresh drinks and dessert. But keep the break short (about five minutes). Participants need to come back and review the task one more time. If you have not been video-taping the session before, now is the best time to capture the information. (Refer to Chapter 6, During Your User Requirements Activity, "Recording and Note-taking" section, page 226.)

Reviewing the task is one of the most important aspects of the GTA. It is critical that you save 10–15 minutes at the end for this part of the activity. It is your last chance to:

- Make sure that you have a good understanding of the flow
- Make sure that all participants agree with the flow
- Make any last additions or changes.

Ask a participant to volunteer, or pick the quietest user to explain the task flow from trigger to end point. Make sure that you understand everything that has been written down. If you cannot read the handwriting or do not understand what the group has done, stop the walkthrough and get clarification. Also, watch the other participants' faces. Does someone shake his/her head in disagreement? Does someone look confused? If so, stop the walkthrough and ask that participant what he/she thinks about the flow. A participant will rarely speak up to make changes at this point. It is important to encourage participants to make changes if they disagree. If everyone agrees on the flow, you can now tape it down. Also make sure arrows connecting the steps are drawn in. Nothing should have been taped down prior to this point because participants will be reluctant to make changes since it appears "permanent."

Thank the participants for their time and send them on their way. If you are providing an honorarium, now is the time to distribute it (refer to Chapter 5, Preparing for Your User Requirements Activity, "Determining Participant Incentives" section, page 159). See Figure 11.6 for an actual GTA flow.

Figure 11.6:

An actual GTA flow

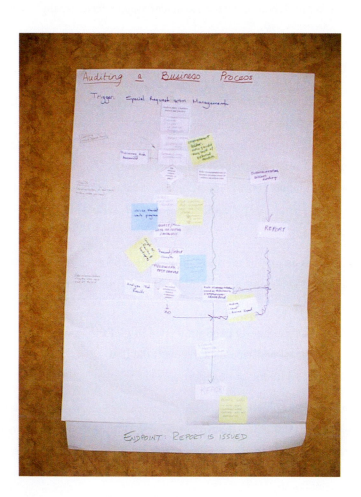

Tip

When you tape the steps down, make sure that you also tape the stickies down. They are guaranteed to fall off if you don't.

Debrief

Immediately after the session it is a good idea to hold a short debrief meeting with those who observed the activity. In most cases it is difficult for observers to see exactly what participants are writing on the flow as it is being created, so they are sure to want to see it up close. You always want to encourage the team's interest, so take a few minutes to let them examine the flows and ask any questions.

Data Analysis and Interpretation

Before you can begin analyzing the results, you need to recreate the task flow and, if appropriate, combine flows from multiple groups into one flow that represents everyone. Once this is done, you are ready to analyze the data. Below, we provide a checklist of questions to help you with the analysis, and walk you through an example.

At a Glance

> Recreate the flow within 24 hours
> Deal with multiple flows
> Analyze the data

Recreate the Flow within 24 Hours

Within 24 hours, while the information is still fresh in your mind, take the task flow back to your desk and replicate it with an illustration or flow chart program (e.g., Visio, Illustrator, PaintShop Pro). Figure 11.7 shows a recreated task flow. We cannot emphasize enough how important it is to do this sooner rather than later. The longer you leave the flow, the more difficult it becomes to recall and discern all

Figure 11.7:

Sample travel flow for booking a hotel online

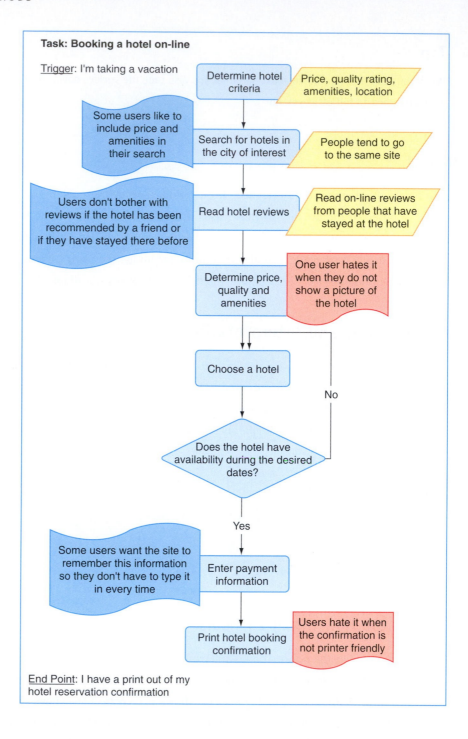

Task: Booking a hotel on-line

Trigger: I'm taking a vacation

Determine hotel criteria

Price, quality rating, amenities, location

Some users like to include price and amenities in their search

Search for hotels in the city of interest

People tend to go to the same site

Users don't bother with reviews if the hotel has been recommended by a friend or if they have stayed there before

Read hotel reviews

Read on-line reviews from people that have stayed at the hotel

Determine price, quality and amenities

One user hates it when they do not show a picture of the hotel

Choose a hotel

No

Does the hotel have availability during the desired dates?

Yes

Some users want the site to remember this information so they don't have to type it in every time

Enter payment information

Print hotel booking confirmation

Users hate it when the confirmation is not printer friendly

End Point: I have a print out of my hotel reservation confirmation

of the subtleties. This will give you a much cleaner, portable version of the data, and it can be inserted into a usability report (refer to Chapter 14, Concluding Your Activity, "Reporting Your Findings" section, page 652).

If you conducted the activity with a co-worker, we recommend discussing the flow with him/her as you work. The discussion can trigger things you might have forgotten otherwise. It is also valuable to have someone with you to confirm your impressions, thoughts, and recollections.

Use different shapes to denote the different types of sticky notes. Do not rely solely on color when recreating the flow because people often like to print things out and not everyone has a color printer or copier. Clean up and clarify the flow when you recreate it. Spell out the shorthand notes and abbreviations; get rid of any errors or redundancies, etc. Also, you may discover during this process that you need to go back and watch the videotape. If you have left the flow for a long time, you will most certainly have to do this. Even if you create an electronic flow immediately, there can still be some areas of confusion that the walkthrough section of the video can help you to clarify.

Deal with Multiple Flows

If you captured multiple flows for the same task and same user type (i.e., ran multiple groups), the task flow created by each group should be similar with only slight differences in details. Each of the major steps identified should be the same, but one group may have provided more sticky notes. You may notice that one group identified areas they hate but the other group did not. Another group may have felt that a certain area of the flow was particularly critical and therefore provided more "additional information" sticky notes. Or you may notice that one group provided more "exception" sticky notes because they were unable to compromise on the flow. All of these kinds of differences are acceptable.

If the flows are similar, you can either combine them into one generic flow or keep them as separate flows. Combining the flows takes additional time and effort but is easier for the product development team to understand. All the detailed notes are located in one place and the team does not have to decide which flow to pay attention to.

As with the wants and needs analysis, combining two sets of data is more of an art than a science. Start out by identifying areas where the flows are the same. Then examine the areas where it differs. If steps are in different sequences, this indicates that the task flow in your product must be flexible. Compile all the additional information, actors, disliked steps, and exceptions to document all the information uncovered. If you uncover conflicting information or if the flows are not at all similar between groups, you need to examine the users recruited. Were they all the same user type? Did each group receive the same instructions? What other differences could exist between the groups? You may need to review the tapes to see differences in instructions, users, etc. Unfortunately, you may not be able to pinpoint the reason why the flows are different. The fact is, there is no research on the reliability of this method and there may be differences between the flows that are independent of anything the usability professional has done (e.g., recruiting, instructions). We recommend running another group and comparing the flows again; however, in our experience, we have never come across a situation where flows between two groups are so different that we need to run another group.

Analyze the Data

Now it is time to analyze your results. Figure 11.8 is a checklist of some questions to ask when examining your flow(s). Let's use Figure 11.7 (presented earlier) from our travel example and analyze the results.

Figure 11.8:

Checklist of questions to ask when examining your flow(s)

☐ 1. What steps did users take to complete the task? You need to provide functionality that allows for the completion of the specified steps.

☐ 2. What information do users indicate they need to complete a step? When designing a website, you need to decide what information must be presented first and what can be a mouse-click away. Providing everything up-front will mean slower download times, which is frustrating. However, placing information deeper in the product may mean users cannot find it.

☐ 3. Are there a series of steps that are linearly dependent? If so, you will need to provide a mechanism to walk your users through those steps so they do not make unnecessary errors.

☐ 4. Did users across multiple groups all dislike or have difficulty with the same steps? If so, these steps should be improved, automated, or removed all together in your product.

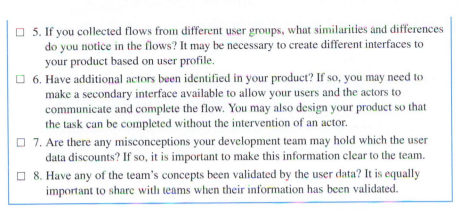

Figure 11.8

– Cont'd

☐ 5. If you collected flows from different user groups, what similarities and differences do you notice in the flows? It may be necessary to create different interfaces to your product based on user profile.

☐ 6. Have additional actors been identified in your product? If so, you may need to make a secondary interface available to allow your users and the actors to communicate and complete the flow. You may also design your product so that the task can be completed without the intervention of an actor.

☐ 7. Are there any misconceptions your development team may hold which the user data discounts? If so, it is important to make this information clear to the team.

☐ 8. Have any of the team's concepts been validated by the user data? It is equally important to share with teams when their information has been validated.

What steps did users take to complete the task? What information do users indicate they need to complete a step?

Begin by comparing the steps users listed to the features available (or planned) in your product. If there are steps that users take, or pieces of information that users need and your product does not support, it will be of little value to users. In our example, there are specific criteria that users judge a hotel by when deciding they want to stay there: price, quality rating, amenities, and location. Later in the flow, we see that participants also want to see a photo of the hotel and its availability. Does our current product provide all of those pieces of information about each hotel? If not, we better include them. If users do not have enough information to judge a hotel by, they will likely leave our site to find the information elsewhere. That could also mean they do not make a reservation via our site and we will lose business.

Other steps that users take which our product will need to support are searching, hotel reviews by customers, the ability to store payment information for future use, and the ability to print hotel confirmation information. Again, these are steps our product must support. With the search feature we need to decide how many of the criteria users should be able to search on initially. Speak with the development team to determine whether there is any reason why you could not provide a particular criterion or all of the criteria for users to search on. It is important to understand technical constraints that the development team must work with and balance those with the user requirements.

Since not all of the users read hotel reviews all of the time, this is a feature that we can place one-click down. We want to make it easy for users to find the link, but it is not necessary to provide it with the search results or on each hotel information page. Removing this additional text will mean faster download times.

Are there a series of steps that are linearly dependent?

Now we want to examine if the flow is linear or if many of the steps are done in parallel. Although none of the steps are shown as being completed in parallel, we believe that users may alter their criteria and perform additional searches if they do not like the hotel results returned from previous searches. Since this is only a suspicion, we do not want to make it difficult for users to conduct new searches; but we also do not want to make it part of our linear flow. At this point, we recommend providing a user interface that begins with a search engine, allowing users to search by price, quality rating, amenities, location, and availability. Next, we want to provide an option to read hotel reviews but not make this a mandatory "stop." When users select a particular hotel to view, we want to provide a photo, along with price, quality rating, amenities, location, and availability. If users do not like the particular hotel they are viewing, they should be provided with the option to go back to the results and select a new hotel. Once users have found a hotel they like, they should be able to select it, provide payment information, store it for later use, and print a hotel confirmation.

Did users across multiple groups all dislike or have difficulty with the same steps?

None of the users mentioned entire steps that he/she disliked, but there are particular aspects of steps that we want to address – specifically, including a photo of the hotel and making the confirmation printer-friendly.

If you collected flows from different user groups, what similarities and differences do you notice in the flows?

Since we did not examine different user types, we do not have information at this time to decide whether different user interfaces are needed for each user type.

Have additional actors been identified in your product?

No additional actors were identified, so a secondary interface is not necessary for communication between users at this time. Since the team is considering adding a chat feature to the site to allow users to communicate with a live travel agent (an additional actor), additional usability activities should be conducted to determine whether users would find this feature worthwhile.

Are there any misconceptions your development team may hold which the user data discounts?

At this point, we should compare the steps and decision points the development team or other research provided us against the steps the participants used. Let's say that you discover that one of the steps that you provided, "look for deals and discounts for the hotel" was left out of the flow by participants. What did users say when they came across that step and decided to leave it out? If you do not remember, you should review the videotape. Let's assume that we have reviewed the tape and the participants stated that they expect discount information to be automatically included in the price of the hotel – they do not want to have to search for it. This is valuable information and should be added as a yellow (additional information) sticky note to the "Determine price, quality, and amenities" step. When designing the web page that presents detailed information for each hotel, deals or discounts should be displayed there as well.

Have any of the team's concepts been validated by the user data?

Based on the proposed steps and decision points, we can see the product development team is on target. The team's understanding of how users expect to book a hotel online has been validated, and additional valuable information has been collected.

Communicate the Findings

Preparing to Communicate Your Findings

The specific data that you communicate to product teams can vary depending upon the activity you conducted, but some elements of *how* you communicate the results are the same regardless of the method. Because these strategies are common to all user requirements activities, they are discussed in detail in Chapter 14, Concluding Your Activity, page 636. We recommend that you read that chapter prior to relaying your results to your stakeholders. Topics discussed include the following:

□ **Prioritization of your findings** (see page 638)
□ **Creating an effective presentation** (see page 644)
□ **Writing valuable reports for different audiences** (see page 652)
□ **Ensuring the incorporation of your findings** (see page 660)

Using the answers to the questions above, it is important to provide the team with a set of design recommendations that they can follow. User data is of no value if the team does not know how to use it (refer to Chapter 14, Concluding Your Activity, "Presenting Your Findings" section, page 644). The recommendations should be in the form of specific instructions. Below are some recommendations to present to the TravelSmart.com development team based on our previous results and analysis:

1. Provide the following information about each hotel: price, quality rating, amenities, location, availability, and a photo of the hotel.

2. Allow users to search by price, quality rating, amenities, location, and availability. Based on performance criteria, determine if users can search on all criteria at once. If they cannot, conduct a survey to determine which criteria should be searched on first and which can be placed in "advanced search."

3. Provide a link to hotel reviews from each hotel page.

4. Provide the following task flow:
   ▪ Search for hotel based on specific criteria (i.e., price, quality rating, amenities, location, availability).
   ▪ Drill down to a specific hotel and view detailed information.
   ▪ Drill down to read reviews about the hotel.
   ▪ Either select a hotel and enter payment information or return to search results.
   ▪ After payment information is entered, provide option to store for later use.
   ▪ Display printer-friendly hotel confirmation.

5. Conduct survey, interview, focus group, or wants and needs analysis to determine if chat feature with live agent would be of value to users.

6. Include any deals or discounts in the price of the hotel room. Do not force users to search for this information separately.

If you are not a designer yourself, we recommend working with a designer to translate the recommendations into designs. Even if you are a designer, if you can work with another designer on the recommendations, you will find a fresh perspective helpful. The other designer may propose designs you had not thought of. In addition to providing a copy of the task flow, we also recommend providing the product development team with line drawings or screen mockups to better illustrate your recommendations. This will vastly improve the uptake of your recommendations by the product development team. You also want to make sure that what you have learned is incorporated into any formal documentation that the team has, such as a functional specification or design documents. Printing large versions of the recreated task flows and any design proposals on a color plotter and then posting them where the team and executives can see them (in the hallway, meeting rooms, kitchen or copy room) can stimulate discussion and keep the results of your activity on their minds.

Modifications

Although there are numerous ways to conduct a task analysis, we have presented the method as we typically use it. In this section, we briefly present four modifications of this particular method. You may find that one of these modifications better fits your product's needs.

Create the Current and the Ideal

The first modification compares current versus ideal task flows. Begin by asking participants to create a flow based on the way they currently work. How do users complete the task today? After completing the first flow, users are given a break and then asked to create a flow that represents the *ideal* way they would like to complete the task. Asking users to complete two task flows in one session can be exhausting. You can ask users to come back a second night to complete the second flow or you can keep both flows at a high level (and therefore shorter). This modification is ideal if you are trying to improve flows that you realize are flawed.

Rank Order Severity of Disliked Steps

The second modification asks users to rank order the severity of the disliked steps. If you find users are indicating they dislike several of the steps throughout the tasks, you may want to understand which steps are the most problematic. You may be limited in your resources and unable to respond to all the issues users are identifying. In that case, it will be helpful to understand where you should concentrate your resources to provide the largest benefit to your users.

Include Multiple User Types

A third modification to this method regards the make-up of the participants in your session. Normally, users of the same type (e.g., database administrators) are brought in to work together on a task. Alternatively, you may wish to bring in different user types to work together on the same task. The key is that each user is responsible for a different part of the task. It works most effectively when everyone is from the same company or group. This provides information about the business process – how do these individuals work together or collaborate to complete a task?

This type of GTA can be a bit more difficult to moderate. Not everyone is contributing at the same time since they may not work in parallel on a task. With this variation, it can be difficult to keep everyone focused and engaged in the activity. However, you can learn a great deal about what people *think* others contribute to a task! You can also reveal some surprising inefficiencies in the process.

Task Survey

Surveys can be added onto any usability activity (see Chapter 7, Interviews, page 246). One type of survey that compliments the GTA well is the "task frequency" survey. If you are aware of a variety of tasks that users might complete with your product or in a certain domain, you can ask users to state how frequently they complete those tasks. The more frequently a task is completed, the more easily accessible those tasks should be in your product. In addition, you can ask users how important those tasks are to them. If a task is not important and is rarely done, you may not want to include it in your product. If you do choose to include it, it should not take up prime real estate.

Lessons Learned

Since we began conducting GTAs, we have learned quite a bit. Sometimes lessons learned are painful. We would like for you to benefit from our experiences.

Training

We witnessed one GTA in which the moderator had seen several GTAs but had never shadowed an experienced moderator or received other training. She was confident that all the GTAs she had seen previously were plenty of training and that the technique is so simple, she didn't need additional help. We watched from a separate room and quickly saw the moderator become a participant. She began by writing down a participant's comment on a sticky note since the participant was reluctant to do it himself. After that point, the moderator kept the pen in her hand and filled out all future sticky notes for the participants. The participants put their pens down one by one and their body language changed from participants to observers. Their arms were crossed or hands in their pockets and were only half facing the flow. Halfway through the session, the moderator was interviewing participants and moving the steps into place herself. When the moderator asked the participants if they should put step X or Y next, one participant responded "I don't know. You're the expert." Later, another participant responded "Whatever you think is best."

The moderator was impressed because the flow turned out just the way she thought it would and she finished in record time. Her colleague on the other side of the room was moderating a different group on the same flow. Her group was only a third of the way through their flow. It was not surprising when, upon comparing the flows, they learned they were different.

It was painful for us to watch because the data were basically worthless. The novice moderator had developed her own flow based on her own expectations. The moment she picked up that pen and began writing for the participants, she owned the flow and took it away from the participants. It is so easy to do – and once you are in the middle of it, you may not even realize it has become *your* flow. Participants look up to you as the expert and will follow your lead. It is your job to pull the information out of participants and to force them to own the flow. This takes practice and the first few GTAs you conduct will not be perfect. Having a co-worker beside you to watch for pitfalls is extremely helpful. Go back later and watch a video of the session to see what you can improve next time.

The Overbearing Participant

Some user types can be more difficult to moderate than others. Highly trained, type A personality individuals will often be uncomfortable in situations where there is not a designated leader. They may feel the need to "fill this power vacuum," or they may want to demonstrate their expertise. These are the sessions that will test your skills as a moderator.

In one particular session, we had a participant who immediately grabbed up the proposed steps and began putting them in order himself. This was halted immediately, the flow taken apart, and the rules of "cooperation" were explained to the group as a whole. For most participants, this is all the moderator needs to do to set the group on track. Unfortunately, the domineering participant grabbed up the steps again and began building his own flow. The other participants just stood and watched. The steps were taken away again and the flow dismantled again. A light-hearted comment was directed at the participant: "You're in a timeout! You have to let everyone play in the sandbox." The domineering participant backed off for a couple of minutes while we asked individual participants to contribute. Unfortunately, the domineering participant jumped up and undid some of the work another participant had down because "it was ridiculous." He then began building his own flow again. We continued tearing down his work, asking the participant to cooperate, and trying to draw out the other participants, but it was not successful. The other participants were getting annoyed with the constant tearing down and rebuilding. They didn't care if the domineering participant wanted to do the whole thing – they were tired and ready to leave. It would have been much better to stop the session and ask the participant to leave. This kind of confrontation is difficult, especially with overbearing individuals, but it needs to be done to save the data.

We recommend role-playing with your co-workers. Take turns being the overbearing participant and try to frazzle the moderator. Practice taking control back and empowering the other participants. You should even practice ejecting participants. This must be done politely and with respect, no matter how rude or annoying the participant may be. Practice will help you stand up to the difficult participants, especially since co-workers bent on frazzling you will likely be more difficult than any participant can be.

Pulling It All Together

In this chapter, we have discussed an effective way to collect task information. When you do not have the time, resources, or access to users in the field, group task analysis is an efficient and valuable alternative to collect task information. We have described how to prepare for and conduct a GTA, as well as how to analyze the data, turn it into design solutions, and present it to the development team. Finally, we have presented several cautions and advice about moderating the activity.

CASE STUDY

This case study describes a pair of group task analyses (GTAs) conducted while I worked at Oracle for a product called iMeeting. It was the first usability activity we conducted for the team and led to a positive relationship between the usability group and the development team.

Capturing Task Information on How People Prepare For and Conduct Online Meetings

Kathy Baxter, eBay, Inc.

When Oracle began developing a product that allows individuals to conduct meetings via the web, the development team felt they needed more information. They believed they had a good idea of the features necessary, but wanted some validation to be sure they were not missing anything.

Our Approach

I conducted a group task analysis to capture information about the steps users take when preparing for, hosting, and attending an online meeting. Two different groups of users participated in two different GTA sessions. The first group consisted of individuals who normally conduct online meetings or teach courses online. They were asked to work together to create a task flow that demonstrated the steps they take when preparing for and hosting an online meeting. The second group of individuals had either attended meetings online or had taken courses online. They were asked to create a flow together that demonstrated the steps they took when preparing to attend and then attending an online meeting.

Analysis and Findings

Portions of both task flows are presented in Figures 11.9 and 11.10. For confidentiality reasons, the entire flows cannot be presented.

Figure 11.9:

Portion of a task flow to prepare for and attend a meeting online

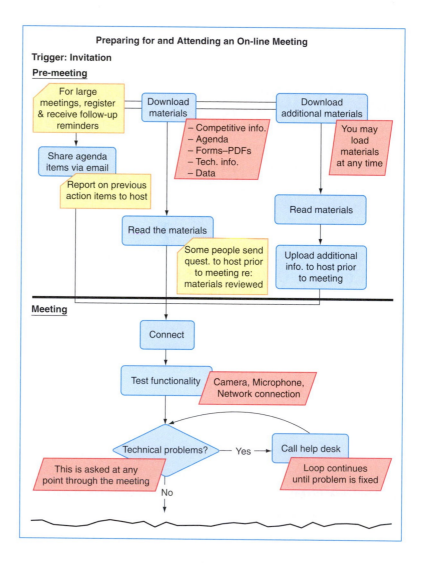

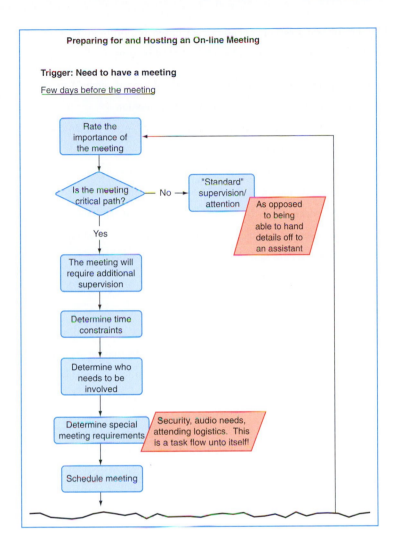

Figure 11.10:

Portion of a task flow to prepare for and host a meeting online

These task flows allowed us to capture a great deal of information that was specific to some companies or common across many companies. After examining these task flows, and using the checklist of questions presented on pages 498–499, Figure 11.8, we made the following design recommendations to the development team:

- Both hosts and attendees need to prepare for meetings on the system (e.g., download materials, read materials, etc.).
- Both hosts and attendees may need to send out materials in advance and/or during the meeting.
- Hosts need to control the presentation and meeting overall.

Note that the following recommendations are based on information in portions of the task flow that have been removed for confidentiality reasons.

- Everyone requires a secure meeting, in terms of who is allowed to attend (e.g., by invitation only), as well as security of data transmission.
- Hosts and attendees need to send messages to each other during a meeting.
- Hosts need to poll attendees.
- Hosts may need to indicate desired versus required attendees in meeting invitations and then check attendance at the time of the meeting.
- Hosts need to check RSVPs to determine whether the minimum number of people can attend or whether the required people can attend. Meetings may have to be canceled if attendance is known to be an issue in advance.

These requirements were presented to the team and were included in the product's functional specification. These requirements were then realized in the product itself. The team was so impressed by what they heard during the sessions, we had no difficulty convincing them to take up our recommendations. This is an ideal situation and one that we were extremely pleased about. Refer to Figures 11.11–11.13 for screenshots of the actual product to see how the findings were included in the design.

Functionality and issues that the development team had never considered were brought to the forefront. This included the amount of time and energy that is spent resolving

Figure 11.11:

iMeeting Home page

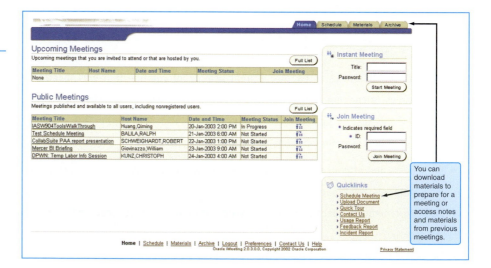

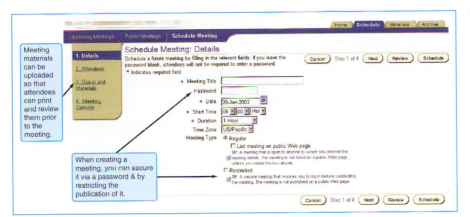

Figure 11.12:

Creating and scheduling a meeting using iMeeting

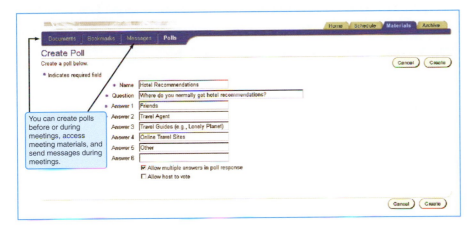

Figure 11.13:

Creating a poll using iMeeting

technical issues and the need to indicate optional versus required attendees. In addition, features that the team originally thought were vital to the users were reevaluated. Finally, resources were allocated to include as many of the features required as technology permitted (which was almost all of them!). For example, the technology was not available at the time of the first release to exchange materials via iMeeting before, during, or after a meeting. It was also not possible to indicate whether everyone was able to view a presentation or whether the network was still up.

The team was extremely satisfied with all of the information they learned in such a short period of time. They did not have to worry that they were designing a product based on best guesses or biases. The team has repeatedly come back to us for usability testing and we have been impressed by their high marks, as was the development team.

Lessons Learned

We were encouraged to include a few Oracle employees in our session. We normally do not include internal employees because they often know Oracle products better than external participants and they may be biased towards Oracle products. However, since the product did not exist and we were capturing user requirements for a product that Oracle employees would be using, we decided to include them. Unfortunately, we cannot pay our own employees for attending a usability activity. We are able to provide them with Oracle logo gear (e.g., sweatshirts) but that was not enough incentive for a couple of the participants to show after a long day at work.

We learned that we are more successful when we contact an employee's manager and ask him/her to recommend some employees for the activity. When we then contact the employees, we always state "Your manager has recommended you for our activity." This alone is typically enough incentive to avoid any no-shows.

CHAPTER 12

FOCUS GROUPS

Introduction

In a focus group, six to ten individuals are brought together to discuss their experiences or opinions around topics introduced by a moderator. The session typically lasts one to two hours and is good for quickly understanding user perception about a particular topic or concept. Focus groups are typically used by marketing professionals, but they have been used in social research since the 1930s. In our experience, the focus group is a valuable methodology when done *correctly*. One of the key benefits is that the group dynamic brings up topics you may never have thought to ask about. In addition, the group discussion can stimulate new ideas or encourage participants to talk about things they wouldn't have thought about if interviewed alone.

In this chapter, we highlight the strengths of this methodology and discuss how it can be used effectively as a part of the **user-centered design** (UCD) process. We present a common method for conducting a focus group, as well as several modifications. Finally, we discuss how to analyze and present the data, along with some of our lessons learned. A case study by Tech-Ed is provided at the end to demonstrate a real-world application of this frequently used methodology.

At a Glance

> When should you use a focus group?

> Things to be aware of when conducting a focus group

> Preparing to conduct a focus group

> Conducting a focus group

> Data analysis and interpretation

> Communicate the findings

> Modifications

When Should You Use a Focus Group?

Focus groups are excellent for the generation of ideas and for quickly gauging user impressions about a topic or concept. They allow you to capture information that might be more expensive to study directly. For example, in a focus group you can learn about activities that span days or weeks, which can be expensive to do via field studies. You can't get information as quickly and from as large a variety of companies/users with individual interviews or field studies as you can with focus groups.

You can also discover problems, challenges, frustrations, likes, and dislikes among users. They help you understand users' opinions, attitudes, preferences, and initial reactions. Focus groups can also be used to discover users' priorities (e.g., must have, nice to have, what they are willing to pay for).

Focus groups are one way to gather information about a target audience that you have very limited information about. You may not have enough information to design a survey (see Chapter 8, page 312) or develop a field study plan (see Chapter 13, page 562), but a focus group with six to ten users can provide the information you need to prepare for other usability activities. Below is a list of ways you can use a focus group to prepare for other usability activities:

- Identify or develop a question for a wants and needs analysis (see Chapter 9, page 370)

- Identify objects to be included in a card sorting activity (see Chapter 10, page 414)

- Identify potential steps for a group task analysis (see Chapter 11, page 458)
- Fine-tune the wording of survey questions and identify the most frequent or likely responses for multiple-choice questions (see Chapter 8, page 312)
- Identify new questions for surveys that you had not considered before (see Chapter 8, page 312)
- Identify scenarios (see Chapter 2, Before You Choose an Activity, "Learn About Your Users" section, page 41).

Focus Group, Individual Interviews, or Surveys?

Focus groups are excellent if you are looking for multiple points of view in a short period. They can be used in the middle or at the end of the development cycle. They can also be a great activity to help you gather initial requirements or ones that can be of benefit at a later stage of development. For example, a focus group can help you understand surprising or contradictory results obtained via surveys (see Chapter 8, page 312) or identify reasons why user satisfaction is so poor with your product. Individual interviews (see Chapter 7, page 246) are a better choice than focus groups if you are looking for detailed information that you cannot obtain from group discussion or via a survey. You are able to follow-up on responses and clarify participants' statements, which is not possible in a survey. Furthermore, you can spend more time understanding a single participant's needs, thoughts, and experiences in an interview than in a focus group. You can also cover more topics and do not have to worry about participants influencing each other's responses. In a focus group, you are typically limited in the number of questions you can ask and the depth of discussion with each participant because you want to hear from each participant equally.

One-on-one interviews can take significant time to conduct and more resources than a survey. However, there may be times when you need to collect large samples of data to feel more confident that the results you have obtained can be applied to the user population as a whole (not just the people you interviewed). This is not typical of most product development, but it may be the case, for example, in government regulated industries. Since you cannot obtain **statistically significant** results with a focus group (or even several focus groups), you cannot be sure that the proportion of responses to a question or topic in a focus group will match the proportion in the general population. In other words, if eight out of ten participants in a focus group state they want a particular feature, you cannot extend that to say 80%

of all users want that same feature. If you are looking for statistically significant results that can be generalized to the population as a whole, surveys are a better choice.

Things To Be Aware of When Conducting a Focus Group

There are a few situations in which we recommend using caution when designing a focus group or suggest using an alternative method instead.

Avoid Predictions

Studies have found that participants are not always good at predicting the features they would find useful in practice (Root & Draper 1983; Karlin & Klemmer 1989; Gray, Barfield, Haselkorn, Spyridakis, & Conquest 1990). This is why we recommend against asking participants to "pretend" about things with which they have no experience. For example, it is completely appropriate for you to ask someone "What is the biggest challenge you face in your job?" and then follow up the user's response with "What would make that part of your job easier to do?" You are not asking the participant to pretend – the participant does that job and may encounter that challenge every day. You can be sure that the participant has thought on many occasions about ways the challenge could or should be addressed. Going back to our travel example in earlier chapters, a travel agent might say that her biggest challenge is when people call her to book a vacation but never have the information needed, like the maximum budget, the dates of travel, and desired destinations.

On the other hand, you should not ask the travel agent whether she would like using voice-activated input, if the agent has never seen or used such a system before. She may think the concept sounds really cool when you describe it, but once she begins using it at work she hates it because everyone in the surrounding cubicles can hear every mistake she makes.

Avoid Sensitive or Personal Topics

It should go without saying, but it is unwise to discuss extremely sensitive or personal topics like politics, sex, or morals in a focus group. Obviously, these are topics that are sometimes uncomfortable or cause heated discussion between friends and family. It is not appropriate for you to ask participants to discuss them in front of strangers and on camera.

Use a Skilled Moderator

As with any group activity, you *must* have a skilled moderator familiar with the domain to contain overbearing users, draw out quiet users, avoid bias, probe to understand users' underlying needs, and limit groupthink (i.e., the tendency for the members of a group to come to a consensus, rather than expressing individual ideas). The moderator must always keep command of the room, be personable, treat even difficult participants with the utmost respect, and never pass judgment on the opinions expressed during the session. (Refer to Chapter 6, During Your User Requirements Activity, "Moderating Your Activity" section, page 220 for a detailed discussion about effective moderation.) If a moderator is not successful at these tasks, the data collected will be biased and should not be used.

If you are not a skilled moderator, you could hire a professional to moderate the group (Appendix B, page 688, has a list of professional moderators and training courses). Contact your marketing department since marketing professionals typically have training and experience running focus groups. One advantage of using an outside moderator is that he/she typically will not share your biases and will be more likely to collect information in a neutral format. Unfortunately, the added expense and time to bring the moderator up to speed on your product or area of concern may not be feasible. Ask for a sample of their work (i.e., quick findings, usability report, presentation) and find out exactly how long it will take to complete the activity from kickoff to report delivery. And don't forget to check those references. Optionally, you may choose to have a member of the product team serving as a co-moderator to follow-up with more detailed questions that the outside moderator would not know to ask.

Observation is Still Best for Understanding Tasks

In one study, participants in three focus groups were asked how they would complete the task of assessing the credibility of a website (Eysenbach & Köhler 2002). Participants provided a number of methods they would use – but when many of those same individuals participated in a usability evaluation and were asked to assess the credibility of a website, they did not use the same methods they described in the focus groups. The takeaway here is that if you want to know exactly how end users go about completing a task, the best method is via direct observation. This applies whether you are conducting focus groups, interviews, or surveys.

Focus Groups are Not Appropriate for Comparative, Competitive, and Benchmarking Data

Focus groups are not appropriate for conducting formal usability tests for your product. Conducting comparative, competitive, and benchmarking studies with a group of users results in co-discovery and doesn't produce individual data. If you want to collect task performance information (i.e., errors, assists, task success), it is best to run individual usability tests. Unless your end users normally work with your product as a group, collecting group performance information does not provide an accurate assessment of the usability of your product. It would, however, provide you information about aspects of your product that participants think are easy or difficult and things that they like or dislike.

SUGGESTED RESOURCES FOR ADDITIONAL READING

Usability evaluations are outside the scope of this book. If you would like to learn more about collecting usability data on your product, please refer to one of the excellent books below:

- Dumas, J. S. & Redish, J. C. (1999). *A Practical Guide to Usability Testing*, 2nd edn. Exeter, England: Intellect Books.
- Rubin, J. (1994). *Handbook of Usability Testing*. New York: John Wiley & Sons.

Preparing to Conduct a Focus Group

Are You Ready?

Before you begin *any* user requirements activity there are a number of things you must be familiar with. Because these elements are common to all user requirements activities they have all been covered in the earlier chapters, but now is a good time to double-check the list. If you are not familiar with one of the items you can refer to the earlier chapter to brush up or familiarize yourself with that element.

Chapter 1: Introduction to User Requirements
- ☐ **Getting stakeholder buy-in for your activity** (see page 14)

Chapter 2: Before You Choose an Activity
- ☐ **Learn about your product** (see page 29)
- ☐ **Learn about your users** (see page 41)

Chapter 3: Ethical and Legal Considerations
- ☐ **Create consent forms** (see page 98)
- ☐ **Create confidential disclosure agreements** (see page 103)

Chapter 4: Setting up Facilities for Your User Requirements Activity
- ☐ **Create or acquire a facility for your activity** (see page 106)

Chapter 5: Preparing for Your User Requirements Activity
- ☐ **Develop an activity proposal** (see page 146)
- ☐ **Determine the time of day and duration of your session** (see page 155)
- ☐ **Recruit participants** (see page 156)
- ☐ **Develop an activity protocol** (see page 191)
- ☐ **Pilot your activity** (see page 193)

Chapter 6: During Your User Requirements Activity
- ☐ **Welcoming participants** (see page 209)
- ☐ **Deal with late and absent participants** (see page 211)
- ☐ **Warm-up your participants** (see page 215)
- ☐ **Invite observers to watch your activity** (see page 216)
- ☐ **Successfully moderate your activity** (see page 220)
- ☐ **Record and take notes during your activity** (see page 226)

Now that you understand what a focus group is and when to use it, we are going to present a fundamental version of a focus group. If you would like to make additions to the method, refer to the "Modifications" section on page 542.

Preparation Timeline

The timeline in Table 12.1 covers in detail the sequence and timing of events to prepare for a focus group. These are *approximate* times based on our personal experience and should be used only as a guide. It could take longer or less time for each step depending on a variety of factors – such as responsiveness of the development team, access to users, and resources available.

Table 12.1:

Preparation timeline for a focus group

When to complete	Approximate time to complete	Activity
As soon as possible	2 weeks	☐ Meet with team to develop the user profile(s) ☐ Meet with team to formulate the question(s) and/or create artifacts to stimulate discussion
After identification of questions and user profile	1 week	☐ Create and distribute proposal
After the proposal has been agreed to by all stakeholders	2 weeks	☐ Identify and recruit users ☐ Assign roles for the activity (e.g., moderator, note-taker, videographer) ☐ Prepare materials ☐ Acquire location ☐ Acquire incentives ☐ Prepare documentation (e.g., confidentiality agreement, consent form)
1 week before the session	2 days	☐ Run a pilot session or rehearse ☐ Make changes in response to the pilot
Day before the focus group	1 hour	☐ Call and confirm with participants
Day of focus group	2–3 hours	☐ Create and place "Welcome" sign in lobby ☐ Pick up food (optional) ☐ Set up location with all materials necessary

At a Glance

> Identify the questions you wish to answer
> Players in your activity
> Inviting observers
> Activity materials

Identify the Questions You Wish to Answer

Begin your preparation by identifying the questions you wish to answer. You may want to have an initial **brainstorming** session with all of your **stakeholders** (members of the product team, the usability group, marketing). You will likely end up with questions that are out of the scope of the proposed activity or questions that are best answered by other activities. You may also end up with more questions than you could possibly cover in a single focus group session. If this is the case, you will either need to conduct multiple sessions or trim down the number of questions to fit into a single session. We do not recommend conducting focus groups sessions beyond two hours, however; dedicated participants or customers may be willing to stay for longer sessions provided you provide regular breaks and keep the session interesting.

Types of Questions You Can Ask

Below are several sample questions you can ask in a focus group:

- A user's "typical" day or the user's last full day at work
- The tasks that users do and how they do them
- The domain in general (e.g., terminology, standard procedures, industry guidelines)
- Users' likes and dislikes
- Users' desired outcomes or goals (refer to Chapter 7, Interviews, "Outcomes Analysis" section, page 252)
- Users' reactions, opinions, or attitudes towards a new product/concept
- Desired outcomes for new products or features.

Asking participants to discuss a "typical" day at work gives you a high-level overview of participants' perceptions about the way they work or activities they may do in general. Asking participants to tell you about their last full day at work gives you specific examples about tasks they have recently done. You can also understand how certain tasks are done at a high level, challenges they face, and things they enjoy. Focus groups also offer the opportunity to learn about standard terminology, guidelines, and industry practices. Participants can additionally describe desired outcomes in their work or goals they want to achieve. Finally, you can gauge user reaction to concepts and brainstorm ideas for new products or features.

Wording Your Questions

Make sure that all questions are open-ended, worded clearly, impartially, and actually ask what you intended to ask. We strongly recommend reviewing the advice given in Chapter 7 before proceeding (refer to Chapter 7, Interviews, "Write the Questions" section, page 262).

The data you collect may be described as either qualitative or quantitative. We describe both types below.

Qualitative data

The majority of your focus group will likely be comprised of open-ended questions (i.e., designed to elicit detailed responses, and free from structure). These types of questions generate **qualitative data**. You may walk away with some quantitative data if you include ranking or polling as a part of your focus group (e.g., "85% of participants want to be able to book cruises online"), but the bulk of your data will be qualitative.

Let's use our online travel website as an example and design some questions for a focus group. You know that college students sometimes attend professional conferences relevant to their major. You also know that college students are usually poor. Your company would like to offer "room sharing" on your website. People who are interested in sharing a hotel room in a particular hotel or city could sign up and specify preferences (e.g., females only, under $50/night, no more than three roommates, non-smoking). Since you are not aware of any travel website that offers this, you would like to learn more about people's attitudes towards signing up on a website to share a hotel room. A focus group seems like the best way to get a general feel for attitudes, biases, and new ideas in this area. This will be followed up with a survey and sent out to a few hundred current and potential customers. With a two-hour focus group and ten participants, you realize you can probably cover only about five or six questions. Some open-ended questions you might ask are:

- How satisfied are you with the kind of accommodations your budget allows?
- How willing would you be to share a hotel room with someone you know to lower your costs and get a nicer room?
- How willing would you be to share a hotel room with someone you didn't know to lower your costs and get a nicer room?
- What would you want to know about a person with whom you might share a room?
- What would make you more likely to share a room with someone you didn't know?

Quantitative data

During a focus group you may ask **closed-ended questions**. These are questions that provide a limited set of responses for participants to choose from (e.g., yes/no, agree/disagree, option a, b, or c). In a focus group you may also ask participants to rank a series of options or to vote for their preferred choice, or you can poll the participants (i.e., determine how many people agree with a statement). These types of questions collect **quantitative data** that can be counted or measured (but see our caution on page 517 about using quantitative measures with small numbers of participants). The benefit of collecting this type of data during a focus group rather than on a survey (where it is typically collected) is that you can ask individuals to discuss *why* they made the selection(s) they did. In fact, it's best to think about ratings and polls as providing an opportunity to have a discussion rather than as a quantitative measure of a preference or attitude. You may also choose to give a survey prior to or following a focus group in order to address questions that you do not have time to address in the focus group itself.

Using our travel example, some closed-ended questions you might ask are:

- How many people have a hotel budget when they travel for work or school? [ask for a show of hands]

- If you had a limited budget to attend a conference/trade show/meeting, and could not stay in the hotel where it was being held, which of the following options would you choose: (a) stay in a hotel you can afford three miles from the hotel; (b) stay in the conference hotel but pay the extra out-of-pocket; (c) share a room at the conference hotel with someone of the same gender you didn't know?

- Do you agree or disagree with the following statement: "I would be willing to share a hotel room with someone I didn't know to lower my costs and get a nicer room."?

It is possible to generate *quantitative* data from open-ended questions by collecting data that reflects the *number* of people who agreed with a specific comment or point of view discussed. However, the bulk of your data collected from open-ended questions will typically focus on the actual responses and overall sentiments of the group. And remember that your quantitative data will not be representative anyway.

Test Your Questions

Use the data from your pilot session to practice your data analysis (see "Data Analysis and Interpretation," page 538). You can prepare to analyze quantitative data by creating spreadsheets and entering in data from your pilot session. Basic analyses such as averages, minimums, maximums, and frequencies can be computed. (Refer to Chapter 8, Surveys, "Types of Calculation" section, page 349, to learn more about analyzing quantitative data.)

There really isn't a lot to do to prepare to analyze qualitative data. Three common methods of data analysis are the **affinity diagram**, simple summarization of user responses to each question, and using qualitative analysis tools. We discuss each of these options later (see "Data Analysis and Interpretation," page 538). If you choose to use a qualitative analysis tool, enter the pilot data into the tool to learn how the tool works and whether it will suit your needs.

Present the analysis of your pilot data to the product development team and state what conclusions you can draw from those results. Is this the type of information that the team is looking for? If not, you need to reword or create new questions to collect the information the team is seeking.

Players in Your Activity

Of course you will need end users to take part in your session, but there are also three additional roles that need to be filled to conduct a successful focus group: moderator, note-taker, and videographer.

You need to decide how many sessions to run, the number of participants per session, and the composition for each session. Below, we address those issues and provide recommendations to help you decide.

Participant mix

Some focus group professionals like to mix different user types in the same session. They feel they can get better discussion when different perspectives are brought together. We do not recommend this approach. With as few as six users per session, you cannot get a large enough sample size to know whether you are getting representative answers from each user type. In addition, the user types may be so different, that you cannot capture quality information to build upon. Finally, some user types should not be placed together. For example, managers and their direct reports should never be placed in the same group because the direct reports may not be honest or may defer to their managers. Managers may even feel it necessary to "take control" of the session and play a more dominant or expert role in the activity to save face in front of their employees. The issues are similar when you mix user types of different levels within a hierarchy, even if one does not report directly to the other (e.g., doctor and nurse). Refer to "Lessons Learned" (page 546) for a discussion of how mixing user types of different levels in a hierarchy can cause real problems.

Lastly, speaking with especially effective or expert users can provide a wealth of ideas since these "lead" users can often be a source of innovation. However, you should also recruit novice and average users since expert users may request features or services that are too sophisticated from the majority of the user population. By speaking with each user type individually, you can quickly understand the needs and issues for a broad spectrum of your population.

How many groups? How many participants?

Since the group dynamic is an important component to this method, we recommend recruiting 6–10 end users per session; however, groups as small as four can still provide valuable information. Groups with more than ten participants can be difficult to manage because you are not focused on one question – as in a wants and needs analysis where we normally have groups of 12 participants (see Chapter 7, Interviews, page 246). The questions in a focus group may be more complex and the answers are more in-depth. As a result, if you have a large group, it is unlikely that everyone will have an opportunity to speak. In addition, since you want to hear from every participant, you can cover very few questions with large groups. It may seem that two additional participants will not make a big difference, but when you are trying to get multiple perspectives to multiple questions, it will.

Although it is excellent to run two or three groups of ten participants, your time and resources may not permit it. If you are restricted on the number of participants you can recruit, it is better to run multiple smaller groups than one large group (e.g., it is better to run two groups with five participants each rather than one group with ten participants). This is because group dynamics can vary. You do not want one dominating user to influence your entire pool of participants. In addition, you may learn information in one focus group that you never thought about and would like the opportunity to develop new questions for a second focus group. If you put all your participants in one basket, you loose the opportunity to revise your questions. If you change your questions between sessions, you cannot compare the answers across groups but you do have the opportunity to cover more ground.

Only you know what resources you have available to conduct your studies and you must weigh the resources available with the questions you need to answer. There is no magic formula for determining the numbers of participants and groups to run – the final answer is: "It depends."

Online Travel Example

Even though your idea for room sharing originally focused on college students, you realize that other people may be traveling on a budget and want to take advantage of this new feature as well. Since students are different from other travelers, you identify them as one user group and identify adult budget travelers as a second user type.

Your research identifies college students as being 18–24 years old, currently enrolled in school, and they travel at least once a year on a tight budget. Adult budget travelers are 25–40 years old. Based on some preliminary research that you have done, it is likely that males and females will have different needs and criteria when deciding whether or not to share a room with a stranger, so you decide to run adult male and female budget travelers in separate groups. So your user composition is:

- **Male and female college students aged 18–24 years**
- **Single female budget travelers aged 25–40**
- **Single male budget travelers aged 25–40**

The moderator

One moderator is needed per session to facilitate the activity. (Refer to "Conducting a Focus Group," page 535, as well as Chapter 6, During Your User Requirements Activity, "Moderating Your Activity" section, page 220, for the details of being an effective moderator.) The moderator will elicit responses from the group, examine each answer to ensure he/she understands what the participant is really asking for, and then paraphrase the response to make sure that the intent of the statement is captured.

The moderator must engage all the participants. This is typically done by containing any overbearing participants and drawing out quiet participants. Finally, the moderator needs to know when to let a discussion go off the "planned path" into valuable areas of discovery and when to bring a fruitless discussion back on track.

The moderator needs to have sufficient domain knowledge to know which discussions are adding value and which are sapping valuable time. He or she also needs to know what follow-up questions to ask on-the-fly to get the details the team needs to make product decisions (see "Lessons Learned," page 546).

If you have never run a focus group before, participate as a user in several different focus groups. You can go to online community boards or search job listings for companies in your area that are looking for focus group participants. Also, observe different moderators in action to learn what worked and what did not. You may also identify a certain style that you would like to emulate. It is essential that you practice moderating a focus group rather than just jumping in feet first. You do not want to learn "on the job" when expensive data collection is at stake.

Figure 12.1 is a moderator's checklist. For a detailed discussion of the art of moderating, refer to Chapter 6, During Your User Requirements Activity, "Moderating Your Activity" section, page 220.

Figure 12.1:

Moderator's checklist

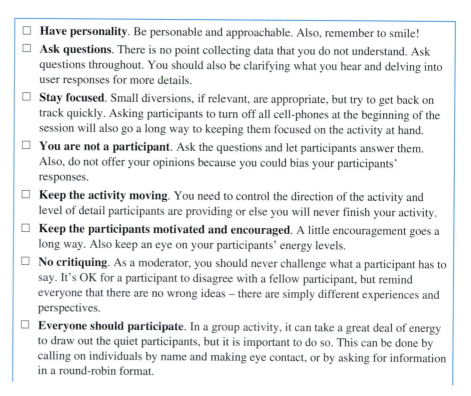

- ☐ **Have personality**. Be personable and approachable. Also, remember to smile!
- ☐ **Ask questions**. There is no point collecting data that you do not understand. Ask questions throughout. You should also be clarifying what you hear and delving into user responses for more details.
- ☐ **Stay focused**. Small diversions, if relevant, are appropriate, but try to get back on track quickly. Asking participants to turn off all cell-phones at the beginning of the session will also go a long way to keeping them focused on the activity at hand.
- ☐ **You are not a participant**. Ask the questions and let participants answer them. Also, do not offer your opinions because you could bias your participants' responses.
- ☐ **Keep the activity moving**. You need to control the direction of the activity and level of detail participants are providing or else you will never finish your activity.
- ☐ **Keep the participants motivated and encouraged**. A little encouragement goes a long way. Also keep an eye on your participants' energy levels.
- ☐ **No critiquing**. As a moderator, you should never challenge what a participant has to say. It's OK for a participant to disagree with a fellow participant, but remind everyone that there are no wrong ideas – there are simply different experiences and perspectives.
- ☐ **Everyone should participate**. In a group activity, it can take a great deal of energy to draw out the quiet participants, but it is important to do so. This can be done by calling on individuals by name and making eye contact, or by asking for information in a round-robin format.

☐ **No one should dominate**. When you notice a participant is beginning to dominate the group, try to call on others in the group to balance things out and use body language to quiet down the dominant participant (e.g., turning your back to the participant, not making eye contact). If things don't improve, gently address the overbearing participant and, in the worst case, escort the participant out.

Figure 12.1:

– Cont'd

The note-taker

A note-taker is needed to help the moderator. The moderator has a big job and should not be worried about taking detailed notes. The sole job of the note-taker is to write down notes from the session. It is important for the note-taker to have domain knowledge so that he/she knows what points are important to capture and what comments can be left off, as well as to ensure that the notes make sense. (See "Lessons Learned," page 546, to read more about the importance of domain knowledge.) You will find a detailed discussion of note-taking tips and strategies in Chapter 6 (refer to Chapter 6, During Your User Requirements Activity, "Recording and Note-taking" section, page 226).

The notes can be displayed for the group (including the moderator) to see. This can be done on a laptop and projecting the image or by writing the notes on flip charts at the front of the room. Obviously, reading someone's handwriting is not an issue when using a laptop, but if your note-taker is not a fast or good typist, you may want to go with the handwritten notes. An obvious advantage of typing the notes during the session is that you can send out the notes to stakeholders immediately following the session.

Taking notes for the group to see has a few advantages and disadvantages. One advantage is that it can help the participants to avoid repeating the same information, and it shows the participants that their comments have been captured (otherwise participants may ramble on to be sure you captured what was said). If the note-taker captured a comment incorrectly, the participant can correct him/her immediately. Finally, the moderator can refer back to the notes during the session to follow-up on a particular comment or to direct the group to a different line of discussion.

One disadvantage to having the notes displayed for all to see is that you may not be able to use a lot of shorthand because the participants won't understand it.

Additionally, the note-taker should not include design ideas or notes about the participants, comments, or session for all to see.

Whether or not the notes are being displayed to the group, the big benefit to having a note-taker is to avoid the need to watch the entire focus group on tape for later data analysis. As soon as the session is over, you have data at hand to begin analyzing. If there are areas where the moderator feels that the notes do not make sense, he or she can go back and watch just that portion of the session. This cuts down significantly on the time it takes to analyze the data. Finally, the note-taker can help you analyze your data. Since the note-taker was there for the entire session, he/she understands the data as well as you and it is always helpful to have an extra pair of eyes and a different perspective to analyze the data.

If a note-taker is not available, you could always go back and take notes while watching a tape of the session. However, we recommend that you do this only as a last resort. A note-taker is extremely helpful and can save a great deal of time.

Some focus group professionals prefer to have their sessions transcribed by professionals. People working in highly regulated fields (e.g., the pharmaceutical industry regulated by the FDA) may be required to have precise documentation of any usability activity they conduct since the information learned in such sessions provides data for making product design decisions. Transcribing focus group sessions is extremely time-consuming and expensive. It can take an average of six hours to transcribe one hour of tape. If multiple voices are involved, it will likely take longer. Companies usually charge per hour of *transcription* time (not per hour of tape). In our experience in the San Francisco Bay area, we have found that they charge about $42/hour. Not only is this expensive, it can take days before you get your information back to begin data analysis. For these reasons, we strongly recommend using a note-taker to note key points and quotes for immediate data analysis.

The videographer

Whenever possible you will want a video record of your session. You will find a detailed discussion of videotaping tips and the benefits of videotape in Chapter 6 (refer to Chapter 6, During Your User Requirements Activity, "Recording and Note-taking" section, page 226). You will need someone to be responsible for recording.

In most cases, this person simply needs to start and stop the tape, insert new tapes as needed, and keep an eye out for any technical issues that arise.

Inviting Observers

If you have the facilities to allow stakeholders to view these sessions, you will find it highly beneficial to get them involved (refer to Chapter 4, Setting up Facilities for Your User Requirements Activity, "Lab Layout" section, page 123). Stakeholders can learn a lot about what users like and dislike about the current product or a competitor's product, the difficulties they encounter, what they want, and why they think they want it.

If you take a break during the session, you can ask the observers if they have any questions they would like answered or areas they want to delve into further. You should not promise you will be able to cover them; but if time and opportunity permit, it is good to have these additional questions available. If the questions the observers suggest are clearly biased or would derail the focus group, you can always state: "Those are questions that we might want to consider for another activity."

As always, we strongly recommend videotaping the sessions for any stakeholder who may not be able to attend, as well as for your own future reference.

Activity Materials

A basic focus group requires a few materials:

- ☐ Laptop/computer or whiteboard or flip chart
- ☐ Computer projector and screen (if using laptop/computer)
- ☐ Blue or black markers (if using whiteboard or flip chart)
- ☐ Materials for creativity exercises
- ☐ Paper and pens for participants to take notes
- ☐ Prototype or other artifact to stimulate discussion (optional)
- ☐ Large room conducive for a group activity
- ☐ Video recording equipment.

We prefer to use a laptop and display each question on a PowerPoint® slide (see Figure 12.2). This looks professional and the questions are easy to read. However,

Figure 12.2:

*A focus group in action.
The question has been
projected so that
everyone can read it
easily. The tables are in
a "U" formation so that
everyone can see each
other and the
moderator easily*

a whiteboard or flip chart will work just as well. Remember to write clearly and with large letters in blue or black marker.

It is valuable to provide paper and pens for the participants. If multiple people wish to speak at the same time, you may have to ask them to "hold their thoughts." Sometimes people forget what they wanted to say when they hear someone else speaking. It can be frustrating for both you and the user if good ideas are lost. Allowing participants to jot a quick note on paper can help save those great ideas.

Tip

Don't throw away those papers at the end of the session! If you can read the handwriting, you may find good nuggets of information that were not discussed during the session.

Finally, presenting a prototype, a competitor's product, or a video (if appropriate) can help encourage discussion and focus thoughts. You do not want to bias participants' answers, but it is often helpful to show examples of the product (yours or a competitor's) during the discussion. Make sure that all participants can easily see whatever you are presenting.

Conducting a Focus Group

You are now prepared to conduct a focus group. In this section, we walk you through the steps to conduct your session.

Activity Timeline

The timeline in Table 12.2 covers in detail the sequence and timing of events to conduct a focus group. It is based on a two-hour session and will obviously need to be adjusted for shorter or longer sessions. These are *approximate* times based on our personal experience and should be used only as a guide.

Now that you know the steps involved in conducting a focus group at a high level, we will discuss each step in detail.

Approximate duration	Procedure
5 minutes	Welcome participants (introductions, forms)
5 minutes	Creative exercise/participant introductions
45–100 minutes	Discussion
5 minutes	Wrap-up (distribute incentives, thank participants, escort them out)

Table 12.2:
Timeline of a focus group session

At a Glance

> Welcome the participants

> Introduce the activity and discussion rule

> The focus group discussion

Welcome the Participants

This is the time during which you greet your participants, allow them to eat some snacks, ask them to fill out paperwork, and get them warmed-up for your activity.

It is helpful to begin with a creative exercise such as designing name tents. Alternatively, you can discuss likes and dislikes of the current system or a competitor's product. The details of these stages are described in Chapter 6 (refer to Chapter 6, During Your User Requirements Activity, "Warm-up Exercises" section, page 215).

Introduce the Activity and Discussion Rule

Once all forms are complete, introductions are made, and the participants are warmed-up, the rule for discussion should be provided. The rule is simple: "All ideas are correct." It is important to explain to participants that their individual experiences may be different, and those differences should be expressed – but they should not critique each other's ideas or perceptions. Write the rule "All ideas are correct" on a flip chart and have it visible during the entire session. If anyone breaks the rule, the moderator can point to it as a polite reminder.

The Focus Group Discussion

Participants should feel that the focus group session is free-flowing and relatively unstructured. You should have a list of questions or topics to be covered during the session, but you may discover interesting insights by allowing a conversation to progress down an unexpected path. Group interaction is the key benefit of focus groups, so it is important to be open to new topics and allow the conversation to flow, otherwise you may as well do a series of individual interviews. If your questions are presented on slides (see Figure 12.3), that does not mean you are locked into asking the questions in that order. As long as all your questions are answered by the end of the session, the order shouldn't matter.

You may wish to begin the session or even each question with a "round-robin" to get everyone comfortable speaking in the group and ensure that everyone has a chance to speak.

As we mentioned earlier, you can ask ranking questions during a focus group or ask participants to vote for their preference. Rather than asking everyone to vote by raising their hand (and risk **groupthink** or **evaluation apprehension**), you can ask people to vote on paper. You can have the questions pre-printed and distribute each

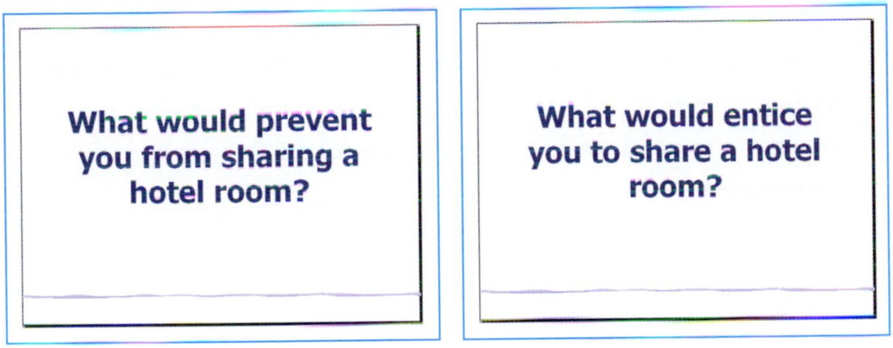

Figure 12.3:
Sample focus group question slides

question at the time you would like to vote. This prevents users from filling out all the questions in advance rather than paying attention to the group discussion. Or worse, users may look at the questions in advance and this could possibly bias the discussions. Alternatively, you can have a survey available for users to complete at the very end. It should be noted that voting on paper, whether it is during the session or on a survey at the end, removes the benefit of group discussion. A compromise is to vote on paper during the session and then ask volunteers to talk about how they voted. If no one feels comfortable sharing his/her vote, you can move on.

A possible component of focus groups is brainstorming. Chapter 9 provides tips for conducting an effective brainstorming session, and ways to ruin a session (refer to Chapter 9, Wants and Needs Analysis, "The Brainstorming" section, page 385, and "Modifications" section, page 401). We recommend reviewing those sections if you plan to have brainstorming during your focus group.

Online Travel Example

You have asked participants to discuss what would encourage them to share a room with a stranger. Obviously, saving money is the number one answer. There are other possible incentives that you would like to learn more about, and several of them have been offered by participants. These include networking, safety, having someone to share dinner in a strange city, and having someone with whom to see the sights. Because none of these really stood out as being more important than the others, you can list the incentives on the board and ask participants to rank them in order of importance or rate them on a scale of one (not at all important) to seven (very important).

Data Analysis and Interpretation

Data analysis and interpretation can be divided into three steps: debriefing, analyzing quantitative data, and analyzing qualitative data.

At a Glance

> Debrief
> Analyzing quantitative data
> Analyzing qualitative data

Debrief

Within 24 hours of the focus group session, we recommend getting together with your note-taker to have a debriefing session. Review the questions asked and note the key points from the session. Were there any unexpected findings? What did each observer identify as the key take-away from the session? Were there any trends that can be identified at this point? Fill in areas of the notes that may not be clear while everything is still fresh in your mind. You should also decide whether another session is necessary with the same user type. If so, determine if you would like to change the questions based on what your learned in the previous session.

Analyzing Quantitative Data

As we mentioned earlier in the chapter, you can collect quantitative as well as qualitative data during a focus group. If you prepared a spreadsheet in advance, you can quickly input the data from your quantitative questions. Complicated statistics are not appropriate with such a small sample. With small numbers of users, all you want to demonstrate is the average response, and perhaps frequency of response, and minimum and maximum responses. The details of these calculations are discussed in Chapter 8 (refer to Chapter 8, Surveys, "Types of Calculation" section, page 349). You should be very cautious about making too much out of the quantitative data from a focus group. As we mentioned earlier, if you ran one focus group and eight out of ten participants said they would buy a product, that data is not the same as having 80% of 100 participants in a survey say the same thing.

Analyzing Qualitative Data

Several software tools are available for purchase to help you analyze qualitative data. Even so, when we surveyed several usability experts, we found that none of them had ever used such a tool. If you are interested in exploring qualitative analysis software tools, refer to Appendix G (page 722) for a description of each tool and the pros and cons of using such tools.

Most professionals who conduct focus groups (including ourselves) find affinity diagrams (see Appendix F, page 714) and simply summarizing users' responses more beneficial. Because this analysis technique applies to a variety of methods, it is located in an appendix for all applicable methods to reference. You may also find it helpful to develop a coding system as you analyze the data to identify trends across a single session or multiple sessions. For example, you might want to code each instance a participant mentions a shortcoming of your current product as "negative" and each positive statement as "positive." This will make it easier to quickly scan your notes and summarize all the positive and negative statements participants made about your product.

There are several sources of information for you to draw upon as you analyze the results:

- Notes taken by the note-taker
- Notes taken by observers (they can have different insights on the participants' comments)
- Notes taken during the debriefing session(s)
- Audio/videotapes of the sessions

- Transcripts of the sessions (if available)
- Notes participants may have made during the sessions.

You may wish to write a summary of the responses to each question and provide some supporting quotes. Use the participants' actual words whenever possible. This will likely require watching the tape(s) but it is worth it. You can group similar responses by user type, age, gender, or other factors you collected during recruitment. (Refer to Chapter 5, Preparing for Your User Requirements Activity, "Recruitment Methods" section, page 173.) Identify themes or frequently made statements. Look for data that support or contradict the thoughts and research already gathered by the development team or marketing. If the purpose of the activity was to create a basis for future usability activities, you should also demonstrate how the focus group results would be used in the next activity. You may also be able to provide guidance to the development team on new areas to investigate further.

Online Travel Example

Your focus group results have provided you with a wealth of information to provide solid multiple-choice questions for a follow-up survey. You would like to conduct this survey so that you can gather information from a large sample of the population. From the results of the focus group sessions, it seems as though students are the primary audience interested in sharing rooms to save money, so that is who you will concentrate your efforts on.

Communicate the Findings

Preparing to Communicate Your Findings

The specific data that you communicate to product teams can vary depending upon the activity you conducted, but some elements of *how* you communicate the results are the same regardless of the method. Because these strategies are common to all user requirements activities, they are discussed in detail in Chapter 14, Concluding Your Activity, page 636. We recommend that you read that chapter prior to relaying your results to your stakeholders. Topics discussed include:

- **Prioritization of your findings** (see page 638)
- **Creating an effective presentation** (see page 644)
- **Writing valuable reports for different audiences** (see page 652)
- **Ensuring the incorporation of your findings** (see page 660)

Depending on the complexity of the data you collected, you can create a simple bullet list of information you learned during the focus group, a table comparing the answers between two or more user types, or a summary paragraph for each of the questions you asked users. Figure 12.4 is an example of a portion of a report.

Question asked:

What would entice you to share a hotel room?

When the concept was initially introduced, participants expressed reluctance at the idea of sharing a hotel room with a stranger. Once participants began discussing possible merits of room sharing, the attitude of each group became more positive. Money was the most obvious benefit, regardless of user type. In addition, all participants wanted to ensure that a reputable agency was responsible for matching the guests. They would feel more comfortable that "dangerous" or "questionable" guests would be screened out, as well as ensuring that people with similar interests and habits (e.g., smoking versus non-smoking) would be matched.

In general, women expressed positive benefits that were more social in nature. This includes having someone to do things with, such as going to dinner, sight-seeing, and sharing common experiences. Female participants stated one of the outcomes of travel was to see and learn about a new city, but they were rarely satisfied they met their goal because they do not like site-seeing alone. They also mentioned increased safety as a positive benefit. Most female participants said they would be more likely to explore new cities and go out in the evening if they had someone to go with. Finally, the majority of female participants made it clear that they would be interested in sharing a room only with other females.

Continued

Figure 12.4:

Portion of a report summarizing the results of one question across multiple sessions and user types

Adult male budget travelers, on the other hand, discussed the networking benefits of sharing a room, particularly if they were on travel for related business (e.g., a common conference). Male college students stated having someone to hang out with would be "cool," but the social aspect was not of primary importance. None of the male participants mentioned increased safety as a possible benefit (or outcome) from sharing a room. Male participants also did not mention the gender of the guest as a concern. This does not mean that the gender of the guest will not matter to male customers; it simply means that gender was not one of the primary concerns for them when deciding whether or not to share a room.

Overall, participants in college (male and female) were much more enthusiastic about the concept of room sharing than people who were not in college because, for them, the outcome of sharing a room is to save money – and that is their primary concern.

Modifications

Because focus groups have been in use for so many years, there are a plethora of different modifications that you can try. Many of them involve providing users with exposure to the product or concept under development in different ways so that users have some base of experience from which to draw. For more information about a particular modification, check out the reference provided.

Task-based Focus Groups

In task-based focus groups, participants are presented with a task (or scenario) and asked to complete it with a prototype or the actual product. Several participants may be working in the same room at the same time but they should be working individually. If your product is software or a web application, this will obviously require several computers. After participants have completed their task(s), they are brought together to discuss their experiences.

It is best to give the participants the same set of core tasks so they can share common experiences. For example, in one study, participants were asked to look up information in a user's manual and describe how confident they were that the answer they gave was right (Hackos & Redish 1998). Similar focus groups have been conducted for car owner's manuals, appliance manuals, and telephone bills (Dumas &

Redish 1999). Keep in mind, however, that a focus group is not a substitute for a usability test.

Similarly, you can present participants with multiple activities or artifacts during a single focus group. Participants may start off with a brief group discussion but then they work individually for the majority of the session. Multiple facilitators are needed for this activity. Each facilitator works with a participant one-on-one and completes a different activity (e.g., brainstorming new ways of solving a problem, view a prototype). After all the participants have gone through all of the activities, the group reconvenes to discuss experiences. Ideally, all participants will have completed all of the activities.

An excellent example of this methodology began with each of five focus groups photographing participants holding phone handsets to assess gripping styles (Dolan, Wiklund, Logan, & Augaitis 1995). Participants then rank-ordered six conventionally designed handsets and six progressively designed handsets according to several ergonomic and emotional attributes (after having experience with each). Finally, participants critiqued the handset designs according to personal preference, and each built a clay model of his/her ideal handset. By giving participants exposure to a wide range of experiences with the potential product or domain area, participants do not need to "imagine" what a product would be like. They can discuss their actual experiences with the product or domain and determine whether or not the product would support their desired outcomes or goals. The activities can also spark new ideas for you to draw upon.

The same type of questions can be asked in task-based and non task-based focus groups. The benefit of task-based focus groups is that follow-up discussions are richer when participants have the opportunity to actually use the product than when they must simply imagine it or remember when they used it last. With this technique, participants can reference the tasks they just completed to provide concrete examples, or the tasks may trigger previous experiences with the product.

The cost of doing such a study is that you must have several sets of your product available so that participants can work with them simultaneously. You will also need several facilitators to help, and the prep time to develop such a focus group will be longer than for traditional focus groups since you need to create the materials for several activities. It can also be more expensive because more materials are needed. However, the added benefit of giving participants something to experience and work with is worth the cost and should be done whenever possible!

Day-in-the-Life

You can create a "day-in-the-life" video to demonstrate how someone would use your product and then discuss participants' impressions of what they have seen. Participants can get a better idea of what the product is really like without having to imagine it. This is perfect for situations where you cannot give participants direct exposure to the product or domain (e.g., requires significant training, safety issues, financially infeasible).

It is important to show someone realistically using the product (warts and all!) since providing an idealized image will not result in valid user impressions. This allows users an opportunity to determine whether what they are seeing would address their desired outcomes. It takes additional time to create the video and may even require you to develop a prototype of the product to work with if a real version does not exist. The benefit of getting all the participants on the same page and enabling them to share your vision is worth it!

Iterative Focus Groups

With iterative focus groups, you begin by presenting a prototype to participants and getting feedback from them. This can be specific design suggestions or just general impressions. Once the prototype is updated to reflect the feedback from users, the same participants are called back to participate in a second focus group. The new prototype is presented and additional feedback is collected. You could continue this iterative process as long as participants return, until you feel comfortable with the design, or until you run out of money.

The benefit is that you can see whether you are on the right track and understood the participants' requests. It also takes less time to recruit since you are not looking for new participants each time. On the other hand, this modification is useful only in cases where you have enough information to build a prototype and you have the time and resources to make regular changes and conduct additional focus groups.

Obviously, it takes time and resources to make changes to a prototype and run additional sessions.

The Focus Troupe

The "focus troupe" is an interesting twist on the focus group (Sato & Salvador 1999). Members of the usability or development group – or even the participants themselves – perform dramatic vignettes demonstrating the new product, feature, or concept in use (participants would follow a script). The play should demonstrate the implications, operations, and expectations of what the product would do. A discussion among the group is then initiated.

As with some of the modifications listed earlier, participants can gain experience with the product or domain and this will limit their need to "pretend." They can think of concrete examples of "using" the product while they provide their reactions, opinions, and alternative suggestions. The additional cost of using this modification is the time it takes to write the script(s), and – if you use co-workers in your troupe – the additional people involved. However, if you are unable to create a working prototype, this is the next best option.

Computer-aided Focus Groups

Computer-based brainstorming tools can be used for focus groups. If you are interested in these tools, please refer to Chapter 9, Wants and Needs Analysis, "The Brainstorming" section, page 385, and "Modifications" section, page 401.

Telefocus Groups

Smaller focus groups (i.e., five or fewer participants) can be conducted over the phone. This is more convenient for participants and you can recruit people from outside your geographic region. You can also save money because participants will often participate for less since they do not have to leave the comfort of their home or office. However, you need a high-quality phone meeting system that allows multiple people to call and clearly hear everyone speak.

There are several disadvantages to this modification. Social loafing (i.e., the tendency for individuals to reduce the effort they make toward some task when working together with others) is potentially high because participants are not held accountable by their peer group or the moderator if they do not contribute. A participant can surf the web or read a book without others seeing it. Doing a "round-robin" can help because everyone knows they will be called on to contribute to the question so they are less likely to slack off. It is also helpful to ask all participants to say their name before responding. It will be more obvious if, during an hour-long focus group, you never hear Bob announce his name. In that case, you call on Bob directly to reply.

Another problem is that the moderator cannot read the body language of the participants. There is no way to know whether a participant is silent out of disagreement, boredom, or because he/she has nothing to add. Queue-jumping by overbearing participants can also be a problem. It is hard to know who is speaking (even if you ask people to announce themselves before the speak) or if someone wants to speak but can't get a word in edgewise!

Figure 7.3 on page 261 can help you further determine whether it is better to conduct the session in person or over the phone. Overall, we recommend telefocus groups when you have geographically diverse users, when you do not need to demonstrate a product, when you are tight on resources, and when you have a high-quality phone conferencing system available.

Lessons Learned

Below are three lessons we have learned with regard to user composition, moderating, and note-taking for focus groups.

We advised earlier not to mix user types of different levels in a hierarchy. The first lesson learned demonstrates why. Also, as we indicated earlier, it is important for a moderator to have good domain knowledge to follow-up on user comments, but it is also important for the note-taker. The moderator also needs to know how to handle difficult users, even to the point of removing a user to save the session.

Mixing User Types

A series of focus groups was conducted to learn about the use of "Patient Problem Lists" (PPL) by nurses and physicians. The goal of a PPL is to bring a provider up to speed regarding a patient's healthcare or medical history without having to review the patient's entire chart. Both doctors and nurses use it, so the development team wanted to combine the two user types in the same session to reduce the number of sessions needed and to hear a discussion of their different perspectives. Because the type of work they do is different, and because the relationship between doctors and nurses can be antagonistic, we insisted on separating the two user types.

During one of the sessions with the physicians, the participants began insulting nurses over the way they maintain their paperwork and the notes they take. A development team member who happened to be a Registered Nurse was watching from another room and nearly leapt through the one-way mirror when she heard the physicians' comments! Although both user types would have likely been on their best behavior if combined, we would not have gotten their *honest* opinions. The physicians' comments may have seemed mean-spirited at the time of the session, but the point was clear that the notes the nurses take (and find valuable in *their* job) clearly do not meet the needs of the physicians. Everyone on the product development team realized that it was far safer and more enlightening to keep those user types separated in future usability activities, even if it meant running additional sessions.

Having Sufficient Domain Knowledge

This may sound obvious but, when conducting a focus group, you need sufficient domain knowledge in order to know which questions to follow-up on and how or when to probe deeper into participant responses. This is also true in a wants and needs analysis (see Chapter 7, page 246) and a group task analysis (see Chapter 9, page 370). We witnessed one colleague's painful two-hour focus group in which he did not have enough knowledge of the discussion topic. The moderator learned a great deal about the domain during his moderation; but because he did not know what information was important to follow-up on and what he should ignore, he could not provide new information and useful insights to the product development team as a result of the focus group.

What is different from a wants and needs analysis is that a focus group *note-taker* must also have domain knowledge to take notes in a focus group. On a separate evening this same individual took notes for a co-worker who was running a focus group on the same topic. Unfortunately, his domain knowledge was so insufficient that the notes were meaningless to his co-worker. He documented statements that were not noteworthy, missed points that were actually of value, and inaccurately summarized other comments. His notes were worthless and his co-worker had to review the session videotape to take proper notes herself.

Not only can you harm your credibility with a product team, you can lose credibility with the participants you are interviewing and your co-workers if you do not know what you are talking about. You need to do your homework before running *any* usability activity – including user requirements gathering activities. (Refer to Chapter 2, Before You Choose an Activity, "Learn About Your Product" section, page 29.)

Removing the Difficult Participant

During the same healthcare focus group discussed in the first lesson learned, we covered an amazing ten questions in each session. Each question was presented and then we completed a "round-robin" so that each participant had adequate time to contribute. After everyone had a chance to speak, people were free to add additional thoughts. This worked extremely well for the nurses. Once we reviewed the ground rules for participation, we never had to refer to them again.

The physician sessions were more difficult to moderate. The participants did not stick to the "round-robin" format, interrupted each other frequently, disagreed with each other, and by the end of the session were speaking quite loudly in order to be easily heard over the others. The ground rules had to be referred to regularly. At one point, the physicians even mocked the way nurses maintained and used the PPL. One outspoken physician in particular insulted the comments and ideas provided by another soft-spoken physician. Despite continued instructions of "everyone is right" and "do not critique the thoughts of others," the domineering physician only got worse and the soft-spoken physician stopped speaking altogether. The amazing thing was that the negative vibe rubbed off on the other participants and they all began criticizing each other's ideas.

We realized that, even with a great deal of experience moderating groups, it is easy to lose control of a session. Once you let one negative or overbearing participant take control of a group, the rest of the group will either behave similarly (e.g., insulting each other) or bow out of participating all together. Sometimes humor and polite reminders will not work. It takes a strong hand to get a session back on track. In this case, it meant taking the participant to the side and asking him to either quit criticizing others or to leave altogether. This is uncomfortable to do; but for the well-being of your participants and for the sake of good data collection, it is critical that you intervene as soon as you realize the session is headed on a downward spiral.

For more tips and information on moderating activities, see Chapter 6, During Your User Requirements Activity, "Moderating Your Activity" section, page 220.

SUGGESTED RESOURCES FOR ADDITIONAL READING

The following handbook contains information to help you design your focus group, design research vendor questionnaires, select an effective moderator, and analyze the data from focus groups. It also includes sample forms, checklists, sample studies, and comprehensive executive summaries of the results:

- Edmunds, H. (1999). *The Focus Group Research Handbook*. Chicago, IL: NTC Business Books.

The next book is filled with multiple, short case studies in every chapter. Each chapter addresses how you can use focus groups to address specific needs (e.g., market research, participatory design, scenario-based discussions):

- Langford, J. & McDonagh, D. (eds) (2003). *Focus Groups: Supporting Effective Product Development*. London: Taylor & Francis.

Thomas Greenbaum is a professional moderator and provides information about conducting market research with focus groups, how to select and evaluate moderators and facilities, and using video-conferencing technology. Below is his latest handbook for people new to focus groups, and a website containing a collection of articles on focus groups and related topics:

- Greenbaum, T. L. (1998). *The Handbook of Focus Group Research*. London: Sage Publications.
- www.groupsplus.com/pages/articles.htm. This site also includes an overview of the focus group process, organized as a calendar of events.

The next guide provides information for the beginning focus group researcher about planning and conducting focus groups, as well as analyzing the data. It is now in its third edition, but the out-of-print second edition (March 1994) is more comprehensive and contains several appendices omitted from the third edition:

- Krueger, R. & Casey, M. A. (2000). *Focus Groups: a Practical Guide for Applied Research*. London: Sage Publications.

The following website is a categorized collection of links assembled by Carter McNamara, on conducting focus groups:

- www.mapnp.org/library/grp_skll/focusgrp/focusgrp.htm.

STC Focus Group Resources – The Society for Technical Communications (STC) has a special interest group devoted to usability. One of their topics is focus groups. On their web site you can find a list of useful resources including articles, books, and web pages that relate to focus groups:

- http://www.stcsig.org/usability/topics/focusgroups.html.

Pulling It All Together

In this chapter, we have discussed what a focus group is, when you should conduct one, and things to be aware of. We also discussed how to prepare for and conduct a focus group, along with several modifications. Finally, we have demonstrated various ways to analyze the data and used our travel example to show you how to interpret and present the results.

CASE STUDY

Stephanie Rosenbaum from Tec-Ed discusses what it is like to be called in as a professional focus group administrator for a product development company. Her consulting team was tasked with collecting data for a complex product in a short span of time. This meant gathering the requisite domain knowledge, recruiting the users, and working with the product team to identify the questions to be answered. In the case study she walks us through the entire process of preparing for the focus group, conducting the activity, and analyzing the data. She even provides some lessons she learned along the way.

Engineering Collaborative Tools: a Different Use

Stephanie Rosenbaum, Tec-Ed, Inc.

The Internet is the catalyst for the design of many new products. Innovation Chain (formerly Analytics Channel) developed collaborative tools for publishing and using engineering design information on a website called an Exchange. The company then engaged my research firm, Tec-Ed, to:

- Learn how engineers currently save and share design information such as models and simulations
- Observe how engineers search for and publish models and simulations
- Gauge engineers' reactions to the Exchange tool and elicit feedback.

To collect this data, we conducted usability focus groups with members of an engineering professional society, the IEEE (Institute of Electrical & Electronics Engineers), that was considering partnering with Innovation Chain to offer the collaborative tools. Innovation Chain approached us on the recommendation of the IEEE, for which Tec-Ed has performed many user experience projects.

The Innovation Chain marketing director had used focus group data at a previous company and suggested this type of research. After exploratory planning discussions, Tec-Ed agreed that usability focus groups were an appropriate method for the project, which sought target audience feedback not only on an early prototype of the Exchange, but also on its underlying business process model. The social quality of interactive discussion in focus groups makes them a useful research method to explore the potential value of a product to its intended users.

Our Approach

In a focus group, people with similar characteristics who do not know one another discuss selected topics with the assistance of a facilitator. The focus group facilitator creates an atmosphere in which participants feel free to express diverse points of view, with no pressure to agree or support particular ideas. Participants develop perceptions and make choices in part by interacting with the other people in the group, just as they do in real life.

Tec-Ed's methodology for usability focus groups differs somewhat from traditional focus groups in that ours are task-based whenever possible, so we can observe the participants' actual behavior with products or websites. These observations add validity to the data, because participants base their opinions on real product use, not on an imprecise (and invisible to researchers) image of how they might use the product.

After an initial group discussion, we typically "break out" into smaller clusters of two to four people who explore a product in a co-discovery manner, each cluster with a facilitator; then we reconvene the full focus group for discussion of the participants' experiences. (In co-discovery, two or more people use a product together; they take turns handling controls and advising the "driver.") Alternatively, we plan smaller focus groups of three or four people, which is the approach we used for Innovation Chain because of budget constraints.

Although these usability focus groups provide the opportunity to observe user task behavior, the findings cannot be treated like individual performance data from usability testing. In the group situation, although one person "drives" the computer, the other focus group members make comments and suggestions, so the task behavior is collaborative. Quantitative task findings (such as "Six out of eight participants had difficulty completing the task") are not an outcome of focus group methodology, although we can and do say things like "The participants found task 1 more difficult than task 2."

Because usability focus groups produce qualitative rather than quantitative data, the data can be challenging to analyze. Differences among the groups – both audience type and discussion content – can further complicate the analysis. Finally, the quality of the results depends heavily on the facilitator's skill.

Participant Selection and Recruiting

In all user research, the value and the validity of the findings depend in part on how well the study participants represent the actual target audience. If the participants do not have the same characteristics as the intended audience for the product or website, we cannot know how well the collected data apply to the real situation. Therefore, Tec-Ed invests thought and time in first identifying the participant criteria and then recruiting people who meet the criteria. Recruiting for specialized areas of expertise, as we did for this project, can take two to four hours per recruited participant.

While Innovation Chain and the IEEE explored their partnering opportunity, we had access to the Boston-area membership list of the Signal Processing Society, one of the IEEE's special-interest groups. We began recruiting using this list, and expanded our efforts to include other IEEE members in Tec-Ed's database of participant candidates. Another reason why participant recruiting is so time-consuming is that customer lists are often out of date, requiring follow-up efforts to track down appropriate candidates; however, the IEEE membership list used in this project was more accurate than most corporate customer lists Tec-Ed has used.

Our goal was to have three or four people in each of three focus group sessions, so we recruited 15 people in all, to provide one or two back-ups for each group in case of no-shows. In studies with engineers and system administrators – or any busy, highly skilled professionals – last-minute cancellations are common. In fact, we had only one no-show; we conducted two focus group sessions with five people and one session with four. All participants were paid honoraria of $200, a typical incentive for technical professionals. However, most technical professionals agree to help with user research out of intellectual curiosity or a desire to improve technical products, not for the incentive payments.

All participants had to be IEEE members and comfortable with the web (use it at least five hours a week). We recruited participants with varying amounts of engineering design experience, ideally three to five participants each with less than 5 years of experience, 5–10 years, and over 10 years. We recruited three to five people each with industry, government, and academic jobs. We screened for diversity in size of employer, from individual consultants to large companies like Nokia, Verizon, and Texas Instruments. Finally, because we began with a list from the Signal Processing Society, we also screened to obtain diversity among the technical areas within that engineering specialty.

Tec-Ed employs participant recruiters on our staff, which enables us to provide training and ongoing feedback to build their recruiting skills. For this study, we expected the professional society involvement to reduce the time required for recruiting, but that was not the case. We believe the IEEE connection did influence candidates to accept calls from our recruiters, and it may have contributed to our excellent no-show rate. When candidates agreed to participate, they actually did so. However, we had the usual difficulty in coaxing busy engineers to leave their office or lab for a user research project.

Focus Group Activities

Conducting usability focus groups requires a team of two researchers: a facilitator and an observer/note-taker. The facilitator must concentrate on drawing out quiet group members, eliciting explanations of ambiguous or incomplete comments, and making sure everyone's opinions are respected. Therefore, the attentiveness and perception of the note-taker are very important. In most focus groups Tec-Ed conducts (including this one), both the facilitator and the note-taker sit in the room with the participants, although the note-taker takes an unobtrusive position.

Tec-Ed also videotapes and audiotapes our focus groups to create an archival record, or to produce "clips" for client executives. Time and budget constraints usually discourage us from reviewing entire recordings during data analysis, although we use them to cross-check our notes as needed.

The facilitator conducts the focus groups from a scripted outline that lists high-level questions and issues, with supplementary "probing questions" for each. However, because of the dynamics of the group environment, focus group scripts are not as detailed as those for laboratory testing. The facilitator must remain flexible, which in turn puts more demands for in-depth note-taking on the observer.

To ensure that the outline addressed the issues of most concern to Innovation Chain, we created and revised several drafts of the outline before the focus group sessions began. The facilitator and note-taker also used the prototype extensively, both to refine our formulation of the questions in the outline and to practice the tasks participants would perform (so that we could provide appropriate remediation during the sessions).

Each two-hour focus group session for Innovation Chain had four parts. We began with a 30-minute group discussion of how the participants currently develop and exchange engineering solutions such as models, simulations, and program code; this discussion provided insights into the environment in which the Exchange tool might be used. Some of the questions (with follow-on probing questions in brackets) the facilitator asked were:

- Do you tend to develop models and simulations from scratch, or modify existing ones from other sources? [What other sources?]
- Once you develop or modify models and simulations, how often do you need to re-use them? [Or do they tend to have limited use?]
- Where do you save your models and simulations? Does your company or organization have a specific place where you save them so that they're available to your co-workers? [If so, do you use it? If not, would you use one if they had one? Names of software? How likely? How often?]
- What other ways do you share models and simulations? [With your co-workers? With clients or vendors? How often do you use them?]
- What are some of the concerns you have when sharing models and simulations with peers, clients, or vendors? [Pitfalls/problems?]
- Could you give an example of an engineering model or simulation that you've developed or used recently? I'm not an engineer, so try to describe it briefly in simple terms.

The participants then used a prototype of the Exchange tool to download an engineering model from the Internet. Different participants performed the tasks in this activity, while the others looked on and made suggestions. After a short break, the participants used the prototype to upload and publish a model, again trading places so that all had a chance to perform some tasks. The downloading and uploading activities were fairly complex, yet they illustrated the power of the Exchange tool.

In the wrap-up 30-minute discussion, the participants were probed for their reactions to the Exchange tool. The facilitator asked questions like:

- How does this process compare with the way you currently share and exchange solutions? [How much would this tool save you time?]

- How do you like the idea of exchanging interactive solutions over the Internet? [How much confidence would you have in a solution that you downloaded from this site?]
- How would you feel about paying to download solutions from this site? [How would you feel about being paid for solutions you submitted? Would you prefer a flat-rate or per-use fee?]
- How likely would you be to use this tool if it were available to you?
- What other comments do you have about the engineering solution exchange tool you've seen today?

Finally, after each facilitated session was over, we invited the Innovation Chain developers to join us and answer technical questions from the participants, as well as ask their own questions. We often use this technique for focus groups and usability testing of highly technical products. It addresses developers' concerns that usability researchers will not understand their products well enough, and it enables us to use session time to learn about agreed-upon research goals rather than field participants' questions about product features. (We say "You can ask the developers after the session.")

In this study, all participants stayed at least 15 minutes after their session to ask technical questions of the developers and answer developers' follow-on questions about the engineers' experiences with the prototype. Most participants indicated that they would be willing to be contacted again by Innovation Chain for further input.

Lessons Learned During the Focus Group Sessions

Innovation Chain originally envisioned its engineering collaborative tools being used over the Internet, through the websites of professional societies. The participants' behavior and comments in the first focus group session caused us to question this usage model; and after the second session, we and the Innovation Chain observers were convinced it had problems.

Although participants liked the idea of using the Exchange tool to access program code or multimedia components of published articles, they said they would not submit models to the Exchange tool on a public website, because most worked for companies with concerns about proprietary information. Even within their companies, they rarely shared models and code with peers outside their own work groups.

One of the benefits of focus groups for the early stages of product design is their flexibility to adjust topics between sessions, unlike controlled surveys or performance-based usability testing. Although this approach reduces comparability between the groups, if the participants' behavior clearly indicates the need for a change in product positioning, we can revise the script outline and collect more relevant qualitative data from the remaining sessions.

Therefore, between the second and third focus group sessions, Tec-Ed's team held an intensive working meeting with Innovation Chain management and then revised the wrap-up discussion questions as follows:

- Under what circumstances would you be interested in sharing models or simulations with your co-workers through the Exchange?
- Who else might you share models with?
- If you encountered a design challenge you did not have the answer to, when would you search the Exchange for a model or simulation that might help your efforts? [How would you apply that model or simulation to your design? How much confidence would you have in a model you found on the site?]
- What projects within your organization do you feel would benefit from the Exchange? [Why?]
- If you were reading a technical brief in an IEEE journal and learned that you could access an interactive component of the article through this Exchange, would you take the time to register and download it? [Why or why not?]
- What would you call this tool? [Model and simulation exchange? Something else?]
- What have you seen that's like it?
- What other comments do you have about the Exchange?

In the third focus group session, we introduced the discussions with a scenario of using the collaborative tools on corporate intranets to share models and simulations with co-workers, rather than on the Internet. The questions thus elicited new issues and concerns about using the Exchange as an internal collaborative tool.

When a company like Innovation Chain considers a major change in product positioning, user research is typically only one of several determinants. Innovation Chain management had been considering the pros and cons of positioning the Exchange as a public publishing tool versus an internal tool for intranets. Discussions with the IEEE had motivated Innovation Chain to explore a public Exchange first, but management was already sensitive to indications – like the data from our first two focus groups – that an internal tool would be more acceptable to their target audience.

Lessons Learned *After* the Focus Group Sessions

After the focus group sessions, the user research team compiled its notes, supplementing them as needed by consulting the videotapes and back-up audiotapes of the sessions. For qualitative research projects like focus groups, Tec-Ed creates a text database of notes (including participant quotes) that reflect various aspects of the answers to the research questions. This method both facilitates the initial data analysis and makes it easier to "mine" the data to address follow-up questions from the design team.

The results of the usability focus groups benefited Innovation Chain in two key ways. They learned about engineers' current use and reuse of models and simulations, which differed considerably from their expectations. And they learned that the collaborative tools needed extensive usability improvements, even for the target audience of engineers. Our findings included:

- After working 50 minutes with the prototype, participants did not gain a good mental model of the Exchange process; they had difficulty understanding how the Exchange tool worked.

- All groups required assistance from the facilitator to successfully download a model and submit a model.

- Engineers do not generally exchange models with peers outside their work group unless the company culture specifically demands it. They tend to reuse their own code, or use portions from established engineering sources and programs.

- One of the main reasons engineers do not share models and code with a wider audience is that it takes time to document a model well enough for other people to understand it, and to figure out how someone else's model works.

- Most engineers do not reuse an entire model or simulation. They are more likely to reuse and modify segments of code in order to create a model that applies directly to their problem.

Overall, while the focus group participants could envision the Exchange being a useful tool in some circumstances, they had reservations about its value in practice. As they worked with the Exchange, they didn't easily discover many of its features and benefits. Although they thought sharing models was a good idea in theory, they had many concerns and were unsure how or whether the Exchange addressed them. Some of the perceived barriers to using an Exchange tool included:

- Time investment to document models well enough for others to understand them
- Time investment to understand how other peoples' models work, when considering whether to use them
- Need for models to be very specific and thus only applicable to a narrow or limited audience
- Need to adapt the source code, because most models apply to a limited audience and cannot be used "as is"
- Proprietary constraints on sharing models, even within a company.

Tec-Ed noted that the Exchange tool needed a more supportive user interface; in particular, we made several recommendations for improving the usability of the Exchange home page. Innovation Chain was implementing the recommendations – and planning further rounds of focus groups targeting technical and business audiences in corporations – when the dot-com recession began and the company failed to receive funding for further development.

The case history remains a good example of the flexibility of focus group research and the kinds of data usability focus groups can collect. The realistic tasks helped participants experience a complex new tool and envision using it in their own workplaces, so their discussions gave more in-depth insight into the tool's strengths and weaknesses. When participants reacted negatively to Innovation Chain's initial positioning of the Exchange as an Internet-based tool, we were able to change focus quickly to describe an intranet context, while continuing to observe the same task behavior.

As always, we learned other lessons that improved our methodology:

- We resolved (again) to allow more time for recruiting participants who are technical users rather than members of the general population.
- We confirmed our decision to assign an especially skilled observer to the project. Note-taking in focus groups is always more demanding than in studies with one participant at a time; and the highly technical subject matter made this project more challenging.

- The user research team obtained coaching in design engineering terminology before conducting the sessions, another practice we will continue in the future. User researchers need not be experts in the product domain, but some familiarity with the users' language helps us collect richer qualitative data.

Above all, these usability focus groups helped Innovation Chain better understand the needs of its target audience while exploring their opinions of its new ideas for engineering collaborative tools.

CHAPTER 13

FIELD STUDIES

Introduction

Collecting data in the field (i.e., in your user's environment) is sometimes referred to as "site visits." However, "site visit" is a broad term and can include other interactions with customers while not necessarily collecting data (e.g., conducting a sales demo). More accurate names for site visits to collect data are "ethnographic study," "field research," or "field studies."

"Field studies" refers to a broad range of data gathering techniques at the user's location – including observation, apprenticeship, and interviewing. A field study can be composed of several visits to the user's environment and can be conducted in any environment in which a user lives or works. For example, researchers observed users in a vineyard to develop a ubiquitous computing system for agricultural environments (Brooke & Burrell 2003). Studies have also been done in people's homes and offices. Field studies can last for a couple hours to a full day or even weeks, depending on the goals and resources of the study. The advantage of this technique is that you get to observe the users completing the tasks in their environment. You can observe their task flows, inefficiencies, and challenges directly. This information can then be used to help you understand the user requirements for your product.

You will notice that this chapter is designed a little differently from the other method-related chapters. In the previous chapters, we presented one primary way to conduct a specific method and then a few modifications. There is no one best way to conduct a field study – it depends on the goals of your study and your access to users. Consequently, we will provide you with several variations from which to choose. In this chapter, we discuss different types of field studies available to enable you to go into your user's environment to collect data, how to select the best method to answer your questions, special considerations, how to analyze the data you collect, and how to present the results to stakeholders. Additional sources for information are provided throughout, as well as lessons learned. Finally, a case study by Bentley College (for Staples) is showcased to demonstrate the value of a field study in the real world.

At a Glance

> When should you conduct field studies?
> Things to be aware of when conducting field research
> Field study methods to choose from
> Preparing for a field study
> Conducting a field study
> Data analysis and interpretation
> Communicate the findings

When Should You Conduct Field Studies?

The purpose of a field study is to understand the end user's natural behavior in the context of his or her everyday environment. You will want to conduct a field study any time you are interested in seeing first-hand how the user works or behaves, the context of the tasks undertaken, and the artifacts used to support those tasks (e.g., checklists, forms to fill out, calendars). It can be more advantageous to observe user behavior than to ask the user to describe how he/she works because of issues with memory, social desirability, acquiescence, and prestige response bias. In addition, users often know more than they say in a single or even several interviews. It is not that they are "holding out" on you, rather that much of what they do has become automatic and, as a result, is difficult to articulate. For example, describe how you balance yourself while riding a bicycle. It's not easy to describe, is it? Alternatively, users may incorrectly explain a behavior because they don't understand it well enough.

You can conduct a field study to learn about an area in general (exploratory) or to answer a specific question or problem. You can also conduct a **longitudinal study** (i.e., a series of visits with the same participant over time) rather than an "out-of-box" or one-time exposure study. Field studies can be used to accomplish a number of goals:

- Identify new features/product
- When the product development team needs to be jolted out of their current way of thinking or to challenge/verify assumptions that you or the stakeholders have about users/tasks/environment
- Identify a mismatch between the way user's work/think and the tools/procedures they are forced to use
- Understand the users' goals
- Identify training materials needed
- Create initial designs
- Develop a task inventory
- Determine task hierarchy
- Collect **artifacts** (i.e., objects or items that users use to complete their tasks or that result from their tasks)
- Verify the user profile (are people using your product who do not match your initial user profile?)
- Develop personas through observations of actual users (refer to Chapter 2, Before You Choose an Activity, "Step 2: Personas" section, page 47)
- Collect necessary information for another **usability** activity (e.g., develop a survey, identify tasks for a usability test).

Field studies are excellent for collecting rich, detailed data and for obtaining a holistic view of the process or domain. Field studies are not a good technique if you want to collect quantitative data or data from large samples. The data collected are usually qualitative and it is too expensive and time-consuming to examine large sample sizes. All in all, field studies allow you to collect data to design based on reality, not assumptions. The goal of a field study is to make the implicit aspects and processes of the user environment explicit.

Things To Be Aware of When Conducting Field Research

There are several challenges you may face when proposing a field study. There are also challenges you could face while conducting the study. Below are some issues to be aware of when deciding to conduct a field study.

Gaining Stakeholder Support

It can be difficult to convince people with limited time and budgets to support field studies. Products must be developed on tight budgets and deadlines. It can be easier to convince product teams or management to support a wants and needs session or focus group, because the materials needed are few and the time frame for delivering results is short. It can be much more difficult to get that same support for longer term, off-site studies with actual customers or end users.

The fact is, no short-term, lab-based study can compare to observing users in their own environment. And the reality is that schedules slip. Even if you cannot get the information in time to influence the upcoming release of the product, there will be future releases where your data can be used. You want your information to make an impact as soon as possible, but do not let schedules prevent you from collecting information altogether.

There are also discount ways to collect information. Write a detailed proposal to demonstrate the information you plan to collect and when. Also include estimated cost, and immediate and long-term benefits. You may also want to show documented cases where products went wrong and could have been saved by conducting a field study. Better understanding of your users can also provide a competitive edge.

SUGGESTED RESOURCES FOR ADDITIONAL READING

If you need some facts to convince your product team why a field study is of tremendous value, check out the following book. The authors share real-world case studies of products that went wrong but which could have been saved by conducting field studies:

- Hackos, J. T. & Redish, J. C. (1998). *User and Task Analysis for Interface Design*. New York: John Wiley & Sons.

Despite sharing the war stories listed by Hackos and Redish, your stakeholders may still offer an abundance of arguments against conducting field studies. Below are just a few you may hear:

"We simply don't have the time or money for such a study."

"Sales owns the customers. We don't want to ruin any potential deals. We don't want to make the customer unhappy by pointing out what our product doesn't do. This will be too time-consuming for our customers."

"You'll make promises we can't keep. You'll let out confidential information."

"We have information already. Why collect more?"

"We're introducing a different process so don't waste your time studying the current process."

"This product/process/service is completely new. There is nothing to observe."

"Everyone does it differently so there is no point studying a few users."

"We're changing just one part of the system/product/environment; we don't need to study more than that."

"We are developing this product for our own company, not for sale, so we don't need a field study."

In Chapter 1, we offer counter-arguments for each of these statements (refer to Chapter 1, Introduction to User Requirements, "Getting Stakeholder Buy-in for

Your Activity" section, page 14). We strongly recommend reviewing these prior to presenting a proposal for a field study.

Finally, you will likely need to educate stakeholders on the empirical nature of usability, how the information you collect on-site with users differs from lab-based data, and how the data you collect in field studies can provide a competitive edge.

Other Things to Keep in Mind

Once you have convinced stakeholders, there are a few other things to keep in mind when designing and conducting field studies.

Types of bias

There are two types of bias to be aware of when conducting field studies. The first is introduced by the investigator and the second by the participant.

If the investigator is a novice to the domain, he or she may have a tendency to conceptually simplify the expert users' problem-solving strategies while observing them. This is not done intentionally, of course, but the investigator does not have the complex mental model of the expert, so a **simplification bias** results. For example, if an investigator is studying database administrators and does not understand databases, he/she may think of a database as nothing more than a big spreadsheet and misinterpret (i.e., simplify) what the database administrator is explaining or demonstrating. It is important for you to be aware of this bias and ask users or a subject matter expert to review your notes/observations. They can identify areas where you have over-simplified or incorrectly captured information.

The other type of bias is called a **translation bias**. Expert users will attempt to translate their knowledge so that the investigator can understand it. The more experts translate, the more there is the potential for them to over-simplify and distort their knowledge/skills/etc. One way to avoid this is to ask the expert user to train you or speak to you as if you had just started the job. If you are missing the background knowledge necessary to understand everything the user is saying, you may either ask probing questions or bring a subject matter expert (SME) with you to "translate." However, it is to your advantage to learn as much as you can prior to your visit so that you have some mental model to begin understanding what you are observing. You should be enthusiastic about learning the domain and become well-versed yourself, but with a "usability hat on" so that you can identify opportunities for improvement. This is different from coming in with preconceived notions. You should have a good base of knowledge but do not think about solutions yet.

The Hawthorne effect

Participants may behave differently when observed; this is known as the **Hawthorne effect**. They will likely be on their best behavior (e.g., observing standard operating procedures rather than using their usual shortcuts). It can take some time for users to feel comfortable with you and reveal their "true behavior." Users can't keep up a façade for long and you'll notice differences between participants. Developing a rapport with the user can lessen this effect.

Logistics can be more challenging

Field studies can be very simple when you are conducting pure observation. All you need is a pen and paper. Depending on the location, you may not need anyone's permission so you are free to come and go as you please.

However, most field studies done for product development are more complex because you are interacting with more people (e.g., recruiter, sales person, site contact, other observers, participants, legal departments, etc.) and because more things can potentially go wrong on-site (e.g., broken equipment, missing forms, late arrival, dead batteries). So, field studies are much more challenging to conduct than most other techniques described in this book. Even though your equipment may fail in the lab, you are in a better position to replace/repair it than when you are traveling to an unfamiliar location. You cannot possibly take duplicates of every piece of equipment. In addition, directions to your site may be poor and driving in unfamiliar areas can be stressful. Being detail-oriented, creating a well thought out plan in advance, and piloting everything can help you avoid many problems but there will always be some surprises along the way.

Field Study Methods to Choose From

Field studies come to us from anthropology. Field studies can last from a few hours to days, weeks, or even months depending on the scope of your study and your resources. Before you can begin preparing, you need to understand the techniques available to you. Methods range from pure observation to becoming a user yourself. Table 13.1 is a chart that provides comparisons between the techniques.

Since there is no standard method, we will consider a range of techniques. The goal of each method is the same: to observe users and collect information about their tasks and the context in which they are done. The cost for each method is also very similar (e.g., your time to collect and analyze the data, recording equipment, potential recruitment fees, and incentives). The differences arise in the way you collect data and some of the information you are able to collect.

The techniques described here are divided into three categories: observation only, interacting with the user, and method supplements. *The most important thing to remember when designing a field study is to be flexible.* Select the method(s) that will best address the goals of your study, as well as the time and resources available to conduct it. Collect several types of data (e.g., notes, audio, video, still pictures, artifacts, sketches, diaries) to obtain a richer data set. Finally, and regardless of the type of study you conduct, do not focus on solutions before or during data collection. Doing that may bias your observations and needlessly limit the information you collect. You can conduct follow-up visits to investigate hypotheses, but – at least in the initial visit – focus on the data collection and keep an open mind.

At a Glance

> Observation only

   Pure observation

   Deep Hanging-Out

> Interacting with the user

   Contextual Inquiry

   Process analysis

   Condensed ethnographic interview

   Discount User Observation (DUO)

> Method supplements

   Artifact walkthroughs

   Incident diaries

   Observing while you are not present

Method	Synopsis	Advantages	Level of effort	
Pure observation	When you are unable or don't wish to interact with the user, you simply observe from a distance.	• Flexible • Low resources	• Minimal. Place yourself in a good vantage point and observe as many users/sites/tasks as you feel appropriate. • You continue to conduct observations until you feel you have a good understanding of the domain or areas of focus.	Observation only
Deep Hanging-Out	This method is similar to pure observation but provides more structure by suggesting focus areas and things to observe.	It has more structured than pure observation so you can do a more detailed level of data analysis and compare data collected across multiple sites.	• Because there is more structure, it takes more effort than pure observation. • You are "on" at all times, which can be tiring. • It is also valuable to become a user yourself (if possible) and collect artifacts along the way.	
Contextual Inquiry	Interview, apprentice with, and interpret the resulting data with users.	• Contextual Inquiry is more focused and context dependent than the previous methods. • At the end, you walk away with actionable items.	The effort level is higher than for observation-only techniques. You must develop an observation guide, observe users, apprentice with them, and discuss your observations with them.	Interacting with users
Process analysis	Capture the task sequence for a process that may span several days	Because it is more focused than Contextual Inquiry, it is also much faster.	You need to stay focused on the process at hand to help users walk you through the process of interest.	
Condensed ethnographic interview	Use the results of semi-structured interviews to guide observations.	This technique is considerably shorter than some of the other techniques described above, because the interviews scope what you observe; but it also limits the data you are able to collect.	It requires a medium level of effort to conduct interviews and then observe users and collect artifacts.	

Table 13.1:

Comparison chart of field study methods

Continued

Table 13.1–
Cont'd

Interacting with users – Cont'd

Method supplements

Method	Synopsis	Advantages	Level of effort
Discount User Observation (DUO)	One facilitator interviews the user and takes notes while another facilitator takes pictures of everything.	You can quickly reconstruct the session through time stamped notes and digital pictures to verify your observations with users.	• It takes two investigators to focus on their specific tasks of either interviewing or taking pictures and notes. • It will take additional time/effort to combine notes with digital photos and put them in a PowerPoint presentation to review with users. • It takes additional effort to validate observations with users afterward.
Artifact walkthroughs	Collect all the artifacts used by participants and determine what triggers their use, when they are used, and for what.	Quick and easy to conduct	Low level of effort to review artifacts with participants and make/collect copies of them
Incident diaries	Worksheets the user takes home or to work to collect ongoing data rather than one-time performance or opinions	No observation is required. You are able to understand more issues than what can be observed in the lab or during a single visit.	• Low effort level to create and distribute diaries • Moderate effort to analyze data across multiple diaries. There will be a time lag between when you distribute the diaries and when you receive the data • You are depending on the participants to follow-through
Observing while you are not present	Recording users in action when space, time, or restrictions prevent you from being there in person	If you have multiple video cameras, you can view several users simultaneously.	• Low effort to set up cameras and record • Moderate effort to meet with user again and review tapes • Moderate effort to categorize and index behavior

Observation Only

Techniques that do not involve interacting with users are ideal when you cannot get permission to interview them or when you do not want the users to know you are observing them. There are also cases when you cannot interact with participants (e.g., a doctor in surgery, a trader on the stock exchange floor). Observation-only techniques have their limits in terms of the information that can be collected but they are typically less resource-intensive. There is no set number of users or sites to observe. You simply continue to observe until you feel you understand the users/tasks/environment and you are no longer gaining new insights with each new user or site.

Pure Observation

Ideally, you would like to begin your field study by simply observing. Classic ethnographic methods require one to enter a situation with an open mind (i.e., no preconceived notions or biases). You must spend significant time building sufficient understanding to know what questions to ask and what issues to research. You begin by observing the user, the tasks, and the environment before you ever formulate your first question or study goal. As we mentioned earlier, do not focus on solutions before or during data collection.

In pure observation studies, users may or may not know they are being studied. If you wanted to observe people's initial reaction to a self-serve kiosk at an airport, you might sit quietly at a well-positioned table and simply record the number of people who saw the kiosk, looked at it, and then used it. You might also capture information such as facial expressions and overheard comments. If you didn't need photographs or interviews from the participants, you would not need to inform them of your presence. In other situations, however, you will likely need to inform individuals that you are observing them (e.g., in office settings). Refer to Chapter 3, Ethical and Legal Considerations, page 94, for information about informed consent and appropriate behavior with participants.

Obviously, with this technique you do not interact with the participant. You do not distribute surveys, interview the user, or ask for artifacts from the user. This is simply about immersing yourself in the environment and developing questions along the way. From here, you may go back to your product team and management to recommend additional areas of focus.

Travel Example

TravelSmart.com has decided that they want to build a travel kiosk at the airport nearby since nearly all of its clients travel in and out of that airport. This kiosk would allow customers to print out their itineraries for their hotel, car, and airline bookings, electronic tickets, and access online help. Before the company actually invests money in such a venture, you would like to better understand travelers' needs and how they behave at the airport. You don't really know what you are looking for at this time, but you feel it is wise to conduct some initial observations. Since there are no significant travel expenses or permissions to obtain, your management has decided to give you a week to conduct this study.

You have spent the week walking around the airport, observing people being dropped off, picked up, checking in bags, picking bags up, asking the information desk for directions, getting stopped by security, and interacting with kiosks offered by the different airlines. During this time, you observed that several people spent a couple of minutes looking at the kiosks and then walked away. This appears to be a trend across the different companies' kiosks. You do not know why they walked away after only a short time, but this clearly provides a question for a follow-up study. What is it about those kiosks that makes some people walk away after only a few minutes, and how can your company avoid that problem?

The pure observation technique is valuable in situations where you cannot interact with the end users. Perhaps you cannot speak with the end user for privacy or legal reasons (e.g., hospital patients), or it is an environment where you cannot distract the user with questions (e.g., emergency room doctors). The information that you can obtain is obviously limited. You cannot find out why the user did a particular action or how the user completed the task. This is particularly challenging in situations where you are new to the domain and you may not understand much of what you are seeing. In addition, you cannot influence events; you get only what is presented and may miss important events as a result. Consequently, it is essential to have a good **sampling plan**. The sampling plan should include days/times you anticipate key events (e.g., the day before Thanksgiving, or bad weather at an airport), as well as "normal" days. However, regardless of how good your sampling plan is, you may still miss out on infrequent but important events (e.g., a bad weather closure at the airport, or multiple traumas in the ER). Nevertheless, the information that you can obtain is worthwhile and will bring you closer to under-standing the user, tasks, and environment than you were when you began. As Yogi Berra said, "You can see a lot just by watching."

Deep Hanging-Out

A more structured form of pure observation is referred to as "Deep Hanging-Out." It involves significant amounts of observation along with involving yourself in the process. In addition, some structure is wrapped around the observation process.

Researchers from Intel developed this method by applying anthropological tech-niques to field research (Teague & Bell 2001). Their method of Deep Hanging-Out includes structured observation, collection of artifacts, and becoming a user yourself. However, you do not interview participants, distribute surveys, or present design ideas for feedback.

To make this data collection manageable, the system/environment is divided up into ten focus areas, as shown in Table 13.2. The foci are intended to help you think about different aspects of the environment. Because these foci are standardized, you can compare data across multiple sites in a structured manner (to be described in detail later).

Breadth can be important, even at the expense of depth, when first learning about an area. One use of the list in Table 13.2 is to remind you to focus on a large number of areas and not focus on just one small (easy to collect) area. This list is particu-larly useful for a novice – to appreciate all the areas to look at and to understand that depth in every area isn't that important.

Focal point	Some questions to ask
Family and kids	Do you see families? How many children are there? What are the age ranges? What is the interaction between the kids? Between the parents and the kids? How are they dressed? Is the environment designed to support families/kids (e.g., special activities, special locations, etc.)?
Food and drinks	Are food and drinks available? What is being served/consumed? Where is it served/consumed? When is it served? Are there special locations for it? Are people doing other things while eating? What is the service like? Are only certain people consuming food and drinks?
Built environment	How is the space laid out? What does it look like? What is the size, shape, decoration, furnishings? Is there a theme? Are there any time or space cues (e.g., clocks on the walls, windows to show time of day or orientation to the rest of the outside)?
Possessions	What are people carrying with them? How often do people access them? How do people carry them? What do they do with them? What are people acquiring?
Media consumption	What are people reading, watching, and listening to? Did they bring it with them or buy it there? Where do they consume the media and when? What do they do with it when they are done?
Tools and technology	What technology is built in? How does it work? Is it for the customers or the company? Is it visible?
Demographics	What are the demographics of the people in the environment? Are they in groups (e.g., families, tours)? How are they dressed? How do they interact with each other? How do they behave?
Traffic	What is the flow of traffic through the space? Was it designed that way? What is traveling through the space (e.g., people, cars, golf carts)? Where are the high/low traffic areas? Why are they high/low traffic areas? Where do people linger?
Information and communication access	What are the information and communication access points (e.g., pay phones, ATMs, computer terminals, kiosks, maps, signs, guides, directories, information desks)? Do people use them, and how often? How do people use them? Where are they located (e.g., immediately visible, difficult to access)? What do they look like?
Overall experience	Don't forget the forest for the trees. What is the overall environment like? What is the first and last thing you noticed? What is it like to be there? How is it similar or different from similar environments? Are there any standard behaviors, rules, or rituals? [Think high level and obtain a holistic view, rather than concentrating on details.]

Another key use of the list is to help teams who are doing research together to come away with better findings. Many times a group of four to five people go out and conduct observations independently but they all come back with pretty much the same findings. This can be frustrating for everyone involved and may cause stakeholders to question the value of having so many people involved in the study or the value of the study *period*. Using the list of foci and giving each person a specific focus area helps to ensure that the team examines multiple areas. In addition, it gives individuals some direction and ownership and makes their insight a unique contribution to the team.

Numerous studies at Intel demonstrated that, regardless of the system, users, or environment they studied, these ten foci represented the domain and supported valuable data collection. The technique is intended to be flexible. There is no minimum number of foci to collect data about or recommended amount of time to spend observing each focus area. However, even if a particular focal point does not seem appropriate to your study, you should still try to collect information about it. The lack of information about that particular focal point can be just as enlightening! For example, you may think that the "Family and kids" focal point is not appropriate when you are studying users in their office environment. Who brings their family to work with them? But, you may observe that a user is constantly getting calls from a spouse and pages from the kids. Perhaps they are complaining because your user is never home or is late for the daughter's recital. Maybe this means that the user is so overwhelmed with work that problems with the family life are spilling over into work, and vice versa. Even if you do not think a particular focal point is applicable to your study, you should remember to go in with an open mind!

Just as with observation only when creating your sampling plan, we recommend collecting data at different times during the day and on different days of the week. For example, you would likely observe different things if you went to the airport at 8 am on Monday, 8 am on Saturday, and 6 pm on Wednesday.

Deep Hanging-Out stresses that you are "on" at all times. Using our earlier travel example, you would begin your observations from the time you travel to the airport. Observe the experience from the very beginning of the process, not just once you are inside the airport. Pay attention to the signs directing you to parking and passenger pick-up. The intention is to obtain a holistic view of the system/environment that goes beyond Contextual Inquiry (discussed on page 580).

While you are observing the users and environment, create maps (see Figure 13.1). Identify where actions occur. If your focus is "Family and kids," identify locations designed for families or kids (e.g., jungle gym, family bathroom). Where do families tend to linger? In addition to creating maps, collect maps that the establishment provides. Collect every artifact you can get your hands on (e.g., objects or items that users use to complete their tasks or that result from their tasks). If allowed, take photos or videos of the environment. You may need to obtain permission first, so keep this in mind.

Figure 13.1:

Map from an airport kiosk study – hot-spot areas and other issues are noted on map

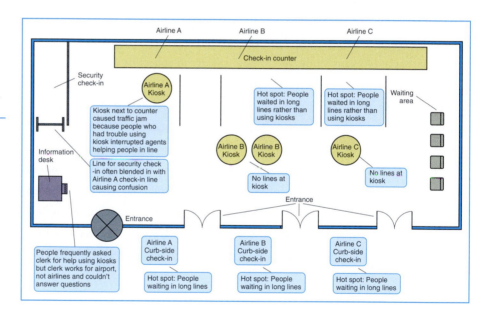

Finally, involve yourself in the process by becoming a user. If you are interested in designing a kiosk at an airport, use each kiosk currently at the airport but never mistake yourself for the actual end user. Involving yourself in the process helps you understand what the users are experiencing, but it does not mean that you *are* the end user.

Tips

Here are some other tips to keep in mind when conducting pure observation or Deep Hanging-Out (Teague & Bell 2001):

- *Maintain a low profile.* Do not announce your presence and what you are doing. Stay out of everyone's way and be quiet.

- *Act like everyone else – or not.* You can either blend in (e.g., clothing, behavior, language) or stand out to see people's reactions. How would people react if you did not observe their rituals (e.g., dressing inappropriately)? Perhaps certain taboos aren't actually taboos. You won't know until you test them.

- *Find an appropriate note-taking method.* You do not want to draw attention to the fact that you are observing people and making notes about their behavior. Find a method that allows you take useable notes but is not obvious. This may be as simple as bringing a pocket-sized notepad, or you may find an isolated corner where you can dictate notes into an audio recorder. Refer to Chapter 7, Interviews (page 307) for a discussion of note-taking methods.

- *Think "big picture."* Don't think about solutions or focus on just one interesting finding. You are going for a holistic understanding of the environment, users, and tasks.

- *Pay attention to signs.* There is a reason why signs are posted. What is the important point that needs to be conveyed, and why?

Interacting with the User

For actual product development (not just learning about a domain or preparing for another usability activity), it is almost *always* better to interact with users rather than just observe them. You will not get enough information to design from observation alone. You frequently need to follow-up an observational study with an interaction study. Several techniques are available to you to accomplish this, including:

- Contextual Inquiry
- Process analysis
- Condensed ethnographic interview
- Discount User Observation.

Contextual Inquiry

Beyer and Holtzblatt (1998) wrote the book on Contextual Inquiry (CI) and Contextual Design. This is a very detailed method and we are unable to cover all of the fine points in this chapter. However, because this is a very popular and useful method, we would like to introduce you to the basics. For more details, please refer to the Suggested Resources box.

SUGGESTED RESOURCES FOR ADDITIONAL READING

Readers who want a more comprehensive understanding of CI should refer to:
- Beyer, H. & Holtzblatt, K. (1998). *Contextual Design: Defining Customer-centered Systems*. San Francisco: Morgan Kaufmann.

There are four main parts to Contextual Inquiry:

- *Context*. You must go to the user's environment in order to understand the context of his/her actions. Contextual Inquiry assumes that observation alone or out-of-context interviews are insufficient.
- *Partnership*. To better understand the user, tasks, and environment, you should develop a master–apprentice relationship with the participant. Immerse yourself in the participant's work and do as he/she does. Obviously, this is not possible with many jobs (e.g., surgeon, fighter pilot).
- *Interpretation*. Observations must be interpreted *with the participant* in order to be used later. Verify that your assumptions and conclusions are correct.
- *Focus*. Develop an observation guide to keep you focused on the subject of interest/inquiry.

Unlike the methods described earlier, the user is very aware of your presence and becomes a partner in the research. Contextual Inquiry is more focused and context dependent than the previous methods. It *can* also be faster, taking only a few hours or a day. At the end, you walk away with actionable items to begin designing a product, your next usability activity (e.g., tasks for a usability test, questions for a survey), or areas for innovation and future research.

Issues:

Sources for travel research available to travel agent

Interactions among coworkers at travel agency

Length of time spent doing research for clients
- Individual Clients
- Groups
- Companies
- Others??

Types of interactions
- Phone
- E-mail
- In-person

Busy and slow periods and breaks

Scheduled versus unscheduled activity
(e.g., appointments versus drop-ins)

The process begins by developing an observation guide (see Figure 13.2). This is a list of general concerns or issues to guide your observations – but it is *not* a list of specific questions to ask. You may want to refer to the foci listed in Table 13.2 to build your observation guide. Using a travel agent observation example, some issues to look out for might be sources for travel research, interactions with co-workers, and length of time spent doing research for an individual client. This observation guide would obviously be influenced by the goals of your study and what you want to learn.

Next, you carefully select a few representative users to observe and apprentice with. Beyer and Holtzblatt recommend 15–20 users, but four to six is more common in industry practice. The number of participants used should be based on the question you are trying to answer. The more focused (or narrow) the question and the more consistency across users, tasks, and environments, the fewer participants are necessary. For example, if you are interested in studying only one particular task that a travel agent does rather than his/her job in general, you could observe fewer participants and feel more confident in the reliability of the results.

Context

Work with participants individually. Begin by observing the participant in action. The goal is to collect ongoing and individual data points rather than a summary or abstract description of the way the participant works. It is best to have one note-taker and one interviewer present. You can ask the participant to think-aloud as he/she works (refer to Chapter 6, During Your User Requirements Activity, "Introducing Your Think-aloud Protocol" section, page 218), or you may choose to ask the participant clarifying questions along the way. You may even decide not to interrupt the participant at all but wait until he or she has completed a task and then ask your questions. Your choice should depend on the environment, task, and user.

For example, travel agents would not be able to think-aloud as they book travel plans for clients over the phone. It would also cause confusion and annoy participants if you interrupted them with questions during the call. It is best in that case to wait until the travel agent has concluded the call and then ask your questions. Task clarification questions in the case of a hotel booking might include: "How did you determine the rate?", "Why did you ask the customer if she had AAA membership?", and "How were you able to pull up the customer's personal profile?"

Partnership

Once the participant is comfortable with your presence and you have developed a rapport, you can introduce the master–apprentice relationship. (Refer to Chapter 7, Interviews, "Monitoring the Relationship with the Interviewee" section, page 290 to learn about developing a rapport with participants.) As long as the company approves it and you are not breaking any laws, the participant becomes the master and instructs you (the apprentice) on how to complete a given task. You could not apprentice next to an emergency room physician unless each patient gave you permission; but considering the nature of emergencies, it is not likely that your presence could be easily accommodated. Despite limitations in some environments, the participant can always instruct you on *some* aspect of his/her activities.

It is easy for certain types of relationships to develop during this time. You should avoid the three relationships listed below because they are not conducive to unbiased data collection.

- *Expert–novice.* Because you are entering the environment as a "specialist," the user may see *you* as the expert. It is important for you to remind the participant that he or she is the expert and you are the novice.

- *Interviewer–interviewee.* Participants may assume that this is an interview and, if you are not asking questions, you already understand everything. Stress to the participant that you are new to the domain and need to be instructed as if you were a new employee starting the job. The user should not wait for questions from you before offering information or instruction.

- *Guest–host.* You are a partner with the user and should be involved with the user's work. The user should not be getting you coffee, and you should not be concerned about invading the user's personal space. Get in there and learn what the user knows.

Tip

This may sound *painfully* obvious, but remember to bring your own water and snacks. Do not let your growling stomach derail the interview. Anticipate if you will need caffeine along the way and schedule coffee breaks. Make sure you have a plan in place for lunch. If you wish to eat lunch with the participant – so that you can fully experience his/her day – ask the participant's permission first. Do not assume that you are welcome at what is considered "personal" time.

Interpretation

Interpretations of the data you collect will drive future decisions, so it is critical that those interpretations are correct. As you work with participants, share your interpretations with them and verify that you are correct. You do not have to worry that users will agree with an incorrect interpretation just to please you. When you create a solid master–apprentice relationship, the user will be keen for you to understand the process and will correct any misconceptions you have. He or she will often add to your interpretations as well, extending your knowledge and understanding of what you have observed.

Remember what your teacher told you: "The only dumb questions are the ones you don't ask." Do not be afraid to ask even simple questions. In addition to increasing your own knowledge, you can make the participants think more about what they would consider "standard practices" or the "that's just the way we have always done it" mentality. (Refer to Chapter 7, Interviews, "Your Role as the Interviewer" section, page 277, for tips about communicating with users and helping them provide the information you are seeking.)

Focus

During the entire process, you want to keep the inquiry focused on the areas of concern. You began by developing an observation guide for the inquiry (see above). Refer to this guide throughout the process. Since the participant is the master, he or she will guide the conversation to points he/she finds of interest. It is essential for you to learn what the participant finds important, but it is also critical that you get the data necessary to guide your design/next usability activity/innovation. The user may find it more interesting to cover all topics at a high level, but your focus should uncover details in the areas that you believe are most important. "The devil is in the details" – if you do not uncover the details, your interpretation of the data will be inadequate to inform design/the next usability activity/innovation. (Refer to Chapter 7, Interviews, "Your Role as the Interviewer" section, page 277, to learn more about guiding the participant's conversation.)

Process Analysis

A process analysis is similar to Contextual Inquiry. Unlike Contextual Inquiry, however, you enter with a series of questions (see below) and you do not necessarily apprentice with the user. It is a focused type of field study targeted at understanding the task sequence for a process that may span several days. At the end, you can develop a process map that visually demonstrates the steps in a process. (Figure 13.3 illustrates a very simple process map for a travel agent.) Because process analysis is more focused than Contextual Inquiry, it is also much faster to conduct.

- When does the first task in the process happen?
- What triggers it?
- Who does it?
- What information does the person have when the task begins?
- What are the major steps in the task?
- What information comes out of it?
- Who is the next person in the chain of the process?

- When does the next task happen? [repeat for each task in the process]
- How do you know when the process is complete?
- Does this process connect to other processes?
- Is this process ever reopened and, if so, under what circumstances?
- What errors can be made? How serious are they? How often do they occur?
- What are the major roadblocks to efficient performance?

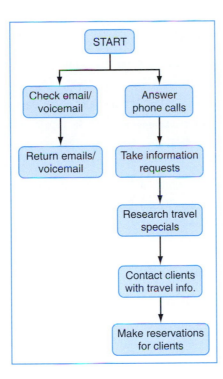

Figure 13.3:

Process map for a travel agent's typical day

Condensed Ethnographic Interview

Based on the cognitive science model of expert knowledge, the condensed ethnographic interview employs the standardization and focus of a **semi-structured interview** (refer to Chapter 7, Interviews, page 246) along with the context of observations and **artifacts**. Users are first interviewed to ask them how they accomplish a task, as well as other information surrounding their work. Users are then observed doing the task(s) in question, focusing on processes and tools. Artifacts are collected and discussed. Rather than a general observation guide, investigators use a standard set of questions to guide the visits but remain flexible throughout. One researcher developed a model of the users' work and then asked experts for validation/correction (Wood 1996).

This approach is characterized as "top-down" – in contrast to Contextual Inquiry's "bottom-up" approach – because the interviews form a general framework from which to interpret specific observations. This technique is considerably shorter than some of the other techniques described above but it also limits the data you are able to collect.

SUGGESTED RESOURCES FOR ADDITIONAL READING

The book chapters below offer two good examples of condensed ethnographic interviewing:

- Bauersfeld, K. & Halgren, S. (1996). You've Got Three Days! Case Studies in Field Techniques for the Time-challenged. In D. R. Wixon & J. Ramey (eds), *Field Methods Casebook for Software Design*, pp. 177–195. New York: John Wiley & Sons.
- Wood, L. (1996). The Ethnographic Interview in User-centered Work/Task Analysis. In D. R. Wixon & J. Ramey (eds), *Field Methods Casebook for Software Design*, pp. 35–56. New York: John Wiley & Sons.

Discount User Observation (DUO)

Three usability professionals created a method of collecting, analyzing, and presenting observational data in a shorter time frame than other methods they were familiar with – such as Contextual Inquiry (Laakso, Laakso, & Page 2001).

"Discount User Observation" (DUO) requires two data collectors. The first is a note-taker and is responsible for taking detailed notes during the visit, as well as asking clarifying questions. The questions should not disrupt the user's activities and should not turn into an interview. It is best to save questions until the end. Also, it is important that all notes be time-stamped. Notes can be taken either by hand or on a laptop. Using Microsoft Excel, you can write a program that automatically time-stamps each data entry. This would be less resource-intensive and error prone. See Figure 13.4 for a sample of time-stamped notes.

The second data collector is a photographer. The key difference between DUO and other methods is the critical aspect of collecting digital photographs of artifacts (e.g.,

Figure 13.4:

Sample of time-stamped notes

```
1:35   looking up hotel availability at clients preferred hotel
1:37   instant message (IM) dialog pops up & user types "hias," user says she
       loves IM but it can be disruptive
1:40   determined hotel availability — client cannot stay at preferred hotel
1:41   calls client to deliver news & propose other hotels instead
1:41   while waiting for client to answer phone, user types into IM dialog "y?"
```

printouts, business cards, notes, day planners) and the environment. Digital cameras typically include automatic time-stamps. Combining the time-stamped notes with the time-stamped photos provides a timeline of the user's work. Following data analysis, a summary of the results is presented to users for verification and correction (see "Data Analysis and Interpretation," page 615).

The goal of this discount method is not to save time by focusing in on any specific area of the user's work or environment, but rather to capture a holistic picture of the user's work, environment, and tasks. The goal is to understand the complex interdependencies of tasks, interruptions, and temporal overlaps (i.e., two actions occurring at the same time) without having to spend significant amounts of time transcribing, watching videos, or confusing raw data with inferences and interpretations.

Method Supplements

There are three activities that you can conduct in addition to the above methods, or use as standalone techniques: artifact walkthroughs, incident diaries, and observing while absent. They all require participation from the user, so they are not useful when conducting observation-only studies.

Artifact walkthroughs

Artifact walkthroughs are quick and easy but provide indispensable data. Begin by identifying each artifact a user leverages to do a particular task. Artifacts are objects or items that users use to complete their tasks or that result from their tasks. These can include the following:

- "Official" documents (e.g., manuals, forms, checklists, standard operating procedures)
- Handwritten notes
- Documents that get printed out as needed and then discarded
- Communications (e.g., inter-office memos, e-mails, letters)
- Outputs of tasks (e.g., confirmation number from travel booking).

You want to understand what triggers the use of each artifact: when is it used, and for what. Whenever possible, get copies of each artifact. If there are concerns about sensitive or private information (e.g., patient information, credit card numbers), ask for a copy of the original, black out the sensitive data, and then make a second copy. This takes a little extra time but most participants are willing to help wherever possible. You can also sign the company's confidential disclosure agreement promising that you will keep all data collected confidential (refer to Chapter 3, Ethical and Legal Considerations, "Legal Considerations" section, page 103). The information obtained during an artifact walkthrough will be essential if you want to conduct an artifact analysis (see "Data Analysis and Interpretation," page 615).

Incident diaries

Another technique that works well in field studies is the **incident diary**. Incident diaries allow you to collect ongoing data from users rather than one-time performance or opinions. They are given to users to keep track of issues they encounter while using a product.

Participants are provided with a notebook containing worksheets to be completed at home or work on their own (i.e., when you are not around to observe). The worksheets may ask users to describe a problem or issue they encountered, how they solved it (if they did), and how troublesome it was (e.g., **Likert scale**). The exact content of the worksheet will depend on the goals of the study. The purpose of incident diaries is to understand infrequent tasks that you might not be able to see even if you observed the user all day. In the example shown (see Figure 13.5), planning a vacation often happens over an extended period and during unplanned times. You cannot possibly be there to observe on all of those occasions and you do not want to interrupt their natural behavior. Finally, incident diaries can also be used while you *are* present to get two different perspectives on the same issue (e.g., during a usability evaluation).

Planning Your Vacation Diary

ID: P1

Date: _____

Describe what your goal was: _____

_____

_____

What web site did you visit? Please provide the URL or address of the web site.

_____

_____

Did you accomplish your goal? _____ Yes _____ No

Please explain: _____

_____

_____

Please describe any difficulties you encountered or anything you would have liked
to do differently. _____

_____

_____

_____

Other comments or thoughts: _____

_____

_____

_____

The appeal of incident diaries is that they require little time or resources on your part. However, there are several issues with using incident diaries which call into question their validity and reliability:

- They are best used when problems or tasks are relatively infrequent. It is important to remember that frequency does *not* equate with importance. Some very important tasks happen very rarely but you need to capture and understand them. Frequent tasks can and should be observed directly, especially since users are usually unwilling to complete worksheets every few minutes for frequent tasks.

- When you are not present, there is a chance that users will not remember (or want) to fill out the diary while they are in the middle of a problem. There is no way of knowing whether the number of entries matches the number of problems actually encountered.

- The user may not provide enough detail or context for the entry to be meaningful.

- The user may lack the technical knowledge to accurately describe the problem.
- User perception of the actual cause or root of the problem may not be correct.

Despite these issues, incident diaries can give you additional insight into the user experience over time that you would not otherwise have. The caution here is not to use incident diaries in isolation. Follow-up with interviews or other usability activities.

Observing while you are not present

You can observe users even when you are not present by setting up a video camera and then leaving. This is an excellent way to understand detailed steps a user takes, especially in small environments where observers cannot fit or critical jobs where you do not want to interrupt/distract the user. In one study, researchers videotaped radiologists at work, viewed the tapes later, and formulated questions (Ramey, Rowberg, & Robinson 1996). They then set up another appointment with the radiologists about three days later to view the tapes together while the radiologists provided a running commentary (called "retrospective think-aloud" or "stimulated recall"). The interviewers inserted questions along the way. They refer to this technique as "stream-of-behavior chronicles." To analyze the data, they categorized and indexed specific behaviors.

In another example of recording user behavior, investigators videotaped the participant's setting and captured the participant's computer screen (Bauersfeld & Halgren 1996). This was recorded as a picture-in-picture image with a video mixer. The user could turn the recording on and off as needed (e.g., turn off the recording to read personal e-mail). The investigators then came back two to three hours later to collect the equipment and analyze the tapes. If you have several cameras, you can record the behavior of several participants simultaneously.

Preparing for a Field Study

Are You Ready?

Before you begin *any* user requirements activity there are a number of things that you must be familiar with. Because these elements are common to all user requirements activities, they have been covered in the earlier chapters – but now is a good time to double-check the list. If you are not familiar with one of the items you can refer to the earlier chapter to brush up or familiarize yourself with that element.

Chapter 1: Introduction to User Requirements

- ☐ **Get stakeholder buy-in for your activity** (see page 14)

Chapter 2: Before You Choose an Activity

- ☐ **Learn about your product** (see page 29)
- ☐ **Learn about your users** (see page 41)

Chapter 3: Ethical and Legal Considerations

- ☐ **Create consent forms** (see page 98)
- ☐ **Create confidential disclosure agreements** (see page 103)

Chapter 5: Preparing for Your User Requirements Activity

- ☐ **Develop an activity proposal** (see page 146)
- ☐ **Recruit participants** (see page 156)
- ☐ **Develop an activity protocol** (see page 191)
- ☐ **Pilot your activity** (see page 193)

Chapter 6: During Your User Requirements Activity

- ☐ **Record and take notes during your activity** (see page 226)

Now that you are familiar with some of the techniques available to you, it is time to plan and prepare for your field study. Although some of the details may vary slightly depending on the data collecting technique selected, the preparation, participants, and materials remain constant.

At a Glance

> Identify the type of study to conduct
> Players in your activity
> Train the players
> Develop your protocol
> Schedule the visits
> Activity materials
> Summary

Identify the Type of Study to Conduct

To identify the type of study you would like to conduct, use the decision diagram in Figure 13.6.

Scope your study appropriately. You may not have time to learn everything you would like to, or be able to visit all the sites you are interested in. It is critical to the success of your study to plan carefully. Create a realistic timetable for identifying the sites, recruiting the users, collecting the data, and then analyzing the data. You will have questions later on (usually during the analysis stage). If possible, leave enough time to conduct follow-up interviews. There is nothing more frustrating than running out of time and not being able to analyze all the data you have! And remember, it always takes longer than you think – so include enough extra time in case you run into snags along the way.

Write a proposal (refer to Chapter 5, Preparing for Your User Requirements Activity, "Creating a Proposal" section, page 146) that establishes the objectives of the study, identifies the user and site profile, the timeline, the resources needed (e.g., budget, materials, contacts, customers) and from whom, as well as how the information you collect will benefit the company/product/design. If you cannot provide this information, you have more research to do. It is *essential* that you get buy-in from all stakeholders on this proposal. You do not want stakeholders changing their focus or disagreeing about the direction of your study halfway through. The proposal will be your stake in the ground.

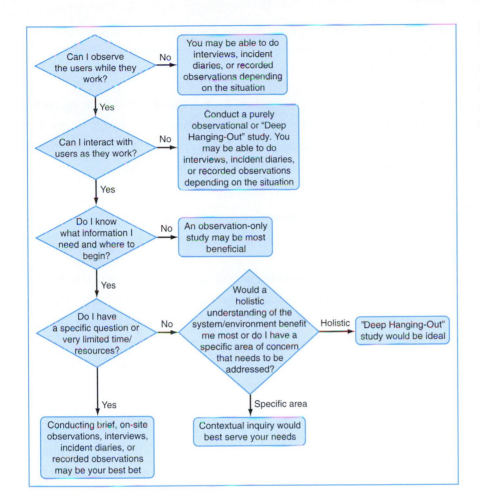

Figure 13.6:

Decision diagram to determine the type of study that would best suit your needs

Players in Your Activity

In addition to participants to observe, there are a few other roles you may need to fill for your study. Each one is described below.

The participants

Once you know the type of study you would like to conduct, you need to identify the user type to investigate (refer to Chapter 2, Before You Choose an Activity, "Learn About Your Users" section, page 41). As with any of the techniques described in this book, the data you collect are only as good as the participants you recruit.

Create a screener to guide your recruitment and make sure everyone is in agreement (refer to Chapter 5, Preparing for Your User Requirements Activity, "Recruitment Methods" section, page 173).

There is no set number of users to recruit. As mentioned earlier, some people recommend 15–20 users, but time and cost restraints mean that four to six (per user type) is more common in industry practice. There are other factors to keep in mind when identifying users and sites for field studies. These include:

- Getting a diverse range of users and sites
- Setting company expectations up-front.

Diverse range of users and sites

Get a broad representation of users and sites. This includes industry, company size, new adopters and long-time customers, as well as geographical diversity. Try to get access to multiple users at each site. They may be doing the same task, but each person may do it differently, have different ideas, challenges, workarounds, etc. You also want a mix of experts and novices. Contacts at a given company will likely introduce you to their "best" employees. Explain to the contacts the value in observing both expert and novice users. In the end, though, politics and people's availability may determine your choice of sites and users to observe. Just make sure the participants and sites meet your profile, otherwise there is no point in collecting the data. Also, try to get stakeholders involved in identifying sites, users, and contacts at those sites. They often have the contacts to help you do this.

When you begin recruiting, start small; do not recruit more users or sites than your schedule will permit. If your first set of visits is successful, you can leverage that success to increase the scope of your study. In addition, you may need to start with local sites for budgeting reasons; but if your study is successful, you could be given the opportunity to expand later.

Setting company expectations up-front

Some companies may insist, as a condition of participating, on seeing the results of your study or receiving a report on their employees. Be clear and set their expectations at the beginning; you are not there to report on the employees – it is unethical and may be a violation of labor laws. In addition, you cannot provide information gained from another company. Most often, companies will ask you to sign a confidential disclosure agreement to ensure that you will keep their data confidential (refer to Chapter 3, Ethical and Legal Considerations, page 94). You may offer to provide a copy of the notes from the sessions conducted at their site, or a very general summary, but first speak with your legal department to get permission.

Do not reveal the names of the people who participated in your study. The actions and comments you observed should not be associated with specific participants.

Some conclusions and design recommendations that you develop as a result of the site visits could be deemed confidential by your company, so you may not be able to share this information with the companies that participated.

Once you explain all this, most site contacts will understand your position. Some may still feel that you are not providing them with enough information to make participation worthwhile. Explain the benefit they will see in a new or improved product. However, if that is not incentive enough, you must move on to another site.

The investigators

Begin by identifying who wants to take part as genuine data collectors, not just as curious onlookers. You may be surprised to discover how many people want to be present during your field visits, particularly those visits in which you intend to interact with customers. In purely observational or Deep Hanging-Out studies (as described above), this is not a big issue. You should welcome some additional help in collecting data. It will speed the process, and an additional set of eyes can bring a fresh perspective to the data analysis. Expect and encourage people to get involved, but be aware of some of the issues surrounding inexperienced investigators.

You may want to establish a rule that anyone present at the site must participate in the data collection and follow a set of ground rules (see "Train the Players," page 598). This is where you must establish yourself as the expert and insist that everyone respect your expertise. Sometimes you need to be diplomatic and tell a stakeholder that he/she cannot attend a particular visit, without ruining your relationship with that stakeholder.

Once you have a list of people who want to take part in the study, look for those who are detail-oriented, and good listeners. We recommend working in teams of just two, because that is less overwhelming for the participant being observed. Each team should consist of an investigator and a note-taker, and a videographer/ photographer (see below). Since the video camera can usually be set up in the beginning and left alone, either the investigator or note-taker can do this. And because three people can be overwhelming for a user, we recommend that either the note-taker or investigator double-up as photographer. Mixed-gender teams can help in cases where a participant feels more comfortable relating to one gender or another.

The job of the investigator is to develop rapport with the participant, and if applicable, conduct the interview and apprentice with him/her. The investigator is the "leader" in the two-person team. In cases where you lack a great deal of domain knowledge, you may not know enough about what you are observing to ask the user follow-up questions later on. You may wish to create more of a partnership with a developer or product manager. You can begin by asking participants each question, but the domain expert would then follow up with more detailed questions. Just be sure that one of you is capturing the data! Alternatively, you can bring a "translator" along with you. This may be a user from the site or an expert from your company who will provide a running commentary while the participant is working. This is ideal in situations where the participant cannot provide **think-aloud** data and cannot be interrupted with your questions. In a healthcare field study we conducted, we asked a member of the product team who was a former Registered Nurse to act as a translator for us. She pointed out observations that were interesting to her and which we would not have noticed. She also explained the purpose of different artifacts when users were not available to discuss them. Her help was priceless on-site!

If you have more potential investigators than you have roles, you may choose different investigators for each site. This can lower **inter-rater reliability** (i.e., the degree to which two or more observers assign the same rating or label to a behavior), but it may also be necessary if individual investigators do not have the time to commit to a series of visits. Having a single person who attends all visits (i.e., yourself) can ensure continuity and an ability to see patterns/trends. Having a new investigator every few visits provides a fresh set of eyes and a different perspective. It also breaks up the workload and allows more people to take part in the study. You are sharing the knowledge, and important stakeholders do not feel excluded.

If time is a serious issue for you, it may be wise to have more than one collection team. This will allow you to collect data from multiple sites at once, but you will need to train several people and develop an explicit protocol for investigators to follow (see "Develop Your Protocol," page 599). If there is more than one experienced usability professional available, pair each one up with a novice investigator. Having more than one collection team will mean that you will lose that consistent pair of eyes, but it may be worthwhile if you are pressed on time but have several sites available to you.

The note-taker

In addition to an investigator, a note-taker is required. The investigator should be focused on asking questions and apprenticing with the user (if applicable), not taking detailed notes. You will find a detailed discussion of note-taking tips and strategies in Chapter 6 (refer to Chapter 6, During Your User Requirements Activity, "Recording and Note-taking" section, page 226). The note-taker can also serve as a timekeeper if that is information you wish to collect. You may also wish to have the note-taker serve as the videographer/photographer (see below). Lastly, it is also important to have an additional pair of hands on-site to set up equipment, and the note-taker can serve this purpose.

Tip

It is extremely beneficial to have your note-taker present during data analysis. Having someone as a sounding board and additional pair of eyes is invaluable!

The videographer/photographer

Whenever possible you will want to video record your field study. You will find a detailed discussion of videotaping tips and the benefits of videotape in Chapter 6 (refer to Chapter 6, During Your User Requirements Activity, "Recording and Note-taking" section, page 226). In most cases, this person simply needs to start and stop the tape, insert new tapes as needed, and keep an eye out for any technical issues that arise.

You may also want someone to take photographs. (Again, the note-taker can often take on the roles of videographer and photographer.) Capturing visual images of the user's environment, artifacts, and tasks is extremely valuable. It helps you remember what you observed, and it helps stakeholders who were not present to internalize the data. Even if you do not plan to include pictures of participants in your reports or presentations, they can help you remember one participant from another. A digital camera is advantageous, because if the user is nervous about what you are capturing, you can show him/her every image and get permission to keep it. If the user is not happy with the image, you can demonstrate that you deleted it.

Account managers

The account manager or sales representative is one person who may insist on following you around until he or she feels secure in what you are doing. Since this is the person who often owns the sales relationship with the customer and must continue to support the customer after you are long gone, you need to respect his/her need for control. Just make sure the account manager understands that this is not a sales demo and that *you* will be collecting the data. We have experienced this ourselves in more than one study. We have found that account managers are so busy that they will often leave you after an hour or less.

Train the Players

You are entering someone's personal space; for some users, this is often more stressful for the user than going to a lab. You will also likely need to leverage multiple skill sets such as interviewing, conducting surveys, observing, and managing groups of people. If you or a co-worker has not conducted a field study before, we recommend reviewing Chapter 6, During Your User Requirements Activity, "Moderating Your Activity" section, page 220, for a foundation in moderating. You may also want to sign up for a tutorial at a conference hosted by a relevant professional organization to get hands-on training for one of the particular techniques. Shadowing an experienced usability professional is another option, but it is more difficult to do since the primary investigator will want to reduce the number of observers to an absolute minimum.

Even if the people available to collect data are all trained usability professionals, you want to ensure that everyone is on the same page – so a planning and/or training session is essential. Begin by identifying roles and setting expectations. If you need the other investigator to help you prep (e.g., copy consent forms, QA equipment), make sure he or she understands the importance of that task. You do not want to get on-site only to find that you don't have the consent forms because of miscommunication or because the other investigator was annoyed at being your "assistant." Also make sure that everyone is familiar with the protocol that you will be using (refer to Chapter 5, Preparing for Your User Requirements Activity, "Creating a Protocol" section, page 190).

If you will be conducting usability evaluations on-site, make it clear to all investigators that they are not there to "help" the participant. It is human nature to want to help someone who is having difficulty, but all the investigators need to remember that they will not be there to help the user later on. One usability professional keeps a roll of duct tape with him and shows it to his co-investigators prior to the visit. He informs them that he will not hesitate to use it should they offer inappropriate help or comments during the visit. It gets a laugh and helps them to remember the point.

If this will be a large field study (rather than a one-time visit), you may want inexperienced investigators to read this chapter, attend workshops, practice during mock sessions, or watch videos of previously conducted field studies. Develop standardized materials (see "Activity Materials," page 603) and review them with all investigators. Additionally, everyone should know how to use each piece of equipment. Practice setting up and packing up equipment quickly. Labeling cords for easy identification will make setting up much faster. Finally, identify a standard note-taking method and shorthand for easy decoding.

Develop your Protocol

By now, you have selected the type of field study you will conduct. Now you need to identify your plan of attack or protocol. This is different from your observation guide (a list of concerns or general areas to observe). A **protocol** can include how you will interact with users (the observation guide is part of that), how much time you plan to spend observing each user/area, and what instructions you will give users (e.g., think-aloud protocol). You should also identify any activities that you want other investigators to participate in. The answers to these and many other questions need to be spelled out in a protocol (refer to Chapter 5, Preparing for Your User Requirements Activity, "Creating a Protocol" section, page 190). Without a protocol, you do not have a script for everyone to follow and each investigator will do his/her own thing. Even if you are doing the study alone, you may end up conducting each visit differently, forgetting some questions, haphazardly adding in others. A protocol allows you to collect the data in the most efficient and reliable manner possible. It also allows you to concentrate on the data collection, not trying to remember what you forgot this time.

Schedule the Visits

After you have selected your investigators, get commitment from each one and include them in scheduling discussions. They must agree to be present at the visits they are scheduled for, and they must be willing to receive training. If they do not have time for either of these, it is best to find someone else.

Below are some things to consider when scheduling your visits. The questions below may seem obvious, but when you are in the middle of creating the schedule, many "obvious" details are forgotten.

- Where is the site? How long it will take to get there? If there will be a significant drive and traffic will likely be a problem, obviously you do not want to schedule early morning appointments.
- Have you checked to see if your contact or the user's manager should be called or scheduled as part of the visit?
- Do you plan to visit more than one site per day? How far apart are they? Will there be traffic? What if you are running behind schedule at the other site? If you must visit more than one location per day, put in plenty of pad time between sites.

- Include breaks between users or sites in your schedule. This will allow you to review your notes, rest, eat a snack, check your messages, etc. You do not want a growling stomach to interrupt your quiet observations.

- Make sure you are refreshed for each visit. If you are not a morning person, do not schedule early morning appointments; or if your energy tends to run out at the end of the day, schedule only one visit per day. Clearly, you do not want the user to see you yawning during the interview.

- Consider the user's schedule:
  - Lunchtime may either be good or bad for users. Find out what they prefer as well as what their workload might be during that time (see next point).
  - Some users want you there when work is slow so you won't disturb them. Obviously, you want to be there when things are busy! Make sure that the time the user suggests for your visit will allow you to observe what you are interested in.
  - Consider the cyclical nature of work. Some tasks are done only during certain times of the year. Going back to the vineyard study mentioned at the beginning of this chapter, if you are interested in observing the harvest, there is a limited window in which you can observe.
  - Some days of the week are worse than others (e.g., Monday and Friday). As a general rule, avoid Monday mornings and Friday afternoons. Also find out if there are standard "telecommuting" days at your user's site?
  - Be prepared to compromise. Your users have lives to live and your study is likely low on their priority list. You may have to change your original plan or schedule, but keep in mind that some data are better than none.

- Do not forget the other investigators. Ask them for their availability. Find out whether they are morning or evening people. It isn't any less offensive for the note-taker to be yawning during an interview.

- Find out how to make copies or print out files. Can you use the user's facilities or will you have to find a local copy shop?

- Finally, consider the haphazard schedule of some occupations (e.g., surgeons, emergency medical technicians). They may agree to participate but be pulled away to activities you cannot observe. Be prepared to wait long periods of time. Bring other work with you to do and/or have a list of things to observe that do not require interacting with participants. Also be prepared to take advantage of sudden opportunities.

Begin your study on a professional foot. When recruiting individuals over the phone, they may be skeptical. You must demonstrate that you are not trying to sell them a timeshare in Florida and you can be trusted. If your company is not well known, point people to your website for legitimacy. Give them your name and call-back information. Obviously, you should be polite even if the person on the other end is not.

If the potential participant or site contact is interested, provide all logistical details up-front (e.g., dates, times, length of stay, etc.). Get names, e-mail addresses, and phone numbers for each person you plan to speak with (not just their supervisor's or the account manager's information). You need this information to follow up, ask questions, and resolve issues that may arise. If the supervisor or account manager is absent, you may be unable to find your next appointment or learn that the person you are supposed to be interviewing went home sick (see "Lessons Learned," page 623). Finally, call the night before to confirm your appointment and answer any last-minute questions the participant or site contact may have.

Tip

Get detailed directions to each site and verify them with the participant. Do not simply trust the directions you download from the web. Ask the participants to warn you about typical traffic conditions and tell you about alternative routes or shortcuts.

The final thing to keep in mind when scheduling is *burnout*. Burnout is a risk for extended studies. Field studies are intense activities where you must be "on" at all times. It is time-consuming to conduct each visit and analyze the data. You can also suffer from information overload. All of the sites or users tend to blur together after a while. And travel can be stressful. Take the "fatigue factor" into consideration when scheduling the visits and determining the timeline for analyzing data. Unfortunately, you may be placed in the situation where you must visit six sites in three days and there is no way around it. Alternating the roles of note-taker and interviewer between yourself and your co-worker can give you a break. At least you will not have to be "on" for every participant (encouraging participants to think-aloud, following up on questions, apprenticing). You will still be exhausted, but since you get a "break" every other participant, the data collected will hopefully not be degraded.

Tip

Find out the appropriate dress code. You cannot assume that most places are business casual these days. If a workplace is quite conservative, you will look out of place in your khakis and people may not take you seriously. On the other hand, if it is an extremely casual environment, people may be afraid to approach you or talk to you if you are dressed in a suit and tie. If in doubt, dress a little nicer than you think is necessary – but wear comfortable shoes. And check with your teammates to make sure you are on the same dress code page.

Activity Materials

You may have many materials to take to each site; it depends on the type of study you are conducting and what is permitted on-site. Below is a list of suggested materials for most types of studies, but you should tailor this for your own study and include more detail in your own checklist. Some of these materials may not be familiar to you, but they are all described later. This is the best way to stay organized and keep your study running smoothly from one site to the next. Without your checklist, you will likely forget at least one thing each time out.

Checklist of all materials and equipment needed

- ☐ Contact information for each participant
- ☐ Directions and map to site
- ☐ Consent forms and confidentiality agreements
- ☐ Protocol
- ☐ Observation guide
- ☐ Visit summary template

☐ Schedule

☐ Method of note-taking (audio recorder and/or paper and pencil)

☐ Peripherals (e.g., batteries, tapes, extension cords, power strip)

☐ Method for collecting artifacts (e.g., accordion folder, notebook, hole puncher)

☐ Method for carrying all the equipment (e.g., small suitcase, luggage cart)

☐ Thank you gift for participant(s)

☐ Business cards for participants to contact you later with questions or additional information

☐ Video recorder or camera and audio recorder (if permission has been obtained to record).

Tips

- Conduct a check of your equipment prior to every visit. Are the batteries still good? Did you bring all the cords back from your last visit? Is everything behaving as it should? Practice to make sure you know how everything works and needs to be set up. Do not wait until you are in the user's cubicle to find out the battery to the video recorder is dead or you did not bring the right power cord.

- Label all cords and make sure they are correct. Many black cords tend to look alike but are not interchangeable.

- Use your checklist!

We recommend providing an incentive for participants (refer to Chapter 5, Preparing for Your User Requirements Activity, "Determining Participant Incentives" section, page 159). We also recommend getting a gift for anyone who helped arrange your access to the site or users (e.g., account/product manager). This individual may have spent significant time finding people in the company to match your user profile, or helping you to arrange your visit. It never hurts to show your appreciation and it can also help if you ever need to access that site again. When selecting the gift, keep in mind that you must carry it along with the rest of your equipment. You don't want to carry around several shirts in each size or heavy, breakable coffee mugs.

Tip

If you are flying from one site to another and you have the time between sites, shipping your materials to your hotel can save your back and your sanity. You do not want to lug 30 pounds of recording equipment onto a plane, only to find there is no overhead bin space left. Watching luggage handlers throw your expensive equipment onto the plane with the rest of the check-in baggage can ruin your entire flight (and visit!). When you ship equipment, you can purchase additional insurance for a small fee. If any damage is done to your equipment, you will be reimbursed with less hassle than the airlines will give you. Make sure you have a tracking number so you can track the progress of your shipment.

After a very painful experience hauling a video recorder, tripod, tapes, laptop, incentives, and paperwork through an airport, we began shipping our materials and equipment out a week prior to our visits. After four years, our shipments have never been lost, damaged, or late. Yes, it costs more but it is worth it!

Tip

Do you really need all that stuff? If you are traveling to six different cities in five days, you can't possibly ship everything from one site to another. You want to be well equipped but you should also pack light. Buying gifts or incentives once you get on-site can lighten the load. Bringing a simple floppy or CD with all your forms on it and then printing them at a local copy shop or business center will further relieve your burden. If you can't pack it all in a bag and comfortably carry it around the office with you for 10 minutes, how will you ever lug it from site to site?

As we mentioned earlier, it is important to develop an observation guide. This is a list of general concerns or issues to guide your observations but it is not a list of specific questions to ask. This will help ensure you address each of the goals of your study. Next, use your observation guide to develop a **visit summary template** (see Figure 13.7). This is a standardized survey or worksheet given to each investigator to complete at the end of each visit. This helps everyone get their thoughts on paper while they are fresh. It also speeds data analysis and avoids reporting *only* odd or

Sample visit summary

template

Airport Kiosk Study

Location: _____

Participant ID: _____

Date: _____

Investigator: _____

Area I observed: __ Curb side check-in__ Ticket counter__ Baggage claim __Gate

Key observations:_____
_____
_____
_____

Participant job title: _____

Years of experience: _____

Summary of main points from interview with participant: _____
_____
_____
_____
_____
_____

Artifacts collected: __ Audio tape of interview __ Digital photos __ Video recording
　　　　　　　　 __ Screenshots 　　　　　 __ Notes/documents from user

List any documents/notes/artifacts you collected from the user:
_____
_____
_____
_____

Recommendations for next visit/lessons learned:
_____
_____
_____
_____
_____

funny anecdotal data. Although this can be the most thought-provoking informa-tion and can bring your users to life for stakeholders, it should not be the *only* data you report. Stakeholders who are eager for immediate results can read the summary worksheets and know what the key points are from each visit. They will appreciate being kept in the loop and will be less likely to insist on being present at each site if they feel you are promptly providing the information.

The template should be flexible enough so that you can record data you hadn't anticipated and avoid losing important insights. You may also further develop the template as you conduct more visits. Just make sure that everyone who views the summaries understands that they are viewing summary data from *one* data point. They should not begin building the product or making changes to their existing product based on their interpretations of that data.

Create any incident diaries, surveys, prototypes, or interview worksheets you may need during your study. You can also create any pre-visit activity materials such as mailing out a survey in advance to help you develop your observation guide. Incident diaries are another valuable tool to send out prior to your visit. The surveys and diaries will be extremely useful if you know you will have limited time with each participant.

Tip

Identify back-up activities. In the event there is nothing to observe (e.g., no customer calls, no emergencies in the emergency room), you will want to do a different activity. Do not waste the precious time you have with users by waiting for a gunshot victim to be wheeled in.

Summary

We have provided a lot of information to help you prepare for your field study. Figure 13.8 now summarizes the main points. Use this checklist when preparing for your study.

☐ Create a proposal that establishes the objectives of the study, identifies the user and site profile, the timeline, the resources needed and from whom, and the benefits of the study.

☐ Get a mix of sites and users.

☐ Start small when recruiting, and use the success of those studies to expand.

☐ Gain the support of stakeholders before accessing a customer site.

☐ Seek the help of at least one other investigator to speed data collection, and get an additional perspective.

☐ Include stakeholders in identifying sites, users, and contacts, as well as data collection so they too have a stake in success of the study and feel part of the process.

Figure 13.8:
Recommendations for preparing for a field study

Continued

Figure 13.8

– *Cont'd*

☐ If you are lacking in domain knowledge, bring along a member of the product team to ask follow-up questions or a "translator" to provide a running commentary.

☐ Train all investigators to collect data in a standardized method, including how to operate all equipment.

☐ Develop standardized materials for all investigators so the data are collected similarly across teams, users, and sites.

☐ Develop a detailed protocol, including an observation guide.

☐ Identify back-up activities in case there is nothing to observe.

☐ Conduct a pilot session to pilot your protocol and timeline, and use that data to practice analysis.

☐ Consider factors like traffic, distance to site, personal breaks, the "fatigue factor," the user's schedule, holidays, and other investigators' schedules when scheduling your visits.

☐ Create a checklist of the required materials and check everything off prior to each site visit.

☐ Use digital cameras and video recorders whenever possible.

☐ Do a QA check of all equipment prior to departing, and have everyone practice setting up the equipment.

☐ Develop a visit summary template for each investigator to complete, and send these out for stakeholders to keep apprised of the progress of your study.

☐ Take extra forms, batteries, tapes, and other materials in case any are lost or damaged.

☐ Burn all your materials on a CD or save them on a floppy disk to make additional copies if necessary.

Conducting a Field Study

The specific procedure for your field study will obviously vary depending on the type of study you conduct. We can offer some high-level tasks to conduct, regardless of the type of study. Just remember to remain flexible.

At a Glance

> Get organized

> Meet the participant

> Begin data collection

> Wrap-up

> Organize your data

> Summary

Get Organized

If the visit has been arranged (i.e., this is not a public location where you can observe users unnoticed), upon arrival meet with your site contact. Familiarize yourself with the environment. Where is the bathroom, kitchen, copier, etc.? Where can you get food (if that hasn't been planned for you already)? If your site contact won't be with you throughout the visit, how will you get to your next appointment, and so forth? If there are multiple investigation teams, decide where and when you will meet up again. Arrive at least 15 minutes before your first scheduled appointment to take care of these details. Be prepared for some extra hand-shaking and time at this point. You may need to say "hello" to the contact's or user's boss. This is another good reason for being early.

Meet the Participant

Again, if your visit is arranged, go to your first scheduled appointment on time. Introduce yourself and any other investigators or observers with you. If you are reviewing prototypes, it may be necessary to ask each participant to sign a confidential disclosure agreement. All participants should be aware of their rights, so ask them to sign a consent form at the beginning. Don't forget to make copies of those forms for the user if he/she wants them. Refer to Chapter 3, Ethical and Legal Considerations, page 94, for information on these forms. (This is one reason you need to check on copying capability ahead of time.)

Tip

When possible it is always best to have all legal forms signed by you and/or the participants beforehand.

Explain what you will be doing and your timeframe. Also, state clearly that the participant is the expert; not you. Remind the participant that he/she is not being evaluated in any way. While you are going over the forms and explaining these points, the other investigator should be setting up the equipment. If you must invade a co-worker's space, ask for permission and treat that person with the same respect you are showing your participant. This may sound obvious, but it is easy to overlook common courtesies when you are wrestling with equipment and trying to remember a million different things. This is when your protocol will come in handy.

Next, get a feel for the user's environment (e.g., take pictures, draw maps, record sticky notes, note lighting, equipment, background sounds, layout, software used). While the note-taker is doing this, the interviewer should begin developing a rapport with the user. Give the participant time to vent any frustrations about your product or his/her job in general. If the user has product-specific questions or enhancement requests, state that you can record these questions and take them back to the product team, but do not attempt to answer them yourself. Participants will be curious about you and the purpose of the study. They may also ask for help. State that you cannot give advice or recommendations and that you are there simply to observe. At the end of the session, you may choose to provide the user with help, both to repay the user and to learn more about why the user needed help in the first place. Through-out, be polite and show enthusiasm. Your enthusiasm will rub off on others and make the participant feel more comfortable.

If you plan to set up recording equipment and leave for a few hours, you should still review the consent form with participants and have a discussion to make sure the participant is comfortable with being recorded. You may think it is not necessary to establish a rapport with the user; but if you want the participant to behave naturally, he or she needs to understand the purpose of your study and have the opportunity to ask questions. Enthusiasm is important, even if you won't be there for more than 10 minutes.

Begin Data Collection

Now it is time to begin your selected data collection technique. Use an appropriate note-taking method. If you do not want people to know you are collecting data about them, select an inconspicuous method (e.g., a small notepad). If it is not necessary to hide your actions, a laptop and tape recorder may be better.

SUGGESTED RESOURCES FOR ADDITIONAL READING

Biobserve (www.biobserve.com) offers a number of tools for observing users and noting their actions. Although we have not used them ourselves, *Spectator* (software that records a large variety of events like movements and behaviors via user-definable keyboard shortcuts as well as recording to .mpg or .avi files) and *Spectator Go!* (a mobile version of *Spectator*) appear to offer a lot of potential for recording observational data.

It is important to know the difference between capturing observations and inferences. Unless you verify your interpretations with the participant, do not record your assumptions as facts. Your interpretations are not raw data points and may be incorrect. Check your interpretations with the participant wherever possible. For example, imagine you are observing an agent interacting with clients and she is always smiling and is very cheery and pleasant. This is good information to record, but do not infer from that observation that she loves her job – she may feel extremely overworked but has learned to hide it with a smile. As another example, imagine you observe the travel agent spending great deal of time on e-mail. Do not infer that she is e-mailing clients – it could be co-workers, friends, family, etc. You must speak with the person to understand what you are observing.

> **Tip**
>
> Give the participant privacy when needed (e.g., personal phone calls, bathroom breaks). Tell the person up-front that he/she can let you know when privacy is needed and that you will gladly respect that request. For example, if you are noting events, you might tell the user that any personal calls that they receive will be noted as just "a personal call," with no further details.

Wrap-up

Once you have completed your selected data collection technique or when your time with the participant is up, wrap-up the session. Make sure you leave time at the end to provide any help that you promised earlier and to answer additional questions the participant may have. While the interviewer thanks the participant, answers questions, and provides the incentive for participation or a thank-you gift, the note-taker should be packing up all materials and equipment. You may wish to leave behind follow-up surveys or incident diaries. This is also a good time to schedule follow-up visits. You will often find during data analysis that you have new questions.

> **Tip**
>
> When you return to your office, always send a simple thank-you note to all participants. It just reminds them that the time they took away from their day is still appreciated. If you ever need to follow-up with those same users, they will be more likely to welcome you since they know you really appreciated their effort.

Organize Your Data

After the session, you will find it useful to compare notes, thoughts, and insights with your fellow investigators. Now is the time to get everything on paper or record the discussion on a tape recorder. You can complete the visit summary template individually or together. You may be tired after the session and just want to move on to the next appointment or go home, but you will be so relieved at the end of the study when you have everything well documented. You can provide quick interim reports and it will make data analysis much easier.

Now is also the time to label all data (e.g., tapes, surveys, artifacts) with a participant ID (but not their name, for confidentiality reasons), date, time, and investigation team. You may want to have a large manila envelope to keep each participant's materials separate. It is a terrible feeling to get back to the office and not know which user provided a set of artifacts or who completed a certain survey.

When you return to the office, scan in artifacts, notes, and photos. In addition to sending out the visit summary report, you can include electronic files or physical copies of the artifacts to stakeholders without worrying about losing the originals. However, this is time-consuming if you have lots of artifacts. (We collected nearly 200 documents from one hospital during our healthcare field study!) Alternatively, you could ask participants for multiple copies of each original artifact – but this can be asking a lot.

Recommendations for Conducting Family/Home Visits

It is just as important to begin on a professional foot when attempting to access users in their home environment as it is when accessing them at work. Stress that you are not attempting to sell them anything, and provide your contact information so they can call you back with additional questions or to verify your legitimacy. Also, provide information about all of the logistics up-front so they can make an educated decision.

When doing home visits, it is best to ask when the individual or family eats meals. You should either avoid those times or offer to bring food for everyone. The latter can provide an opportunity to socialize with your users and develop a rapport (just make sure that you approve the menu with everyone). Feel free to discuss the study and allow the participants to ask questions (if this will not bias the study). This is a time to develop rapport, not interview the participants. Since you are not collecting data at this time, do not tape discussions over dinner – you will kill the laid-back atmosphere.

The initial few minutes are critical to developing rapport and trust with your user(s). Start with introductions and state the purpose of your visit, even if this was stated during recruiting. It helps to find something in common to relate to (e.g., pets, kids' ages, collectables in the house, etc.). Review the consent form and confidentiality agreements (if necessary). Finally, ask permission to record the session and make it clear to the participants that they may ask to have the audio/video recorders turned off at any time. If they are embarrassed by the mess in the living room and do not want it photographed, respect their wishes. If the mess in the living room is important to your study, explain why a photograph of it would be so valuable to your study. If they still object, do not pursue it further. You will only break down any trust you may have developed up to that point.

If your study involves the entire family, begin by interviewing or observing the children. Use their enthusiasm and curiosity to bring out the more reserved parents. Parents will respect your attention to their children. Create an additional activity for the children to participate in while you speak with the parents (e.g., draw a picture of an airplane from the future). Since most kids love being the center of attention, you could have difficulty ending your interaction with the children and then collecting data from the parents. The additional activity will keep them occupied and prevent them from feeling left out for the rest of your visit.

Finally, if you plan to follow-up with the family, it is particularly helpful to send a thank-you note. It is a nice idea to take a family photo at the end of each visit and send a copy to the family along with the card.

- ☐ Bring your own snacks and drinks.
- ☐ Audio record at a minimum.
- ☐ Maintain a low profile.
- ☐ Choose an appropriate note-taking method.
- ☐ Think "big picture" and obtain a holistic understanding of the environment, users, and tasks.
- ☐ Pay attention to signs and notes. Collect multiple types of data for a richer data set.
- ☐ Meet with your site contact upon arrival on-site.
- ☐ Familiarize yourself with the environment (e.g., bathrooms, kitchen, copier).
- ☐ If there are multiple investigation teams, decide where and when you will meet up again.
- ☐ Develop a rapport with the participant before delving into observation or interviews.
- ☐ Treat the participant's coworkers with the same respect you show the participant.
- ☐ If the participant asks for help, wait until the end of the study to provide it to avoid biasing your study.
- ☐ Show your enthusiasm and interest in the participant's work.
- ☐ Know the difference between capturing observations and inferences.
- ☐ Give the participant privacy when needed.
- ☐ Leave time at the end for the participant to ask questions and for you to wrap-up (e.g., distribute incentives, pack up equipment).
- ☐ Send a thank-you note following the study.
- ☐ Take time to organize your data immediately after each visit.
- ☐ Scan in artifacts to share electronically with all stakeholders.

Figure 13.9:

Recommendations for conducting a field study

Summary

We have given a lot of recommendations about how to conduct a successful field study. For easy referral, they are summarized in Figure 13.9.

Data Analysis and Interpretation

At this point, you have a stack of visit summary worksheets and other notes and artifacts from your visits to wade through. The task of making sense out of all the data can seem daunting. Below we present several different ways of analyzing the data. There is no one right way – you have to select the method that best supports your data and the goals of your study. The goal of any of these data analysis techniques is to compile your data and extract key findings. You do this by organizing and categorizing your data across participants. The analysis methods within this section provide you with different approaches for accomplishing this.

Before you begin your analysis, there are few key points to keep in mind:

- *It is all good data.* Some points may not seem to make sense, or it may be difficult to bring it all together, but the more time you spend with the data, the more insight you will gain from it. In other words, your first impression won't be your last.

- *Be flexible.* If you planned to analyze your data with a qualitative data analysis tool but it is not working for you, consider an affinity diagram or another mechanism.

- *Do not present raw data.* It can be quite challenging to take the detailed data from each visit and turn them into actionable recommendations for the product team. However, neither designers nor product developers want the plethora of raw data you collected. You need to compile the information, determine what is really important, and highlight it for your audience.

- *Prioritize.* You will likely end up with a lot of data and may not have the time or resources to analyze it all at first. Analyze the data, first based on the goals of your study, and then you can go back and search for other insights/nuggets/ideas.

- *Frequency does not necessarily mean importance.* Just because a user does a task frequently, that does not necessarily mean it is critical to the user. Keep the context and goals of the user's actions in mind during analysis.

At a Glance

> Debrief
> Affinity diagram
> Analyzing Deep Hanging-Out data
> Analyzing Contextual Inquiry/Design Data
> Analyzing data from Discount User Observations
> Qualitative analysis tools

Debrief

Begin with an initial debriefing session. Once all visits have been conducted, bring all the data collectors together in a large conference room with a whiteboard or laptop and computer projector (that way you can easily save the discussion points and distribute them to the group afterward). Designate a scribe to capture the important points of the discussion. Once you have selected the analysis method (see below), work as a group to analyze the data.

The results and recommendations you obtain in the end are the same regardless of how you analyze the data. However, the method you select to structure/organize data can be easier or more difficult, depending on how you collected it. Regardless of the data collection technique used, you can use any of the analysis techniques below. You do not have to limit yourself to the analysis technique associated with your collection technique. In other words, if you conducted a Contextual Inquiry, you could use the questions from Deep Hanging Out to analyze your data. Pick the analysis method that best fits your data or the goals of your study.

Affinity Diagram

An affinity diagram is probably the most frequently used method for analyzing qualitative data. Similar findings or concepts are grouped together to identify themes or trends in the data. Most of the methods for data analysis listed below use affinity diagrams as part of their technique. A full discussion of affinity diagrams is presented in Appendix F (page 714). The details of this analysis method are located in an appendix as this analysis method is used by other methods such as interviews and focus groups.

Analyzing Deep Hanging-Out Data

It is best to begin by going around the room and asking each person to provide a one-sentence summary for each focus area (refer back to Table 13.2 on page 576). Ask the following questions when analyzing the data:

- What were the biggest/most important findings?
- Immediate impressions?

- What sticks out or really grabs you?
- Are there themes/patterns/coherence?
- What's THE story? What is the key takeaway?
- What surprised you and what didn't?
- What is the disruptive or challenging information?
- If you could go back again, what else would you do or what would you do differently?
- What do you wish you paid more attention to?
- If more than one person studied a focus area or observed a single user, what are the similarities and differences found?

Upon answering these questions, you can begin organizing the data.

Analyzing Contextual Inquiry/Design Data

You may have conducted a Contextual Inquiry to prepare for another usability activity (e.g., identify questions for a survey), to better understand the domain, or as an innovation exercise. If that is the case, you can use any of the data analysis techniques in this chapter. If, however, you conducted a Contextual Inquiry in order to inform your design decisions, you are ready to move into Contextual Design.

Contextual Design is complex and beyond the scope of this book, as we do not delve into design. If you are interested in the data analysis that is specific to Contextual Design, we strongly recommend referring to Beyer and Holtzblatt (1998). The other types of data analysis discussed in this section can be applied to the data collected from Contextual Inquiry.

SUGGESTED RESOURCES FOR ADDITIONAL READING

- Beyer, H. & Holtzblatt, K. (1998). *Contextual Design: Defining Customer-centered Systems.* San Francisco: Morgan Kaufmann.

Analyzing Data from Discount User Observations

Because of the unique nature of DUO's data collection, the creators offer a unique way to analyze the data and present it to stakeholders.

Initial organization

Immediately after the visit has concluded, it is critical for the two data collectors to record the events (actions) observed on a timeline with the help of the notes and photographs. Waiting even three or four days can result in significant loss of data. Group the events observed by task. For each event, identify a task that it is associated with. Some events may be "orphans" in that you are unable to identify tasks for them. Those events may be associated with tasks that were started before you arrived or segments of larger goals that extended beyond your visit. A three to four hour observation can take four to five hours to document.

Communication

The creators of DUO recommend creating your timeline in Microsoft® Power-Point®. On the PowerPoint master slide (i.e., the editable slide template PowerPoint uses to provide the same look for all the slides in your presentation), use the drawing tools to create a timeline along the left side of the slide. Leave ample space to insert a description of the actions, overall task or goal, and corresponding photographs. Create one set of slides per user observed.

Next, take the first task the user began during your visit and identify the associated events. Highlight each event and provide descriptive text and photos in the main content area (see Figure 13.10). Continue until all tasks are completed. Use a separate slide to discuss the orphaned events.

A Gantt chart can also be used to present the timeline data DUO captures.

Figure 13.10:

Sample slide presenting the timeline and description of specific events observed with a travel agent

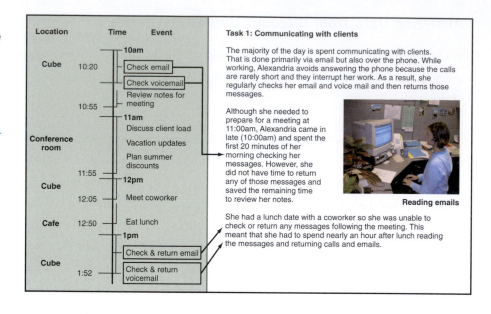

Task 1: Communicating with clients

The majority of the day is spent communicating with clients. That is done primarily via email but also over the phone. While working, Alexandria avoids answering the phone because the calls are rarely short and they interrupt her work. As a result, she regularly checks her email and voice mail and then returns those messages.

Although she needed to prepare for a meeting at 11:00am, Alexandria came in late (10:00am) and spent the first 20 minutes of her morning checking her messages. However, she did not have time to return any of those messages and saved the remaining time to review her notes.

Reading emails

She had a lunch date with a coworker so she was unable to check or return any messages following the meeting. This meant that she had to spend nearly an hour after lunch reading the messages and returning calls and emails.

User verification

Once you have created a first draft of your timeline with associated tasks and photos, you should either visit the participants again and review the slides with them, or send the slides out to the participants to review on their own (e-mail works well, but you may need to physically mail them if the file size is too large). The participants should verify that the identified events are connected to the correct tasks. They will readily point out mistakes and make annotations.

Tip

It is best to ask participants to make the annotations directly on a hard copy, rather than within PowerPoint. It can be difficult to create the timeline, insert pictures, and format all the information in each slide. Participants can spend a great deal of time trying to figure out how to edit the slides and end up causing more confusion, especially if they are not familiar with PowerPoint. We strongly recommend e-mailing or physically mailing participants the slides and then they can either mail or fax back hard copies to you with their comments.

Uses for documentation

There are numerous uses for the PowerPoint slides following your field study. The creators recommend using them not only to communicate the results to the users and product development, but also to leverage them during design. They use the resulting scenarios during prototype design and review. They also use the tasks they observed to provide real-world tasks during usability and system testing. Finally, they have found that the documentation helps create end user educational materials, task-based search, and a user guide organized by task.

Qualitative Analysis Tools

Several software tools are available for purchase to help you analyze qualitative data. Even so, when we surveyed several usability experts, we found that none of them had ever used such a tool. If you are interested in exploring qualitative analysis software tools, refer to Appendix G (page 722) for a description of each tool and the pros and cons of using such tools.

Communicate the Findings

Preparing to Communicate Your Findings

The specific data that you communicate to product teams can vary depending upon the activity you conducted, but some elements of *how* you communicate the results are the same regardless of the method. Because these strategies are common to all user requirements activities, they are discussed in detail in Chapter 14, Concluding Your Activity, page 636. We recommend that you read that chapter prior to relaying your results to your stakeholders. Topics discussed include:

- ☐ **Prioritization of your findings** (see page 638)
- ☐ **Creating an effective presentation** (see page 644)
- ☐ **Writing valuable reports for different audiences** (see page 652)
- ☐ **Ensuring the incorporation of your findings** (see page 660)

Because the data collected during field studies is so rich, there are a wide variety of ways in which to present the data. Leveraging several of the techniques below will help bring stakeholders closer to the data and get them excited about your study. There is no right or wrong answer; it all depends on the goals of your study, how your data stacks up, and the method you feel best represents your data. In the end, a good report illuminates all the relevant data, provides a coherent story, and tells the stakeholders what to do next. Below, we offer some additional presentation techniques that work especially well for field study data. For a discussion of standard presentation techniques for any requirements method, refer to Chapter 14, Concluding Your Activity, page 636.

Two frequently used methods for presenting or organizing your data are the artifact notebook and **storyboards**.

- *Artifact notebook.* Rather than storing away the artifacts you collected in some file cabinet where people will not see them, create an artifact notebook. Insert each artifact collected, along with information about how the artifact is used, the purpose, and the implications for design. Keep this notebook in an easily accessible location. You can create several of these and include them as another educational material for the product development team.
- *Storyboards.* You can illustrate a particular task or a "day-in-life" of the user through **storyboards** (using representative images to illustrate a task/scenario/story). Merge data across your users to develop a generic, representative description. The visual aspect will draw stakeholders in and demonstrate your point much faster.

Hackos & Redish (1998) provided a table summarizing some additional methods for organizing or presenting data from a field study. A reduced version is reproduced here as Table 13.3.

Analysis method	Brief description
Lists of users	Examine the types and range of users identified during your study, including estimates of their percentages in the total user population and a brief description of each.
Lists of environments	Examine the types and range of environments identified during your study, including a brief description of each.
Task hierarchies	Tasks are arranged in a hierarchy to show their interrelationships, especially for tasks that are not performed in a particular sequence.
User/task matrix	Matrix to illustrate the relationship between each user type identified and the tasks they perform.
Procedural analysis	Step-by-step description examining a task including the objects, actions, and decisions.
Task flowcharts	Drawings of the specifics of a task including objects, actions, and decisions.
Insight sheets	List of issues identified during the field study and insights about them that may affect design decisions.
Artifact analysis	Functional descriptions of the artifacts collected, their use, and implications/ideas for design.

Table 13.3: *Methods for presenting/organizing data. (Hackos & Redish 1998)*

Lessons Learned

In the course of conducting field studies over the years, we have learned some painful lessons. These include working with customers, account managers, and product managers.

Surprise Guests

Several years ago, Kathy and another co-worker went on-site to several customers in the Atlanta area. It took about two to three months to arrange the visits. The product team was invited to participate in the field study from the very beginning, but declined. We later learned that they were conducting their own "site visits" with customers along the east coast during the same time as our field study in Atlanta.

We were fortunate that our company's account manager for the Atlanta customers was open to our study, but it was clear that she was a bit nervous about our presence. She was relieved to hear that only two people would be conducting the visits (less people to manage and fret over). Upon arriving at our first site, the account manager came up to us and fumed, "I thought you said there were only two of you!"

We were stunned and didn't understand what she was talking about. She replied that four other members of "our team" had already arrived and were waiting. When we walked around the corner, four product managers greeted us. Needless to say, we were astonished. They decided that, since they were so close, they might as well fly down and join us. Because we had sent the product team copies of all documents (including our agenda) they knew exactly where to go and who to contact. Unfortunately, they felt no need to inform us of their change in plans.

Since we did not expect the additional guests, we had not conducted any training sessions or even discussed the appropriate protocol. Our intended activity was a focus group with about eight database administrators. We knew we could not delve into each question deeply but we wanted to get an overall impression. We could then use the upcoming individual interviews to delve into the important issues that arose from the focus group. Unfortunately, the product managers were not on the same wavelength. They drilled down into each question in such painful detail that a couple of users actually walked out of the session. We then decided to split up for the individual interviews. We suggested that the product managers interview one user while we interviewed another. It allowed the product managers to be involved but they were not able to influence the data we were collecting during our interviews. The data the product managers collected were not incorporated into our data analysis because the questions they asked were quite different, being feature-oriented.

Considering our close relationship to the team before this activity, it was all the more shocking that they did not understand the inappropriateness of their behavior. The lesson learned here is that you should be prepared for anything! Have a back-up plan. In this case, we split up so that the team could interview some participants while we interviewed others. We got the data we needed without alienating the product team, although our credibility with the account manager was a bit scuffed at the end.

Missing Users

At another location in Atlanta, we had difficulty finding our participants. The supervisor who had arranged for his employees to speak with us had an emergency at home and had to leave early. Unfortunately, no one knew which of his employees he wanted us to speak with. We walked around the floor, asking people whether they had been asked to participate in our study. We found only one participant. We now know to insist on getting the names and contact information for all participants, even if there is one point of contact that will take you to each participant.

Pulling It All Together

In this chapter, we have discussed the best uses for field studies and things to keep in mind when proposing them. We have presented a plethora of techniques for collecting, analyzing, and presenting the data. Considering the complexity of field studies, tips and recommendations have been provided throughout. Finally, painful lessons learned illuminate common mistakes we are all capable of making.

SUGGESTED RESOURCES FOR ADDITIONAL READING

The first book has a detailed discussion of how to prepare for, conduct, and analyze data from field studies. It includes success stories and challenges throughout:

- Hackos, J. T. & Redish, J. C. (1998). *User and Task Analysis for Interface Design.* New York: John Wiley & Sons.

This second book provides 14 detailed case studies to demonstrate how practitioners adapted field methods to meet their needs:

- Wixon, D. R. & Ramey, J. (eds) (1996). *Field Methods Casebook for Software Design.* New York: John Wiley & Sons.

CASE STUDY

Beth Loring and Kelly GordonVaughn describe field studies they conducted for Staples. As employees of American Institutes for Research (AIR), they describe the process of working as consultants for Staples. They provide detailed information about how they prepared for and conducted the field studies, as well as how they analyzed the data and presented it to the company. Practical lessons learned are presented at the end.

Understanding the Staples Delivery Experience

Beth Loring, Bentley College, and Kelly GordonVaughn, American Institutes for Research

Staples is an $11.6 billion retailer of office supplies, business services, furniture, and technology. Staples provides its products and services to a wide variety of customers in North America and Europe, from home-based businesses to Fortune 500 companies. American Institutes for Research (AIR) is a not-for-profit human sciences research firm whose Concord, MA, office is considered one of the country's leading usability engineering groups.

Staples partnered with the usability engineering group at AIR to conduct both internal and external user needs research targeted at improving the Staples customer experience. The overarching goals of this "life of an order" project included understanding the process of placing an office supply delivery order from a business customer's perspective; identifying opportunities to improve the ease-of-use of Staples' catalog, website, and customer service; and stimulating ideas for future research.

AIR worked closely with Staples to develop a research plan that addressed the goals of the study. As the plan evolved, the study segmented into two phases, internal and external. In the internal phase, AIR conducted research (including field studies and shadowing) with Staples' employees who interact directly with business customers. The purpose of this phase was to identify opportunities to improve the ordering and delivery process from "behind the scenes," and to obtain an internal point of view on ways to improve existing levels of customer satisfaction. The second (external) research phase involved conducting 23 field studies with small to medium-sized Staples business customers in their workplaces. The purpose of the second phase was to obtain feedback about the Staples customer experience and to identify "points of pain" in the current ordering and delivery process. The second phase was of primary importance to Staples.

As described in the following sections, the research provided Staples with a thorough understanding of the life of an order. Specifically, it provided valuable qualitative information and a rich set of video and photographic evidence that proved particularly compelling to stakeholders within the Staples organization. The final result was a set of detailed recommendations for enhancing the Staples customer experience.

Our Approach

As is common with many research projects, the schedule was tight – the AIR team had slightly over four months to complete the study. The first two months were spent planning the study, preparing the materials, and conducting the internal research. The third month was spent conducting the external research, and the fourth month was spent analyzing the data and preparing the final report. Due to the responsiveness and commitment of the project manager on the Staples side, there were no unwanted gaps in the schedule. Also, AIR employed a core team of four usability specialists (including the project manager), as well as occasional help from other staff members, in order to accomplish the work in four months.

Internal Research

Planning the Research

Planning for the internal research phase included determining the appropriate individuals to interview, scheduling participants, and developing interview scripts for the field studies and shadowing activities. AIR and Staples managers collaborated to accomplish these tasks. We determined that the most valuable Staples participants would be those who interact most frequently with business customers, and that the timeframe for the internal phase would have to be limited in order to maintain primary focus on the external research. Ultimately, the internal research participants included several Staples delivery drivers (one Staples fleet driver and one contract delivery service), and six customer service representatives at the Staples customer service center in Halifax, Nova Scotia.

To prepare for the internal research, AIR created two separate interview scripts, one for the delivery drivers and one for the customer service representatives. The scripts contained structured data collection forms that incorporated areas for interviewer notes. AIR also created checklists of materials to bring into the field, such as interviewees' contact information, clipboards, video camera, digital videotapes, digital camera, and extra batteries.

Shadowing the Delivery Drivers

AIR shadowed a Staples fleet delivery driver for one day. We selected a driver whose schedule included different types of small to medium-sized businesses, as well as several residences and a hospital.

Two AIR team members rode with the driver as he made scheduled deliveries in the Greater Boston area. During the course of the day, we interviewed the driver about his job and his impressions of how the Staples customer experience could be improved. Due to the long duration of the shadowing, both team members participated in the interviewing, note-taking, and handling of the video camera and digital camera. We took turns noting any usability issues the driver encountered with the delivery forms and equipment, as well as any ergonomic issues regarding the handling of the boxes.

Several days later, the same AIR team shadowed a contract delivery company in New Hampshire for one day as its team of two men delivered Staples office supplies to small to medium-sized businesses and residences. We followed the same procedure with the contract delivery company as was used with the fleet driver.

Conducting Field Studies with Customer Service Representatives

At the customer service center in Halifax, the same two AIR team members spent one day interviewing six phone representatives. This time, we conducted separate interviews simultaneously in order to maximize the number of customer service representatives included. We observed, videotaped, and photographed the representatives as they worked, and listened to their conversations with customers via headsets.

During the course of the day, we were able to observe representatives taking orders, handling calls about existing orders, and taking information from customers who wanted to establish Staples accounts (see Figure 13.11). Using our interview scripts, we noted any usability issues the representatives experienced, such as difficulties using the software interfaces, as well as any suggestions they made for ways to improve customer service.

Figure 13.11: (a) *One of the authors videotaping the Staples fleet delivery driver.* (b) *Contract delivery drivers delivering Staples office furniture.* (c) *Customer service representative taking a customer's order*

a   b   c

External Research

Planning the Field Studies

To plan the external phase of the study, the AIR/Staples team began by determining the appropriate number and types of business customers to target for the field studies. We decided that the sample should include participants from two of Staples' major markets, Boston and Los Angeles. Further, we developed a detailed profile for the type of customer that would provide the most appropriate feedback in relation to the project goals.

After carefully weighing many factors, we targeted our recruiting toward individuals who placed office supply orders at small to medium-sized businesses. Potential participants were further segmented according to factors such as their Staples ordering history, ordering volume, and primary ordering channel (e.g., website vs. catalog-and-phone). AIR created a detailed participant matrix, ensuring that the appropriate number of participants was represented in each cell.

Using lists provided by the Staples marketing group, AIR recruited 24 participants (12 from each city) who met the predetermined criteria. Even with such a targeted list of potential participants, the recruiting required hundreds of phone calls over the course of two weeks. Many customers were interested in participating, but they were reluctant or unable to have their workday interrupted. In addition to ordering office supplies, these customers were typically responsible for office administration, reception, answering phones, and other key office activities. As such, it was difficult for them to make even a short time commitment during work hours (9 am to 5 pm), even though they were interested in the $100 cash incentive offered. In spite of these obstacles, AIR was successful in recruiting 24 participants who matched the research criteria.

AIR prepared a script for the field studies that included an introduction, a semi-structured interview, an observation section (used to record observations as the customer placed a delivery order via their preferred channel), and a debriefing section (see Figure 13.12). As with the internal research, the script also incorporated areas for interviewer notes. As we had completed the internal research phase by this time, the findings from that phase informed the script development for the external phase. For example, we incorporated issues identified by the delivery drivers or customer service representatives, such as how customers communicate with Staples regarding a problem with a shipment, into the interview questions for the business customers.

6. How do you typically gather orders from the staff? **Probe:** do they email you with requests, do you send out reminders, approach everyone physically, or order basic stuff according to office supply levels unless someone requests otherwise?

7. How do you typically order office supplies? Why? **Probe:** phone, web, store, combination?

8. What types of products do you normally order through Staples? What types of products do you order through other suppliers? Why? **Probe:** do they ever order break room or sanitary supplies, food, plastic utensils, etc.

The AIR team pilot-tested the field study script with their own office manager, who matched the customer profile. We then refined the script based on the results of the pilot test, for example, reorganizing some of the interview questions.

Conducting Field Studies with Business Customers

A three-person research team, including two AIR team members and one Staples observer, conducted each field study. Staples felt that it was important to have an observer attend each field study in order to hear customers' comments first-hand. During the visit, one AIR team member conducted the interview while the other handled the cameras, although the roles were alternated from visit to visit. The Staples observer listened and took notes, asking occasional probing questions on particular points of interest. Prior to the visits, we set ground rules with the Staples observer for interacting with customers to ensure that the interviews would stay on track and remain unbiased.

We began the field studies by explaining the purpose of the research and obtaining written consent from the customers. Next, we interviewed customers about their office supply ordering process and associated activities (e.g., gathering orders, selecting items, storing items, and returns and exchanges). We conducted most of the interviews at the customers' desks. However, some customers preferred to be interviewed in a conference room or other quiet area so as not to disrupt office activities.

After the interview, we asked customers to place an office supply order as they normally would (see Figure 13.13). All customers had been asked to reserve their office supply order until the field study. However, we found that several had already placed their normal order and therefore they placed a smaller order while being observed.

After customers had placed their order, we asked them for a tour of their workplace, specifically indicating where office supplies were delivered, unpacked, sorted, and stored. We asked them to show us where they stored office supply catalogs, how they filed their

a   b   c   d

Figure 13.13:

Office manager (a) checking for an item in her catalog; (b) using the catalog in conjunction with the website to order supplies; (c) calling Staples to check on the availability of an item for next-day delivery; (d) checking delivered goods against the Staples invoice

receipts, and how they paid their invoices. We collected interesting artifacts during this portion of the field study, such as examples of re-ordering checklists and notes from co-workers indicating what supplies were needed.

Following the tour, we asked the customers for any final comments or suggestions for simplifying ordering processes, and then compensated them for their valuable time.

Analysis

To analyze the data from both the internal and external research, the AIR team first compiled a comprehensive list of findings. Each team member typed up his or her notes, which included customers' answers to the interview questions. The Boston team then read the notes from the Los Angeles field studies, and vice versa. Next, AIR built a database and entered observed usability issues and reported incidents (both positive and negative) that affected customers' experiences with Staples. The database allowed us to sort the issues and incidents according to the area of Staples service that was impacted, allowing the various groups within Staples to focus on the findings that mattered most to them. Thus, the database had categories for catalog-related findings, website-related findings, and delivery-related findings, among others.

Because the field studies generated such a large number of digital images, the AIR team found it difficult to locate specific photos. To solve this problem, we created an HTML-based photo archive that made browsing the photos much easier.

Over the course of several weeks, the AIR/Staples team worked closely to prioritize the list of over 50 findings and brainstorm creative ways to address each issue. We organized the findings to correspond with stages of the ordering process, from planning the order through to billing. Each finding was assigned an urgency rating (high, medium, or low), an impact assessment (such as "Will increase customer retention") and an "owner," which was the person within Staples who would be responsible for addressing the issue.

Findings

AIR presented the findings from the study in a multimedia format using Macromedia® Director®. Director was selected, rather than a presentation tool such as Microsoft PowerPoint, for its ability to handle large numbers of video clips. Director also allowed us to add custom controls for navigating back and forth through the presentation and for playing the video clips. Each finding was presented on a slide along with a customer quote and one or more video clips to stimulate discussion from the audience. The multimedia presentation proved highly effective and AIR was asked to repeat the presentation several times to various audiences within Staples.

Overall, the research showed a high level of satisfaction with Staples' customer service. Because of this, the first finding in the presentation was "Customers had mostly positive things to say about Staples' delivery." Examples of other findings generated by the study were:

- Many customers shopped using more than one channel. For instance, Web users often referred to their catalogs for item numbers in order to expedite the process of placing an order online.
- Customers personalized their catalogs by flagging frequently ordered items with sticky notes, by circling items, or by folding page corners. This required them to transfer their flags when a new catalog arrived.

These findings, as well as numerous similar findings, gave Staples a clear understanding of the life of an order. Additionally, it provided opportunities to enhance the Staples customer experience, and generated many ideas for future research.

Lessons Learned

Looking back on this project, we have identified the following lessons regarding field studies:

- Close collaboration and a true team approach with an invested client yields the best results.

- Whenever possible, schedule field studies in adjacent ZIP codes during the same day to minimize travel time between sites.

- When scheduling the field studies, ask participants to be prepared to carry out the activities you are interested in observing. In this case, we asked customers to place actual orders, which made the observation portion of the field studies more authentic.

- Flexibility is important. In this case, if participants naturally began with a tour of their office, we asked questions from the section of the script that required movement within the work environment. Similarly, if more than one individual placed office supply orders, we interviewed both of them.

- When necessary, briefly suspend the interview to allow the customer to continue working.

- Be aware that some participants will express concern about being videotaped. In this case we offered a few options: (1) audiotaping and taking digital photographs; (2) audiotaping only; or (3) hand-written notes only. Most participants who declined to be videotaped allowed us to videotape their computer screen if they placed an order via the website.

- Finally, it is important to be as unobtrusive as possible during field studies. This particular study involved three-person teams, which AIR typically considers a maximum.

This case study proved that field studies are a unique and effective means of gathering customer data. This method provides an inside look at customers' environments, behaviors, and use patterns that is impossible to achieve with other user research methods.

Acknowledgments. The authors wish to acknowledge the major contribution of Colin Hynes, Director of Usability at Staples, for sponsoring this research and providing input into this case study.

PART 4

WRAPPING UP

CHAPTER 14

CONCLUDING YOUR ACTIVITY

Introduction

In earlier chapters we have presented a variety of user requirements activities to fit your needs. After conducting a user requirements activity, you have to effectively relay the information you have collected to the **stakeholders** in order for it to impact your product. If your findings are not communicated clearly and successfully, you have wasted your time. There is nothing worse than a report that sits on a shelf, never to be read. In this, the concluding chapter, we show you how to prioritize and report your findings, present your results to stakeholders, and ensure that your results get incorporated into the product.

In addition, we have included a case study from a usability specialist at Sun Microsystems, Inc. Tim McCollum discusses the resistance he encountered at a previous company when planning user requirements activities and promoting the results – and, more importantly, how he overcame that resistance.

At a Glance

> Prioritization of findings
> Presenting your findings
> Reporting your findings
> Ensuring the incorporation of your findings

Prioritization of Findings

Clearly, you would never want to go to your stakeholders with a flat list of 400 user requirements. It would overwhelm them and they would have no idea where to begin. You must prioritize the issues and requirements you have obtained and then make recommendations based on those priorities. Prioritization conveys your assessment of the impact of the findings uncovered by your user requirements activity. In addition, this prioritization shows the order in which requirements should be addressed by the product team.

It is important to realize that usability prioritization is not suitable for all types of user requirements activities. In methods such as a card sort or task analysis, the findings are presented as a whole rather than as individual recommendations. For example, if you have completed a card sort to help you understand the necessary architecture for your product (see Chapter 10, page 414), typically, the recommendation to the team is a whole architecture. As a result the entire object (the architecture) has high priority. On the other hand, interviews (Chapter 7, page 246), surveys (Chapter 8, page 312), wants and needs analyses (Chapter 9, page 370), focus groups (Chapter 12, page 514), and field studies (Chapter 13, page 562) typically generate data that are conductive to prioritization. For example, if you conducted a focus group to understand users' issues and new requirements for the current product so that you could use this information to improve the next version, you would likely get a long list of issues and requests each having varying degrees of support from the participants. Rather than just handing over the list of findings to the product team, you can help the team understand what findings are the most important so that they can allocate their resources effectively. We discuss how to do this. We also

distinguish between usability prioritization and prioritization that takes into consideration not only the usability perspective but also the product development perspective. The typical sequence of the prioritization activities is shown in Figure 14.1.

This section discusses both types of prioritization, but note that the presentation of your findings (discussed later) typically takes place *prior to* the second prioritization.

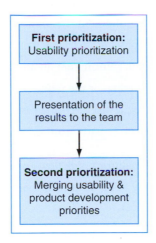

Figure 14.1:

Prioritization sequence

First Prioritization: Usability Perspective

There are two key criteria (from a usability perspective) to take into consideration when assigning priority to a recommendation: impact and number.

- *Impact* refers to your judgment of the impact of the usability finding on users. Information about consequence and frequency is used to determine impact. For example, if a particular user requirement is not addressed in your product so that users will be unable to do their jobs, clearly this would be rated as "high" priority.
- *Number* refers to the number of users who identified the issue or made a particular request. For example, if you conducted 20 interviews and two participants stated they would *like* (rather than need) a particular feature in the product, it will likely be given a "low" priority. Ideally, you also want to assess how many of your true users this issue will impact. Even if only a few users

mentioned it, it may still *affect* a lot of other users. For example, if an issue arose from two users regarding logging in to the product, this issue – although mentioned by only a small number of users – would impact *all* users.

The reality is that prioritization tends to be more of an art than a science. Requirement priorities are sometime gray as opposed to black and white. We do our best to use guidelines to determine these priorities. They help us decide how the various combinations of the *impact* and *number* translate into a rating of "high," "medium," or "low" for a particular user requirement. To allow stakeholders and readers of your report to understand the reasons for a particular priority rating, the description of the requirement should contain information about the impact of the finding (e.g., the issue is severe and re-occurring, or the requested function is cosmetic) and the number of participants who requested the feature or identified the issue during the requirements activity (e.g., 20 of 25 participants).

Guidelines for the "high," "medium," and "low" priorities are as follows (keep in mind that these may not apply to the results of every activity):

High:

- The finding/requirement is extreme. It will be difficult for the *majority* of users to use the product, and will likely result in task failure without the requirement.
- The finding/requirement is *frequent and re-occurring.*
- The finding/requirement is broad in scope, has interdependencies, or is symptomatic of an underlying infrastructure issue.

Medium:

- The finding/requirement is moderate. It will be difficult for *some* participants to use the product without it.
- It will be difficult for *some* participants to complete their work without the requirement.
- A *majority* of participants will experience frustration and confusion when completing their work (but not an inability to get their work done) without the requirement.
- The requirement is less broad in scope and its absence *might* affect other tasks.

Low:

- A *few* participants might experience frustration and confusion without the requirement.
- The requirement is slight in scope and its absence will not affect other tasks.
- Only a *few* participants will be affected without the requirement.
- It is a cosmetic requirement, mentioned by only a *few* participants.

If a requirement meets the guidelines for more than one priority rating, then it is typically assigned the highest rating.

Of course, when using these rating guidelines you will also need to consider your domain. If you work in a field when any error can lead to loss of life or an emergency situation (e.g., a nuclear power plant, hospital) you will likely need to modify these guidelines to make them more stringent.

Tip

Because assessing the priority of user requirements can be subjective, it is ideal to have at least two usability professionals independently assess a finding's importance. You can then compare and modify your ratings accordingly.

Second Prioritization: Merging Usability and Product Development Priorities

The previous section described how to prioritize recommendations of a user requirements activity from a usability perspective. The focus for this kind of prioritization is, of course, on how each finding impacts the user. In an ideal world, we would like the product development team to make changes to the product by dealing with all of the high-priority issues first, then the medium-priority, and finally the low-priority issues. However, the reality is that factors such as budgets, contract commitments, resource availability, technological constraints, marketplace pressures, and deadlines often prevent product development teams from implementing your recommendations. They may really want to implement all of your recommendations but are simply unable to. Frequently, usability professionals do not have insight into the true cost to implement a given recommendation. By understanding the cost to implement your recommendations and the constraints the product development team is working under, you not only ensure that the essential recommendations are likely to be incorporated, you also earn allies on the team.

As mentioned earlier, this type of prioritization typically occurs after you have presented the findings to the development team. After the presentation meeting (described later), schedule a second meeting to prioritize the findings you have just discussed. You may be able to cover it in the same meeting if time permits, but we find it is best to schedule a separate meeting. At this second meeting you can determine these priorities and also the status of each recommendation (i.e., accepted, rejected, or under investigation). A detailed discussion of recommendation status can be found below (see "Ensuring the Incorporation of Your Findings," page 660).

It can be a great exercise to work with the product team to take your prioritizations to the next level and incorporate cost. The result is a cost–benefit chart to compare the priority of a usability recommendation to the cost of implementing it.

After you have presented the list of user requirements or issues and their impact on the product development process, ask the team to identify the cost associated with implementing each change. Because developers have substantial technical experience with their product, they are usually able to make this evaluation quickly.

The questions in Figure 14.2 are designed to help the development team determine the cost. These are based on questions developed by MAYA Design (McQuaid 2002).

Average the ratings that each stakeholder gives these questions to come up with an overall cost score for each usability finding/recommendation. The closer the average score is to 7, the greater the cost for that requirement to be implemented. Based on the "cost" assignment for each item in the list and the usability priority you have provided, you can determine the final priority each finding or requirement should be given. The method to do this is described below.

In Figure 14.3, the x-axis represents the importance of the finding from the usability perspective (high, medium, low), while the y-axis represents the difficulty or cost to the product team (rating between 1 and 7). The further to the right you go, the

The degree to which the finding (issue/requirement) is widespread or pervasive:

None   A great deal

1   2   3   4   5   6   7

The requirement requires more research or a major restructuring (information architecture, hardware, system architecture):

None   A great deal

1   2   3   4   5   6   7

The product development team has adequate resources to include the requirement:

A great deal   None

1   2   3   4   5   6   7

The key corporate stakeholders are interested in including the requirement:

Extremely   Not at all

1   2   3   4   5   6   7

The key product management stakeholders are interested in including the requirement:

Extremely   Not at all

1   2   3   4   5   6   7

The key marketing stakeholders are interested in including the requirement:

Extremely   Not at all

1   2   3   4   5   6   7

Figure 14.2:

Questions to help with the cost prioritization of user requirements. (McQuaid 2002)

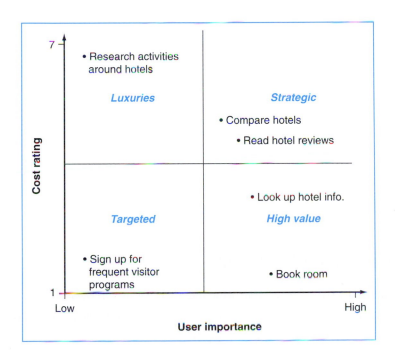

Figure 14.3:

Example of a cost–benefit chart for results obtained during a wants and needs analysis (see the results on page 400). (McQuaid 2002)

greater the importance is to the user. The higher up you go, the greater the difficulty to implement the recommendation. This particular figure shows a cost–benefit chart for the wants and needs travel example conducted in Chapter 9, Wants and Needs Analyses (see page 400 for the table of results).

The chart quadrants

As you can see, there are four quadrants into which your recommendations can fall:

- *High value*. Quadrant contains high-impact issues/recommendations that require the least cost or effort to implement. Recommendations in this quadrant provide the greatest return on investment and should be implemented first.
- *Strategic*. Quadrant contains high-impact issues/recommendations that require more effort to implement. Although it will require significant resources to implement, the impact on the product and user will be high and should be tackled by the team next.
- *Targeted*. Quadrant contains recommendations with lower impact and less cost to implement. This may be referred to as the "low-hanging fruit": they are tempting for the product development team to implement because of the low cost; however, because the impact is lower, these should be addressed third, only after the team has tackled the "high-value" and "strategic" recommendations.
- *Luxuries*. Quadrant contains low-impact issues/recommendations that require more effort to implement. This quadrant provides the lowest return on investment and should be addressed only after recommendations in the other three quadrants have been completed.

By going through the extra effort of working with the product team to create this chart, you have provided them with a plan of attack. In addition, the development team will appreciate the fact that you have worked with them to take their perspective into account.

Presenting Your Findings

Now that you have collected your data and analyzed it, you need to showcase the results to all stakeholders. This presentation will often occur prior to the prioritization exercise with the product development team (i.e., you will have a usability prioritization, but it will not factor in the product team's priorities yet). The reality is that writing a usability report, posting it to a group website, and e-mailing out the link to the report is just not enough. Usability reports fill an important need (e.g., documenting your findings and archiving the detailed data for future reference), but you must present the data verbally as well.

You really need to have a meeting to discuss your findings. This meeting will likely take one to two hours, and ideally should be done in person. Yes, we realize that the meeting could be conducted remotely using application-sharing tools, but we find that the meeting tends to run smoother with face-to-face interaction. Then there are no technical issues to contend with, and – more importantly – you can see for yourself the reaction of your audience to the results. Do they seem to understand what you are saying? Are they reacting positively with smiles and head nods, or are they frowning and shaking their heads?

Tip

If you are an external consultant (i.e., not a full-time employee of the company) you will likely have to depend on an internal contact to set up the meeting and to set expectations about the meeting's scope. Be sure that your contact is clear about the agenda. Also, although the meeting room is important, as a consultant you may have no control over its layout. You may not even know where it is. It important to get there early and set it up the way you want it and to figure out how to run the equipment.

At a Glance

> Why the verbal presentation is essential
> Presentation attendees
> Ingredients of a successful presentation

Why the Verbal Presentation is Essential

Since your and the stakeholders' time is valuable, it is important to understand why a meeting to present your results and recommendations is so critical. No one wants unnecessary meetings in his/her schedule. If you do not feel the meeting is essential, neither will your stakeholders. What follows are some reasons for having a meeting and for scheduling it as soon as possible.

Tip

If there is time, you should go over all your recommendations with a key member of the team *before* this meeting – to make sure that they are realistic and do-able. Otherwise, at the meeting, it may appear that you don't understand the findings or their complexity – which can set the meeting off course. It deteriorates into a discussion about why the recommendations cannot be followed. A pre-meeting can also enable you to get a sense of the team's other priorities.

Dealing with the issues sooner rather than later

Product teams are very busy. They are typically on a very tight timeline and they are dealing with multiple sources of information. You want to bring your findings to the attention of the team as soon as possible. This is for your benefit and theirs. From your perspective, it is best to discuss the issues while the activity and results are fresh in your mind. From the product team's perspective, the sooner they know what they need to implement based on your findings, the more likely they are to actually be able to do this.

Ensuring correct interpretation of the findings and recommendations

You may have spent significant time and energy conducting the activity, collecting and analyzing the data, and developing recommendations for the team. The last thing you want is for the team to misinterpret your findings and conclusions. The best way to ensure that everyone is on the same page is to have a meeting and walk through the findings. Make sure that the implications of the findings are clearly understood and why they are important to stakeholders. The reality is that many issues are too complex to describe effectively in a written format. A face-to-face presentation is key.

Dealing with recommendation modifications

It may happen that one or more of your recommendations are not appropriate. This often occurs because of technical constraints that you were unaware of. Users sometimes request things that are not technically possible to implement. You want to be aware of the constraints and to document them. There may also be the case where the product is implemented in a certain manner because a key customer or contract agreement requires it. By having the stakeholders in the room, you can brainstorm a new recommendation that fulfills the users' needs and fits within the product or technological constraints. Alternatively, stakeholders may offer better recommendations than what you considered. We have to admit that we don't always have the best solutions, so a meeting with all the stakeholders is a great place to generate them and ensure everyone is in agreement.

Presentation Attendees

Invite all the stakeholders to your presentation. These are typically the key people who are going to benefit and/or decide what to do with your findings. Do not rely on one person to convey the message to the others, as information will often get lost in the translation. In addition, stakeholders who are not invited may feel slighted and you do not want to lose allies at this point. We typically meet with the product manager, the development manager, and sometimes the business analysts. The product manager can address any functional issues, the schedule, and budget issues that relate to your recommendations, while the development manager can address issues relating to technical feasibility and the time and effort required to implement your proposals. You may need to hold follow-up meetings with individual developers to work out the technical implementation of your recommendations. Keep the presentation focused on the needs of your audience.

Tip

If executives are also interested in the presentation, you may want to hold a separate high-level presentation for them. They are not necessarily interested in all of the nitty-gritty details that the product team needs to hear.

Ingredients of a Successful Presentation

The format and style of the presentation can be as important as the content that you are trying to relay. You need to convey the importance of your recommendations. Do not expect the stakeholders to automatically understand the implications of your findings. The reality is that product teams have demands and requirements to meet from a variety of sources, such as marketing, sales, and customers. User requirements are just one of these many sources. You need to convince them that your user findings are significant to the product's development. There are a variety of simple techniques that can help you do this.

Tip

Do a quick dry run to make sure you have enough time to cover your material. The biggest mistake presenters of requirements activities make is trying to cover too much detail. Force yourself to set priorities and to leave plenty of time for questions.

At a Glance

> Keep the presentation focused
> The delivery medium
> Start with the good stuff
> Use visuals
> Prioritize and start at the top
> Avoid discussion of implementation or acceptance
> Avoid jargon

Keep the presentation focused

You will typically have only one or two hours to meet with the team, so you need to keep your presentation focused. If you need more than two hours, you are probably going into too much detail. If necessary, schedule a second meeting rather than conducting a three-hour meeting (people become tired, irritable, and lose their concentration after two hours).

You may not have time to discuss all of the details, but that's fine because a detailed usability report can serve this function (discussed later). What you should cover will depend on who you are presenting to. Hopefully, the product team has been involved from the very beginning (refer to Chapter 1, Introduction to User Requirements, "Getting Stakeholder Buy-in for Your Activity" section, page 14), so you will be able to hit the ground running and dive into the findings and recommendations (the meat of your presentation). The team should be aware of the goal of the activity, who participated, and the method used. Review this information at a high level and leave time for questions. If you were not able to get the team involved early on, you will need to provide a bit of background. Provide an "executive summary" of what was done, who participated, and the goal of the study. This information is important to provide context for your results.

Tip

Keep the meeting on track! You will have a lot of material to cover and you will not have time to get sidetracked. If someone moves away from the focus (e.g., discussing all of the detailed technical requirements necessary to implement a particular recommendation), table it for a follow-up discussion.

The delivery medium

The way that you choose to deliver your presentation can have an effect on its impact. We have found PowerPoint slides can be an effective way to communicate your results. In the past, we used to come with photocopies of our table of recommendations and findings. The problem was that people often had trouble focusing on the current issue being discussed. If we looked around the room, we would find people flipping ahead to read about other issues. This is not what you want. By using slides, you can place one finding per slide so the group is focused on the finding at hand. Also, you are in control so there is no flipping ahead. As the meeting attendees leave, you can hand them the paper summary of findings to take with them.

Start with the good stuff

Start the meeting on a positive note; begin your presentation with positive aspects of your findings. You do not want to be perceived as someone who is there to deliver bad news (e.g., this product stinks or your initial functional specification is incorrect). Your user requirements findings will always uncover things that are perceived "good news" to the product team.

For example, let's say you conducted a card sort to determine whether an existing travel website needed to be restructured. If you uncovered that some of the site's architecture matched users' expectations and did not need to be changed, while other aspects needed to be restructured, you would start out your discussion talking about the section of the product that can remain unchanged. The team will be thrilled to hear that they do not need to build from scratch! Also, they work hard and they deserve a pat on the back. Obviously, putting the team in a good mood can help soften the potential blow that is to come.

Product teams also always love to hear the positive things that participants have to say. So, when you have quotes that give praise to the product, be sure to highlight them at the beginning of the session.

Use visuals

Visuals can really help to get your points across. Screenshots, photographs, results (e.g., **dendrogram** from a card sort), proposed designs or architecture are all examples of visuals you can use. Insert them wherever possible to help convey your message. They also make your presentation more visually appealing. Video and highlights tapes can be particularly beneficial. Stakeholders who could not be present at your activities can feel a part of the study when watching video clips or listening to audio highlights. This can take some significant time and resources on your part, so choose when to use these carefully. For example, if the product team holds an erroneous belief about their end users and you have data to demonstrate it, there is nothing better than visual proof to drive the point home (done tactfully, of course).

Prioritize and start at the top

It is best to prioritize your issues from a usability perspective prior to the meeting (refer to "First Prioritization: Usability Perspective," page 639). It may sound obvious, but you should begin your presentation with the high-priority issues. It is best to address the important issues first because this is the most critical information that you need to convey to the product team. It also tends to be the most interesting. In case you run out of time in the meeting, you want to make sure that the most important information has been discussed thoroughly.

Avoid discussion of implementation or acceptance

The goal of this meeting is to present your findings. At this point you do not want to debate what can and cannot be done. This is an important issue that must be debated, but typically there is simply not enough time in the presentation meeting. It will come in a later meeting as you discuss the status of each recommendation (discussed later). If the team states "No, we can't do it," let them know that you would like to find out why, but that discussion will be in the next step. Remind them that you do not expect the user requirements data to replace the data collected from other sources (e.g., marketing and sales), but rather that the data should complement and support those other sources and you will want to have a further discussion of how all the data fits together. A discussion of when and how to determine a status for each recommendation can be found below (see "Ensuring the Incorporation of Your Findings," page 660).

Avoid jargon

This sounds like a pretty simple rule, but it can be easy to unknowingly break it. It is easy to forget that terms and acronyms that we use on a daily basis are not common vocabulary for everyone else (e.g., "UCD," "think-aloud protocol," "transfer or training"). There is nothing worse than starting a presentation with jargon that no one in the room understands. If you make this mistake you are running a serious risk of being perceived as arrogant and condescending. As you finalize your slides, take one last pass over them to make sure that your terminology is appropriate for the audience. If you must use terminology that you think will be new to your audience, define it immediately.

Reporting Your Findings

By this point, you have conducted your activity, analyzed the results, presented the recommendations to the team, and now it is time to archive your work. It is important to compile your results in a written format for communication and archival purposes. After the report is created and finalized, you should post it on the web for easy access (either as a link to the document, or convert the text document to HTML). You do not want to force people to contact you to get the report or to find out where they can get it. The website should be well known to all stakeholders. The more accessible your report is, the more it will be viewed. In addition to making your report accessible from the web, we recommend sending an e-mail to all stakeholders with the executive summary (discussed below) and a link to the full report as soon as it is available.

Report Format

The format of the report should be based on the needs of your audience. Your manager, the product development team, and executives are interested in different information. It is critical to give each reader what he or she needs. In addition, there may be different methods in which to convey this information (e.g., the web, e-mail, paper). In order for your information to be absorbed, you must take content and delivery into consideration. There are three major types of report:

- The complete report
- The recommendations report
- The executive summary.

The complete report is the most detailed, containing information about the users, the method, the results, the recommendations, and an executive summary. The other "reports" are different or more abbreviated methods of presenting the same information. You can also include items such as educational materials and posters to help supplement the report. These are discussed in the "Report Supplements" section later (see page 659). Table 14.1 provides an "at a glance" view of the different report types, their contents, and audiences.

Presentation format	Type of content	Audience
Complete report	• All details pertaining to the activity and findings: executive summary, background, method, participants, findings, recommendations, conclusions	• Everyone • For those that want ALL the details • Very important for your own archival purposes
Recommendations report	• Focuses on the findings and recommendations from your activity • Can be qualitative (e.g., list of observations from a field study) or quantitative (e.g., % of users giving a certain response on a survey)	• Serves as a great checklist for those who need to implement the requirements (e.g., product team members) or as a preview of results for any stakeholder
Executive summary	• Contains high-level information: – Method conducted – Purpose – High-level summary of the participants – Key, high-level findings	• Perfect for executives or those who want to learn about the study at a glance • Don't make it longer than two pages
Educational materials	• Create booklets, handouts, or a website containing a description of the end user(s), the requirements gathering activity, and the findings • Ideal to begin building a website or notebook over time and add your findings with each activity	• Best for product development managers and their team members • Also helps members of the usability group
Posters	• Depends on the activity: You can give quantitative results for a survey or present a collage of photos from a field study • Especially powerful for ongoing field studies • They tend to be very visual	• Works well for all stakeholders, especially those who were not involved in your activity

Table 14.1:

Comparison of the various reporting methods

Tip

Usability test your reports. Your report will often need to communicate some visual and/or complex findings. As a result, it can sometimes be difficult to clearly and accurately make your point on paper. Have a second set of eyes review your report to make sure that it is clear and logical before you send it out to the stakeholders. It is ideal to have someone who was not involved in the activity do this. You want your report to makes sense to anyone who picks it up.

The Complete Report

Ideally, each user requirements gathering activity that you conduct should have a complete report as one of your deliverables. This is the most detailed of the reports. It should be comprehensive, describing all aspects of the activity (e.g., recruiting, method, data analysis, recommendations, conclusion).

At a Glance

> Value of the complete report
> Key sections of the complete report
> Complete report template

Value of the Complete Report

You may be thinking "No one will read it!" or "It takes too much time." It really is not much extra work to pull a complete report together once you have a template (discussed later). Plus, the proposal for your activity will supply you with much of the information needed for the report. (Refer to Chapter 5, Preparing for Your User Requirements Activity, "Creating a Proposal" section, page 146.) Even if the majority of people do not read the full report, it still serves some important functions. Also, regulated industries (e.g., drug manufacturers) may be required for legal reasons to document everything they learned and justify the design recommendations that were made.

Archival value

The complete report is important for archival purposes. If you are about to begin work on a product, it is extremely helpful to review detailed reports that pertain to the product and understand exactly what was done for that product in the past. What was the activity? Who participated? What were the findings? Did the product team implement the results? You may not be the only one asking these questions. The product manager, your manager, or other members of the usability group may need these answers as well. Having all of the information documented in one report is the key to finding the answers quickly.

Another benefit is the prevention of repeat mistakes. Over time, stakeholders change. Sometimes when new people come in with a fresh perspective they suggest designs or functionality that have already been investigated and demonstrated as unnecessary or harmful to users. Having reports to review before changes are incorporated can prevent making unnecessary mistakes.

The detail of a formal, archived report is also beneficial to people that have never conducted a particular user requirements activity before. By reading a report for a particular type of activity, they can gain an understanding of how to conduct a similar activity. This is particularly important if they want to replicate your method.

Tip

Put all the reports in a searchable database. You can then search by a feature or a question and pull up all surveys/reports that contain keywords to find out whether that feature/question has ever been the subject of an activity.

Certain teams want the details

Complete reports are important if the product team that you are working with wants to understand the details of the method and what was done. This is particularly important if they were unable to attend any of the session or view videotapes. They may also want those details if they disagree with your findings and/or recommendations.

Consulting

Experienced usability professionals working in a consulting capacity know that a detailed, complete report is expected. The client wants to ensure that they are getting what they paid for. It would be unprofessional to provide anything less than a detailed report.

Key Sections of the Complete Report

The complete report should contain at least the following sections.

Executive summary:

In this summary, the reader should have a sense of what you did and the most important findings. Try not to exceed one page, or two pages maximum. Try to answer a manager's simple question: "Tell me what I need to know about what you did and what you found." This is one of the most important sections of the report and it should be able to stand alone. Key elements include:

- Statement of the method that was conducted
- Purpose of the activity
- The product and version number your research is intended to impact (if applicable)
- High-level summary of the participants (e.g., number of participants, job roles)
- The key, high-level findings in one or two pages at most.

Background:

This section should provide background information about the product or domain of interest.

- What product was the activity conducted for? Or what domain/user type/question were you investigating?
- What is the purpose of the product?
- Were there any past activities for this product? Who conducted them, and when?
- What was the goal of this activity?

Method:

Describe in precise detail how the activity was conducted and who participated.

- *Participants.* Who participated in the activity? How many participants? How were they recruited? What were their job titles? What skills or requirements did an individual have to meet in order to qualify for participation? Were participants paid? Who contributed to the activity from within your company?
- *Materials.* What materials were used to conduct the session (e.g., survey, cards for a card sort)?
- *Procedure.* Describe in detail the steps that were taken to conduct the activity. Where was the session conducted? How long was it? How were data collected? It is important to disclose any shortcomings of the activity. Did only eight of your 12 participants show up? Were you unable to complete the session(s) due to unforeseen time restraints? Being up-front and honest will help increase the level of trust between you and the team.

Tip

Do not to reveal participants' names as this is considered confidential information. Refer to participants by a unique ID (e.g., user 1, P1, user's initials).

Results:

This is where you should delve into the details of your findings and recommendations. It is ideal to begin the results section with an overview – a couple of paragraphs summarizing the major findings. It acts as a "mini" executive summary.

- What tools, if any, were used to analyze the data (e.g., *EZSort* to analyze card sort data)? Show visual representations of the data results, if applicable (e.g., a dendrogram).
- Include quotes from the participants. Quotes can have a powerful impact on product teams. If the product manager reads quotes like "I have gone to TravelSmart.com before and will never go back" or "It's my least favorite travel site," you will be amazed at how he/she sits up and takes notice.

- Present a detailed table of all findings and recommendations. Include a status column to track what the team has agreed to. Document what recommendations they have agreed to and what they have rejected. Also, if appropriate, prioritize your recommendations, as described earlier (see page 638).

> **Tip**
>
> Just as in a presentation, you want to highlight positive findings in your report as well. Often we just think to deliver a laundry list of things to change or modify.

Conclusion:

Provide the reader with a summary of the activity and indicate the next steps.

- How will this information aid the product?
- What do you expect the team to do with the data?
- Are there any follow-up activities planned or recommended?
- Are there any limitations to how the data can be used?

Appendices:

Here, include any documents that were a part of the process (e.g., the participant screener, the protocol that was used for the activity, any surveys that were given, etc.).

Complete Report Template

Appendix H (page 726) provides a report template. This gives a clear sense of the sections of the report and their contents. This template can be easily modified for any user requirements activity.

The Recommendations Report

This is a version of the report that focuses on the findings and recommendations from the activity. This report format is ideal for the audience that is going to be implementing the findings – typically the product manager or developer manager. In our experience, developers are not particularly interested in the details of the method we used. They want an action list that tells them what was found and what they need to do about it (i.e., issues and recommendations). To meet this need we simply take the results section of the complete report (discussed above) and save it as a separate document.

We find that visuals such as screen shots or proposed architecture flows, where appropriate, are important for communicating recommendations. A picture is truly worth a thousand words. We find that developers appreciate that we put the information that is important to them in a separate document, saving them the time of having to leaf through a 50-page report. Again, the more accessible you make your information, the more likely it is to be viewed and used. You should also provide your developers with access to the complete report in case they are interested in the details.

The Executive Summary Report

The audience for this report is typically executive vice-presidents and senior management (your direct manager will likely want to see your full report). The reality is that executives do not have time to read a formal usability report; however, we do want to make them aware of the activities that have been conducted for their product(s) and the key findings. The best way to do this is via the executive summary (see page 656). We typically insert the executive summary into an e-mail and send it to the relevant executives, together with a link to the full report. (The reality is that your executives still may not take the time to read the full report, but it is important to make it available to them.) This is especially important when the changes you are recommending are significant or political. Copy yourself on the e-mail and you now have a record that this information was conveyed. The last thing you want is a product VP coming back to you and saying "Why was I not informed about this?" By sending the information you can say "Actually, I e-mailed you the information on June 10."

Report Supplements

You can create additional materials to enhance your report. Different people digest information best in different formats, so think of what will work best for your audiences. Educational materials and posters are two ways to help relay your findings in an additional format.

Educational materials

The product manager or development manager may have been involved in your study and attended a presentation of the results, but it is unlikely that every member of the product development team will be similarly aware. To educate team members, including new employees, you can create booklets, handouts, or a website containing a description of the end user(s), the requirements gathering activity, and the findings. This ensures that what you have learned will continue to live on. Ask the team to post links to these materials on the product team's website.

Posters

Posters are an excellent lingering technique that can grab stakeholders' attention and convey important concepts about your work quickly. You can create a different poster for each type of user, activity conducted, or major finding. It obviously depends on the goals of your study and the information you want the stakeholder to walk away with. The poster can contain a photo collage, user quotes, artifacts collected, results from the activity (e.g., dendrogram from a card sort, task flow from group task analysis), and recommendations based on what was learned (see Figure 14.4 on page 661). Display posters in the hallways where the product team works so that people will stop and read them. It is a great way to make sure that everyone is aware of your findings.

Ensuring the Incorporation of Your Findings

You have delivered your results to the stakeholders, and now you want to do everything you can to make sure the findings are acted upon. You want to make sure that the data are incorporated into user profiles, personas, functional documentation, and ultimately the product. As mentioned in the previous section, presenting the results rather than simply e-mailing a report is one of the key steps in making sure your results are understood and are implemented *correctly*. There are some key things you can do to help to ensure your findings are put to use. These include involving stakeholders from beginning to end, becoming a team player, making friends at the top, and keeping a scorecard.

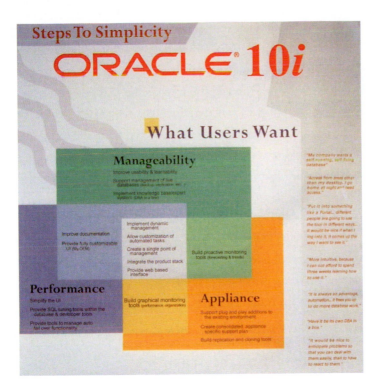

Figure 14.4:
Real-world example of a poster

At a Glance

> Stakeholder involvement

> Be a virtual member of the team

> Obtain a status for each recommendation

> Ensure the product team documents your findings

> Keep a scorecard

Stakeholder Involvement

A theme throughout this book has been to get your stakeholders involved from the inception of your activity and to continue their involvement throughout the process. (Refer to Chapter 1, Introduction to User Requirements, "Getting Stakeholder Buy-in for Your Activity" section, page 14). Their involvement will have the biggest payoff at the recommendations stage. Because of their involvement, they will understand what the need was for the activity, the method used, and the users who were recruited. In addition, they should have viewed the session(s) and should not be surprised by the results of your study. By involving the product team from the beginning, they feel as though they made the user requirements discoveries with you. They have seen and heard the users' requirements first hand. Teams that are not involved in the planning and collection processes may feel as though you are trying to shove suspect data down their throats. It can sometimes be a tough sell to get them to believe in your data.

If the team has not been involved in the user requirements process at all, start to include them now – better late than never! Work with them to determine the merged usability and development prioritization (see "Prioritization of Findings," page 638), and continue to do so as the findings are implemented. Also, be sure to involve them in the planning for future activities.

Be a Virtual Member of the Team

As was mentioned earlier in this book, if at all possible you will want to be an active, recognized member of the product team from the moment you are assigned to the project. (Refer to Chapter 1, Introduction to User Requirements, "Getting Stakeholder Buy-in for Your Activity" section, page 14.) Take the time to become familiar with the product as well as with the product team priorities, schedule, budget, and concerns. You need to do your best to understand the big picture. You should be aware that usability data are only one of the many factors the team must consider when determining the goals and direction of their product. (Refer to Chapter 1, Introduction to User Requirements, "A Variety of Requirements" section, page 8.)

Recognizing this time investment, the product team will trust you and acknowledge you as someone who is familiar with their product and the development issues. This knowledge will not only earn you respect; it will also enable you to make informed recommendations which are executable because you are familiar with all the factors that impact the product's development processes. The team will perceive you as someone who is capable of making realistic recommendations to improve the product. In contrast, if you are viewed as an outsider with the attitude "You must implement all of the users' requirements and anything less is unacceptable," you will not get very far.

Obtain a Status for Each Recommendation

Document the team's response to your recommendations (e.g., accept, reject, needs further investigation). This shows that you are serious about the finding and that you are not simply presenting them as suggestions. We like to include a "status" column in all of our recommendations tables (refer to Appendix H, page 734). After the results presentation meeting (discussed above) we like to hold a second meeting where we can determine the priority of the results in terms of development priorities (see "Second Prioritization: Merging Usability and Product Development Priorities," page 641) as well as the status of each recommendation. If the team agrees to implement the recommendation, we document the recommendation as "Accepted." If the recommendation is pending because the product team needs to do further investigation (e.g., resource availability, technical constraints), we note this and state why. No matter how hard you try, there will be a few recommendations that the product development team will reject or not implement. You should expect this, nobody wins all the time. In these cases, we note their rejection and indicate the team's reasoning. Perhaps they disagree with what the findings have indicated, or they do not have the time to build what you are requesting. Whatever their reason is, document it objectively and move on to the next recommendation. We also like to follow-up with the team after the product has been released to do a reality check on the status column. We let them know ahead of time that we will follow-up to see how the findings were implemented. Did they implement the recommendations they agreed to? If not, why? Be sure to document what you uncover in the follow-up.

Ensure the Product Team Documents Your Findings

As mentioned in Chapter 1, Introduction to User Requirements, "A Variety of Requirements" section, page 8, there are a variety of different kinds of product requirements (e.g., marketing, business, usability). Typically someone on the product team is responsible for creating a document to track all of these requirements. Make sure your usability requirements get included in this document. Otherwise, they may be forgotten.

As a reader of this book, you may not be a product manager, but encouraging good habits within the team you are working with can make your job easier. The product team should indicate each requirement's justification, the source(s), and the date it was collected. This information is key to determining the direction of the product, so it is important to have the documentation to justify the decisions made. If certain user requirements are rejected or postponed to a later release, this should also be indicated within the document. By referring to this document you will be able to ensure that the user requirements are acknowledged – and if they are not incorporated, you will understand why. This is similar to the document that you own that tracks the status of each recommendation, but a product team member will own this document and it will include all of the product requirements, not just user requirements. If the team you work with uses a formal enhancement request system, make sure that your findings are entered into the system.

Tip

Encourage the team to have a date on which the requirements document is closed. The closure of the document indicates that you have completed all requirements collection and that you can move on to the design phase. Adding additional requirements during the design phase should be avoided as it creates the need for designs to be reworked to accommodate new features.

Keep a Scorecard

As was just discussed above, you should track the recommendations that the product development team has agreed to implement. If you are working as an external consultant, you may not be so concerned about this; but if you are an internal employee, it is important. We formally track this information in what we refer to as "the usability scorecard." Figure 14.5 illustrates the information that we maintain in our scorecard.

We use scorecard information for a number of purposes. If a product is getting internal or customer complaints regarding usability and the team has worked with us before, we like to refer to our scorecard to determine whether they implemented our recommendations. In some cases they have not, so this information proves

Product/ version #	Activity	Risk	Recommendations:			Product VP	Notes
			Given	Accepted	Implemented		
SmartTravel .com v1 – hotel UI	Card Sort	High	38	10	5	John Adams	Team feels the user requirements do not match the marketing requirements of the product
SmartTravel .com v1– airline reservation UI	Interviews	Medium	35	25	22	Karen McGuire	None
SmartTravel .com v2 airline reservation UI	Wants & Needs	Medium	50	33	33	Karen McGuire	Technical investigations being conducted to assess unaddressed issues
SmartTravel .com v2 – car rental UI	Interviews	Low	42	40	39	Jennifer Crosbie	None

Figure 14.5:

A usability scorecard

invaluable. Executives may ask why the usability group (or you) has not provided support or why your support failed. The scorecard can save you or your group from becoming involved in the blame-game. If the product development team has implemented the recommendations, however, we need to determine what went wrong. The scorecard helps to hold the product team and us accountable.

We also find that the scorecard is a great way to give executives an at-a-glance view of the state of usability for their products. It helps them answer questions such as "Who has received usability support?", "When and how often?", and "What has the team done with the results?" We assign a "risk" factor to each of the activities, based on how many of the recommendations have been implemented. When a VP sees the red coding (indicating high risk), he or she quickly picks up the phone and calls the product manager to find out why they are at that risk category. It is a political tactic to get traction, but it works.

It is important for us to note that this approach has worked well for us, due in large part to the fact that we have worked with a vice-president in charge of usability and UI. If you don't have a strong VP or a strong CEO who can back you up, a bad score can kill the usability function at a company. Anytime the score is low, it fingers someone as either not doing their job or as ignoring the recommendations of the study. If that person being blamed is powerful, he or she can do harm to the usability studies. If this is a concern at your particular company, use the scorecard simply for *your* tracking purposes at first, to record the state of things, and make it public only when there is an important need.

Lastly, the reality of many usability departments is that they are understaffed. As a result, you want to track who is making use of your data versus who is using your services but not your data. The scorecard is an ideal way to do this. Obviously, you will want to use your limited resources to help the teams that are utilizing both your services and the data you collect.

Pulling It All Together

In this chapter, we have described the steps to take after you have conducted your user requirements activity and analyzed the data. You may have conducted several activities or only one. In either case, the results and recommendations need to be prioritized based on the user impact and cost to the product development to incorporate them. In addition, we have described various formats for showcasing your data, presenting the results, and documenting your data. It is not enough to collect and analyze user requirements; you must communicate and archive them so they can live on long after the activity is done. Good luck in your user requirements ventures!

CASE STUDY

Tim McCollum of Sun Microsystems, Inc. has provided a case study from his days at Calico Commerce. This study clearly illustrates the kinds of challenges you may encounter as you plan and deliver the results of your user requirements activity. He had to overcome resistance from disciplines that we often bump heads with: engineering and marketing. He was also unable to initially obtain support for the task analysis project without making significant modifications to address concerns from other stakeholders – a common dilemma with that method. He presents an honest assessment of his success and what he would change next time.

Calico Configuration Modeling Workbench

Tim P. McCollum, Sun Microsystems, Inc.

Calico Commerce, Inc. was a privately held company whose core product enabled companies to sell customizable configurations of complex products (e.g., personal computers, hi-tech bicycles, mainframe computers, cellphone plans). By using Calico's products, companies could greatly reduce their cost of sales and increase customer satisfaction by automating the sales process and eliminating returns resulting from erroneous orders. The company's founder and core engineering team did an outstanding job creating an approach and a set of features innovative enough to win several Fortune 100 customers and have one of the most successful IPOs in NASDAQ history.

Web-based sales applications built by Calico enabled consumers to create and purchase valid configurations of complex products. For example, if someone wanted to buy a personal computer via the Web, he or she might go to a computer vendor's website to place the order. The consumer would "build" the PC by selecting from a variety of PC components. The Calico-created website prevented consumers from selecting incompatible components, which eliminated erroneous orders and costly product returns. The website used to configure the PC, and ultimately to place the order, would have been created by Calico professional services using the Calico Configuration Modeling Workbench.

The Challenge

The original Calico modeling workbench was created during a time when graphical user interface (GUI) applications were the predominate paradigm. As the predominate application paradigm shifted to the Web, new competitors were able to develop their architectures from the ground up to better suit Web-based application development.

In order to compete, Calico had to update its core offering quickly or risk becoming out of date and irrelevant. The Calico Workbench needed to address the primary customer values of initial time to market and the cost of maintaining the application following initial deployment.

Our Approach

To successfully update the workbench, the product team (the engineering architect, engineering manager, product marketing, and myself) needed to:

- Determine the list of modifications needed
- Establish the priority of those changes
- Determine how to best "design in" some new functionality.

Working closely with the workbench engineering manager and architect, we pored through previous bug reports and lists of feature improvement requests from marketing. The most important questions, however, were how to improve the features and in what priority. These questions required understanding the contexts in which the problems occurred. We therefore planned to conduct a task analysis to identify the workbench shortcomings and their contexts. What we found, however, was significantly more fundamental and important to the overall product strategy.

Resistance in the Proposal Phase

The original task analysis proposal was met with significant resistance for many legitimate reasons:

- The plan required several hours from the most productive field service people we had. Their work was measured in billable hours and this was not billable time, so their management was hesitant to free up their time.
- Mid/upper level engineering management was already behind schedule and they felt that this activity would take too much time. They were forging ahead, so whatever we found would be irrelevant.
- Some marketing factions maintained: "We already have the list of what we need done. Just implement that."
- Some powerful executives believed: "This workbench is good enough. Let's just attach it to a more modern runtime."

Field Service People

The professional services billable-hours issue was resolved by utilizing people who were going to be at headquarters anyway. There were times at which they would be "out of the field" for training or organizational meetings. When they came into headquarters, we requested a four-hour time slot while they were in town. This meant the task analysis took a little longer, but we were still able to fully de-brief six professional services people over the course of three weeks.

Engineering and Marketing

For the most part, marketing was very supportive. The biggest challenge in getting buy-in for this activity from marketing was overcoming their fear that we might undermine their position of authority regarding product requirements.

As is often the case, the marketing requirements for this release were pretty "clear" but also pretty high-level (e.g. new Web-based architecture, faster run-time, fix the known usability problems with the workbench). The marketing requirements document (MRD) is rarely detailed enough to sufficiently explain what engineering must do to deliver a successful product. Often, when the user interface designer and an engineer start working on a new product feature, they discover that it impacts the user interface of a variety of other existing features/attributes – all of which engineering views as new, un-promised "features" with significant schedule impacts. The set of "in-between" requirements that are both too low-level to show up in the MRD, but big enough for engineering to view them as schedule-impacting features, were the class of requirements we used to illustrate, and justify, the need for "user experience requirements."

The biggest challenge with engineering management was that they didn't see the value of the exercise. Many engineering staff members had worked with "usability" people before and, in all honestly, didn't feel that usability work contributed useful information in a timely fashion. The results came in too late, the importance of the findings was often overstated, and the net result was a lot of noise that could not or should not be acted on. To resolve the marketing and engineering issues, we leveraged the traditional gap that exists between marketing requirements and engineering planning.

Engineering was all too familiar with this scenario and was frustrated from receiving blame for late deliveries due to "feature creep" in the development cycle. I made the argument that the real culprit was not feature creep later in the cycle, it was poor planning based upon insufficient design assumptions early in the cycle. I successfully argued that the product is ultimately defined by three primary influences:

- Feature requirements
- Engineering constraints
- User experience requirements.

In most cases, only two of these influences are accounted for in the planning phases of a project, which leads to seriously slipped schedules, and/or products that may meet the letter of the marketing requirements, but still not satisfy the true customer needs. In order to deliver a successful product in a realistic timeframe, we needed to run user requirement activities parallel with marketing and engineering activities.

Successfully articulating this information and committing to provide user requirements in an effective timeframe did a couple of things for us. First, it established user requirements on a level playing field with marketing and engineering requirements. Next, it illustrated that user requirements gathering is related to, but distinct from, marketing requirements and thereby eliminated many of marketing's political issues. In addition, this level of design detail is too time-involved for the typical marketer to work through, so marketing saw us as extending their work rather than competing with it. Engineering also saw user requirements as a means for getting the level of detail they needed to make more accurate forecasts. Lastly, because this work would also prioritize user requirements, engineering saw this as an important resource for assessing the costs of slipping a ship date or sticking to the date and cutting features. Having now acquired an understanding of how user requirements fit in and could help solve some existing pain points, the other stakeholders were willing to entertain proposals for user requirement activities.

Resistance in the Planning Phase

The first user requirement activity the product team undertook was a task analysis of workbench users. In this case, I encountered some resistance to my task analysis protocol because I stepped back and took a broader look at the space than what many believed was necessary. When designing the interview script, you must make sure the time is filled with useful information gathering, but you also need be flexible enough to follow lines of discovery not originally anticipated. You have to develop a protocol that allows the story to unfold rather than imposes preconceived biases and assumptions.

Issues with the Proposed Execution of the Activity

While we were simply trying to capture the broader perspective in these interviews, we were pressured by others to modify our interview script so it was "more efficient and didn't cover ground that everyone already knew the answers to." Most of the other stakeholders were much more comfortable with directly targeted questions like:

- Name the top 5 problems you encountered with the workbench.
- When do you use feature X and what problems do you encounter when using it?
- Rate the importance of fixing feature X.

While these are certainly clear, useful, and efficient questions, they assume that all the problems with the workbench are relatively small and well known. Making this assumption minimizes the opportunity to uncover more fundamental, and potentially more productive, insights about the true nature of the product's user experience and competitiveness. While we listened to everyone's feedback and incorporated many of their specific questions into the protocol, we stuck to our guns and framed the interviews within a broader user experience perspective. Instead of simply interviewing with "efficient," targeted questions, we designed the protocol in two pieces. We started with a much broader perspective by asking questions like:

- What projects did you work on in the last 18 months?
- What were the customer goals on each project?
- Describe the project architecture.
- Draw a picture of the project organization (who did what jobs and how they interacted).

The second section of the interview protocol included the specific questions the other stakeholders wanted answered plus quite a few targeted questions of our own. As it turned out, the broader questions proved very effective and we rarely had to utilize the targeted questions to uncover necessary information. Devising the script in this manner ensured that, at a minimum, we would get answers to the specific questions people thought we should be asking. This helped garner initial support for the project, but it also would have enabled us to claim project success even if the broader, more risky, questioning did not yield any directly actionable results.

Issues from Executives and Key Stakeholders

Perhaps even more importantly, modifying our approach to obtain buy-in *prior* to the investigation was key to successfully "selling" the results to the organization after the study was complete. If this initial step is done correctly, the other stakeholders will feel some ownership for the study's results and thereby some responsibility for acting upon the findings. One of the last things done in the "buy-in" process before the activity was to show a Microsoft PowerPoint slide of the key findings we would obtain during the study. This was actually a minimal subset of all the things we hoped to accomplish, but we correctly assumed this small list of concrete findings would be sufficient for the other stakeholders to approve the investigation. When the time came to present the findings, we then led the presentation with the same slide and proceeded through the findings. This enabled us to remind people why we did the study, and their part in determining the questions we would answer. It also demonstrated that we had successfully accomplished what we set out to do. Providing a clear simple link between what we said we would do and what we actually delivered established a credibility baseline for any messages we wanted to convey later in the presentation.

It also enabled us to add a little drama by essentially saying: "Not only did we do what we set out to do and find answers to *your* important questions, but we also found some things we believe are even more important." This gets people's attention and enhances the credibility of all the findings.

In sum, setting understandable, achievable expectations, bestowing some ownership of the results upon others during the buy-in phase, and creating continuity between the study proposal and presentation of findings, was critical for obtaining actionable commitments from other stakeholders.

Presenting the Results

The original workbench had a very "panels-based" UI. In the original UI most of the critical model elements were presented in the form of separate dialogs ("panels") with each containing several data entry fields. This forced users to deal with very small elements of the model in isolation from one another. The panels UI paradigm did not allow users to easily understand how the model worked overall. In addition, the panels-based UI also made it extremely difficult to debug and modify the model because there was no simple way to see how the individual elements of the model affected one another. These combined influences meant that it was unnecessarily difficult to deploy and maintain a sales application using the original Calico Modeling Workbench.

During the task analysis we observed several of the field personnel drawing pictures of how they thought the model elements interacted. Upon further investigation we found that these hand-written pictures were often the most used part of a project's documentation. Based upon these critical observations during the task analysis, it became clear that the panels UI model was a huge productivity problem and that we needed a new workbench paradigm that visually depicted the overall model structure and enabled users to directly interact with the model elements.

Convincing Stakeholders and Getting Buy-in for Change

Discovering this insight was not enough. We now had to make the insight relevant to various stakeholders who were already feeling pressure to get an updated product into the market as soon as possible. Fortunately, and in part due to their roles in the task analysis, both the engineering architect and engineering manager immediately understood the importance of the finding. This cleared the way to put together some early concept prototypes of the new model visualization workbench. Of course, getting people to understand that a problem exists and getting their commitment to do something about it are two different things. Even though our proposal had support in many quarters, there was still a significant leadership group who believed that our proposal would introduce too much risk into the schedule. Fortunately, due to the way we handled the buy-in phase and worked successfully with field personnel, we had established some credibility with, and access to, a variety of "influencers."

In addition to being well-versed in their own skill set, usability professionals must also be well-versed in the language and needs of marketing and engineering. I began working on a concept prototype to show the internal engineering and marketing audiences some of the core advantages of the new model visualization concept. To make our findings even more relevant to marketing, I also translated our design proposal into a pseudo-marketing white paper. The intent was, in a light-hearted way, to articulate how the kinds of features we were proposing might be valued by a customer or used in marketing messaging. The "marketing" write-up, the prototype, and the results of the task analysis formed a cohesive package that enabled others to see the power of the ideas for which we were recommending action.

Getting Feedback on Proposed Changes from Customers

There was an opportunity to test drive our prototype and our value propositions with some real customers. Once internal users saw a tool which allowed them to graphically depict and interact with models, they immediately appreciated how it could positively impact many of their modeling tasks, reduce time-to-market, and decrease cost-of-ownership issues. Similarly, once customers saw the prototype and understood how this would impact their time-to-market, cost-of-ownership, and maintenance issues, they became very enthusiastic for our proposal. Gaining access to customers with a value proposition and a prototype in hand was a huge step that would not have been possible if we had not established credibility during the user requirements activity. When customers are clearly enthused by something that engineering management considers possible, most serious objections disappear.

Obtaining Buy-in during Development

Obtaining support from marketing, sales, service, and engineering leadership was only part of the user requirements battle; we also needed buy-in from the individual engineers who would implement the requirements-based designs. Translating user requirements into actionable product designs can be a significant bottleneck which, if not handled correctly, can result in an insufficient implementation of the requirement. In my experience, engineers resent being told how to design. The best practice is collaboration, and making them an integral part of the design process.

Low-fidelity prototyping is a great tool for obtaining engineering buy-in. Due to the success of the user requirements and prototyping work, we obtained approval to conduct a three-day low-fidelity prototyping session. After participating in the session, all the engineers had a personal interest in making the designs a reality and a greater appreciation for the time and effort required to create good designs. For the remainder of the project, the engineers and user experience personnel collaborated very effectively to produce a product whose design matched both the letter and the spirit of the user experience requirements.

Lessons Learned

In this case, I wish I had done a couple of things differently. First, I should have initially presented a more conservative task analysis plan that focused more on a small set of important, specific questions rather than one that focused on the process of the technique. While I would have conducted the study in the same manner, I now think that presenting a plan with more nebulous objectives only served to reinforce opinions that this was a fluffy, esoteric usability activity that was unlikely to yield useful results. If I had it to do over, I would have focused on the concrete things we were most likely to uncover and would not have presented so much detail about the process we would use to uncover them. Overcoming this slight misstep required significant time and rework.

In addition, I would have planned to get the resulting design ideas in front of actual customers as soon as possible. Garnering positive customer feedback for the feature set was invaluable in convincing the organization to act on the findings. In all honesty, it was fortune rather than insight that enabled us to get customer feedback. The transition from an old code base (that didn't make sense to update with new functionality) to a new code base (that wasn't yet ready to show in a sales situation) had left sales and marketing with little new material to demo. This happenstance, and the "marketing-ese" write-up that we had done, opened the door for marketing to see how the vision painted by our findings and prototype would fly with customers. As more customers and field service personnel continued to express enthusiasm for the design direction, even the most resistant stakeholders adopted an "OK, we'll try it" stance. Creating ways to obtain further customer feedback and enabling other internal groups to confirm the findings with real customers are the most powerful means for persuading an organization to act on user requirements.

Conclusion

The bottom line is that even important, strongly substantiated, results do not speak for themselves. Obtaining clear results is ultimately of little value if they are not communicated effectively up, down, and across the organization. Each important stakeholder must often be approached using a different message style and/or technique to obtain his/her necessary support. Determining how to approach each stakeholder requires one to understand the vernacular of the skill-set, the social-political context, and their past history with usability groups.

In the end, the user requirements gathering activities provided the foundation for a credible user experience team and established a set of effective user experience design processes that led to significantly better products. This was accomplished by:

- Educating the company about how user experience activities extend and ease the work of marketing and engineering
- Including other stakeholders in the user requirements planning and making them co-owners of the results
- Conducting an effective, collaborative, user requirements activity that brought new, meaningful, and actionable insights to the company
- Creating an effective set of user experience process and deliverables synchronized with engineering and marketing deliverables

- Taking time to make our findings relevant to each audience by trying to talk in their terms (e.g. sketching a valid business model, potential marketing value propositions, and engineering impacts)
- Validating our findings and designs with customers and users in collaboration with other skill-sets
- Creating good, mutually beneficial relationships with other customer facing groups by demonstrating that we could, and would, listen and act.

Insights gained through user requirements activities contributed greatly to Calico's development of innovative tools that enabled it to win multiple technical bake-offs against competitors. In fact, if imitation is the sincerest form of flattery, then Calico was paid the highest compliment by its competitors as many modified their workbenches and laid claim to similar visualization capabilities in their products within the 12 months following the Visual Workbench's release.

However, Calico's ultimate fate also provides a cautionary perspective. While it is important to articulate the value of good customer requirements activities, it is just as important not to over-sell its ultimate impact. Be certain you know the upper and lower limits of user requirements impacts because you must often gain buy-in for user requirements activities based upon the *least* you will learn. If you make your justification on more than this, you run the risk of losing credibility during the pitch, or possibly worse, failing to meet expectations once the research is complete. On the other hand, if you don't understand and plan for potential discoveries, you can wind up eliminating potentially important insights before you even start the user requirements activity. In Calico's case, the company released a technically advanced product with innovative features based upon insightful user requirements, but it ultimately failed as a company. The moral of the story: Good user requirements can be the competitive difference that enables a company to outperform the competition, but no amount of design or technical superiority can overcome the influences of a poor corporate strategy, failed customer management, and a shrinking economy.

PART 5

APPENDICES

APPENDIX A

LEARN ABOUT USABILITY

Introduction

Usability is an evolving field, so it is always a good idea to keep up to date with the latest and greatest in this profession. This can include anything from new techniques to modifications of existing theories and beliefs. If you are going to conduct a usability activity, it is advisable to find out whether there is any new research about the activity that interests you. If you are new to the field, you will want to do some research to learn about the fundamental practices of usability. In this appendix we point you to some of the key resources that will help keep you informed. You may also want to hire a professional to provide training or to consult on your project. Refer to Appendices B–D for lists of companies that offer training courses on user requirements gathering, companies that will help you build or rent facilities, as well as consultants that can do the work for you.

Caution

Please note the information contained within Appendices A–D is provided as a starting point. The content is based on our research at the time of the publication of this book. Offerings from vendors and organizations may change with time, so we advise that you check with the sources directly to learn about their current offerings.

The Web

There are a plethora of websites that can provide information about usability and human factors research, or answer specific usability questions. Below is a sampling of some of the many valuable resources available on the web.

- **ACM Digital Library** (http://portal.acm.org):

  When you sign up for access to the ACM portal, you can search a database of abstracts, articles, conference proceedings, magazines, and newsletters in the HCI field.

- **CHI-WEB** (http://sigchi.org):

  The ACM's Special Interest Group on Computer–Human Interaction (SIGCHI) provides an international, interdisciplinary forum for the exchange of ideas about the field of human–computer interaction (HCI).

- **Cooper** (http://www.cooper.com/content/insights/newsletters.asp):

  This consulting organization offers a free newsletter featuring insights and tips on topics including design, personas, innovation, and training. Alan Cooper, the founder, is the author of two best-selling books: *About Face: The Essentials of User Interface Design* and *The Inmates are Running the Asylum*.

- **HCIbib.org**:

  This no-frills search engine scours HCI articles, conference proceedings, and books in response to your search criteria.

- **Sensible.com**:

  Steve Krug's (author of *Don't Make Me Think*) website. You can read interviews he's given and download useful documents like a sample test script and video consent form.

- **UIWizards.com**:

  Jeff Johnson's website; author of *GUI Bloopers* and *Web Bloopers*. The "Suggested Reading" section is an incredible repository of interface design and usability-related books.

- **Usability.gov**:

  This US Department of Health and Human Services website provides a vast array of usability information, including guidelines, checklists, accessibility resources, and usability methods.

- *Usability News* by Software Usability Research Lab (SURL) (http://psychology.wichita.edu/surl):

  SURL is a service division to the Human–Computer Interaction (HCI) Laboratory at Wichita State University. It provides an online newsletter called *Usability News.*

- Usableweb.com:

  This website states that it is no longer being updated, but it contains lists of links to different usability resources that are still useful.

- Useit.com:

  Jakob Nielsen's website. You can read current and previous editions of his newsletter *Alertbox*, as well as read about the latest usability news, book reviews, usability reports, and information about the Nielsen/Norman Tour.

- UTEST:

  "The UTEST community originally began as a space where a small group of colleagues could collaborate and share ideas about usability testing and user-centered design projects. The goal then and now was to create a 'safe' space where practicing professionals could work on the problems and issues they confronted in their professional experiences. Then and now, the list was intended to be a place where researchers could test out unpolished, inchoate ideas without fear that their ideas would be used out of context or attacked in other media. For this reason, it was decided very early on that UTEST's messages would never be archived, that UTEST's subscribers would not redistribute the list's messages in other groups and/or media, that membership on the list would be closed to the general public, and that new members would be allowed to join by invitation only. These practices are still followed today. For subscription information, please contact Dr Tharon Howard at tharon@hubcap.clemson.edu."

Tip

When all else fails, typing in your usability search criteria into any search engine will often result in articles available for print or download from researchers' own websites.

Professional Societies, Journals, and Conferences

If you are interested in the latest research related to human factors, usability, and human–computer interaction (HCI), there are a variety of organizations that offer publications and conferences to keep you up to date. Below are organizations and publications found predominately in the US, as well as international resources.

Societies in the US

Some of the best known US-based societies are: Computer–Human Interaction (ACM SIGCHI), Human–Computer Interaction International (HCII), Human Factors and Ergonomics Society (HFES), The Society for Technical Communication (STC), and the Usability Professionals' Association (UPA). The URLs to each website are given below:

- **CHI** (www.acm.org/sigchi):

  This is the special interest group (SIG) for the Association of Computing Machinery (ACM). They hold an annual conference each year that primarily focuses on the latest research in the field, but also includes case studies from industry. Their publications – *Interactions, Communications of the ACM*, and *SIGCHI Bulletin* – are of great value and read by many in the usability field. Their academic journal is *Transactions on Computer Human–Interactions* (TOCHI).

- **HCII**:

  The website and its URL changes every year to reflect the upcoming conference. We recommend that you conduct a general web search to find the most current URL. Their newsletter can be found at www.hci-international.org/press-room. It offers information about the upcoming conference and interesting usability articles published in a variety of sources.

- **HFES** (www.hfes.org):

  This organization focuses on human factors as a whole and includes all disciplines, such as HCI, ergonomics, communications, transportation, etc. It is more academic (research-oriented). It also has several technical groups, including Internet, communications, computer systems, and test and evaluation. Each technical group has their own publication. HFES also publishes the newsletter *HFES Bulletin*, the journal *Human Factors*, and the magazine *Ergonomics in Design*.

- **STC** (www.stcsig.org/usability):

  Most documentation writers belong to the STC. They also have several SIGs, including one for usability. They offer a great quarterly newsletter, *Usability Interface*, a list of the most recommended books on usability and design, a usability toolkit, and an annual conference.

- **UPA** (www.upassoc.org):

  This organization is focused on practitioners of usability, rather than academics. It is a smaller organization than the ones mentioned above, and the annual conference focuses on helping the community network and learn from each other. UPA publishes a newsletter, *Common Ground*, and an excellent magazine, *User Experience*.

International Societies

UPA, CHI, and HFES all have some international chapters. You can locate them from the websites provided above. There are some additional non-US usability and HCI organizations to be aware of. The largest one is the International Ergonomics Association – **IEA** (www.iea.cc/index.cfm). It is "the federation of ergonomics and human factors societies from around the world." IEA holds a Triennial Congress (i.e., conference every three years) in a different country. The organization offers a quarterly newsletter, *Ergonomics International*, and you can view archived issues on the website.

Table A.1 lists a few more country-specific organizations. Visit their websites to learn more about their missions, memberships, events, and publications.

We would also like to mention the journal *International Journal of Human–Computer Interaction*, published three or four times a year by Lawrence Erlbaum Associates, Inc. It isn't sponsored by a particular usability or human factors organization but is recommended by many of them. You can find out more at www.catchword.com/erlbaum/10447318/contp1-1.htm.

Table A.1: *Partial list of usability and human factors (ergonomics) organizations, with their websites*

Organization and country	Website
Asociación Interacción Persona Ordenador – AIPO (Spain)	griho.udl.es:8080/aipo
Associação Portuguesa de Ergonomia (Portugal)	www.apergo.pt
Association of Canadian Ergonomists/ Association Canadienne d'Ergonomie	www.ace.ergonomist.ca (English) www.ace.ergonome.ca (French)
Belgian Ergonomics Society	www.md.ucl.ac.be/hytr/bes
British HCI Group	www.bcs-hci.org.uk
Computer Society of India	www.csi-india.org/indobr.html
Chinese Academy of Sciences	english.cas.ac.cn/Eng2003/page/home.asp
Dutch Ergonomics Society (Nederlandse Vereniging voor Ergonomie – NVvE)	www.ergonoom.nl
Ergonomics Society of Korea	esk.or.kr
Ergonomics Society of South Africa	www.ergonomics-sa.org.za
Ergonomics Society of Taiwan	www.est.org.tw
European Research Consortium for Information and Mathematics (ERCIM)	www.ercim.org
Finnish Ergonomics Society	www.ergonomiayhdistys.fi
Gesellschaft für Informatik e.V. – GI (Germany)	www.gi-ev.de
Hong Kong Ergonomics Society (HKES)	www.ergonomics.org.hk
Human Factors & Ergonomics Society of Australia Inc. (HFESA)	www.ergonomics.org.au
Human Interface Society (Japan)	www.his.gr.jp
Irish Ergonomics Society	www.ul.ie/~ies
New Zealand Ergonomics Society	www.ergonomics.org.nz
SELF – the Société d'Ergonomie de Langue Française (France)	www.ergonomie-self.org
Società Italiana di Ergonomia – SIE (Italy)	www.societadiergonomia.it
Spanish Ergonomics Association (Asociación Española de Ergonomía)	www.prevencionintegral.com/aee
Swedish Interdisciplinary Interest Group for Human Computer Interaction (STIMDI)	www.stimdi.se
The Ergonomics Society (UK)	www.ergonomics.org.uk

Standards

The International Standards Organization and International Electrotechnical Commission (ISO/IEC) have developed a number of standards that aim to improve the usability of a product under development. They range from usability of everyday products to mobile products to icons and dialogs. Below is a list of some key standards you should be familiar with. For more detail on any of them, visit the ISO website at www.iso.ch/iso/en/ISOOnline.frontpage.

- The definition of usability: ISO 9241.
- Human-centered design processes for interactive systems. This includes a standard for usability plans: ISO 13407.
- Evaluation of software products: ISO/IEC 14598.
- Usability methods supporting human-centered design: ISO TR 16982.
- Human-centered lifecycle process: ISO TR 18529.
- Usability for everyday products: ISO 20282.

Tip

Standards should not be followed blindly. Good standards are hard to come by and often become outdated quickly. In addition, they promote consistency of both good designs *and* bad. They can also be misinterpreted by those who don't fully understand them and/or do not understand their limitations. Finally, standards can work against usability activities because those who do not understand their limitations may believe that usability activities are unnecessary since they follow good standards. Know the limitations of the standards you develop and implement and *never* use them as a substitute for usability activities.

SUGGESTED RESOURCES FOR ADDITIONAL READING

Information about ISO and the catalog of standards is available from the ISO home page at www.iso.ch and the American National Standards Institute at web.ansi.org.

Some other great resources regarding the standards and their use are:

- Bevan, N. (1999). Quality in Use: Meeting User Needs for Quality. *Journal of System and Software* 49(1), 89–96.
- Dick, D. (1999). Achieving Usability Beyond ISO 9001. *Usability Interface* 5(4). Available at: www.stcsig.org/usability/newsletter/9904-beyond-9001.html.
- Additional information about the standards listed above can be found at www.usability.serco.com/trump/resources/standards.htm.

APPENDIX B

VENDORS THAT OFFER TRAINING IN USABILITY ACTIVITIES

Throughout the book we have mentioned vendors for a variety of purposes. Here we present the vendors that offer training in usability activities. We do not have experience with all of these vendors. These are companies that we were able to find the most information about. They are placed in alphabetical order and it is not a complete list. You can always do a web search to find other references, but we recommend speaking with other people in the Human–Computer Interaction (HCI) industry to get recommendations. Additional usability consultants can be found on the Usability Professionals' Association (UPA) Consultant List (www.upassoc.org/people_pages/consultants_directory/index.html). Also check out usability-related conferences (e.g., CHI, UPA, HCII – see Appendix A, page 678); they offer a range of tutorials at the beginning of each conference.

Caution

Please note the information contained within Appendices A–D is provided as a starting point. The content is based on our research at the time of the publication of this book. Offerings from vendors and organizations may change with time, so we advise that you check with the sources directly to learn about their current offerings.

■ **Bentley College Usability Boot Camp**, 175 Forest Street, Waltham, MA 02452-4705, USA

This intensive five-day course covers requirements gathering and scenario building, prototyping, usability testing, heuristic reviews, and cognitive walkthroughs.

Contact: Suzanne Lefebvre

Phone: (781) 891-2000

E-mail: slefebvre@bentley.edu

Web: www.bentley.edu/professional/programs/
   usability.cfm?program=in&pagetitle=infodesign&
   CFID=3134960&CFTOKEN=37745411

■ **Cooper**, 49 Stevenson Street #1200, San Francisco, CA 94105, USA

This consulting organization provides training in all aspects their GOAL-DIRECTED® methodology. Classes include Interaction Design Practicum and Documenting Research, Requirements, and Design. At the time of publication of this book, a certification program was in the works.

Phone: (415) 267-3500

Fax: (415) 267-3501

E-mail: business@cooper.com

Web: http://www.cooper.com/content/cooperu/overview.asp

■ **Effortmark Ltd**, 11 Bridge Street, Leighton Buzzard LU7 1AH, United Kingdom

Effortmark offers a half-day workshop called "Interviewing skills for usability testing." It is most suitable for a mixed group, most of whom have experience of between one and five usability tests. Caroline Jarrett has taught it at CHI 2000 and HF2002 in Melbourne, Australia. You can find a brief description at www.iceaustralia.com/HF2002/Programs-Workshops.htm. An introductory course to usability testing is also available.

Contact: Caroline Jarrett

Phone: +44 (0) 1525 370379

E-mail: enquiries@effortmark.co.uk

Web: www.effortmark.co.uk/services.html

- **Ennis Information Age Services**, Information Age Centre, Ballymaley Business Park, Ennis, County Clare, Ireland

  Ennis provide a training course specifically on user requirements gathering including interviewing and persona development. They also provide services for expert reviews, user testing, and persona development.

  Phone: +353 (0) 65 68 69 200

  Fax: +353 (0) 65 68 69 244

  E-mail: info@eias.ie

  Web: www.eias.ie/index.php

- **Human Factors International, Inc.**, 410 West Lowe, PO Box 2020, Fairfield, IA 52556, USA

  HFI Inc. teach a two-day seminar called "How to Conduct User-Centered Analysis." It covers creating user profiles, developing interview questions and surveys, performing task analysis, developing scenarios, and translating design solutions to interface solutions. HFI also offer courses in web design and usability testing, as well as offering services in expert review, usability testing, and design. In addition, they offer certification. By passing an examination that demonstrates your comprehension of the fundamental principles of user-centered design you can become a "Certified Usability Analyst."

  Phone: (800) 242-4480 or (641) 472-4480

  Fax: (641) 472-5412

  E-mail: hfi@humanfactors.com

  Web: www.humanfactors.com

- **Lextant Corporation**, 580 North 4th St, Suite 610, Columbus, OH 43215, USA

  Lextant teach a short course in moderator training, interviewing, and contextual inquiry techniques.

  Phone: (800) 324-1613 or (614) 228-9711

  Fax: (614) 228-9715

  E-mail: info@lextant.com

  Web: www.lextant.com

- **Nielsen Norman Group**, 48921 Warm Springs Boulevard, Fremont, CA 94539-7767, USA

  Nielson Norman offer full-day tutorials in field studies, user testing, interaction design, fast prototyping, accessibility, intranet usability, useful websites, usability of PR sites, and discount usability engineering. They also offer guidelines development, process mentoring, and usability evaluation.

  Phone: (408) 720-8808

  E-mail: info@nngroup.com

  Web: www.nngroup.com

- **OTIVO, Inc.**, 451 Hayes St, Floor 3, San Francisco, CA 94102, USA

  Otivo have given numerous one-day workshops, to the general public, to their specific clients, and at conferences. The workshops focus on planning/preparing for usability activities, test plan development, moderation of sessions, and how to summarize reports.

  Phone: (415) 626-2604

  Fax: (415) 626-2605

  E-mail: contact@otivo.com

  Web: www.otivo.com

- **Tec-Ed, Inc.**, 4300 Varsity Drive, Suite A, PO Box 1905, Ann Arbor, MI 48106, USA

  Tec-Ed. are headquartered in Ann Arbor, but they also have offices in Palo Alto, CA, and Rochester, NY. They provide training in heuristic (expert) evaluation, usability testing, field studies, focus groups, participatory design, user interviews, and customer surveys/questionnaires.

  Phone: (734) 995-1010

  Fax: (734) 995-1025

  E-mail: info@teced.com

  Web: www.teced.com/ue-ust.html

- **University of Michigan Human Factor's Short Course**, Center for Professional Development, University of Michigan College of Engineering, Chrysler Center, Room 273, 2121 Bonisteel Blvd, Ann Arbor, MI 48109-2092, USA

  This two-week course covers the design of systems, products, and services to make them easier, safer, and more effective for human use. The first week discusses human factors concepts and the second week covers human–computer interaction. Most people register to attend both weeks, but you can register for a single week only.

Phone: (734) 647-7200, then press 2

Fax: (734) 647-7182

E-mail: shortcourses@umich.edu

Web: www.umich.edu/~driving/shortcourse

- **User Interface Engineering**, 4 Lookout Lane, Unit 4D, Middleton, MA 01949, USA

  They offer a variety of public and on-site corporate training courses targeted towards the entire development team. Topics include: how to design for website usability, paper prototyping techniques, and tricks for including usability testing in the product design process.

  Phone: (800) 588-9855

  Fax: (978) 777-9894

  E-mail: webmaster@uie.com

  Web: www.uie.com

- **The Usability Training Centre**, Userfocus Ltd, 211 Piccadilly, London W1J 9HF, United Kingdom

  The Usability Training Centre offers a plethora of courses including moderating usability tests, the user centered design process, discount usability techniques (heuristic evaluation, cognitive walkthrough), building a usability lab, and British standards and UK legislation relevant to usability and accessibility.

  Phone: +44 (0) 20 7917 9535

  E-mail: helpdesk@userfocus.co.uk

  Web: www.userfocus.co.uk/training/index.html

- **User-Centered Design, Inc.**, 20548 Deerwatch Place, Ashburn, VA 20147, USA

  User-Centered Design offer a one-day course in facilitation techniques for moderators. They also offer courses in usability testing, GOMS modeling techniques for interface analysis, and video capture and editing techniques for usability professionals.

  Phone: (703) 729-0998

  Fax: (703) 729-0998

  E-mail: info@user-centereddesign.com

  Web: www.user-centereddesign.com

APPENDIX C

VENDORS THAT CONSULT ON USABILITY LAB DESIGN, SELL OR RENT LAB EQUIPMENT, OR BUILD LABS

Throughout the book we have mentioned vendors for a variety of purposes. Here we present the vendors that consult on the design of labs, sell or rent lab equipment, and/or build usability labs. The specific service offered by these companies varies. We do not have experience with all of these vendors. These are companies that we were able to find the most information about. They are placed in alphabetical order and it is not a complete list. You can always do a web search to find other references, but we recommend speaking with other people in the Human–Computer Interaction (HCI) industry to get recommendations. Additional usability consultants can be found on the Usability Professionals' Association (UPA) Consultant List (www.upassoc.org/people_pages/consultants_directory/index.html).

Caution

Please note the information contained within appendices A–D is provided as a starting point. The content is based on our research at the time of the publication of this book. Offerings from vendors and organizations may change with time, so we advise that you check with the sources directly to learn about their current offerings.

- **American Institutes for Research**, 490 Virginia Road, Floor One, Concord, MA 01742-2747, USA

  Phone: (978) 371-5885
  Fax: (978) 371-5884
  Web: www.air.org

- **Noldus Information Technology**, International HQ: P.O. Box 268, 6700 AG, Wageningen, The Netherlands

  Phone: +31 (317) 497677
  Fax: +31 (317) 424496
  E-mail: info@noldus.nl
  Web: www.noldus.com

  North American HQ: 751 Miller Drive, Suite E-5, Leesburg, VA 20175, USA

  Phone: (800) 355-9541
  Fax: (703) 771-0441
  E-mail: info@noldus.com
  Web: www.noldus.com

- **Norm Wilcox Associates**, 4507 Metropolitan Court, Suite F, Frederick, MD 21704-9452, USA

  Phone: (301) 874-1191
  Fax: (301) 874-1194
  E-mail: info@normwilcox.com
  Web: www.normwilcox.com/default.htm

- **OTIVO, Inc.**, 451 Hayes St, Floor 3, San Francisco, CA 94102, USA

  Phone: (415) 626-2604
  Fax: (415) 626-2605
  E-mail: contact@otivo.com
  Web: www.otivo.com

- **Ovo Studios**, Cleveland, OH, and Pittsburgh, PA
  They offer portable usability labs as well as full service usability lab design and installation.

  Phone: [OH] (440) 247-2501; [PA] (412) 401-5598
  E-mail: [OH] scott@ovostudios.com; [PA] rich@ovostudios.com
  Web: www.ovostudios.com

- **Snader and Associates**, Multiple locations in Northern California

  In northern CA, they consult on lab design, selling the equipment, and installing it. They also rent lab equipment.

  Phone: (415) 257-8480

  Fax: (415) 257-8990

  E-mail: customerservice@snader.com

  Web: www.snader.com

- **Triangle Research Collaborative, Inc.**, PO Box 12167, Research Triangle Park (RTP), NC 27709-2167, USA

  They design and implement complete lab solutions for both portable and permanent labs.

  Phone: (919) 549-9093

  Fax: (919) 549-0493

  E-mail: info@TRCtech.com

  Web: http://trctech.com

- **Alucid Solution, Inc.** (formerly **Usability Systems, Inc.**), 6845 Shiloh Road East, Suite D-10, Alpharetta, GA 30005, USA

  Phone: (770) 889-6475

  Fax: (770) 889-6875

  E-mail: jimmy@usabilitysystems.com

  Web: www.usabilitysystems.com

APPENDIX D

VENDORS THAT RECRUIT PARTICIPANTS, CONDUCT USABILITY ACTIVITIES FOR YOU, AND/OR RENT FACILITIES TO YOU

Throughout the book we have mentioned vendors for a variety of purposes. Here we present the vendors available to recruit participants for you, conduct usability activities for you, and those that will rent facilities so that you can conduct your own activities. The services offered by each company vary. We do not have experience with all of these vendors. These are companies that we were able to find the most information about. They are placed in alphabetical order and it is not a complete list. You can always do a web search to find other references, but we recommend speaking with other people in the Human–Computer Interaction (HCI) industry to get recommendations. Additional usability consultants can be found on the Usability Professionals' Association (UPA) Consultant List (www.upassoc.org/people_pages/consultants_directory/index.html).

Caution

Please note the information contained within appendices A–D is provided as a starting point. The content is based on our research at the time of the publication of this book. Offerings from vendors and organizations may change with time, so we advise that you check with the sources directly to learn about their current offerings.

- **American Institutes for Research** (AIR), 490 Virginia Road, Floor One, Concord, MA 01742-2747, USA

  Phone: (978) 371-5885
  Fax: (978) 371-5884
  E-mail: airwebmaster@air.org
  Web: www.air.org

- **Bernett Research**, 1505 Commonwealth Ave, Boston, MA 02135, USA

  Phone: (617) 746-2600
  E-mail: bernyce@bernett.com
  Web: www.bernett.com

- **Consumer Surveys Company**, Northpoint Shopping Center, 304 East Rand Road, Arlington Heights, IL 60004, USA

  Phone: (847) 394-9411
  Fax: (847) 394-0001
  E-mail: consumersurveys1@aol.com
  Web: Unknown

- **Delve**, 1355 North Highway Drive, Fenton, St Louis County, MO 63099, USA

  Phone: (800) 325-3338
  Fax: (636) 827-6761
  E-mail: postmaster@delve.com
  Web: www.delve.com/delvemain.asp

- **Ennis Information Age Services**, Information Age Centre, Ballymaley Business Park, Ennis, County Clare, Ireland

  Phone: +353 (0) 65 68 69 200
  Fax: +353 (0) 65 68 69 244
  E-mail: info@eias.ie
  Web: www.eias.ie/index.php

- **Fieldwork**

  Locations all across the USA

  Phone: (800) 863-4353

  Fax: (312) 923-7405

  E-mail: info@network.fieldwork.com

  Web: www.fieldwork.com

- **Fieldwork Services**, PO Box 5616, Inverness IV3 8YZ, UK

  Phone: +44 (0) 1463 236288

  Fax: +44 (0) 1463 716988

  E-mail: info@fieldworkservices.com

  Web: www.fieldworkservices.com

- **Focus Pointe**

  Offices all across the USA

  Phone: 888-US-FOCUS

  E-mail: OneCall@focuspointe.net

  Web: www.focuspointe.net

- **Human Factors International, Inc.**, 410 West Lowe, PO Box 2020, Fairfield, IA 52556, USA

  Phone: (800) 242-4480 or (641) 472-4480

  Fax: (641) 472-5412

  E-mail: hfi@humanfactors.com

  Web: www.humanfactors.com

- **Merrill Research Headquarters:**

  Merrill Consulting [MC] (provides full-service consulting and analysis), 1300 S. El Camino Real, Suite 370

  Merrill Field & Tab [MFT] (provides data collection and data processing services) 1300 S. El Camino Real, Suite 380, San Mateo, CA 94402, USA

  Phone: [MC] (650) 341-4411; [MFT] (650) 358-1480

  Fax: (650) 341-2678

  E-mail: info@merrill.com

  Web: www.merrill.com

- **Nichols Research, Inc.**, 333 W. El Camino Real, Suite 180, Sunnyvale, CA 94087-1968, USA

  Phone: (408) 773-8200
  Fax: (408) 733-8564
  E-mail: sunnyvale@nicholsresearch.com
  Web: www.nichols-research.com

- **Nielsen Norman Group**, 48921 Warm Springs Bvd, Fremont, CA 94539-7767, USA

  Phone: (408) 720-8808
  E-mail: info@nngroup.com
  Web: www.nngroup.com

- **Noldus Information Technology**, International HQ: P.O. Box 268, 6700 AG, Wageningen, The Netherlands

  Phone: +31 (317) 497677
  Fax: +31 (317) 424496
  E-mail: info@noldus.nl
  Web: www.noldus.com

  North American HQ: 751 Miller Drive, Suite E-5, Leesburg, VA 20175, USA

  Phone: (800) 355-9541
  Fax: (703) 771-0441
  E-mail: info@noldus.com
  Web: www.noldus.com

- **Tec-Ed, Inc.**, 4300 Varsity Drive, Suite A, PO Box 1905, Ann Arbor, MI 48106, USA

  Phone: (734) 995-1010
  Fax: (734) 995-1025
  E-mail: info@teced.com
  Web: www.teced.com/ue-ust.html

- **Usable Solutions, LLC**, 4610 S. Ulster Street, Suite 150, Denver, CO 80237, USA

  Phone: (303) 364-0446
  E-mail: karen@usables.com
  Web: www.usables.com

APPENDIX E

DEVELOP A QUESTIONNAIRE FOR POTENTIAL PARTICIPANTS

DISTRIBUTE YOUR QUESTIONNAIRE

TECHNICAL REQUIREMENTS FOR A PARTICIPANT DATABASE

REQUIREMENTS FOR CREATING A PARTICIPANT RECRUITMENT DATABASE

There are several things you should know if you want to set up your own participant database for recruiting people for your activity. Unfortunately, the creation of a participant database does not happen overnight. It will take some work on your part to create and maintain it.

Develop a Questionnaire for Potential Participants

There are a variety of avenues you can pursue to add people to your database. The first thing you will want to do is develop a questionnaire for potential participants to complete. This is the information that you will enter into your database and use to query when you have an activity (Refer to Chapter 8, Surveys, page 312, to learn how to develop an effective survey.)

Some basic information you will want to include is:

- Name
- Address
- E-mail address
- Phone numbers (work, home, cell)
- Job title
- Years of experience in that role
- Company name
- Company size
- Industry
- How the person found out about your questionnaire (this can help you track the most effective methods for signing people up).

The rest of the details really depend on what is for you important to know when you are trying to recruit participants.

Figure E.1 is a sample participant database questionnaire. In 12-point font, the questions fit across both sides of an 8.5 in × 11 in sheet of paper.

Usability Participation Questionnaire

If you are interested in participating in our Usability Program, please complete this questionnaire. It should take approximately 10–15 minutes to complete. All information will remain confidential. This information will not be sold to a third party vendor. Thank you for your participation. If you have any questions please e-mail usability@travelsmart.com or call (800) 999-2222.

Contact Information

First Name: _____

Last Name: _____

Mailing Address:
    Street or PO Box   _____
                                       _____
    City   _____
    State   _____
    Zip   _____

Phone Numbers:
    Daytime #   (   ) _____ Ext: _____
    Evening #   (   ) _____ Ext: _____

Email Address: _____

Background Information

Highest Level of Education (*please choose one*):
    ○ High School or Less
    ○ Some College

    O Associate Degree
    O Bachelor's Degree
    O Graduate Degree

Age Group:
    O Under 18
    O 18–29
    O 30–44
    O 45–60
    O Over 60

Gender:
    O Male
    O Female

Do you own a cellphone?
    O Yes   O No
    If yes, is it Web-enabled?
    O Yes   O No

Do you own a PDA (Personal Digital Assistant)?
    O Yes   O No
    If yes, what type:
    ☐ Palm   ☐ Windows CE

Occupational Information

Industry (*please choose one*):

O Advertising / Marketing / PR
O Aerospace
O Architecture
O Biotechnology
O Chemical / Petroleum / Mining / Lumber / Agriculture
O Education
O Entertainment / Media / Film
O Finance / Banking / Accounting
O Government Services
O Health / Medical
O Insurance

O Internet Provider
O Legal
O Manufacturing Design: Computer /
O Communications Equipment
O Manufacturing / Design: Software
O Manufacturing Design: Other
O Non-profit Organization
O Pharmaceuticals
O Real Estate
O Retail
O Services: Business (non-computer)

Continued

Figure E.1 – *Cont'd*

○ Services: Data processing / Computer

○ System Integrator

○ Telecommunications

○ Transportation / Freight / Shipping

○ Travel

○ Utilities / Energy-related

○ VAR / Distributor / Other Reseller

○ Wholesale

○ Other: _____

Company's Name: _____

Size of Company:

○ Small (1–49)   ○ Medium (50–500)   ○ Large (500+)

Job Function (*please choose one*):

○ Executive / Senior Mgmt

○ HR / Personal / Benefits

○ Finance / Accounting

○ Administration / Clerical

○ Shipping / Receiving

○ Marketing / Sales / PR

○ Operations / General Mgmt

○ Facilities / General Mgmt

○ Manufacturing

○ Purchasing / Procurement

○ Consulting

○ Other: _____

Are you a Manager?

○ Yes   ○ No

Job Title: _____

Job Description: _____

_____

Job Experience (*years*): _____

Employment Status (*please choose one*):

○ Full Time

○ Part Time

○ Self Employed

○ Temp / Contract

○ Unemployed

Thank you for your time!

Distribute Your Questionnaire

Now that you have your questionnaire, you need to distribute it to potential participants. We recommend creating both a web-based and a paper-based version of the questionnaire for distribution. Some distribution methods are described below.

Buy a mailing or e-mail list

There are companies that sell you the home addresses and/or e-mail addresses of people. You can tell them some criteria about the people that you are interested in and they can tell you (before you purchase) how many addresses they have that match your criteria. If you like what you hear, you can make the purchase. In the past, we have used such companies as Names in the News (www.nincal.com) and InfoCore (www.info-core.com).

The main disadvantage of this method is that there is only about a 1% response rate. In other words, you need to buy a *lot* of these addresses in order for this to be successful.

Physical mailing addresses

When you purchase mailing addresses, you can physically mail your questionnaire to each address with a return address envelope (postage pre-paid). It will cost you about $1.00 per address, including postage. (Refer to Chapter 8, Surveys, page 312, to learn about response rates.)

E-mail addresses

Purchasing e-mail addresses will cost about 50 cents per address. You can e-mail an invitation, asking people to join your participant database. You should describe your company and potential activities, as well as provide the URL to sign up for your database.

Attend tradeshows

Attending tradeshows or conferences where you think your users might be provides the opportunity to speak with end users in person and hand out your questionnaire. For example, if you are looking for Mac users, go to Mac World. If you are looking for electronics users, go to the Consumer Electronics Show. It is ideal if you can get a booth and offer people goodies for signing up, or enter their name in a prize drawing if they sign up.

Put a link on your company website

Place a link to your web-based questionnaire on your company's website. A couple of great places for a link would be on a page the talks about your company's usability program, and on a page that links to jobs within your company. If you can get space on your company's homepage, that's even better!

Put a link on an electronic community bulletin board

Just like an ad that you put up to recruit people for a specific activity, place an ad to invite people to sign up for your participant database. It won't cost much to place the ad, and you can get a lot of responses by doing so.

Recruit people who participate in your activities

If you have participants who come in for activities from a source other than your participant database, invite them to join your database. (This may not be possible if the participants come from a recruiting agency – refer to Chapter 5, Preparing for Your User Requirements Activity, "Use a Recruiting Agency" section, page 175.) You can do this by distributing your questionnaire while participants are at your session, or you can send them a thank you note after the session and invite them to sign up.

Technical Requirements for a Participant Database

There are some technical requirements to consider when planning your participant database. As with usability labs, you can build your participant database on the cheap or you can create an ideal participant database. Like everything else, there are pros and cons to each choice.

On the Cheap

You can create a very simple participant database in Microsoft Excel or Microsoft® Access®. Most offices have access to this software so it is easy to acquire. You will notice it has several limitations, however.

Pros:

- It is cheap.
- It is relatively quick and easy to construct a simple table of participants and their information.

Cons:

- If multiple people in your group will be leveraging the participant database, versioning may become a problem.
- You will need to write macros to conduct searches for participants, based on certain criteria.
- You will need an Apache server to post a survey externally and have the information imported to your database.
- You will also need a scripting engine like Perl/CGI to import the results of your survey from the web to your database.

More Extensive and Expensive

If your company has an enterprise database (e.g., Oracle 9iAS, IBM WebSphere, Microsoft SQL Server), many of the problems listed above will be solved, but new ones arrive.

Pros:

- Everything is included in one package (the database, scripting tools, the web server, and management, monitoring and tuning tools).
- Versioning is no longer an issue.
- You can easily post your survey on the web and upload the results into your database.
- You can quickly and easily search through your database for participants based on specific criteria.
- You can create you infrastructure in the language of your choice (e.g., Perl, Java, SQL/PLSQL, C++) to run your form and get its contents into the database.

Cons:

- It is expensive.
- You will need the time of your company's database administrator (DBA) or system administrator to maintain your database and applications.

Maintenance Requirements for Any Solution

Regardless of which database you go with, you will need to keep it up to date. This is critical; information that is out of date is useless. Maintenance includes:

- Removing or updating people whose contact information is no longer valid
- Removing people who no longer want to participate
- Adding new entries on a regular basis (from paper-based and web-based questionnaires)
- Tracking when each participant came in and how much he/she was paid (refer to Chapter 5, Preparing for Your User Requirements Activity, "Determining Participant Incentives" section, page 159)
- Adding comments about certain participants after activities ("great participant," "arrived late," etc.)
- Moving people to a Watch List (refer to Chapter 5, Preparing for Your User Requirements Activity, "Create a Watch List" section, page 190).

APPENDIX F

AFFINITY DIAGRAM

Introduction

A Japanese anthropologist, Jiro Kawakita, developed a method of synthesizing large amounts of data into manageable chunks based on themes that emerge from the data itself. It is known as the "K-J method," following the Japanese custom of placing the family name first. It has become one of the most widely used of the Japanese management and planning tools.

In the west, a very similar method known as "affinity diagramming" has been developed based on the K-J method. An **affinity diagram** is probably the most useful method for analyzing qualitative data including participant responses from an interview (Chapter 7, page 246), focus group (Chapter 12, page 514), field study (Chapter 13, page 562), or even a wants and needs analysis (Chapter 9, page 370). It can also be used to group characteristics when building personas (refer to Chapter 2, Before You Choose an Activity, "Learn About Your Users" section, page 41) or to analyze findings from a **usability** test.

Take the data from each participant and pull out key points (e.g., participant comments, observations, questions, design ideas), and write each one individually on an index card or sticky note. You may want to indicate other things on the cards like the participant number, task, or site (in the case of a field study) associated with that data point. The cards are then shuffled to avoid any pre-existing order and each card is placed on a wall or whiteboard. Similar findings or concepts are physically grouped together (on the wall or whiteboard) to identify themes or trends in the data.

It is important to enter the analysis with an open mind and not preconceived categories for the data to fit into. The structure and relationship will *emerge* from the data. Once the groups have emerged, you should label each group. What do these comments have in common? Why do they belong together?

When Should You Use an Affinity Diagram?

There are a plethora of uses for an affinity diagram and benefits you get from this analysis method:

- The affinity diagram is an excellent method for sharing the results of your study with **stakeholders** as the study progresses. They can look at the physical diagram to see evolving trends, as well as individual pieces of data. It also allows for quick data analysis once the study is complete (see step 7 below).

- It can add structure to a large or complicated issue. You are able to break down a complicated issue into broader categories or more specific, focused categories.

- It helps you to identify issues that affect multiple areas because those same issues belong in multiple groups. It can also help you identify areas where you are missing information, and the scope of issues that needs to be addressed.

- When using an affinity diagram, you can see that the design/product ideas are based on direct user data. If you recommend solution A, you can point to a group of data points (each with an associated participant ID) that informed your recommendation.

- Because individual issues, requests, or problems are grouped into higher-level themes, the team can respond on a broader scale rather than trying to address each one individually. This leads to a holistic rather than piecemeal solution.

- It can help with innovation because you are not working from preconceived categories. New ideas emerge from the data.

- By working as a team with the raw data, you can gain agreement on an issue. It can also help unify a team because the product development team can take part in the analysis, alongside the person who led the study.

Things to Consider When Using an Affinity Diagram

Using an affinity diagram requires one to enter with an open mind and be creative. Some people are uncomfortable with using the gut feeling and feel more comfortable adding in structure. This often results in an attempt to create categories *a priori* (i.e., before the sorting). That defeats the purpose of using an affinity diagram. Make sure your team members understand the purpose of affinity diagram and the benefits to its approach before the analysis begins.

Creating an Affinity Diagram

Below are the steps to create your own affinity diagram. The process is slow at first, but with each analysis session the team will get faster.

Step 1: Find a Space

You can create an affinity diagram on any wall or whiteboard in your office, lab, or a conference room. Obviously, the amount of space needed depends on the amount of data you collected. Since you will likely work on it for the duration of your study, be sure the diagram is in a secure location where co-workers or cleaning staff won't undo your hard work.

Step 2: Assemble Your Team

Following each user requirements session, bring together the members of the team that took part in the session (e.g., moderator, scribe, videographer). We strongly recommend updating your diagram after each session while the data are fresh in your mind; however, if this is not possible then complete the diagram as soon as you have finished running all sessions for your activity.

As with the K-J method, affinity diagramming works best as a team approach. Your scribe, videographer, and/or fellow field study investigator(s) should take part in this exercise. If a product team member was a part of the session, be sure to get him/her involved as well. Not only will that speed data analysis, the additional point of view is essential. This is information that should be discussed, examined from multiple angles, and hypotheses posed. Creativity should be encouraged and there should be no criticism of people's ideas or hypotheses.

Ground Rules for Creating an Affinity Diagram

1. Everyone is equal – there is no leader.
2. There will be no criticism of ideas – all ideas have merit.
3. There are no preconceived categories – they will emerge from the data.
4. Small groups can be merged and large groups can be broken apart, as appropriate.
5. Cards can be duplicated to live in multiple groups, if necessary.
6. Cards or groups of cards can be moved, if necessary. Cards are not locked in once place.

Tip

Write the ground rules for creating an affinity diagram on the board. Make sure everyone understands them and agrees to them. Then if anyone breaks them, you can simply point the offender back to the rules. This will save a good deal of bickering.

Step 3: Create the Cards

As a team, write key points of information from the data on index cards or sticky notes. Participant quotes, observations, hypothesis, questions, design ideas, pain points, etc., can all be included. You may choose to color-code your data by using different colored cards or notes for each participant or for each type of data (e.g., quotes are green, hypothesis are blue, questions are pink). Depending on the length of your usability session and/or number of participants, you can generate around 50–100 cards.

Step 4: Sort the Cards

Once all the cards are created for a session, the cards should be shuffled and divided among the members of the team. As each card is posted to the wall, the team member should call it out. You can also duplicate cards if you feel the item belongs in more than one group. To indicate that one issue or data point lives in multiple groups (and therefore affects multiple areas), you may want to create that duplicate issue on a different colored index card or sticky note. This will help the duplicated issues stand out.

When grouping similar cards, you do not have to state *why* you think those cards belong together. This can be a gut feeling. Do not try to label your categories early on. If you find an identical (or very similar) issue, problem, request, or quote is made, stack those cards on top of each other. You will be able to tell at a glance that the thicker stacks indicate recurring issues.

Tip

Placing a time limit on the sorting phase (e.g., one hour) can prevent team members from over-analyzing every placement. You *can* move cards or groups of cards later on. Place the card either by itself, near another card, or with a card quickly and move on to the next card.

Step 5: Label the Groups

After about three usability sessions (e.g., interviews, focus groups, field study visits) you will see the categories emerging. At this point, you can begin to label each group with a title or description.

Step 6: Regroup

As the sorting proceeds with data from more sessions, look for duplicate groups. If you have a lot of data, sometimes duplicate groups are created. Also, look for smaller groups. Do they belong with larger groups? They may not, but it is useful as you progress to look for higher-level groups emerging. Conversely, larger groups may need to be broken down into more meaningful, sub-groups.

Step 7: Walk through the Diagram

After all usability sessions have been run, the team should verbally walk through the diagram together. You may want to audio-record this discussion or have a scribe take notes, because the discussion will be useful when writing up the results of your study. The team should take a last stab at identifying higher-level groups and breaking larger groups into more meaningful sub-groups. They should also make sure they are in agreement with descriptions for each group. Members are free to add cards with clarifying information, new insights, design ideas, and questions for further investigation.

Tip

Take a digital picture of the final affinity diagram. It can demonstrate to stakeholders the wealth of data you collected and how it all came together. Include this in your usability report to better describe how you analyzed your data. Many product developers and executives will be unfamiliar with affinity diagramming and a picture of the final result can better convey what it is. They won't be able to read all the details, but it helps to give them a sense of what you did.

Figure F.1 shows an affinity diagram for a series of six TravelSmart.com interviews conducted during a hypothetical airport kiosk field study. The intention of this figure is to give you a visual sense of what an affinity diagram might look like. As a result we have not focused on the details of what could be written on each sticky note. The squares represent sticky notes with participant responses. Each participant is a different color. When the same participant made similar comments, the sticky notes were stacked on top of each other yielding rectangles, rather than squares. You will notice that some sticky notes cross the lines between categories. This means that the comment fell into more than one category and demonstrates related issues. The actual affinity diagram can be recreated in any drawing application so that the high-level groupings can be visually displayed in a usability report. More detail can be added than is shown here so that a poster can be created to display the results for all to see.

Figure F.1: *Fictional affinity diagram for TravelSmart.com airport kiosk field study*

APPENDIX G

COMPUTERIZED QUALITATIVE ANALYSIS TOOLS

Several tools are available for purchase to help you analyze qualitative data (e.g., interviews, focus groups, field study notes). They look for patterns or trends in your data. Some allow you to create categories and then search for data that matches those categories. A few can even search multimedia files (e.g., graphics, video, audio). However, since these programs require practice and for the data to be typed up, they are best used only when you have complex data (i.e., unstructured interviews) and lots of it. If you have a small number of data points and/or the results are from a very structured interview, these tools would be overkill and unnecessary. A simple spreadsheet or affinity diagram (refer to Appendix F, page 714) would better serve your purposes. (Refer to Chapter 8, Surveys, "Data Analysis and Interpretation" section, page 348 for a discussion of tools to analyze closed-ended questions.)

Prior to purchasing any tool, you should investigate each one and be familiar with its limitations. For example, many of the products make statements like "no *practical* limit on the number of documents you can analyze" or "*virtually* unlimited number of documents." By "documents," they mean the number of transcripts or notes the tool is able to analyze. The limits may be well outside the range of your study, but do the investigation to be sure. The last thing you want to is to enter in reams of data only to hit the limit and be prevented from doing a meaningful analysis. In addition, a program may analyze *text* but not *content*. This means that it may group identical words but is not intelligent enough to categorize similar or related concepts. That job will be up to you.

Below is a list of a few of the more popular tools on the market today. For more information, please go to the individual product's URL.

- *NVivo*™ and *N6*™ by QSR are the latest incarnations of *NUD*IST*™ (Non-numerical Unstructured Data-Indexing, Searching, & Theorizing), a leading content analysis tool. You can learn more about *NVivo* and *N6* at www.qsr.com.au/products/productoverview/product_overview.htm.

- *Qualrus*™ by Idea Works has several nice features including full multimedia support (text, graphics, video, and audio). For more information, see www.qualrus.com/Qualrus.shtml.

- *The Ethnograph* by Qualis Research Associates analyzes data from text-based documents. For more information, see www.qualisresearch.com.

- *Atlas.ti*® supports qualitative analysis of large amounts of textual, graphical, audio, and video data. For more information, see www.atlasti.de/features.shtml.

- *HyperQual3* for Macintosh is a tool for storing, managing, organizing, and analyzing qualitative text data. For more information, see home.satx.rr.com/hyperqual.

- *TextSmart*™ is SPSS's module for coding and analyzing open-ended survey questions but could be used to analyze interview data. For more information, see www.spss.com/spssbi/textsmart/index.htm.

APPENDIX H

REPORT TEMPLATE

This document is a sample report template. Its purpose is to demonstrate sample layout and content for a complete report. This particular template illustrates a card sort report, but the same basic sections can be used so that it can be modified and used for any requirements activity.

CARD SORT

Product Name (*version number, if applicable*)

<Department Name>

Author:

Creation Date:

Test Dates: *<mm/dd/yy – mm/dd/yy>*

Version: *<Draft or Final>*

Last updated: *<Month, yyyy>*

Report Contributor(s)

Name	Position	Role
		Co-moderator
		Videographer
		Designer

Report Reviewer(s)

Name	Position

Supporting Documents

Document title	Owner

Usability History

Activity	Author	Date of study

Executive Summary

Briefly introduce the product and the motivation for conducting this activity. Provide an overview of the number of participants, dates, purpose of the session(s), and number of sessions.

If a particular menu or tab structure or information architecture is being proposed as a design recommendation, include an image of the proposed design

Proposed Information Architecture or Menu structure <optional>

[Insert figure if available]

Travel Card Sort Table of Recommendations

Tab name	Objects to be located within the tab
Resources	Tipping information
	Languages
	Currency
	Family-friendly travel information
News	Travel deals
	Travel alerts
	Featured destinations
	Weekly travel polls
Opinions	Read reviews
	Post and read questions on bulletin boards
	Chat with travel agents
	Chat with travelers
	Rate destinations
Products	Travel games
	Luggage
	Books
	Links to travel gear sites

Background

Provide a brief description of the product and the anticipated tasks that users will accomplish with it.

State the number and dates of the sessions. You can use the following paragraph to describe the purpose and goals of the card sort. You can also describe the rationale for conducting a card sort (e.g., to derive a new tab or menu structure for an application). Modify the following to your own specific needs.

Card sorting is a common usability technique used to discover the users' mental model of an information space (e.g., a website, a product, or a menu). It generally involves representing each piece of information from the information space on an individual card and then asking target users to arrange these cards into groupings that make sense to them.

Method

Participants

Briefly describe the participants who were recruited, the number of participants, the method of recruitment (e.g., internal participant database, customers, recruiting agency), and the incentive (e.g., $100 in AMEX gift checks, or a company logo mug). If conducting multiple group sessions, discuss the number of groups and composition of each group. Also include recruitment criteria with an optional reference to the phone screener in Appendix 1. Below is an example.

Recruitment was based on specific criteria. The screening profile required that users:

- Could not work for a competitor
- Were over 18 years of age
- Demonstrated proficiency in the language used in the card sort.

Detailed user profiles can be found in Appendix 2. Participants were recruited via Ideal Recruiting and were compensated with a $100 gift check for their time.

Materials

Describe the cards. For example, did the cards contain a description and/or a line for an alternative label? Descriptions and space for an alternative label are optional. Next, show a sample card. Below is an example.

Each card contained a label, a short description of the concept/label, and space for participants to write in an alternative label. Figure X shows a sample card from this activity.

Figure X: Sample Card

Airline deals

These are deals or discounts that airlines are currently offering.

Alternative label

____

Procedure

Participants read and signed informed consent forms and non-disclosure agreements.<*If you did a warm up activity, mention it here.*> <*Insert number*> members of the UI group acted as moderators for the session. Moderators answered participants' questions and handed out and collected card sorting materials.

Participants worked individually throughout the session. Each participant was given an envelope containing a set of <*Insert number*> cards in random order representing the concepts included in <*insert product name here*> – see Appendix 3.

<*Optional: The following text can be used as a boilerplate procedure for defining the subtasks. Customize it to your own needs.*>

The card sort activity involved three subtasks: card sort read/rename, card sort initial grouping, and card sort secondary grouping. Card sort subtasks were presented to the participants as separate and discrete steps. Instructions specific to each subtask were given separately. Participants were not told what they would be doing in the later steps because this might have biased their decisions. Details of each subtask are summarized below.

Part 1. Card Sorting Read/Rename

- Participants read through each card to make sure they understood the meaning of the function. The test facilitator instructed participants not to order the cards.
- Participants renamed any cards they found unfamiliar or inappropriate by crossing out the original name and writing in an alternative(s).

Part 2. Card Sorting Initial Grouping

First, participants sorted the cards into logical groups. When everyone had finished reading the cards, participants were instructed to:

> **"Arrange the cards into groups in a way that makes sense to you. There is no right or wrong arrangement. We are interested in what you perceive to be the most logical or intuitive arrangement of the cards."**

<Optional: Typically there are no constraints on the number and size of groups that participants can create. If there are constraints, provide them here.> Participants were told that they should make no more than *<Insert number>* groups, each with no more than *<Insert number>* cards.

After finishing the groupings, participants named each group on a Post-it note and attached the note to the groups.

Part 3. Card Sorting Secondary Grouping

- Participants sorted the grouped cards into higher-level groups if any were apparent.
- Participants named each of the higher-level groups on a Post-it note and attached the note to the groups.

<Optional> See Appendix 4 for the complete instructions provided to the participants.

Results

Note that authors may choose to divide the Results into several subsections dealing with sorting data, terminology, and user comments. Customize what follows according to your needs.

Sorting Data

The card sorting data were analyzed using a cluster analysis program called *EZCalc* to derive the overall sort shown in Figure X. The figure shows the composite sort of all *<Insert number>* cards for all *<Insert number>* participants. The closer the concepts are to each other on the sorting diagram, the more conceptually related they are. *EZCalc* generates groups based on relationship strength between items.

Figure X: Sorting Results Diagram

<Optionally, include more images as needed>

<Optional: Insert callouts in the image to show the groupings and their names. Discuss how the sorting results can be translated into a UI design. For example:>

The yellow and white bands can be used as a guide for determining the new menu structure. Figure X shows the suggested menu labels and menu content derived from these card sorting data.

If the recommendations deviate from the EZSort results, explain why. When appropriate, make your results as visual as possible. You can also use other kinds of images (schematics, tab layouts, etc.) to communicate your design recommendations.

Travel Card Sort Table of Recommendations

This table provides the recommended architecture for the subtabs of the planning tab. The proposed architecture is considered high priority.

Tab name	Objects to be located within the tab	Status of recommendation
Resources	Tipping information Languages Currency Family-friendly travel information	Accepted
News	Travel deals Travel alerts Featured destinations Weekly travel polls	Accepted
Opinions	Read reviews Post and read questions on bulletin boards Chat with travel agents Chat with travelers Rate destinations	Accepted
Products	Travel games Luggage Books Links to travel gear sites	Pending. The team may not be adding this functionality to the first release.

Terminology Data <section optional>

Optionally, add a subsection about terminology issues discovered during the card sort activity (e.g., relabeling, questions from participants to the session moderator). If relabeling occurred, include a table (see below) showing which concepts were relabeled, with what frequencies, and what the participant-generated labels were. A column with terminology recommendations should also be included.

Alternative Labels for Concepts <optional>

Current label	Concept description	Label provided by participants	Recommendations
Airline deals	These are deals or discounts that airlines are currently offering.	Flight deals (6 of 10 participants)	Flight deals
.....			
.....			
.....			

Participant Comments <section optional>

If a think-aloud protocol was used, or if you allowed users to make comments at the end of the activity, include a section highlighting participants' comments. Only include participant comments if those comments affected the UI recommendations.

Conclusion

Discuss the implications of the card sort data on the information architecture of the product. Do the data validate the current direction of the product? If not, discuss how the product team should change their designs to be more consistent with the users' mental model of the domain.

<Optional: Discuss future usability activities to be conducted as a follow up.>

Appendix 1

Insert your screening questionnaire. For a sample, refer to Chapter 5, Preparing for Your User Requirements Activity, "Sample Screener" section, page 166.

Appendix 2

Participant Profiles

Participant #	Employer	Job title	<Other requirement>	<Other requirement>	<Other requirement>

Some information to consider including in the table:

- *Company size*
- *Industry*
- *Line of business*
- *Experience with a particular domain, application, or product.*

If applicable, gender, age, and disability may be included.

Appendix 3

Card Set

Show the complete set of cards used in the study. List the card names and definitions listed on the cards. Below are some examples:

Travel news

Definition: The latest news that relates to traveling

Travel deals

Definition: Travel specials or discounts offered by the website

Children's promotions

Definition: Travel specials or discounts offered by the website that relate to children

Vacations packages

Definition: Travel packages that include combinations of transportation, accommodations and other features

Appendix 4

Participant Instructions

Show the complete instructions provided to the participants, including rules about relabeling, grouping, etc. Below is an example.

"The cards in front of you have pieces of objects/information that might be contained within a travel website.

1. Look over all of the cards.
2. If something is confusing, make a note on the card.
3. Sort the cards into groups that you would want or expect to find together.
4. Try to reduce them to 4 or fewer groups.
5. Each group cannot have less than 3 cards or more than 11 cards.
6. Use a blank card to give each group a name.
7. Staple each of the groups together.
8. Take the provided envelope and write your initials on the front. Put the stack of stapled cards in the envelope."

APPENDIX I

GLOSSARY

A

Account manager—Within large corporations an account manager is often someone who is devoted to managing a customer's relationship with their company. For example, if IXG Corporation is a large customer of TravelSmart.com, an account manager would be responsible for ensuring that that IXG Corporation is satisfied with the services they are receiving from TravelSmart.com and determining whether they require further services.

Acknowledgment tokens—Words like "oh," "ah," "mm hm," "uh huh," "OK," and "yeah" that carry no content. They reassure participants that you hear them, understand what is being said, and want them to continue.

Acquiescence—In this context, acquiescence means to easily give in to what the experimenter (or group) suggests, despite one's own true feelings. This often happens because a participant wants to please the experimenter (or group).

Affinity diagram—Similar findings or concepts are grouped together to identify themes or trends in the data.

Anti-user—Someone who would not buy or use your product in any circumstances.

Artifacts—Objects or items that users use to complete their tasks or that result from their tasks.

B

Brainstorming—A technique by which a group attempts to find a solution for a specific problem or generate ideas about a topic by amassing all the ideas together without initial concern of their true worth.

C

Cache—Location where information is stored temporarily. The files you request are stored on your computer's hard disk in a cache subdirectory under the directory for your browser. When you return to a page you've recently visited, the browser can retrieve the page from the cache rather than the original server. This saves you time and the network the burden of some additional traffic.

CDA—See *Confidential disclosure agreement*.

Click stream—Sequence of pages requested as a visitor explores a website.

Closed-ended question—A question that provides a limited set of responses for participants to choose from (e.g., yes/no, agree/disagree, answer a/b).

Cognitive interference—The ability of one idea to interfere with another's ability to generate ideas.

Cognitive interview testing—This involves asking the target population to describe all the thoughts, feelings, and ideas that come to mind when examining specific questions or messages, and to provide suggestions to clarify wording as needed.

Color-blind—Congenital defect in vision that prevents an individual from distinguishing two or more colors that people without the defect can distinguish easily. Total color blindness (achromatopsia and monochromacy) is quite rare. Red/green dichromats (those who confuse red and green wavelengths) are more common. About 1 in 15 males and 1 in 100 females have some type of color vision defect.

Communication speed—Whether one is speaking, writing, or typing, one can communicate an idea only as fast as he/she can speak, write, or type.

Confidential disclosure agreement (CDA)—A legal agreement, which the participant signs and thereby agrees to keep all information regarding the product and/or session confidential for a predefined time.

Consent form—A document that informs a participant of the purpose of the activity he/she is involved in, the expected duration, procedures, use of information collected (e.g., to design a new product), incentives for participation, and his/her rights as a participant. The participant signs this form to acknowledge that he/she has been informed of these things and agrees to participate.

Convenience sampling—The sample of the population used reflects those who were available (or those that you had access to), as opposed to selecting a truly representative sample of the population. Rather than selecting participants from the population at large, you recruited participants from a convenient subset of the population. For example, research done by college professors often uses college students for participants instead of representatives from the population at large.

D

Dendrogram—A visual representation of a cluster analysis. Consists of many U-shaped lines connecting objects in a hierarchical tree. The height of each U represents the distance between the two objects being connected. The greater the distance, the less related the two objects are.

Double-barreled questions—A single question that addresses more than one issue at a time.

Double negatives—The presence of two negatives in a sentence, making it difficult for the participant to understand the true meaning of the question.

E

Evaluation apprehension—The fear of being evaluated by others. Individuals with evaluation apprehension may not perform a specific task or speak truthfully for fear of another's negative opinion. The larger the group, the larger the affect.

F

Feature-creep—The tendency for developers to add more and more features into a product as time goes by without clear need or purpose for them.

Feature-shedding—The tendency for developers to remove features from a product because of time constraints, limited resources, or business requirements.

Firewall—Computer software that prevents unauthorized access to private data on your computer or a network by outside computer users.

Free-listing—Participants write down every word or phrase that comes to their mind in association with a particular topic, domain, etc.

G

Gap analysis—A competitive analysis technique in which your product/service is compared against a competitor's to determine gaps in functionality. A value of "importance" and "satisfaction" is assigned to each function by end users. A single score is then determined for each function by subtracting the satisfaction from importance. This score is used to help determine whether resources should be spent incorporating each feature into the product.

Groupthink—Within group decision-making procedures, it is the tendency for the various members of a group to try to achieve group consensus. The need for agreement takes priority over the motivation to obtain accurate knowledge to make appropriate decisions.

H

Hawthorne effect—Participants may behave differently when observed. They will likely be on their best behavior (e.g., observing standard operating procedures rather than using their usual shortcuts).

Heuristic—A rule or guide based on the principles of usability.

Hits—The number of times a particular web page is visited.

I

Incident diary—Participants are provided with a notebook containing worksheets to be completed on their own. The worksheets may ask users to describe a problem or issue they encountered, how they solved it (if they did), and how troublesome it was (e.g., via a Likert scale.). They are given to users to keep track of issues they encounter while using a product.

Information architecture—The organization of a product's structure and content, the labeling and categorizing of information, and the design of navigation and search systems. A good architecture helps users find information and accomplish their tasks.

Internet protocol (IP)—This is the method or protocol by which data are sent from one computer to another on the Internet.

Internet service provider (ISP)—A company that provides individuals or companies access to the Internet and other related services. Some of the largest ISPs include AT&T WorldNet, IBM Global Network, MCI, Netcom, UUNet, and PSINet.

IP address—Every computer connected to the Internet is assigned a unique number known as an Internet protocol (IP) address. Since these numbers are usually assigned in country-based blocks, an IP address can often be used to identify the country from which a computer is connecting to the Internet.

Inter-rater reliability—The degree to which two or more observers assign the same rating or label to a behavior. In field studies, it would be the amount of agreement between observers coding the same user's behavior. High inter-rater reliability means that different observers coded the data in the same way.

Interviewer prestige bias—The interviewer informs participants that an authority figure feels one way or another about a topic and then asks the participant how he/she feels.

L

Leading questions—Questions that assume the answer and may pass judgment on the participant. They have the ability to influence a participant's answers.

Likert scale—A scale developed by Rensis Likert to measure attitudes. Participants are given a statement and five to seven levels along a scale to rate their agreement/disagreement, satisfaction/dissatisfaction, etc., with the statement.

Loaded questions—Questions that typically provide a "reason" for a problem listed in the question. This frequently happens in political campaigns to demonstrate that a majority of the population feels one way or another on a key issue.

Log files—When a file is retrieved from a website, server software keeps a record of it. The server stores this information in the form of text files. The information contained in a log file varies but can be programmed to capture more or less information.

Longitudinal study—Research carried out on the same participants over an extended period.

M

Markers—Key events to the participant that you can probe into for richer information.

Median—A measure of central tendency. When data points are ordered by magnitude, the median is the middlemost point in the distribution.

Mental model—A person's mental representation or organization of information.

N

Negative user—See *Anti-user*.

Non-responder bias—People who do not respond to surveys (or participate in studies) can be significantly different from those who do. Consequently, missing the data from non-responders can bias the data you collect, making your data less generalizable.

O

Observation guide—A list of general concerns or issues to guide your observations in a field study – but it is *not* a list of specific questions to ask.

Open-ended question—A question designed to elicit detailed responses and free from structure (i.e., you do not provide options for the participant to choose from).

Outlier—A data point that has an extreme value and does not follow the characteristics of the data in general.

P

Persona—An exemplar of a particular user type designed to bring the user profile to life during product development.

Prestige response bias—The participant wants to impress the facilitator and therefore provides answers that enhance his/her image.

Primary users—Those individuals who work regularly or directly with the product.

Procedural knowledge—Stored information that consists of knowledge of how to do things.

Production blocking—In verbal brainstorming, people are asked to speak one at a time. By having to wait in a queue to speak, ideas are sometimes lost or suppressed. Attention is also shifted from listening to other speakers towards trying to remember one's own idea.

Protocol—A script that outlines all procedures you will perform as a moderator and the order in which you will carry out these procedures. It acts as a checklist for all of the session steps.

Proxy—Server that acts as a mediator between a user's computer and the Internet so that a company can ensure security, administrative control, and caching service.

Q

Qualitative data—Represents verbal or narrative pieces of data. These types of data are collected through focus groups, interviews, opened-ended questionnaire items, and other less structured situations.

Quantitative data—Numeric information that includes things like personal income, amount of time, or a rating of an opinion on a scale from 1 to 5. Even things that you do not think of as quantitative, like feelings, can be collected using numbers if you create scales to measure them.

R

Reliable/reliability—Reliability is the extent to which the test or measurement yields the same approximate results when used repeatedly under the same conditions.

Response bias—In any study in which responses of some sort (e.g., answers to set questions) are required of participants, *response bias* exists if, independently of the effect of any experimental manipulation, the participants are more likely to respond in one way than in another (e.g., more likely, in a multiple-choice task, to choose Option A than Option B).

S

Sample—A portion of the population selected to be representative of the population as a whole. Since it is typically unfeasible to collect data from the entire population of users, you must select a smaller subset.

Sampling bias—The tendency of a sample to exclude some members of the sampling population and over-represent others.

Sampling plan—A list of days/times to observe users. This should include days/times when you anticipate key events (e.g., the day before Thanksgiving, or bad weather at an airport), as well as "normal" days.

Scenario—A story about a user. It provides a setting, has actors, objectives or goals, a sequence of events, and closes with a result. It is used to illustrate how an end user works or behaves.

Secondary users—They would utilize the product infrequently or through an intermediary.

Self-selection bias—Bias that results because a certain type of person has volunteered or "self-selected" to be a part of your study (e.g., those people who have a special interest in the topic, those who really just want your incentive, those who have a lot of spare time on their hands, etc.). If those who volunteered differ from those who did not, there will be bias in your sample.

Semi-structured interview—The interviewer may begin with a set of questions to answer (closed- and open-ended) but deviate from that set of questions from time to time. It does not have quite the same conversational approach as an unstructured interview.

Significant event—A specific experience in a participant's past that either exemplifies specific experiences or that is particularly noteworthy.

Simplification bias—If the researcher is a novice to the domain, he/she may have a tendency to conceptually simplify the expert user's problem-solving strategies while observing the expert. This is not done intentionally, of course, but the researcher does not have the complex mental model of the expert.

Social desirability—Participants provide a response to your questions that they believe are more socially desirable or acceptable than the truth.

Social loafing—The tendency for individuals to reduce the effort that they make toward some task when working together with others. The larger the group, the larger the affect.

Stakeholder(s)—An individual or group with an interest (or stake) in your user requirements activity and its results. Stakeholders typically influence the direction of the product (e.g., product managers, developers, business analysts, etc.).

Statistically significant—The probability that the results you obtained were unlikely to have occurred by chance.

Storyboards—Illustrate a particular task or a "day-in-life" of the user using representative images to illustrate a task/scenario/story. Merge data across your users to develop a generic, representative description.

Surrogate products—These are products that may or may not compete directly with your product. They have similar features to your product and should be studied to learn about the strengths and weaknesses.

Synergy—An idea from one participant positively influences another participant, resulting in an additional idea that would not have been generated without the initial idea.

T

Task allocation—The process of determining who or what should be responsible for completing various tasks in a system. This may be dividing tasks among different humans or between human and machine based on specific criteria.

Telescoping—People have a tendency to compress time. So, if you are asking about events that happened in the last six months, people may unintentionally include events that happened in the last nine months. Over-reporting of events will result.

Tertiary users—Those who are affected by the system or the purchasing decision makers.

Think-aloud protocol—A technique used during usability activities. The participant is asked to vocalize his/her thoughts, feelings, and opinions while working or interacting with the product.

Transfer of training—Transfer of learned skills from one situation to another. You are leveraging the users' current skill set so they do not have to learn everything new to use your product.

Translation bias—Expert users will attempt to translate their knowledge so that the researcher can understand it. The more experts translate, the more there is the potential for them to oversimplify and distort their knowledge/skills/etc.

U

Usability—The effectiveness, efficiency, and satisfaction with which users can achieve tasks when using a product. A usable product is easy to learn and remember; efficient, visually pleasing and pleasant to use. Usability enables users to recover quickly from errors and accomplish their tasks with ease.

User-centered design (UCD)—A product development approach that focuses on the end users of a product. The philosophy is that the product should suit the user, rather than making the user suit the product. This is accomplished by employing techniques, processes, and methods throughout the product lifecycle that focus on the user.

User profile—A list of characteristics and skills that describe the end user. It should provide the range of characteristics or skill levels that a typical end user may fall in, as well as the most common ones.

User requirements—The features/attributes your product should have or how it should perform from the users' perspective.

V

Vague questions—Questions that include imprecise terms like "rarely," "sometimes," "usually," "few," "some," or "most." Individuals can interpret these terms in different ways, affecting their answers and your interpretation of the results.

Valid/validity—The question or task actually measures the desired trait.

Visit summary template—A standardized survey or worksheet used in field studies. It is given to each investigator to complete at the end of each visit. This helps everyone get their thoughts on paper while fresh in their minds. It also speeds data analysis and avoids reporting only odd or funny anecdotal data.

APPENDIX J

REFERENCES

Chapter 1: Introduction to User Requirements

Bias, R. G. & Mayhew, D. J. (eds) (1994). *Cost-justifying Usability*. San Francisco: Morgan Kaufmann.

Gould, J. D. & Lewis, C. (1985). Designing for Usability: Key Principles and What Designers Think, *Communications of the ACM* 2(3), 300–311.

IBM (2001). Cost Justifying Ease of Use: Complex Solutions Are Problems. Available (October 9, 2001) at www-3.ibm.com/ibm/easy/eou_ext.nsf/Publish/23.

Lederer, A. L. & Prasad, J. (1992). Nine Management Guidelines for Better Cost Estimating, *Communications of the ACM* 35(2), 51–59.

Marcus, A. (2002). Return on Investment for Usable UI Design, *User Experience*, Winter, 25–31. (Bloomingdale, IL: Usability Professionals' Association.)

Pressman, R. S. (1992). *Software Engineering: a Practitioner's Approach*. New York: McGraw-Hill.

Standish Group (1995). Chaos Research Report. In Donahue, G. M., Weinschenk, Dr S., & Nowicki, J., *Usability Is Good Business*. Available (October 15, 2001) at www.compuware.com. As cited in Marcus, A. (*q.v.*).

Weinberg, J. (1997). *Quality Software Management. Vol. 4: Anticipating Change*. New York: Dorset House.

Chapter 2: Before You Choose an Activity: Learning About Your Product and Users

Brinck, T., Ha, S., Pritula, N., Lock, K., Speredelozzi, A., & Monan, M. (2003). Making an iMpact: Redesigning a Business School Web Site around Performance Metrics. In *DUX 2003, Designing User Experiences*, San Francisco, CA,

June, pp. 1–15. Available at http://www.aiga.org/resources/content/9/7/8/documents/brinck.pdf.

Carroll, J. M. (2000). *Making Use: Scenario-based Design of Human–Computer Interactions*. Cambridge, MA: MIT Press.

Cooper, A. (1999). *The Inmates are Running the Asylum: Why High Tech Products Drive Us Crazy and How To Restore The Sanity*. Indianapolis, IN: Sams.

Cooper, A. & Reimann, R. (2003). *About Face 2.0: The Essentials of Interaction Design*, 2nd ed. New York: John Wiley & Sons.

Fuller, R. & de Graaff, J. J. (1996). Measuring User Motivation from Server Log Files. Available at www.microsoft.com/usability/webconf/fuller/fuller.htm.

Kantner, L. (2001). Accessing Web Site Usability from Server Log Files. In Branaghan, R. (ed.), *Design by People for People: Essays on Usability*, pp. 245–261. Chicago: Usability Professionals' Association.

McInerney, P. (2003). Getting More from UCD Scenarios. Paper for IBM MITE. Available at www-306.ibm.com/ibm/easy/eou_ext.nsf/Publish/50?OpenDocument&../Publish/1111/$File/paper1111.pdf.

Rosson, M. B. & Carroll, J. M. (2002). *Usability Engineering: Scenario-based Development of Human–Computer Interaction*. San Francisco: Morgan Kaufmann.

Chapter 3: Ethical and Legal Considerations

American Psychological Association (1995). *Publication Manual of the American Psychological Association*, 4th ed., pp. 46–60. Washington, DC: APA.

Chapter 4: Setting Up Facilities for Your User Requirements Activity

Jones, J. & Bullara, F. (2003). Building Blocks for a Digital Solution to Usability Testing. In *Proceedings of the Usability Professionals' Association 2003 Conference*. Scottsdale, AZ, 23–27 June (CD-ROM).

Chapter 5: Preparing for Your User Requirements Activity

Dray, S. & Mrazek, D. (1996). A Day in the Life of a Family: an International Ethnographic Study. In Wixon, D. R. & Ramey, J. (eds), *Field Methods Casebook for Software Design*. New York: John Wiley & Sons.

Chapter 6: During Your User Requirements Activity

Dumas, J. S. & Redish, J. C. (1999). *A Practical Guide to Usability Testing*, 2nd ed. Exeter, England: Intellect Books.

Chapter 7: Interviews

Alreck, P. L. & Settle, R. B. (1995). *The Survey Research Handbook*, 2nd ed. Burr Ridge, IL: Irwin Professional Publishing.

Argyle, M. (1988). *Bodily Communication*, 2nd ed. London: Methuen.

Boren, M. T. & Ramey, J. (2000). Thinking Aloud: Reconciling Theory and Practice, *IEEE Transactions on Professional Communication*, 43, pp. 261–278. Available at http://ieeexplore.ieee.org/xpl/tocresult.jsp?isNumber=18778&puNumber=47.

Cadiz, J., Venolia, G., Jancke, G., & Gupta, A. (2002). Designing and Deploying an Information Awareness Interface. *Proceedings of the 2002 ACM Conference on Computer Supported Cooperative Work* (CSCW 2002), New Orleans, LA, 16–20 November, pp. 314–323. Available at http://research.microsoft.com/research/pubs/view.aspx?msr_tr_id=MSR-TR-2002-87.

Dumas, J. S. & Redish, J. C. (1999). *A Practical Guide to Usability Testing*, 2nd ed. Exeter, England: Intellect Books.

Johnson, T., Hougland, J., & Clayton, R. (1989). Obtaining Reports of Sensitive Behavior: a Comparison of Substance Use Reports from Telephone and Face-to-Face Interviews, *Social Science Quarterly* 70(1), 173–183.

Nance, J. (2001). *Conquering Deception*. Irvin-Benham Group, LLC.

Ulwick, A. W. (2002). Turn Customer Input into Innovation, *Harvard Business Review*, January, 5–11. Available at harvardbusinessonline.hbsp.harvard.edu/b01/en/common/item_detail.jhtml?id=R0201H.

Weiss, R. S. (1994). *Learning From Strangers: The Art and Method of Qualitative Interview Studies*. New York: Free Press.

Chapter 8: Surveys

Alreck, P. L. & Settle, R. B. (1995). *The Survey Research Handbook*, 2nd ed. Burr Ridge, IL: Irwin Professional Publishing.

Dumas, J. (2001). Usability Testing Methods. Subjective Measures – Measuring Attitudes and Opinions. In *Design by People for People: Essays on Usability*, pp. 107–117. Chicago: Usability Professionals' Association.

Salant, P. & Dillman, D. (1994). *How to Conduct Your Own Survey*. New York: John Wiley & Sons.

Schaefer, E. (2001). *Web Surveying: How to Collect Important Assessment Data Without Any Paper*. Office of Information and Institutional Research, Illinois Institute of Technology.

Chapter 9: Wants and Needs Analysis

Dennis, A. R. & Williams, M. L. (2003). Electronic Brainstorming: Theory, Research, and Future Directions. In Paulus, P. B. & Nijstad, B. A. (eds), *Group Creativity. Innovation through Collaboration*, pp. 160–178. New York: Oxford University Press.

Kass, S. J., Inzana, C. M., & Willis, R. P. (1995). The Effects of Team Member Distribution and Accountability on a Brainstorming Task. *Proceedings of the Human Factors and Ergonomics Society 39th Annual Meeting*, Vol. 2, San Diego, CA, 9–13 October, pp. 882–886.

Kelly, T. (2001). *The Art of Innovation*. New York: DoubleDay.

Mullen, B., Johnson, C., & Salas, E. (1991). Productivity Loss in Brainstorming Groups: A Meta-analytic Integration, *Basic and Applied Psychology* 12, 2–23.

Paulus, P. B., Larey, T. S., & Ortega, A. H. (1995). Performance and Perceptions of Brainstormers in an Organizational Setting, *Basic and Applied Psychology* 17, 249–265.

Ulwick, A. W. (2002). Turn Customer Input into Innovation, *Harvard Business Review*, January, 5–11. Available at harvardbusinessonline.hbsp.harvard.edu/b01/en/common/item_detail.jhtml?id=R0201H.

Chapter 10: Card Sorting

Aldenderfer, M. S. & Blashfield, R. K. (1984). *Cluster Analysis*. Sage University paper series on Quantitative Applications in the Social Sciences, #07-044. Beverly Hills, CA.

Lewis, S. (1991). Cluster Analysis as a Technique to Guide Interface Design. *Journal of Man–Machine Studies* 10, 267–280.

Nielsen, J. & Sano, D. (1994). SunWeb: User Interface Design for Sun Microsystem's Internal Web. *Proceedings of the 2nd World Wide Web Conference '94: Mosaic and the Web*, Chicago, IL, 17–20 October, pp. 547–557. Available at http://archive.ncsa.uiuc.edu/SDG/IT94/Proceedings/HCI/nielsen/sunweb.html.

Romesburg, C. H. (1984). *Cluster Analysis for Researchers*. Belmont, CA: Lifetime Learning Publications (Wadsworth).

Tullis, T. S. (1985). Designing a Menu-based Interface to an Operating System. *CHI '85 Proceedings*, San Francisco, CA, pp. 79–84.

Tullis, T. & Wood, L. (2004). How Many Users are Enough for a Card-sorting Study? *Proceedings of the Usability Professionals' Association 2004 Conference*, Minneapolis, MN, 7–11 June (CD-ROM).

Zavod, M. J., Rickert, D. E. & Brown, S. H. (2002). The Automated Card-sort as an Interface Design Tool: A Comparison of Products. In *Proceedings of the Human Factors and Ergonomics Society 46th Annual Meeting*, Baltimore, MD, 30 September–4 October, pp. 646–650.

Chapter 11: Group Task Analysis

Dayton, T., McFarland, A., & Kramer, J. (1998). Bridging User Needs to Object Oriented GUI Prototype via Task Object Design. In L. Wood (ed.), *User Interface Design: Bridging the Gap from Requirements to Design*, pp. 15–56. Boca Raton, FL: CRC Press.

Hackos, J. T. & Redish, J. C. (1998). *User and Task Analysis for Interface Design*. New York: John Wiley & Sons.

Chapter 12: Focus Groups

Dolan, W., Wiklund, M., Logan, R., & Augaitis, S. (1995). Participatory Design Shapes Future of Telephone Handsets. *Proceedings of the Human Factors and Ergonomics Society 39th Annual Meeting*, San Diego, CA, 9–13 October, pp. 331–335.

Dumas, J. S. & Redish, J. C. (1999). *A Practical Guide to Usability Testing*, 2nd ed. Exeter, England: Intellect Books.

Edmunds, H. (1999). *The Focus Group Research Handbook*. Chicago: NTC Business Books.

Eysenbach, G. & Köhler, C. (2002). How Do Consumers Search for and Appraise Health Information on the World Wide Web? Qualitative Study using Focus Groups, Usability Tests, and In-depth Interviews, *British Medical Journal 324*, 573–577.

Gray, B. G., Barfield, W., Haselkorn, M., Spyridakis, J., & Conquest, L. (1990). The Design of a Graphics-based Traffic Information System Based on User Requirements. *Proceedings of the Human Factors and Ergonomics Society 34th Annual Meeting*, Orlando, FL, 8–12 October, pp. 603–606.

Hackos, J. T. & Redish, J. C. (1998). *User and Task Analysis for Interface Design*. New York: John Wiley & Sons.

Karlin, J. E. & Klemmer, E. T. (1989). An Interview. In Klemmer, E. T. (ed.), *Ergonomics: Harness the Power of Human Factors in Your Business*, pp. 197–201. Norwood, NJ: Ablex.

Root, R. W. & Draper, S. (1983). Questionnaires as a Software Evaluation Tool. *Proceedings of the ACM CHI Conference*, Boston, MA, 12–15 December, pp. 83–87.

Sato, S. & Salvador, T. (1999). Playacting and Focus Troupe: Theater Techniques for Creating Quick, Intense, Immersive, and Engaging Focus Groups Sessions. *Interactions* 6(5), September–October, 35–41.

Chapter 13: Field Studies

Bauersfeld, K. & Halgren, S. (1996). You've Got Three Days! Case Studies in the Field Techniques for the Time-challenged. In Wixon, D. R. & Ramey, J. (eds), *Field Methods Casebook for Software Design*, pp. 177–195. New York: John Wiley & Sons.

Brooke, T. & Burrell, J. (2003). From Ethnography to Design in a Vineyard. In *DUX 2003 Proceedings*, San Francisco, CA, pp. 1–4. Available at http://www.aiga.org/resources/content/9/7/8/documents/brooke.pdf.

Hackos, J. T. & Redish, J. C. (1998). *User and Task Analysis for Interface Design*. New York: John Wiley & Sons.

Laakso, S. A., Laakso, K., & Page, C. (2001). DUO: A Discount Observation Method. Available at www.cs.helsinki.fi/u/salaakso/papers/DUO.pdf.

Ramey, J., Rowberg, A. H., & Robinson, C. (1996). Adaptation of an Ethnographic Method for Investigation of the Task Domain in Diagnostic Radiology. In Wixon, D. R. & Ramey, J. (eds), *Field Methods Casebook for Software Design*, pp. 1–15. New York: John Wiley & Sons.

Teague, R. & Bell, G. (2001). Getting Out Of The Box. Ethnography Meets Life: Applying Anthropological Techniques to Experience Research. In *Proceedings of the Usability Professionals' Association 2001 Conference*, Las Vegas, NV (Tutorial).

Wixon, D. R., Ramey, J., Holtzblatt, K. et al. (2002). Usability in Practice: Field Methods Evolution and Revolution. In *Proceedings of CHI*, Minneapolis, MN, pp. 880–884.

Wood, L. (1996). The Ethnographic Interview in User-centered Work/Task Analysis. In Wixon, D. R. & Ramey, J. (eds), *Field Methods Casebook for Software Design*, pp. 35–56. New York: John Wiley & Sons.

Chapter 14: Concluding Your Activity

McQuaid, H. L. (2002). Developing Guidelines for Judging the Cost and Benefit of Fixing Usability Problems. *Proceedings of the Usability Professionals' Association 2002 Conference* (CD-ROM).

McQuaid, H. L. & Bishop, D. (2001). An Integrated Method for Evaluating Interfaces. *Proceedings of the Usability Professionals' Association 2001 Conference* (CD-ROM).

INDEX

G

H

I

T

V

W

FIGURE AND TABLE CREDITS

Figures 1.1, 2.1, 3.2, 4.1–4.3, 4.6–4.10, 5.1–5.3, 5.5, 5.6, 6.1, 9.2, 9.4, 10.2, 10.3, 11.5, 11.6, 11.9–11.13, 12.2, 14.4, E.1, and Appendix H courtesy of Daniel Rosenberg, Oracle Corporation.

Figures 1.2 and 1.3 based on illustrations in *Software Requirements* by K. E. Weigers (1999), Microsoft Press.

Figure 2.4 Copyright © 2004 Getty Images. Reprinted with permission.

Figure 2.6 produced using the template proposed by McInerney (2003). Paper for IBM MITE, www-306.ibm.com/ibm/easy/cou_ext.nsf/Publish/50?OpenDocument &../Publish/111/$File/paper111.pdf.

Figures 2.7–2.13 courtesy of Derren Hermann and Tom Brinck.

Figures 2.14–2.19 courtesy of John Pruitt and Microsoft Corporation.

Figure 4.4 reprinted with permission. Copyright © 2004, Virtual Ink Corporation. http://www.mimio.com.

Figure 4.5 reprinted with permission. Copyright © 2004, Solutions for Humans. http://www.SforH.com.

Figures 4.11 and 4.12 courtesy of James Jones and David Mitropoulos-Rundus.

Figures 4.12–4.20 courtesy of Aimee McCabe.

Figures 5.7–5.11 courtesy of Elaine Ann and Eastman National IDSA Education Conference Proceedings.

Figures 7.1, 7.3, and 7.4, and Tables 7.1 and 7.3, adapted from *The Survey Research Handbook,* 2nd ed., by P. L Alreck and R. B. Settle (1995). Irwin Professional Publishing, A Division of the McGraw Hill Companies. Reprinted with permission.

Table 7.4 adapted from *A Practical Guide to Usability Testing* by J. Dumas and J. Redish (1999). Reprinted with permission from Intellect Ltd.

Figure 7.7 courtesy of Donna Bosworth Andrews.

Figures 8.11A and B courtesy of Kelly Braun.

Figures 10.10–10.13 courtesy of Ginny Redish.

Figures 13.11–13.13 courtesy of Beth Loring and Kelly Gordon Vaughn.

Table 13.2 redrawn from Teague & Bell (2001), *Proceedings of the Usability Professionals' Association 2001 Conference,* Las Vegas, NV.

Table 13.3 redrawn from Hackos & Redish (1998), *User and Task Analysis for Interface Design,* John Wiley & Sons.

Figures 14.2 and 14.3 redrawn from McQuaid (2002), *Proceedings of the Usability Professionals' Association 2002 Conference* (CD-ROM).

Cartoon on page 5 based on cartoon #5 at http:www.usability.uk.com.

Cartoon on page 324 based on an illustration from The Christian Science Monitor, www.csmonitor.com.

DILBERT cartoons (pages 11, 373, and 638). Reprinted with permission of United Features Syndicate, Inc.

New Yorker cartoons (pages 48, 163, and 263) © The New Yorker Collection. All rights reserved.

ABOUT THE AUTHORS

Kathy Baxter is a Senior User Experience Researcher in eBay's User Experience and Design (UED) group in San Jose, CA. She supports multiple areas of eBay's website through the user-centered design lifecycle, focusing primarily on Community, Trust and Safety, and Help. Previously, she worked as a usability engineer for five years in Oracle Corporation's Usability and Interface Design Group. She received her Masters of Science degree in Engineering Psychology with an emphasis on Human–Computer Interaction from the Georgia Institute of Technology. Kathy is an active member of the Usability Professionals' Association (UPA), Human Factors and Ergonomics Society (HFES), the Computer–Human Interaction (CHI) special interest group of the Association for Computing Machinery, and BayCHI. She has presented papers, posters, and tutorials – including a tutorial on which this book is based – to the Human Factors and Usability Community since 1997.

Catherine Courage is a Principal Usability Engineer in the Usability and Interface Design Group at Oracle Corporation, where she is responsible for driving usability initiatives for enterprise resource planning and customer relationship management applications. In addition to planning and leading usability activities throughout the product lifecycle, Catherine plays a key role in educating product teams on the subject of user-centered design. She also manages Oracle's Design Partners Program, a program focused on engaging strategic customers in usability and design initiatives. Catherine is an active member in the Usability and Human–Computer Interaction communities and regularly shares her knowledge and experiences via paper presentations, panels, and tutorials. She received a Masters of Applied Science degree specializing in Human Factors from the University of Toronto. Catherine currently resides in San Francisco, California.